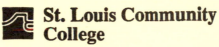

HISTORICAL DICTIONARY OF CENSORSHIP IN THE UNITED STATES

HISTORICAL DICTIONARY OF CENSORSHIP IN THE UNITED STATES

LEON HURWITZ

Greenwood Press
Westport, Connecticut • London, England

Library of Congress Cataloging in Publication Data

Hurwitz, Leon.
  Historical dictionary of censorship in the United
States.

  Bibliography: p.
  Includes index.
  1. Censorship—United States—History—Dictionaries.
I. Title.
KF4770.A68H87   1985   344.73′0531′0321   84-15796
ISBN 0-313-23878-2 (lib. bdg.) 347.3045310321

Library of Congress Catalog Card Number: 84-15796
ISBN: 0-313-23878-2

First published in 1985

Greenwood Press
A division of Congressional Information Service, Inc.
88 Post Road West
Westport, Connecticut 06881

Printed in the United States of America

10 9 8 7 6 5 4 3 2 1

To my nieces and nephews
Cheryl, Jeff, Scott, Taila, and Lauren

Congress shall make no law . . . abridging the freedom of speech, or of the press.

Amendment I, The Bill of Rights
United States Constitution

Now, Mr. Justice [Black], your construction of . . . [the First Amendment] is well known, and I certainly respect it. You say that no law means no law, and that should be obvious. I can only say, Mr. Justice, that to me it is equally obvious that 'no law' does not mean 'no law,' and I would seek to persuade the Court that that is true. . . . There are other parts of the Constitution that grant power and responsibilities to the Executive, and . . . the First Amendment was not intended to make it impossible for the Executive to function.

U.S. Solicitor General Erwin N. Griswold
New York Times v. United States
403 U.S. 713 (1971) at 717-718
[The Pentagon Papers]

CONTENTS

PREFACE

This historical dictionary of censorship in the United States does not pretend to be exhaustive; the subject is simply too vast for a single volume. Rather, it attempts to present an overview of the types of censorship and the types of speech and press that have been subjected to censorship, repression, and punishment.

The Introductory Essay identifies the four main categories of censorship: (1) political censorship in the name of national security; (2) community censorship in order to preserve public order and safety; (3) constitutional censorship of speech and press when these First Amendment rights conflict with other constitutionally protected rights; and (4) moral censorship over what is considered offensive material and sin.

The body of the book is organized alphabetically, each main entry standing alone. Cross-references to other main entries are noted by the symbol *, and although the cross-references contain information relevant to the original entry, they need not be read in conjunction with the original. The appendices include a Chronology, a Table of Cases, and a Selected Bibliography.

I am a political scientist and this book has been compiled from a political public policy point of view; legal terminology and legal concepts most certainly are present, but no claims are offered that the material is a guide to the legal profession. I also believe that my own view of censorship should be stated at the outset: I cannot find any intellectual justification for political censorship in the name of national security and, other than protecting unconsenting adults and minors, I likewise see no justification for censoring sexually explicit material. Censorship of speech and press in order to preserve public safety—the prevention of an imminent riot—and censorship in order to protect other rights—individual privacy, for example—can find intellectual justification in certain specific situations.

Several people aided and abetted this project and I thank them here (each will know what I am thanking him or her for): Robert Charlick, Paul Dommel, Marc Fishel, Pat Foy, Rodger Govea, John Holm, Susan Lindsley, Carol Patrick, Carol Smith, and Jim Woods. I also thank the editorial and production staff at Greenwood Press for their encouragement and most professional assistance: Jim Sabin, Margaret Brezicki, Cynthia Harris, Mary Sive, Arlene Belzer, Barbara Hodgson, and Mildred Vasan. Finally, my wife, Fran, and my children, Elise and Jonathan, have been most understanding of the demands of academic pursuits.

INTRODUCTORY ESSAY

The First Amendment to the U.S. Constitution, proposed in 1789 and adopted in 1791, states that "Congress shall make no law respecting an establishment of religion, or prohibiting the free exercise thereof, or abridging the freedom of speech, or of the press; or the right of the people peaceably to assemble, and to petition the Government for a redress of grievances." If these words—"Congress shall make no law . . . abridging the freedom of speech, or of the press"—meant exactly what they say, there would be no censorship over thought, speech, or the press in the United States.

But First Amendment rights are not absolute; even Justices Douglas and Black, two of the most outspoken, consistent, and intellectual defenders of the First Amendment against censorship attacks, have recognized that no one has the unfettered right to say or print whatever he wants, whenever he wants, wherever he wants, to whomever he wants. The exercise of First Amendment rights frequently collides with the exercise of other rights and objectives in an organized society, and although these societal rights and objectives are only imagined in many cases, sometimes speech and press must be accommodated to other, equally valid and important considerations (the right to a fair trial, for example, or the right to individual privacy). As Justice Jackson wrote (*Terminiello v. Chicago**) in a 1949 dissenting opinion: "The choice is not between order and liberty. It is between liberty with order and anarchy without either."

It is difficult to argue with Justice Jackson's view, but most of the censorship activity in the United States did not (and still does not) present the bald choice between "liberty with order and anarchy without either." Although not insignificant, there have been relatively few instances in which speech and press were subject to censorship or punishment because governmental authorities believed—rightly or wrongly—that a clear, present, immediate, and imminent danger of riot and violence would be a direct consequence of the speech or press or that the particular communication would harm another person's constitutionally protected rights and freedoms. Such situations have been few and far between, and the courts have generally approached them on an individual basis, attempting to balance the conflicting claims to protect liberties.

Rather, the majority of censorship, repression, and punishment of ideas, speech, and press was (and still is) due to the fact that the content of the specific expression or communication "angers" or "offends"—it offends the listener's or the viewer's or the reader's sense of nationalism or patriotism, of morality or ethics, of decency or propriety. This type of censorship has nothing to do with Justice Jackson's fear of anarchy; it is, purely and simply, the mind-set of insecurity and intolerance. Speech and press that offend the sensitivities of the self-appointed guardians standing watch over the political and moral health of other people will be repressed. This is the real nature of censorship, and it should not be confused with prohibitions against inciting a riot or interfering with the right to a fair trial.

The following historical overview does not claim to cover the entire range of censorship in the United States. The subject is too vast even to make the attempt. Rather, this essay identifies the four basic categories into which most governmental censorship activities fall: (1) political censorship: speech, press, and national security; (2) community censorship: speech, press, and public order/safety; (3) constitutional censorship: speech, press, and conflicting rights; and (4) moral censorship: speech, press, and sin.

POLITICAL CENSORSHIP: SPEECH, PRESS, AND NATIONAL SECURITY

The rights guaranteed in the First Amendment have generally come out second best in most confrontations with the claimed requirements of national security during periods of international crises, tensions, warfare, and imagined domestic subversion and sedition. Wartime in particular brings with it the overriding governmental objective to create and maintain national unity and, by so doing, frequently punishes with severity those individuals who refuse to stay within the artificial boundaries of accepted political expression. Such people have been punished not so much for what they might have done as overt behavior or conduct (selling military secrets to the enemy, for example, or engaging in sabotage), but for what they believe, say, or publish.

Wartime, however, is not the only period when the claimed needs of national security and national unity permit censorship and punishment for the wrong political ideology and expression. Since 1917 the U.S. government (and many states as well) has insisted that "internal enemies" and "subversives" (read "political dissidents"), even during peacetime, need to be shown the errors of their ways and led back to the path of correct thinking and righteousness. The following comments review briefly some of the political censorship activities by various governmental levels within the United States over thought, speech, and press—all of which was done in the name of "national security."

The story begins with the infamous Sedition Act* of 1798, passed by Congress on July 14, 1798, with a three-year life; the act did in fact expire on March 3, 1801. This act's formal title was "An Act for the punishment of certain crimes against the United States." It contained the following prohibitions and penalties: a $5,000 fine (an *extraordinary* amount in 1798) and five years in prison for opposing "any measure or measures of the government of the United States"; $2,000 and two years for "publishing any false, scandalous and malicious writing" against the government or the president or for bringing the government or the president into "contempt or disrepute" or for exciting "hatred of the good people" against the government or the president.

John Adams was president at the time (1797–1801) and was a Federalist; his political rivals were the Jeffersonian Republicans who attacked, in press and speech, Adams, his policies, and the Federalists. Congress at the time was dominated by the Federalists and wanted to put an end to the Jeffersonian broadsides; the 1798 Sedition Act thus made it a crime to "oppose" the government or to bring the president into "contempt or disrepute." John C. Miller (*Crisis in Freedom: The Alien and Sedition Acts*, pp. 74–75) writes that "the Federalists thought that the existing common law of seditious libel wouldn't support prosecutions so its authority had to be affirmed by a specific statute" and that the Sedition Act "was an implied acknowledgment by the Federalists that force and coercion rather than reason and argument were to be the ultimate arbiters of political controversy in the United States. Differences of opinion were to be erased and the American mind was to be forced into an intellectual strait jacket."

Some twenty-five people, mostly Jeffersonian Republican newspaper editors, were arrested under the Sedition Act; ten were ultimately convicted by the Federalist-dominated courts. John Daly Burk was arrested in July 1798 on a warrant signed by President Adams himself, for the crime of "seditious libel" (Adams did not appreciate Burk's comments in his New York newspaper, *Time Piece*). The government first wanted to deport Burk to his native Ireland but then decided that a hefty fine would be better (it was obvious to everyone that had Burk been deported, he would not have sent in his fine from Ireland). Burk eventually fled to Virginia, a state that gave refuge to fugitives from the Sedition Act. A Jeffersonian Republican member of Congress from Vermont, Matthew Lyon, was found guilty under the act and received four months in jail and a $1,000 fine (again, quite a large sum at that time). Lyon was convicted for writing certain articles in the *Vermont Journal* and for publishing a letter in which the author urged Congress "to commit President Adams to the madhouse." Anthony Haswell received two months and a $200 fine for publishing an advertisement in the *Vermont Gazette* that solicited contributions to pay off Matthew Lyon's fine. In 1800, Charles Holt, editor of the New Haven *Bee*, received six months in jail and a $200 fine for being "a wicked, malicious, seditious and ill-disposed person."

Thomas Jefferson was eventually elected president. After he took office, he pardoned those still serving jail terms under the act and used public monies to reimburse those who had had to pay a fine. Miller (p. 231) cites Jefferson to the effect that he considered the Sedition Act of 1798 "to be a nullity as absolute and as palpable as if Congress had ordered us to fall down and worship a golden image.'' The 1798 Sedition Act expired on March 3, 1801; the country was well rid of it.

There was relatively little activity in the area of suppression and punishment of political expression in the subsequent 116 years after the Sedition Act expired. The United States was in a bucolic era, and all levels of government, especially the federal level, had a limited and mundane role to play. Such modern-day agencies as the Central Intelligence Agency, the Federal Bureau of Investigation, the National Security Council, military intelligence agencies, loyalty review boards, and Attorney-General's Lists did not exist—no one saw the need for them during the 1800s. Even if the government wanted to investigate and punish deviant and subversive political thought and press (a questionable assumption in the first place), it lacked the ability to do so.

Obviously, the Civil War (1861–1865) did not leave First Amendment rights unscathed. President Lincoln, in the attempt to preserve the Union, resorted to several questionable applications of military tribunals, especially in the "Copperhead" section of southern Indiana, to try people suspected of rebellion or sedition. This is not an apology for Lincoln, but the reader must be reminded that there was an immense difference between U.S. society during the Civil War and U.S. society during the war in Viet Nam. The Civil War threatened the very existence of the country and was fought on U.S. soil, brother against brother; Viet Nam was 8,000 miles distant and only the unrepentant hawks argued the specious claim that Viet Nam was vital to U.S. national security. Be that as it may, President Lincoln most assuredly violated the First Amendment in many instances, but on the whole, the rights guaranteed by the First Amendment survived the Civil War relatively intact. Lincoln did not ask Congress for a contemporary version of the 1798 Sedition Act, and press and speech freedoms generally were honored.

By 1917, the United States had returned in earnest to the practice of punishing people for having the wrong political ideas. World War I brought political censorship and repression back into vogue. At that time, the United States was an industrialized nation; the war required massive mobilization and the draft; the government participated in the direction and planning of a wartime economy; a concerted war effort was needed. No longer were just a few soldiers involved in faraway places, such as during the Indian wars; the entire population had to be mobilized and politically motivated. All these factors, but especially the claimed need for mass political motivation, inexorably led to severe censorship and punishment of people not so much for what they might have done (the reference here is not to German spies), but for what they thought, wrote, or said. The Espionage Act* of 1917 was the U.S. government's answer to political dissidence during World War I.

The federal Espionage Act was passed on June 15, 1917, and was amended on May 16, 1918. The main problem with the act was that it did not deal with espionage; rather, it dealt with political opposition. The relevant sections of the act provided the following:

Whoever, when the United States is at war, shall willfully make or convey false reports or false statements with intent to interfere with the operation or success of the military or naval forces of the United States or to promote the success of its enemies and whoever, when the United States is at war, shall willfully cause or attempt to cause insubordination, disloyalty, mutiny, or refusal of duty, in the military or naval forces of the United States, or shall willfully obstruct the recruiting or enlistment service of the United States, to the injury of the service or of the United States, shall be punished by a fine of not more than $10,000 or imprisonment for not more than twenty years, or both.

Read in its literal terms, a person who sent the Kaiser a birthday card wishing long life would be liable for $10,000 and twenty years, for such a card "promote[s] the success of [our] enemies."

The following represents only a few of the instances in which the U.S. government severely punished people under the 1917 Espionage Act; clearly these individuals' crimes were that they opposed U.S. involvement in World War I and ascribed to the hated doctrine that international disputes and the resolution of conflict ought not to be managed by force of arms. Jacob Abrams (*Abrams v. United States**) received twenty years for circulating a pamphlet in Yiddish ("Workers—Wake Up!") that only a handful of people ever read. The Supreme Court characterized Abrams' pamphlet as "obviously intended to provoke and to encourage resistance to the United States in the war." The editor of the *Missouri Staats Zeitung* was convicted (*Frohwerk v. United States**) because "the circulation of the paper was in quarters where a little breath would be enough to kindle a flame."

Another unfortunate pamphleteer (*Pierce v. United States**) was convicted for describing in "The Price We Pay" the horrors of trench warfare and what would probably happen to the new army recruits: "Into that seething, heaving swamp of torn flesh and floating entrails they will be plunged, in regiments, divisions and armies, screaming as they go. Agonies of torture will rend their flesh from their sinews, will crack their bones and dissolve their lungs." The Supreme Court, seeing the obvious—that such descriptions would certainly make young men think twice before enlisting—judged this to be a blatant violation of the Espionage Act:

"The Price We Pay" was intended to interfere with the conscription and recruitment services; to cause men eligible for the service to evade the draft; to bring home to them, and especially to their parents, sisters, wives, and sweethearts, a sense of impending personal loss, calculated to discourage the young men from entering the service.

The entire philosophy can be summed up by a statement by Justice Holmes relating to yet another conviction under the Espionage Act (*Schenck v. United States**): "When a nation is at war many things that might be said in time of peace are such a hindrance to its effort that their utterance will not be endured so long as men fight and that no court could regard them as protected by any constitutional right."

In what is perhaps the most infamous conviction under the 1917 Espionage Act, Eugene Debs received a ten-year prison term. On Sunday, June 16, 1918, at Nimisilla Park in Canton, Ohio, Eugene Debs delivered a speech in which he advocated the aims of international political socialism and expressed his opposition to U.S. involvement in World War I. Debs received a ten-year prison term (*Debs v. United States**), Justice Holmes of the Supreme Court saying that Debs' speech opposed the war effort and thus was intended to obstruct the recruiting service. It was irrelevant whether or not such obstruction actually happened; imputed intent was sufficient. President Harding commuted Debs' sentence in 1921 but his citizenship was not restored. Eugene Debs was a national political figure who was respected in many circles as an intelligent and articulate spokesman of democratic socialism—he received some 900,000 votes in the 1920 presidential election—but he had the misfortune to espouse a political creed that the majority detested and to oppose a war that the majority supported. The only real difference between Eugene Debs in 1918 and George McGovern in 1972 was that the U.S government did not brand McGovern a felon and put him in jail for his political opposition to the war in Viet Nam.

The political censorship arising from World War I was not limited to the federal Espionage Act; many states entered the fray, showing that they, too, could command patriotism and punish political heresy and political blasphemy. One such example (*Gilbert v. Minnesota**) had the Supreme Court affirming a conviction under a Minnesota statute entitled "Discouraging the War Effort." This statute punished anyone who espoused the political doctrine of pacifism. In affirming Gilbert's $500 fine and one year in prison, Justice McKenna stated explicitly that those who do not follow the accepted political line during wartime deserve to be punished. Justice McKenna:

The Nation was at war with Germany, armies were recruiting, and the speech was the discouragement of that. . . . It was not an advocacy . . . that a citizen had the right to make. The war was flagrant; it had been declared by the power constituted by the Constitution to declare it. . . . It was not declared in aggression, but in defense, in defense of our national honor, in vindication of the "most sacred rights of our Nation and our people." This was known to Gilbert . . . and every word that he uttered in denunciation of the war was false [and] deliberate misrepresentation of the motives which impelled it.

To paraphrase Justice McKenna: "There is a war going on and if you do not support the government, even in thought and speech, you will be put into jail." The First Amendment most certainly came out second best during World War I when it confronted the claim for political orthodoxy.

The above examples were tragic because people were branded felons and sent to jail. This irrational search for political consensus also had its absurd manifestations. One such absurdity—although it wasn't very absurd for the defendant because he, too, was sent to jail—concerned the 1917 American film *The Spirit of '76*. The film was about the Revolutionary War, and presumably, its intent was to encourage patriotism and national unity during World War I. Several historical events were dramatized in the film: Patrick Henry's speech on "Liberty or Death," Paul Revere's classic ride to Lexington and Concord, the somber signing of the Declaration of Independence, and Washington's painful winter at Valley Forge. *The Spirit of '76* also contained some scenes that were not flattering to the British soldiers; one such scene had the redcoats shooting and bayoneting American women and children. The scenes that portrayed the British in a bad light did in the producer because the U.S. government did not like such scenes exhibited—although factually correct—during a war in which the British were now U.S. allies. The film was seized by federal agents; further exhibition was prevented; and the producer, Robert Goldstein, was convicted under the Espionage Act (*United States v. Motion Picture Film The Spirit of '76*, 252 F. 946 [1917]). The logic was unassailable: The United States was at war; Britain was a U.S. ally; the film was "calculated to arouse antagonism and hatred" against the British; this would hurt the war effort; and finally, hurting the war effort was a clear violation of the Espionage Act! Goldstein received a prison term for producing and exhibiting *The Spirit of '76* and a federal appeals court affirmed the sentence (*Goldstein v. United States*, 258 F. 908 [1919]). Goldstein did not appeal his conviction to the Supreme Court, but considering how the Court reacted in other cases under the Espionage Act, Goldstein would not have had his conviction reversed.

Soon after World War I, there was a concerted governmental effort to crack down on and suppress those who exhibited any left-wing political tendencies or ideas. Socialists, Communists, anarchists, criminal syndicalists—any variety of left-wing political ideology—became subject to repression. This can perhaps be called the first Red Scare; the second Red Scare exploded after World War II with Senator Joseph McCarthy, the House Un-American Activities Committee, loyalty review boards, guilt by association, and loyalty oaths. The 1920s witnessed several states passing "criminal syndicalism" or "criminal anarchy" statutes (for example, California, Kansas, New York, Ohio, Oregon). All these statutes were similar in content. In general, they made it a crime for anyone to advocate, advise, or teach the duty, necessity, or propriety of overthrowing organized government by force or violence or to attempt to effectuate industrial change by force or violence or to publish anything that advanced such doctrines. Just as the courts during World War I would not countenance any political opposition to the war effort, the 1920s witnessed the courts punishing any left-wing thought that had the temerity and audacity to question the values of the majority concerning private property and bourgeois exploitation of the working class.

One of the best-known cases in this area was the 1925 *Gitlow v. New York** decision. Benjamin Gitlow was convicted of violating the New York criminal anarchy statute for having published and circulated his "Left Wing Manifesto." The "Manifesto" was a turgid and rambling political tract on the necessity of accomplishing the Communist revolution through dialectical materialism, the dictatorship of the proletariat, and the class struggle. Although there was *no* evidence of any effect resulting from the publication and circulation of the "Manifesto" (probably one hundred persons at most ever read it and, among these, few, if any, understood what Gitlow was talking about), the Supreme Court affirmed Gitlow's conviction. The Court believed that the very thoughts and ideas that the "Manifesto" expressed—thoughts and ideas devoid of any conduct or action—were in and by themselves a danger to national security.

Justice Sanford delivered the majority opinion in the *Gitlow* case:

That utterances inciting to the overthrow of organized government by unlawful means, present a sufficient danger of substantive evil to bring their punishment within the range of legislative discretion, is clear. Such utterances, by their very nature, involve danger to the public peace and to the security of the State. They threaten breaches of the peace and ultimate revolution. And the immediate danger is none the less real and substantial, because the effect of a given utterance cannot be accurately foreseen. The State cannot reasonably be required to measure the danger from every such utterance in the nice balance of a jeweler's scale. A single revolutionary spark may kindle a fire that, smouldering for a time, may burst into a sweeping and destructive conflagration. It cannot be said that the State is acting arbitrarily or unreasonably when in the exercise of its judgment as to the measures necessary to protect the public peace and safety, it seeks to extinguish the spark without waiting until it has enkindled the flame or blazed into the conflagration. It cannot reasonably be required to defer the adoption of measures for its own peace and safety until the revolutionary utterances lead to actual disturbances of the public peace or imminent and immediate danger of its own destruction; but it may . . . suppress the threatened danger in its incipiency.

A conviction under the California criminal syndicalism statute was affirmed by the Supreme Court in 1927 (*Whitney v. California**). Anita Whitney had assisted in the organization of a Communist Labor party, and the Supreme Court agreed with the government prosecutors that her "advocacy" of the outlawed political doctrine was as reprehensible and as evil as the conduct itself. In other words, not only did the state have the power to punish certain activity, but it could also punish people who merely believed that such conduct was desirable and that it should take place sometime in the vague and distant future. This punishment lasted until 1969 (1969!), when the Supreme Court, in dealing with Ohio's criminal syndicalism statute in *Brandenburg v. Ohio*,* ruled that the "freedoms of speech and press do not permit a State to forbid advocacy of the use of force or of law violation except where such advocacy is directed to inciting or producing imminent lawless action and is likely to incite or produce such action."

If one discounts a massive use of governmental authority to restrict and control war news and information, World War II witnessed relatively few assaults on domestic free speech and press. The government still had recourse to the 1917 Espionage Act, but the act was employed against real spies, not against people who voiced political opposition to the war. In fact, the Supreme Court (*Hartzel* *v. United States**) refused to sanction a conviction under the Espionage Act of someone who wrote intemperate and malicious diatribes against the British, the Jews, and President Roosevelt. After the war, another wave of political hysteria, repression, and censorship appeared—the second Red Scare. This was fostered by the psychological view that America's problems in the world—the cold war, the "loss" of eastern Europe and China, the loss of U.S. nuclear monopoly— could not be due to lack of power, since at the time the United States was the most powerful country in the world, but to internal enemies, spies, subversives, and traitors. From the mid-1940s and lasting well over twenty years, the second Red Scare produced loyalty oaths, McCarthyism, the House Un-American Activities Committee, loyalty review boards, Attorney-General's Lists, guilt by association, and Communist (read "left-wing") witch-hunts across the country.

The Smith Act,* originally passed in 1940 and amended in 1948, provided the means by which the government could repress all these new left-wingers. The Smith Act provided a punishment of a $10,000 fine or ten years in prison or both for anyone who:

advocates, abets, advises, or teaches the duty, necessity, desirability, or propriety of overthrowing or destroying the government of the United States or the government of any State . . . by force or violence . . . or Whoever . . . prints, publishes, edits, issues, circulates, sells, distributes, or publicly displays any written or printed matter advocating . . . or Whoever . . . organizes or helps to organize any society, group, or assembly of persons who teach, advocate, or encourage the overthrow or destruction of any such government by force or violence.

The Supreme Court, in 1951, ruled that the Smith Act was constitutional and did not present a violation of the First Amendment (*Dennis v. United States**). The Court saw no need for the government to have to wait until the actual overthrow was about to begin before punishing the people involved; if the government learns that a group of people are organizing to talk about some future activity, the government can then punish the thought itself. Justices Black and Douglas registered a strong dissent to this decision, seeing it was a "virulent form of prior censorship of speech and press." Justice Black commented that:

Public opinion being what it now is, few will protest the conviction of these Communist petitioners. There is hope, however, that in calmer times, when present pressures, passions and fears subside, this or some later Court will restore the First Amendment liberties to the high preferred place where they belong in a free society.

Passions and fears did not totally subside but, in 1957, the Supreme Court refined its *Dennis* decision in *Yates v. United States.** The Court ruled that the Smith Act does not prohibit advocacy and teaching of the forcible overthrow of the government as an abstract principle; only incitement to direct and immediate action and conduct could be punished. The *Yates* decision reversed some convictions but sent several other people back to the lower courts to be retried. Justice Black, again joined by Justice Douglas, dissented from this latter decision:

In essence, petitioners were tried upon the charge that they believe in and want to foist upon this country a different and to us a despicable form of authoritarian government in which voices criticizing the existing order are summarily silenced. I fear that the present type of prosecutions are more in line with the philosophy of authoritarian government than with that expressed by our First Amendment. Doubtlessly, dictators have to stamp out causes and beliefs which they deem subversive to their evil regimes. But governmental suppression of causes and beliefs seems to me to be the very antithesis of what our Constitution stands for. The choice expressed in the First Amendment in favor of free expression was made against a turbulent background by men such as Jefferson, Madison, and Mason—men who believed that loyalty to the provisions of this Amendment was the best way to assure a long life for this new nation and its Government. Unless there is complete freedom of expression for all ideas, whether we like them or not, concerning the way government should be run and who shall run it, I doubt if any views in the long run can be secured against the censor. The First Amendment provides the only kind of security system that can preserve a free government—one that leaves the way wide open for people to favor, discuss, advocate, or incite causes and doctrines however obnoxious and antagonistic such views may be to the rest of us.

Another manifestation of the second Red Scare at the federal level was the creation of the Loyalty Review Board.* Established by executive order, issued by President Truman on March 21, 1947, the board was mandated to circulate the Attorney General's List to all governmental departments and agencies in order to weed out subversives from the federal civil service. The infamous Attorney General's List contained the names of all organizations that were judged to be subversive. Any individual who was—or had been—a member of any of the listed organizations was therefore guilty by association.

Even the U.S. Postal Service got into the act, doing its share to keep track of subversives and attempting to monitor the reading habits of U.S. citizens. Certain postal regulations (Postal Regulations, Communist Political Propaganda*) permitted the postmaster general to determine which unsealed foreign-origin mailings were "communist political propaganda," and before such mail would be delivered to the addressee, the addressee had to return a card to the post office stating that, yes indeed, the subversive publication was wanted. This was one of the few federal governmental schemes against political subversives that the Supreme Court refused to sanction (*Lamont v. Postmaster General**), but this was in 1965, well after the excesses of McCarthyism. Justice Douglas delivered the opinion of the court in this case:

This requirement [the addressee having to request delivery] is almost certain to have a deterrent effect, especially as respects those who have sensitive positions. Their livelihood may be dependent on a security clearance. Public officials, like schoolteachers who have no tenure, might think they would invite disaster if they read what the Federal Government says contains the seeds of treason. Apart from them, any addressee is likely to feel some inhibition in sending for literature which federal officials have condemned as "communist political propaganda." The regime of this Act is at war with the "uninhibited, robust, and wide-open" debate and discussion that are contemplated by the First Amendment.

The Immigration and Nationality Act of 1952 employed political criteria to determine which aliens could receive a visa to enter the United States and, once here, which aliens could be deported. Certain sections of this act gave the U.S. attorney general the sole discretion to refuse to grant visas to aliens who advocate or publish on "the economic, international, and governmental doctrines of world communism or the establishment in the United States of a totalitarian dictatorship." The Supreme Court, in 1972 (*Kleindienst v. Mandel**), ruled that these regulations were not a violation of freedom of speech or of the press and they have been frequently employed by the government to prevent "undesirable" people from visiting and lecturing in the United States. This ability to deny visas was used throughout the 1950s, the 1960s, and the 1970s to prevent people from entering the country on "national security" grounds, but a brief review of the process (Immigration and Nationality Act, Visa Regulations*) shows that most of the people were denied entry because they did not support U.S. foreign policy objectives—there were no terrorists, dope pushers, or plague carriers in the lot. One example will suffice: Nino Pasti, a former NATO general and a member of the Italian Senate, was denied entry for "national security" reasons, but it was obvious that Pasti's opposition to the deployment of Pershing and cruise missiles in Europe had something to do with the refusal. The Reagan administration attempted to make explicit what had been the past practice; in addition to the "national security" justification for a visa denial, the government wanted to add "foreign policy factors" as well.

The Immigration and Nationality Act of 1952 also authorizes the deportation of a resident alien if the alien ever belonged to a Communist party anywhere, even if such membership was terminated before the act was passed (once a subversive, always a subversive). In 1952, the Supreme Court sanctioned this process, seeing no difference between being a former member of an organization that advocated the abstract doctrine of the overthrow of the government in the vague and distant future and being a current member, inciting to immediate and imminent riot and revolution (*Harisiades v. Shaughnessy**).

The history of the House Un-American Activities Committee is too long to deal with in this essay; suffice it to say that when the Committee was on the trail of subversives, the First Amendment guarantees of speech and press were all too often ignored. One witness before the committee refused to answer questions as to whether he was then or had ever been a member of the Communist party, apparently believing that his political beliefs (his actual conduct was not at issue) were not the committee's concern. He was fined and sentenced to six months in jail for "contempt" of Congress; in 1959, the Supreme Court affirmed the conviction (*Barenblatt v. United States**). Justice Black dissented, recognizing that Barenblatt was being punished for what he thought and not for what he might have done. Justice Black:

I cannot agree with the Court's notion that First Amendment freedoms must be abridged in order to "preserve" our country. That notion rests upon the unarticulated premise that this Nation's security hangs upon its power to punish people because of what they think, speak or write about, or because of those with whom they associate for political purposes. The Government, in its brief, virtually admits this proposition when it speaks of the "communication of unlawful ideas." I challenge this premise, and deny that ideas can be proscribed under our Constitution.

Individual state governments wanted to demonstrate that they, too, could fight communism and left-wing subversives just as resolutely as was done at the federal level. Strangely, the Supreme Court did not sanction these state activities to the same extent as it did the repression at the federal level. The following are a few of the many political censorship schemes attempted by the states during the second Red Scare.

In 1950, the state of Oklahoma passed a statute that required each state officer and employee, as a condition for current or future employment, to take a "loyalty" oath, stating, among other things, that the employee was not, and had not been for the preceding five years, a member of any organization listed by the U.S attorney general (the Attorney General's List) as "communist front" or "subversive." The Oklahoma Supreme Court interpreted the statute as excluding people from state employment solely on the basis of membership in such listed organizations, regardless of their knowledge concerning the activities and purposes of the organizations. The oath also prohibited from state employment any person who believed in the political doctrine of pacifism, for one of the clauses in the oath read: "I will take up arms in the defense of the United States in time of war." The Supreme Court ruled this loyalty oath to be unconstitutional in 1952 (*Wieman v. Updegraff**), and as in many instances, a concurring (or dissenting) opinion is often more significant and relevant than the majority decision. Justice Black wrote such a concurring opinion in this case:

The present period of fear seems more ominously dangerous to speech and press than was that of the Alien and Sedition Laws. Suppressive laws and practices are the fashion. The Oklahoma oath statute is but one manifestation of a national network of laws aimed at coercing and controlling the minds of men. Test oaths are notorious tools of tyranny. When used to shackle the mind, they are, or at least they should be, unspeakably odious to a free people. . . . Governments need and have ample power to punish treasonable acts. But it does not follow that they must have a further power to punish thought and speech as distinguished from acts. Our own free society should never forget that laws which stigmatize and penalize thought and speech of the unorthodox have a way of reaching, ensnaring and silencing many more people than at first intended. We must have freedom of speech for all or we will in the long run have it for none but the cringing and the craven.

The state of California, in 1952, adopted a statute prohibiting anyone from receiving a standard property tax exemption unless the taxpayer first signed a statement on the tax return saying that he or she didn't "advocate the overthrow of the Government by force or violence or other unlawful means" and that the taxpayer swore that he or she would not support "a foreign government against the United States in the event of hostilities or war." In 1958, the Supreme Court ruled (*Speiser v. Randall**) that the California oath requirement was unconstitutional and was aimed solely at the suppression of unpopular ideas. The Court saw the oath as being the equivalent of the state fining a taxpayer for such speech.

In 1969, the state of Indiana passed its own version of a loyalty oath directed not at taxpayers, but at politicians. The Indiana statute provided that no political party would be listed on the ballot unless and until it had furnished a signed statement attesting to the fact that the party, and all its candidates, did not advocate the overthrow of any government at any level and that the party did not advocate a program of sedition. The Supreme Court, in 1974 (*Communist Party of Indiana v. Whitcomb**), ruled that the First Amendment prohibits such requirements except when such advocacy is directed to inciting or producing imminent lawless action; the thought is *not* the father to the action and Indiana could not suppress access to the ballot because of political nonconformity.

The state of Louisiana passed a series of statutes, collectively known as the Louisiana Subversive Activities and Communist Control Law.* These statutes relied on the infamous Attorney General's List and made it a *felony* for anyone to participate in any "subversive" organization or to belong to any "Communist front" organization. As usual, these terms were defined in reference not to what the organizations might have actually done, but in terms of their political beliefs (advocating the overthrow of the government or advocating desegregation).

The state of Pennsylvania passed its own version of the 1798 Sedition Act and made sedition a felony, punishable by a fine of $10,000 or twenty (twenty!) years in prison or both for anyone doing the following: advocating the overthrow of the government or—and this clause must have been copied from the 1798 Act—"to incite or encourage any person to commit any overt act with a view to bringing the Government of this State or the United States into hatred or contempt." To bring the government into "hatred or contempt" doesn't take much; a vote for the opposition candidate would probably be sufficient. The question of the constitutionality of the Pennsylvania statute reached the Supreme Court in 1956 (*Pennsylvania v. Nelson**), and the Court ruled that, indeed, the Pennsylvania Sedition Act was unconstitutional. But the reasons for the decision are more significant in this discussion of political censorship than the actual decision. The Supreme Court ruled that the Smith Act, at the federal level, took precedence over any state sedition law and that if anyone was going to be prosecuted and punished for having the wrong ideas, it would be the federal government that would do the repressing and not the state. This decision, although ruling that the Pennsylvania statute was not viable, did not do much for the First Amendment.

In 1951, the state of New Hampshire passed a Subversive Activities Act, a comprehensive scheme of regulation of alleged subversive persons and activities. Subversive organizations were declared unlawful and ordered dissolved, and subversive persons were made ineligible for state employment. Included in the disability were those who were employed as teachers or in other capacities by any public educational institution. A loyalty program was instituted to eliminate all subversive persons from public employment, and employees were required to make sworn statements that they were not subversive persons. The New Hampshire attorney general was authorized to carry on investigations under the act. One such investigation led to a contempt citation because the alleged subversive person would not furnish the names of people thought to be subversive (*Uphaus v. Wyman* [1959]*). The Supreme Court affirmed Uphaus' contempt conviction with the following comments, which, when read carefully, present a chilling view of the Red Scare's impact on freedom of thought:

What was the interest of the State? The Attorney General was commissioned to determine if there were any subversive persons within New Hampshire. The obvious starting point of such an inquiry was to learn what persons were within the state. It is therefore clear that the requests relate directly to the Legislature's area of interest, i.e., the presence of subversives in the State, as announced in its resolution. . . . While . . . guilt by association remains a thoroughly discredited doctrine, it is with a legislative investigation—not a criminal prosecution—that we deal here. Certainly the investigatory power of the State need not be constricted until sufficient evidence of subversion is gathered to justify the institution of criminal proceedings.

One last example of the states' activities in cracking down on subversive and political dissidents concerned the application of several New York statutes (the New York Civil Service Law,* the New York Education Law,* and the so-called New York Feinberg Law*). These statutes dealt with the eligibility of who could be state employees (including public school teachers and university employees) and contained the usual prohibitions: advocacy of the violent overthrow of the government, publishing on such a doctrine, membership in certain organizations (the Communist party, obviously, was included), and criminal anarchy. A loyalty oath was also required. The Supreme Court, in 1952 (*Adler v. Board of Education**), saw nothing wrong with these statutes, Justice Minton delivering the majority opinion:

It is equally clear that they [public school teachers] have no right to work for the State in the school system on their own terms. They may work for the school system upon the reasonable terms laid down by the proper authorities of New York. If they do not choose to work on such terms, they are at liberty to retain their beliefs . . . and go elsewhere. Has the State thus deprived them of any right to free speech or assembly? We think not.

Justices Black, Frankfurter, and Douglas most certainly *did* think that New York had deprived these people of their First Amendment rights and that the entire scheme was an unacceptable censorship over political ideas and thought. Justice Black commented, in his dissent: "This is another of those rapidly multiplying legislative enactments which make it dangerous—this time for school teachers—to think or say anything except what a transient majority happen to approve at the moment." The dissent in *Adler* eventually became the majority, for in 1967 (*Keyishian v. Board of Regents**), the Supreme Court overturned the *Adler* decision and ruled that advocacy, apart from any overt public action or behavior, cannot be employed as a criterion to fire public employees.

The years of the Viet Nam War were entirely different when compared with the 1917 Espionage Act and World War I. So many people were opposed to the war that they all couldn't be branded as felons, traitors, subversives, or internal enemies. The jails were not large enough to hold even a fraction of those who expressed political opposition to the war in Viet Nam! This does not mean that various governmental levels did not attempt to punish such thought and instead followed a policy of laissez faire; on the contrary, many attempts were made to censor and punish political speech. But by this time the Supreme Court had finally recognized the crucial difference between espionage/treason/sabotage and political thought and speech. The Court, in most cases, did not allow the political dissidents to be punished. Again, it must be emphasized that the government attempted to punish these people not for what they did, but because what they said or published "offended" the sense of nationalism, patriotism, and national unity in a time of war.

One example of such censorship concerned Julian Bond, an outspoken civil rights activist. Several months after being elected to the Georgia House of Representatives, in 1965, Bond made certain statements regarding the government's policies in Viet Nam and the operation of the Selective Service laws. Bond was quoted as saying:

I think it is sorta hypocritical for us to maintain that we are fighting for liberty in other places and we are not guaranteeing liberty to citizens inside the continental United States. . . . I think that the fact that the United States Government fights a war in Viet Nam, I don't think that I as a second class citizen of the United States have a requirement to support that war. I think my responsibility is to oppose things that I think are wrong if they are in Viet Nam or New York, or Chicago, or Atlanta, or wherever.

The Georgia House of Representatives did not appreciate Bond's remarks—the house thought the comments, and thus Bond himself, were disloyal—and Bond was denied his seat. The Supreme Court did not sanction this exclusion (*Bond v. Floyd**), seeing that Bond was punished only for speech, and ordered the Georgia house to seat Bond.

A Baltimore court convicted a group of anti-war protesters under a disorderly conduct statute for having a peaceful demonstration and for carrying placards with the slogans "Make Love Not War" and "Peasant Emancipation, Not Escalation." The jury convicted them after the trial judge defined "disorderly conduct" for it: "Disorderly conduct is the doing or saying or both of that which offends, disturbs, incites or tends to incite a number of people gathered in the same area. It is conduct of such nature as to affect the peace and quiet of persons who may witness it and who may be disturbed or provoked to resentment because of it." The Supreme Court (*Bachellar v. Maryland**) sliced right to the heart of the matter when it reversed the convictions: It saw that the protesters were convicted not for "disorderly conduct," but because the message on the placards "offended," "disturbed," and "provoked to resentment." The content of the ideas was being punished by Maryland, and the Supreme Court ruled that political offensive ideas have the same degree of First Amendment protection as do politically innocuous ideas.

Three public school pupils in Des Moines, Iowa, were suspended from school for wearing black arm bands as a symbolic protest against the government's policies in Viet Nam. There was no evidence that the arm bands had provoked any disorder or disturbance: The arm bands represented symbolic speech without any accompanying conduct. The students found an ally in the Supreme Court (*Tinker v. Des Moines School District**), and the Des Moines authorities were ordered to reinstate the students and not to interfere with the wearing of the arm bands. Justice Fortas delivered the majority opinion of the Court:

School officials do not possess absolute authority over their students. Students in school as well as out of school are "persons" under our Constitution. They are possessed of fundamental rights which the State must respect, just as they themselves must respect their obligations to the State. . . . They may not be confined to the expression of those sentiments that are officially approved . . . [and] school officials cannot suppress "expressions of feelings with which they do not wish to contend."

Certain military regulations prohibited the wearing of military uniforms by civilians unless used for a "theatrical" performance or in a film. The regulations, however, read that such actors can wear a uniform "only if the portrayal does not tend to discredit that armed force" (Military Regulations, Wearing Uniforms—Non-Military Personnel*). The government attempted to use this regulation to punish someone who, while wearing a uniform, gave a sidewalk skit that clearly portrayed the army as murderers of pregnant women in Viet Nam. The Supreme Court (*Schacht v. United States**) saw the obvious: The "actor" would have been left alone by the government if he had praised the role of the military in Viet Nam, but since he spoke out against the role of the army and the country, he was liable for punishment. The Court saw this as blatant censorship over the content of political speech and reversed the conviction.

*The Pentagon Papers** concerned the now-famous attempt by the U.S. government during the Nixon administration to prevent the *New York Times* and the *Washington Post* from publishing the contents of a classified study formally entitled *History of United States Decision-Making Process on Viet Nam Policy*, but commonly referred to as *The Pentagon Papers*. The *Papers* did not contain any "secret" documents, although the government alleged that its publication would "harm the national interest" and tried to get an injunction against its publication. The Supreme Court would have nothing to do with this attempt at a prior restraint and freed the newspapers to print as they saw fit. The Court's decision was a three-paragraph per curiam decision; several justices, however, added their own concurring opinions. Justice Black, joined by Justice Douglas, made the following comments:

Now, for the first time in the 182 years since the founding of the Republic, the federal courts are asked to hold that the First Amendment does not mean what it says, but rather means that the Government can halt the publication of current news of vital importance to the people of this country. In seeking injunctions against these newspapers and in its presentation to the Court, the Executive Branch seems to have forgotten the essential purpose and history of the First Amendment. . . . The press was to serve the governed, not the governors. The Government's power to censor the press was abolished so that it could bare the secrets of government and inform the people. Only a free and unrestrained press can effectively expose deception in government. And paramount among the responsibilities of a free press is the duty to prevent any part of the government from deceiving the people and sending them off to distant lands to die of foreign fevers and foreign shot and shell. . . . The word "security" is a broad, vague generality whose contours should not be invoked to abrogate the fundamental law embodied in the First Amendment. The guarding of military and diplomatic secrets at the expense of informed representative government provides no real security for our Republic.

One anti-war activist was not as fortunate as the others, however, but his conviction rested on the assertion that it was his actual, overt conduct that was punished and not the political ideas or thoughts behind the behavior. In 1968, the Supreme Court affirmed (*United States v. O'Brien**) a conviction for burning a draft card, a violation of a statute that prohibited intentional mutilation or destruction of a draft card. The Supreme Court was careful to emphasize the difference: The defendant was punished for the overt conduct of destroying his draft card and *not* for his opposition to the war, which was behind his actions.

The above comments referred to non-military personnel, to civilians. The U.S. government most certainly did not appreciate the anti-war sentiment and seeing Jane Fonda travel to Hanoi, but the government could not repress the political dissidence. Opposition to the war in Viet Nam, however, and the expression of political blasphemy and deviance within the military itself was dealt with in an entirely different manner. The subversives within the military could be identified with ease—there were't that many of them—and the government claimed that military personnel had a special duty to proclaim loyalty. Military justice meted out draconian punishments to anyone who was opposed to the war.

An army physician received a dishonorable discharge, forfeiture of all pay and allowances, and a three-year jail term at hard labor from a court-martial for making public statements urging black enlisted men to refuse to obey orders to go to Viet Nam and referring to special forces personnel as "liars and thieves," "killers of peasants," and "murderers of women and children." The conviction was based on Article 133 of the Uniform Code of Military Justice that can punish a commissioned officer for "conduct unbecoming an officer and a gentleman." The court-martial most certainly believed that such statements were unbecoming an officer, and the Supreme Court agreed and affirmed the conviction (*Parker v. Levy**). As with most cases dealing with military personnel, the courts placed the claimed needs of morale, discipline, obedience, fighting readiness, and loyalty above the First Amendment, and the doctor learned, as did many other people before him, that political deviance is often punished quite severely.

The Uniform Code of Military Justice (Article 88) is a reincarnation of the 1798 Sedition Act: Article 88 prohibits the use of "contemptuous words" against the president of the United States and is punishable as "conduct unbecoming an officer and a gentleman." An army officer received a dishonorable discharge and one year at hard labor (*United States v. Howe**) for taking part in an antiwar demonstration and for carrying a placard that categorized President Johnson as a "fascist." It made no difference to the court-martial that the demonstration was not on military property or that the officer was not wearing his uniform or that he was off duty: The placard was "contemptuous" of the president and such speech is simply not allowed in the military.

Article 134 of the Uniform Code of Military Justice punishes "all conduct of a nature to bring discredit upon the armed forces," and one unfortunate navy man received a dishonorable discharge for bringing such discredit on the armed forces (*United States v. Priest**). It appears that he wrote and distributed some pamphlets that opposed the war in Viet Nam. The court-martial found that the publications were disloyal to the United States and he suffered the full weight of the military's interpretation of the First Amendment.

The Central Intelligence Agency (CIA) is another governmental agency for which the rights guaranteed by the First Amendment appear to have a different meaning and interpretation. Owing to the secrecy agreements that all CIA agents sign regarding the publication of classified information, the CIA has been able to exert a prior restraint on the writings of former CIA agents. The courts have consistently agreed that such pre-publication review and censorship does not violate the First Amendment.

One such example concerned the book *Decent Interval*, written by Frank W. Snepp, a former CIA agent (*Snepp v. United States**). The book was about certain CIA activities in Viet Nam, but Snepp did not submit the manuscript to the agency for pre-publication review. Snepp, however, had signed an agreement, promising that he would "not publish any information or material relating to the Agency, its activities or intelligence activities generally, either during or after the term of [his] employment without specific prior approval by the Agency." Snepp had actually promised not to divulge *any* classified information and not to publish *any* other information without pre-publication clearance.

The Supreme Court readily accepted Snepp's argument that the agreement was a prior restraint, but such a restraint, as it deals with the CIA, was permissible in view of the national interest in maintaining an effective intelligence service. The Court ruled that Snepp had breached a fiduciary obligation, and the Court then imposed a constructive trust for the government's benefit on all profits Snepp might earn from publishing the book—the profits ran into thousands of dollars.

The courts, as noted above, have been consistent in allowing prior restraints and prohibitions on publishing when the CIA is involved, as can also be seen in the cases of *United States v. Marchetti** and in 1983, *McGehee v. Casey.** Both these cases involved the same principle: The CIA has the right to demand pre-publication review and censorship of any material a former agent may wish to write.

The 1980s have witnessed a new assault—again, in the name of national security—on the rights guaranteed by the First Amendment. The Reagan administration apparently did not believe that a full-scale dissemination of political information was of any benefit and that democracy did not require an informed population. As Floyd Abrams wrote in "The New Effort to Control Information" (*New York Times Sunday Magazine*, September 25, 1983, pp. 22–28, 72–73), the Reagan administration has:

(1) Consistently sought to limit the scope of the Freedom of Information Act*; (2) Barred the entry into the country of foreign speakers, including Hortensia Allende, widow of Chilean President Salvador Allende, because of concern about what they might say; (3) Inhibited the flow of films into and even out of our borders: neither Canada's Academy Award-winning *If You Love This Planet* [categorized as "propaganda"] nor the acclaimed ABC documentary about toxic waste, *The Killing Ground*, escaped Administration disapproval; (4) Rewritten the classification system [Classified Information*] to assure that *more* rather than less information will be classified; (5) Subjected governmental officials to an unprecedented system of lifetime censorship; and (6) Flooded universities with a torrent of threats relating to their right to publish and discuss unclassified information— usually of a scientific or technological nature—on campus.

One obvious manifestation of this new secrecy was the government's role vis-à-vis the press during the U.S. invasion of Grenada. The press was not allowed access to the war zone and the news that did filter out was managed and censored by the military authorities.

The Reagan administration's policies were a bit different from the usual political censorship in the name of national security. The usual schemes severely punish the political dissidents after the speech or publication; Reagan's schemes applied more to the withholding of government information from the public. It is more governmental secrecy and prior restraint than punishment after the fact. The process may be different, but the nature of the censorship is the same: Certain ideas do not mesh with the current accepted views of national unity and national security and such speech and press must be limited. The United States has, beginning with the 1798 Sedition Act and continuing well into the 1980s with the Reagan administration, insisted that the claims of national security take precedence over the rights guaranteed in the First Amendment.

COMMUNITY CENSORSHIP: SPEECH, PRESS, AND PUBLIC ORDER/SAFETY

A second type of censorship over speech and press can be termed "community censorship"—restrictions on the free exercise of First Amendment rights in order to maintain public safety and public order. Of the four categories of censorship discussed in this essay, it is only with this second type that Justice Jackson's fear of anarchy without liberty and order is present. With this category, governmental authorities attempt to regulate, censor, suppress, or punish speech and press on the ground that such expression, rightly or wrongly, will lead to a disruption in the social fabric, will incite to riot and violence, or will prevent the orderly maintenance of public services.

It is with this type of censorship that the concepts of "time-place-manner" restrictions and "public forums" apply. The courts have consistently allowed various restrictions on the exercise of First Amendment rights if such restrictions are based on a valid time-place-manner rationale. This term relates to the circumstances of the speech or press: A political candidate most certainly has the right to use a marching band complete with dancing elephants to publicize his or her candidacy; a municipality has the power to prevent the use of such a band in a residential area at 3:00 A.M. People most certainly have the right to distribute pamphlets to passersby; a municipality has the power to restrict the location of such distribution in order to maintain the sidewalks for pedestrian traffic.

The term "public forum" concerns those places that are usually considered open to the public, and in general, the exercise of First Amendment rights in such forums cannot be made a crime. But the fact that property is publicly owned does not necessarily turn it into a public forum; military bases, jails, courtrooms, transit system cars are not totally open to free speech and press. But most other public places—parks, sidewalks, streets, the doorbell or knocker on a private residence, the area around public buildings—are public forums and, in the absence of valid time-place-manner restrictions, are open to individuals to pursue their First Amendment rights.

As noted above, one reason employed in community censorship is the view that such speech or press will incite to violence and riot and thus can be restrained before the fact; another facet of community censorship is the punishment of speech or press if such expression did, in fact, lead to violence or incite a riot. One such example of a prior restraint on First Amendment freedoms, a restraint based on a fear by governmental authorities that the speech would incite to violence, happened in Philadelphia in 1968.

In the aftermath of the assassination of Martin Luther King, Jr., the mayor of Philadelphia, James Tate, declared a state of emergency that, among other provisions, prohibited the gathering of more than twelve people in any public place. Several people were arrested for violating this measure: They were arrested and convicted *not* for any violent conduct, but because they were engaged in peaceful picketing, petitioning, speechmaking in public parks, and similar First Amendment activities. The Pennsylvania court, fully aware of the volatile situation at the time, did not see the police actions as a violation of the First Amendment (*Commonwealth of Pennsylvania v. Stotland**). The court explained its reasons with the following comments, reasons that the Supreme Court also thought were justified because the Supreme Court refused to hear an appeal of the convictions:

The question posed relates to the power of the State to impose time, size and area limitations upon peaceful public assemblies. A State may under its police powers regulate these aspects of assembly although the conduct which is the subject of regulation is intertwined with expression. . . . In ordinary times and at ordinary places, large public assemblies, especially for the purpose of peacefully communicating controversial ideas and minority viewpoints, must be given the greatest possible protection. However, in the highly charged atmosphere prevailing when the danger of a large scale riot is present, large public assemblies, although peaceful to all appearances, may inflame passions or promote clashes between persons or groups with divergent views and ignite the violence which may quickly become a full scale riot. The purpose of the limitation upon assembly is to eliminate the possibility of these dangerous confrontations at times and places where there is a clear and present danger of a large scale riot. The effect of the limitation is merely to delay assemblies until they can be held without endangering the entire community.

Another example of restricting speech in order to prevent an anticipated riot concerned a person who disobeyed a court restraining order not to interfere with the court's desegregation order (*Kasper v. Brittain**). The person was convicted for contempt of court when he made a speech inciting people to disobey the court order. An appeals court affirmed the conviction, believing that the prevention of violence took precedence of the man's First Amendment right to free speech. The court made the following comments:

The right to speak is not absolute and may be regulated to accomplish other legitimate objectives of the government. The First Amendment does not confer the right to persuade others to violate the law. The speech here enjoined was clearly calculated to cause a violation of law and speech of that character is not within the protection of the First Amendment. [The speech] . . . was not a mere exposition of ideas. It was advocacy of immediate action to accomplish an illegal result. . . . The clear and present danger test is here met by the mob violence that followed the urgings of the appellant. Danger that calls for the presence of the State Patrol and the National Guard, with the use of bayonets and tear gas, is, we think, within the narrowest limits of the concept and cries aloud for such court action as was here taken.

The two examples above notwithstanding, finding a general standard that the courts apply to such situations is difficult. The Supreme Court heard two cases, one in 1949 (*Terminiello v. Chicago**) and the other in 1951 (*Feiner v. New York**), that dealt with speech and incitement to violence, but the Court, in rather similar circumstances, reached opposite conclusions.

Arthur Terminiello, a fascist defrocked Catholic priest, gave a speech in Chicago under the auspices of the Christian Veterans of America. The hall was filled to capacity and there was a large crowd milling outside. The speech was an anti-Semitic fascist diatribe and the crowd became angry and turbulent. Terminiello was then arrested, tried, and convicted for disturbing the peace, an ordinance defined by the trial judge as any behavior that "stirs the public to anger, invites dispute, brings about a condition of unrest, or creates a disturbance." Terminiello's speech most certainly stirred the public to anger and created disturbances, but the Supreme Court reversed the conviction on the ground that the state cannot punish someone whose speech "invites dispute" or "stirs people to anger," for in the Court's view, that is the very essence of speech and the communication of ideas. The Court did not see any clear and present danger in the situation, although this was not a unanimous view. It was in this case that Justice Jackson expressed his fears about anarchy:

This Court has gone far toward accepting the doctrine that civil liberty means the removal of all restraints from these crowds and that all local attempts to maintain order are impairments of the liberty of the citizen. The choice is not between order and liberty. It is between liberty with order and anarchy without either. There is danger that, if the Court does not temper its doctrinaire logic with a little practical wisdom, it will convert the constitutional Bill of Rights into a suicide pact.

The Supreme Court reversed itself two years later when it affirmed a conviction (*Feiner v. New York*) for breach of the peace of someone who made an equally intemperate speech in Syracuse. The speech caused some pushing and shoving in the crowd, and one listener even said to a police officer, "If you don't get that son of a bitch off, I will go over and get him off there myself." The police then ordered the speaker to stop speaking; he was arrested when he refused. Rather than approaching this case as one in which the police should have protected the speaker from the threats of the crowd, the Court reasoned that the speech was leading to violence and thus affirmed the conviction. Chief Justice Vinson stated that the state has the power to prevent and punish speech when it appears likely that riot or disorder is imminent and that the Court will respect "the interest of the community in maintaining peace and order on its streets."

The power of municipalities to regulate First Amendment activities, activities such as parades and mass meetings, by requiring permits or licenses before such activity can take place in public forums (parks, streets, sidewalks) has been affirmed time and again by the Supreme Court. The procedural nature of the permit/license scheme is often struck down but not the substantive issue of the permit itself. That is to say, if the courts perceive that the permit scheme is only a guise to censor or prevent speech and press, the scheme is usually invalidated. If the scheme is seen as an impartial time-place-manner regulation, the courts usually affirm convictions of people who engaged in the First Amendment activities without the permits or licenses.

One example of a licensing scheme that the Supreme Court saw as a blatant form of government censorship involved a New York City ordinance requiring a permit before anyone could use the streets and sidewalks for religious meetings (*Kunz v. New York**). The problem with this scheme was that the permit could be revoked at any time and for any reason. The Court believed that this power of revocation gave too much discretion to the licensing authorities because they were free to revoke the permit not for any real breach of peace or for disorderly conduct, but for the simple reason that the authorities did not like the content of what was said at these meetings.

Many cities have a permit scheme before allowing mass meetings in public parks, but as above, the permits must be issued in an impartial manner. The Supreme Court invalidated two such licensing requirements (*Niemotko v. Maryland** and *Fowler v. Rhode Island**) because it was shown that the municipal authorities issued permits as a matter of course to just about every applicant except the Jehovah's Witnesses. Such discrimination was not seen as a valid time-place-manner restriction, for the evidence showed that the licensing authorities didn't like the Jehovah's Witnesses and would not issue the required permit to use the public facility.

Licensing/permit requirements are generally upheld if the process is impartial, if the licensing authorities have no discretion over the granting or the revocation of the permit, if the content of the proposed speech is not relevant to its issuance (the question is the orderly use of the park, not the content of the speech), if the process is seen as a valid time-place-manner ordinance for the comfort, convenience, and safety of the community (*Poulos v. New Hampshire**).

An illustration of the validity of permits/licenses can be seen in *Cox v. New Hampshire.** A New Hampshire regulation required anyone who wanted to hold a parade or procession on the public streets to first obtain a license from the municipal authorities. Cox and others, Jehovah's Witnesses, marched along the sidewalks in a New Hampshire city, carrying placards with certain messages. The march was peaceful, the sidewalk was not obstructed, and there was no threat of violence. But Cox did not have the required permit because he never applied for one. He was convicted for violating the licensing ordinance and the Supreme Court affirmed the conviction. Chief Justice Hughes delivered the Court's opinion:

The sole charge against appellants was that they were taking part in a parade or procession on public streets without a permit as the statute required. . . . Civil liberties, as guaranteed by the Constitution, imply the existence of an organized society maintaining public order without which liberty itself would be lost in the excesses of unrestrained abuses. The authority of a municipality to impose regulations in order to assure the safety and convenience of the people in the use of public highways has never been regarded as inconsistent with civil liberties but rather as one of the means of safeguarding the good order upon which they ultimately depend. . . . If a municipality has authority to control the use of its public streets for parades or processions, as it undoubtedly has, it cannot be denied authority to give consideration, without unfair discrimination, to time, place and manner in relation to the other proper uses of the streets. We find it impossible to say that the limited authority conferred by the licensing provisions of the statute in question as thus construed by the state court contravened any constitutional right.

Licensing and permit requirements for the distribution of literature by individuals have been treated quite differently by the courts than have similar schemes relating to the use of public facilities by groups of people. In general, a municipality cannot require the prospective distributor to apply and receive in advance a permit or license before distributing the literature or pamphlets or handbills or circulars. There have been dozens of attempts by various localities to hinder the distribution of literature by imposing license fees and special taxes, prohibiting the ringing of doorbells, allowing total discretion to the licensing authorities whether to issue the permit, prohibiting anonymous handbills, requiring character references, and other similar provisions.

The courts have generally viewed that the distribution of literature is part and parcel of the freedom of speech and press; the First Amendment would be a hollow statement if the government could prevent the distribution of literature because freedom of press also entails freedom to circulate the information. This view was first stated in 1938 (*Lovell v. City of Griffin**), when the city of Griffin, Georgia, passed an ordinance that required permission from the city manager before anyone could distribute any pamphlets, leaflets, or circulars within the city. Alma Lovell ignored this requirement and was sentenced to fifty days in jail. The Supreme Court reversed her conviction, holding that since the ordinance was void on its face, Lovell did not have to apply for the required permission. Chief Justice Hughes delivered the Court's opinion:

Legislation of the type of the ordinance in question would restore the system of license and censorship in its baldest form. The liberty of the press is not confined to newspapers and periodicals. It necessarily embraces pamphlets and leaflets. These indeed have been historic weapons in the defense of liberty, as the pamphlets of Thomas Paine and others in our own history abundantly attest. The press in its historic connotation comprehends every sort of publication which affords a vehicle of information and opinion. The ordinance cannot be saved because it relates to distribution and not to publication. "Liberty of circulating is as essential to that freedom as liberty of publishing; indeed, without the circulation, the publication would be of little value."

CONSTITUTIONAL CENSORSHIP: SPEECH, PRESS, AND CONFLICTING RIGHTS

As mentioned at the beginning of this Introductory Essay, the rights guaranteed by the First Amendment may be in a "preferred position," but they are not absolutes. Individuals have constitutionally protected rights other than speech and press and when the exercise of First Amendment rights clashes with the exercise of these other rights, the courts must necessarily attempt to balance them. The courts are hesitant to use general standards here, and each case is usually approached on an individual basis in order to balance and accommodate the conflicting claims.

Some of these conflicting rights can be seen as (1) the right to protect children from what would be, for adults, acceptable; (2) the right to a fair trial and the orderly administration of the judicial process; (3) the right of individuals not to be libeled, slandered, or defamed; (4) the right to individual privacy; and (5) the right not to be verbally abused or to be subject to personal slurs and epithets.

The First Amendment guarantees concerning free speech and press do not always apply totally when the speech or press is directed at children and minors. The Supreme Court has ruled in several instances that minors can be treated differently than adults; there have been an equal number of situations in which the Court has ruled that, although the specific regulation has the honorable purpose of protecting minors, it either violates the minors' First Amendment rights or violates the rights of adults.

One example in which the assumed protection of minors took precedence over First Amendment rights was *Prince v. Massachusetts** in 1944. A Massachusetts statute provided that no minor (boys under twelve or girls under eighteen) could sell or distribute literature on the public streets and also made it unlawful for any adult to permit a minor to sell or distribute the publications. That the distribution of literature is protected by the First Amendment is not at issue here; this case concerned the clash between this First Amendment right and the state's view of what constituted the best interests of children. Prince, a Jehovah's Witness, was convicted under the statute for allowing a minor to distribute religious publications and the Supreme Court affirmed the conviction. The Court felt that the state's power to regulate the activities of children—at least in this case—took precedence over any First Amendment claim to freedom of speech and the press. Justice Rutledge delivered the Court's opinion:

Parents may be free to become martyrs themselves. But it does not follow they are free, in identical circumstances, to make martyrs of their children before they have reached the age of full and legal discretion when they can make that choice for themselves. Massachusetts has determined that an absolute prohibition, though one limited to streets and public places and to the incidental uses proscribed, is necessary to accomplish its legitimate objectives. Its power to attain them is broad enough to reach these peripheral instances in which the parent's supervision may reduce but cannot eliminate entirely the ill effects of the prohibited conduct. We think that with reference to the public proclaiming of religion, upon the streets and in other similar public places, the power of the state to control the conduct of children reaches beyond the scope of its authority over adults, as is true in the case of other freedoms, and the rightful boundary of its power has not been crossed in this case.

The "rightful boundary" of the state to protect children and minors was also seen not to be crossed when, in 1978, the Supreme Court sanctioned a Federal Communications Commission's (FCC) reprimand to a New York City radio station for having broadcast an "indecent" but not "obscene" program at a time when children were likely to be in the listening audience ["Filthy Words"*]. The radio station had broadcast George Carlin's "Filthy Words" monologue at about 2:00 P.M. in the afternoon and a listener complained that his young son heard the "indecent" broadcast. Carlin's monologue was not "obscene," but the FCC and the courts characterized it as "indecent": Carlin's monologue started with the comment that he was going to talk about the words one couldn't say over the air (Carlin was not at issue here; he gave his monologue in a night club—the radio station broadcast a tape recording), and then he proceeded to list those words (fuck, shit, piss, cunt, tits, cocksucker, motherfucker, fart, turd, cock, twat, ass) and repeated them over and over in various colloquialisms. The Supreme Court agreed that such broadcasting should not be done in the afternoon, when children are likely to have unsupervised access to the radio; such a program could be aired at night, when, presumably, parents could exercise some control over the listening habits of their children.

A 1982 Supreme Court decision (*New York v. Ferber**) established that different criteria can be applied to sexual activity of minors than are applied to adults. In an attempt to control the problem of child pornography, a New York statute prohibited the use of minors in any sexual performance and made it unlawful for anyone to distribute any material depicting minors engaged in such activity; the sexual conduct prohibited was just about all types and it need not have been legally "obscene" under the standards used by the courts. The Supreme Court affirmed a conviction under this statute, holding that it did not violate the First Amendment. Several opinions were filed in this case, but the thread of general agreement was that states could prohibit certain types of activity involving children notwithstanding the fact that the activity in question is not seen as "obscene" under any of the tests or standards for obscenity.

The majority of the Court ruled that states are entitled to great leeway in the regulation of the depiction of children engaged in sexual activities for the following reasons: (1) The legislative judgment that the use of children as subjects of sexual materials is harmful to the psychological, emotional, and mental health of the child, easily passes muster under the First Amendment; (2) the Miller Standard* for determining what is legally obscene is not a satisfactory solution to the child pornography problem; and (3) the value of permitting live performances and photographic reproductions of children engaged in lewd exhibitions is modest at best.

But as noted above, the courts have not accepted many governmental schemes to censor or repress speech or press in the name of the protection of minors or, in terms that are usually employed, to prevent the corruption of morals of youth. The state of Michigan had a statute that prohibited the sale of any book to any person—not just the sale to children but the sale to *any* person, including adults— that contained language "tending to the corruption of the morals of youth." The Supreme Court, in *Butler v. Michigan*,* did not accept this, seeing it to be a blatant form of censorship. Justice Frankfurter delivered the now-famous decision in this case:

It is clear on the record that [Butler] was convicted because Michigan . . . made it an offense for him to make available for the general reading public . . . a book that the trial judge found to have a potentially deleterious influence upon youth. The State insists that, by thus quarantining the general reading public against books not too rugged for grown men and women in order to shield juvenile innocence, it is exercising its power to promote the general welfare. Surely, this is to burn the house to roast the pig. . . . The incidence of this enactment is to reduce the adult population of Michigan to reading what is only fit for children. It thereby arbitrarily curtails one of those liberties of the individual . . . that history has attested as the indispensable conditions for the maintenance and progress of a free society.

The Rhode Island state legislature created a Commission on Youth Morality in the late 1950s whose mandate was to "educate the public concerning any book . . . or other thing containing obscene, indecent or impure language, or manifestly tending to the corruption of the youth and to investigate and recommend the prosecution of all violations." The commission soon had more than one hundred publications on its "objectionable" list; the commission then notified distributors and retailers that if the offending publications were not withdrawn, it would recommend the institution of legal proceedings. The Supreme Court, in 1963 (*Bantam Books, Inc. v. Sullivan**), ruled that the entire scheme was an unconstitutional administrative censorship attempt. The Court offered the following comment: "Although the Commission's supposed concern is limited to youthful readers, the 'cooperation' it seeks from distributors invariably entails the complete suppression of the listed publications; adult readers are equally deprived of the opportunity to purchase the publications in the State."

The right to a fair trial and the orderly administration of justice within the courtroom are additional constitutionally protected rights that often clash with the First Amendment guarantees of free speech and press. As noted above, the courts are hesitant to apply blanket standards over such cases, and each is evaluated on its own merits. One such clash in this area (although it also dealt with the protection of minors and individual privacy) concerned a Massachusetts statute that mandated the judge to close the courtroom to everyone—including the media—except those who were parties to the case when the case concerned a minor involved as either the victim or the assailant in any sex crime. The Supreme Court saw this blanket exclusion as an invalid abridgment on the right to a free press, and that in this particular situation, the First Amendment took precedence over any claims to privacy or the protection of minors because public access to trials was an accepted doctrine ever since colonial times (*Globe Newspaper Company v. Superior Court**).

The First Amendment often clashes with the orderly administration of justice, both within and without the courtroom, and judges have frequently resorted to the contempt power to ensure such orderly administration. Courts of review, however, have usually insisted on an immediate, imminent, clear, and present danger to the administration of justice; if such a danger is lacking, the First Amendment usually receives priority. The relationship between the First Amendment and the right to an impartial and orderly administration of justice was well stated by Justice Reed when the Supreme Court reversed (*Pennekamp v. Florida**) a conviction for contempt:

Whether the threat to the impartial and orderly administration of justice must be a clear and present or a grave and immediate danger, a real and substantial threat, one which is close and direct or one which disturbs the court's sense of fairness depends upon a choice of words. Under any one of the phrases, reviewing courts are brought in cases of this type to appraise the comment on a balance between the desirability of free discussion and the necessity for fair adjudication, free from interruption of its processes. Free discussion of the problems of society is a cardinal principle of Americanism—a principle which all are zealous to preserve. Discussion that follows the termination of a case may be inadequate to emphasize the danger to public welfare of supposedly wrongful judicial conduct. It does not follow that public comment of every character upon pending trials or legal proceedings may be as free as a similar comment after complete disposal of the litigation. Between the extremes there are areas of discussion which an understanding writer will appraise in the light of the effect on himself and of the public of creating a clear and present danger to fair and orderly judicial administration. Courts must have power to protect the interests of prisoners and litigants before them from unseemly efforts to pervert judicial action. In the borderline instances where it is difficult to say upon which side the alleged offense falls, we think the specific freedom of public comment should weigh heavily against a possible tendency to influence pending cases. Freedom of discussion should be given the widest range compatible with the essential requirement of the fair and orderly administration of justice.

In one of the most publicized cases (*Sheppard v. Maxwell**), the Supreme Court ruled that the defendant's right to a fair and impartial trial was violated by the activities of the press. Sam Sheppard's trial took place in a circus-like atmosphere, with the judge either unwilling or unable to control the excesses of the press within the courtroom. The Court ruled that the massive, pervasive, and prejudicial publicity prevented Sheppard from receiving a fair trial and ordered Sheppard's release unless he was tried again within a reasonable time. The Court's opinion was two-fold: The first part extolled the virtues of a free press and reiterated that the proceedings in a courtroom belonged in the public domain; the second part castigated the media's (and the judge's) activities that led to the circus-like atmosphere. The Court, in ruling that in this particular case the right to a fair trial took precedence over the free exercise of First Amendment rights, made the following comments:

We have consistently required that the press have a free hand, even though we sometimes deplored its sensationalism. But the Court has also pointed out that legal trials are not like elections, to be won through the use of the meeting-hall, the radio, and the newspaper. ... We [previously] set aside a federal conviction where the jurors were exposed through news accounts to information that was not admitted at trial. We held that the prejudice from such material may indeed be greater than when it is part of the prosecution's evidence for it is then not tempered by protective procedures. ... With his life at stake, it is not requiring too much that [Sheppard] be tried in an atmosphere undisturbed by so huge a wave of public passion [generated and abetted by the media].

The First Amendment guarantees the right of free speech and press; individuals also have the right *not* to be libeled, slandered, or defamed by the exercise of these rights. The Supreme Court has created two categories of people in this area: public figures*/public officials* and private individuals. The application of the libel law differs according to the type of person making the complaint; it is more difficult for a public official or a public figure to prosecute successfully for libel or slander. Public officials are those people who occupy a decision-making position at any level of government; public figures are those people who are well known or who have injected themselves into public controversy (all candidates for political office are considered either public officials or public figures).

The *New York Times* Rule,* announced by the Supreme Court in its 1964 *New York Times Company v. Sullivan* decision, is the test or standard applied in cases dealing with public officials or public figures. This rule holds that the constitutional guarantee of a free press and of free speech requires a public official or a public figure who sues for libel or defamation to prove malice on the part of the defendant. Malice, in this context, is the publishing of the material knowing it to be false or with a reckless disregard of whether it was true or false. The law with respect to libel and defamation of public officials and public figures was much simpler before this 1964 decision—libelous utterances were not protected by the First Amendment. The rationale for the Court's 1964 view started from the initial premise of the profound national commitment to the principle that debate on public issues should be uninhibited, robust, and wide open. Because the threat of defamation suits possesses a great potential for intrusion into the zone of protected public speech, the Court declared that the traditional principles of defamation law were incompatible with the First Amendment.

The following examples represent two such libel cases decided under the *New*

York Times Rule and the need to prove express malice when dealing with a public figure or public official. Both cases upheld the libel judgment: the first because the public official was able to prove express malice and the second because the person defamed was not a public official/public figure and thus did not have to prove express malice.

During the 1964 presidential campaign, Ralph Ginzburg published an article that severely questioned Senator Barry Goldwater's sanity and mental capacity. Goldwater then brought suit, alleging that the article was written with "express malice" and subjected him to "public scorn, contempt, obloquy and ridicule" (*Goldwater v. Ginzburg**). The courts found that Ginzburg, indeed, had published the article with a reckless disregard of whether the information contained in it was true or false (some of the material was shown to have been fabricated) and Ginzburg stood convicted of employing express malice.

The second case also had the defendant judged guilty, but here the requirement of express malice was not needed because the plaintiff, a university professor, was neither a public official nor a public figure (the defendant was most certainly a public official). The case concerned Senator William Proxmire and some of his comments made in relation to his "Golden Fleece" awards (*Hutchinson v. Proxmire**). Proxmire's "Awards" publicize what he thinks is wasteful spending by governmental agencies and one such award was given Professor Ronald Hutchinson. Hutchinson received some $500,000 in government research grants to study the aggressive behavior of monkeys, and Proxmire made several nasty comments about the research and Hutchinson himself (e.g., "The good doctor has made a fortune from his monkeys and in the process made a monkey out of the American taxpayer"). The court ruled that Hutchinson was not a public figure/public official and that express malice was not required. Proxmire was protected by the Speech and Debate Clause for whatever comments he might have made on the floor of the Senate, but this protection did not extend to his defamation of Hutchinson in comments contained in various newsletters and interviews.

The right to individual privacy is another constitutionally protected right that often clashes with the First Amendment; here, as above, the courts are hesitant to apply a standard and attempt to evaluate each situation in order to balance the conflicting claims. Two examples follow: One represents a situation in which the Supreme Court ruled that the privacy interests of an individual took precedence over another individual's speech and press rights; the second represents a situation in which the courts ruled that speech and press rights outweighed privacy interests.

The first case, *Lehman v. City of Shaker Heights,** decided in 1974, concerned Harry J. Lehman, a candidate for Ohio state representative. He was refused available advertising space on the city's rapid transit system; the refusal of space was based on a municipal policy of not allowing any political advertising but permitting other types of public transit advertising. Lehman brought suit, arguing that this exclusion violated his First Amendment rights, but the Supreme Court did not agree. The Court ruled that the transit passengers were a captive audience and were using the system only for public transportation. The passengers brought with them a "zone of privacy," and if the municipality wanted to shield them from political ads, it was free to do so. In an uncharacteristic departure from strong and traditional support of the freedoms of speech and press, Justice Douglas agreed with this decision: "Lehman is free to express his views to a willing audience but has no constitutional right to force his message upon a captive audience which uses public transportation not as a place for discussion, but only as a means of transport."

The second case of an obvious clash between the First Amendment and the right to individual privacy and dignity concerned the film *Titicut Follies.** This film is a documentary about the conditions in a Massachusetts state prison for the criminally insane, and it contains several scenes of "mentally incompetent patients in the nude and in the most personal and private situations." The Massachusetts attorney general ruled that the film constituted an invasion of the patients' privacy and tried to prevent further exhibition of it. A trial judge agreed and ruled that the film was an "unwarranted intrusion into the right of privacy of each inmate pictured, degrading those persons in a manner clearly not warranted by any legitimate public concern," and that it was the responsibility of the state to "protect the right of privacy of those committed to its custody." The Massachusetts Supreme Judicial Court, however, did not sanction this blanket prohibition against the film's exhibition. The court recognized that it was an invasion of privacy, but that the concerned public had a right to know about the conditions in the prison. The Massachusetts court attempted to reach a balance, a compromise: The film could be shown only to audiences having a professional interest in penology and mental illness (legislators, judges, lawyers, sociologists, social workers, doctors, psychiatrists, etc.); it could not be shown to satisfy "general public curiosity." The Supreme Court refused to hear the case, thus affirming the compromise reached by the Massachusetts court. In a dissent filed from the Court's refusal to hear the case, Justice Harlan went to the heart of the matter:

[*Titicut Follies*] is at once a scathing indictment of the inhumane conditions that prevailed at the time of the film and an undeniable infringement of the privacy of the inmates filmed, who are shown nude and engaged in acts that would unquestionably embarrass an individual of normal sensitivity.... [The film highlighted the conflict] between the constitutional commitment to the principle that debate on public issues should be uninhibited, robust, and wide-open and the individual's interest in privacy and dignity.

Although not explicit in the Constitution, the courts have generally ruled that another right that individuals have is the right not to be subjected to verbal abuse and slurs. This doctrine was announced by the Supreme Court in 1942, in *Chaplinsky v. New Hampshire*,* when the Court affirmed a conviction for the use of "fighting words." A New Hampshire statute made it unlawful for any person to address "any offensive, derisive or annoying word to any other person [or] to call him by any offensive or derisive name." It appears that Chaplinsky called certain individuals "God damned racketeers" and "Fascists." Justice Murphy delivered the Court's opinion in this now-famous case:

It is well understood that the right of free speech is not absolute at all times and under all circumstances. There are certain well-defined and narrowly limited classes of speech, the prevention and punishment of which have never been thought to raise any Constitutional problem. These include the lewd and obscene, the profane, the libelous, and the insulting or "fighting" words—those which by their very utterance inflict injury....It has been well observed that such utterances are no essential part of any exposition of ideas, and are of such slight social value as a step to truth than any benefit that may be derived from them is clearly outweighed by the social interest in order and morality. Resort to epithets or personal abuse is not in any proper sense communication of information or opinion safeguarded by the Constitution.

The doctrine of "fighting words"—abusive personal insults and epithets— was advanced in 1942 with Chaplinsky, but later decisions by the Supreme Court have narrowed the meaning of this category of unprotected speech. "God damned racketeer" and "damned Fascist" may have been seen to be fighting words in 1942, but considering what the Court has subsequently ruled *not* to be fighting words, one can only surmise that the category no longer exists. The following abusive insults and epithets have not been seen to be fighting words: "Fuck the Draft" (*Cohen v. California**); "Get out of my way, you fucking prick-ass cops" (*Cincinnati v. Karlan**); "You God-damn mother-fucker police" (*Lewis v. City of New Orleans**); "Mother-fucking fascist pig cops" (*Brown v. Oklahoma**); and "Look at the chicken shit mother fucker hide over there behind that sign" (*Lucas v. Arkansas**).

One last example of this clash of rights and interests concerned the right of free speech against the rights of individuals to be free from ethnic and religious slurs and hatred. The crux of this controversy (*Smith v. Collin**) in 1978 was that Frank Collin, who was then head of the American Nazi party, wanted to strut down the streets of Skokie, Illinois, with his men dressed in the full regalia of the Nazis with swastikas and the Death Head; Skokie had a large Jewish population, many of whom were survivors of the Nazi extermination camps in Europe. The village of Skokie hastily passed several ordinances that would have had the effect of preventing the Nazi parade. The ordinances were declared unconstitutional as a violation of the First Amendment. Collin and his Nazi friends eventually marched but not in Skokie; Chicago was more amenable to the parade.

The Supreme Court refused to hear the various appeals in this long and confusing controversy, but Justice Blackmun offered the following comments in his dissent to the refusal to grant a hearing:

These facts and this chronology demonstrate, I believe, the pervading sensitivity of the litigation. On the one hand, we have precious First Amendment rights vigorously asserted and an obvious concern that, if those asserted rights are not recognized, the precedent of a ''hard'' case might offer a justification for repression in the future. On the other hand, we are presented with evidence of a potentially explosive and dangerous situation, enflamed by unforgettable recollections of traumatic experiences in the second world conflict. . . . The present case affords the Court an opportunity to consider whether. . .there is no limit whatsoever to the exercise of free speech. There indeed may be no such limit, but when citizens assert, not casually but with deep conviction, that the proposed demonstration is scheduled at a place and in a manner that is taunting and overwhelmingly offensive to the citizens of that place, that assertion, uncomfortable though it may be for judges, deserves to be examined.

MORAL CENSORSHIP: SPEECH, PRESS, AND SIN

Moral censorship is different than political censorship or censorship in the name of public safety/public order or censorship in order to protect another equally valid and constitutionally protected right. It does not entail any claim—however specious and imagined or real and imminent—that the thought, word, or press will harm vital national security interests, that it will disturb public order by inciting a riot, or that it encroaches on other individual rights. This type of censorship, moreover, has nothing to do with Justice Jackson's fears of anarchy.

Moral censorship takes place because the very content of the specific expression or communication ''offends''—it offends people's sense of morality, their sensitivities; that the content is ''improper'' or ''indecent'' or ''vile'' or ''corrupting'' or ''disgusting'' or ''filthy'' or ''lewd'' or ''lascivious'' or ''obscene''; that ''pure-minded'' and ''right-thinking'' people should not have to see or hear or read or even think about the information.

But moral censorship goes far beyond the individual's not liking the content or being disgusted by it. There would be relatively few problems if these individuals simply avoided speech and press by not reading the book or by not seeing the film: One can always avert the eye and it is a short trip from the mailbox to the trash can. But because this area of censorship deals with morality and sin, such people cannot be content to avoid the material themselves; the very knowledge that some other person, somewhere, may have access to such information or is in contact with such speech or press is as harmful to their psyches as if they themselves were immersed in the literature.

Moral censorship goes beyond the individual's proclivities and extends to the attempt to prevent everyone else from coming into contact with such vile and disgusting ideas. The entire history of U.S. anti-vice movements, such as the New York Society for the Suppression of Vice and the Boston-based New England Watch and Ward Society (Comstockery*), illustrates this censorship activity. It was not sufficient for Anthony Comstock (and his modern-day counterparts) to be opposed to what he considered filth and sin; his moral standards had to be extended to everyone. This is the true nature of censorship and the mentality of the censor: the self-appointed guardians of other people's morality and the pseudo-intellectual claim of the censor that society must be protected from corrupting and vile ideas.

One such area of moral censorship and "sin" relates to religion and the view of many people that if speech or press is not "reverent" enough, it must be censored and punished. Most of the early prosecutions in England and colonial America—before the claims of national security and public safety—were for "blasphemy," "heresy," or for "sacrilegious" speech or press. This type of speech and press is no longer punished by the U.S. government, but it was not that long ago that religious sensitivities played an active role in censorship and in the repression of First Amendment rights.

One such example was *The Miracle*,* a film that New York authorities denied permission to be exhibited because it was "sacrilegious"—it "offended." This film did *not* affect national security or infringe on other people's rights or incite to riot. (This last phrase is not entirely correct: The film's opponents did resort to some rather questionable demonstrations and bomb threats.) *The Miracle* was simply, but not simplistically, a situation in which a certain group of people did not like the ideas expressed in the film, and rather than just staying away from the theaters that exhibited the film, they decided that no one else ought to see it.

The New York motion picture censorship statute required that an exhibition permit be granted before any film could be shown, and the permit had to be granted unless a film "or a part thereof is obscene, indecent, immoral, inhuman, sacrilegious, or is of such a character that its exhibition would tend to corrupt morals or incite to crime." *The Miracle* received an exhibition permit but was promptly attacked as "a sacrilegious and blasphemous mockery of Christian religious truth" by the Legion of Decency,* a private Catholic organization dedicated to ridding the motion picture industry of filth, corruption, and immorality. Francis Cardinal Spellman condemned the picture, calling on all people with a sense of decency to stay away. The right-thinking people did more than just stay away; the theater was picketed several times (one such demonstration had more than 1,000 persons), and there were even two bomb threats that forced the theater's evacuation. The New York Board of Regents then had second thoughts and reviewed the film again; it concluded that *The Miracle* was indeed "sacrilegious" and ordered the immediate revocation of its exhibition permit. The distributor of the film appealed this decision, and the Supreme Court, in 1952, ruled that a film could not be censored for any alleged sacrilegious content. Justice Clark commented that "it is not the business of government in our nation to suppress real or imagined attacks upon a particular religious doctrine, whether they appear in publications, speeches, or motion pictures."

Another intolerant thread running through moral censorship in this general area of religion is the anti-evolutionist, anti-Darwin school of fundamentalism, which believes in a literal interpretation of the book of Genesis. It is not a question of these people's right to believe in anything they wish to consider as the Truth and to instruct their children about the errors and falsity of competing views; the problem arises when these people capture the machinery of the government and employ the police power to censor—and to punish—any mention of competing views. It is not sufficient that these individuals protect their own children from falsehood; everyone else's children must also be shielded.

This controversy has existed ever since Charles Darwin published his *Origin of Species*; its contemporary incarnation is the bitter antagonism between the school of thought termed "scientific creationism" and the new version of the Devil, the Communist secular humanists. The classic case in this area is the infamous 1927 "monkey trial," also known as *Scopes v. State.** John Scopes was convicted and fined $100 (his fine was later rescinded) in Tennessee for teaching "a certain theory that denied the story of the divine creation of man, as taught in the Bible, and did teach instead thereof that man had descended from a lower order of animals." The Tennessee Supreme Court affirmed Scopes' conviction, seeing nothing wrong with the anti-evolution statute:

Our school authorities are...quite free to determine how they shall act in this state of the law. Those in charge of the educational affairs of the state are men and women of discernment and culture. If they believe that the teaching of the [theory of evolution is not to be done in Tennessee, this court will accept their judgment].

The anti-evolution philosophy did not end with Scopes' conviction. The Tennessee statute was not repealed until 1967. Approximately twenty state legislatures entertained anti-evolution statutes in the 1920s; one such statute, in Arkansas, lasted until 1968. The Arkansas statute was finally declared a violation of the First Amendment by the Supreme Court in 1968 (*Epperson v. Arkansas**). The Court record in the *Epperson* case contained some revealing advertisements surrounding the original adoption of the Arkansas statute in 1928, information that clearly illustrates the linkage between this form of censorship, religion, and the need to protect everyone's children:

THE BIBLE OR ATHEISM, WHICH? All atheists favor evolution. If you agree with atheism vote against Act No. 1. If you agree with the Bible vote for Act No. 1. Shall conscientious church members be forced to pay taxes to support teachers to teach evolution which will undermine the faith of their children?

Now let the mothers and fathers of our state that are trying to raise their children in the Christian faith arise in their might and vote for this anti-evolution bill that will take it out of our tax supported schools. When they have saved the children, they have saved the state.

The children of Tennessee and Arkansas might have been affected during the period in which the above statutes were in force; a far more damaging anti-evolution censorship affected most schoolchildren throughout the United States from 1974 to 1984. The Texas State Textbook Committee,* the agency that approves all the textbooks for all the public schools in Texas, is a powerful and influential force in textbook publishing: It spends about $65 million a year on texts and the state is the fourth largest unified market in the country. In 1974, the committee notified publishers that, if they wanted their books to be considered for adoption, the following two guidelines had to be observed: (1) "Textbooks that treat the theory of evolution shall identify it as only one of several explanations of the origins of humankind and avoid limiting young people in their search for meanings of their human existence" and (2) "Each textbook must carry a statement on an introductory page that any material on evolution included in the book is clearly presented as theory rather than fact."

In light of these guidelines and in view of maintaining the Texas market, several publishers watered down their coverage of evolution. This satisfied the Texans, but the same books were also distributed throughout the rest of the United States, thus inflicting fundamentalist beliefs on other, unconsenting people. These guidelines were finally rescinded in April 1984.

Moral censorship in the area of religion is not limited to the above examples. Religion encompasses a whole set of moral values, world outlook and behavior, views toward "corruption" and "proper development"; it is an entire philosophy of life and there have been many censorship activities directed at speech and press that are perceived to be antagonistic to this philosophy of life. Again, it is not sufficient for these censors to be God-fearing people; they have to put the fear of God into everyone else. One such example took place in 1952, in Marshall, Texas. The local Board of Censors refused to issue an exhibition permit for the film *Pinky** because the board thought the film was "of such character as to be prejudicial to the best interests of the people" of the city. The film was exhibited without the required permit and the exhibitor was duly convicted. The conviction was affirmed by the Court of Criminal Appeals of Texas but was subsequently reversed by the Supreme Court. The comments of the Texas judge are of interest here, for they show the linkage between censorship and a world outlook/philosophy of life, based partly on religious sensitivities. Judge Beauchamp of the Texas Court of Criminal Appeals:

If some [people] are exposed to evil, if evil it be, there is within such fact no argument that other and all evil should be strewn in the path of our youth. The desire of a great industry to reap greater fruits from its operations should not be indulged at the expense of Christian character, upon which America must rely for its future existence. Every boy and every girl reaching manhood or womanhood is, to an extent, the product of the community from which he comes. If the citizens of that community are divested of all power to surround them with wholesome entertainment and character building education, then their product will go forth weak indeed.

The Massachusetts legislature was so concerned about the proper observance of Sunday as the "Lord's Day" that it passed a statute requiring the commissioner of public safety to issue an opinion that any prospective public event (speeches, movies, assemblies, parades, etc.) that was to be held on a Sunday was "in keeping with the character of the day and not inconsistent with its due observance." If the event did not meet the solemnity of the day, the commissioner would not allow it to take place. This obvious prior restraint on the exercise of First Amendment rights was declared to be unconstitutional in 1955 (*Brattle Films v. Commissioner of Public Safety**).

Even as recently as 1982 have there been censorship attempts on grounds that the speech or press offended religious sensitivities. The Board of Education of the Island Trees Union Free School District, in New York, attempted to remove several books from the school libraries. Among the books were *Slaughterhouse Five*, by Kurt Vonnegut, Jr., and *The Fixer*, by Bernard Malamud. The board characterized these books as "anti-American, anti-Christian, anti-Semitic, and just plain filthy." The Supreme Court (*Board of Education v. Pico**) ruled, however, that the board could not simply remove books from the school library because some people thought they were "anti-Christian" and "anti-Semitic."

A second general area of moral censorship over imputed sin deals with the human body and some aspects of sex—not sex as in sexual activities as in masturbation, fellatio, cunnilingus, sodomy, bestiality, etc., but with the human body as a living organism and with human sexual biology and reproductive capacities. This entire area was (and still is) seen by so many people to be so vile and disgusting and filthy and horrible (e.g., the very mention of condoms would lead to immediate illicit sexual activities) that it has had a long history in the United States of suppression and punishment for speech and press. The moralists considered any such expression equivalent to pornography and used the police power of the state to restrict and punish the perpetrators of such abominations.

Fortunately—but this was not always true—the courts have come around to the enlightened view that human sexual biology, reproductive functions, and the emotional side of sexual development are *not* the equivalent of pornography and such speech and press are now protected by the First Amendment. Although such expression is protected, the entire subject still meets with so much revulsion and disgust that, for example, few school districts have sex education courses built into the curriculum. For most of our history, the very mention of abortion, contraception and birth control, conception and childbirth, venereal disease, sex education, homosexuality and lesbianism was seen as the first step into the immediate and total disintegration of the family and Western civilization. The government, aided and abetted by private individuals and groups, censored such expression but, as noted above, the courts slowly extended the protection of the First Amendment to such speech and press.

One such example of censorship in this area concerned a Virginia statute that made it unlawful to "encourage or prompt the processing of an abortion" by the sale or circulation of any publication. In 1975, a weekly newspaper published in Virginia carried an advertisement from a New York City organization; the ad announced that the organization would arrange low-cost abortions in accredited hospitals and clinics in New York (abortions were legal in New York in 1975 and there were no residence requirements). The editor of the Virginia newspaper was duly convicted for "encouraging" the processing of an abortion, but the Supreme Court (*Bigelow v. Virginia**) ruled that the Virginia statute violated the First Amendment and reversed the conviction.

The Court ruled that the advertisement conveyed information of potential interest and value to a diverse audience consisting of not only the readers possibly in need of the services offered, but also those concerned with the subject matter or the law of another state, and readers seeking reform in Virginia. The Court felt that an individual state does not acquire power or supervision over another state's internal affairs merely because its own citizens' welfare and health may be affected when they travel to the other state, and although a state may seek to disseminate information so as to enable its citizens to make better informed decisions when they leave, it may not bar a citizen of another state from disseminating information about an activity that is legal in that state. The opinion concluded with the remark that Virginia's interest in regulating what Virginians may hear or read about the New York services or in shielding its citizens from information about activities outside its borders was not entitled to any weight.

The Virginia statute, an attempt to prevent Virginia citizens from reading anything about abortions from any source, was changed after the 1975 decision. The statute now makes it unlawful for anyone to publish information encouraging the processing of an abortion in Virginia; information about abortions in other states cannot be punished.

The complete story of the American birth control movement, led by Margaret Sanger, is too vast to review here; it will be sufficient to say that the subject of birth control and contraception was another filthy and disgusting topic that was repressed for most of the country's history. U.S. Customs regulations (Tariff Act*) prohibit the importation into the United States of any obscene or immoral book, device, or matter (the importation of contraceptives themselves was prohibited under a separate section, although this prohibition has since been rescinded) and permit Customs to seize the offensive matter. The government must then file suit in a federal district court for a judicial determination as to the material's obscenity. If the court rules that it is not obscene, the material can then enter the United States; if it is ruled to be obscene, Customs then destroys the seized material. In 1931, a book by Marie Stopes entitled *Contraception** was seized by Customs because the inspectors determined that the book was obscene, immoral, and disgusting and, as such, was subject to destruction. District Judge Woolsey (the same judge who later would rule on James Joyce's *Ulysses*) determined that *Contraception* was not obscene and thus could be sold in the United States. Judge Woolsey's comments illustrate the views of the government censors who believed that any information about birth control and contraception was obscene and thus should be suppressed:

I have read *Contraception* and I find that it does not fall, in any respect, within these definitions of the words "obscene" or "immoral." *Contraception* is written primarily for the medical profession....It is a scientific book written with obvious seriousness and with great decency, and it gives information to the medical profession regarding the operation of birth control clinics and the instruction necessary to be given at such clinics to women who resort thereto....Such a book, although it may run counter to the views of many persons who disagree entirely with the theory underlying birth control...would not stir the sex impulses of any person with a normal mind.

   The state of Wisconsin, in the early 1930s, passed a statute that prohibited the sale of contraceptives except in a few and limited circumstances. (The original legislation wanted to prohibit birth control in toto but this failed; the prohibition against the sale of such devices was the compromise.) Coin-operated vending machines in gas station restrooms that dispensed condoms were *not* among the few permissible ways that condoms could be sold. The rest should be self-explanatory: The operator of a Milwaukee gas station had such a vending machine and the vice squad arrested him; he was duly convicted in 1935 (*State of Wisconsin v. Arnold**).

   The gas station operator's defense was that he provided the vending machine and the condoms only "for the prevention of disease" and not for the illegal purpose of selling them to prevent conception. The Wisconsin court dismissed his arguments, ruling that the condoms were being sold as contraceptive devices. Because such a sale was illegal, the gas station operator received the full penalty of the law.

   The state of Connecticut had on its books since 1879 a law that made it illegal for anyone to use contraceptives; subsequent amendments also made it illegal for anyone to give out information about birth control devices or to prescribe or distribute such devices. It was not until 1965 (*Griswold v. Connecticut**) that this statute was ruled unconstitutional. The executive director of the Planned Parenthood League of Connecticut was convicted for giving a married couple information on how to prevent conception; his conviction was affirmed by the Connecticut Supreme Court. But in 1965, the U.S. Supreme Court ruled that such information is protected by the First Amendment and that a state cannot punish someone who provides information on birth control.

   A section of the New York Education Law made it a crime for anyone to advertise or display contraceptives. The sale and use of such devices were permissible—only the advertising and display of them were illegal. It was not until 1977 (*Carey v. Population Services International**) that the Supreme Court ruled that this prohibition was unconstitutional. Justice Brennan's decision clearly shows that the state of New York thought that the very sight of condoms was so offensive that they had to be hidden under the counter and, moreover, that the sight of a condom would lead to an increase in illicit sexual behavior. Justice Brennan:

[The State of New York contends]...that advertisements of contraceptive products would be offensive and embarrassing to those exposed to them, and that permitting them would legitimize sexual activity of young people. But these are classically not justifications validating the suppression of expression protected by the First Amendment. At least where obscenity is not involved, we have consistently held that the fact that protected speech may be offensive to some does not justify its suppression. As for the possible "legitim-ization" of illicit sexual behavior, whatever might be the case if the advertisements directly incited sexual activity among the young, none of the advertisements in this record can even remotely be characterized as "directed to inciting or producing imminent lawless action and...likely to incite or produce such action." They merely state the availability of products and services that are not only entirely legal but constitutionally protected.

Certain postal regulations prohibited the mailing of advertisements for con-traceptives. Youngs Drug Products, one of the largest U.S. manufacturers of condoms, wished to use a direct mass-mailing campaign to increase sales. Youngs wanted to mail flyers discussing the desirability and availability of condoms and several pamphlets (*Condoms and Human Sexuality* and *Plain Talk About Ve-nereal Disease*). Youngs brought suit against the Postal Service to prevent the government from applying the prohibition against mailing such material. The government still believed that such information—Youngs wished to mail only printed information; the actual condoms had to be bought at the local drugstore— was so offensive that it resisted. But the Supreme Court, in 1983 (*Bolger v. Youngs Drug Products Corporation**), ruled that the Postal Service had to carry and deliver such information. Justice Marshall delivered the Court's opinion:

[The] proposed commercial speech is clearly protected by the First Amendment. Neither of the interests asserted by the Government—that [the regulations] shield recipients of mail from materials that they are likely to find offensive and aid parents' efforts to control the manner in which their children become informed about birth control—is sufficient to justify the sweeping prohibition on the mailing of unsolicited contraceptive advertise-ments. The fact that protected speech may be offensive to some persons does not justify its suppression, and, in any event, recipients of objectionable mailings can avoid further offensiveness simply by averting their eyes or disposing of the mailings in a trash can. The statute's marginal degree of protection afforded those parents who desire to keep their children from confronting such mailings is improperly achieved by purging all mailboxes of unsolicited material that is entirely suitable for adults.

Just as abortion and birth control were seen as offensive, so too was any representation or discussion of conception and childbirth. One (of many) ex-amples of this can be seen with the film *Mom and Dad.** This film describes and illustrates the conception and delivery of an infant, both in a normal manner and by caesarean operation; it also depicts the ravages of untreated venereal diseases. In 1948, the public safety director of Newark, New Jersey, attempted to censor this film because he thought that the subject matter was "too delicate" to be exhibited by the usual theaters open to the general public. The director would issue the required exhibition permit only if *Mom and Dad* were shown under "educational, medical, or social welfare supervision." A New Jersey court could not understand why the film was seen to be objectionable if exhibited in the usual manner but not objectionable if shown under "educational" supervision. The court ordered the public safety director to issue the exhibition permit and not to interfere with the presentation of *Mom and Dad*.

A 1924 American silent film (*The Naked Truth**) was the object of two censorship attacks. One (unsuccessful) in New Jersey, in 1926, and one (successful) in New York, in 1928. *The Naked Truth* depicted the ravages of untreated venereal disease, argued for sex education, and was clearly against extramarital sex. The public safety director of Newark, New Jersey, sent his vice squad to view the film and, not surprisingly, sent a notice to the film's distributor to the effect that the presentation of the film was prohibited, that he would prevent the exhibition by force, that he would revoke the theater's license if it attempted to show the film, and that he would arrest all persons connected with the exhibition. A New Jersey judge, in reviewing the process, ordered the public safety director not to interfere with the film's exhibition. The judge commented that "no one is more anxious than I to see that the city of Newark is and remains a clean city, and no one is more opposed to indecent exhibitions than I," but the judge commented that the director did not have the authority to prevent the showing of the film. *The Naked Truth*, however, was banned in New York in 1928, and the New York courts sanctioned the refusal of the New York censorship board to issue the required exhibition permit.

Information and publications dealing with sex education have always been seen as filthy and disgusting, and the obscenity statutes have frequently been employed to repress such speech and press. The number of local community-action groups that protest any sex education courses in the public schools is legion; the opposition is based on the fear that if young people learn about sex, they will resort to immediate activity. But the U.S. government has also been involved in this anti-sex education crusade. Two agencies in particular—the Customs Service, with its mandate to prevent the importation of any obscene or immoral thing into the country, and the Postal Service, with its mandate to prosecute anyone who uses the mails to send obscene or immoral material—have consistently made the linkage between sex education materials and pornography and have attempted several times to suppress and punish such publications.

One such example concerned a Ms. Dennett, the mother of two boys. When her sons reached the ages of eleven and fourteen, she concluded that she ought to teach them about sex. After examining about sixty publications on the subject, Dennett wrote and distributed through the mails her own publication, *The Sex Side of Life.** She was duly convicted in a federal district court for sending through the mails an "obscene, lewd, or lascivious" publication and was fined $300 (quite a large sum in 1930). The trial judge said the pamphlet "has a tendency to deprave and corrupt the morals'' and arouses ''lewd and obscene thought or desire.'' Dennett's conviction was reversed, however, by an appeals court. This court characterized *The Sex Side of Life* in the following terms:

The pamphlet. . .purported to give accurate information concerning the sex side of life and the functions of the sex organs. The pamphlet then proceeded to explain sex life in detail, both physically and emotionally, and it described the sex organs and their operation and the way children are begotten. It negatived the idea that sex impulse was base passion and treated it as normal and its satisfaction as great and justifiable joy when accompanied by love between two human beings. It warned against perversion, venereal disease, and prostitution, and argued for continence and healthy mindedness and against promiscuous sex relations.

In reversing Dennett's conviction for sending through the mail what the government prosecutors (and the jury at the district court level) claimed to be obscene and lewd, the appeals court held that a little sex education for adolescents might not be a bad thing:

It may be assumed that any article dealing with the sex side of life and explaining the functions of the sex organs is capable in some circumstances of arousing lust. The sex impulses are present in every one, and without doubt cause much of the weal and woe of human kind. But it can hardly be said that, because of the risk of arousing sex impulses, there should be no instruction of the young in sex matters, and that the risk of imparting instruction outweighs the disadvantages of leaving them to grope about in mystery and morbid curiosity and of requiring them to secure such information, as they may be able to obtain, from ill-informed and often foul-mouthed companions, rather than from intelligent and high-minded sources.

Another example of the Postal Service's equating sex education with obscenity was in 1945, with a pamphlet entitled *Preparing for Marriage.** This pamphlet contained information about the physical and emotional aspects of marriage, but the postmaster general thought it was ''obscene, lewd, and lascivious.'' The courts dismissed this contention and ordered the postmaster general to carry *Preparing for Marriage* in the mails.

A similar publication, *Married Love,** ran afoul of the Customs Service's view of obscenity and was seized in 1931. It would appear that for both the Postal Service and the Customs Service *anything* that had to do with sex was obscene and thus subject to suppression. Judge Woolsey did not agree with this characterization of *Married Love* and ordered the Customs Service to release the pamphlet. Judge Woolsey offered the following comment: ''I do not find anything exceptional anywhere in the book, and I cannot imagine a normal mind to which this book would seem to be obscene or immoral within the proper definition of these words or whose sex impulses would be stirred by reading it.''

A section of the New York Penal Law made it a crime to sell or distribute or make available ''obscene'' material to a minor under eighteen years of age. The problem with the statute, however, was that some of the definitions of "obscenity" effectively prevented any sex education materials from being made available to minors. Among the things prohibited by the statute were material or publications "which would appeal to the lust of persons under the age of eighteen years or to their curiosity as to sex or to the anatomical differences between the sexes." The Supreme Court, in 1968 (*Rabeck v. New York**), saw the obvious: The prohibition against information that would appeal to a minor's "curiosity as to sex or to the anatomical differences between the sexes" did not deal with obscenity but would ban all publications that are used in sex education classes.

Homosexuality and lesbianism, perhaps more than sex education or contraception, have been topics that offend and thus are subjected to censorship and repression. The reference here is not to actual homosexual conduct—in private or in public—but to the thought, the speech, and the publications that deal with such topics. The activity itself is seen to be so vile and perverted that just the mention of it is offensive to public decency and morals.

One such example of this occurred in New York in 1929 and concerned a book, *The Well of Loneliness*,* whose plot concerned the emotional character of a lesbian (the court used the term "female invert"). The distributors of the book were found guilty under a New York statute that made it a crime to sell "obscene" publications. Again, this case did not involve public displays of lesbianism; it involved a novel that had lesbianism as its theme. New York City Magistrate Bushel was appalled by the book's content because the very thought of lesbianism was:

too perverted for public consumption....I am convinced that *The Well of Loneliness* tends to debauch public morals, that its subject-matter is offensive to public decency, and that it is calculated to deprave and corrupt minds open to its immoral influences and who might come into contact with it and...I hold that the book...is violative of the statute.

The discussion of male homosexuality has also been seen as a perversion that should be repressed at the outset. An example of this can be seen in a case that concerned the University of Missouri's refusal to grant official campus recognition to Gay Lib (*Ratchford, President, University of Missouri v. Gay Lib**). The organization stated that it was to be a discussion group dealing with the emotional needs of homosexuals and that it did not plan to encourage people to violate a Missouri statute that made certain activities (sodomy and fellatio) crimes. A district court, in 1978, ruled that the university was justified in not granting recognition, but an appeals court reversed that decision, holding that Gay Lib's First Amendment rights were violated. Judge Lay delivered the majority opinion of the appeals court:

In the present case, none of the purposes or aims of Gay Lib evidences advocacy of present violations of state law or of university rules or regulations. . . . It is of no moment, in First Amendment jurisprudence, that ideas advocated by an association may to some or most of us be abhorrent, even sickening. The stifling of advocacy is even more abhorrent, even more sickening. . . . Once used to stifle "the thought that we hate," in Holmes' phrase, it can stifle the ideas we love. It signals a lack of faith in people, in its supposition that they are unable to choose in the market place of ideas.

The above represented the majority opinion; there was a sharp dissent from Judge Regan. Judge Regan appears to have been so appalled by homosexuality that he was of the view that any discussion of it in the abstract, not linked to any overt behavior, should be suppressed:

Here, the officials' denial of recognition to Gay Lib was not based on "mere disagreement" with the group's "philosophy." State University officials have a responsibility not only to taxpayers but to *all* students on campus, and that responsibility encompasses a right to protect latent or potential homosexuals from becoming overt homosexual students. . . . In my opinion, the University was entitled to protect itself and the other students on campus, in this small way, against abnormality, illness and compulsive conduct.

Another general category of moral censorship over sin deals with nudity—the depiction or representation of the nude male and female bodies. Here, as above, the reference is not to overt sexual activities; this area deals simply with pictures of people without clothes on. The controlling standard for many years was simple: The publication would be censored if it contained any nudity whatsoever because nudity was the equivalent of obscenity. Nudity, however, did not always mean nudity to the point of depicting genitals or breasts; nudity as indecency at one time referred to female arms and legs. This view is well evidenced by a short comment from Judge Cotillo, who, in 1938, was appalled by some pictures in magazines (*Silk Stocking Magazine/Silk Stocking Stories**) that, from the judge's description, sound like the advertisements appearing in current issues of the *New York Times Sunday Magazine*:

Upon reading the minutes of the trial and after an examination of the exhibits consisting of the magazines themselves, an entirely new atmosphere was thrown around the case. A prudent caution required that this examination of the exhibits be made in my own room, and the examination compelled me to place the exhibits under lock and key in order to prevent them from falling into the hands of my young daughter. Why was this necessary? . . . Each one of these issues bears on its cover the picture of a young and attractive woman in a state of dishabille, and permissible only in the sanctum of a woman's boudoir. Each picture features nakedness, particularly as to her lower limbs. . . . [and] pictures of girls clad with nothing but underwear and stockings, and make a featured display of their arms. . . . We face a current drive today against sex perverts, all forms of vice engendered by loose morals, and even positive degeneracy. . . . [We must] protect the minds of our growing boys and girls from this pestilence and noisome filth.

The courts, as with human sexual biology, *slowly* came to the realization that nudity per se was not obscene and thus protected expression under the First Amendment. But this was a long process because nudity was equated with obscenity by the Postal Service and publications containing nudes were prohibited from the mails; the Customs Service seized such publications because they were obscene; and motion picture censorship boards refused to issue exhibition permits for films that contained nudity.

In one case, copies of the book *Nudism in Modern Life** was seized in 1940 by U.S. Customs, which ruled that the book was obscene because it contained four small photographs of nude men and women. Although the judge equated nudity with cancer, leprosy, and syphilis, the book was found not to be obscene:

Nudity in art has long been recognized as the reverse of obscene. Art galleries and art catalogues contain many nudes, ancient and modern....The use of nude figures and photographs in medical treatises and textbooks is also commonly practiced today....It is apparent, therefore, that civilization has advanced far enough, at last, to permit picturization of the human body for scientific and educational purposes....And....it may be well to repeat that the question is not whether nudity in practice is justifiable or desirable. All would agree that cancer, leprosy, and syphilis are highly undesirable; still, it is recognized, generally, by normal, intelligent persons, that there is a need for scientific study, exposition and picturization of their manifestations.

Various local motion picture censorship boards refused to issue exhibition permits to films if the film contained nudity. Some of the more absurd censorship activities concerned the revulsion against certain documentary films—one of them produced under the auspices of the American Museum of Natural History—that contained scenes of people without clothes on. Two such examples concerned *Naked Amazon** and *Latuko.** *Naked Amazon* was a quasi-documentary of some Amazon Indian tribes and *Latuko* dealt with the Latuko tribe in Africa. Although each film did show some nudity, the people weren't engaged in any sexual activity and it was obvious that nudity was part of their culture and life-style. Only after a long judicial process were the censors forced to issue exhibition permits for these films.

Exhibition permits were also refused for nudist films—films that dealt with nudism as a life-style rather than as an irrelevant part of a larger documentary. Two such examples concerned the films *Have Figure—Will Travel** (the plot is contained in the film's title) and *The Garden of Eden** (again, the plot is not difficult to imagine). These films simply showed nude people engaging in everyday activities but, and this must be emphasized, sexual activities were not included. As above, exhibition permits were finally granted but not until the distributors and exhibitors resisted the censorship through a long and costly court process.

The depiction of female nudity appears to have been treated a bit differently by the male-dominated court system than has male nudity. Pictures showing bare breasts and female pubic areas seem to be part of the American culture, and although frequently subject to censorship, the courts have generally ruled that female nudity per se is not the same as obscenity. The judges appear to have a different impression when penises are shown; such publications are seen to be directed at deviant sexual groups (read "homosexuals") and the magazines are often declared obscene.

One such example of the treatment given male nudity concerned the magazine *Hellenic Sun.** Copies of the magazine were seized by Customs in 1967, and both a federal district court and an appeals court ruled that *Hellenic Sun* was obscene because the pictures were "patently offensive, without redeeming social value, and appealed exclusively to a clearly defined deviant group (male homosexuals)." Again, the photographs contained no hint whatsoever of sexual activities; they were simply pictures of naked men. But the judges, apparently feeling more comfortable with breasts than with penises, ruled *Hellenic Sun* to be obscene. The magazine was described in the court records:

The magazine . . . is a collection of photographs of undressed men. Some are in color. There is one of a group of boys. They are posed in the out-of-doors, but the generally languid models are not engaged in outdoor activity. In the composition of the photographs, the genitals of the models are made the focal points of the pictures. The camera's interest is languished upon the penis, and, if the general pose of each model be languid, the penis in some of the pictures appears not in complete repose. . . . The pictures would have a prurient appeal for a large proportion of male homosexuals, particularly juvenile males with homosexual tendencies. The one picture of the boys would have a prurient appeal for paedophiles. Adolescent girls would find them frightening as well as shocking, but with some exceptions, mature women would find little stimulation in such material.

Hellenic Sun notwithstanding, the representation of nudity without any accompanying sexual activity is now seen as protected speech and press under the First Amendment because nudity as such is no longer equated with obscenity and pornography. The Supreme Court has ruled on this question of nudity several times, and its view can be summed up with one sentence taken from its decision in the *Carnal Knowledge** case (1974): "There are occasional scenes of nudity, but nudity alone is not enough to make material legally obscene under the [current] standards."

Moral censorship over speech and press in the name of fighting sin becomes a lot more complicated when actual sexual activities and conduct are described or depicted because this now spills over to the area of obscenity and pornography. The reference here is not, for example, to a pamphlet describing venereal diseases or a book of nude Greek statues; this area concerns publications that contain, for example, pictures of a naked woman attempting to guide a horse's penis into her mouth (*Illustrated Report**) or a film (*Un Chant d'Amour**) whose plot seems to revolve around two males engaging in fellatio and sodomy. This type of speech and press most certainly offends, and obscene speech and press have been declared to be "unprotected" by the First Amendment and thus open to censorship, suppression, and punishment.

Obscenity and pornography have always been punished in the United States on the grounds—rightly or wrongly—that they corrupt and cheapen the individual; that they lead to increased crime and illicit sexual activity; that they serve no known socially useful purpose; and that they are devoid of any viable communicative element in the search for truth. Although such expression has always been punished, it was not until 1957, in *Roth v. United States,** that the Supreme Court ruled that obscene speech and press, like libel and selling military secrets to the enemy, are *unprotected* by the First Amendment and that, indeed, Congress and the states can pass laws abridging the freedom of such speech and press. Justice Brennan delivered the Court's majority opinion in this now-famous case:

The dispositive question is whether obscenity is utterance within the area of protected speech and press. Although this is the first time the question has been squarely presented to the Court. . .expressions found in numerous opinions indicate that this Court has always assumed that obscenity is not protected by the freedoms of speech and press. . . .It is apparent that the unconditional phrasing of the First Amendment was not intended to protect every utterance. . . .All ideas having even the slightest redeeming social importance—unorthodox ideas, controversial ideas, even ideas hateful to the prevailing climate of opinion—have the full protection of the guaranties, unless excludable because they encroach upon the limited area of more important interests. But implicit in the history of the First Amendment is the rejection of obscenity as utterly without redeeming social importance.

Obscene speech and press were thus subject to censorship. Before 1957, censorship was based on some implicit understanding that such material could be suppressed; after 1957, it was based on the explicit ruling that obscenity is unprotected by the First Amendment. The problem was to define obscenity. The term really is not susceptible to a precise definition, and there have been changing standards over the years as to what constitutes this class of unprotected speech and press.

The first general standard employed to determine what was—and what was not—obscene was the so-called Hicklin Rule.* The Hicklin Rule was announced in Great Britain by Lord Chief Justice Cockburn. In dealing with a pamphlet entitled *The Confessional Unmasked*, Cockburn announced in *Regina v. Hicklin* (L.R. 3 Q.B., 360 [1868]): "The test of obscenity is this, whether the tendency of the matter charged as obscenity is to deprave and corrupt those whose minds are open to such immoral influences and into whose hands a publication of this sort may fall." The Hicklin Rule basically declared a publication to be obscene if isolated passages or paragraphs—not the work taken as a whole—could corrupt the most susceptible person. This guide then became the standard for all obscenity cases in the United States and in Great Britain.

The Hicklin Rule was absurd: One paragraph's effect on a moron would render the entire book obscene and thus open for censorship. The Hicklin Rule was the weapon employed by the anti-vice societies (Comstockery*) to weed out the vile, disgusting, and immoral literature: The crusaders would review books line by line, and if, by chance, they found an isolated passage that offended, the entire book could then be suppressed (the Bible is an obvious candidate under the Hicklin Rule). There have been too many censorship activities based on the Hicklin Rule to discuss them here; two such examples concerned attempts to ban *If I Die*,* André Gide's autobiography, and Gautier's *Mlle de Maupin*.* One of the most trenchant comments on the rule was given by Judge Curtis Bok: "Strictly applied, this rule renders any book unsafe, since a moron could pervert to some sexual fantasy to which his mind is open the listings of a seed catalogue."

The Hicklin Rule was applied in the United States until 1934, but there were some intimations before 1934 that the rule was unworkable. In 1913 (*United States v. Kennerley**), Judge Hand affirmed a conviction of someone charged with sending an obscene book through the mail and employed the Hicklin Rule in so doing:

That test [the Hicklin Rule] has been accepted by the lower federal courts until it would be no longer proper for me to disregard it. Under this rule, such parts of this book as pages 169 and 170 might be found obscene, because they certainly might tend to corrupt the morals of those into whose hands it might come and whose minds were open to such immoral influences. Indeed, it would be just those who would be most likely to concern themselves with those parts alone, forgetting their setting and their relevancy to the book as a whole.

But Judge Hand was not pleased with having to apply the Hicklin Rule, and he began the slow process of demolition, which was not completed until 1934:

I hope it is not improper for me to say that the rule as laid down, however consonant it may be with mid-Victorian morals, does not seem to me to answer to the understanding and morality of the present time, as conveyed by the words "obscene, lewd, or lascivious."...Indeed, it seems hardly likely that we are even to-day so lukewarm in our interest in letters or serious discussion as to be content to reduce our treatment of sex to the standard of a child's library in the supposed interest of a salacious few....Should not the word "obscene" be allowed to indicate the present critical point in the compromise between candor and shame at which the community may have arrived here and now?...To put thought in leash to the average conscience of the time is perhaps tolerable, but to fetter it by the necessities of the lowest and least capable seems a fatal policy.

The Hicklin Rule was in effect until 1934, when, in the *Ulysses** case (*United States v. One Book Entitled Ulysses*), Judge Woolsey formulated the "Ulysses Standard."* This standard now required that the entire book or publication be evaluated—not just isolated passages—in terms of its dominant effect on people with average sex instincts—not its effect on the most susceptible person. In finally ending the applicability of the absurd Hicklin Rule, Judge Woolsey made the following comments:

We think the same immunity should apply to literature as to science, where the presentation, when viewed objectively, is sincere, and the erotic matter is not introduced to promote lust and does not furnish the dominant note of the publication. The question in each case is whether a publication taken as a whole has a libidinous effect.

The Ulysses Standard has not been overruled; it has been made only more precise by subsequent decisions. In essence, obscenity was now to be determined by judging the entire publication's dominant effect in appealing to the prurient interest (lust) of an average reader in the community. This standard or test was refined in 1957 in the *Roth* decision, which created the Roth Standard.* This test was to last until 1966, when, in turn, it was further refined. The Roth Standard stated the test to be "whether to the average person, applying contemporary community standards, the dominant theme of the material taken as a whole appeals to prurient interest."

The Roth Standard was refined in 1966 in the now-famous *Memoirs v. Massachusetts* case (*Memoirs of a Woman of Pleasure/Fanny Hill** by John Cleland). In ruling that *Memoirs* was not obscene, the Supreme Court created the Memoirs Standard: "It must be established that (a) the dominant theme of the material taken as a whole appeals to a prurient interest in sex; (b) the material is patently offensive because it affronts contemporary community standards . . .; and (c) the material is utterly without redeeming social value." To be judged obscene, a work had to meet all three of the requirements independently. A book (and *Memoirs* fell into this category) could not be judged obscene if it had *any* redeeming social value; the degree of its prurient appeal or its offensiveness could not cancel out its social value.

The Memoirs Standard was itself refined in 1973 (*Miller v. California**), and the resulting Miller Standard* is now the current standard or test of obscenity. It appears that the Supreme Court was not comfortable with the dictum "utterly without redeeming social value"; it is difficult to prove that a book or film is *utterly* without *any* redeeming social value. The Miller Standard rejected this requirement and substituted "lacks serious literary, artistic, political, or scientific value." The current test for obscenity, the Miller Standard, has three criteria that have to be met independently; a work that has political value is protected under the First Amendment, regardless of its prurient appeal and offensive depiction of sexual activities. The current standard now reads:

The basic guidelines must be: (a) whether the average person, applying contemporary community standards, would find that the work, taken as a whole, appeals to the prurient interest; (b) whether the work depicts or describes, in a patently offensive way, sexual conduct specifically defined by the applicable state law; and (c) whether the work, taken as a whole, lacks serious literary, artistic, political, or scientific value.

One example of the Miller Standard can be seen with the 1980 American film *Caligula*.* This film has been described as "a dizzying display of bodies, genitals, orgies, heterosexual and homosexual activity, masturbation, bodily functions, and sexual content and excesses of all varieties.'' The film faced several censorship attempts on the ground that it was obscene, but in March 1984, the Supreme Court ruled that *Caligula* was not obscene under the Miller Standard. *Caligula* might have been patently offensive, but it failed to meet the remaining two criteria. Rather than appealing to the viewer's prurient interest in sex— arousing desire or lustful feelings—the film sickened and disgusted the viewer. In addition, *Caligula* was seen to have serious "political value," showing the effects of the use of unrestrained political power on a society.

Other publications and films have, however, been seen to meet the Miller requirements and have been declared obscene. One such example was the film *Deep Throat*.* This film, produced in 1972, has received more publicity perhaps than any X-rated film. The film was attacked and censored in more than twenty-five states, but the finding of obscenity by the Supreme Court, in 1976, did not prevent its exhibition in most localities. *Deep Throat* relates the story of one unfortunate woman whose clitoris is located in her throat; fellatio is the only way she can reach orgasm. This film was judged to have prurient appeal, patent offensiveness, and to be lacking in serious artistic, political, literary, or scientific value.

Space here does not allow a full review of all the publications and films subjected to censorship on grounds of obscenity. Some of the more well-known cases are discussed in greater detail below, but they at least deserve mention here: Henry Miller's classic *The Tropic of Cancer** was banned for thirty years, and it was not until 1964 that the book was de-criminalized; Edmund Wilson's *Memoirs of Hecate County** was declared obscene; *Lady Chatterley's Lover*,* by D. H. Lawrence, was vilified for years; Schnitzler's classic *Hands Around** (*Reigen*) was characterized as "disgusting" and Schnitzler himself was judged to be a "degenerate." The list is almost endless.

There is one last comment to be made in this Introductory Essay. Although the Supreme Court attempted to bring some order and understanding to this area of obscenity by establishing the various tests or standards to be applied—Roth, Memoirs, Miller—some judges still ignore these standards and formulate their own particular and often peculiar standards. One such example of this happened in 1976 (*Liles v. Oregon**); it appears that the trial judge employed his mother's sensitivities as to what determined obscenity. Alexander Portnoy was alive and well in Oregon in 1976. The following comments are by Justice Brennan, who filed a dissent to the Supreme Court's refusal to grant certiorari:

I note that this case particularly exemplifies the difficulty and arbitrariness inherent in any attempt to articulate a standard of obscenity. I need only quote the standard applied by the judge before whom [Liles'] case was tried: "Well, what is patently offensive? And, frankly, I had to kind of apply my own standard, which, I believe, corresponds with the standards of the community. And the standard probably, simply stated and boiled down, is the same one which was taught to me by my mother from the day I was a small child. If there was something of which I would not want her to know, then don't do it.

Pretty simple. Applying that standard I would think that I wouldn't get any quarrel out of anyone in this room, that they wouldn't want their mothers sitting next to them while they looked at either one of these movies. They are patently offensive.

THE DICTIONARY

A

ABC BOOKS, INC. v. BENSON (1970). This case concerned the constitutionality of the Tennessee Obscenity Statute.* The statute allowed for a prior restraint and ABC Books argued that the statute was unconstitutional, since the state of Tennessee had "no power to enact any statute regulating what Tennessee citizens may write, print, distribute, sell, or read." The district court held that the relevant statutes were constitutional because the temporary restraining order was for a limited period with a trial and decision to be rendered as to the obscenity of the matter within a period of days. Although the obscenity of the contested matter was not at issue, Judge Miller, in a concurring opinion, wrote: "I would only add that I am prepared at this time...to hold and conclude that the film *The Bushwhacker*, personally viewed by all the members of the court, is obscene within the meaning of the Tennessee statute and should be so declared." *ABC Books, Inc. v. Benson*, 315 F. Supp. 695 (1970).

ABRAMS v. UNITED STATES (1919). Jacob Abrams and others were convicted of conspiring to violate provisions of the Espionage Act* of June 15, 1917. The defendants argued that their activities were not unlawful because the First Amendment protected their rights of freedom of speech and press. The Supreme Court rejected their arguments and affirmed twenty-year prison sentences. Abrams and the others printed and distributed two circulars that in the words of Justice Clarke, who wrote the majority opinion for the Court, were described as "obviously intended to provoke and to encourage resistance to the United States in the war...and the defendants...plainly urged and advocated a resort to a general strike of workers in ammunition factories for the purpose of curtailing the production of ordnance and munitions necessary and essential to the prosecution of the war." The circulars were titled "The Hypocrisy of the United States and Her Allies" and (in Yiddish) "Workers—Wake Up." The Court record contains some excerpts from the circulars: "His [the President's] shameful, cowardly silence about the intervention in Russia reveals the hypocrisy of the plutocratic gang in Washington and vicinity....Workers, Russian emigrants, you who had the least belief in the honesty of *our* Government, must now throw away all confidence, must spit in the face the false, hypocritic, military propaganda which has fooled you so relentlessly, calling forth your sympathy, your help, to the prosecution of the war.''

Justice Holmes, joined by Justice Brandeis, dissented from the majority opinion: ''In this case sentences of twenty years' imprisonment have been imposed for the publishing of two leaflets that I believe the defendants had as much right to publish as the Government has to publish the Constitution of the United States now vainly invoked by them. I think that we should be eternally vigilant against attempts to check the expression of opinions that we loathe and believe to be fraught with death, unless they so imminently threaten immediate interference with the lawful and pressing purposes of the law that an immediate check is required to save the country. I wholly disagree with the argument of the Government that the First Amendment left the common law as to seditious libel in force. History seems to me against the notion. I had conceived that the United States through many years had shown its repentance for the Sedition Act of 1798,* by repaying fines that it imposed. Only the emergency that makes it immediately dangerous to leave the correction of evil counsels to time warrants making any exception to the sweeping command, 'Congress shall make no law...abridging the freedom of speech.' Of course I am speaking only of expressions of opinion and exhortations, which were all that were uttered here, but I regret that I cannot put into more impressive words my belief that in their conviction...the defendants were deprived of their rights under the Constitution of the United States.'' *Abrams v. United States*, 250 U.S. 616 (1919).

ADAMS THEATRE CO. v. KEENAN (1953). The Adams Theatre applied for a license from the director of public safety of Newark, New Jersey, to stage a ''burlesque'' show. The director refused to issue the license because he felt that the burlesque would be ''lewd and indecent.'' The New Jersey Supreme Court ruled that the director had no way of knowing what type of performance would be staged, and therefore, the refusal to issue the license was an unconstitutional prior restraint. Judge Brennan delivered the Court's opinion: ''Plaintiff's application stated merely that it intended to stage 'burlesque' shows. 'Burlesque' today is descriptive of two very different kinds of show. Legitimate burlesque, and once the only kind, is clean and wholesome entertainment defined...as 'a type of theatrical entertainment, developed in the United States in the late nineteenth century, characterized by broad humor and slapstick presentation, at first consisting of a musical travesty, but later of turns, as songs, ballet dancing, and caricatures of well-known actors and plays.' In contrast, that which has been termed 'modern burlesque' has been described as 'a plotless musical entertainment consisting of a series of unrelated episodes and dances, all with the purpose of depicting or suggesting sexual subjects or objects. The one outstanding characteristic of modern burlesque is the fact that it is completely sex-centered. It has some low comedy and occasionally some humor, but the principal subject of both is sex....The *piece de resistance* is the girl who disrobes, partially or entirely, and this act varies with the political season and the locality.'' *Adams Theatre Co. v. Keenan*, 96 A. 2d 519 (1953).

ADDERLY v. FLORIDA (1966). Adderly and some thirty other persons blocked a jail driveway and demonstrated (singing and dancing) against what they thought was segregation in the jail. The local sheriff told them that they were on county property and would have to leave or be arrested for violating a Florida Trespass Statute.* They were duly arrested, tried, and convicted; the Supreme Court upheld the convictions. The Court ruled that there was no evidence that the group was arrested or convicted for their views or objectives, but, rather, a jail is not open to the public and that the convictions rested on a valid time, place, and manner regulation. Justice Douglas registered a strongly worded dissent: "A tragic consequence happens today when a trespass law is used to bludgeon those who peacefully exercise a First Amendment right to protest to government against one of the most grievous of all modern oppressions which some of our States are inflicting on our citizens. The greater the importance of safeguarding the community from incitements to the overthrow of our institutions by force and violence, the more imperative is the need to preserve inviolate the constitutional rights of free speech, free press and free assembly in order to maintain the opportunity for free political discussion, to the end that government may be responsive to the will of the people and that changes, if desired, may be obtained by peaceful means. Therein lies the security of the Republic, the very foundation of constitutional government." *Adderly v. Florida*, 385 U.S. 39 (1966).

ADLER v. BOARD OF EDUCATION (1952). The New York Civil Service Law,* supplemented by the New York Education Law* and the so-called New York Feinberg Law,* made any person ineligible for employment in any public school if he or she were a member of any organization advocating the overthrow of the government by force, violence, or any unlawful means. The constitutionality of these regulations was upheld by the Supreme Court in 1952, but this decision was later overruled in *Keyishian v. Board of Regents*.* Justice Minton delivered the majority opinion in 1952: "It is clear that such persons have the right under our laws to assemble, speak, think and believe as they will. It is equally clear that they have no right to work for the State in the school system on their own terms. They may work for the school system upon the reasonable terms laid down by the proper authorities of New York. If they do not choose to work on such terms, they are at liberty to retain their beliefs and associations and go elsewhere. Has the State thus deprived them of any right to free speech or assembly? We think not. . . . A teacher works in a sensitive area in a schoolroom. There he shapes the attitude of young minds towards the society in which they live. In this, the state has a vital concern. It must preserve the integrity of the schools. That the school authorities have the right and the duty to screen the officials, teachers, and employees as to their fitness to maintain the integrity of the schools as a part of ordered society, cannot be doubted. One's associates, past and present, as well as one's conduct, may properly be considered in determining fitness and loyalty. From time immemorial, one's reputation has been determined in part by the company he keeps. In the employment of officials and teachers of the school system, the state may very properly inquire into the company they keep, and we know of no rule . . . that prevents the state, when determining the fitness and loyalty of such persons, from considering the organizations and persons with whom they associate.''

This decision was not unanimous, for Justices Black, Douglas, and Frankfurter each offered a strong dissent. Justice Black: "This is another of those rapidly multiplying legislative enactments which make it dangerous—this time for school teachers—to think or say anything except what a transient majority happen to approve at the moment. Basically these laws rest on the belief that the government should supervise and limit the flow of ideas into the minds of men. . . . Public officials cannot be constitutionally vested with powers to select the ideas people can think about, censor the public views they can express, or choose the persons or groups people can associate with. Public officials with such powers are not public servants; they are public masters." Justice Douglas: "The [New York] law inevitably turns the school system into a spying project. Regular loyalty reports on the teachers must be made out. The principals become detectives; the students, the parents, the community become informers. What was the significance of the reference of the art teacher to socialism? Why was the history teacher so openly hostile to Franco Spain? Who heard overtones of revolution in the English teacher's discussion of *Grapes of Wrath*? . . . The framers knew the danger of dogmatism; they also knew the strength that comes when the mind is free, when ideas may be pursued wherever they lead. We forget these teachings of the First Amendment when we sustain this law.'' *Adler v. Board of Education*, 342 U.S. 485 (1952).

ADULT FILM ASSOCIATION OF AMERICA. This organization was founded in 1969. Its members are producers, distributors, and exhibitors of sexually explicit adult films (X-rated). It was formed to combat censorship of such films and has filed several amicus curiae briefs in court cases supporting the anti-censorship position. The association bestows annual Erotic Film Awards in sixteen categories and is located in Los Angeles, California.

ADVOCACY. In 1925, Benjamin Gitlow was convicted for advocating the violent overthrow of the government (*Gitlow v. New York**). The Supreme Court, in the *Gitlow* case, stated: "That utterances inciting to the overthrow of organized government by unlawful means, present a sufficient danger of substantive evil to bring their punishment within the range of legislative discretion, is clear. Such utterances, by their very nature, involve danger to the public peace and to the security of the State. They threaten breaches of the peace and ultimate revolution. And the immediate danger is none the less real and substantial, because the effect of a given utterance cannot be accurately foreseen. The State cannot reasonably be required to measure the danger from every such utterance in the nice balance of a jeweler's scale. A single revolutionary spark may kindle a fire that, smouldering for a time, may burst into a sweeping and destructive conflagration. It cannot be said that the State is acting arbitrarily or unreasonably when in the exercise of its judgment as to the measures necessary to protect the public peace and safety, it seeks to extinguish the spark without waiting until it has enkindled the flame or blazed into the conflagration. It cannot reasonably be required to defer the adoption of measures for its own peace and safety until the revolutionary utterances lead to actual disturbances of the public peace or imminent and immediate danger of its own destruction; but it may, in the exercise of its judgment, suppress the threatened danger in its incipiency." But in a much later decision, in 1957 (*Yates v. United States**), the Supreme Court ruled that mere "advocacy" seen as the "teaching of any prohibited activities as an abstract principle, even if the advocacy or teaching is done with an evil intent and with the hope that a violent overthrow of the government might eventually occur" was a form of protected speech under the First Amendment. The urging of *action*—direct, imminent, immediate, and clear and present danger action—can be punished; the mere advocacy or teaching the necessity or goodness of such action falls within the area of "protected speech."

ALABAMA, CORRUPT PRACTICES ACT. Alabama Code, 1940, Title 17, §§ 268–286, esp. § 285 (599): "Corrupt practices at elections enumerated and defined. —It is a corrupt practice for any person on any election day to intimidate or attempt to intimidate an elector or any of the election officers; or, obstruct or hinder or attempt to obstruct or hinder, or prevent or attempt to prevent the forming of the lines of the voters awaiting their opportunity or time to enter the election booths; or to hire or to let for hire any automobile or other conveyance for the purpose of conveying electors to or from the polls; or, to do any electioneering or to solicit any votes for or against the election or nomination of any candidate, or in support of or in opposition to any proposition that is being voted on the day on which the election affecting such candidates or propositions is being held." This regulation was held to be unconstitutional by the Supreme Court in *Mills v. Alabama,** 384 U.S. 214 (1966).

ALABAMA, LOITERING AND PICKETING. Section 3448 of the State Code of 1923: "Loitering or picketing forbidden. —Any person or persons, who, without a just cause or legal excuse therefor, go near to or loiter about the premises or place of business of any other person, firm, corporation, or association, of people, engaged in a lawful business, for the purpose, or with the intent of influencing, or inducing other persons not to trade with, buy from, sell to, have business dealings with, or be employed by such persons, firm, corporation, or association, or who picket the works or place of business of such other persons, firms, corporations, or associations of persons, for the purpose of hindering, delaying, or interfering with or injuring any lawful business or enterprise of another, shall be guilty of a misdemeanor; but nothing herein shall prevent any person from soliciting trade or business from a competitive business." This regulation was declared to be overbroad and thus unconstitutional by the Supreme Court in *Thornhill v. Alabama,** 310 U.S. 88 (1940).

ALASKA, TEACHERS IMMORALITY. In the face of a challenge to its statutes describing reasons for dismissing a public school teacher (*Watts v. Seward School Board,** 381 U.S. 126 [1965]), the state of Alaska amended the statute to allow public school teachers to criticize the governing body of any school. The amended statute now reads: "No rule or regulation of the commissioner of education, a local school board, or local school administrator may restrict or modify the right of a teacher to engage in comment and criticism outside school hours, relative to school administrators, members of the governing body of any school or school district, any other public official, or any school employee, to the same extent that any private individual may exercise the right." Alaska Statute, Title 14, c. 20, § 14.20.095. Right to Comment and Criticize Not to be Restricted.

ALBERTS v. CALIFORNIA (1957). Alberts conducted a mail-order business in Los Angeles and was convicted for violating a California statute (California, Obscenity Statute*) by offering for sale obscene and indecent books and by publishing an obscene advertisement for them. The Supreme Court upheld his conviction on the grounds that the California statute does not violate the First Amendment. This case was decided together with *Roth v. United States,** 354 U.S. 476 (1957).

ALEXANDRIA (LA), ANTI-SOLICITING ORDINANCE. "Section 1. Be it Ordained by the Council of the City of Alexandria, Louisiana, in legal session convened that the practice of going in and upon private residences in the City of Alexandria, Louisiana by solicitors, peddlers, hawkers, itinerant merchants or transient vendors of merchandise not having been requested or invited so to do by the owner or owners, occupant or occupants of said private residences for the purpose of soliciting orders for the sale of goods, wares and merchandise and/or disposing of and/or peddling or hawking the same is declared to be a nuisance and punishable as such nuisance as a misdemeanor." The Supreme Court, in *Breard v. Alexandria,** 341 U.S. 622 (1951), ruled that this ordinance was not unconstitutional as an abridgment of free press when applied to the door-to-door sale of magazine subscriptions.

AMERICAN BOOKSELLERS ASSOCIATION. This organization was founded in 1900 and has more than 5,500 members, most from retail bookstores. It is basically a trade organization but has taken part in several campaigns against censorship and strongly supports the right of a free press.

AMERICAN CIVIL LIBERTIES UNION. The American Civil Liberties Union was founded in 1920 and now has·approximately 250,000 members in all fifty states. It is perhaps the leading civil rights/civil liberties group in the United States and has a long history in supporting freedom of inquiry, expression, speech, and press. Its activities include test court cases in opposition to what it sees as repressive legislation, and it has filed numerous amicus curiae briefs in support of the anti-censorship position.

AMERICAN COMMUNICATIONS ASSOCIATION v. DOUDS (1950). Certain sections of the 1957 National Labor Relations Act deny certain benefits to any labor organization whose officers do not file a so-called "non-Communist" affidavit. The Supreme Court ruled that this did not violate the First Amendment. Justice Vinson delivered the Court's opinion: "Legitimate attempts to protect the public, not from the remote possible effects of noxious ideologies, but from present excesses of direct, active conduct, are not presumptively bad because they interfere with and, in some of its manifestations, restrain the exercise of First Amendment rights. In essence, the problem is one of weighing the probable effects of the statute upon the free exercise of the right of speech and assembly against the congressional determination that political strikes are evils of conduct which cause substantial harm . . . and that Communists . . . pose continuing threats to that public interest when in positions of union leadership. It is important to note what this Act does not do. No individual is forbidden to be or to become a philosophical Communist or a full-fledged member of the Party. No one is penalized for writing or speaking in favor of the Party or its philosophy. Also, the Act does not require or forbid anything whatever to any person merely because he is a member of, or is affiliated with, the Communist Party. It applies only to one who becomes an officer of a labor union." *American Communications Association v. Douds*, 339 U.S. 382 (1950).

AMERICAN LIBRARY ASSOCIATION. The American Library Association is one of the largest professional associations in the United States. Founded in 1876, it has close to 40,000 members, comprising librarians, libraries, trustees, and other people who are interested in the responsibilities that libraries have for society. One of its committees is on Intellectual Freedom, concerned with the rights of free press and anti-censorship. One of its publications, the *Newsletter on Intellectual Freedom*, documents contemporary attempts to suppress free press as it relates to libraries.

ARIZONA, SUPREME COURT DISCIPLINARY RULE. Disciplinary Rule 2-101(B), incorporated in Rule 29(a) of the Supreme Court of Arizona, 17A Arizona Revised Statutes, p. 26 (Supp. 1976): "(B) A lawyer shall not publicize himself, or his partner, or associate, or any other lawyer affiliated with him or his firm, as a lawyer through newspaper or magazine advertisement, radio or television announcements, display advertisements in the city or telephone directories or other means of commercial publicity, nor shall he authorize or permit others to do so in his behalf.'' This statute was declared to be violative of the First Amendment guarantee of free speech by the Supreme Court in *Bates v. State Bar of Arizona** (1977): As long as the advertisements were not misleading or fraudulent, commercial speech fell under the protection of the First Amendment.

ARKANSAS, ANTI-EVOLUTION STATUTE. The state of Arkansas adopted this statute in 1928 to prohibit the teaching in its public schools and universities of the theory that man evolved from other species of life. The statute was a product of the fundamentalist fervor of the 1920s and was based on the [in]famous Tennessee ''monkey law'' that Tennessee adopted in 1925 and that was upheld in *Scopes v. State.** The text of the Arkansas statute read: ''§ 80-1627. — Doctrine of ascent or descent of man from lower order of animals prohibited. —It shall be unlawful for any teacher. . .to teach the theory or doctrine that mankind ascended or descended from a lower order of animals and also it shall be unlawful for any teacher, textbook commission, or other authority. . .to adopt or use in any such institution a textbook that teaches the doctrine or theory that mankind descended or ascended from a lower order of animals.'' Anyone convicted under this statute faced a fine of $500 and dismissal from his or her position. Arkansas Stat. Ann. §§ 80-1627-28. The Supreme Court, in 1968, ruled that this ''anti-evolution'' statute violated the First Amendment (*Epperson v. Arkansas**). The Court record in *Epperson v. Arkansas* contained the following comments about the adoption of the 1928 statute: ''The following advertisement is typical of the public appeal which was used in the campaign to secure adoption of the statute: 'THE BIBLE OR ATHEISM, WHICH? All atheists favor evolution. If you agree with atheism vote against Act No. 1. If you agree with the Bible vote for Act No. 1. Shall conscientious church members be forced to pay taxes to support teachers to teach evolution which will undermine the faith of their children? The *Gazette* said Russian Bolshevists laughed at Tennessee. True, and that sort will laugh at Arkansas. Who cares? Vote FOR ACT NO. 1.' (The *Arkansas Gazette*, November 4, 1928, p. 12.) Letters from the public expressed the fear that teaching of evolution would be 'subversive of Christianity' and that it would cause school children 'to disrespect the Bible.' One letter read: 'The cosmogony taught by [evolution] runs contrary to that of Moses and Jesus, and as such is nothing, if anything at all, but atheism. Now let the mothers and fathers of our state that are trying to raise their children in the Christian faith arise in their might and vote for this anti-evolution bill that will take it out of our tax supported schools. When they have saved the children, they have saved the state.' ''

ARKANSAS, INSULTING LANGUAGE. Arkansas Stat. Ann. § 41-1412 (1964) reads: ''If any person shall make use of any profane, violent, vulgar, abusive or insulting language toward or about any other person in his presence or hearing, which language in its common acception is calculated to arouse to anger the person about or to whom it is spoken or addressed, or to cause a breach of the peace or an assault, shall be deemed guilty of a breach of the peace, and upon conviction thereof shall be punished by a fine of not less than $5.00 nor more than $200.00 or by imprisonment in the county jail for not less than one nor more than six months.'' The Supreme Court, in *Lucas v. Arkansas** (1974), ruled that such language as ''chicken shit'' and ''mother fucker'' were not fighting words and thus could not be used to convict under this statute.

ASHTON v. KENTUCKY (1966). Ashton was convicted for violating a Kentucky statute on criminal libel in that he published material that was calculated ''to create disturbances of the peace.'' The Supreme Court reversed the conviction, recognizing ''that to make an offense of conduct which is 'calculated to create disturbances of the peace' leaves wide open the standard of responsibility. It involves calculations as to the boiling point of a particular person or a particular group, not an appraisal of the nature of the comments *per se*. This kind of criminal libel 'makes a man a criminal simply because his neighbors have no self-control and cannot refrain from violence.' '' *Ashton v. Kentucky*, 384 U.S 195 (1966).

ASSOCIATED PRESS v. NATIONAL LABOR RELATIONS BOARD (1937). A section of the National Labor Relations Act requires that employees dismissed for union activities and for advocacy of collective bargaining be restored to employment with back pay. The Associated Press (AP) discharged an employee who, eventually, the National Labor Relations Board decided was fired because of union activities. The board tried to force the AP to reinstate the employee. The AP brought suit, alleging that such action violated the First Amendment guarantee against abridging freedom of the press.

The Supreme Court did not accept the AP's logic: ''Does the statute, as applied to the petitioner, abridge the freedom of speech or of the press, safeguarded by the First Amendment? We hold that it does not.... The conclusion which the petitioner draws is that whatever may be the case with respect to employees in its mechanical departments it must have absolute and unrestricted freedom to employ and to discharge those who...edit the news, and there must not be the slightest opportunity for any bias or prejudice personally entertained by an editorial employee to color or to distort what he writes, and that the Associated Press cannot be free to furnish unbiased and impartial news reports unless it is equally free to determine for itself the partiality or bias of editorial employees. We think the contention not only has no relevance to the circumstances of the instant case but is an unsound generalization. The business of the Associated Press is not immune from regulation because it is an agency of the press. The publisher of a newspaper has no special immunity from the application of general laws. He has no special privilege to invade the rights and liberties of others. He must answer for libel. He may be punished for contempt of court. He is subject to the anti-trust laws. Like others he must pay equitable and nondiscriminatory taxes on his business. The regulation here in question has no relation whatever to the impartial distribution of news. The order of the Board in nowise circumscribes the full freedom and liberty of the petitioner to publish the news as it desires it published or to enforce policies of its own choosing with respect to the editing and rewriting of news for publication, and the petitioner is free at any time to discharge...any editorial employee who fails to comply with the policies it may adopt [but it cannot discharge employees for union activity].'' *Associated Press v. National Labor Relations Board*, 301 U.S. 103 (1937).

ASSOCIATED PRESS v. UNITED STATES (1945). This case was similar to *Associated Press v. National Labor Relations Board.** The United States charged that certain bylaws of the Associated Press (AP), relating to the prohibitions of distributing AP news to non-members of the association, restrained trade under the Sherman Antitrust Act. The AP brought suit, alleging that the government's action abridged freedom of the press.

The Supreme Court did not accept the arguments of the AP. Justice Black read the Court's decision: ''It would be strange indeed, however, if the grave concern for freedom of the press which prompted adoption of the First Amendment should be read as a command that the government was without power to protect that freedom. The First Amendment, far from providing an argument against application of the Sherman Act, here provides powerful reasons to the contrary. That Amendment rests on the assumption that the widest possible dissemination of information from diverse and antagonistic sources is essential to the welfare of the public, that a free press is a condition of a free society. Surely a command that the government itself shall not impede the free flow of ideas does not afford non-governmental combinations a refuge if they impose restraints upon that constitutionally guaranteed freedom. Freedom to publish means freedom for all and not for some. Freedom to publish is guaranteed by the Constitution, but freedom to combine to keep others from publishing is not. Freedom of the press from governmental interference under the First Amendment does not sanction repression of that freedom by private interests. The First Amendment affords not the slightest support for the contention that a combination to restrain trade in news and views has any constitutional immunity.'' *Associated Press v. United States*, 326 U.S 1 (1945).

ASSOCIATION OF COLLEGE BOOKSTORES. This organization is basically a trade association, founded in 1923 and now with about 3,500 members, designed to provide specific services to college and university bookstores. The association has taken a consistent anti-censorship position and frequently mounts a ''Banned Book Week''—an exhibition of those books subjected to censorship in the past year.

ATLANTA (GA), FILM CENSORSHIP. The city of Atlanta passed an ordinance that attempted to regulate (and thus prevent) the showing of obscene or licentious films that may affect the peace, health, morals, and good order of the city by making it "unlawful for any person to exhibit or cause to be exhibited within the city or within any other territory over which the city exercises police jurisdiction, any pictures or moving pictures unless the same has been approved by the censor or board of censors." This ordinance was ruled a prior restraint,* and thus unconstitutional under the Georgia Constitution, by a Georgia court in 1962 (*K. Gordon Murray Productions, Inc. v. Floyd**).

AVERAGE PERSON. The concept of the "average person" is used as an element in the definition of obscenity,* including the tests or standards laid down by the Supreme Court in the Roth*/Miller*/Memoirs* standards. The "average person," to whom the material in question must have prurient interest,* does not include particularly susceptible or sensitive people (the Hicklin Rule*), but it can include specific groups, such as homosexuals, sexual deviants, or minors, as distinguished from the average adult. But if the material is not aimed at a specific deviant group, the material's obscenity is to be judged by its impact on an average adult person applying contemporary community standards.

B

BACHELLAR v. MARYLAND (1970). Bachellar and others were convicted
by a Baltimore court for violating Maryland's disorderly conduct statute. This
statute prohibits "acting in a disorderly manner to the disturbance of the public
peace, upon any public street...in any [Maryland] city." (Maryland Ann. Code,
Article 27, § 123). The prosecution and conviction arose out of a demonstration
protesting the Viet Nam War.

On appeal, the Supreme Court reversed the convictions, deciding that Bachellar and the others were convicted *not* for disturbing the peace, but for disturbing
the sensibilities and political views of several onlookers. Justice Brennan delivered the opinion of the Court: "There is general agreement regarding the nature
of the facts...[and] the trial judge instructed the jury that 'disorderly conduct
is the doing or saying or both of that which offends, disturbs, incites or tends
to incite a number of people gathered in the same area. It is a conduct of such
nature as to affect the peace and quiet of persons who may witness it and who
may be disturbed or provoked to resentment because of it.' Baltimore law enforcement authorities had advance notice of the demonstration, and a dozen or
more police officers and some United States marshals were on hand when approximately 15 protesters began peacefully to march in a circle on the sidewalk
in front of the [recruiting] station. The marchers carried or wore signs bearing
such legends as: 'Peasant Emanicipation, not Escalation,' 'Make Love not War,'
'Stop in the Name of Love,' and 'Why are We in Vietnam?' The number of
protesters increased to between 30 and 40 before the demonstration ended. A
crowd of onlookers gathered nearby and across the street. From time to time
some of the petitioners and other marchers left the circle and distributed leaflets
among and talked to persons in the crowd.... Clearly the wording of the placards
was not within that small class of 'fighting words'* that, under *Chaplinsky v.
New Hampshire*,* are 'likely to provoke the average person to retaliation, and
thereby cause a breach of the peace,' nor is there any evidence that the demonstrators' remarks to the crowd constituted 'fighting words.' Any shock effect
caused by the placards, remarks, and peaceful marching must be attributed to
the content of the ideas being expressed, or to the onlookers' dislike of demonstrations as a means of expressing dissent. But '[it] is firmly settled that under

our Constitution the public expression of ideas may not be prohibited merely because the ideas are themselves offensive to some of their hearers,' or simply because bystanders object to peaceful and orderly demonstrations. Plainly nothing that occurred during this period could constitutionally be the ground for conviction under § 123.'' *Bachellar v. Maryland*, 397 U.S. 564 (1970).

BANTAM BOOKS, INC. v. SULLIVAN (1963). The Rhode Island legislature created a commission ''to educate the public concerning any book. . .or other thing containing obscene, indecent or impure language, or manifestly tending to the corruption of the youth. . .and to investigate and recommend the prosecution of all violations.'' (Rhode Island, Commission on Youth Morality*). The commission began its job, and by 1960, more than one hundred publications were seen to be objectionable to youths under eighteen. The commission notified distributors and retailers that it would recommend prosecution if the material were not withdrawn. Among the paperback books listed by the commission as objectionable were *Peyton Place*, by Grace Metalious, and *The Bramble Bush*, by Charles Mergendahl. Most of the other publications were magazines, such as *Playboy*, *Rogue*, *Frolic*, and several issues of ''horror'' comics.

The Supreme Court ruled that this system of informal censorship violated the Constitution: ''The Commission's operation is a form of effective state regulation superimposed upon the State's criminal regulation of obscenity and making such regulation largely unnecessary. In thus obviating the need to employ criminal sanctions, the State has at the same time eliminated the safeguards of the criminal process. Criminal sanctions may be applied only after a determination of obscenity has been made in a criminal trial hedged about with the procedural safeguards of the criminal process. The Commission's practice is in striking contrast, in that it provides no safeguards whatever against the suppression of nonobscene, and therefore constitutionally protected, matter. It is a form of regulation that creates hazards to protected freedoms markedly greater than those that attend reliance upon the criminal law. What Rhode Island has done, in fact, has been to subject the distribution of publications to a system of prior administrative restraints. . .[and] although the Commission's supposed concern is limited to youthful readers, the 'cooperation' it seeks from distributors invariably entails the complete suppression of the listed publications; adult readers are equally deprived of the opportunity to purchase the publications in the State (*Butler v. Michigan**).'' *Bantam Books, Inc. v. Sullivan*, 372 U.S. 58 (1963).

BARENBLATT v. UNITED STATES (1959). Barenblatt was summoned to testify before a subcommittee of the House of Representatives Committee on Un-American Activities, which was investigating alleged Communist infiltration into the field of education. Barenblatt refused to answer questions as to whether he was then or had ever been a member of the Communist party, objecting to the right of the subcommittee to inquire into his political beliefs. For refusing to answer, he was convicted of a violation of 2 U.S.C. § 192 (United States

Congress, Contempt*), which makes it a misdemeanor for any person summoned as a witness by either house of Congress to refuse to answer any question pertinent to the inquiry. Barenblatt was fined and sentenced to six months' imprisonment.

On appeal, the Supreme Court sustained the conviction. Justice Harlan delivered the majority opinion: "On the record in this case, the balance between the individual and the governmental interest here at stake must be struck in favor of the latter, and, therefore, the provisions of the First Amendment were not transgressed by the Subcommittee's inquiry into petitioner's past or present membership in the Communist Party.... Investigatory power in this domain is not to be denied Congress solely because the field of education is involved, and the record in this case does not indicate any attempt by the Committee to inquire into the content of academic lectures or discussions, but only to investigate the extent to which the Communist Party had succeeded in infiltrating into our educational institutions persons and groups committed to furthering the Party's alleged objective of violent overthrow of the Government."

There was, however, a vigorous and eloquent dissent by Justice Black: "I cannot agree with the Court's notion that First Amendment freedoms must be abridged in order to 'preserve' our country. That notion rests on the unarticulated premise that this Nation's security hangs upon its power to punish people because of what they think, speak or write about, or because of those with whom they associate for political purposes. The Government, in its brief, virtually admits this proposition when it speaks of the 'communication of unlawful ideas.' I challenge this premise, and deny that ideas can be proscribed under our Constitution. I agree that despotic governments cannot exist without stifling the voice of opposition to their oppressive practices. The First Amendment means to me, however, that the only constitutional way our Government can preserve itself is to leave its people the fullest possible freedom to praise, criticize or discuss, as they see fit, all governmental policies and to suggest, if they desire, that even its most fundamental postulates are bad and should be changed; 'Therein lies the security of the Republic, the very foundation of constitutional government.' On that premise this land was created, on that premise it has grown to greatness. Our Constitution assumes that the common sense of the people and their attachment to our country will enable them, after free discussion, to withstand ideas that are wrong. To say that our patriotism must be protected against false ideas by means other than these is, I think, to make a baseless charge. Unless we can rely on these qualities—if, in short, we begin to punish speech—we cannot honestly proclaim ourselves to be a free Nation and we have lost what the Founders of this land risked their lives and their sacred honor to defend." *Barenblatt v. United States*, 360 U.S 109 (1959).

BARTELS v. IOWA (1923). An Iowa statute (Iowa, Teaching in a Foreign Language*) prohibited teaching in any school in a language other than English. The statute was seen to be unconstitutional by the Supreme Court; the decision is contained in *Meyer v. Nebraska.* *Bartels v. Iowa*, 262 U.S. 404 (1923).

BATES v. STATE BAR OF ARIZONA (1977). John Bates and Van O'Steen, members of the Arizona State Bar, were charged in a complaint by the State Bar's president with violating the Arizona Supreme Court Disciplinary Rule,* which prohibited attorneys from advertising in newspapers and other media. The Arizona Supreme Court upheld the conclusion of a bar commission that Bates violated the rule and it rejected Bates' claim that the rule infringed on his First Amendment rights. On appeal, the Supreme Court reversed: "Commercial speech, which serves individual and societal interests in assuring informed and reliable decision making, is entitled to some First Amendment protection. Because Bates' ads were not misleading, false, or fraudulent, they fall within the scope of First Amendment protection." *Bates v. State Bar of Arizona*, 433 U.S. 350 (1977).

BAXLEY (GA), SOLICITING ORDINANCE. "Section I. Before any person or persons, firms or organizations shall solicit membership for any organization, union or society of any sort which requires from its members the payments of membership fees, dues or is entitled to make assessment against its members, such person or persons shall make application in writing to Mayor and Council of the City of Baxley for the issuance of a permit to solicit members in such organization from among the citizens of Baxley. . . . Section IV. In passing upon such application the Mayor and Council shall consider the character of the applicant, the nature of the business of the organization for which the members are desired to be solicited, and its effects upon the general welfare of citizens of the City of Baxley." This ordinance was judged to be an unconstitutional prior restraint by the Supreme Court in *Staub v. City of Baxley* (1958).*

BEAUHARNAIS v. ILLINOIS (1952). Beauharnais was convicted by an Illinois court for distributing on the streets of Chicago anti-black leaflets in violation of Illinois Rev. Stat., 1949, c. 38, § 471 (Illinois, Group Libel*), which made it a crime to exhibit in any public place any publication that "portrays depravity, criminality, unchastity, or lack of virtue of a class of citizens, of any race, color, creed or religion" and that "exposes the citizens of any race, color, creed or religion to contempt, derision, or obloquy."

The Supreme Court, Justice Frankfurter delivering the majority opinion, affirmed the conviction: "The lithograph complained of was a leaflet setting forth a petition calling on the Mayor and City Council of Chicago 'to halt the further encroachment, harassment and invasion of white people, their property, neighborhoods and persons, by the Negro.' Below was a call for 'One million self respecting white people in Chicago to unite' with the statement added that 'If persuasion and the need to prevent the white race from becoming mongrelized by the negro will not unite us, then the aggressions. . .rapes, robberies, knives, guns and marijuana of the negro, surely will.' This. . .concluded with an attached application for membership in the White Circle League of America, Inc. In the face of. . .history and its frequent obligato of extreme racial and religious propaganda, we would deny experience to say that the Illinois legislature was without reason in seeking ways to curb false or malicious defamation of racial and religious groups, made in public places and by means calculated to have a powerful emotional impact on those to whom it was presented....Libelous utterances not being within the area of constitutionally protected speech, it is unnecessary, either for us or for the State courts, to consider the issues behind the phrase 'clear and present danger.'* Certainly no one would contend that obscene speech, for example, may be punished only upon a showing of such circumstances. Libel, as we have seen, is in the same class.''

Justice Black, joined by Justice Douglas, dissented from the majority opinion, viewing the conviction as a violation of the First Amendment and an example of state censorship: "The conviction rests on the leaflet's contents, not on the time, manner or place of distribution....This act sets up a system of state censorship at war with the kind of free government envisioned by those who forced adoption of our Bill of Rights. The motives behind the state law may have been to do good. But the same can be said about most laws making opinions punishable as crimes. History indicates that urges to do good have led to the burning of books and even to the burning of 'witches.' No rationalization on a purely legal level can conceal the fact that state laws like this one present a constant overhanging threat to freedom of speech, press and religion. Today Beauharnais is punished for publicly expressing strong views in favor of segregation. Ironically enough, Beauharnais, convicted of crime in Chicago, would probably be given a hero's reception in many other localities, if not in some parts of Chicago itself. Moreover, the same kind of state law that makes Beauharnais a criminal for advocating segregation in Illinois can be utilized to send people to jail in other states for advocating equality and nonsegregation. What Beauharnais said in his leaflet is mild compared with usual arguments on both sides of racial controversies....To say that a legislative body can, with this Court's approval, make it a crime to petition for and publicly discuss proposed legislation seems as farfetched to me as it would be to say that a valid law could be enacted to punish a candidate for President for telling the people his views....If there be minority groups who hail this holding as their victory, they might consider the possible relevancy of this ancient remark: 'Another such victory and I am undone.' " *Beauharnais v. Illinois*, 343 U.S. 250 (1952).

BELL, ATTORNEY GENERAL v. WOLFISH (1979). Wolfish and others, inmates, brought this class action challenging the constitutionality of numerous conditions of confinement and practices in the Metropolitan Correctional Center, a federally operated short-term custodial facility in New York City designed primarily to house pretrial detainees. One practice was the "publisher-only" rule* prohibiting inmates from receiving hardcover books that were not mailed directly from publishers, book clubs, or bookstores. The Supreme Court held that the publisher-only rule did not violate the First Amendment rights of the detainees, but rather, it was a rational response by prison officials to the obvious security problem of preventing the smuggling of contraband in books sent in from the outside. In addition, the Court judged that the rule operated in a neutral fashion, without regard to the content of the books; there were alternative means of obtaining reading material; and the rule's impact on the pretrial detainees was minimal, since most inmates did not stay in the facility longer than sixty days. *Bell, Attorney General v. Wolfish*, 441 U.S. 520 (1979).

BERKELEY (CA), ORDINANCE ON POLITICAL CONTRIBUTIONS.
The voters of Berkeley adopted the Election Reform Act of 1974, Ordinance No. 4700-NS, by initiative. The campaign ordinance so enacted placed limits on expenditures and contributions in campaigns involving both candidates and ballot measures. Section 602 of the ordinance provided: "No person shall make, and no campaign treasurer shall solicit or accept, any contribution which will cause the total amount contributed by such person with respect to a single election in support of or in opposition to a measure to exceed two hundred and fifty dollars ($250)." The Supreme Court, in 1981, in *Citizens Against Rent Control v. City of Berkeley*,* ruled that such an ordinance violated the First Amendment.

BIGELOW v. VIRGINIA (1975). Bigelow was the managing editor of a weekly newspaper published in Virginia. As the result of publishing a New York City organization's advertisement announcing that it would arrange low-cost placements for women with unwanted pregnancies in accredited hospitals and clinics in New York (where abortions were legal and there were no residency requirements), Bigelow was convicted of violating the Virginia Abortion Advertising Statute.* This statute made it a misdemeanor, by the sale or circulation of any publication, to encourage or prompt the processing of an abortion.

The Supreme Court ruled that the statute violated the First Amendment: The Virginia courts erred in assuming that advertising, as such, was entitled to no First Amendment protection and that Bigelow had no legitimate First Amendment interest, since speech is not stripped of First Amendment protection merely because it appears in the form of a paid commercial advertisement. The fact that the advertisement in question had commercial aspects or reflected the advertiser's commercial interest did not negate all First Amendment guarantees. The Court ruled that the advertisement conveyed information of potential interest and value to a diverse audience consisting not only of readers possibly in need of the services offered, but also those concerned with the subject matter or the law of another state, and readers seeking reform in Virginia. The Court felt that an individual state does not acquire power or supervision over another state's internal affairs merely because its own citizens' welfare and health may be affected when they travel to the other state. Although a state may seek to disseminate information so as to enable its citizens to make better-informed decisions when they leave, it may not bar a citizen of another state from disseminating information about an activity that is legal in that state. The opinion concluded with the remark that Virginia's interest in regulating what Virginians may hear or read about the

New York services or in shielding its citizens from information about activities outside its borders is not entitled to any weight. *Bigelow v. Virginia*, 421 U.S. 809 (1975).

BIRMINGHAM (AL), PARADE ORDINANCE. Section 1159 of the General Code of Birmingham read: "It shall be unlawful to organize or hold, or to assist in organizing or holding, or to take part or participate in, any parade or procession or other public demonstration on the streets or other public ways of the city, unless a permit therefor has been secured from the commission. To secure such a permit, written application shall be made to the commission, setting forth the probable number of persons, vehicles and animals which will be engaged in such parade, procession or other public demonstration, the purpose for which it is to be held or had, and the streets or other public ways over, along or in which it is desired to have or hold such parade, procession or other public demonstration. The commission shall grant a written permit for such parade...prescribing the streets or other public ways which may be used therefor, unless in its judgment the public welfare, peace, safety, health, decency, good order, morals or convenience require that it be refused. It shall be unlawful to use for such purposes any other streets or public ways than those set out in said permit. The two preceding paragraphs, however, shall not apply to funeral processions." This ordinance was used by the city of Birmingham to prevent any civil rights demonstrations, but the Supreme Court, seeing it as a prior restraint (the issuance of the permit did not have narrow and well-defined standards), ruled it a violation of the First Amendment in *Shuttlesworth v. City of Birmingham* (1969).*

BLOUNT v. RIZZI (1971). Certain regulations of the U.S. Postal Service (Postal Regulations, Unlawful Mail*), 39 U.S.C. §§ 4006-4007, permitted the postmaster general to stamp as "unlawful" and return to the sender letters addressed to any person and to prohibit the payment of postal money orders to that person if he finds, on "evidence satisfactory to [him]," that the person is obtaining or seeking money through the mails for "an obscene...matter" or is using the mails to distribute information about how such items may be obtained. Under departmental regulations, following a complaint and a notice of hearing, a judicial officer holds a hearing and renders his opinion "with all due speed," from which there is an administrative appeal (§ 4006). Section 4007 permitted district courts to order the defendant's incoming mail detained pending completion of the § 4006 proceedings.

The Supreme Court held that this administrative censorship scheme violated the First Amendment, since it lacked adequate safeguards against undue inhibition of protected expression. Justice Brennan delivered the opinion of the Court: "To avoid constitutional infirmity a scheme of administrative censorship must: place the burdens of initiating judicial review and of proving that the material is unprotected expression on the censor; require 'prompt judicial review'—and a final judicial determination on the merits within a specified, brief period—to prevent the administrative decision of the censor from achieving an effect of finality; and limit to preservation of the *status quo* for the shortest, fixed period compatible with sound judicial resolution, any restraint imposed in advance of the final judicial determination. These safeguards are lacking in the administrative scheme created by §§ 4006-4007 and the regulations.'' *Blount v. Rizzi*, 400 U.S. 410 (1971).

BLUE MOVIE/FUCK. This 1969 film, produced and directed by Andy Warhol and starring Viva Waldon and Louis Waldon, was the subject of several court cases as to the film's obscenity. Edward de Grazia and Roger K. Newman (*Banned Films*, p. 316) write that ''this movie depicts an afternoon in a Manhattan apartment where Viva and Louis discuss current social issues while lying in bed. Louis makes sexual advances and Viva giggles; they indulge in sexual foreplay and then intercourse. They talk about the Vietnam War, watch television, get dressed, eat, discuss Louis' unhappy marriage, and finally take a shower, more and more aware of the presence of a camera. After more sex play in and out of the shower, Viva stares at the camera and asks, 'Is it on?' ''† The New York Court of Appeals, in *People v. Heller*, 277 N.E. 2d 651 (1971), ruled that the film was obscene and thus a violation of the New York Obscenity Statute.* But on appeal to the Supreme Court (*Heller v. New York*, 413 U.S. 483 [1973]), the case was remanded back to New York to reconsider the film's obscenity in light of the Miller Standard.* In the rehearing, the New York Court of Appeals (*People v. Heller*, 307 N.E. 2d 805 [1973]) again ruled that *Blue Movie/Fuck* was obscene.

BOARD OF EDUCATION v. PICO (1982). The Board of Education of the Island Trees Union Free School District No. 26, in New York, characterized a number of books as ''anti-American, anti-Christian, anti-Semitic, and just plain filthy'' and ordered their removal from the junior and senior high school libraries. The board then appointed a commission of parents and members of the school staff to review the books and to make recommendations about them. The board largely ignored the recommendations and decided that several books should be removed from the school libraries and should not be used in the school curriculum. A group of students brought suit, claiming that the board's actions—taken because the books offended their social, political, and moral tastes—violated the students' First Amendment rights. A federal district court gave summary judgment for the board, but an appeals court remanded the case for a trial on the students' allegations.

The Supreme Court affirmed the appeal court's ruling. This case resulted in a sharply divided Supreme Court: A majority could not agree on a single decision,

---

†Reprinted from *Banned Films* with permission of the R. R. Bowker Company. Copyright © 1982 by Edward de Grazia and Roger K. Newman.

but five members did agree that the students' allegations were such that the board could not receive summary judgment. Justice Brennan announced the decision of the Court's plurality: "Local school boards have broad discretion in the management of school affairs but this discretion must be exercised in a manner that comports with the transcendent imperatives of the First Amendment; the First Amendment rights of students may be directly and sharply implicated by the removal of books from the shelves of a school library; and local school boards may not remove books from school library shelves simply because they dislike the ideas contained in those books."

Chief Justice Burger, joined by Justices Powell, Rehnquist, and O'Connor, dissented: "If the plurality's view were to become the law, the court would come perilously close to becoming a 'super censor' of school board library decisions and the Constitution does not dictate that judges, rather than parents, teachers, and local school boards, must determine how the standards of morality and vulgarity are to be treated in the classroom."

The Court record contained the objectionable passages from the books involved: *The Best Short Stories by Negro Writers*, edited by Langston Hughes: "You need some pussy. Come on, let's go up to the whore house on the hill. She first became aware of the warm tense nipples on her breasts. Her hands went up gently to calm them. In profile, his penis hung like a stout tassel. She could even tell that he was circumcised"; *Black Boy*, by Richard Wright: "We black children—seven or eight or nine years of age—used to run to the Jew's store and shout:. . . Bloody Christ Killers/Never trust a Jew/Bloody Christ Killers/ What won't a Jew do/Red, white and blue/Your pa was a Jew/Your ma a dirty dago/What the hell is you?"; *The Fixer*, by Bernard Malamud: "What do you think goes on in the wagon at night: Are the drivers on their knees fucking their mothers?/Who else would do anything like that but a motherfucking Zhid?/No more noise out of you or I'll shoot your Jew cock off/Also there's a lot of fucking in the Old Testament, so how is that religious?"; *Go Ask Alice*, by Anonymous: "shitty, goddamned, pissing, ass, goddamned beJesus, screwing life's, ass, shit. Doris was ten and had humped with who knows how many men in between/but now when I face a girl its like facing a boy. I get all excited and turned on. I want to screw with the girl"; *A Hero Ain't Nothing but a Sandwich*, by Alice Childress: "Hell, no! Fuck the society./They can have back the spread and curtains, I'm too old for them fuckin bunnies anyway"; *Laughing Boy*, by Oliver LaFarge: "I was frightened when he wanted me to lie with him, but he made me feel all right. He knew all about how to make women forget themselves, that man"; *The Naked Ape*, by Desmond Morris: "If either males or females cannot for some reason obtain sexual access to their opposite numbers, they will find sexual outlets in other ways. They may use other members of their own sex, or they may even use members of other species, or they may masturbate"; *Slaughterhouse Five*, by Kurt Vonnegut, Jr.: "But the Gospels actually taught this: Before you kill somebody, make absolutely sure he isn't well connected/ The flaw in the Christ stories, said the visitor from outer space, was that Christ who didn't look like much, was actually the son of the Most Powerful Being in the Universe/So the people amused themselves one day by nailing him to a cross and planting the cross in the ground. There couldn't possibly be any repercussions, the lynchers thought. . . since the new Gospel hammered home again and again what a nobody Jesus was. And then just before the nobody dies. . . the voice of God came crashing down. He told the people that he was adopting the bum as his son''; *Soul on Ice*, by Eldridge Cleaver: "There are white men who will pay you to fuck their wives. They approach you and say, 'How would you like to fuck a white woman?' 'What is this?' you ask. 'On the up-and-up,' he assures you. 'It's all right. She's my wife. She needs a black rod, is all. She has to have it. It's like a medicine or drug to her. She has to have it. I'll pay you. It's all on the level, no trick involved. Interested?' '' *Board of Education v. Pico*, 73 L. Ed. 2d 435 (1982).

BOHNING v. OHIO (1923). An Ohio statute (Ohio, Teaching in a Foreign Language*) prohibited teaching in any school in any language other than English. The Supreme Court ruled that this statute violated the First Amendment. The decision is contained in *Meyer v. Nebraska* (1923).* *Bohning v. Ohio*, 262 U.S. 404 (1923).

BOLGER v. YOUNGS DRUG PRODUCTS CORPORATION (1983). Certain postal regulations (Postal Regulations, Advertising Contraceptives*) prohibit the mailing of unsolicited advertisements for contraceptives. Youngs decided to undertake a campaign of unsolicited mass mailings to members of the public and attempted to mail three types of materials: (1) multipage, multi-item flyers promoting a large variety of products available at a drugstore, including prophylactics; (2) flyers exclusively or substantially devoted to promoting prophylactics; and (3) informational pamphlets discussing the desirability and availability of prophylactics in general and Youngs' products in particular. One pamphlet, titled *Condoms and Human Sexuality*, described the use, manufacture, desirability, and availability of condoms and provided detailed descriptions of various Trojan-brand condoms manufactured by Youngs; another, *Plain Talk About Venereal Disease*, discussed at length the problem of venereal disease and the use and advantages of condoms in aiding the prevention of venereal disease. Youngs brought suit to enjoin the Postal Service from preventing these mailings, arguing that the regulations violated the First Amendment.

The Supreme Court, Justice Marshall delivering the opinion of the Court, agreed: "Advertising for contraceptives not only implicates 'substantial individual and societal interests' in the free flow of commercial information, but also relates to activity that is protected from unwarranted governmental interference. . . [the] proposed commercial speech is clearly protected by the First Amendment. Neither of the interests asserted by the Government—that [the regulations] shield recipients of mail from materials that they are likely to find offensive and aid parents' efforts to control the manner in which their children

become informed about birth control—is sufficient to justify the sweeping prohibition on the mailing of unsolicited contraceptive advertisements. The fact that
protected speech may be offensive to some persons does not justify its suppression, and, in any event, recipients of objectionable mailings can avoid further
offensiveness simply by averting their eyes or disposing of the mailings in a
trash can. . . . The statute's marginal degree of protection afforded those parents
who desire to keep their children from confronting such mailings is improperly
achieved by purging all mailboxes of unsolicited material that is entirely suitable
for adults.'' *Bolger v. Youngs Drug Products Corporation*, 77 L. Ed. 2d 469
(1983).

BONDAGE BOOKS. Irving Klaw and Jack Kramer were convicted in a U.S.
district court for mailing obscene matter (Postal Regulations, Mailing Obscene
Material*), but the convictions were reversed in a court of appeals (*United States
v. Klaw*, 350 F. 2d 155 [1965]). Klaw was the owner of Nutrix Co., a New
York-based establishment that printed and distributed, mostly through the mails,
materials known in the trade as ''bondage'' books. The court record contained
a description of some of this material: ''These 'bondage' booklets usually contain
some twenty to twenty-five photographs or crude drawings of females—some
scantily clad, some tightly trussed, and all voluptuous—subjecting other women
and men to various tortures and indignities, including violent and forcible de-
formation of the body, while being gagged, fettered, and bound in bizarre pos-
tures. The booklets bore such titles as *Female Doctor Forced into Bondage* and
Men in the Ladies Room. A text in each booklet described in puerile and asinine
fashion the activity depicted in the drawings. . . . The captives and tormentors
are drawn with exaggerated female physical characteristics, clothed in tight-
fitting garments, wearing black leather shoes with very high heels, and posed
in unusual positions.''

In reversing the lower court's conviction, Judge Moore wrote: ''Indeed, vulgarity seems to be in vogue. But it is doubtful whether our jails would be well
used if convictions were to be based on material that is just 'disgusting and
revolting.'. . . . The courts may have opened the floodgates for horror and filth,
but if they are to be closed it should be done by the careful drafting of proper
laws by our duly elected representatives, and not by a combination of zealous
governmental inspectors, prosecutors, and uninformed juries. . . . Otherwise it
would be altogether too easy for any prosecutor to stand before a jury, display
the exhibits involved, and merely ask in summation: 'Would you want your son
or daughter to see or read this stuff?' A conviction in every instance would be
virtually assured.''

BOND v. FLOYD (1966). Several months after being elected to the Georgia
House of Representatives in 1965, Julian Bond, an outspoken civil rights advocate, made certain statements regarding the government's policies in Viet Nam
and the operation of the Selective Service laws. Bond was quoted as saying: ''I

think it is sorta hypocritical for us to maintain that we are fighting for liberty in other places and we are not guaranteeing liberty to citizens inside the continental United States''; and ''Well, I think that the fact that the United States Government fights a war in Viet Nam, I don't think that I as a second class citizen of the United States have a requirement to support that war. I think my responsibility is to oppose things that I think are wrong if they are in Viet Nam or New York, or Chicago, or Atlanta, or wherever.''

The Georgia House of Representatives did not appreciate Bond's comments and refused to seat him; a district court sanctioned the exclusion. The Supreme Court, however, saw this as a blatant violation of the First Amendment. Chief Justice Warren delivered the Court's opinion: ''The State argues that the exclusion does not violate the First Amendment because the State has a right...to insist on loyalty to the Constitution as a condition of office...[but] that is not the issue in this case....Certainly there can be no question but that the First Amendment protects expressions in opposition to national foreign policy in Vietnam and to the Selective Service System. The State does not contend otherwise. But it argues that Bond went beyond expressions of opposition, and counseled violations of the Selective Service laws, and that advocating violation of federal law demonstrates a lack of support for the Constitution. The State declines to argue that Bond's statements would violate any law if made by a private citizen, but it does argue that even though a citizen might be protected by his First Amendment rights, the State may nonetheless apply a stricter standard to its legislators. We do not agree.'' *Bond v. Floyd*, 385 U.S. 116 (1966).

BOSTON (MA), PUBLIC SPEAKING PERMIT. In what would today be most assuredly classified as an unconstitutional prior restraint, the Supreme Court, in *Davis v. Massachusetts* (1897),* upheld the following Boston ordinance: ''No person shall, in or upon any of the public grounds, make any public address, discharge any cannon or firearm, expose for sale any goods, wares or merchandise, erect or maintain any booth, stand, tent or apparatus for the purposes of public amusement or show, except in accordance with a permit from the mayor.''

BOWDEN v. FORT SMITH (1942). A Fort Smith, Arkansas, Book Sellers' License* was required before any person could peddle any article door to door within the city. Bowden was convicted for selling religious pamphlets door to door without such license and appealed the conviction to the Supreme Court on grounds that the city ordinance was an unconstitutional restriction of freedom of the press. The Supreme Court sustained the conviction; its decision is reported below, in *Jones v. Opelika* (1942).* But just one year later, in a rehearing in 1943, the Court vacated its original decision in light of *Jamison v. Texas* (1943)* and *Largent v. Texas* (1943).* *Bowden v. Fort Smith*, 316 U.S. 584 (1942).

BRANDENBURG v. OHIO (1969). Brandenburg, a Ku Klux Klan leader, was convicted under the Ohio Criminal Syndicalism* statute for "advocating the duty, necessity, or propriety of crime, sabotage, violence, or unlawful methods of terrorism as a means of accomplishing industrial or political reform" and for "voluntarily assembling with any society, group or assemblage of persons formed to teach or advocate the doctrines of criminal syndicalism." He was fined $1,000 and sentenced to one to ten years' imprisonment. Brandenburg was charged with stating the following: "How far is the nigger going to—yeah/This is what we are going to do to the niggers/A dirty nigger/Send the Jews back to Israel/Let's give them back to the dark garden/Save America/Let's go back to constitutional betterment/Bury the niggers/We intend to do our part/Give us our state rights/Freedom for the whites/Nigger will have to fight for every inch he gets from now on."

On appeal, the Supreme Court reversed the conviction, stating: "Since the statute, by its words and as applied, purports to punish mere advocacy and to forbid, on pain of criminal punishment, assembly with others merely to advocate the described type of action, it falls within the condemnation of the First Amendment. Freedoms of speech and press do not permit a State to forbid advocacy of the use of force or of law violation except where such advocacy is directed to inciting or producing imminent lawless action and is likely to incite or produce such action." This decision overruled *Whitney v. California* (1927).* *Brandenburg v. Ohio*, 395 U.S. 444 (1969).

BRANZBURG v. HAYES (1972). This particular case was decided by the Supreme Court along with *In the matter of Paul Pappas* and *United States v. Earl Caldwell*. These three cases concerned a claimed constitutional privilege of newsreporters, based on the First Amendment, not to appear or give testimony before a grand jury. The briefs for the reporters argued that freedom of the press protects all activities necessary for the press to fulfill its First Amendment functions and that state action that discourages the flow of information between confidential informants and newsgatherers violates the First Amendment.

The Supreme Court did not agree: "The First Amendment does *not* relieve a newspaper reporter of the obligation that all citizens have to respond to a grand jury subpoena and answer questions relevant to a criminal investigation and, therefore, the First Amendment does not afford him a constitutional testimonial privilege for an agreement he makes to conceal facts relevant to a grand jury's investigation of a crime or to conceal the criminal conduct of his source or evidence thereof." *Branzburg v. Hayes*, 408 U.S 665 (1972).

BRATTLE FILMS v. COMMISSIONER OF PUBLIC SAFETY (1955). Brattle Films, a movie theater, wished to exhibit a film (*Miss Julie*) on a Sunday, but the Massachusetts Sunday Exhibitions/Entertainment* statute required that the commissioner of public safety issue an opinion that the activity was "in keeping with the character of the day and not inconsistent with its due observ-

ance.'' Judge Wilkins of the Supreme Judicial Court of Massachusetts ruled that
the statute was an unconstitutional prior restraint: ''That the present controversy
concerns exhibitions on only one day a week, and that day Sunday, does not
seem to us to alter the governing rules of law. It is unthinkable that there is a
power, absent as to secular days, to require the submission to advance scrutiny
by governmental authority of newspapers to be published on Sunday, of sermons
to be preached on Sunday, or public addresses to be made on Sunday.'' *Brattle
Films v. Commissioner of Public Safety*, 127 N.E. 2d 891 (1955).

BREARD v. ALEXANDRIA (1951). An Alexandria, Louisiana, Anti-Soliciting Ordinance* prohibited the practice of door-to-door soliciting of private
residences for the purpose of selling goods without the prior consent of the owner
or occupant. Breard was selling subscriptions to nationally known magazines
and periodicals but was convicted under the ordinance because he did not obtain
the required prior consent. The Supreme Court affirmed the conviction, Justice
Reed delivering the Court's opinion: ''The First Amendment has never been
treated as [an] absolute. Freedom of speech or press does not mean that one can
talk or distribute where, when and how one chooses. Rights other than those of
the advocates are involved. By adjustment of rights, we can have both full liberty
of expression and an orderly life.''

Justice Black dissented from this decision: ''Today's decision marks a revi-
talization of the judicial views which prevailed before this Court embraced the
philosophy that the First Amendment gives a preferred status to the liberties it
protects. I adhere to that preferred position philosophy. It is my belief that the
freedom of the people of this Nation cannot survive even a little governmental
hobbling of religious or political ideas, whether they be communicated orally
or through the press. The constitutional sanctuary for the press must necessarily
include liberty to publish and circulate. In view of our economic system, it must
also include freedom to solicit paying subscribers. Of course homeowners can
if they wish forbid newsboys, reporters or magazine solicitors to ring their
doorbells. But when the homeowner himself has not done this, I believe that
the First Amendment, interpreted with due regard for the freedoms it guarantees,
bars laws like the present ordinance which punish persons who peacefully go
from door to door as agents of the press.'' *Breard v. Alexandria*, 341 U.S. 622
(1951).

BRENNEMAN v. MADIGAN (1972). Brenneman and others were confined
in the Santa Rita Rehabilitation Center, a jail in Alameda County, California,
as pretrial detainees because they were unable to post bond. They brought a civil
rights class action suit, alleging that their treatment violated the First Amendment's guarantee of free speech (their ability to have visitors, make telephone
calls, and to have uncensored correspondence was restricted).

Judge Zirpoli, of the district court, agreed that the pretrial detainees had the
constitutional right, protected by the First Amendment, to communicate with

friends, relatives, attorneys, and public officials by means of visits, correspondence, and telephone calls: "While a convicted prisoner may have no right to make any telephone calls at all . . . a pretrial detainee does. In apparent recognition of this right, the defendants have recently installed pay telephones . . . for the use of detainees confined there, and such telephones receive heavy use. Needless to say, eavesdropping, accomplished either by means of electronic equipment or the presence of a custodial officer, would raise serious constitutional questions. While prison officials may inspect incoming correspondence for contraband, it is difficult to justify any restrictions at all on the amount or content of a pretrial detainee's outgoing correspondence. . . . The following standards [should apply]: 1. There shall be no censorship of outgoing mail. 2. There shall be no limitation on the persons to whom outgoing mail may be directed. 3. There shall be no censorship of incoming letters from the prisoner's attorney, or from any judge or elected public official. 4. Incoming parcels or letters may be inspected for contraband, but letters may not be read. 5. Proper arrangements shall be made to insure that prisoners may freely obtain writing materials and postage. 6. Indigent prisoners shall be furnished at public expense writing materials and ordinary postage for their personal use in dispatching a maximum of five (5) letters per week. . . . Enough has been said to establish the right of pretrial detainees to be free from any privations and restrictions which are not absolutely necessary to insure their presence at trial. Pretrial detainees do not stand on the same footing as convicted inmates. For the latter, punishment, rehabilitation and deterrence are appropriate adjuncts of incarceration, and the courts will be loathe to interfere with the means adopted to accomplish these goals. For pretrial detainees, however, the only constitutional purpose of incarceration is the detention itself, and the courts must intervene in appropriate cases to insure that the means adopted to accomplish that purpose are not unduly restrictive." *Brenneman v. Madigan*, 343 F. Supp. 128 (1972).

BRIDGES v. CALIFORNIA (1941). Harry Bridges, a long-time labor union organizer and activist connected with the Marine Workers' Industrial Union, was found guilty of contempt of a California state court when he published in a newspaper the text of a telegram he had sent to the U.S. secretary of labor. The telegram criticized the decision of a judge in a labor dispute case and hinted that the decision would lead to a strike.

On appeal, the Supreme Court reversed the conviction, saying it was a violation of Bridges' constitutional rights of freedom of speech and of the press. Justice Black delivered the opinion of the Court: "In brief, the state courts asserted and exercised a power to punish petitioners for publishing their views concerning cases not in all respects finally determined, upon the following chain of reasoning: California is vested with the power and duty to provide an adequate administration of justice; by virtue of this power and duty, it can take appropriate measures for providing fair judicial trials free from coercion or intimidation; included among such appropriate measures is the common law procedure of punishing certain interferences and obstructions through contempt proceedings; this particular measure, devolving upon the courts of California by reason of their creation as courts, includes the power to punish for publications made outside the courtroom if they tend to interfere with the fair and orderly administration of justice in a pending case; the trial court having found that the publications had such a tendency, and there being substantial evidence to support the finding, the punishments here imposed were an appropriate exercise of the state's power; in so far as these punishments constitute a restriction on liberty of expression, the public interest in that liberty was properly subordinated to the public interest in judicial impartiality and decorum.... No suggestion can be found in the Constitution that the freedom there guaranteed for speech and the press bears an inverse ratio to the timeliness and importance of the ideas seeking expression. Yet, it would follow as a practical result of the decisions below that anyone who might wish to give public expression to his views on a pending case involving no matter what problem of public interest, just at the time his audience would be most receptive, would be as effectively discouraged as if a deliberate statutory scheme of censorship had been adopted. Indeed, perhaps more so, because under a legislative specification of the particular kinds of expressions prohibited and the circumstances under which the prohibitions are to operate, the speaker or publisher might at least have an authoritative guide to the permissible scope of comment, instead of being compelled to act at the peril that judges might find in the utterance a 'reasonable tendency' to obstruct justice in a pending case." *Bridges v. California*, 314 U.S. 252 (1941).

BRIDGES v. WIXON (1945). Harry Bridges, a long-time labor union organizer and activist, was ordered to be deported because he was seen to be "affiliated" with an organization (the Communist Party) that believed in, advised, advocated, or taught the overthrow of the government by force or violence.

On appeal, the Supreme Court ruled that the deportation order was unlawful. Justice Douglas delivered the opinion of the Court: "We cannot assume that Congress meant to employ the term 'affiliation' in a broad, fluid sense which would visit such hardship on an alien for slight or insubstantial reasons. It is clear that Congress desired to have the country rid of those aliens who embraced the political faith of force and violence. But we cannot believe that Congress intended to cast so wide a net as to reach those whose ideas and program, though coinciding with the legitimate aims of such groups, nevertheless fell far short of overthrowing the government by force and violence. Freedom of speech and of press is accorded aliens residing in this country. So far as this record shows the literature published by Harry Bridges, the utterances made by him were entitled to that protection.... When the evidence underlying these findings is examined it is found to be devoid of any showing that the *Waterfront Worker* advocated overthrow of the government by force. It was a militant trade-union journal. It aired the grievances of the longshoreman. It discussed national affairs affecting the interests of working men. It declared against war. But we have found no evidence whatsoever which suggests that it advocated the overthrow of the government by force. Nor is there any finding that Bridges took over this project with the view of doing more than advancing the lawful cause of unionism." *Bridges v. Wixon*, 326 U.S.135 (1945).

BROADCASTING. Although broadcasting (radio and television) is a means of communication and speech protected by the First Amendment, Congress, the Federal Communications Commission (FCC), and the courts have applied somewhat different standards to broadcasting than those applied to other forms of communication. The Supreme Court, in its "Filthy Words"* decision (*Federal Communications Commission v. Pacifica Foundation* [1978]), advanced several reasons for treating broadcast speech (especially radio) differently from other forms of expression: "Broadcasting requires special treatment because of four important considerations: (1) children have access to radios and in many cases are unsupervised by parents; (2) radio receivers are in the home, a place where people's privacy interest is entitled to extra deference; (3) unconsenting adults may tune in a station without any warning that offensive language is being or will be broadcast; and (4) there is a scarcity of spectrum space, the use of which the government must therefore license in the public interest. Of special concern to the Commission as well as parents is the first point regarding the use of radio [and television] by children."

The courts have ruled that various principles and applications dealing with the FCC's interpretation of the Communication Act does not violate the First Amendment: reasonable access rule,* Federal Communications Commission Regulations, Fairness Doctrine,* and the public interest, convenience, and necessity.* In addition, the courts have tried to balance the rights of the broadcast media and the rights of due process and a fair trial. In general, the broadcast media can report and publicize matters already in the public record, but in *Estes v. Texas*,* the Supreme Court ruled that failure to regulate the conduct of the news media in the courtroom and to insulate the trial from the effects of massive publicity violated the fair trial guarantees of the defendants. *Annotation: Broadcast Regulation*, 69 L. Ed. 2nd 1110.

BROADERICK v. OKLAHOMA (1973). A group of Oklahoma state employees filed a suit challenging the constitutionality of certain sections of the state's Merit System Act (Oklahoma, State Hatch Act*), patterned after the federal Hatch Act,* which placed limits on civil servants' First Amendment rights. The Supreme Court ruled that the states did have the authority to limit the freedom of expression by civil servants, but Justice Douglas dissented: "I do not see how government can deprive its employees the right to speak, write, assemble, or petition once the office is closed and the employee is home on his own....I would not allow the bureaucracy in the State or Federal Government to be deprived of First Amendment rights." *Broaderick v. Oklahoma*, 413 U.S 601 (1973).

BROWN, SECRETARY OF DEFENSE v. GLINES (1980). Air force regulations (Military Regulations, Air Force*) require members of that service to
obtain approval from their commanders before circulating petitions on air force
bases. Glines was removed from active duty for distributing on an air force base
petitions to members of Congress and the secretary of defense that complained
about air force grooming standards without having obtained approval of the base
commander, as required by the regulations.

The Supreme Court ruled that the regulations are not invalid: "Such regulations
do not violate the First Amendment. They protect a substantial Government
interest unrelated to the suppression of free expression—the interest in maintaining the respect for duty and discipline so vital to military effectiveness—and
restrict speech no more than is reasonably necessary to protect such interest.
Since a military commander is charged with maintaining morale, discipline, and
readiness, he must have authority over the distribution of materials that could
affect adversely these essential attributes of an effective military force. . . . Such
regulations do not violate 10 U.S.C. § 1034 [Military Regulations, Petitioning
Congress*], which proscribes unwarranted restrictions on a serviceman's right
to communicate with a member of Congress. As § 1034's legislative history
makes clear, Congress enacted the statute to ensure than an individual member
of the Armed Services could write to his elected representatives without sending
his communication through official channels, and not to protect the circulation
of collective petitions within a military base. Permitting an individual serviceman
to submit a petition directly to any member of Congress serves § 1034's legislative
purpose without unnecessarily endangering a commander's ability to preserve
morale and good order among his troops." *Brown, Secretary of Defense v.
Glines*, 444 U.S. 348 (1980).

BROWN v. HARTLAGE (1982). A Kentucky statute (Kentucky, Corrupt Practices Act*) prohibited candidates for public office from offering benefits to voters
in exchange for votes. Brown, running for Hartlage's seat as a county commissioner, made a campaign pledge that, if elected, he would work at a reduced
salary to save some of the taxpayers' money. Brown won the election, but
Hartlage then charged him with violating the state's Corrupt Practices Act; the
Kentucky courts agreed. On appeal, the Supreme Court reversed the decision,
saying that, as applied, the act violated Brown's First Amendment freedoms.
Justice Brennan delivered the opinion of the Court: "The application in this case
cannot be justified as a prohibition on buying votes. Petitioner's statements,
which were made openly and were subject to the criticism of his political op-
ponent and to the scrutiny of the voters, were very different in character from
corrupting private agreements and solicitations historically recognized as unprotected by the First Amendment. There is no constitutional basis upon which his
pledge to reduce his salary may be equated with a candidate's promise to pay
voters privately for their support from his own pocketbook. A candidate's promise

to confer some ultimate benefit on the voter, qua taxpayer, citizen, or member of the general public, does not lie beyond the pale of First Amendment protection.'' *Brown v. Hartlage*, 456 U.S 45 (1982).

BROWN v. OKLAHOMA (1972). Wilbert Brown was convicted in a Tulsa court for uttering obscene language and was fined one hundred dollars with thirty days in the county jail. The court record contains part of the indictment: ''that Wilbert Montell Brown...did unlawfully, and wilfully and knowingly, utter and speak obscene and lascivious words and language, to-wit: 'Mother-fucking fascist pig cops' and 'that black mother-fucking pig McIntosh,' in the Sharp Chapel on the campus of the University of Tulsa...the same being a public place where numerous female persons were then and there assembled.'' The Supreme Court vacated the decision and remanded the case back to Oklahoma in the light of its decisions relating to offensive language in *Cohen v. California** and *Gooding v. Wilson.** Brown v. Oklahoma*, 492 P. 2d 1106 (1972).

BROWN v. SOCIALIST WORKERS '74 CAMPAIGN COMMITTEE (1982). An Ohio statute (Ohio, Campaign Expense Reporting Law*) requires every candidate for political office to file a statement identifying each contributor and each recipient of a disbursement of campaign funds. The object or purpose of each disbursement must also be disclosed. The lists of names and addresses of contributors and recipients are open to public inspection for at least six years, and violations are punishable by fines of up to $1,000 for each day of violation. The Ohio Socialist Workers party—a rather unsuccessful party with less than 2 percent of the 1980 vote and with about only $15,000 in campaign expenditures— brought suit, claiming that the statute was used to harass the party. The Supreme Court agreed: ''The First Amendment prohibits a State from compelling disclosures by a minor political party that will subject those persons identified to the reasonable probability of threats, harassment, or reprisals....Here, the District Court, in upholding appellees' challenge to the constitutionality of the Ohio disclosure provisions, properly concluded that the evidence of private and government hostility toward the SWP and its members establishes a reasonable probability that disclosing the names of contributors and recipients will subject them to threats, harassment, and reprisals.'' *Brown v. Socialist Workers '74 Campaign Committee*, 74 L. Ed. 2d 250 (1982).

BUCKLEY v. VALEO (1976). The Federal Election Campaign Act* of 1971 (amended in 1974) set limits on the amount of contributions that individuals and groups could give to political candidates, set limits on the amounts candidates could spend from personal and family funds, and set reporting requirements with the Federal Election Commission. The Supreme Court held that the act's contribution provisions were constitutional, but the expenditure provisions violated the First Amendment: ''The contribution provisions, along with those covering disclosure, are appropriate legislative weapons against the reality or appearances of improper influence stemming from the dependence of candidates on large campaign contributions, and the ceilings imposed accordingly serve the basic governmental interest in safeguarding the integrity of the political process without directly impinging upon the rights of individual citizens and candidates to engage in political debate and discussion.... The First Amendment requires the invalidation of the Act's independent expenditure ceiling, its limitation on a candidate's expenditures from his own personal funds, and its ceilings on overall campaign expenditures, since those provisions place substantial and direct restrictions on the ability of candidates, citizens, and associations to engage in protected political expression, restrictions that the First Amendment cannot tolerate." *Buckley v. Valeo*, 424 U.S. 1 (1976).

BURNSIDE v. BYARS (1966). A federal district court in Mississippi held that high school officials could prohibit students from wearing in school buttons that read "One Man One Vote" and "SNCC" even though the buttons did not appear to hamper school activities or discipline. On appeal, a court of appeals ruled that this was an arbitrary and unreasonable infringement of students' protected right of free expression. Judge Gewin delivered the opinion of the court: "We wish to make it quite clear that we do not applaud any attempt to undermine the authority of the school. We support all efforts made by the school to fashion reasonable regulations for the conduct of their students and enforcement of the punishment incurred when such regulations are violated. Obedience to duly constituted authority is a valuable tool, and respect for those in authority must be instilled in our young people. But, with all of this in mind, we must also emphasize that school officials cannot ignore expressions of feelings with which they do not wish to contend. They cannot infringe on their students' right to free and unrestricted expression as guaranteed to them under the First Amendment to the Constitution, where the exercise of such rights in the school buildings and schoolrooms do not materially and substantially interfere with the requirements of appropriate discipline in the operation of the school." *Burnside v. Byars*, 363 F. 2d 744 (1966).

BUTLER v. MICHIGAN (1957). Butler was charged with violating § 343 of the Michigan Penal Code (Michigan, Protection of Minors*), which made it a misdemeanor to sell a book to anyone that contained language "tending to the corruption of the morals of youth" (the specific book was *The Devil Rides Outside*, by John Griffin). Butler was found guilty and fined one hundred dollars, but the Supreme Court, Justice Frankfurter delivering the opinion, reversed the conviction: "It is clear on the record that appellant was convicted because Michigan, by Section 343, made it an offense for him to make available for the general reading public (and he in fact sold to a police officer) a book that the trial judge found to have a potentially deleterious influence upon youth. The State insists that, by thus quarantining the general reading public against books not too rugged for grown men and women in order to shield juvenile innocence, it is exercising its power to promote the general welfare. Surely, this is to burn the house to roast the pig. . . . We have before us legislation not reasonably restricted to the evil with which it is said to deal. The incidence of this enactment is to reduce the adult population of Michigan to reading what is only fit for children. It thereby arbitrarily curtails one of those liberties of the individual. . . that history has attested as the indispensable conditions for the maintenance and progress of a free society. We are constrained to reverse this conviction.'' *Butler v. Michigan*, 352 U.S. 380 (1957).

C

CAFETERIA EMPLOYEES UNION v. ANGELOS (1943). This case involved the right of union picketing and that when such picketing is peaceful, a state cannot infringe on the constitutional guarantee of freedom of speech. The Court also ruled that the right to peaceful picketing cannot be taken away merely because in the course of the picketing there may have been isolated incidents of abuse falling far short of violence. Justice Frankfurter delivered the opinion of the Court: "That the picketing under review was peaceful is not questioned. And to use loose language or undefined slogans that are part of the conventional give-and-take in our economic and political controversies—like 'unfair' or 'fascist'—is not to falsify facts. In a setting like the present, continuing representations unquestionably false and acts of coercion going beyond the mere influence exerted by the fact of picketing, are of course not constitutional prerogatives. But here we have no attempt by the state through its courts to restrict conduct justifiably found to be an abusive exercise of the right to picket." *Cafeteria Employees Union v. Angelos*, 320 U.S. 293 (1943).

CALIFORNIA, CRIMINAL SYNDICALISM ACT. This act is California Penal Code §§ 11400 and 11401. Section 11400—Definition: " 'Criminal syndicalism' as used in this article means any doctrine or precept advocating, teaching or aiding and abetting the commission of crime, sabotage (which word is hereby defined as meaning willful and malicious physical damage or injury to physical property), or unlawful acts of force and violence or unlawful methods of terrorism as a means of accomplishing a change in industrial ownership or control, or effecting any political change." Section 11401—Offense and Punishment: "Any person who: 1. By spoken or written words or personal conduct advocates, teaches or aids and abets criminal syndicalism or the duty, necessity or propriety of committing crime, sabotage, violence or any unlawful method of terrorism as a means of accomplishing a change in industrial ownership or control, or effecting any political change; or 2. Willfully and deliberately by spoken or written words justifies or attempts to justify criminal syndicalism . . . ; or 3. Prints, publishes, edits, issues or circulates or publicly displays any books, paper, pamphlet, document, poster or written or printed matter in any form...teaching...criminal syndicalism; or 4. Organizes or assists in organizing...any organization...assembled to advocate...criminal syndicalism...is guilty of a felony and punishable by imprisonment in the state prison not less than one nor more than 14 years.'' This act was seen *not* to be a violation of the First Amendment protections in *Whitney v. California* (1927),* and the Supreme Court, in *Younger v. Harris* (1971),* refused to block a California prosecution under the act.

CALIFORNIA, DEPARTMENT OF ALCOHOLIC BEVERAGE CONTROL REGULATIONS. Rules 143.3 and 143.4 prohibited the following kinds of entertainment on licensed premises: ''(a) The performance of acts or simulated acts, of sexual intercourse, masturbation, sodomy, bestiality, oral copulation, flagellation or any sexual acts which are prohibited by law; (b) The actual or simulated touching, caressing or fondling of the breasts, buttocks, anus or genitals; (c) The actual or simulated displaying of the pubic hair, anus, vulva or genitals; (d) The permitting by a licensee of any person to remain in or upon the licensed premises who exposes to public view any portion of his or her genitals or anus; and (e) The displaying of films or pictures depicting a live performance which was prohibited by the regulations quoted above.'' Deciding that the Twenty-first Amendment had precedence over the First Amendment, the Supreme Court, in *California v. LaRue* (1972),* upheld these regulations as not ''repugnant'' to the First Amendment protection of free speech.

CALIFORNIA MEDICAL ASSOCIATION v. FEDERAL ELECTION COMMISSION (1981). The Federal Election Campaign Act* prohibits individuals and unincorporated associations from contributing more than $5,000 to multicandidate political committees. The California Medical Association brought suit, claiming that the prohibition violated their rights to free expression in the political process. Although unable to agree on a single decision, the Supreme Court ruled that the contribution limit did not violate the First Amendment. Justice Marshall, joined by other justices in sections, gave the Court's opinion: ''Nothing in the Act limits the amount the medical association or its members could independently expend in order to advocate political views, but rather the statute restrains only the amount the association may contribute to its political action committee; the speech by proxy that the medical association sought to achieve through its contributions to the political action committee was not the type of political advocacy entitled to full First Amendment protection, the political action committee being instead a separate legal entity that receives funds from multiple sources and engages in independent political advocacy; the rights of a contributor are not impaired by limits on the amount he may give to a multicandidate political committee which advocates the views and candidacies of a number of candidates; and the prohibition is an appropriate means by which Congress sought to protect the integrity of other statutory restrictions on contributions which individuals and multicandidate political committees may make to candidates and their political committees.'' This decision is related to *Buckley v. Valeo.* California Medical Association v. Federal Election Commission*, 453 U.S. 183 (1981).

CALIFORNIA, OBSCENITY STATUTE. Section 311 of the California Penal Code reads: ''Every person who willfully and lewdly, either... writes, composes, stereotypes, prints, publishes, sells, distributes, keeps for sale, or exhibits any obscene or indecent writing, paper, or book; or designs, copies, draws, engraves, paints, or otherwise prepares any obscene or indecent picture or print; or molds, cuts, casts, or otherwise makes any obscene or indecent figure; or writes, composes, or publishes any notice or advertisement of any such writing, paper, book, picture, print or figure... is guilty of a misdemeanor.'' Obscene matter means ''matter, taken as a whole, the predominant appeal of which to the average person, applying contemporary community standards, is to prurient interest, i.e., a shameful or morbid interest in nudity, sex, or excretion; and is matter which taken as a whole goes substantially beyond customary limits of candor in description or representation of such matters; and is matter which taken as a whole is utterly without redeeming social importance.'' This statute has been sustained by the Supreme Court on several occasions (*Alberts v. California* [1957]*).

CALIFORNIA, OFFENSIVE LANGUAGE. California Penal Code, § 415, reads: ''Every person who maliciously and willfully disturbs the peace and quiet of any neighborhood or person, by loud or unusual noise, or by tumultuous or offensive conduct... or use[s] any vulgar, profane, or indecent language within the presence or hearing of women or children, in a loud and boisterous manner, is guilty of a misdemeanor.'' In *Cohen v. California* (1971),* the Supreme Court ruled that this statute could not be applied to convict someone who wore in a public place a jacket on which were the words ''Fuck the Draft.'' The Court ruled that the California courts did not limit the meaning of the ''vulgar'' language component of the statute and juries had been instructed that ''vulgar'' means ''coarse, ill-bred, ill-mannered, rude... [and] profane means serving to debase or defile that which is holy or worthy of reverence.'' The Court noted that ''it hardly needs stating that States are not free to penalize speech merely because it is 'coarse,' 'ill-bred,' or 'hardly suitable.' ''

CALIFORNIA, PRISON DIRECTOR'S RULES ON CORRESPON-DENCE. Rule 2401 provided: ''The sending and receiving of mail is a privilege, not a right, and any violation of the rules governing mail privileges either by you or by your correspondents may cause suspension of the mail privileges.'' Rule 1201: ''Inmate Behavior—Do not agitate, unduly complain, magnify grievances'' (the terms ''unduly complain'' and ''magnify grievances'' were applied to the content of personal correspondence). Rule 1205: ''The following is contraband: Any writing or voice recordings expressing inflammatory political, racial, religious or other views or beliefs.'' The Supreme Court, in *Procunier v.*

Martinez (1974),* ruled that these regulations relating to prisoner mail authorized censorship of protected expression without adequate justification in violation of the First Amendment and that they were void for vagueness. In addition, the Court noted that the regulations failed to provide minimum procedural safeguards against error and arbitrariness in the censorship of inmate correspondence.

CALIFORNIA, PRISON REGULATIONS. Regulation § 415.071 of the California Department of Corrections Manual provides that "press and other media interviews with specific inmates will not be permitted." The Supreme Court, in *Pell v. Procunier* (1974),* ruled that such a regulation did not abridge the freedom of the press: "The First Amendment does not guarantee the press a constitutional right of special access to information not available to the public generally."

CALIFORNIA, PROPERTY TAX EXEMPTION. Article XX, § 19, of the California Constitution, adopted at the general election of November 4, 1952, provided: "Notwithstanding any other provision of this Constitution, no person or organization which advocates the overthrow of the Government of the United States or the State by force or violence or other unlawful means or who advocates the support of a foreign government against the United States in the event of hostilities shall:...receive any exemption from any tax imposed by this State or any county, city or county, city, district, political subdivision, authority, board, bureau, commission or other public agency of this State." To operationalize this constitutional amendment, the California legislature enacted § 32 of the Revenue and Taxation Code, which required the claimant, as a prerequisite to qualification for any property-tax exemption, to sign a statement on his tax return declaring that he does not engage in the activities described in the constitutional amendment. The entire scheme was ruled to be a violation of free speech by the Supreme Court, in *Speiser v. Randall* (1958).*

CALIFORNIA, RED FLAG STATUTE. California Penal Code § 403-a provided: "Any person who displays a red flag, banner or badge or any flag, badge, banner, or device of any color or form whatever in any public place or in any meeting place or public assembly, or from or on any house, building or window as a sign, symbol or emblem of opposition to organized government or as an invitation or stimulus to anarchistic action or as an aid to propaganda that is of a seditious character is guilty of a felony." The Supreme Court, in *Stromberg v. California* (1931),* ruled that this statute violated expression protected by the First Amendment.

CALIFORNIA, STATE BAR CODE. Under California procedure, the state supreme court may admit a person to the bar on certification by the Committee of Bar Examiners that the candidate meets the necessary requirements. California Business and Professions Code, 1937, § 6060(c) required that an applicant must have "good moral character" before he could be certified, and § 6064.1 provided that no person "who advocates the overthrow of the Government of the United States or of this State by force, violence, or other unconstitutional means, shall be certified to the Supreme Court for admission and a license to practice law." The U.S. Supreme Court, in *Konigsberg v. State Bar of California* (1957)* ruled that advocacy of the above cannot be used to refuse admission to the bar.

CALIFORNIA v. LaRUE (1972). California Department of Alcoholic Beverage Control regulations* prohibit explicit sexual live entertainment and films in bars and other establishments licensed to serve liquor. A district court held that the regulations were invalid under the First Amendment, concluding that some of the proscribed activity could not be classified as obscene or lacking a communicative element. On appeal by the state, the Supreme Court reversed the lower court's decision, saying that the regulations were valid: "In the context, not of censoring dramatic performances in a theatre, but of licensing bars and nightclubs to sell liquor by the drink, the states have broad latitude under the Twenty-first Amendment to control the manner and circumstances under which liquor may be dispensed, and here the conclusion that sale of liquor by the drink and lewd and naked entertainment should not take place simultaneously in licensed establishments was not irrational nor was the prophylactic solution unreasonable."

Justice Brennan did not agree with the Court's reasoning: "The State points out. . . that the regulation does not prohibit speech directly, but speaks only to the condition under which a license to sell liquor by the drink can be granted and retained. But. . . by requiring the owner of a nightclub to forgo the exercise of certain rights guaranteed by the First Amendment, the State has imposed an unconstitutional condition on the grant of a license. . . . Nothing in the language or history of the Twenty-first Amendment authorizes the States to use their liquor licensing power as a means for the deliberate inhibition of protected, even if distasteful, forms of expression." *California v. LaRue*, 409 U.S. 109 (1972).

CALIGULA. Novelist Gore Vidal wrote the original screenplay to this 1980 American film, and some internationally known and respected actors—Peter O'Toole, Malcolm McDowell, and Sir John Gielgud—appeared in various roles. These four (Vidal, O'Toole, McDowell, and Sir John) and others stated, however, that they wished to be "dissociated" from the film. The producer of *Caligula* did not submit the film to the Motion Picture Association of America (MPAA)* for a rating; the MPAA nevertheless assigned the film an X rating. The producer assigned the film his own rating—MA for mature audiences.

The film has been described (de Grazia and Newman, *Banned Films*, p. 378) in the following terms: "The film is based on Suetonius's biography of Caligula. It tells the story of the bloody reign of the fourth of the 12 Caesars of the Roman Empire. We follow the mad ruler and his companions through a great variety of explicit sexual activities, as well as assorted decapitations, dismemberments, and disembowelings. These set the scene for the film's climax—the bloody assassination of Caligula himself. 'The film is a dizzying display of bodies, genitals, orgies, heterosexual and homosexual activity, masturbation, bodily functions, and sexual content and excesses of all varieties.... Violence is as much a part of the film as is promiscuity.' ''†

Caligula faced censorship attempts in several localities, most notably in Boston in 1980 (*Massachusetts v. Saxon Theater*, 6 Media Law Rep. 1979 [1980]) and in Atlanta in 1981 (*Penthouse v. McAuliffe*, 7 Media Law Rep. 1978 [1981]); both attempts failed to have *Caligula* judged obscene. The Boston trial was before Judge Elam with a jury; Judge Elam applied the Miller Standard* and found the film not to be obscene. As de Grazia and Newman (pp. 149-150) comment, the judge ''decided that the film appealed to the prurient interest, depicted and described sexual conduct in a patently offensive way, and lacked serious literary, artistic, and scientific value. He went on to observe, however, that political science professor Andrew Hacker 'articulated rather effectively' that a 'serious political theme ran throughout the film': 'namely that absolute power corrupts absolutely. He was able to show the frightening effect of power in the hands of a single person, how power was used to emasculate, debase, and exploit sexually. And he was able to relate convincingly all of this to its historical context, as reported by ancient Roman historians. He projected the sobering thought that it was important to be aware of this and other such degrading periods in the history of our world, lest they are allowed to repeat themselves.' When the prosecution neglected to rebut this testimony, thereby failing to prove 'beyond a reasonable doubt' that *Caligula* lacked 'serious political value,' the court held the film not obscene and thus constitutionally protected.''†

The result in Atlanta was similar to the decision in Boston: *Caligula* was not obscene, for it had, under the Miller Standard, artistic and political value.

The U.S. Supreme Court ruled on *Caligula* in March 1984, and they, too, felt that the film was not obscene under the Miller Standard. The Court agreed with the previous finding that the film had ''political and artistic value'' and thus was protected, but they did not agree that the film appealed to the prurient interest. Rather than appealing to the viewer's prurient interest in sex—arousing desire and lustful feelings—*Caligula* sickened and disgusted the viewer. Eroticism was absent and thus *Caligula* could not be prohibited. De Grazia and Newman comment that *Caligula* has since become the ''largest grossing independently produced X-rated film ever made in the United States,''† even surpassing the all-time classic *Deep Throat*.*

CAMMARANO V. UNITED STATES (1959). Certain Internal Revenue Service regulations prohibit the deduction of funds as ordinary and necessary business expenses if the expenditures were made in connection with efforts to promote

†Reprinted from *Banned Films* with permission of the R. R. Bowker Company. Copyright © 1982 by Edward de Grazia and Roger K. Newman.

or defeat legislation by persuasion of the general public as well as efforts to influence legislative bodies directly through lobbying activities.

The Supreme Court ruled that these regulations were not aimed at the suppression of dangerous ideas and thus did not violate the First Amendment. Justice Douglas, a strong supporter of free speech, concurred in the Court's judgment: "I find it impossible to say that the owners of the present business, who were fighting for their lives in opposing these initiative measures, were not exercising First Amendment rights. If Congress had gone so far as to deny all deduction for 'ordinary and necessary business expenses' if a taxpayer spent money to promote or oppose initiative measures, then it would be placing a penalty on the exercise of First Amendment rights. That was in substance what a State did in *Speiser v. Randall.** 'To deny an exemption to claimants who engage in certain forms of speech is in effect to penalize them for such speech.' Congress, however, has taken no such action here. It has not undertaken to penalize taxpayers for certain types of advocacy; it has merely allowed some, not all, expenses as deductions. Deductions are a matter of grace, not of right. To hold that this item of expense must be allowed as a deduction would be to give impetus to the view favored in some quarters that First Amendment rights must be protected by tax exemptions. But that proposition savors of the notion that First Amendment rights are somehow not fully realized unless they are subsidized by the State. Such a notion runs counter to our decisions and may indeed conflict with the underlying premise that a complete hands-off policy on the part of government is at times the only course consistent with First Amendment rights." *Cammarano v. United States*, 358 U.S. 498 (1959).

CANDID. On July 19, 1965, at the instigation of Operation Yorkville, seventeen-year-old Anthony Sciacovelli entered Tannenbaum's cigar store and bought, at $2.25, a copy of *Candid* magazine, one of the many types of "girlie" magazines available in the store. Tannenbaum was subsequently convicted in a New York state court (*People v. Tannenbaum*, 220 N.E. 2d 783 1966]) of violating § 484-i of the New York Penal Law (New York, Sale of Obscene Material to Minors*). Tannenbaum appealed his conviction to the Supreme Court, but his appeal was dismissed per curiam (*Tannenbaum v. New York*, 388 U.S. 439 [1967]).

The New York court described *Candid* as follows: "*Candid*'s cover shows a girl seductively posed beside a couch wearing the skimpiest of undergarments. In addition, the cover describes the contents: 'Smut for Women Only'/'How to Undress With Class'/'Sex with a Twist'/'Picadilly Prostitute' and 'Should She or Shouldn't She.' The lower left-hand corner states: 'Sale to Minors Forbidden.' What the cover promises, the contents delivers. *Candid* is devoted purely to sex, told pictorially by nudes in almost every conceivable pose and by tales of sex orgies in picture and prose. The advertisements, in line with the over-all theme, are for mail-order photographs and motion pictures of nudes, lingerie, and sexual devices and handbooks. We have no difficulty concluding...that *Candid* falls within the ban of the statute and that [Tannenbaum], with knowledge of its contents, sold the magazine to a person under the age of 18 years.''

There was a dissenting opinion, however: ''Section 484-i proscribes sale to minors of photographs and other representations of certain parts of the human body if such material appeals to the 'curiosity' of children 'as to sex or to the anatomical differences between the sexes.' These criteria, standing by themselves, are patently insufficient and impermissible predicates for penal liability. Quite apart from the fact that the statute would improperly cover both married teenagers and children of tender years, it would indiscriminately punish the dissemination of material that stimulates healthy, as well as morbid, curiosity about sex and sexual differences. Taken literally, the provision would outlaw every course in sex education and feminine hygiene taught in the schools and would bar access by children to reproductions of, for example, the paintings by Michelangelo in the Sistine Chapel as well as the works of other great masters.'' This dissent eventually was heard, for one year later, in 1968, the Supreme Court, in *Rabeck v. New York** held that the New York statute was unconstitutionally vague and that it was no answer to say that it was adopted for the salutary purpose of protecting children.

CANTWELL v. CONNECTICUT (1940). A Connecticut anti-soliciting statute* forbade any person to solicit money or valuables for any alleged religious cause unless a license was first obtained. The statute was held to be an unconstitutional prior restraint as applied to Cantwell, when he was distributing literature claimed to be religious in nature and soliciting contributions to be used for the publication of the literature. Justice Roberts delivered the opinion of the Court: The defendant, while on a public street endeavoring to interest passersby in the purchase of publications, or in making contributions, in the interest of what he believed to be true religion, induced individuals to listen to the playing of a phonograph record describing the publications. The record contained a verbal attack on the religious denomination of which the listeners were members, provoking their indignation and a desire on their part to strike the defendant, who thereupon picked up his books and phonograph and went on his way. There was no showing that the defendant's deportment was noisy, truculent, overbearing, or offensive; nor was it claimed that he intended to insult or affront the listeners by playing the record; nor was it shown that the sound of the phonograph disturbed people living nearby, drew a crowd, or impeded traffic. The defendant's conviction of the common law offense of breach of the peace was violative of the constitutional guarantee of freedom of speech. *Cantwell v. Connecticut*, 310 U.S. 296 (1940).

CAREY v. BROWN (1980). An Illinois statute on picketing* prohibited the picketing of residences or dwellings but exempted peaceful picketing of a place of employment involved in a labor dispute regardless of whether it was a residence or a dwelling. Brown and others were convicted under the statute when they picketed the mayor of Chicago's home in protest against his alleged failure to support the busing of schoolchildren to achieve racial integration. The Supreme Court held that the statute was unconstitutional, since it made an impermissible distinction between peaceful labor picketing and other peaceful picketing: In prohibiting peaceful picketing on the public streets and sidewalks in residential neighborhoods, the statute regulates expressive conduct that falls within the First Amendment's preserve, and in exempting peaceful labor picketing from its general prohibition, the statute discriminates between lawful and unlawful conduct based on the content of the demonstrator's communication. On its face, the statute accords preferential treatment to the expression of views on one particular subject; information about labor disputes may be freely disseminated, but discussion of all other issues is restricted. *Carey v. Brown*, 447 U.S. 455 (1980).

CAREY v. POPULATION SERVICES INTERNATIONAL (1977). Section 6811(8) of the New York Education Law (New York, Advertising Contraceptives*) made it a crime for anyone to advertise or display contraceptives. The Supreme Court held that this prohibition was unconstitutional, Justice Brennan delivering the Court's opinion: "[The State contends]. . .that advertisements of contraceptive products would be offensive and embarrassing to those exposed to them, and that permitting them would legitimize sexual activity of young people. But these are classically not justifications validating the suppression of expression protected by the First Amendment. At least where obscenity is not involved, we have consistently held that the fact that protected speech may be offensive to some does not justify its suppression. As for the possible 'legitimization' of illicit sexual behavior, whatever might be the case if the advertisements directly incited sexual activity among the young, none of the avertisements in this record can even remotely be characterized as 'directed to inciting or producing imminent lawless action and. . .likely to incite or produce such action.' They merely state the availability of products and services that are not only entirely legal but constitutionally protected." *Carey v. Population Services International*, 431 U.S. 678 (1977).

CARLSON v. CALIFORNIA (1940). A Shasta County, California, ordinance on picketing* made it unlawful for any person to carry or display any sign, banner, or badge in the vicinity of any place of business for the purpose of inducing others to refrain from buying or working there, or for any person to "loiter" or "picket" in the vicinity of any place of business for such purpose. The ordinance was held to be unconstitutional by the Supreme Court, for it made an impermissible distinction based on the content of the communication: "In brief, the ordinance does not regulate all carrying of signs, but, on the contrary, proscribes the carrying of signs only by persons directly interested who approach the vicinity of a labor dispute to convey information about the dispute. The sweeping and inexact terms of the ordinance disclose the threat to freedom of speech inherent in its existence. The carrying of signs and banners, no less than the raising of a flag, is a natural and appropriate means of conveying information on matters of public concern. . . . The power and duty of the State to take adequate steps to preserve the peace and protect the privacy, the lives, and the property of its residents cannot be doubted. But the ordinance in question here abridges liberty of discussion under circumstances presenting no clear and present danger of substantive evils within the allowable area of state control.'' *Carlson v. California*, 310 U.S. 106 (1940).

CARNAL KNOWLEDGE. This 1971 American film, directed by Mike Nichols and starring Jack Nicholson, Candice Bergen, Art Garfunkel, Ann-Margret, and Rita Moreno, was nominated for an Oscar (Best Supporting Actress). It received favorable reviews in *Newsweek*, *Washington Post* (by George F. Will), *Time*, *Saturday Review*, and the *New York Times*; it was also banned as obscene in Albany, Georgia, in 1972. A synopsis of the film is given by de Grazia and Newman (*Banned Films*, pp. 351-352): ''During the postwar 1940s, two college room-mates who are best friends discuss the ideal woman. Knowledgeable Jonathan wants only physically perfect girls; nice, bumbling Sandy considers intellect and sensitivity to be of primary importance. Although both are attracted to a lovely student, Susan, whom they spot at a college mixer, Jonathan declares her breasts are too small and leaves her to Sandy. When Sandy confides that Susan, despite her virginity, engaged in bold sexual foreplay, Jonathan pursues her and, pretending an unhappy childhood, seduces her. Next, Sandy, by dint of clumsy advances, seduces Susan too, and both friends continue to date her. When Jonathan insists that Susan choose between them, Susan, being unwilling to hurt Sandy, rejects Jonathan. Years later, we find Sandy, a well-established New York doctor married to Susan, and Jonathan, running through a dozen women a year in search of the perfect female bedmate. Now Jonathan thinks he has found her in Bobbie, a voluptuous 29-year-old model, with whom he has a dreadful relationship. They break up only after Jonathan rejects Bobbie's request for marriage and a child, and she barely survives an overdose of pills. A decade later, dressed as a member of the 'Now Generation,' Sandy visits Jonathan at his luxurious bachelor pad with an 18-year-old hippie named Jennifer, who he claims has shown him true love. Jonathan presents slides of the women in his life, revealing that he married and had a child with Bobbie and is now being bled for alimony. When he reduces Jennifer to tears, Sandy takes her home. And Jonathan is visited by his hundred-dollar prostitute, who performs her regular sexual ritual, reassuring him of his virility.''†

The film was rated R, but it ran afoul of Georgia's obscenity statute* and the exhibitor was found guilty of showing an obscene film. The Supreme Court, however, in *Jenkins v. Georgia* (418 U.S. 153 [1974]), ruled that the film was

†Reprinted from *Banned Films* with permission of the R. R. Bowker Company. Copyright © 1982 by Edward de Grazia and Roger K. Newman.

not obscene under the Miller Standard.* Justice Rehnquist delivered the opinion of the Court: "Our own viewing of the film satisfies us that *Carnal Knowledge* could not be found under the Miller standards to depict sexual conduct in a patently offensive way. Nothing in the movie falls within either of the two examples given in Miller of material which may constitutionally be found to meet the 'patently offensive' element of those standards, nor is there anything sufficiently similar to such material to justify similar treatment. While the subject matter of the picture is, in a broader sense, sex, and there are scenes in which sexual conduct including 'ultimate sexual acts' is to be understood to be taking place, the camera does not focus on the bodies of the actors at such times. There is no exhibition whatever of the actors' genitals, lewd or otherwise, during these scenes. There are occasional scenes of nudity, but nudity alone is not enough to make material legally obscene under the Miller standards."

CARROLL v. PRINCESS ANNE (1968). Carroll and others, members of the white supremacist National States Rights party, held a public rally in Princess Anne, Maryland, on August 6, 1966. The public rally contained aggressive and militant racist speeches. It was announced that a second rally would be held the next day, but the local authorities obtained a restraining order from a local court that prohibited Carroll for ten days from holding rallies that "would tend to disturb and endanger the citizens of the County."

The Supreme Court held that the action was an unconstitutional prior restraint on the activities of the rally organizers. Justice Fortas delivered the opinion of the Court: "The underlying question persists and is agitated by the continuing activities and program of petitioners: whether, by what processes, and to what extent the authorities of the local governments may restrict petitioners in their rallies and public meetings. . . . The petitioners urge that the injunction constituted a prior restraint on speech and that it therefore violated the principles of the First Amendment which are applicable to the States by virtue of the Fourteenth Amendment. In any event, they assert, it was not constitutionally permissible to restrain petitioners' meetings because no 'clear and present danger' existed. Respondents, however, argue that the injunctive order in this case should not be considered as a 'prior restraint' because it was based upon the events of the preceding evening and was directed at preventing a continuation of those events, and that, even if considered a 'prior restraint,' issuance of the order was justified by the clear and present danger of riot and disorder deliberately generated by petitioners. . . . The Court has emphasized that '[a] system of prior restraints of expression comes to this Court bearing a heavy presumption against its constitutional validity.' And even where the presumption might otherwise be overcome, the Court has insisted upon careful procedural provisions, designed to assure the fullest presentation and consideration of the matter which the circumstances permit. . . . A noncriminal process of prior restraints upon expression 'avoids constitutional infirmity only if it takes place under procedural safeguards designed to obviate the dangers of a censorship system.' Measured against these standards, it is clear that the 10-day restraining order in the present case, issued *ex parte*, without formal or informal notice to the petitioners or any effort to advise them of the proceeding, cannot be sustained." *Carroll v. Princess Anne*, 393 U.S. 175 (1968).

CASA GRANDE (AZ), BOOKSELLERS' LICENSE. An ordinance of Casa Grande read as follows: "It shall be unlawful for any person. . .to carry on any trade, calling, profession, occupation or business. . .without first having procured a license from the City of Casa Grande to do so. . . .All persons coming within the definition of the occupations defined herein shall pay a quarterly license fee of Twenty Five Dollars ($25.00), in advance." This ordinance was held to be valid under the First Amendment by the Supreme Court as applied to itinerant booksellers in *Jobin v. Arizona* (1942).* But one year later, in a rehearing, the *Jobin* decision was vacated by the Court in light of its decisions in *Largent v. Texas* (1943)* and *Jamison v. Texas* (1943).* *Jobin v. Arizona*, 316 U.S. 584 (1942).

CENTRAL HUDSON GAS AND ELECTRIC CORPORATION v. PUBLIC SERVICE COMMISSION OF NEW YORK (1980). The New York Public Service Commission advertising regulations* completely prohibited an electric utility company from advertising to promote the use of electricity. The state of New York argued that its interest in energy conservation and in preventing inequities in electric rates—successful promotion of electricity consumption in off-peak hours would create extra costs that would have to be paid for by all the customers—were sufficient reasons to prevent such commercial speech.* The Supreme Court recognized the legitimacy of these interests but ruled that such a sweeping prohibition on protected speech violated the First Amendment: "In applying the First Amendment to this area, we have rejected the 'highly paternalistic' view that government has complete power to suppress or regulate commercial speech. 'People will perceive their own best interests if only they are well enough informed, and. . .the best means to that end is to open the channels of communication, rather than to close them.' Even when advertising communicates only an incomplete version of the relevant facts, the First Amendment presumes that some accurate information is better than no information at all [*Bates v. State Bar of Arizona**].'' *Central Hudson Gas and Electric Corporation v. Public Service Commission of New York*, 447 U.S. 557 (1980).

CENTRAL INTELLIGENCE AGENCY, PUBLISHING AGREEMENTS. The Central Intelligence Agency requires that all employees sign an agreement on appointment to the effect that the employee would "not. . .publish. . .any information or material relating to the Agency, its activities or intelligence activities generally, either during or after the term of [his] employment. . .without specific prior approval by the Agency." This agreement was seen not to be a prior restraint by the Supreme Court in *Snepp v. United States* (1980)* and in

McGehee v. Casey (1983).* Snepp published a book entitled *Decent Interval* and ran afoul of the agency's regulations. Snepp claimed that the regulations imposed an invalid prior restraint, but the Court did not accept his reasoning. The Court ruled that Snepp had promised not to publish any information without pre-publication clearance and the government could keep any profits that Snepp might make by the sale of his book.

CENTRAL INTELLIGENCE AGENCY, SECRECY AGREEMENTS. The Central Intelligence Agency (CIA) requires each new employee to sign on appointment a secrecy agreement: "I, _____, understand that by virtue of my duties in the CIA, I may be or have been the recipient of information and intelligence which concerns the present and future security of the United States....I do solemnly swear that I will never divulge, publish or reveal either by word, conduct, or by any other means, any classified information, intelligence or knowledge except in the performance of my official duties and in accordance with the laws of the United States, unless specifically authorized in writing, in each case, by the Director of Central Intelligence or his authorized representatives."

On leaving CIA employment, each (former) employee swears to the following secrecy oath: "I, _____, ...solemnly swear, without mental reservation or purpose of evasion, and in the absence of duress, as follows: I will never divulge, publish, or reveal by writing, word, conduct, or otherwise, any information relating to the national defense and security and particularly information of this nature relating to intelligence sources, methods and operations, and specifically Central Intelligence Agency operations, sources, methods, personnel, fiscal data, or security measures to anyone, including but not limited to, any future governmental or private employer, private citizen, or other Government employee or official without the express written consent of the Director of Central Intelligence or his authorized representative." These restrictions on former CIA employees to publish, even though a prior restraint, were seen by the Supreme Court not to be a violation of the First Amendment. *United States v. Marchetti* (1972)* and *McGehee v. Casey* (1983).*

CHAPLINSKY v. NEW HAMPSHIRE (1942). Chapter 378, § 2, of the Public Laws of New Hampshire (New Hampshire, Offensive Conduct*) prohibited any person to address "any offensive, derisive or annoying word to any other person who is lawfully in any street or other public place" or "call him by any offensive or derisive name."

In one of the most famous cases, the Supreme Court refined the doctrine of "fighting words"* and sustained Chaplinsky's conviction for breach of the peace when he called certain individuals "God damned racketeers" and "Fascists." Justice Murphy delivered the opinion of the Court: "The complaint charged that appellant, 'with force and arms, in a certain public place in said city of Rochester, to wit, on the public sidewalk...did unlawfully repeat, the words following, addressed to the complainant, that is to say, "You are a God damned racketeer" and "a damned Fascist and the whole government of Rochester are Fascists or agents of Fascists," the same being offensive, derisive and annoying words and names.' It is now clear that freedom of speech and freedom of the press, which are protected by the First Amendment from infringement by Congress, are among the fundamental personal rights and liberties which are protected by the Fourteenth Amendment from invasion by [the] state. . . . Allowing the broadest scope to the language and purpose of the Fourteenth Amendment, it is well understood that the right of free speech is not absolute at all times and under all circumstances. There are certain well-defined and narrowly limited classes of speech, the prevention and punishment of which have never been thought to raise any Constitutional problem. These include the lewd and obscene, the profane, the libelous, and the insulting or 'fighting' words—those which by their very utterance inflict injury or tend to incite an immediate breach of the peace. It has been well observed that such utterances are no essential part of any exposition of ideas, and are of such slight social value as a step to truth that any benefit that may be derived from them is clearly outweighed by the social interest in order and morality. Resort to epithets or personal abuse is not in any proper sense a communication of information or opinion safeguarded by the Constitution, and its punishment as a criminal act would raise no question under that instrument. On the authority of its earlier decisions, the state court declared that the statute's purpose was to preserve the public peace, no words being 'forbidden except as have a direct tendency to cause acts of violence by the persons to whom, individually, the remark is addressed.' It was further said: 'The word offensive is not to be defined in terms of what a particular addressee thinks. The test is what men of common intelligence would understand would be words likely to cause an average addressee to fight. The English language has a number of words and expressions which by general consent are fighting words when said without a disarming smile. Such words, as ordinary men know, are likely to cause a fight. So are threatening, profane or obscene revilings. Derisive and annoying words can be taken as coming within the purview of the statute. . . . The statute, as construed, does no more than prohibit the face-to-face words plainly likely to cause a breach of the peace by the addressee, words whose speaking constitutes a breach of the peace by the speaker—including classical fighting words, words in current use and less classical but equally likely to cause violence, and other disorderly words, including profanity, obscenity and threats.' ''

The doctrine of fighting words as being unprotected speech was thus advanced with Chaplinsky, but later decisions have narrowed the meaning of fighting words. "God damned racketeer" and "damned Fascist" may have been seen to be fighting words in 1942, but the following have *not* been construed as fighting words: "Fuck the Draft" (*Cohen v. California* [1971]*) and "Get out of my way you fucking prick-ass cops" (*Cincinnati v. Karlan* [1973]*). *Chaplinsky v. New Hampshire*, 315 U.S 568 (1942).

CHICAGO (IL), DISTURBING THE PEACE. Municipal Code of Chicago, 1939, § 193-1, read: "All persons who shall make, aid, countenance, or assist in making any improper noise, riot, disturbance, breach of the peace, or diversion tending to a breach of the peace, within the limits of the city...shall be deemed guilty of disorderly conduct, and upon conviction thereof, shall be severally fined not less than one dollar nor more than two hundred dollars for each offense.'' The City of Chicago applied this statute to Father Terminiello (*Terminiello v. Chicago* [1949]*), when he made a speech that the authorities thought tended to a breach of the peace, but the Supreme Court ruled that the Chicago ordinance, as applied, violated free speech. *Terminiello v. Chicago*, 337 U.S. 1 (1949).

CHICAGO (IL), MOTION PICTURE CENSORSHIP. The Chicago motion picture censorship ordinance, § 155 of the Municipal Code, reads: "It shall be unlawful for any person to show or exhibit in a public place [any motion picture] without first having secured a permit therefor from the commissioner of police....Before any such permit is granted, an application in writing shall be made and the...films...shall be shown to the commissioner of police, who shall inspect such...and within three days after such inspection he shall either grant or deny the permit....If a picture or series of pictures, for the showing or exhibition of which an application for a permit is made, is immoral or obscene, or portrays depravity, criminality, or lack of virtue of a class of citizens of any race, color, creed, or religion and exposes them to contempt, derision, or obloquy, or tends to produce a breach of the peace or riots, or purports to represent any hanging, lynching or burning of a human being, it shall be the duty of the commissioner of police to refuse such permit; otherwise it shall be his duty to grant such permit.'' There have been several court challenges to this prior censorship scheme; most have dealt with the definitions, right of appeal, judicial intervention, or the time frames (*Times Film Corporation v. City of Chicago* [1961]*). The substantive issue itself, the requirement of a permit, is still in place.

CHICAGO (IL), ORDINANCE ON PICKETING. Chapter 193-1(i) of the Municipal Code of Chicago read: "A person commits disorderly conduct when he knowingly...(i) pickets or demonstrates on a public way within 150 feet of any primary or secondary school building while the school is in session and one-half hour before the school is in session and one-half hour after the school session has been concluded, provided that this subsection does not prohibit the peaceful picketing of any school involved in a labor dispute.'' This ordinance was ruled unconstitutional by the Supreme Court in *Police Department of Chicago v. Mosley* (1972)* because it made an impermissible distinction between labor picketing (permitted) and other forms of peaceful picketing (prohibited). *Police Department of Chicago v. Mosley*, 408 U.S. 92 (1972).

CHILD PORNOGRAPHY STATUTES/KIDDIE PORN. In *New York v. Ferber* (1982),* the Supreme Court ruled that a state could prohibit the dissemination of material depicting children engaged in sexual conduct regardless of whether the material in question was obscene (the *Ferber* decision involved films of young boys masturbating). In addition to New York, nineteen states have prohibited the dissemination of material depicting children engaged in sexual conduct regardless of whether the material in question meets the constitutional test of obscenity: Arizona, Colorado, Delaware, Florida, Hawaii, Kentucky, Louisiana, Massachusetts, Michigan, Mississippi, Montana, New Jersey, Oklahoma, Pennsylvania, Rhode Island, Texas, Utah, West Virginia, and Wisconsin. Fourteen states prohibit the dissemination of such material only if it is obscene: Alabama, Arkansas, California, Indiana, Maine, Minnesota, Nebraska, New Hampshire, North Dakota, Ohio, Oregon, South Dakota, Tennessee, and Washington. The federal statute also prohibits dissemination only if the material is obscene. Two states prohibit dissemination only if the material is obscene as to minors: Connecticut and Virginia. Twelve states prohibit only the use of minors in the production of the material: Alaska, Georgia, Idaho, Iowa, Kansas, Maryland, Missouri, Nevada, New Mexico, North Carolina, South Carolina, and Wyoming. *New York v. Ferber*, 73 L. Ed. 2d 1113 (1982).

THE CHINESE ROOM. Sometime in 1950, Melko, then the prosecutor of the pleas of Middlesex County, New Jersey, formed and accepted the services of a so-called Committee on Objectionable Literature, composed of citizens of the county. The purpose of the committee was to review publications offered for sale in the county, determine whether they were "fit and suitable" reading for the public, inform the prosecutor about those "unsuitable" books, and then the prosecutor would threaten legal action if the offensive publications were not removed from circulation. Justice Goldmann of the Superior Court found that Melko's actions were a direct violation of the constitutional guarantee of freedom of the press: "The proceedings center upon the committee's ban of *The Chinese Room*, a novel by Vivian Connell, but involved here is the larger question of extra-legal censorship.... I hold that neither the prosecutor nor the committee constituted by him had authority to proscribe the distribution or sale in Middlesex County of books deemed by them, or either of them, to be objectionable. The action of the prosecutor in issuing the letters [requesting withdrawal from circulation] was illegal and beyond the scope of his official authority."

The specific book, *The Chinese Room*, was first published in 1942 and then reprinted by Bantam Books in 1948 at twenty-five cents a copy. There were some ten additional printings before Bantam Books brought suit, and the court record commented that more than 2,5000,000 copies of the novel had been sold throughout the United States and Canada. H. C. Lewis, in *Books* (November 1, 1942): "*The Chinese Room* has a lot of sex in it, and Mr. Connell writes about sex with the same lack of restraint, if not the same warmth and perception, that characterized the writing of D. H. Lawrence." Another reviewer, writing in the *New Republic* (November 9, 1942): "As a mystery it is only fair, with real mental suspense built up, but an unfair solution based upon unrevealed clues.

As a clinical study of marriage it is honest, earthy and sometimes moving. As a what-not shelf it is overloaded with bric-a-brac: a slinky mistress with a heart of stone and black silk pajamas, an elderly bank employee who goes home evenings and becomes a Chinese mandarin, a man with hands that have independent personalities, opium smoking, much lechery and tag-ends of philosophy and psychiatry." *Bantam Books, Inc. v. Melko*, 96 A. 2d 47 (1953).

CHRISTIAN CRUSADE. Founded in 1948 and now headed by Billy James Hargis, the Christian Crusade is one of the largest (250,000 families) Christian educational ministries in the United States. The Crusade states as its objective: "to safeguard and preserve the Conservative Christian ideals upon which America was founded; to protect our cherished freedoms, the heritage of every American; to oppose persons or organizations who endorse socialist or Communist philosophies and to expose publicly the infiltration of such influences into American life; and to defend the Gospel of Jesus Christ; oppose U.S. participation in the United Nations, federal interference in schools, housing and other matters constitutionally belonging to the states, and government competition with private business." *Encyclopedia of Associations* (#14220). Among the "socialist and Communist" influences that the Crusade has attempted to oppose through censorship have been rock and roll music and "indecent" literature. The American courts have not yet been influenced by the Christian Crusade.

CINCINNATI (OH), ANNOYING BEHAVIOR. Cincinnati Municipal Code § 901-D4 provided: "No person shall willfully conduct himself or herself in a noisy, boisterous, rude, insulting or other disorderly manner, with the attempt to abuse or annoy any person or the citizens of the city." This ordinance was seen to be unconstitutional by the Supreme Court in *Karlan v. Cincinnati* (1974), for it prohibited words that were merely "rude" (i.e., "Get out of my way you fucking prick-ass cops!") and was not limited to words that by their very utterance inflict injury or tend to incite an immediate breach of the peace (i.e., "fighting words"*). *Cincinnati v. Karlan.**

CINCINNATI (OH), PUBLIC ANNOYANCE ORDINANCE. Section 901-L6, Code of Ordinances of the city of Cincinnati, read: "It shall be unlawful for three or more persons to assemble, except at a public meeting of citizens, on any of the sidewalks, street corners, vacant lots, or mouths of alleys, and there conduct themselves in a manner annoying to persons passing by, or occupants of adjacent buildings. Whoever violates any of the provisions of this section shall be fined not exceeding fifty dollars ($50.00), or be imprisoned not less than one (1) nor more than thirty (30) days or both." This ordinance was seen to be too vague—"annoying" behavior could be defined as just about any type of behavior—and thus it was held as a violation of the First Amendment. *Coates v. City of Cincinnati*, 402 U.S. 611 (1971).*

CINCINNATI v. KARLAN (1973). Karlan was convicted for violating the Cincinnati, Ohio, annoying behavior* ordinance, which prohibited rude or annoying behavior. His conviction was later reversed by the Supreme Court because even though certain behavior could be seen as "rude," such behavior does not necessarily fall under that narrow class of fighting words* as pronounced in *Chaplinsky v. New Hampshire.** Justice Herbert of the Ohio Supreme Court delivered the opinion that upheld the Hamilton County court's decision (Herbert's decision, as noted above, was eventually reversed by the U.S. Supreme Court): "It is obvious to us that the epithets shouted by the appellant were unmistakably in the 'fighting' category. Even recalling that in 1941 Fascism was considered among the ultimate of evils, it is difficult to imagine more inflammatory and personally abusive insults than those emitted by the appellant.... Appellant nevertheless maintains that the officer's own testimony establishes his failure to be moved to anger or violence, though his face did become flushed. Hence, runs appellant's theory, these were not fighting words to this particular individual and the speech was constitutionally protected. We disagree with this reasoning."

The court record contained the following exchange between the prosecutor and the arresting officer: "As you approached the defendant, who spoke first? The defendant did. What did he say to you? He asked me what I was looking at. What was your response? I asked him if he had permission to tamper with this car. What was his response to that? He said I hate all of you fucking cops. Demonstrate to the jury, repeating the conversation, the initial conversation, demonstrate exactly how loud he said it to you. Just shout it out the way he shouted it out. [Demonstrating] He said, I hate all you fucking cops. After he said that to you, what did you do. I said, Wait a minute. I said, Do you have permission to fool with this automobile? What did he say at this point? He said, Get out of my way you fucking, prick-ass cops. What was your response to this? At this time I stopped him from going to the car and I warned him about his language. Then, what did he say? He called me a prick-ass cop again. Now this was the second time? This was the third time. Then what did you do? Then I told him, I warned him again, and he called me a prick-assed cop again." *Cincinnati v. Karlan*, 298 N.E. 2d 34 (1973).

CINDY AND DONNA. In 1970, the sheriff of Pulaski County, Kentucky, accompanied by the district prosecutor, went to a drive-in and saw the film *Cindy and Donna*, an X-rated American film. The sheriff, viewing nudity and various love scenes, concluded that the film was obscene, and thus its exhibition violated the Kentucky obscenity statute.* At the end of the film (the sheriff apparently stayed for the complete showing), the sheriff arrested the manager of the drive-in and seized a copy of the film to use in evidence. The sheriff had no warrant when he made the arrest and seizure, and there had been no prior judicial determination that the film was obscene. Convicted for exhibiting an obscene film, the manager of the drive-in appealed to the Supreme Court. The case did not concern whether or not *Cindy and Donna* was obscene; rather, the case concerned whether the arrest and seizure here were valid. Chief Justice Burger, delivering the Court's opinion, held that a warrant was a prior requirement and that there had to be a formal, judicial determination as to the film's obscenity— the sheriff's views were not sufficient—before the film could be seized. *Roaden v. Kentucky*, 413 U.S. 496 (1973).

De Grazia and Newman (*Banned Films*, p. 339) give an outline of the plot: "Fifteen-year-old Cindy is curious about but afraid to discover her own sexual nature. After she sees her half-sister Donna, 17, make love to Cindy's father while high on marijuana, Cindy decides to experiment. With both parents gone one weekend, Donna has sex with three young men, Cindy and her friend Karen get high on marijuana, and Cindy has a sex experience with Karen. When Cindy later tries to have sex with Donna's boyfriend, he throws Donna out of the house and she is hit by a car. Cindy's sexual adventures end."†

CITIZENS AGAINST RENT CONTROL v. CITY OF BERKELEY (1981).

A Berkeley, California, ordinance on political contributions* set a limit of $250 on contributions to committees formed to support or oppose ballot measures. The city's fair campaign practices commission ordered an unincorporated association, formed to oppose a particular ballot measure, to pay into the city treasury the amount of contributions it received in excess of the permitted amount. The Supreme Court of California held that the ordinance was not a violation of the First Amendment: The ordinance furthered compelling governmental interests because it ensured that special interest groups could not corrupt the initiative process by spending large amounts to support or oppose a ballot measure and that the ordinance accomplished its goal by the least restrictive means available.

The U.S. Supreme Court reversed on appeal, Chief Justice Burger delivering the opinion: The restraint imposed by the ordinance on rights of association and in turn on individual and collective rights of expression contravened both the right of association and the speech guarantees of the First Amendment, the ordinance not advancing a legitimate governmental interest significant enough to justify its infringement on First Amendment rights, since the public interest allegedly advanced by the ordinance—identifying the sources of support for and opposition to ballot measures—was insubstantial, since contributors were required to make their identities known under another provision, and there being no significant state or public interest in curtailing debate and discussion of a ballot measure, whatever may be the state interest or degree of that interest in regulating and limiting contributors to or expenditures of a candidate or a candidate's committee. *Citizens Against Rent Contol v. City of Berkeley*, 454 U.S. 290 (1981).

CITIZENS FOR DECENCY THROUGH LAW. Founded in 1957 and with headquarters in Phoenix, Arizona, this group is active in trying to censor what it considers obscene material. The *Encyclopedia of Associations* (#11998) contains the following description of Citizens for Decency Through Law, provided by the group itself: "To assist law enforcement agencies and legislatures to enact and enforce Constitutional statutes, ordinances, and regulations controlling obscenity and pornography and materials harmful to juveniles. Works to create an awareness in the American public of the extent and harms associated with the distribution of pornography through newsstands, bookstores, theaters, and television. Provides free legal assistance in the form of legal research, briefs, model legislation, and courtroom assistance for obscenity prosecutions and civil actions. Conducts seminars for police and prosecutors on search and seizure, trial tactics, evidence and proof, and appeals. Enters appellate cases with friend of the court briefs in support of law enforcement." Its major publication is the *National Decency Reporter*, and it was known as Citizens for Decent Literature until 1973. The founder of the original Citizens for Decent Literature was Charles H. Keating, Jr., of Cincinnati, Ohio (known as "Mr. Clean" in his hometown for his efforts to rid the Queen City of what he considered to be smut). Keating was later appointed by President Nixon to the Commission on Obscenity and Pornography,* a commission whose recommendations were ignored by the president.

CITY OF CHICAGO v. UNIVERSAL PUBLISHING AND DISTRIBUTING CORPORATION (1966). The Universal Publishing and Distributing Corporation was convicted in the city of Chicago for a violation of the city's obscenity statute, but on appeal, the Illinois Supreme Court reversed the conviction for distributing obscene books: "The revolting language and 'dirty' words of *Tropic of Cancer** are not present here...no cunnilingus or oral-genital contact is described and apparently none is involved; there is no masturbation, flagellation, masochism or acts of sadism; no male homosexual conduct is involved, and no voyeurism is discussed. There are no transvestite episodes and several of the incidents of lesbianism are 'disgusting' to the neophyte partner. The books now before us do, to a limited extent, deal with common social or marital problems although they certainly are not the type of writing which we would voluntarily read or recommend. Obviously their publication on the basis of literary merit would be unjustified, and they are clearly inappropriate for other than adults. However, it is established that 'sex and obscenity are not synonymous' and that 'the portrayal of sex is not itself sufficient reason to deny material the constitutional protection of freedom of speech and press. We may not weigh the objectionable features of these publications against their affirmative values, and we cannot say they are utterly without redeeming social importance.' "

The court record contained a brief description of the seven books. *Cheater's Paradise* "revolves chiefly about the marital difficulties in which a resort hotel employee and his wife become enmeshed. It includes numerous sexual episodes involving other partners, an incident of lesbianism and concludes with a reconciliation of the married couple.'' *Her Young Lover* ''involves a happily married couple who are returning home from an anniversary dinner when they are assaulted by three young men each of whom rapes the wife. The ensuing dissolution of their marriage is caused by the husband's impotency induced by his feeling of guilt in failing to protect his wife from rape. Both engage in extramarital sexual activity. She learns the identity of one of her attackers, and thereafter engages in numerous sexual episodes with him. The book ends with indications that the husband and wife will be divorced and that each will marry a paramour.'' *High-School Scandal* ''depicts a respectable, attractive widow in her mid-thirties, who becomes enamored of a seventeen-year-old student in one of the classes she teaches. Her seduction of him, and her sexual experience with two other faculty members, one a lesbian, are the dominant theme of the book. The ultimate exposure of her affair with the boy leaves her friendless except for the brother of her deceased husband with whom it appears she will attempt to rebuild her life.'' *Instant Love* ''portrays a motel owner facing financial ruin who finally agrees to an arrangement whereby a panderer places three prostitutes at the motel and operates a poker game there. The owner's problems include his alcoholic wife, and sexual adventures with the motel maid, the prostitutes and a nurse. He finally, although threatened with physical harm and bankruptcy, seeks assistance from law enforcement authorities in terminating the illegal activities and places his wife in a sanatorium. The book ends with indications of an agreed divorce from his wife, her cure from alcoholism and his marriage to the nurse.'' *Love Hostess* ''portrays the experiences of a young actor who obtains employment as a tour guide and eventually marries the niece of the tour director. The operations of the tour staff and the tourists involve considerable sexual activity among the staff and the tourists with an episode of lesbianism.'' *The Marriage Club* ''deals with a young woman whose husband is intolerably brutal in their sexual relationships. She leaves him and goes to the home of an aunt, a rather frank and bawdy person who operates a matrimonial agency in a building where private rooms are available for such use as the members desire. Two of the aunt's secretaries are in fact prostitutes. The niece has several sexual experiences with agency patrons. Her husband attempts to persuade her to return by fraudulent threats against the aunt's property. One of the patrons, with whom the niece has had a sexual relationship, exposes the fraud, and the final sentence indicates her resumption of their sexual activity and probable marriage.'' *The Shame of Jenny* ''portrays a secretary, fearful of spinsterhood, who engages in sexual intercourse with a fellow-employee, is sexually assaulted by her superior, rooms with a lesbian narcotic addict, has numerous sexual experiences with a musician, and ultimately attempts suicide, but is rescued therefrom and decides to marry the musician. Also portrayed are the frustrations involved in her superior's marriage to an abnormally fat wife, his secret desire for the secretary and his ultimate mental breakdown.'' *City of Chicago v. Universal Publishing and Distributing Corporation*, 215 N.E. 2d 251 (1966).

CITY OF CORONA v. *CORONA DAILY INDEPENDENT* (1953). The city of Corona, California, passed an ordinance levying a "business tax" of eight dollars per year on all businesses wishing to do business in the city. The *Corona Daily Independent* filed suit challenging the ordinance, arguing that it was an unconstitutional abridgment of freedom of the press. A California district court of appeals held that the tax was not a violation of freedom of the press. Justice Griffin: "While the ordinary business tax here in issue is levied in form upon the privilege of engaging in or transacting business, it is, on its face and in fact, a tax for revenue purposes only, and does not grant or take away any right to do business, does not subject business to withdrawal or control by the city, is not regulatory in any manner, and in substance has been recognized by the weight of authority. We conclude that a nondiscriminatory tax, levied upon the doing of business, for the sole purpose of maintaining the municipal government, without whose municipal services and protection the press could neither exist nor function, must be sustained as being within the purview and necessary implications of the Constitution and its amendments." *City of Corona v. Corona Daily Independent*, 252 P. 2d 56 (1953).

CITY OF ST. LOUIS v. MIKES (1963). This case involved a prosecution for violating a St. Louis, Missouri, indecent behavior* ordinance in that a burlesque performance was judged to be lewd and indecent. The court's opinion was delivered by Judge Wolfe: "The performance took place in a room described by the police officer as being about 50 feet by 50 feet in area. There was a bar at which customers could be seated for service and a smaller bar for preparing drinks to be served at tables. The room was otherwise furnished with tables and chairs, except for a small space used for social dancing by the customers of the establishment. There was a three-piece orchestra provided. The floor show was conducted in the dancing area, which consisted of an entertainer telling jokes for about a half hour and the performance by defendant Ware. Her act started from a small, round, revolving platform which looked like the top of a rather large bird bath, with simulated spouts of water which arched upward from its rim. This platform was located about 10 feet from the nearest tables. Defendant Ware started her performance by mounting the platform. The platform revolved slowly as the three-piece orchestra played. When the defendant mounted the platform she was fully clothed. She was wearing an evening gown, with a scarf covering her head. As the music played and the platform slowly revolved, the defendant assumed various simple poses with her hands and arms. She also displayed her leg through a drape or slit in her dress. She then started to remove her clothing. She proceeded slowly to remove the scarf about her head. Then she removed part of her dress covering the upper part of her torso. As she removed the various parts of clothing, she dropped them into a container near the platform. She slowly removed her skirt, and after holding it at arm's length, dropped it into a container. At this point in her disrobing, she was wearing a brassiere and a scant pair of underpants. Attached to the top of the pants, or to a belt of sorts, were transparent panels, one in front and two in the rear. She then went through some gyrations in time to the music, and assumed some poses. This was followed by her descent from the platform to the dance floor. She sat on the floor close to the customers and went through some more body gyrations. After this she went to the side of the platform and simulated pouring water from a jug. She then removed an outer brassiere, which she dropped into a container. Under this outer brassiere she was wearing another one, sheer but bespangled and scant. She then returned to the dance floor and went through some more gyrations, after which she returned to the platform and removed the panels which were attached to her costume. The tempo of the music changed, and in a standing position she grasped her ankles and shook her buttocks from side to side. Then standing erect, she did some hip movements. Returning again to the dance floor, she assumed a semi-kneeling position in front of the platform and moved her torso in an up-and-down motion. At this time she was clad in what might best be described as a very scant brassiere and pants. She turned facing the audience, and some of those present yelled, 'More, more—take it off. More, more.' This ended the performance. . . . We have viewed and considered objectively the pictures of the performance here in question, and find the performance nothing more than modern burlesque. It was as devoid of art and beauty as a garbage pail, and was just 'dirt for dirt's sake.' The defendants violated the ordinances in question." *City of St. Louis v. Mikes*, 372 S.W. 2d 508 (1963).

CIVIL SERVICE COMMISSION v. LETTER CARRIERS (1973). Some federal employees, an employees union, and some local Democratic and Republican political committees filed this suit challenging the constitutionality of certain sections of the Hatch Act.* These sections placed limits on civil servants' First Amendment rights, specifically those rights concerned with partisan political activity, speech, press, and assembly. But similar to the Supreme Court's decision in *Broaderick v. Oklahoma* (1973),* the Court upheld the Hatch Act, saying that Congress has the authority to limit certain activity by federal employees and that the prohibition against partisan political activity was in pursuit of a legitimate governmental interest. Justice Douglas, joined by Justices Brennan and Marshall, dissented: "We deal here with a First Amendment right to speak, to propose, to publish, to petition Government, to assemble. . . . I would strike [those sections of the Hatch Act]. . . as unconstitutional." *Civil Service Commission v. Letter Carriers*, 413 U.S. 548 (1973).

CLASSIFIED INFORMATION. The disclosure of classified or secret information has been—and remains—a sensitive issue for the government and the courts. One major distinction between censorship in this area and in other areas is that the publication or communication of classified information is often subject to a prior restraint* as well as to post-publication punishment. Although the courts have looked askance at most prior restraint schemes, they have in general accepted such schemes when classified or secret information was concerned. As

Chief Justice Hughes wrote in *Near v. Minnesota ex rel. Olson* (1931),* striking down a prior restraint on a newspaper: "No one would question but that a government might prevent...the publication of the sailing dates of transports or the number and location of troops."

The courts have usually sustained prior restraints/pre-publication censorship in this area in view of the assumed national interest in maintaining an effective intelligence service (*Haig v. Philip Agee* [1981],* *Snepp v. United States* [1980],* *United States v. Marchetti* [1972],* and *McGehee v. Casey* [1983]*). The courts, however, have not been that pleased with the decisions that they reached. In the *McGehee* case, Judge Wald of the U.S. Court of Appeals for the District of Columbia, while upholding the Central Intelligence Agency's (CIA's) censorship of sections of a highly critical article by a former agent about alleged CIA activities in Latin America, made the following comments: "I write separately to stress, however, that neither the agency's nor our analysis takes account of any separate public right to know critical albeit classified facts about the activities of our intelligence agencies. It would of course be extremely difficult for judges to 'balance' the public's right to know against an acknowledged national security risk, and I do not believe we are currently authorized to do so. However, it seems important in view of recent revelations about past indiscretions in the name of national security, for some governmental institution, if not the classification system itself, to conduct such a balance. As Emerson explained, 'history...give[s] value to the present hour and its duty.' By not weighing the value to the public of knowing about particularly relevant episodes in the intelligence agencies' history, we may undermine the public's ability to assess the government's performance of its duty. Economic and criminal sanctions against agents who violate the preclearance and agency classification scheme are justifiable. But with no mechanism in the system for balancing the public's right to know with possible risks to security, those sanctions can also result in the permanent loss of information critical to public debate. Our decision today, reflecting current restraints on our authority, cannot and does not fill the public's need for such a balance."

In one much publicized case, however—the *Pentagon Papers** (*New York Times v. United States* and *United States v. Washington Post*, 403 U.S. 713 [1971])—the Supreme Court did *not* permit the government to apply a prior restraint on what was alleged to be critical information. In the *Pentagon Papers* case, the government attempted to restrain the *New York Times* and the *Washington Post*. This attempt derived from some vague notion of national security based on the executive's claim to determine national interest in his role as commander in chief and as focal point for the formulation of foreign policy. As noted, the Supreme Court refused to enjoin the publication of the *Pentagon Papers*.

The following is a sample of some of the regulations in force regarding classified/secret information: Title 18 U.S.C. § 797: "On and after thirty days from the date upon which the President defines any vital military or naval installation or equipment as being within the category contemplated under § 795 of this title, whoever reproduces, publishes, sells, or gives away any photograph, sketch, picture, drawing, map, or graphical representation of the vital military or naval installations or equipment so defined, without first obtaining permission of the commanding officer of the military or naval post, camp, or station concerned, or higher authority, unless such photograph, sketch, picture, drawing, map, or graphical representation has clearly indicated thereon that it has been censored by the proper military or naval authority, shall be fined not more than $1,000 or imprisoned not more than one year, or both.''

In relevant part, 18 U.S.C. § 798 provides: ''(a) Whoever knowingly and willfully communicates, furnishes, transmits, or otherwise makes available to an unauthorized person, or publishes, or uses in any manner prejudicial to the safety or interest of the United States or for the benefit of any foreign government to the detriment of the United States any classified information—(1) concerning the nature, preparation, or use of any code, cipher, or cryptographic system of the United States or any foreign government; or (2) concerning the design, construction, use, maintenance, or repair of any device, apparatus, or appliance used or prepared or planned for use by the United States or any foreign government for cryptographic or communication intelligence purposes; or (3) concerning the communication intelligence activities of the United States or any foreign government; or (4) obtained by the process of communication intelligence from the communications of any foreign government, knowing the same to have been obtained by such processes—shall be fined not more than $10,000 or imprisoned not more than ten years, or both.''

Title 18 U.S.C. § 793(e) provides: ''Whoever having unauthorized possession of, access to, or control over any document, writing, code book, signal book, sketch, photograph, photographic negative, blueprint, plan, map, model, instrument, appliance, or note relating to the national defense or information relating to the national defense which information the possessor has reason to believe could be used to the injury of the United States or to the advantage of any foreign nation, willfully communicates, delivers, transmits or causes to be communicated...or attempts to communicate...to any person not entitled to receive it, or willfully retains the same and fails to deliver it to the officer or employee of the United States entitled to receive it; is guilty of an offense punishable by 10 years in prison, a $10,000 fine, or both.''

The Carter administration attempted to refine the types of information that may be considered for classification, and when reasonable doubt was present, the matter either would be classified at a lower level or it would not be classified at all. Executive Order No. 12,065 § 1-301, 3 C.F.R. 190, 193 (1979): ''Information may not be considered for classification unless it concerns: (a) military plans, weapons, or operations; (b) foreign government information; (c) intelligence activities, sources or methods; (d) foreign relations or foreign activities of the United States; (e) scientific, technological, or economic matters relating to the national security; (f) United States Government programs for safeguarding nuclear materials or facilities; or (g) other categories of information which are related to national security and which require protection against unauthorized disclosure as determined by the President, by a person designated by the President...or by an agency head."

The Reagan administration broadened this list and took the point of view that if in doubt, classify. Executive Order No. 12,356 § 1.3(a), 3 C.F.R. 166, 168-169 (1983) contains the Carter list and adds "cryptology; a confidential source; and the vulnerabilities or capabilities of systems, installations, projects, or plans relating to the national security." The Intelligence Identities Protection Act* was signed into law by President Reagan in June 1982, after passage by wide margins in the House and the Senate. This statute makes it a crime ($15,000 or three years or both) to publish "any information that identifies an individual as a covert agent" of the CIA or the FBI, even if the information is unclassified, a matter of public record, or is derived entirely from public sources. The Reagan administration postponed a plan that would have subjected all federal employees who might have had access to classified or secret information while employed to submit to a pre-publication approval scheme for any writing they might do after they leave government service. This prior restraint/approval would not have been limited to publication of the classified information, but to *any* writing they may wish to do during their lifetimes. But the Senate, on October 20, 1983, voted 56 to 34 to delay this scheme for six months. President Reagan announced that the delay would be for a longer time in order to work out a satisfactory agreement with Congress. Reagan's original plan would have subjected approximately 130,000 federal employees to a lifetime of prior restraint and pre-publication approval for any of their writings.

CLASS OF '74. A Jacksonville, Florida, city ordinance (Jacksonville [FL], Nudity in Drive-Ins*) made it a public nuisance and punishable offense for a drive-in movie theater to exhibit films containing nudity when the screen is visible from a public street or place. The operator of a drive-in was convicted under the ordinance for showing *Class of '74*, but the Supreme Court, in *Erznoznik v. City of Jacksonville* (422 U.S. 205 [1975]), held that the ordinance infringed First Amendment rights and that it could not be justified as an exercise of the city's police power for the protection of children against viewing the films. Justice Powell delivered the opinion of the Court: "In this case, assuming the ordinance is aimed at prohibiting youths from viewing the films, the restriction is broader than permissible. The ordinance is not directed against sexually explicit nudity, nor is it otherwise limited. Rather, it sweepingly forbids display of all films containing *any* uncovered buttocks or breasts, irrespective of context or pervasiveness. Thus it would bar a film containing a picture of a baby's buttocks, the nude body of a war victim, or scenes from a culture in which nudity is indigenous. The ordinance might also prohibit newsreel scenes of the opening of an art exhibit as well as shots of bathers on a beach. Clearly all nudity cannot be deemed obscene as to minors."

The *Class of '74* was an American film, produced in 1972 and rated R. De Grazia and Newman (*Banned Films*, p. 368) present a brief review: "A young college woman of the early 1970s looks to three aggressively unconventional fellow coed friends for guidance in her search for her own social and sexual identity. Following their lead, she gleefully cavorts with a handsome young photographer, introduced to her by her 'free-thinking' friend; a young stud, provided by her yearning black friend; and a jet-set married couple looking for a *ménage à trois*, thanks to another friend of exotic taste. Returning, finally, to campus, she determines to put her well-earned sexual prowess at the disposal of a new freshman coed."†

CLEAN UP TV CAMPAIGN. This group was founded in 1978 and describes itself as: "Religious groups, civic groups, and churches; other interested parties. Purpose is to insist that television programs be revised so that they are no longer an insult to decency and a negative influence on young people. Has initiated campaign to boycott products advertised on programs which depict scenes of adultery, sexual perversion or incest or which treat immorality in a joking or otherwise favorable light. Campaign emphasizes that 'this is clearly not censorship, but simply responsible action since companies remain free to sponsor any programs they choose.' " *Encyclopedia of Associations* (# 11959).

CLEAR AND PRESENT DANGER. One criterion for determining the validity of laws preventing or punishing freedom of speech and press is the "clear and present danger" test. This test was first stated by Justice Holmes, in *Schenck v. United States**: "The question in every case is whether the words used are used in such circumstances and are of such a nature as to create a clear and present danger that they will bring about the substantive evils that Congress has the right to prevent." Although it was not until 1969 (*Brandenburg v. Ohio**) that the Court held that the danger had to be "imminent" and not just "probable," Justice Brandeis and Holmes, in *Whitney v. California*,* wrote that the danger had to be "imminent": "No danger flowing from speech can be deemed clear and present, unless the incidence of the evil apprehended is so imminent that it may befall before there is opportunity for full discussion. If there be time to expose through discussion the falsehood and fallacies, to avert the evil by the processes of education, the remedy to be applied is more speech, not enforced silence."

But Justice Frankfurter, in *Pennekamp v. Florida*,* remarked that " 'clear and present danger' was never used by Mr. Justice Holmes to express a technical legal doctrine or to convey a formula for adjudicating cases. It was a literary phrase not to be distorted by being taken from its context. In its setting it served

†Reprinted from *Banned Films* with permission of the R. R. Bowker Company. Copyright © 1982 by Edward de Grazia and Roger K. Newman.

to indicate the importance of freedom of speech to a free society but also to emphasize that its exercise must be compatible with the preservation of other freedoms essential to a democracy and guaranteed by our Constitution. When those other attributes of a democracy are threatened by speech, the Constitution does not deny power to the States to curb it.''

COALITION FOR BETTER TELEVISION. Founded in 1981 by the Rev. Donald Wildman, in Tupelo, Mississippi, the Coalition for Better Television describes itself as an organization, representing approximately five million families, united to fight ''excessive and gratuitous violence, vulgarity, sex and profanity'' on commercial television. *Encyclopedia of Associations* (# 11960).

COATES v. CITY OF CINCINNATI (1971). A Cincinnati, Ohio, public annoyance ordinance* made it a criminal offense for ''three or more persons to assemble. . .on any of the sidewalks. . .and there conduct themselves in a manner annoying to persons passing by.'' Coates and others were involved as pickets in a labor dispute but were convicted for violating the ordinance. In affirming the convictions, the Ohio Supreme Court stated: ''The ordinance prohibits 'conduct annoying to persons passing by.' The word 'annoying' is a widely used and well understood word: it is not necessary to guess its meaning. 'Annoying' is the present participle of the transitive verb 'annoy' which means to trouble, to vex, to impede, to incommode, to provoke, to harass or to irritate.''

On appeal, the U.S. Supreme Court reversed the conviction. Justice Douglas: ''In our opinion this ordinance is unconstitutionally vague because it subjects the exercise of the right of assembly to an unascertainable standard, and unconstitutionally broad because it authorizes the punishment of constitutionally protected conduct. Conduct that annoys some people does not annoy others. Thus, the ordinance is vague, not in the sense that it requires a person to conform his conduct to an imprecise but comprehensible normative standard, but rather in the sense that no standard of conduct is specified at all. As a result, 'men of common intelligence must necessarily guess at its meaning.' It is said that the ordinance is broad enough to encompass many types of conduct clearly within the city's constitutional power to prohibit. And so, indeed, it is. The city is free to prevent people from blocking sidewalks, obstructing traffic, littering streets, committing assaults, or engaging in countless other forms of anti-social conduct. It can do so through the enactment and enforcement of ordinances directed with reasonable specificity toward the conduct to be prohibited. It cannot constitutionally do so through the enactment and enforcement of an ordinance whose violation may entirely depend on whether or not a policeman is annoyed.'' *Coates v. City of Cincinnati*, 402 U.S. 611 (1971).

COHEN v. CALIFORNIA (1971). Cohen was convicted (and received a jail sentence of thirty days) of violating that part of the California Penal Code, § 415 (California, Offensive Language*), that prohibited ''maliciously and willfully disturb[ing] the peace or quiet of any neighborhood or person...by...offensive conduct.'' Cohen wore a jacket bearing the words ''Fuck the Draft'' in a corridor of a Los Angeles courthouse.

The Supreme Court reversed Cohen's conviction on appeal, ruling that a state, consistent with the First Amendment, may not make the simple public display of this single four-letter expletive a criminal offense. Justice Harlan delivered the Court's opinion: ''This conviction quite clearly rests upon the asserted offensiveness of the *words* Cohen used to convey his message to the public. The only 'conduct' which the State sought to punish is the fact of communication. Thus, we deal here with a conviction resting solely upon 'speech,' not upon any separately identifiable conduct.... The State certainly lacks power to punish Cohen for the underlying content of the message the inscription conveyed.... This is not an obscenity case. Whatever else may be necessary to give rise to the State's broader power to prohibit obscene expression, such expression must be, in some significant way, erotic. It cannot plausibly be maintained that this vulgar allusion to the Selective Service System would conjure up such psychic stimulation in anyone likely to be confronted with Cohen's crudely defaced jacket. Can California excise, as 'offensive conduct,' one particular scurrilous epithet from the public discourse, either upon the theory that its use is inherently likely to cause violent reaction or upon a more general assertion that the States, acting as guardians of public morality, may properly remove this offensive word from the public vocabulary? We have been shown no evidence that substantial numbers of citizens are standing ready to strike out physically at whoever may assault their sensibilities with execrations like that uttered by Cohen. How is one to distinguish this from any other offensive word? Surely the State has no right to cleanse public debate to the point where it is grammatically palatable to the most squeamish among us.... While the particular four-letter word being litigated here is perhaps more distasteful than most others of its genre, it is nevertheless often true that one man's vulgarity is another's lyric. Finally...we cannot indulge the facile assumption that one can forbid particular words without also running a substantial risk of suppressing ideas in the process. Indeed, governments might soon seize upon the censorship of particular words as a convenient guise for banning the expression of unpopular views.'' *Cohen v. California*, 403 U.S. 15 (1971).

COMMERCIAL SPEECH. Even though the First Amendment protections of speech and press are in part applicable to advertisements and commercial speech, the Supreme Court has ruled that ''commercial'' speech has less protection than does speech or press directed at public issues and that ''reasonable'' regulations can be applied to commercial speech: ''Despite the conceptual difficulties in articulating a test to distinguish commercial from noncommercial expression, the decision to deny [total] protection to commercial expression reflects the Court's sound judgment about the function of the First Amendment. Put simply, the use of speech to sell products or promote commercial ventures bears little, if any, relation to the discussion of politics, religion, philosophy, art, and other more mundane subjects which the Supreme Court believes the First Amendment was historically designed to protect. Where the government is often barred from interfering with an individual's free choice on those subjects where expression is protected, it has taken an active role in regulating individual behavior in the commercial market place. That commercial activity takes the form of speech does not necessarily immunize it from regulation." Annotation: *Advertisements: Free Speech and Press*, 37 L. Ed. 2d 1124; Redish, "The First Amendment in the Market Place," 39 *George Washington Law Review* 429 (1971).

COMMISSION ON OBSCENITY AND PORNOGRAPHY. Public Law 90-100, October 3, 1967, 81 Stat. 253, as amended by Public Law 90-350, Title V, § 502, June, 19, 1968, 82 Stat. 197; Public Law 91-74, Title V, § 503, September 29, 1969, 83 Stat. 123, provided for the establishment of the President's Commission on Obscenity and Pornography, its membership, compensation of the members, powers, functions, and duties of the commission; required the commission to report to the president and to the Congress its findings and recommendations no later than September 30, 1970; and provided for its termination ten days after the submission of the report. The commission was duly established, gathered evidence, made several recommendations, submitted its report, and then went out of business. The entire affair was an *opera buffo*.

The commission began its work in a low-key fashion (William B. Lockhart was the chairman) by holding its first meeting at the Kinsey Institute at the University of Indiana, where they viewed classic "blue" movies. One year later, in June 1969, President Nixon appointed to the commission Charles H. Keating, Jr., the founder of Citizens for Decent Literature (now called Citizens for Decency Through Law*). In his hometown of Cincinnati, Keating was known as "Mr. Clean" owing to his unflinching efforts to rid the Queen City of filth, smut, and immorality. He did not get along particularly well with Lockhart, viewing Lockhart as pro-smut, and the commission was wracked with controversy and discord. Keating didn't even want the commission to hold its meetings in public—this would only publicize and make more available the material he wanted to suppress—and thus he boycotted the meetings until the final report was being prepared.

Be that as it may, the commission, after much study and research, issued several recommendations that were in line with dominant American public attitudes as shown in survey research. The recommendations included the following (it should be obvious that these recommendations were not passed unanimously): "(1) A massive sex education effort be launched; (2) Continued open discussion, based on factual information, on the issues regarding obscenity and pornography; (3) Citizens organize themselves at local, regional, and national levels to aid in the implementation of the foregoing recommendations. The aim of citizen groups should be to provide a forum whereby all views may be presented for thoughtful consideration. We live in a free, pluralistic society which places its trust in the competition of ideas in a free market place. Persuasion is a preferred technique.

Coercion, repression and censorship in order to promote a given set of views are not tolerable in our society; (4) Federal, state, and local legislation prohibiting the sale, exhibition, or distribution of sexual materials to consenting adults should be repealed; (5) The Commission believes that there is no warrant for continued governmental interference with the full freedom of adults to read, obtain or view whatever such material they wish. Our conclusion is based upon the following considerations: [a] Extensive empirical investigation, both by the Commission and by others, provides no evidence that exposure to or use of explicit sexual materials plays a significant role in the causation of social or individual harms such as crime, delinquency, sexual or nonsexual deviancy or severe emotional disturbances; [b] On the positive side, explicit sexual materials are sought as a source of entertainment and information by substantial numbers of American adults; [c] Public opinion in America does not support the imposition of legal prohibitions upon the rights of adults to read or see explicit sexual materials. While a minority of Americans favors such prohibitions, a majority of the American people presently is of the view that adults should be legally able to read or see explicit sexual materials if they wish to do so; [d] The foregoing considerations take on added significance because of the fact that adult obscenity laws deal in the realm of speech and communication. Americans deeply value the right of each individual to determine for himself what books he wishes to read and what pictures or films he wishes to see. Our traditions of free speech and press also value and protect the right of writers, publishers, and booksellers to serve the diverse interests of the public. The spirit and letter of our Constitution tell us that government should not seek to interfere with these rights unless a clear threat of harm makes that course imperative. Moreover, the possibility of the misuse of general obscenity statutes prohibiting distribution of books and films to adults constitutes a continuing threat to the free communication of ideas among Americans—one of the most important foundations of our liberties; [e] The Commission has also taken cognizance of the concern of many people that the lawful distribution of explicit sexual materials to adults may have a deleterious effect upon the individual morality of American citizens and upon the moral climate in America as a whole. This concern appears to flow from a belief that exposure to explicit sexual materials may cause moral confusion which, in turn, may induce antisocial or criminal behavior. As noted above, the commission has found no evidence to support such a contention. Nor is there any evidence that exposure to explicit sexual materials adversely affects character or moral attitudes regarding sex and sexual conduct; and (6) The Commission takes the view that parents should be free to make their own conclusions regarding the suitability of explicit sexual material for their children and that it is appropriate for legislation to aid parents in controlling the access of their children to such materials during their formative years.''

Keating was incensed with these recommendations and even tried to get a court order barring the publication of the report. President Nixon, in an attempt to dissociate his administration from the report, remarked that it was President

Johnson who appointed most of the members (Nixon took credit for Keating), and Vice-President Agnew used the report to flay away at "radical liberals" and the "permissive society." The U.S. Senate denounced the report, and Nixon called the conclusions "morally bankrupt," saying that the commission performed a "disservice" to the country and that "American morality is not to be trifled with." The Report of the President's Commission on Obscenity and Pornography thus died a largely unmourned death. *The Report of the Commission on Obscenity and Pornography*, Introduction by Clive Barnes (New York: Bantam Books, 1970).

COMMITTEE ON INTERNATIONAL FREEDOM TO PUBLISH. Founded in 1975, this committee states that it is "pledged to protect and promote the rights of publishers and authors throughout the world by every available means and especially where they are persecuted by oppressive and tyrannical governments. Monitors relations between writers and publishers and their governments and takes action to remove such barriers to the freedom to publish as may be raised by governments. Works closely with publisher groups and author groups throughout the world. Discusses the issue of freedom to publish with the U.S. government, other governments and international organizations having responsibilities for protecting writers." *Encyclopedia of Associations* (# 11999).

COMMITTEE TO DEFEND THE FIRST AMENDMENT. Founded in 1979, this committee is a non-profit corporation with a board of directors and a national advisory board of professionals in law, education, media, and religion whose common interest is First Amendment rights. The committee describes itself as a group that: "Raises and provides funds necessary to secure adequate legal services and assistance to individuals whose First Amendment rights are jeopardized by federal, state and local courts. Provides a forum for the exchange of opinions. Disseminates information to the general public, governmental agencies and other interested organizations concerning abridgments, limitations and encroachments on the exercise of First Amendment rights, their role in contemporary society, and the importance of advocating their preservation." *Encyclopedia of Associations* (#12039).

COMMONWEALTH OF PENNSYLVANIA v. STOTLAND (1969). This case was decided along with *Commonwealth v. Countryman* and *Commonwealth v. Achtenberg*. A Philadelphia, Pennsylvania, state of emergency* ordinance authorized the mayor to declare a state of emergency within the city and to impose certain measures for the duration of the emergency period. On April 5, 1968, Mayor James Tate declared such a state of emergency, and Stotland, Countryman, and Achtenberg were arrested and convicted by a Pennsylvania court for certain violations. Stotland was arrested on the campus of the University of Pennsylvania while a member of a gathering of 250 people demonstrating against the proclamation of the state of emergency. The demonstration consisted of several speeches and was peaceful, without disruptive or disorderly conduct. An order to disperse was read by the police, and Stotland was arrested when he refused.

Countryman and forty-nine other persons gathered in Roosevelt Park and held a tree-planting ceremony to protest the recommissioning of the battleship *New Jersey*. The ceremony was held under a permit issued by the Park Commission and was peaceful. The gathering was then ordered to disperse—a group of more than twelve persons violated a measure of the state of emergency—but Countryman refused.

Achtenberg led a march (with eleven other persons), petitioning for passage of civil rights legislation. There were no incidents, but soon thereafter, another member joined the group, which made it a gathering of more than twelve persons. They were ordered to disperse, but Achtenberg refused.

The Pennsylvania court, fully aware of the volatile situation in the aftermath of the assassination of Martin Luther King, Jr., did not see the police actions as a violation of the First Amendment. The court explained: "The question posed relates to the power of the State to impose time, size and area limitations upon peaceful public assemblies. A State may under its police powers regulate these aspects of assembly although the conduct which is the subject of regulation is intertwined with expression and association. . . . The time, place and manner of speech and assembly may constitutionally be regulated by a precise and narrowly drawn regulatory statute evincing a legislative judgment that certain specific conduct should be limited or proscribed. In ordinary times and at ordinary places, large public assemblies, especially for the purpose of peacefully communicating controversial ideas and minority viewpoints, must be given the greatest possible protection. However, in the highly charged atmosphere prevailing when the danger of a large scale riot is present, large public assemblies, although peaceful to all appearances, may inflame passions or promote clashes between persons or groups with divergent views and ignite the violence which may quickly become a full scale riot. The purpose of the limitation upon assembly is to eliminate the possibility of these dangerous confrontations at times and places where there is a clear and present danger of a large scale riot. The effect of the limitation is merely to delay assemblies until they can be held without endangering the entire community. The alternative conditions that the city be 'suffering' or be 'in imminent danger of suffering' a riot indicate that the emergency powers may be employed as a preventive measure as well as a control device. . . . Both the ordinance and its history indicate that the only danger defined by the language 'civil disturbance, disorder, riot or other occurrence' is a large scale urban riot. In 1964, a large scale riot occurring in Philadelphia resulted in scores of injuries and extensive property damage. . . . The ordinance was enacted to give the Mayor more effective power to restore order or prevent disorder in future outbreaks of this kind."

Stotland, Countryman, and Achtenberg appealed their convictions to the Supreme Court, but the Court dismissed the appeal "for want of a substantial federal question" (*Stotland v. Commonwealth of Pennsylvania*, 398 U.S. 916 [1970]). *Commonwealth of Pennsylvania v. Stotland*, 251 A. 2d 701 (1969).

COMMONWEALTH v. BLANDING (1825). This was one of the earliest cases of libel. Blanding published in a newspaper, the *Providence Gazette*, a "scandalous and libelous paragraph concerning one Enoch Fowler, he then being an innholder in that county, and a good and peaceful citizen, &c." Blanding offered to give in evidence information that his remarks were true, but this evidence was not admitted. Justice Wilde of the Massachusetts court delivered the opinion: "The provision in the constitution securing the liberty of the press was intended to prevent any previous restraints upon publications, and not to affect prosecutions for the abuse of such liberty. The general rule is, that upon indictment the truth of a libel is not admissible in evidence. . . [and] publishing a correct account. . . but with comments and insinuations tending to asperse a man's character, is libellous." *Commonwealth v. Blanding*, 3 Pick. [20 Mass.] 304 (1825).

COMMONWEALTH v. TARBOX (1848). Tarbox was indicted for "he did print, publish, and distribute a certain printed paper, containing obscene language and descriptions manifestly tending to the corruption of the morals of youth, which printed paper was distributed and left at the doors. . . of one hundred of the citizens of Boston." Tarbox was duly convicted but complained that the indictment was not sufficient; it said only that he printed and distributed an "obscene" paper and did not describe the matter itself. The court refused to accept the complaint, believing that to put the actual description of the "disgusting" material in the indictment or even in the court record would be improper and indecent. The courts were squeamish in the early days, refusing to "debase the record" with what they considered inappropriate language. This can be compared with the contemporary courts, whose decisions in obscenity cases print and distribute the same graphic descriptions of explicit sexual activity as do the defendant's material. One no longer has to patronize the adult bookstores; the official court records will suffice! The *Tarbox* case should be compared with the *Illustrated Report** case. *Commonwealth v. Tarbox*, 1 Cush. [55 Mass.] 66 (1848).

COMMUNIST PARTY OF INDIANA v. WHITCOMB (1974). The Communist party of Indiana was refused a place on the Indiana ballot for the 1972 general election because it failed to submit a statement (Indiana, Loyalty Oath*) stating that the party "does not advocate the overthrow of local, state or national government by force or violence." The Supreme Court ruled that the loyalty oath requirement of the Indiana statute violated the First Amendment: "The constitutional guarantees of free speech and free press do not permit a State to forbid or proscribe advocacy of the use of force or of law violation except where such advocacy is directed to inciting or producing imminent lawless action and is likely to produce such action.'' *Communist Party of Indiana v. Whitcomb*, 414 U.S 441 (1974).

COMSTOCKERY. The term "comstockery," coined by George Bernard Shaw, is a pejorative epithet meaning a "self-appointed protector of other people's morals." It was inspired by the activities of Anthony Comstock (1844–1915), the epitome of someone who could not exist with the thought that someone, someplace was having a good time in ways that Comstock thought immoral. Comstock fought an incessant battle against what he considered vice; he was quite unsubtle and couldn't distinguish good art from bad art or art from morals. The original vice squads were sired by Comstock: He founded in 1873 and was the secretary of the New York Society for the Suppression of Vice (later renamed the New York Society for the Improvement of Morals and headed by John S. Sumner, a latter-day Comstock) and inspired the creation, in 1876, of the Boston-based New England Watch and Ward Society. Comstock was the person mainly responsible for the passage, in 1873, of the federal obscenity statute, otherwise known as the Comstock Act (Postal Regulations, Mailing Obscene Material*), which barred from the mails any obscene, lewd, or indecent material. Comstock once remarked that his greatest accomplishments in life were that he started some 3,600 prosecutions for obscenity and destroyed some 160 tons of obscene material.

One of the problems was that Comstock's definition of "obscene" ensnared in its net what most normal people today would consider material fit for a G-rated Walt Disney film. Justice Douglas, one of the strongest anti-censorship justices ever to sit on the U.S. Supreme Court, added some remarks on Comstock to his dissenting opinion in *Ginsberg v. New York* (1968).* His comments bear citing: "There is a view held by many that the so-called 'obscene' book or tract or magazine has a deleterious effect upon the young, although I seriously doubt the wisdom of trying by law to put the fresh, evanescent, natural blossoming of sex in the category of 'sin.' That, however, was the view of our preceptor in this field, Anthony Comstock, who waged his war against 'obscenity' from the year 1872 until his death in 1915. Some of his views are set forth in his book *Traps for the Young*, first published in 1883. . . . The title of the book refers to 'traps' created by Satan 'for boys and girls especially.' Comstock, of course, operated on the theory that every human has an 'inborn tendency toward wrongdoing which is restrained mainly by fear of the final judgment.' In his view any book which tended to remove that fear is part of the 'trap' which Satan created. Hence, Comstock would have condemned a much wider range of literature than the present Court is apparently inclined to do. It was Comstock who was responsible for the Federal Anti-Obscenity Act of March 3, 1873. It was he who was also responsible for the New York Act which soon followed. He was responsible for the organization of the New York Society for the Suppression of Vice, which by its act of incorporation was granted one-half of the fines levied on people successfully prosecuted by the Society or its agents.'' Comstockery is still alive and well in the United States, as is evidenced by this manuscript. Charles Trumbull, *Anthony Comstock: Fighter* (1913); Heywood Broun and Margaret Leech, *Anthony Comstock: Roundsman of the Lord* (1927); Robert Haney, *Comstockery in America* (1960).

CONNECTICUT, ANTI-CONTRACEPTIVE STATUTE. General Statutes of Connecticut (1958), §§ 53-32 and 54-196, provided: ''Any person who uses any drug, medicinal article or instrument for the purpose of preventing conception shall be fined not less than fifty dollars or imprisoned not less than sixty days nor more than one year or be fined and imprisoned,'' and ''Any person who assists, abets, counsels, causes, hires or commands another to commit any offense may be prosecuted and punished as if he were the principal offender.'' This statute, when applied to a physician who prescribed contraceptives, was seen to be a violation of the First Amendment by the Supreme Court in *Griswold v. Connecticut* (1965).*

CONNECTICUT, ANTI-SOLICITING STATUTE. General Statutes of Connecticut (1937), § 6294 as amended by § 860d, provided: ''No person shall solicit money, services, subscriptions or any valuable thing for any alleged religious, charitable or philanthropic cause...unless such cause shall have been approved by the secretary of the public welfare council. Upon application of any person...the secretary shall determine whether such cause is...bona fide and conforms to reasonable standards of efficiency and integrity....Any person violating any provision of this section shall be fined not more than one hundred dollars or imprisoned not more than thirty days or both.'' This statute was ruled to be a violation of the First Amendment by the Supreme Court in *Cantwell v. Connecticut* (1940).*

CONNICK v. MEYERS (1983). Meyers, an assistant district attorney in Louisiana for five years, serving at the pleasure of the district attorney, was informed that she would be transferred to a different section. She objected to this transfer and then prepared and distributed to her fellow employees a questionnaire concerning their views on office policy, the need for a grievance committee, and whether or not the employees felt pressured to work in political campaigns. Her boss, Harry Connick, then fired her for insubordination.

The Supreme Court held that the firing did not violate Meyers' First Amendment rights. Justice White delivered the majority opinion of a sharply divided (5 to 4) Court: ''When a public employee speaks not as a citizen upon matters of public concern, but instead as an employee upon matters only of personal interest, absent the most unusual circumstances, a federal court is not the appropriate forum in which to review the wisdom of a personnel decision taken by a public agency allegedly in reaction to the employee's behavior and here, except for one question regarding pressure upon employees to work in political campaigns, the questions posed were not matters of public concern. . .[and] the limited First Amendment interest involved here did not require the employer to tolerate action that he reasonably believed would disrupt the office, undermine his authority and destroy the close working relationships within the office.''

Justice Brennan, joined by three others, dissented: "Speech about the manner in which the government is operated or should be operated is an essential part of the communications necessary for self-governance the protection of which was a central purpose of the First Amendment, and because the questionnaire addressed such matters and its distribution did not adversely affect the operations. . .her dismissal violated the First Amendment.'' *Connick v. Meyers*, 75 L. Ed. 2d 708 (1983).

CONSOLIDATED EDISON COMPANY v. PUBLIC SERVICE COMMISSION OF NEW YORK (1980). A New York Public Service Commission insert ban* prohibited public utility companies from including with the monthly bills any inserts that discussed controversial issues of the day. Con Ed did include such an insert that advocated the increased use of nuclear power ("Independence Is Still a Goal, and Nuclear Power is Needed to Win the Battle"). Con Ed then brought suit, challenging the constitutionality of the insert ban.

The Supreme Court ruled that the ban violated the free speech guarantee of the First Amendment: (a) The restriction on bill inserts cannot be upheld on the grounds that appellant, as a corporation, is not entitled to freedom of speech. "The inherent worth of the speech in terms of its capacity for informing the public does not depend upon the identity of its source, whether corporation, association, union, or individual" (*First National Bank of Boston v. Francis X. Bellotti**); (b) Nor is the state action here a valid time, place, or manner restriction. Such regulations may not be based on either the content or subject matter of speech; (c) The prohibition is not a permissible subject-matter regulation. The First Amendment's hostility to content-based regulation extends not only to restrictions on particular viewpoints, but also to prohibition of public discussion of an entire topic; and (d) The prohibition cannot be justified as being necessary to avoid forcing Con Ed's views on a captive audience, since customers may escape exposure to objectionable material by throwing the bill insert into a wastebasket. *Consolidated Edison Company v. Public Service Commission of New York* 447 U.S. 530 (1980).

CONTEMPORARY COMMUNITY STANDARDS. The concept of "contemporary community standards" is used as an element in the definition of obscenity,* including the tests laid down by the Supreme Court in the Roth*/ Memoirs*/Miller* standards. Contemporary community standards, as used in the Court's guidelines for determining obscenity, are whether the average person,* applying contemporary community standards, would find that the work, taken as a whole, appeals to the prurient interest.* The contemporary community standards are local or statewide standards, not national standards. The reliance on local or statewide standards was emphasized by the Court in *Miller v. California**: "Nothing in the First Amendment requires that a jury consider 'hypothetical and unascertainable' national standards and it is neither realistic nor constitutionally sound to read the First Amendment as requiring that the people of Maine or Mississippi accept public depiction of conduct found tolerable in Las Vegas or New York City."

CONTEMPT. The protections of the First Amendment are not absolute when the judicial process or the administration of justice is involved. Individuals are not free to say whatever they choose when, if in the view of a court, such expressions would unreasonably interfere in an immediate sense with the administration of justice. Inside the courtroom, judges have the power to punish as contempt of court acts or speech that is directed at the judge or at another officer of the court and that is seen as an imminent threat to the administration of justice. Outside the courtroom, the use of the contempt power is more limited; the act or speech must constitute a clear and present danger to the administration of justice.

CONTRACEPTION. Title 19 U.S.C. § 1305 (Tariff Act*) prohibits the importation into the United States of any obscene or immoral book, device, or matter. A book entitled *Contraception* by Marie Stopes, was seized by U.S. Customs on the grounds that it fell under the prohibitions of the Tariff Act, and the government sought a court order allowing for its destruction. District Judge Woolsey heard the case in 1931: "I have read *Contraception* and I find that it does not fall, in any respect, within these definitions of the words 'obscene' or 'immoral.' *Contraception* is written primarily for the medical profession. It is stated, in an introduction written by an eminent English doctor, to be the first book dealing fully with its subject-matter—the theory, history, and practice of birth control. It is a scientific book written with obvious seriousness and with great decency, and it gives information to the medical profession regarding the operation of birth control clinics and the instruction necessary to be given at such clinics to women who resort thereto. It tells of the devices used, now and in the past, to prevent conception, and expresses opinions as to those which are preferable from the point of view of efficiency and of the health of the user. Such a book, although it may run counter to the views of many persons who disagree entirely with the theory underlying birth control . . . would not stir the sex impulses of any person with a normal mind. Actually the emotions aroused by the book are merely feelings of sympathy and pity, evoked by the many cases instanced in it of the sufferings of married women due to ignorance of its teachings. This, I believe, will be the inevitable effect of reading it on all persons of sensibility unless by their prejudices the information it contains is tabooed. . . . The libel brought in this case . . . must be dismissed." *United States v. One Book Entitled Contraception*, 51 F. 2d 525 (1931).

COOPER v. PATE (1964). Cooper, an inmate in an Illinois prison, brought suit against Pate, the warden, because the latter did not allow Cooper to purchase certain religious publications disseminated by the Black Muslims, although the warden allowed other inmates to receive the Bible. The district judge found no violation of the First Amendment protection here: "The Attorney General of the State of Illinois asks us to take judicial notice of certain social studies which show that the Black Muslim Movement, despite its pretext of a religious facade, is an organization that, outside of prison walls, has for its object the overthrow of the white race, and inside prison walls, has an impressive history of inciting riots and violence. Under the ruling of the *Beauharnais** case, it seems clear that Illinois may suppress movements that would otherwise be constitutionally protected when they have violence as their object or an even reasonably likely consequence; further, that the Supreme Court of the United States will take judicial cognizance of authoritative racial studies [a direct reference to the Court's decision in *Brown v. Board of Education*] precisely as though their content had been admitted as evidence in this case." *Cooper v. Pate*, 324 F. 2d 165 (1963). The Supreme Court, however, did *not* take "judicial cognizance" of the district judge's decision: It reversed the judgment without comment (378 U.S. 546 [1964]).

CORINTH PUBLICATIONS, INC. v. WESBERRY (1967). Some members of the Georgia State Literature Commission filed a petition under the Georgia obscenity statute,* seeking a judgment that the book entitled *Sin Whisper* was obscene. The state Supreme Court apparently agreed with the commission, saying that the book contained "sexual misbehavior between its main characters" but that additional description was not necessary, for "we do not wish to sully the pages of the reported opinions of this court" with filthy and disgusting material. *Corinth Publications, Inc. v. Wesberry*, 146 S.E. 2d 764 (1966). By a per curiam opinion, the Supreme Court reversed the finding that *Sin Whisper* was obscene (388 U.S. 448 [1967]).

CORPORATE SPEECH. The Supreme Court has yet to rule on whether business corporations, as legal entities, have the same broad spectrum of rights that individuals have under the First Amendment. But in *First National Bank of Boston v. Francis X. Bellotti*,* the Court ruled that a Massachusetts statute prohibiting the expression of corporate views unrelated to the corporation's major business or product was unconstitutional, and in *Consolidated Edison Company v. Public Service Commission of New York*,* the Court ruled as unconstitutional a ban on bill inserts that discussed issues of public controversy. In both cases, the Court wrote that the expression on issues of national interest and importance is "indispensable to decision-making in a democracy" and the source of such expression—whether corporations, associations, unions, or individuals—was not relevant.

COX BROADCASTING CORPORATION v. COHN (1975). A reporter, during a televised news report, broadcast a deceased rape victim's name that he had obtained from the indictments (public records are available for inspection). The victim's father, relying on a Georgia statute (Georgia, Rape Victims' Privacy*), making it a misdemeanor to broadcast a rape victim's name, claimed that his right to privacy had been invaded. The Georgia Supreme Court agreed, declaring that the state policy was that a rape victim's name was not a matter of public concern and sustained the statute as a legitimate limitation on the First Amendment's freedom of expression.

On appeal, the U.S. Supreme Court reversed: "The State may not, consistently with the First Amendment, impose sanctions on the accurate publication of a rape victim's name obtained from judicial records that are maintained in connection with a public prosecution and that themselves are open to public inspection. Here, under circumstances where the reporter based his televised report upon notes taken during court proceedings and obtained the rape victim's name from official court documents open to public inspection, the protection of freedom of the press provided by the First Amendment bars Georgia from making the broadcast the basis of civil liability. . . . The commission of a crime, prosecutions resulting therefrom, and judicial proceedings arising from the prosecutions are events of legitimate concern to the public and consequently fall within the press' responsibility to report the operations of the government. . . . The interests of privacy fade when the information involved already appears on public record, especially when viewed in terms of the First Amendment and in light of the public interest in a vigorous press." *Cox Broadcasting Corporation v. Cohn,* 420 U.S. 469 (1975).

COX v. LOUISIANA (1965). Cox was the leader of a civil rights demonstration in Baton Rouge protesting segregation in general and the arrest of some black students who participated in a previous civil rights demonstration. The demonstration was in the vicinity of a courthouse, and the police chief ordered the crowd of some 2,000 persons to disperse. Tear gas was used to achieve the dispersal, and Cox was arrested for violating several ordinances (Louisiana, Obstructing Public Passages,* Louisiana, Breach of the Peace,* and Louisiana, Courthouse Picketing*). Cox was found guilty of all charges (four months and $200 for breach of the peace/five months and $500 for obstructing public passages/one year and $5,000 for picketing near a courthouse; the sentences were cumulative), and the Louisiana Supreme Court affirmed all three convictions.

The U.S. Supreme Court reversed the convictions and concluded that the state of Louisiana deprived Cox of his constitutional guarantee of free speech. Justice Goldberg delivered the Court's opinion: "Our conclusion that the record does not support the contention that the students' cheering, clapping and singing constituted a breach of the peace is confirmed by the fact that these were not relied on as a basis for conviction by the trial judge, who, rather, stated as his reason for convicting Cox of disturbing the peace that '[i]t must be recognized to be inherently dangerous and a breach of the peace to bring 1,500 people, colored people, down in the predominantly white business district . . . and congregate across the street from the courthouse and sing songs as described to me by the defendant as the CORE national anthem carrying lines such as black and white together and to urge those 1,500 people to descend upon our lunch counters and sit there until they are served. That has to be an inherent breach of the peace.' There is no doubt from the record in this case that the sidewalk [opposite the courthouse] was obstructed, and thus, as so construed, appellant violated the statute. . . . But here it is clear that the practice in Baton Rouge allowing unfettered discretion in local officials in the regulation of the use of the streets for peaceful parades and meetings is an unwarranted abridgment of appellant's freedom of speech and assembly secured to him by the First Amendment, as applied to the States by the Fourteenth Amendment. . . . Cox was in effect advised by the city's highest police officials that the demonstration was not 'near' a courthouse and it was only after the order to disperse was refused did the officials decide it was too near the courthouse. To permit Cox to be convicted for exercising a privilege they told him was available would be to allow a type of entrapment." *Cox v. Louisiana*, 379 U.S. 536 (1965) and 379 U.S. 559 (1965).

COX v. NEW HAMPSHIRE (1941). A New Hampshire regulation (New Hampshire, Licensing of Parades*) required anyone who wanted to hold a parade or procession on the public streets to first obtain a license from the municipal authorities. Cox and others, Jehovah's Witnesses, marched along the sidewalks in a New Hampshire city carrying placards with informational inscriptions. The march was peaceful, the sidewalk was not obstructed, there was no threat of violence, but Cox and his group did not apply for—and thus did not have—the required permit.

The New Hampshire courts then convicted Cox for violating the license ordinance; the U.S. Supreme Court affirmed the conviction. Chief Justice Hughes delivered the Court's opinion: "The sole charge against appellants was that they were taking part in a parade or procession on public streets without a permit as the statute required. They were not prosecuted for distributing leaflets, or for conveying information by placards or otherwise, or for issuing invitations to a public meeting, or for holding a public meeting, or for maintaining or expressing religious beliefs. Their right to do any one of these things apart from engaging in a parade or procession upon a public street is not here involved. . . . Civil liberties, as guaranteed by the Constitution, imply the existence of an organized society maintaining public order without which liberty itself would be lost in the excesses of unrestrained abuses. The authority of a municipality to impose regulations in order to assure the safety and convenience of the people in the use of public highways has never been regarded as inconsistent with civil liberties but rather as one of the means of safeguarding the good order upon which they ultimately depend. . . . If a municipality has authority to control the use of its public streets for parades or processions, as it undoubtedly has, it cannot be denied authority to give consideration, without unfair discrimination, to time, place and manner* in relation to the other proper uses of the streets. We find it impossible to say that the limited authority conferred by the licensing provisions of the statute in question as thus construed by the state court contravened any constitutional right." *Cox v. New Hampshire*, 312 U.S. 569 (1941).

CRAIG v. HARNEY (1947). Craig was convicted of contempt of court after publishing in a newspaper a series of articles that attacked the trial judge in a still-pending case. The Supreme Court reversed the conviction, ruling that Craig's actions did not constitute a clear and present danger to the administration of justice. Justice Douglas: "This was strong language, intemperate language, and, we assume, an unfair criticism. But a judge may not hold in contempt one who ventures to publish anything that tends to make him unpopular or to belittle him. The vehemence of the language used is not alone the measure of the power to punish for contempt. The fires which it kindles must constitute an imminent, not merely a likely, threat to the administration of justice. The danger must not be remote or even probable; it must immediately imperil.... The law of contempt is not made for the protection of judges who may be sensitive to the winds of public opinion. Judges are supposed to be men of fortitude, able to thrive in a hardy climate.... Judges who stand for reelection run on their records. That may be a rugged environment. Criticism is expected. Discussion of their conduct is appropriate, if not necessary. The fact that the discussion at this particular point of time was not in good taste falls short of meeting the clear and present danger test."

Justice Murphy filed a concurring opinion: "In my view, the Constitution forbids a judge from summarily punishing a newspaper editor for printing an unjust attack upon him or his method of dispensing justice. The only possible exception is in the rare instance where the attack might reasonably cause a real impediment to the administration of justice. Unscrupulous and vindictive criticism of the judiciary is regrettable. But judges must not retaliate by a summary suppression of such criticism for they are bound by the command of the First Amendment.... The liberties guaranteed by the First Amendment are too highly prized to be subjected to the hazards of summary contempt procedure." *Craig v. Harney*, 331 U.S. 367 (1947).

CRIMINAL APPEALS ACT. Title 18 U.S.C. § 3731 (the Criminal Appeals Act of 1907), provides in part: "It is unlawful for any national bank, or any corporation organized by authority of any law of Congress, to make a contribution or expenditure in connection with any election to any political office, or in connection with any primary election or political convention or caucus held to select candidates for any political office, or for any corporation whatever, or any labor organization to make a contribution or expenditure in connection with any election at which Presidential and Vice Presidential electors or a Senator or Representative... are to be voted for, or in connection with any primary election or for any candidate, political committee, or other person to accept or receive any contribution prohibited by this section." This statute was held not to be a violation of the First Amendment's guarantee of free speech in *United States v. Auto Workers* (1957).*

CRIMINAL SYNDICALISM. Several states have enacted "criminal syndicalism" laws that, among other things, attempted to prohibit and punish terroristic anarchism, the advocacy of criminal anarchism, violent overthrow of the government, and other forms of rebellion and revolution. One of the more important decisions in this area was *Gitlow v. New York* (1925),* in which the Supreme Court upheld a New York criminal anarchy* statute. Justice Sanford delivered the *Gitlow* decision: "That utterances inciting to the overthrow of organized government by unlawful means, present a sufficient danger of substantive evil to bring their punishment within the range of legislative discretion, is clear. Such utterances, by their very nature, involve danger to the public peace and to the security of the State. They threaten breaches of the peace and ultimate revolution. And the immediate danger is none the less real and substantial, because the effect of a given utterance cannot be accurately foreseen. The State cannot reasonably be required to measure the danger from every such utterance in the nice balance of a jeweler's scale. A single revolutionary spark may kindle a fire that, smouldering for a time, may burst into a sweeping and destructive conflagration. It cannot be said that the State is acting arbitrarily or unreasonably when in the exercise of its judgment as to the measures necessary to protect the public peace and safety, it seeks to extinguish the spark without waiting until it has enkindled the flame or blazed into the conflagration. It cannot reasonably be required to defer the adoption of measures for its own peace and safety until the revolutionary utterances lead to actual disturbances of the public peace or imminent and immediate danger of its own destruction; but it may, in the exercise of its judgment, suppress the threatened danger in its incipiency."

The *Gitlow* decision was also important because the Court (1) assumed that freedom of speech and of the press were among the personal rights and liberties protected by the due process clause of the Fourteenth Amendment (Incorporation*) and (2) in dissent, Justices Holmes and Brandeis voiced the "clear and present danger"* test. In a more recent decision (*Brandenburg v. Ohio* [1969]*), the Court refined its view and held that a state criminal syndicalism statute violated the First Amendment because it punished mere "advocacy"* without any showing of imminent danger: "The constitutional guarantees of free speech and free press do not permit a state to forbid or proscribe advocacy of the use of force or of law violation except where such advocacy is directed to inciting or producing imminent lawless action, and is likely to incite or produce such action."

CRUSADE FOR DECENCY. Founded in 1969 but presently inactive, this organization was a loosely knit anti-pornography, anti-abortion, and anti-sex-education-in-the-schools group. Its most memorable achievement was the "Petition of Decency"—a petition with some 250,000 signatures sent to Congress and the Federal Communications Commission protesting pornography, abortion, and sex education. *Encyclopedia of Associations* (# 13089).

CUSTOMS REGULATIONS. 19 C.F.R. § 145.3, Opening of Letter Class Mail; Reading of Correspondence Prohibited, provides in part: "(a). . .Customs officers and employees may open and examine sealed letter class mail subject to Customs examination which appears to contain matter in addition to, or other than, correspondence, provided they have reasonable cause to suspect the presence of merchandise or contraband. (b) No Customs officer or employee shall open sealed letter class mail which appears to contain only correspondence unless prior to the opening—(1) A search warrant authorizing that action has been obtained from an appropriate judge. . .or (2) The sender or the addressee has given written authorization for the opening. (c) No Customs officer or employee shall read, or authorize or allow any other person to read, any correspondence contained in any letter class mail, whether or not sealed, unless prior to the reading—(1) A search warrant. . .has been obtained. . .or (2) The sender or the addressee has given written authorization. . . .(d) The provisions of paragraph (c) shall also apply to correspondence between school children." This ability of U.S. Customs to inspect incoming mail on "reasonable cause" was not seen as a violation of the First Amendment in *United States v. Ramsey* (1977).*

D

DALLAS (TX), DISTRIBUTION AND SCATTERING OF HANDBILLS.
"Scattering handbills, etc.—It shall be unlawful for any person to carry or hold
by hand or otherwise, any billboard, show card, placard or advertisement, or to
wear any costume for the purpose of attracting attention of the public, or to
scatter or to throw any handbills, circulars, cards, newspapers or any advertising
device of any description, along or upon any street or sidewalk in the city of
Dallas. Any person violating any of the provisions of this article shall be deemed
guilty of a misdemeanor, and upon conviction, may be fined in any sum not
exceeding one hundred dollars." This ordinance was seen to violate the First
Amendment in *Jamison v. Texas* (1943).*

DALLAS (TX), MOTION PICTURE CLASSIFICATION BOARD. Chapter
46A of the 1960 Revised Code of Civil and Criminal Ordinances of the City of
Dallas, as amended, provides: "Section 46A-1: "(a) 'Film' means any motion
picture film or series of films, whether full length or short subject, but does not
include newsreels portraying actual current events or pictorial news of the day.
(b) 'Exhibit' means to project a film at any motion picture theatre or other public
place within the City of Dallas to which tickets are sold for admission. (c)
'Exhibitor' means any person, firm or corporation which exhibits a film. (d)
'Young person' means any person who has not attained his sixteenth birthday.
(e) 'Board' means the Dallas Motion Picture Classification Board established by
Section 46A-2 of this ordinance. (f) 'Not suitable for young persons' means: (1)
Describing or portraying brutality, criminal violence or depravity in such a
manner as to be, in the judgment of the Board, likely to incite or encourage
crime or delinquency on the part of young persons; or (2) Describing or portraying
nudity beyond the customary limits of candor in the community, or sexual
promiscuity or extra-marital or abnormal sexual relations in such a manner as
to be, in the judgment of the Board, likely to incite or encourage delinquency
or sexual promiscuity on the part of young persons or to appeal to their prurient
interest. A film shall be considered 'likely to incite or encourage' crime, delinquency or sexual promiscuity on the part of young persons, if, in the judgment
of the Board, there is a substantial probability that it will create the impression

on young persons that such conduct is profitable, desirable, acceptable, respectable, praiseworthy or commonly accepted. A film shall be considered as appealing to 'prurient interest' of young persons, if in the judgment of the Board, its calculated or dominant effect on young persons is substantially to arouse sexual desire. In determining whether a film is 'not suitable for young persons,' the Board shall consider the films as a whole, rather than isolated portions, and shall determine whether its harmful effects outweigh artistic or educational values such film may have for young persons. (g) 'Classify' means to determine whether a film is: (1) Suitable for young persons, or; (2) Not suitable for young persons."

Section 46A-2. Establishment of Board: "There is hereby created a Board to be known as the Dallas Motion Picture Classification Board which shall be composed of a Chairman and Eight Members to be appointed by the Mayor and City Council of the City of Dallas, whose terms shall be the same as members of the City Council. The Chairman and all Members of the Board shall be good, moral, law-abiding citizens of the City of Dallas, and shall be chosen so far as reasonably practicable in such a manner that they will represent a cross section of the community. Insofar as practicable, the members appointed to the Board shall be persons educated and experienced in one or more of the following fields: art, drama, literature, philosophy, sociology, psychology, history, education, music, science or other related fields."

Section 46A-4. Offenses. "(a) It shall be unlawful for any exhibitor or his employee:....(4) Knowingly to sell or give to any young person a ticket to any film classified 'not suitable for young persons.' (5) Knowingly to permit any young person to view the exhibition of any film classified not suited for young persons."

This censorship scheme was seen by the Supreme Court to violate the First Amendment in the *Viva Maria** case (*Interstate Circuit v. Dallas*, 390 U.S. 676 [1968]).

DAVIS v. MASSACHUSETTS (1897). A Boston ordinance (Boston [MA], Public Speaking Permit*) provided that "no person shall, in or upon any of the public grounds, make any public address...except in accordance with a permit from the mayor." This ordinance was not seen to be a violation of the freedom of speech. Justice White delivered the opinion of the Supreme Court: "It is argued that Boston Common is the property of the inhabitants of the city of Boston, and dedicated to the use of the people of that city and the public in many ways, and the preaching of the gospel there has been, from time immemorial to a recent period, one of these ways. For the making of this ordinance in 1862 and its enforcement against preaching since 1885, no reason whatever has been or can be shown....[But] for the legislature absolutely or conditionally to forbid public speaking in a highway or public park is no more an infringement of the rights of a member of the public than for the owner of a private house to forbid it in his house. The finding of the court of last resort of the State of Massachusetts being that no particular right was possessed by the plaintiff in error to the use of the common, is in reason...entirely aside from the fact that the power conferred upon the chief executive officer of the city of Boston by the ordinance in question may be fairly claimed to be a mere administrative function vested in the mayor in order to effectuate the purpose for which the common was maintained and by which its use was regulated." *Davis v. Massachusetts*, 167 U.S. 43 (1897).

DEARBORN PUBLISHING CO. v. FITZGERALD (1921). The Dearborn Publishing Co. published a weekly newspaper (the *Dearborn Independent*) and sold it on the streets of Cleveland, Ohio. Frank Smith, the Cleveland chief of police, arrested four of the vendors, charging them with selling an indecent and scandalous publication having a tendency to create breaches of the peace. The mayor of Cleveland then announced that anyone selling copies of the newspaper on Cleveland streets would be arrested. It appears that the city officials objected to a certain issue of the paper (March 12, 1921), which contained an anti-Semitic article titled "Jewish Rights Clash With American Rights."

Judge Westenhaver of the district court ruled that Mayor Fitzgerald's actions were an unconstitutional prior restraint: "The article in the issue of March 12 has been examined. Earlier issues have not been exhibited or offered in evidence, but it may be assumed that they are of the same general type, and equally vicious or equally harmless, according to the personal views of the reader. An examination of the evidence convinces me that the defendants' action was taken with the intent and purpose of preventing sales of the plaintiff's newspaper on the streets only because it contained these articles; that such action was not with a view to preventing the sale of indecent, obscene, or scandalous publications...that such action was not directed towards preserving the public peace of the city, and was not in any wise necessary to prevent any breach of the peace. The necessary effect of such action is to censor in advance the contents of the newspaper, by preventing its sale in the same manner as all other newspapers are sold, so long as it contains articles of like character....That the publication has a tendency to create breaches of the peace is equally without foundation....The affidavits conclusively show that no disorder or excitement was created on the streets by the sales in question. Nothing appears to indicate who were or might be excited by its sale to break the peace. It would be a libel, it seems to me, on people of the Jewish race to assume that they are imbued with such a spirit of lawlessness. If it be assumed that the article might tend to excite others to breaches of the peace against people of the Jewish race, the reply is plain. It is the duty of all officials charged with preserving the peace to suppress firmly and promptly all persons guilty of disturbing it, and not to forbid innocent persons to exercise their lawful and equal rights." *Dearborn Publishing Co. v. Fitzgerald*, 271 F. 479 (1921).

DEBS v. UNITED STATES (1919). On Sunday, June 16, 1918, at Nimisilla Park in Canton, Ohio, Eugene Debs delivered a speech in which he advocated the aims of political socialism and in which he expressed his opposition to the world war. As compared with more recent political rhetoric and harangues, Debs' comments were relatively low key and mild. Some excerpts: "I realize that, in speaking to you this afternoon, that there are certain limitations placed upon the right of free speech. I must be exceedingly careful, prudent, as to what I say, and even more careful and more prudent as to how I say it. I may not be able to say all I think; but I am not going to say anything that I do not think. But, I would rather a thousand times be a free soul in jail than to be a sycophant and coward on the streets. They may put those boys in jail—and some of the rest of us in jail—but they can not put the Socialist movement in jail."

Unfortunately for Debs, however, he was not as prudent or careful as he should have been, and he was convicted for violating the Espionage Act* of 1917. He received a ten-year jail sentence; President Harding commuted the sentence in 1921, but Debs' citizenship was not restored. Debs was a national political figure—he received some 900,000 votes in the 1920 presidential election—but he had the extreme misfortune to espouse a political creed that the majority detested and to oppose a war that the majority supported. The only real difference between Eugene Debs and George McGovern was that the U.S. government did not attempt to put McGovern in jail for his opposition to the Viet Nam War.

Debs appealed his original conviction to the Supreme Court, but he did not receive a sympathetic hearing. Justice Holmes delivered the opinion of the Court: "The main theme of the speech was socialism, its growth, and a prophecy of its ultimate success. With that we have nothing to do, but if a part or the manifest intent of the more general utterances was to encourage those present to obstruct the recruiting service and if in passages such encouragement was directly given, the immunity of the general theme may not be enough to protect the speech.... Evidence that the defendant accepted this view [opposition to the war] and this declaration of his duties [to oppose the war effort] at the time that he made his speech is evidence that if in that speech he used words tending to obstruct the recruiting service he meant that they should have that effect. The principle is too well established and too manifestly good sense to need citation of the books." Ernst Freund, in "The Debs Case and Freedom of Speech," *The New Republic* (May 3, 1919), wrote that to "stamp a man like Debs...as [a] felon...you dignify the term felony." *Debs v. United States*, 249 U.S. 211 (1919).

DEEP THROAT. This film, produced in 1972 in the United States and starring Linda Lovelace and Harry Reems, has received perhaps the most publicity of any X-rated film. The film was attacked, censored, banned, and vilified in more than twenty-five states but became a classic of the genre by which all subsequent films are evaluated. The film was reviewed by such staid publications as *Saturday Review*, *New York Times*, *Variety*, and *Newsweek*. Even the film's title has entered the public domain: The anonymous source during the Watergate scandal had as a *nom de guerre* "Deep Throat." Edward de Grazia and Roger K. Newman, in *Banned Films*, give a synopsis of the so-called plot: "Frustrated by her inability to 'hear bells' in orgasm during her many sexual encounters, even with 14 men at once, a young woman [Linda Lovelace] consults a promiscuous, accommodating doctor, who diagnoses her problem as having her clitoris in her throat. In search of relief, she tries her mouth out on as many male members as she can, finally settling on one [Harry Reems] measuring 13 inches, which is said to be 4 inches more than adequate to make her 'hear bells.' Miss Lovelace is at once youthful, passably pretty, and has a lithe and supple body."†

Deep Throat was judged to be obscene in *Sanders v. Georgia* (216 S.E. 2d 838 [1975]), and the Supreme Court (424 U.S. 931 [1976]) affirmed, without written opinion, the lower court's finding that the film was obscene. The finding of obscenity did not prevent its exhibition, but Miss Lovelace has since regretted her role and is no longer practicing her art.

DEFAMATION. Defamation is any printing or writing (libel) or any spoken words (slander) that tend to injure the reputation of someone, thereby exposing the person to public hatred, contempt, ridicule, financial injury, or that impeaches someone's character, honesty, integrity, or morality. But there is a conflict between the need for a full disclosure and debate on matters of public interest (protected by the First Amendment) and the need to protect personal reputations from libelous and slanderous attacks. The Supreme Court has tried to resolve this conflict by giving First Amendment protection to certain kinds of defamation. The terms public official,* public figure,* *New York Times* Rule,* and malice* are all related to defamation. *Words and Phrases* (West Publishing Co.), Vol. 25, Libel.

DE JONGE v. OREGON (1937). De Jonge and others were convicted of violating the Oregon criminal syndicalism* law. This law allowed for criminal punishment for participation in the conduct of a public meeting, otherwise lawful, merely because the meeting was held under the auspices of an organization that taught or advocated the use of violence or other unlawful acts to effect industrial or political change.

The Supreme Court, Justice Hughes delivering the opinion, ruled that the Oregon statute violated the constitutional principle of free speech: "The greater the importance of safeguarding the community from incitements to the overthrow of our institutions by force and violence, the more imperative is the need to preserve inviolate the constitutional rights of free speech, free press and free assembly in order to maintain the opportunity for free political discussion, to the end that government may be responsive to the will of the people and that

---

†Reprinted from *Banned Films* with permission of the R. R. Bowker Company. Copyright © 1982 by Edward de Grazia and Roger K. Newman.

changes, if desired, may be obtained by peaceful means. Therein lies the security of the Republic, the very foundation of constitutional government. . . . Consistent with the Federal Constitution, peaceable assembly for lawful discussion cannot be made a crime. The holding of meetings for peaceable political action cannot be proscribed. Those who assist in the conduct of such meetings cannot be branded as criminals on that score. The question, if the rights of free speech and peaceable assembly are to be preserved, is not as to the auspices under which the meeting is held but as to its purpose; not as to the relations of the speakers, but whether their utterances transcend the bounds of the freedom of speech which the Constitution protects. If the persons assembling have committed crimes elsewhere, if they have formed or are engaged in a conspiracy against the public peace and order, they may be prosecuted for their conspiracy or other violation of valid laws. But it is a different matter when the State, instead of prosecuting them for such offenses, seizes upon mere participation in a peaceable assembly and a lawful public discussion as the basis for a criminal charge." *De Jonge v. Oregon*, 299 U.S. 353 (1937).

DELAWARE, OBSCENITY STATUTE. Volume 43, Chapter 239, Laws of Delaware, reads: "Whoever. . .exhibits. . .or has in his possession with intent to. . .exhibit. . .or knowingly advertises. . .any obscene, lewd, lascivious, filthy, indecent drawing, photograph, film, figure or image. . .is guilty of a misdemeanor." This statute was used to convict John Scope (*State of Delaware v. Scope*, 86 A. 2d 154 [1952]) for showing a film titled *Hollywood Peep Show** to teenagers.

DENNIS v. UNITED STATES (1951). The Smith Act* makes it a crime for any person knowingly or willfully to advocate the overthrow or destruction of the government of the United States by force or violence, to organize or help to organize any group that does so, or to conspire to do so. The Supreme Court held that the act does not violate the First Amendment, and Dennis (and others), a leader of the American Communist party, was convicted for advocating the overthrow of the U.S. government: "In this case we are squarely presented with the application of the 'clear and present danger'* test, and must decide what the phrase imports. . . . Obviously, the words cannot mean that before the Government may act, it must wait until the *putsch* is about to be executed, the plans have been laid and the signal is awaited. If Government is aware that a group aiming at its overthrow is attempting to indoctrinate its members and to commit them to a course whereby they will strike when the leaders feel the circumstances permit, action by the Government is required. The argument that there is no need for Government to concern itself, for Government is strong, it possesses ample powers to put down a rebellion, it may defeat the revolution with ease needs no answer. For that is not the question. Certainly an attempt to overthrow the Government by force, even though doomed from the outset because of inadequate numbers or power of the revolutionists, is a sufficient evil for Congress to prevent.''

There was some vigorous and eloquent dissent, however, from this majority opinion by Justices Black and Douglas. Justice Black: ''At the outset I want to emphasize what the crime involved in this case is, and what it is not. These petitioners were not charged with an attempt to overthrow the Government. They were not charged with overt acts of any kind designed to overthrow the Government. They were not even charged with saying anything or writing anything designed to overthrow the Government. The charge was that they agreed to assemble and to talk and publish certain ideas at a later date; the indictment is that they conspired to organize the Communist Party and to use speech or newspapers and other publications in the future to teach and advocate the forcible overthrow of the Government. No matter how it is worded, this is a virulent form of prior censorship of speech and press, which I believe the First Amendment forbids. I would hold § 3 of the Smith Act authorizing this prior restraint unconstitutional on its face and as applied. . . .Public opinion being what it now is, few will protest the conviction of these Communist petitioners. There is hope, however, that in calmer times, when present pressures, passions and fears subside, this or some later Court will restore the First Amendment liberties to the high preferred place where they belong in a free society.'' *Dennis v. United States*, 341 U.S. 494 (1951).

DEPARTMENT OF AIR FORCE v. ROSE (1976). Rose and others were denied access to certain files of the U.S. Air Force Academy's Honor Board, files they thought necessary for them to write a journal article. The academy claimed that Exemption 6 of the Freedom of Information Act* allowed it to withhold the case summaries because they were ''personnel files. . .the disclosure of which would constitute a clearly unwarranted invasion of personal privacy.'' The Supreme Court did not agree with the academy's reasoning and held that Rose's request for access to the case summaries ''with personal references or other identifying information deleted'' respected the confidentiality interests in Exemption 6 and did not violate the academy's tradition of confidentiality. *Department of Air Force v. Rose*, 425 U.S. 352 (1976).

DETROIT (MI), ANTI–SKID ROW ORDINANCE. The city of Detroit, in order to regulate the location of adult motion picture theaters, passed an ordinance specifying that certain types of activities had to be separated from one another by a precise number of feet. An adult movie theater could not be within 1,000 feet of any two other regulated uses or within 500 feet of a residential area. The other regulated uses applied to adult bookstores, cabarets, bars, pawn shops, shoeshine parlors, pool halls, and the like. The classification of a theater as ''adult'' was based on the content of the motion pictures that it exhibited. If the theater presented films that emphasized ''Specified Sexual Activities'' or ''Specified Anatomical Areas,'' it would be classified as an adult theater. ''Specified

Sexual Activities'' were defined as ''1. Human genitals in a state of sexual stimulation or arousal; 2. Acts of human masturbation, sexual intercourse or sodomy; 3. Fondling or other erotic touching of human genitals, pubic region, buttock or female breast.'' ''Specified Anatomical Areas'' were defined as ''1. Less than completely and opaquely covered: (a) human genitals, pubic region, (b) buttock, and (c) female breast below a point immediately above the top of the areola; and 2. Human male genitals in a discernibly turgid state, even if completely and opaquely covered.'' These ordinances were seen as a valid time-place-manner* regulation by the Supreme Court in *Young, Mayor of Detroit v. American Mini Theatres, Inc.* (1976).*

DICKEY v. ALABAMA STATE BOARD OF EDUCATION (1967). Dickey, the student editor of a college newspaper, brought suit to prevent the college from expelling him for having written and published in the paper an article criticizing the governor of the state and the state legislature. Judge Johnson of the district court agreed with Dickey's complaint: ''There could be no editorials written in the school paper which were critical of the Governor of the State of Alabama or the Legislature. The rule did not prohibit editorials of a laudatory nature....The theory of the rule, as this Court understands it, is that Troy State College is a public institution, owned by the State of Alabama, that the Governor and the legislators...control the purse strings, and for that reason...could [not] be criticized....This Court recognizes that the establishment of an educational program requires certain rules and regulations necessary for maintaining an orderly program and operating the institution in a manner conducive to learning. However...it is clear that the maintenance of order and discipline of the students attending Troy State College had nothing to do with the rule that was invoked against Dickey.'' *Dickey v. Alabama State Board of Education*, 273 F. Supp. 613 (1967).

DOMBROWSKI v. PFISTER (1965). Dombrowski, executive director of a civil rights organization, appealed to the Supreme Court to restrain the state of Louisiana from prosecuting or threatening to prosecute under Louisiana's Subversive Activities and Communist Control Law* and Louisiana's Communist Propaganda Control Law. Dombrowski contended that the application of the laws would violate his right of free speech. The Supreme Court ruled that certain sections of the laws (the definitions of a subversive organization and of a Communist front organization) were too vague and an overly broad regulation of protected speech. The Court then instructed the district court (the court that refused initially to restrain the prosecution) to enjoin the prosecution of Dombrowski, ordered the immediate return of all documents seized, and prohibited further enforcement of the sections of the two laws that were found to be void. *Dombrowski v. Pfister*, 380 U.S 479 (1965).

DORAN v. SALEM INN (1975). A North Hempstead, New York, ordinance on topless dancing* prohibited topless dancing in public places, and several watering places complained that the ordinance restricted the right of expression as guaranteed by the First Amendment. The Supreme Court ruled that the ordinance was overbroad* in its application to protected activities at places that do not serve liquor as well as to places that do: "Although the customary 'barroom' type of nude dancing may involve only the barest minimum of protected expression, we recognized in *California v. LaRue* (1972)* that this form of entertainment might be entitled to First and Fourteenth Amendment protection under some circumstances. In *LaRue*, however, we concluded that the broad powers of the States to regulate the sale of liquor, conferred by the Twenty-first Amendment, outweighed any First Amendment interest in nude dancing and that a State could therefore ban such dancing as a part of its liquor license program. In the present case, the challenged ordinance applies not merely to places which serve liquor, but to many other establishments as well. The District Court observed, we believe correctly: 'The local ordinance here attacked not only prohibits topless dancing in bars but also prohibits any female from appearing in any public place with uncovered breasts. There is no limit to the interpretation of the term any public place. It could include the theater, town hall, opera house, as well as a public market place, street or any place of assembly, indoors or outdoors. Thus, the ordinance would prohibit the performance of the *Ballet Africains* and a number of other works of unquestionable artistic and socially redeeming significance.' We have previously held that even though a statute or ordinance may be constitutionally applied to the activities of a particular defendant, that defendant may challenge it on the basis of overbreadth if it is so drawn as to sweep within its ambit protected speech or expression of other persons not before the Court." *Doran v. Salem Inn*, 422 U.S. 922 (1975).

DRAFT CARDS, DESTRUCTION/MISUSE. In general, challenges to the constitutionality of various provisions of 50 U.S.C. § 462-b (pertaining to the possession, misuse, forgery, alteration, destruction, or mutilation of draft cards) have been unsuccessful. In *United States v. O'Brien*,* the Supreme Court rejected a challenge to the constitutionality of the prohibition in § 462-b-3 against knowingly destroying or mutilating a draft card and ruled that the section did not violate a person's First Amendment freedom of speech. O'Brien and some companions publicly burned their draft cards and stated that they were doing it in order to influence others to adopt their opposition to the Viet Nam War. The Court, while ruling that O'Brien could not be punished for his beliefs or for his speech could, however, be punished for his conduct—knowingly destroying the draft card. Here the Court separated speech and nonspeech elements and ruled that even though the burning of the card was a form of symbolic speech or symbolic protest, it nonetheless was conduct open to governmental regulation. *Annotation: Draft Cards*, 20 L. Ed. 2d 1576 (1969).

E

EAGLE FORUM. Founded in 1975 by Phyllis Schlafly (one of the leaders against the adoption of the Equal Rights Amendment—she saw it as being anti-women and anti-family), the Eagle Forum stands for God, Country, and Family. It is also quite unsubtle in its Comstockery*—a self-appointed group to monitor the morality and behavior of other people. The forum claims that the "Holy Scriptures provide the best code of moral conduct yet devised," and it opposes groups that it considers anti-family, anti-religion, anti-morality, anti-children, anti-life, and anti-defense (it is one of the strongest supporters of President Reagan's military buildup and supports a strong nuclear arsenal). The forum is also engaged in the censorship of textbooks—one of its committees is named, curiously, Stop Textbook Censorship—for it wishes to rid the books of what it considers immoral content. The *Phyllis Schlafly Report* is its monthly publication. *Encyclopedia of Associations* (# 13358).

EATON v. CITY OF TULSA (1974). While Eaton was on the witness stand in a Tulsa courtroom, being cross-examined at his trial for violating a Tulsa ordinance, he referred to his alleged assailant as "chicken shit." The judge then convicted him for criminal contempt of court. The Supreme Court reversed the conviction: "This single isolated usage of street vernacular [chicken shit], not directed at the judge or any officer of the court, cannot constitutionally support the conviction of criminal contempt since, under the circumstances, it did not constitute an imminent threat to the administration of justice." *Eaton v. City of Tulsa*, 415 U.S. 697 (1974).

EDUCATIONAL RESEARCH ANALYSTS. The Educational Research Analysts are simply Mel and Norma Gabler of Longview, Texas, who work out of their home in "checking" textbooks for various school boards. They provided the following information about the organization's purposes: "Reviews and analyzes public school textbooks in order to expose those that conflict with traditional values including the Judeo-Christian ethic. Disseminates information through publications and reviews which identify questionable portions of textbooks by page, paragraph, and line. Provides speakers on 'textbooks and their influence upon our nation.' Maintains textbook review library of 7,000 volumes." *Encyclopedia of Associations* (# 6334). Their publication is the *MEL GABLERs Newsletter*, and they also distribute *Textbooks on Trial*. The *New York Times Book Review* of October 23, 1983 (p. 47), wrote that "According to 'As Texas Goes, So Goes The Nation: A Report On Textbook Selection in Texas,' which was prepared by Texas college professors for People for the American Way,* the Gablers determine much of what is—and is not—printed in textbooks on history, biology and English for schools in Texas and elsewhere in the country." The Gablers, modern-day proponents of Comstockery,* have objected to any changes in the traditional sex roles, such as depicting women holding what used to be considered male jobs; their view of history ignores any negatives (slavery, the depression, poverty, discrimination); they have forced several textbook publishers, in order to have the books accepted by the Texas State Textbook Committee,* to put in a disclaimer that evolution is only a theory; and sex (of whatever variety) is strictly taboo.

EDWARDS v. SOUTH CAROLINA (1963). Edwards and some 180 other black high school and college students assembled peacefully at the South Carolina State Capitol to express their grievances. There was no violence, but they were arrested under the South Carolina breach of the peace* statute when they refused to disperse when ordered by the police. The South Carolina Supreme Court upheld their convictions, saying that the crime of breach of the peace is not susceptible of exact definition, and Edwards and the others were guilty.

The U.S. Supreme Court reversed the conviction: "In arresting, convicting, and punishing the petitioners under the circumstances disclosed by this record, South Carolina infringed upon the petitioners' constitutionally protected rights of free speech, free assembly, and freedom to petition for redress of their grievances. . . . A State [cannot] make criminal the peaceful expression of unpopular views. A function of free speech under our system of government is to invite dispute. It may indeed serve its high purpose when it induces a condition of unrest, creates dissatisfaction with conditions as they are, or even stirs people to anger. Speech is often provocative and challenging. It may strike at prejudices and preconceptions and have profound unsettling effects as it presses for acceptance of an idea. That is why freedom of speech is protected against censorship or punishment, unless shown likely to produce a clear and present danger of a serious substantive evil that rises far above public inconvenience, annoyance, or unrest. There is no room under our Constitution for a more restrictive view." *Edwards v. South Carolina*, 372 U.S. 229 (1963).

EPPERSON v. ARKANSAS (1968). Epperson, a public school teacher in Arkansas, brought suit challenging the constitutionality of the Arkansas anti-evolution statute.* This statute made it unlawful for a teacher in any state-supported school or university to teach or to use a textbook that teaches "that mankind ascended or descended from a lower order of animals" and was based on the Tennessee statute that was involved in the famous "monkey trial" of *Scopes v. State*.* The Arkansas Supreme Court, in a two-sentence opinion, sustained the statute as within the state's power to specify the public school curriculum.

The U.S. Supreme Court saw the statute as a blatant violation of the First Amendment. Although this case dealt mainly with the establishment of religion clause, there were elements of free speech and censorship involved: "It is of no moment whether the law is deemed to prohibit mention of Darwin's theory, or to forbid any or all of the infinite varieties of communication embraced within the term 'teaching.' Under either interpretation, the law must be stricken because of its conflict with the constitutional prohibition of state laws respecting an establishment of religion or prohibiting the free exercise thereof. The overriding fact is that Arkansas' law selects from the body of knowledge a particular segment which it proscribes for the sole reason that it is deemed to conflict with a particular religious doctrine; that is, with a particular interpretation of the Book of Genesis by a particular religious group. Arkansas' law cannot be defended as an act of religious neutrality. Arkansas did not seek to excise from the curricula of its schools and universities all discussion of the origin of man. The law's effort was confined to an attempt to blot out a particular theory because of its supposed conflict with the Biblical account, literally read. Plainly, the law is contrary to the mandate of the First Amendment."

Justice Stewart, in a concurring opinion, stressed the free speech and censorship aspects of the case: "The States are most assuredly free to choose their own curriculums for their own schools. A State is entirely free, for example, to decide that the only foreign language to be taught in its public school system shall be Spanish. But would a State be constitutionally free to punish a teacher for letting his students know that other languages are also spoken in the world? I think not. It is one thing for a State to determine that the subject of higher mathematics, or astronomy, or biology shall or shall not be included in its public school curriculum. It is quite another thing for a State to make it a criminal offense for a public school teacher so much as to mention the very existence of an entire system of respected human thought. That kind of criminal law, I think, would clearly impinge upon the guarantees of free communication contained in the First Amendment." *Epperson v. Arkansas*, 393 U.S. 97 (1968).

ESPIONAGE ACT. The federal Espionage Act was passed on June 15, 1917, and was amended on May 16, 1918 (40 Stat. 553). The provisions of the act have been employed in prosecutions against several people, including the cases (all *v. United States*) of *Debs*,* *Hartzel*,* *Schaeffer*,* *Pierce*,* *Abrams*,* *Schenck*,* *Frohwerk*,* and *Sugarman*.* The relevant sections of this act are as follows: Section 3: "Whoever, when the United States is at war, shall willfully make or convey false reports or false statements with intent to interfere with the operation or success of the military or naval forces of the United States or to promote the success of its enemies and whoever, when the United States is at war, shall willfully cause or attempt to cause insubordination, disloyalty, mutiny, or refusal of duty, in the military or naval forces of the United States, or shall willfully obstruct the recruiting or enlistment service of the United States, to the injury of the service or of the United States, shall be punished by a fine of not more than $10,000 or imprisonment for not more than twenty years, or both.'' Section 4: ''If two or more persons conspire to violate the provisions of section. . .three. . .each of the parties to such conspiracy shall be punished.''

ESQUIRE. Certain postal regulations (Postal Regulations, Second-Class Mail*) provide that, in order to be admitted as second-class mail, a publication ''must be originated and published for the dissemination of information of a public character, or devoted to literature, the sciences, arts.'' In 1943, certain issues of *Esquire* magazine offended the aesthetic sense of the postmaster general, and he then revoked the magazine's second-class mailing permit. He was quoted as saying: ''A publication to enjoy these unique mail privileges and special preferences [second class] is bound to do more than refrain from disseminating material which is obscene or bordering on the obscene. It is under a positive duty to contribute to the public good and the public welfare.'' *Esquire* brought suit, seeking its second-class status back.

The Supreme Court, in *Hanegan v. Esquire* (327 U.S. 142 [1946]), ruled that the postmaster general is without power to determine whether the contents of a periodical meet some standard of the public good or welfare. Justice Douglas described the magazine: ''The issues of *Esquire* magazine under attack are those for January to November, inclusive, of 1943. The material complained of embraces in bulk only a small percentage of those issues. Regular features of the magazine (called 'The Magazine for Men') include articles on topics of current interest, short stories, sports articles or stories, short articles by men prominent in various fields of activities, articles about men prominent in the news, a book review department headed by the late William Lyon Phelps, a theatrical department headed by George Jean Nathan, a department on the lively arts by Gilbert Seldes, a department devoted to men's clothing, and pictorial features, including war action paintings, color photographs of dogs and water colors or etchings of game birds and reproductions of famous paintings, prints and drawings. There was very little in these features which was challenged. But [the postmaster general] found that the objectionable items, though a small percentage of the total bulk, were regular recurrent features which gave the magazine its dominant tone or characteristic. These include jokes, cartoons, pictures, articles, and poems. They were said to reflect the smoking-room type of humor, featuring, in the main, sex. Some witnesses found the challenged items highly objectionable, calling them salacious and indecent. Others thought they were only racy and risque. Some condemned them as being merely in poor taste. Other witnesses could find no objection to them.''

Justice Douglas continued with the Court's opinion: ''It is plain, as we have said, that the favorable second-class rates were granted periodicals meeting the requirements...so that the public good might be served through a dissemination of the class of periodicals described. But that is a far cry from assuming that Congress had any idea that each applicant for the second-class rate must convince the Postmaster General that his publication positively contributes to the public good or public welfare. Under our system of government there is an accommodation for the widest varieties of tastes and ideas. What is good literature, what has educational value, what is refined public information, what is good art, varies with individuals as it does from one generation to another. There doubtless would be a contrariety of views concerning Cervantes' *Don Quixote*, Shakespeare's *Venus and Adonis* or Zola's *Nana*. But a requirement that literature or art conform to some norm prescribed by an official smacks of an ideology foreign to our system. The basic values implicit in the requirements...can be served only by uncensored distribution of literature. From the multitude of competing offerings the public will pick and choose. What seems to one to be trash may have for others fleeting or even enduring values. But to withdraw the second-class rate from this publication today because its contents seemed to one official not good for the public would sanction withdrawal of the second-class rate tomorrow from another periodical whose social or economic views seemed harmful to another official. The validity of the obscenity laws is recognition that the mails may not be used to satisfy all tastes, no matter how perverted. But Congress has left the Postmaster General with no power to prescribe standards for the literature or the art which a mailable periodical disseminates.''

ESTES v. TEXAS (1965). Billy Sol Estes was on trial in Texas, having been indicted for swindling. There was massive media coverage of the trial, including telecasting of the proceedings, radio broadcasts, news photography; camera crews and their equipment were in the courtroom causing considerable disruption; film clips of the trial were shown on newscasts. Estes claimed that such behavior violated his right to a fair trial, but both the trial court and a Texas appeals court denied his motion.

The U.S. Supreme Court agreed that televising of the courtroom proceedings over Estes' objections infringed on his right to a fair trial: ''It is said, however, that the freedoms granted in the First Amendment extend a right to the news media to televise from the courtroom, and that to refuse to honor this privilege is to discriminate between the newspapers and television. This is a misconception of the rights of the press. The free press has been a mighty catalyst in awakening public interest in governmental affairs, exposing corruption among public officers and employees and generally informing the citizenry of public events and occurrences, including court proceedings. While maximum freedom must be allowed the press in carrying on this important function in a democratic society its exercise must necessarily be subject to the maintenance of absolute fairness in the judicial process. While the state and federal courts have differed over what spectators may be excluded from a criminal trial...neither [the First or Sixth Amendments] speaks of an unlimited right of access to the courtroom on the part of the broadcasting media. . . . Nor can the courts be said to discriminate where they permit the newspaper reporter access to the courtroom. The television and radio reporter has the same privilege. All are entitled to the same rights as the general public. The news reporter is not permitted to bring his typewriter or printing press. When the advances in these arts permit reporting by printing press or by television without their present hazards to a fair trial we will have another case." *Estes v. Texas*, 381 U.S. 532 (1965).

EVERGREEN REVIEW. As the court record relates it, "On April 24, 1964, Albert Anderson, a detective in the Nassau County Police Depart-ment. . . submitted an affidavit to a Nassau County judge predicated upon in-formation furnished him by 'a confidential informant employed. . .where the magazine *Evergreen Review* was being bound, to the effect that she had informed Anderson that while working in the bindery she observed black and white pho-tographs in the magazine. . .which showed nude human forms, possibly male and female, but reputed by fellow workers to be two females, and that the forms portrayed various poses and positions indicating sexual relations,' and that the printed material accompanying the photographs consisted of four lettered obscene language. 'Based upon the foregoing reliable information,' Anderson concluded, 'there is probable cause to believe that obscene, indecent and pornographic magazines' are being used or possessed with intent to be used for the purpose of committing a crime in violation of Section 1141 of the Penal Code" (New York, Obscenity Statute*). The warrant was duly issued and some 21,000 copies of the magazine were seized. A U.S. district court ruled, however, that seizure of alleged obscene material cannot be undertaken unless there is a full judicial hearing in advance; the conclusion of one police officer based on confidential information cannot determine whether material is obscene. *Evergreen Review v. Cahn*, 230 F. Supp. 498 (1964).

EXCLUSIVE/REVIEW INTERNATIONAL/INTERNATIONAL NUDIST SUN. The Tariff Act* allows U.S. Customs to seize what it perceives to be obscene material and then to seek a court determination as to the material's destruction. Such was the situation in 1966, when certain issues of the magazines *Exclusive*, *Review International*, and *International Nudist Sun* were confiscated. The court records described the magazines in the following words: "*Exclusive* is a collection of photographs of young women. In most of them, long stockings and garter belts are employed to frame the pubic area and to focus attention on it. A suggestion of masochism is sought by the use in many of the pictures of chains binding the model's wrists and ankles. Some of the seated models, squarely facing the camera, have their knees and legs widespread in order to reveal the genital area in its entirety. In one of the pictures, all of these things are combined: The model, clad only in a framing black garter belt and black stockings is chained to a chair upon which she is seated, facing the camera, with one knee elevated and both spread wide. *International Nudist Sun* and *Review International* each contain pictures of well-developed nude men, with the focus in most instances on the penis, which is flagrantly displayed. On the other hand, the few pictures in which two men are shown do not directly suggest homosexual activity, unless there are some esoteric ritual positions of which the Court is not advised. Although posed in outdoor settings, in few of the pictures are the models engaging in any normal outdoor activities. The articles in both magazines are innocuous, dreary and puerile, and bear little relation to the illustrations...and no one, however moronic, would pay a high price for the innocuous written material.''

A district court found that, indeed, these magazines were obscene and that decision was affirmed by an appeals court. The courts found that the publications were patently offensive, would appeal to the prurient interest, and were utterly without any redeeming social value or importance. The two nude-male magazines were also seen to appeal to a specific deviant group: ''Though the psychiatrists differed somewhat in their estimates of the proportion of the 37% of all adult males, who are estimated to have had at least one homosexual contact after adolescence, for whom these magazines would have a prurient appeal, they were in general agreement that the magazines would have such an appeal for practicing male homosexuals.... The magazines would have a prurient appeal to many adolescent males and to some females, though the proportion of women who would be strongly stimulated by such erotica is small, while adolescent females would find the material shocking and frightening.'' *United States v. Exclusive*, 253 F. Supp. 485 (1966) and 373 F. 2d 633 (1967).

But in *Central Magazine Sales, Ltd. v. United States*, 389 U.S. 50 (1967), the Supreme Court, in a per curiam decision citing the cases of *Redrup,** *Roth,** and *Memoirs,** reversed the lower courts' decisions and ruled that *Exclusive*, *Review International*, and *International Nudist Sun* were not obscene.

EX PARTE JACKSON (1877). In 1877, Jackson was fined one hundred dollars and sent to jail until the fine was paid, for mailing a circular about a lottery in violation of certain post office regulations (Postal Regulations, Lotteries*). The Supreme Court affirmed his conviction, but this case is noted for some comments on the use of the mails and freedom of the press: (1) ''The power vested in Congress to establish post-offices and post-roads embraces the regulation of the entire postal system of the country. Under it, Congress may designate what shall be carried in the mail, and what excluded''; (2) ''In the enforcement of regulations excluding matter from the mail, a distinction is to be made between what is intended to be kept free from inspection such as letters, and sealed packages subject to letter postage, and what is open to inspection, such as newspapers, magazines, pamphlets, and other printed matter, purposely left in a condition to be examined''; (3) ''Letters and sealed packages subject to letter postage, in the mail can be opened and examined only under like warrant, issued upon similar oath or affirmation, particularly describing the thing to be seized, as is required when papers are subject to search in one's own household. The constitutional guarantee of the right of the people against unreasonable searches and seizures

extends to their papers, thus closed against inspection, wherever they may be'';
(4) ''Regulations against transporting in the mail printed matter, which is open
to examination, cannot be enforced so as to interfere in any manner with the
freedom of the press. Liberty of circulating is essential to that freedom. When,
therefore, printed matter is excluded from the mail, its transportation in any
other way as merchandise cannot be forbidden by Congress.'' The last admonition
is not quite correct. The prohibition against transporting obscene material by
common carrier has been upheld as constitutional in *United States v. Orito.* *Ex
parte Jackson*, 96 U.S. 727 (1877).

EX PARTE NEILL (1893). The city council of Seguin, Texas, passed an
ordinance stating that the *Sunday Sun*, a newspaper published in Chicago, was
a public nuisance and that the paper could not be circulated or sold in the city.
The Texas court ruled the ordinance unconstitutional as a violation of the freedom
of the press with the terse statement that ''we are not informed of any authority
which sustains the doctrine that a municipal corporation is invested with the
power to declare the sale of newspapers a nuisance.'' *Ex parte Neill*, 22 S.W.
923 81893).

F

FARMERS UNION v. WDAY (1959). Section 315(a) of the Federal Communications Act of 1934 (Federal Communications Commission Regulations, Defamatory Statements*) provides that if anyone licensed to operate a radio station permits a candidate for public office to broadcast over the station, the licensee shall provide equal opportunities for other candidates for that office, but that the licensee "shall have no power of censorship" over whatever is broadcast. The Farmers Union brought suit against WDAY, alleging that a political broadcast under this section contained defamatory statements and that the licensee was liable.

The Supreme Court ruled that the licensee may not delete material from a candidate's radio speech on the ground that the material might be defamatory, and in any case, the licensee is not liable for any defamatory statements made in a speech broadcast over the station by a candidate for public office under § 315(a): "Petitioner argues that § 315's prohibition against censorship leaves broadcasters free to delete libelous material from candidates' speeches, and that therefore no federal immunity is granted a broadcasting station by that section. The term censorship, however, as commonly understood, connotes *any* examination of thought or expression in order to prevent publication of 'objectionable' material. We find no clear expression of legislative intent, nor any other convincing reason to indicate Congress meant to give 'censorship' a narrower meaning in § 315. In arriving at this view, we note that petitioner's interpretation has not generally been favored in previous considerations of the section. Although the first, and for years the only judicial decision dealing with the censorship provision did hold that a station may remove defamatory statements from political broadcasts, subsequent judicial interpretations of § 315 have with considerable uniformity recognized that an individual licensee has no such power. And while for some years the Federal Communications Commission's views on this matter were not clearly articulated, since 1948 it has continuously held that licensees cannot remove allegedly libelous matter from speeches by candidates.

"Similarly, the legislative history of the measure both prior to its first enactment in 1927, and subsequently, shows a deep hostility to censorship either by the Commission or by a licensee. More important, it is obvious that permitting a broadcasting station to censor allegedly libelous remarks would undermine the basic purpose for which § 315 was passed—full and unrestricted discussion of political issues by legally qualified candidates. That section dates back to, and was adopted verbatim from, the Radio Act of 1927. In that Act, Congress provided for the first time a comprehensive federal plan for regulating the new and expanding art of radio broadcasting. Recognizing radio's potential importance as a medium of communication of political ideas, Congress sought to foster its broadest possible utilization by encouraging broadcasting stations to make their facilities available to candidates for office without discrimination, and by insuring that these candidates when broadcasting were not to be hampered by censorship of the issues they could discuss. Thus, expressly applying this country's tradition of free expression to the field of radio broadcasting, Congress has from the first emphatically forbidden the Commission to exercise any power of censorship over radio communication. It is in line with this same tradition that the individual licensee has consistently been denied 'power of censorship' in the vital area of political broadcasts.

"The decision a broadcasting station would have to make in censoring libelous discussion by a candidate is far from easy. Whether a statement is defamatory is rarely clear. Whether such a statement is actionably libelous is an even more complex question, involving as it does, consideration of various legal defenses such as 'truth' and the privilege of fair comment. Such issues have always troubled courts. Yet, under petitioner's view of the statute they would have to be resolved by an individual licensee during the stress of a political campaign, often, necessarily, without adequate consideration or basis for decision. Quite possibly, if a station were held responsible for the broadcast of libelous material, all remarks even faintly objectionable would be excluded out of an excess of caution. Moreover, if any censorship were permissible, a station so inclined could intentionally inhibit a candidate's legitimate presentation under the guise of lawful censorship of libelous matter. Because of the time limitation inherent in a political campaign, erroneous decisions by a station could not be corrected by the courts promptly enough to permit the candidate to bring improperly excluded matter before the public. It follows from all this that allowing censorship, even of the attenuated type advocated here, would almost inevitably force a candidate to avoid controversial issues during political debates over radio and television, and hence restrict the coverage of consideration relevant to intelligent political decision. We cannot believe, and we are certainly unwilling to assume, that Congress intended any such result." *Farmers Union v. WDAY*, 360 U.S. 525 (1959).

FEDERAL COMMUNICATIONS COMMISSION REGULATIONS, DE-FAMATORY STATEMENTS. Section 315(a) of the Federal Communications Act of 1934 reads: "If any licensee shall permit any person who is a legally qualified candidate for any public office to use a broadcasting station, he shall afford equal opportunities to all other such candidates for that office in the use of such broadcasting station: Provided, That such licensee shall have no power of censorship over the material broadcast under the provisions of this section. No obligation is imposed upon any licensee to allow the use of its station by any such candidate." The Supreme Court, in *Farmers Union v. WDAY* (1959),* held that the licensee cannot censor any of the material broadcast under this section and that the licensee cannot be held liable for any libelous or defamatory statements made during such broadcasts.

FEDERAL COMMUNICATIONS COMMISSION REGULATIONS, EQUAL TIME. Section 313(a) of the Federal Communications Act of 1934, as amended, 47 U.S.C. § 315(a) (1958 ed., Supp. V), provides: "If any licensee shall permit any person who is a legally qualified candidate for any public office to use a broadcasting station, he shall afford equal opportunities to all other such candidates for that office in the use of such broadcasting station: Provided, That such licensee shall have no power of censorship over the material broadcast under the provisions of the section. No obligation is imposed upon any licensee to allow the use of its station by any such candidate. Appearance by a legally qualified candidate on any—(1) bona fide newscast, (2) bona fide news interview, (3) bona fide news documentary (if the appearance of the candidate is incidental to the presentation of the subject or subjects covered by the news documentary), or (4) on-the-spot coverage of bona fide news events (including but not limited to political conventions and activities incidental thereto), shall not be deemed to be use of a broadcasting station within the meaning of this subsection. Nothing in the foregoing sentence shall be construed as relieving broadcasters, in connection with the presentation of newscasts, news interviews, news documentaries, and on-the-spot coverage of news events, from the obligation imposed upon them under this chapter to operate in the public interest and to afford reasonable opportunity for the discussion of conflicting views on issues of public importance." The interpretation of this section—what actually constitutes a "bona fide newscast," etc., and what is campaign use of a station's facilities—is not an easy distinction, especially when an incumbent, whose activities are covered by the media, is also a candidate.

In *Goldwater v. Federal Communications Commission* (1964),* the Supreme Court let stand a lower court's ruling that certain coverage of President Johnson was not a "political use" of the broadcasting facilities and thus candidate Barry Goldwater could not receive "equal time."

FEDERAL COMMUNICATIONS COMMISSION REGULATIONS, FAIRNESS DOCTRINE. The Federal Communications Commission has for many years imposed on radio and television broadcasters the requirement that discussion of public issues be presented on broadcast stations, and that each side of those issues must be given fair coverage. This is known as the fairness doctrine and it is distinct from the equal-time provision of the Federal Communications Act of 1934 (Federal Communications Commission Regulations, Equal Time*).

As they now stand amended, the fairness doctrine regulations read as follows: "Personal attacks; political editorials. (a) When, during the presentation of views on a controversial issue of public importance, an attack is made upon the honesty, character, integrity or like personal qualities of an identified person or group, the licensee shall, within a reasonable time and in no event later than 1 week after the attack, transmit to the person or group attacked (1) notification of the date, time and identification of the broadcast; (2) a script or tape (or an accurate summary if a script or tape is not available) of the attack; and (3) an offer of a reasonable opportunity to respond over the licensee's facilities. (b) The provisions of paragraph (a) of this section shall not be applicable (1) to attacks on foreign groups or foreign public figures; (2) to personal attacks which are made by legally qualified candidates, their authorized spokesmen, or those associated with them in the campaign, or other such candidates, their authorized spokesmen, or persons associated with the candidates in the campaign; and (3) to bona fide newscasts, bona fide news interviews, and on-the-spot coverage of a bona fide news event (including commentary or analysis contained in the foregoing programs, but the provisions of paragraph (a) of this section shall be applicable to editorials of the licensee). Note: The fairness doctrine is applicable to situations coming within [(3)], above, and, in a specific factual situation, may be applicable in the general area of political broadcasts [(2)], above. See, section 315(a) of the Act, 47 U.S.C. 315(a); Public Notice: 'Applicability of the Fairness Doctrine in the Handling of Controversial Issues of Public Importance.' 29 F.R. 10415. The categories listed in [(3)] are the same as those specified in section 315(a) of the Act. (c) Where a licensee, in an editorial, (i) endorses or (ii) opposes a legally qualified candidate or candidates, the licensee shall, within 24 hours after the editorial, transmit to respectively (i) the other qualified candidates for the same office or (ii) the candidate opposed in the editorial (1) notification of the date and the time of the editorial; (2) a script or tape of the editorial; and (3) an offer of a reasonable opportunity for a candidate or a spokesman of the candidate to respond over the licensee's facilities: Provided, however, That where such editorials are broadcast within 72 hours prior to the day of the election, the licensee shall comply with the provisions of this paragraph sufficiently far in advance of the broadcast to enable the candidate or candidates to have a reasonable opportunity to prepare a response and to present it in a timely fashion." 47 C.F.R. § § 73.123, 73.300, 73.598, 73.679. These regulations mandating the opportunity for someone who has been attacked to be heard were upheld and not seen as a violation of freedom of the press in *Red Lion Broadcasting Company v. Federal Communications Commission*, 395 U.S. 367 (1969).*

FEDERAL COMMUNICATIONS COMMISSION REGULATIONS, GIVE-AWAY PROGRAMS. Title 18 U.S.C. § 1304 provides: "Whoever broadcasts by means of any radio station for which a license is required by any law of the United States, or whoever, operating any such station, knowingly permits the broadcasting of any advertisement of or information concerning any lottery, gift enterprise, or similar scheme, offering prizes dependent in whole or in part upon lot or chance, or any list of the prizes drawn or awarded by means by any such lottery, gift enterprise, or scheme, whether said list contains any part or all of such prizes, shall be fined not more than $1,000 or imprisoned not more than one year, or both. Each day's broadcasting shall constitute a separate offense.''

Pursuant to this statute, the Federal Communications Commission issued some rules (Commission's Rules and Regulations, § § 3.192, 3.292, and 3.656) designed to prevent the broadcast of such programs. The rules are worded identically and apply to standard radio broadcasting (AM), FM radio broadcasting, and television broadcasting. Paragraph (a) of each rule provides that ''an application for construction permit, license, renewal of license, or any other authorization for the operation of a broadcast station, will not be granted where the applicant proposes to follow or continue to follow a policy or practice of broadcasting'' programs of a sort forbidden by § 1304. Paragraph (b) provides that a program will fall within the ban ''if in connection with such program a prize consisting of money or thing of value is awarded to any person whose selection is dependent in whole or in part upon lot or chance, if as a condition of winning or competing for such prize: (1) Such winner or winners are required to furnish any money or thing of value or are required to have in their possession any product sold, manufactured, furnished or distributed by a sponsor of a program broadcast on the station in question; or (2) Such winner or winners are required to be listening to or viewing the program in question on a radio or television receiver; or (3) Such winner or winners are required to answer correctly a question, the answer to which is given on a program broadcast over the station in question or where aid in answering the question correctly is given on a program broadcast over the station in question. For the purposes of this provision the broadcasting of the question to be answered over the radio station on a previous program will be considered as an aid in answering the question correctly; or (4) Such winner or winners are required to answer the phone in a prescribed manner or with a prescribed phrase, or are required to write a letter in a prescribed manner or containing a prescribed phrase, if the prescribed manner of answering the phone or writing the letter or the prescribed phrase to be used over the phone or in the letter (or an aid in ascertaining the prescribed phrase or the prescribed manner of answering the phone or writing the letter) is, or has been, broadcast over the station in question.'' These rules were seen to be invalid as going beyond the scope of 18 U.S.C. § 1304 by the Supreme Court, in *Federal Communications Commission v. American Broadcasting Company* (1954),* and today, radio and television broadcasting is inundated with such give-away programs.

FEDERAL COMMUNICATIONS COMMISSION REGULATIONS, IN-DECENCY AND CENSORSHIP. Title 18 U.S.C. § 1464 reads: ''Indecency: Whoever utters any obscene, indecent, or profane language by means of radio communication shall be fined not more than $10,000 or imprisoned not more than two years, or both''; 47 U.S.C. § 326 reads: ''Censorship: Nothing in this

Act [Federal Communications Act of 1934] shall be understood or construed to give the Commission the power of censorship over the radio communications or signals transmitted by any radio station, and no regulation or condition shall be promulgated or fixed by the Commission which shall interfere with the right of free speech by means of radio communication.''

Although § 326 prohibits any censorship and interference with the right of free speech, the Supreme Court, in the "Filthy Words"* decision (*Federal Communications Commission v. Pacifica*, 438 U.S. 726 [1978]), held that the Federal Communications Commission could place in a licensee's file information that "indecent" language was in fact broadcast and that such information could be taken into consideration when the license was up for renewal.

FEDERAL COMMUNICATIONS COMMISSION REGULATIONS, LOTTERIES.

Title 18 U.S.C. § 1304 provides: "Whoever broadcasts by means of any radio station for which a license is required by any law of the United States, or whoever, operating any such station, knowingly permits the broadcasting of any advertisement of or information concerning any lottery, gift enterprise, or similar scheme, offering prizes dependent in whole or in part upon lot or chance, or any list of the prizes drawn or awarded by means of any such lottery, gift enterprise, or scheme, whether said list contains any part or all of such prizes, shall be fined not more than $1,000 or imprisoned not more than one year, or both.''

After the briefing and oral arguments to the Supreme Court in *United States v. New Jersey Lottery* (1975),* but before the Court could announce its decision, Congress passed and the president signed Public Law 93-583, 88 Stat. 1916, codified at 18 U.S.C. § 1307: "(a) The provisions of section...1304 shall not apply to an advertisement, list of prizes, or information concerning a lottery conducted by a State acting under the authority of State law...(2) broadcast by a radio or television station licensed to a location in that State or an adjacent State which conducts such a lottery.''

FEDERAL COMMUNICATIONS COMMISSION REGULATIONS, PUBLIC INTEREST, CONVENIENCE, AND NECESSITY.

Title 47 U.S.C. §§ 309(a) and 310(d) read: "Subject to the provisions of this section, the Commission shall determine, in the case of each application filed with it...whether the public interest, convenience, and necessity will be served by the granting of such application....No...station license...shall be...disposed of in any manner...to any person except upon application to the Commission and upon finding by the Commission that the public interest, convenience, and necessity will be served thereby.'' The Supreme Court, in *Federal Communications Commission v. WNCN Listeners Guild* (1981),* ruled that the public interest, convenience, and necessity are best served by promoting diversity through market forces and competition and that a review of a station's format changes was not necessary.

FEDERAL COMMUNICATIONS COMMISSION v. AMERICAN BROADCASTING COMPANY (1954). Title 18 U.S.C. § 1304 and subsequent regulations (Federal Communications Commission Regulations, Give-Away Programs*) issued by the Federal Communications Commission (FCC) prohibited certain types of radio and television give-away programs. One example of the type of program the FCC wanted to stop was *Stop the Music*. This program was described in the court records as follows: "The home contestants are called on the telephone during the program. On the radio version, home contestants are selected at random from telephone directories. On the television version, home contestants are selected by lot from among those listeners who express in advance, through postcards sent to the network, their desire to participate. On both the radio and television versions, however, the home contestant is not required to be listening to the broadcast at the time he is called in order to participate. When called, the home contestant is asked to give the title of a musical selection that has just been played. In the event he was not listening, or for some other reason desires to have the tune repeated, the master of ceremonies hums or sings it to him over the telephone. If he answers correctly, he receives a merchandise prize; if not, he gets a less valuable 'consolation' prize and a member of the studio audience is then given an opportunity to win the merchandise prize by identifying the same tune. If the home contestant answers correctly, he receives, in addition to the merchandise prize, an opportunity to identify another tune, called the 'Mystery Melody.' If he identifies this tune, he wins the 'jackpot' prize, usually valued at several thousand dollars. Should he fail to identify the 'Mystery Melody,' another home contestant is called and the process is repeated. Additions to the 'jackpot' prize are made each week so long as the 'Mystery Melody' remains unidentified."

Other programs singled out by the FCC included *What's My Name* (NBC) and *Sing It Again* (CBS). The Supreme Court ruled that such programs did not come under § 1304's general prohibition and that the commission's regulations exceeded their rule-making powers. *Federal Communications Commission v. American Broadcasting Company*, 347 U.S. 284 (1954).

FEDERAL COMMUNICATIONS COMMISSION v. NATIONAL CITIZENS COMMITTEE FOR BROADCASTING (1978). After a lengthy rule-making procedure, the Federal Communications Commission (FCC) adopted regulations barring the initial licensing or the transfer of newspaper-broadcast combinations in which there was common ownership of a radio or television broadcast station and a daily newspaper located in the same community. Divestiture of existing combinations was not required except in sixteen cases in which the combination involved the sole daily newspaper published in a community and either the sole broadcast station or the sole television station providing that entire community with a clear signal.

The Supreme Court ruled that these regulations did not violate the First Amendment: "The contention that the First Amendment rights of newspaper owners are violated by the regulations ignores the fundamental proposition that there is no 'unbridgeable First Amendment right to broadcast comparable to the right of every individual to speak, write, or publish' '' (*Red Lion Broadcasting Company v. Federal Communications Commission* [1969]).* ''In view of the limited broadcast spectrum, allocation and regulation of frequencies are essential. Nothing in the First Amendment prevents such allocation as will promote the 'public interest' in diversification of the mass communications media. A newspaper owner need not forfeit his right to publish in order to acquire a station in another community; nor is he singled out for more stringent treatment than other owners of mass media under already existing multiple-ownership rules. Far from seeking to limit the flow of information, the F.C.C. has acted to enhance the diversity of information heard by the public without on-going government surveillance of the content of speech. The regulations are a reasonable means of promoting the public interest in diversified mass communications, and thus they do not violate the First Amendment rights of those who will be denied broadcasting licenses.'' *Federal Communications Commission v. National Citizens Committee for Broadcasting*, 436 U.S. 775 (1978).

FEDERAL COMMUNICATIONS COMMISSION v. WNCN LISTENERS GUILD (1981). Sections 309(a) and 310(d) of the Federal Communications Act of 1934 (Federal Communications Commission Regulations, Public Interest, Convenience, and Necessity*) allow the Federal Communications Commission (FCC) to grant an application for renewal or transfer of a radio broadcast license only if it determines that the public interest, convenience, and necessity will be served. The FCC issued a policy statement to the effect that the public interest is best served by promoting diversity through market forces and competition and that a review of a station's format changes was not necessary.

The WNCN Listeners Guild then filed suit, but the Supreme Court upheld the FCC's policy statement: ''The Policy Statement does not conflict with the First Amendment rights of listeners, since the F.C.C. seeks to further the interests of the listening public as a whole and the First Amendment does not grant individual listeners the right to have the F.C.C. review the abandonment of their favorite entertainment programs.'' *Federal Communications Commission v. WNCN Listeners Guild*, 450 U.S. 582 (1981).

FEDERAL ELECTION CAMPAIGN ACT (OF 1971). The Federal Election Campaign Act of 1971, 86 Stat. 11, as amended, 2 U.S.C. § 431ff. (1976 ed. and Supp. III) (2 U.S.C.S. § 431ff.), was a comprehensive reform legislation concerning the election of the president, vice-president, and members of Congress. The entire act and provisions can be found in *Buckley v. Valeo*,* 424 U.S. 1 (1976) at 144–235. The following represents a summary of the act's provisions: (1) Individual political contributions are limited to $1,000 to any single candidate per election, with an annual overall limitation of $25,000 by any contributor; (2) Independent expenditures by individuals and groups relative to a clearly identified candidate are limited to $1,000 a year; (3) Campaign spending by candidates for various federal offices and spending for national conventions by political parties are subject to prescribed limits; (4) Contributions and expenditures above certain threshold levels must be reported and disclosed publicly; (5) A system for public funding of presidential campaign activities was established by Subtitle H of the Internal Revenue Code (the one-dollar check-off); and (6) A Federal Election Commission was established to administer and enforce the legislation.

The act's contribution limits, as well as its reporting requirements, were upheld by the Supreme Court, but the act's limits on expenditures by a candidate were seen to violate the candidate's First Amendment right of free speech (*Buckley v. Valeo*, 1976).

FEDERAL REGULATION OF LOBBYING ACT. This act, among other provisions, contains the following section: "Any person who shall engage himself for pay or for any consideration for the purpose of attempting to influence the passage or defeat of any legislation by the Congress of the United States shall...file with the Clerk and Secretary a detailed report under oath...the names of any papers, periodicals, magazines, or other publications in which he has caused to be published any articles or editorials; and the proposed legislation he is employed to support or oppose." This sweeping requirement of full disclosure of one's writings and publications was seen not to be in violation of the right to a free press by the Supreme Court, in *United States v. Harriss* (1954).*

FEINER v. NEW YORK (1951). Feiner delivered a speech in a small shopping area in a predominantly black residential section of Syracuse, New York. He stood on a large box and spoke over loudspeakers mounted on a car. His audience was composed of about seventy-five persons, black and white. A few minutes after he started, two police officers arrived. The speech (continuing with the court record) was mainly devoted to publicizing a meeting scheduled for that evening and protesting the revocation of a permit. It also touched on various public issues. The following are the only excerpts revealed by the record: "Mayor Costello [of Syracuse] is a champagne-sipping bum; he does not speak for the negro people/The 15th Ward is run by corrupt politicians, and there are horse rooms operating there./President Truman is a bum./Mayor O'Dwyer is a bum./ The American Legion is a Nazi Gestapo./The negroes don't have equal rights; they should rise up in arms and fight for their rights."

There was some pushing and shoving in the crowd and some angry muttering— that was the testimony of the police—but there were no fights and no disorder. But after Feiner had been speaking for about twenty minutes, a man said to the police officers: "If you don't get that son of a bitch off, I will go over and get him off there myself." It was then that the police ordered Feiner to stop speaking. When he refused, they arrested him for violating § 722 of the Penal Code of New York (New York, Breach of the Peace*). Feiner was convicted, and his conviction was affirmed by two New York courts. The U.S. Supreme Court affirmed the conviction, holding that it did not violate Feiner's right of free speech. Chief Justice Vinson delivered the majority opinion: "The language of *Cantwell v. Connecticut** is appropriate here. 'The offense known as breach of the peace embraces a great variety of conduct destroying or menacing public order and tranquillity. It includes not only violent acts but acts and words likely to produce violence in others. No one would have the hardihood to suggest that the principle of freedom of speech sanctions incitement to riot or that religious liberty connotes the privilege to exhort others to physical attack upon those belonging to another sect. When clear and present danger of riot, disorder, interference with traffic upon the public streets, or other immediate threat to public safety, peace, or order, appears, the power of the State to prevent or punish is obvious.' The findings of the New York courts as to the condition of the crowd and the refusal of petitioner to obey the police requests . . . are persuasive that the conviction of petitioner for violation of public peace, order and authority does not exceed the bounds of proper state police action. This Court respects, as it must, the interest of the community in maintaining peace and order on its streets. . . . We are well aware that the ordinary murmurings and objections of a hostile audience cannot be allowed to silence a speaker, and are also mindful of the possible danger of giving overzealous police officials complete discretion to break up otherwise lawful public meetings. . . . But we are not faced here with such a situation. . . . The findings of the state courts as to the existing situation and the imminence of greater disorder coupled with petitioner's deliberate defiance of the police officers convince us that we should not reverse this conviction in the name of free speech."

Vinson spoke only for the majority; Justices Black and Douglas filed eloquent dissents. Justice Black: "I think this conviction makes a mockery of the free speech guarantees of the First and Fourteenth Amendments. The end result of the affirmance here is to approve a simple and readily available technique by which cities and states can with impunity subject all speeches, political or otherwise, on streets or elsewhere, to the supervision and censorship of the local police. I will have no part or parcel in this holding which I view as a long step toward totalitarian authority. Moreover, assuming that the 'facts' did indicate a critical situation, I reject the implication of the Court's opinion that the police had no obligation to protect petitioner's constitutional right to talk. The police of course have power to prevent breaches of the peace. But if, in the name of preserving order, they ever can interfere with a lawful public speaker, they first must make all reasonable efforts to protect him. Here the policemen did not even pretend to try to protect petitioner. According to the officers' testimony, the crowd was restless but there is no showing of any attempt to quiet it; pedestrians were forced to walk into the street, but there was no effort to clear a path on the sidewalk; one person threatened to assault petitioner but the officers did nothing to discourage this when even a word might have sufficed. Their duty was to protect petitioner's right to talk, even to the extent of arresting the man who threatened to interfere. Instead, they shirked that duty and acted only to suppress the right to speak.''

Justice Douglas: ''Public assemblies and public speech occupy an important role in American life. One high function of the police is to protect these lawful gatherings so that the speakers may exercise their constitutional rights. When unpopular causes are sponsored from the public platform, there will commonly be mutterings and unrest and heckling from the crowd. When a speaker mounts a platform it is not unusual to find him resorting to exaggeration, to vilification of ideas and men, to the making of false charges. But these extravagances. . .do not justify penalizing the speaker by depriving him of the platform or by punishing him for his conduct. A speaker may not, of course, incite a riot any more than he may incite a breach of the peace by the use of 'fighting words.'* But this record shows no such extremes. It shows an unsympathetic audience and the threat of one man to haul the speaker from the stage. It is against that kind of threat that speakers need police protection. If they do not receive it and instead the police throw their weight on the side of those who would break up the meetings, the police become the new censors of speech.'' *Feiner v. New York*, 340 U.S. 315 (1951).

FIGHTING WORDS. The constitutional protection of freedom of speech is not absolute at all times and under all circumstances; there are well-defined and narrowly limited classes of speech the prevention and punishment of which does not raise any constitutional problem. The Supreme Court has consistently held or recognized that the utterance of ''fighting words'' is beyond the protection of the First Amendment and that, along with slander, libel, and obscenity,* fighting words are unprotected speech.* Fighting words have been defined by the Supreme Court to mean those personally abusive epithets that, when addressed to the ordinary citizen, are, as a matter of common knowledge, inherently likely to inflict injury or tend to incite an immediate breach of the peace. The landmark decision here is *Chaplinsky v. New Hampshire* (1942),* in which the Court ruled that the words ''God damned racketeer'' and ''damned Fascist'' were indeed fighting words and upheld Chaplinsky's conviction of breach of the peace. But in many cases the Court has ruled that specific utterances were not fighting words and thus protected by the First Amendment: ''We don't need no damn flag'' (*Street v. New York**), ''Make Love Not War'' (*Bachellar v. Maryland**), ''Fuck the Draft'' (*Cohen v. California**), and ''Fucking Prick-Assed Cop'' (*Cincinnati v. Karlan**).

FILM ADVISORY BOARD. This organization, founded in 1975 and with approximately 500 members, describes itself in the following terms: ''To preview and evaluate films and to promote better family entertainment on television and in motion pictures. Bestows Awards of Excellence at monthly luncheons. Advocates the use of symbols describing film content, including L for Language; S for Sex; N for Nudity; V for Violence; and FR for Frightening on PG films." *Encyclopedia of Associations* (# 8270).

FILM CENSORSHIP. In 1913, Ohio passed a statute (Ohio, Motion Picture Censorship*) that created a board of censors that had to approve any motion picture before it could be shown in the state. The statute said that only films of "moral, educational or amusing and harmless character" would be approved by the board. This occurred when the motion picture industry in the United States was just becoming established, and the Court's decision, in *Mutual Film Corporation v. Industrial Commission of Ohio* (1915),* upheld the constitutionality of the statute. The Court saw no violation of freedom of speech or of the press with the Ohio censorship scheme and treated films as a simple business, thus open to government regulation. Justice McKenna wrote: "It cannot be put out of view that the exhibition of moving pictures is a business, pure and simple, originated and conducted for profit, like other spectacles, not to be regarded as part of the press of the country, or as organs of public opinion." This view of the nature of films set the stage for decades of state and municipal regulation and suppression by refusing to issue exhibition permits/licenses to films that the censorship boards did not like.

The following comments, written by Chief Justice Warren (*Times Film Corporation v. City of Chicago* [1961]),* note some of the films that were subjected to such censorship attempts: "A revelation of the extent to which censorship has recently been used in this country is indeed astonishing. The Chicago licensors have banned newsreel films of Chicago policemen shooting at labor pickets and have ordered the deletion of a scene depicting the birth of a buffalo in Walt Disney's *Vanishing Prairie*. Before World War II, the Chicago censor denied licenses to a number of films portraying and criticizing life in Nazi Germany including the *March of Time*'s *Inside Nazi Germany*. Recently, Chicago refused to issue a permit for the exhibition of the motion picture *Anatomy of a Murder* based upon the best-selling novel of the same title, because it found the use of the words 'rape' and 'contraceptive' to be objectionable. The Chicago censor bureau excised a scene in *Street With No Name* in which a girl was slapped because this was thought to be a 'too violent' episode. *It Happened in Europe* was severely cut by the Ohio censors who deleted scenes of war orphans resorting to violence. The Memphis censors banned *The Southerner* which dealt with poverty among tenant farmers because 'it reflects on the south.' *Brewster's Millions*, an innocuous comedy of fifty years ago, was recently forbidden in Memphis because the radio and film character Rochester, a Negro, was deemed 'too familiar.' *No Way Out*, the story of a Negro doctor's struggle against race prejudice, was banned by the Chicago censor on the ground that 'there's a possibility it could cause trouble.' Memphis banned *Curley* because it contained scenes of white and Negro children in school together. Atlanta barred *Lost Boundaries*, the story of a Negro physician and his family who 'passed' for white, on the ground that the exhibition of said picture 'will adversely affect the peace, morals and good order' in the city. *Witchcraft*, a study of superstition through the ages, was suppressed for years because it depicted the devil as a genial rake with amorous leanings, and because it was feared that certain historical scenes, portraying the excesses of religious fanatics, might offend religion. The New York censors banned *Damaged Lives*, a film dealing with venereal disease, although it treated a difficult theme with dignity and had the sponsorship of the American Social Hygiene Society. The picture of Lenin's tomb bearing the inscription 'Religion is the opiate of the people' was excised from *Potemkin*. From *Joan of Arc* the Maryland board eliminated Joan's exclamation as she stood at the stake: 'Oh, God, why hast thou forsaken me?' and from *Idiot's Delight*, the sentence: 'We, the workers of the world, will take care of that.' *Professor Mamlock* was produced in Russia and portrayed the persecution of the Jews by Nazis. The Ohio censors condemned it as 'harmful' and calculated to 'stir up hatred and ill will and gain nothing.' The police refused to permit its showing in Providence, Rhode Island, on the ground that it was communistic propaganda. *Millions of Us*, a strong union propaganda film, encountered trouble in a number of jurisdictions. *Spanish Earth*, a pro-loyalist documentary picture, was banned by the board in Pennsylvania. During the year ending June 30, 1938, the New York board censored, in one way or another, over five percent of the moving pictures it reviewed. Charlie Chaplin's satire on Hitler, *The Great Dictator*, was banned in Chicago, apparently out of deference to its large German population. Ohio and Kansas banned newsreels considered pro labor. Kansas ordered a speech by Senator Wheeler opposing the bill for enlarging the Supreme Court to be cut from the *March of Time* as 'partisan and biased.' An early version of *Carmen* was condemned on several different grounds. The Ohio censor objected because cigarette-girls smoked cigarettes in public. The Pennsylvania censor disapproved the duration of a kiss. The New York censors forbade the discussion in films of pregnancy, venereal disease, eugenics, birth control, abortion, illegitimacy, prostitution, miscegenation and divorce. A member of the Chicago censor board explained that she rejected a film because 'it was immoral, corrupt, indecent, against my . . . religious principles.' A police sergeant attached to the censor board explained, 'Coarse language or anything that would be derogatory to the government—propaganda' is ruled out of foreign films. 'Nothing pink or red is allowed,' he added. The police sergeant in charge of the censor unit has said: 'Children should be allowed to see any movie that plays in Chicago. If a picture is objectionable for a child, it is objectionable period.' And this is but a smattering produced from limited research.''

The courts, however, slowly came around to the view that films were a mode of speech and thus protected by the First Amendment. As Justice Douglas commented in *Superior Films v. Department of Education of Ohio, Division of Film Censorship* (1953) (*M**): ''Motion pictures are of course a different medium of expression than the public speech, the radio, the stage, the novel, or the magazine. But the First Amendment draws no distinction between the various methods of communicating ideas. On occasion one may be more powerful or effective than another. The movie, like the public speech, radio, or television, is transitory—here now and gone in an instant. The novel, the short story, the poem in printed form are permanently at hand to reenact the drama or to retell the story over and again. Which medium will give the most excitement and have the most enduring effect will vary with the theme and the actors. It is not for the censor to determine in any case. . . . In this Nation every writer, actor, or producer, no matter what medium of expression he may use, should be freed from the censor.''

The courts began to whittle away at the abuses of censorship and suppression—not by saying that exhibition permits/licenses were not required, but by mandating that the grounds on which such a permit was refused could not be a violation of the First Amendment guarantees of free speech and press. The courts have ruled that the following reasons, which represent only a sample, cannot be used to censor or ban a film: "sacrilegious" (*The Miracle**); "prejudicial to the best interests of the people of the city" (*Pinky**); "tend to corrupt morals" (*La Ronde**); "harmful and not educational" (*M**); and "undermining confidence that justice can be carried out" (*Native Son**). Concomitant with the rise in government suppression and the wide discrepancy of standards applied, the Motion Picture Association of America* established its production and rating code and system. The rating code has undergone several revisions, and the present one, basically an age-classification scheme, was devised mainly to head off the age-classification schemes proposed by several individual states. At present, the ratings are G—general audience; PG—parental guidance; R—restricted (no one under sixteen to eighteen admitted without parent or guardian); and X—no one under eighteen admitted, period (porno films are X-rated). Most of the previously active state and municipal censor boards/licensing agencies have abdicated to the association's rating scheme. Although an exhibition license is still a requirement, there has been relatively little censorship, and attempts at suppression in recent years, except for the X-rated sexually explicit films, have been few. Because the Supreme Court has ruled time and again that obscene expression is not protected by the First Amendment, and because practically every state and municipality has anti-obscenity statutes, many adult theaters and X-rated films continue to be harassed. There have been too many such cases to list here, but two of the more publicized films that encountered problems are *I Am Curious— Yellow** and the all-time classic *Deep Throat.** For what is probably the best discussion of this entire area of film censorship, see Edward de Grazia and Roger K. Newman, *Banned Films: Movies, Censors, and the First Amendment* (Bowker: 1982).

"FILTHY WORDS." George Carlin, a satiric humorist, recorded a twelve-minute monologue entitled "Filthy Words" before a live audience in a California theater. He began by referring to his thoughts about "the words you couldn't say on the public, ah, airwaves, um, the ones you definitely wouldn't say, ever." He then proceeded to list those words (fuck, shit, piss, cunt, tits, cocksucker, motherfucker, fart, turd, cock, twat, ass) and repeated them over and over again in a variety of colloquialisms. About 2:00 P.M. on Tuesday, October 30, 1973, a New York radio station broadcast the "Filthy Words" monologue. A man then complained to the Federal Communications Commission (FCC) that he heard the broadcast while driving with his young son. The FCC, citing various regulations (Federal Communications Commission Regulations, Indecency and Censorship*), issued an order characterizing the monologue not as "obscene," but as "indecent" and "patently offensive," and stated that the order would be associated with the station's license file and in the event that subsequent complaints were received, the commission would decide whether it would use any of the available sanctions.

The Supreme Court, in *Federal Communications Commission v. Pacifica Foundation*, 438 U.S. 726 (1978), after examining the context of the broadcast, ruled that even though the broadcast was not obscene, it was indecent and the FCC could maintain this information in the files and such records would not constitute "censorship." Justice Stevens stated that "we simply hold that when the Commission finds that a pig has entered the parlor, the exercise of its regulatory power does not depend on proof that the pig is obscene." There were several dissents (Justices Stewart, Brennan, White, and Marshall), based on the belief that the FCC's order was not authorized because the relevant regulations prohibited only "obscene" speech and not merely "indecent" speech.

FIRST AMENDMENT CONGRESS. Founded in 1979, the First Amendment Congress is a journalism and communications-related association with some 50,000 members. Its objectives, as contained in the *Encyclopedia of Associations* (# 13100), are to "enhance the awareness of all Americans that the First Amendment to the U.S. Constitution guarantees them the rights of free speech and a free press; convey the belief that a free press is not the special prerogative of print and broadcast journalists, but a basic right that assures a responsive government; establish a dialogue between the press and people across the country; encourage better education in schools about the rights and responsibilities of citizenship; and obtain broader support from the public against all attempts by government to restrict the citizen's right to information. Conducts local, state, and national First Amendment Congresses that involve the public in efforts to find solutions to problems of media credibility and public perceptions about the media's accuracy, fairness, objectivity, and thoroughness."

FIRST AMENDMENT LAWYERS ASSOCIATION. Founded in 1970, this association is a group of lawyers who support and defend cases involving the First Amendment to the Constitution. It has in the past both provided legal counsel to those people involved in First Amendment cases and filed amicus curiae briefs in behalf of those people.

FIRST NATIONAL BANK OF BOSTON v. FRANCIS X. BELLOTTI (1978).
The First National Bank of Boston, along with other banking associations and business corporations, wanted to spend money to publicize their views opposing a referendum proposal to amend the Massachusetts Constitution to authorize the legislature to enact a graduated personal income tax. They brought suit against the Massachusetts attorney general, challenging the constitutionality of a Massachusetts statute (Massachusetts, Corporate Political Contributions*) that prohibited them and certain other business corporations from making contributions or expenditures "for the purpose of influencing or affecting the vote on any question submitted to the voters, other than one materially affecting any of the property, business or assets of the corporation."

The Supreme Judicial Court of Massachusetts upheld the constitutionality of the statute, but on appeal, the Supreme Court reversed, holding that it was an impermissible restriction on the right of free speech. Justice Powell delivered the opinion of the Court: "If the speakers here were not corporations, no one would suggest that the State could silence their proposed speech. It is the type of speech indispensable to decision-making in a democracy, and this is no less true because the speech comes from a corporation rather than an individual. The inherent worth of the speech in terms of its capacity for informing the public does not depend upon the identity of its source, whether corporation, association, union, or individual.... We thus find no support in the First or Fourteenth Amendment, or the decisions of this Court, for the proposition that speech that otherwise would be within the protection of the First Amendment loses that protection simply because its source is a corporation that cannot prove, to the satisfaction of a court, a material effect on its business or property. The 'materially affecting' requirement is not an identification of the boundaries of corporate speech etched by the Constitution.... If a legislature may direct business corporations to 'stick to business,' it may also limit other corporations—religious, charitable, or civic—to their respective 'business' when addressing the public. Such power in government to channel the expression of views is unacceptable under the First Amendment. Especially where, as here, the legislature's suppression of speech suggests an attempt to give one side of a debatable public question an advantage in expressing its views to the people.... In short, the First Amendment does not 'belong' to any definable category of persons or entities. It belongs to all who exercise its freedoms." *First National Bank of Boston v. Francis X. Bellotti*, 435 U.S. 765 (1978).

FISKE v. STATE OF KANSAS (1927). A Kansas criminal syndicalism* statute defined criminal syndicalism as "the doctrine which advocates crime, physical violence, arson, destruction of property, sabotage . . . as a means of accomplishing industrial or political ends or revolution." Fiske was indicted and then convicted under this statute for soliciting members in an organization that the state determined to be a criminal syndicalist organization.

The Supreme Court reversed the lower court's decision: "The information charged that the defendant did 'by word of mouth and by publicly displaying and circulating certain books and pamphlets and written and printed matter, advocate, affirmatively suggest and teach the duty, necessity, propriety and expediency of crime, criminal syndicalism, and sabotage by...knowingly and feloniously persuading, inducing, and securing certain persons to sign an application for membership in and by issuing to them membership cards in a certain Workers' Industrial Union, a branch and component part of the Industrial Workers of the World organization.' The result is that the Syndicalism Act has been applied in this case to sustain the conviction of the defendant, without any charge or evidence that the organization in which he secured members advocated any crime, violence or other unlawful acts or methods as a means of effecting industrial or political changes or revolution. Thus applied the Act is an arbitrary and unreasonable exercise of the police power of the State, unwarrantably infringing the liberty of the defendant...[and] the judgment is accordingly reversed.'' *Fiske v. State of Kansas*, 274 U.S. 380 (1927).

FLAG DESECRATION/DISRESPECT. The constitutionality of prohibitions against defiance, disrespect, mutilation, or abuse of the American flag has depended on the nature of the particular conduct proscribed. On one hand, the Supreme Court has upheld the constitutionality of a prohibition against the use of the flag in advertisements (*Halter v. Nebraska**—the use of a flag in a beer advertisement). Although the lower federal courts and a majority of the Supreme Court have not expressed their views as to the constitutionality of prohibitions against the destruction or mutilation of the flag, four members of the Supreme Court have written that it is constitutional to convict a person for burning a flag in public (*Street v. New York**). On the other hand, the Supreme Court has held it unconstitutional to prohibit a person from speaking defiant or contemptuous words about the flag (''We don't need no damn flag''—*Street v. New York*), and convictions for showing disrespect for the flag have not been upheld (*Spence v. Washington**—hanging the flag upside down with a peace symbol attached—and *Smith v. Goguen**—sewing the flag to the seat of one's pants).

Prohibitions against the refusal to salute or pledge allegiance to the flag have generally been held unconstitutional by the federal courts. There are only two federal flag statutes: one dealing with the use of the flag with advertisements and the other dealing with public mutilation of the flag. One act, approved February 20, 1905 (33 Stat. 724, § 5), authorized the registration of trademarks in commerce with foreign nations and among the states and provided that no mark would be refused ''unless such mark...consists of or compromises the flag or coat of arms or other insignia of the United States, or any simulation thereof or of any State or municipality or of any foreign nation.'' The desecration/mutilation statute, 18 U.S.C. § 700(a), provides: ''Whoever knowingly casts contempt upon any flag of the United States by publicly mutilating, defacing, defiling, burning, or trampling upon it shall be fined not more than $1,000 or imprisoned for not more than one year, or both.''

Most of the state statutes are patterned after the following: "No person shall publicly mutilate, deface, defile, defy, trample upon, or by word or act cast contempt upon such flag, standard, color, ensign or shield." The problems with this enter with the use of "by word...cast contempt," because such expression has been seen to be protected by the First Amendment's guarantee of free speech. Action and conduct against the flag may (or may not be) punished; words directed against the flag are protected. *Annotation: American Flag Disrespect*, 22 L. Ed. 2d 972.

FLORIDA, RIGHT OF REPLY. § 104.38 of the Florida Statutes, enacted in 1913, provided: "Newspaper Assailing a Candidate in an Election; Space for Reply—If any newspaper in its columns assails the personal character of any candidate for nomination or for election in any election, or charges said candidate with malfeasance or misfeasance in office, or otherwise attacks his official record, or gives to another free space for such purpose, such newspaper shall upon request of such candidate immediately publish free of cost any reply he may make thereto in as conspicuous a place and in the same kind of type as the matter that calls for such reply, provided such reply does not take up more space than the matter replied to. Any person or firm failing to comply with the provisions of this section shall be guilty of a misdemeanor of the first degree." The Supreme Court, in *Miami Herald Publishing v. Tornillo* (1974),* saw this statute as a blatant governmental interference in the right of a free press and held the statute to be a violation of the First Amendment.

FLORIDA, TRESPASS STATUTE. Florida Statutes, § 821.18 (1965), provides: "Every trespass upon the property of another, committed with a malicious and mischievous intent, the punishment of which is not specially provided for, shall be punished by imprisonment not exceeding three months, or by fine not exceeding one hundred dollars." This statute was applied in a conviction for a demonstration on a non-public jail driveway, and the Supreme Court sustained the conviction (*Adderly v. Florida* [1966]).*

FLOWER v. UNITED STATES (1972). Flower was sentenced to six months in prison on charges of violating 18 U.S.C. § 1382 (Military Regulations, Access to Military Bases*). He was arrested by military police while distributing leaflets within the limits of Fort Sam Houston, in San Antonio, Texas. The Supreme Court reversed the conviction, not on grounds that § 1382 was unconstitutional, but that the First Amendment protected Flower under the particular conditions of the situation. The street that Flower was using to distribute the leaflets—although within the limits of the base—was an "open" street: There was no sentry post, traffic used it twenty-four hours a day (about 33,000 vehicles a day), the street was a major civilian artery for buses and cabs, and both civilian and military personnel used the sidewalks. The Court ruled that under these circumstances, the post commander had "abandoned" any claim that he had special interests in who walks, talks, or distributes leaflets on the avenue, for the street was a public forum. *Flower v. United States*, 407 U.S. 197 (1972).

FOLLETT v. TOWN OF McCORMICK (1944). The town of McCormick, South Carolina, had a municipal ordinance (McCormick [SC], License Tax on Book Agents*) that imposed a flat license tax on book agents for the privilege of doing business in the town. Follett was an evangelist who distributed religious tracts and made his livelihood from the sale of such material. The town convicted him, but the Supreme Court, in a short decision similar to *Largent v. Texas* (1943)* and *Jamison v. Texas* (1943)* reversed the decision. Justice Douglas: "This does not mean that religious undertakings must be subsidized. The exemption from a license tax of a preacher who preaches or a parishioner who listens does not mean that either is free from all financial burdens of government, including taxes on income or property. . . . But to say that they, like other citizens, may be subject to general taxation does not mean that they can be required to pay a tax for the exercise of that which the First Amendment has made a high constitutional privilege." *Follett v. Town of McCormick*, 321 U.S. 573 (1944).

FORSHAM v. HARRIS, SECRETARY OF HEW (1980). The Freedom of Information Act (FOIA)* empowers federal courts to order an agency to produce "agency records improperly withheld" from an individual requesting access. This case dealt less with access to government records and more with what constitutes a government "agency." Forsham, under the FOIA, requested data that a private research group generated with federal research grant funds, but Harris refused. The Supreme Court ruled that written data generated, owned, and possessed by a privately controlled organization receiving federal research grants are not "agency records" within the meaning of the FOIA. Receipt of federal grants does not make the private organization a federal agency. Although the Department of Health, Education, and Welfare had a right of access to the data and a right to obtain permanent custody of the data, the FOIA applies to records that have been in fact obtained and not to records that merely could have been obtained. *Forsham v. Harris, Secretary of HEW*, 445 U.S. 169 (1980).

FORT SMITH (AR), BOOK SELLERS' LICENSE. Fort Smith City Ordinance No. 1172 read: "That the license hereinafter named shall be fixed and imposed and collected at the following rates and sums and it shall be unlawful for any person or persons to exercise or pursue any of the following vocations of business in the city. . . without first having obtained a license therefor from the city clerk and having paid for the same. . . . For each person peddling dry goods, notions, wearing apparel, household goods or other articles not herein or otherwise specifically mentioned $25 per month, $10 per week, $2.50 per day. A person, firm or corporation using two or more men in their peddling business $50 per annum.'' This ordinance was originally upheld by the Supreme Court in *Bowden v. Fort Smith* (1942),* but Bowden's conviction was vacated one year later, in a 1943 rehearing.

FORT v. CITY OF MIAMI (1967). Fort created six fiberglass statues, which he then offered for sale from the backyard of his Miami home. Two police officers arrived, but they didn't buy the statues; they confiscated the statues and arrested Fort for violating a municipal ordinance (Miami [FL], Sale of Obscene Material*) that prohibited knowing possession of obscene figures or images for sale (the court records did not disclose the nature of the statues).

Fort was convicted, and the Supreme Court refused to hear his appeal. But Justice Stewart, joined by Justices Black and Douglas, dissented from the denial of certiorari: ''It is clear that the ordinance under which he was convicted is unconstitutional on its face. That ordinance adopts the definition of obscenity embodied in a Florida statute: 'For the purposes of this section, the test of whether or not material is obscene is: Whether to the average person, applying contemporary community standards, the dominant theme of the material taken as a whole appeals to prurient interest.' Members of this Court have expressed differing views as to the extent of a State's power to suppress 'obscene' material through criminal or civil proceedings. But it is at least established that a State is without power to do so upon the sole ground that the material 'appeals to prurient interest.' The petitioner in this case was charged, tried, and convicted under a statutory provision which contains no other criterion of 'obscenity.' This conviction therefore rests upon a law incompatible with the guarantees of the First and Fourteenth Amendments of the United States Constitution.'' *Fort v. City of Miami*, 389 U.S. 918 (1967), *cert. denied*.

FORT WORTH (TX), CHARITABLE SOLICITING. Section 32-3, Fort Worth City Code (1964), Ordinance No. 4753, § 6 and Ordinance No. 4768, § 4, read as follows: ''It shall be unlawful for any person, organization, society, association or corporation...to solicit property or financial assistance of any kind...unless such person...shall have first obtained a permit in compliance with the terms of this chapter.''

The following are reasons given for a denial of the permit: ''(a) That one or more of the statements in the application is not true; (b) That the applicant is not a responsible person of good character and reputation for honesty and integrity, or if the applicant is not an individual person, that any officer or agent of the applicant is not a responsible person of good character and reputation for honesty and integrity; (c) That the control and supervision of solicitations on behalf of the applicant will not be under responsible and reliable persons; (d) That the applicant is or has engaged in a fraudulent transaction or enterprise; (e) That a solicitation on behalf of the applicant would be a fraud upon the public; (f) That the cost of solicitation for a charitable purpose in the city during any of the three years immediately preceding the date of application has been excessive in relation to the gross amount raised; (g) That the expected cost of solicitation will be excessive in relation to the expected gross amount to be raised. Any such cost in excess of twenty per cent of the amount collected shall be deemed to be unreasonable unless special facts or circumstances are presented showing that a cost higher than twenty per cent is not unreasonable; or (h) That such solicitation will be incompatible with the protection of the health, life, property, safety, welfare or morals of the citizens of the city.''

The National Foundation, an organization that was denied a permit to solicit, brought suit, alleging that the ordinance was both too vague and an unconstitutional prior restraint on its First Amendment right of free speech. A lower federal court ruled that the ordinance did not violate the First Amendment rights of any group that wanted to solicit. The Supreme Court affirmed this ruling by denying certiorari. *National Foundation v. Fort Worth* (1969)* and 396 U.S. 1040 (1970), *cert. denied.*

FOUNDATION TO IMPROVE TELEVISION. This organization was founded in 1969 and is based in Boston. This group describes itself as: ''Individuals who wish to increase and promote the proper utilization of television, particularly for children. Sponsors research on the psychological effects of television on its viewers, especially children. Carries out various legal and administrative actions to help promote better television programming. These include court challenges to the right of television stations and sponsors to present violence-oriented programming before 10 p.m. Maintains library of legal briefs and related source material and brochures'' *Encyclopedia of Associations* (# 11962).

491. The Tariff Act* permits U.S. Customs officials to seize what they think is obscene material and then apply to a federal district court for a judicial determination as to the material's obscenity. If the court deems the material is indeed obscene, the seized material is then destroyed. This 1964 Swedish film directed by Vilgot Sjoman (*I Am Curious—Yellow**) was impounded by Customs, ruled obscene by the court, and U.S. viewers were spared having to see it. District court judge Graven: ''The evidence presented by the Government clearly establishes as to the film *491* the following: (a) To the average person applying contemporary community (national) standards, its dominant theme as a whole appeals to the prurient interest; (b) It is characterized by patent offensiveness; (c) It goes substantially beyond the customary limits of candor in description and representation; (d) It is utterly without redeeming social importance; and, therefore, that the film *491* is an obscene matter within the purview of Section 305 of the Tariff Act.''

The film was reviewed in *Variety* (January 22, 1964), *New York Times* (December 21, 1967), and *Box Office* (January 8, 1968), but the following description of the film is taken from the district court records: ''[Vilgot Sjoman] was a protégé of Ingmar Bergman, a director with an international reputation. The film came to the attention of the Claimant at the annual Film Festival at Cannes,

France. It appears that the film has been exhibited in Sweden and Germany. The film has to do with several youthful delinquents who had been in difficulty with the law. Krister, a bachelor, had a very good and well-furnished home and made it available for a social agency to make use of for the housing of the boys under the supervision of that agency. The social worker who had supervision of the boys was referred to as the Inspector. It developed that the Inspector was a homosexual. He had one of the boys come to his private office. He then engaged in what one witness described as homosexual lovemaking which consisted of stroking and fondling of the boy. The Inspector is shown with his head between the thighs of the boy.... The boys proceeded to steal and pawn furniture and books belonging to Krister [and] he insists that the property be redeemed. The boys engage a prostitute and secure sufficient customers to raise the amount required. The boys then get angry with her and vented their anger by holding her and forcing a large dog they had picked up into position to have sexual relations with her. The movie ends with the youngest of the boys committing suicide.''

Judge Graven's decision was remarkable in the sense that the court record contained a full recapitulation of the evidence given for both sides, but as is usual in these cases, the government witnesses claimed that the film was dominated by degeneracy, debauchery, sadism, brutality, adolescent homosexuality, and sexual bestiality. The witnesses for the claimant, on the other hand, although admitting that there might be a few scenes as described above, claimed that the movie's dominant theme was a criticism of the Swedish welfare state, a criticism of social welfare methods and social welfare workers, and that the film had a religious significance (Krister was Christ). A psychiatrist gave testimony for the government, saying that the film would excite and stimulate adolescents in the matter of erotic sexual behavior and that the homosexual activities in the film would act as a special stimulus to latent and active homosexuals. The judge found for the government on all questions, and *491* was denied entry into the United States. *United States v. One Carton Positive Motion Picture Film Entitled 491*, 247 F. Supp. 450 (1965).

FOWLER v. RHODE ISLAND (1953). A municipal ordinance (Pawtucket [RI], Public Speeches in Parks*) was applied in such a manner as to allow most religious sects to hold services in a public park but denied permission to the Jehovah's Witnesses. This case deals with religious freedom but also involves an attempt by government to suppress certain speech that it did not favor. The Supreme Court reversed Fowler's conviction for holding a peaceful [religious] meeting in a public park without the required permit. Justice Douglas: ''Appellant's sect has conventions that are different from the practices of other religious groups. Its religious service is less ritualistic, more unorthodox, less formal than some. But . . . it is no business of courts to say that what is a religious practice or activity for one group is not religion under the protection of the First Amendment. Nor is it in the competence of courts under our constitutional scheme to approve, disapprove, classify, regulate, or in any manner control sermons delivered at religious meetings. Sermons are as much a part of a religious service as prayers. They cover a wide range and have as great a diversity as the Bible or other Holy Book from which they commonly take their texts. To call the words which one minister speaks to his congregation a sermon, immune from regulation, and the words of another minister an address, subject to regulation, is merely an indirect way of preferring one religion over another. . . . Baptist, Methodist, Presbyterian, or Episcopal ministers, Catholic priests, Moslem mullahs, Buddhist monks could all preach to their congregations in Pawtucket's parks with impunity. But the hand of the law would be laid on the shoulder of a minister of this unpopular group for performing the same function.'' *Fowler v. Rhode Island*, 345 U.S. 67 (1953).

FOX v. WASHINGTON (1915). Fox was convicted for violating a Washington statute (Washington, Disrespect for the Law*) that prohibited, not conduct that was in violation of a law, but speech or press that had a tendency to lead others to have ''disrespect for the law.'' Fox was convicted for publishing an article (''The Nude and the Prudes'') that encouraged ''disrespect'' for a state law against indecent exposure (nude bathing). Excerpts from his article follow: ''Home is a community of free spirits, who came out into the woods to escape the polluted atmosphere of priest-ridden conventional society/One of the liberties enjoyed by Homeites was the privilege to bathe in evening dress, or with merely the clothes nature gave them, just as they chose/Eventually a few prudes got into the community and proceeded in the brutal, unneighborly way of the outside world to suppress the people's freedom.''

The Supreme Court sustained the constitutionality of the statute and affirmed Fox's conviction. Justice Holmes delivered the opinion of the Court: ''In this present case the disrespect for the law that was encouraged was disregard of it— an overt breach and technically criminal act. It would be in accord with the usages of English to interpret disrespect as manifested disrespect, as active disregard going beyond the line drawn by the law. . . . By indirection but unmistakably the article encourages and incites a persistence in what we must assume would be a breach of the state laws against indecent exposure.'' *Fox v. Washington*, 236 U.S. 273 (1915).

FRANKIE AND JOHNNIE. This case involved the state of New York prosecuting, under the New York Obscenity Statute,* for the suppression of the play *Frankie and Johnnie*, which told the tale of the adventures of Johnnie, a country boy, in a St. Louis resort for drinking, gambling, and prostitution in the mid-1800s. The New York judge dismissed the prosecution with these words: ''We do not purpose to sanction indecency on the stage by this decision or to let down the bars against immoral shows or to hold that the depiction of scenes of bawdry on the stage is to be tolerated. We hold merely that the fact that Frankie and Johnnie were not nice people does not in itself make the play obscene. A history of prostitution or of sexual life is not per se indecent, although such a book might easily be so written as to offend decency.''

The court record contained some description of the play and the judge's reactions: "The language of the play is coarse, vulgar and profane; the plot cheap and tawdry. As a dramatic composition it serves to degrade the stage where vice is thought by some to lose 'half its evil by losing all its grossness.' That it is 'indecent' from every consideration is entirely clear but the court is not a censor of plays and does not attempt to regulate manners. The question is not whether the scene is laid in a low dive where refined people are not found or whether the language is that of the barroom rather than the parlor. The question is whether the tendency of the play is to excite lustful and lecherous desire. The play is said to 'tend to corrupt the morals of youth.' Here again the question is not whether it would tend to coarsen or vulgarize the youth who might witness it, but whether it would tend to lower their standards of right and wrong, specifically as to the sexual relation. Unless the mere representation on the stage of prostitutes and their patrons would tend to have the effect of stimulating sexual impulses, the performance should not be barred. Unless we say that it is obscene to use the language of the street rather than that of the scholar the play is not obscene under the Penal Law although it might be so styled by the censorious." *People v. Wendling*, 180 N.E. 169 (1932).

FREEDOM OF INFORMATION ACT. The Freedom of Information Act (FOIA), 5 U.S.C. § 552, which became law in 1966, was designed to make available to the public more information from most federal agencies (Congress and the judiciary are exempt from the provisions of the act). The FOIA says that all records in the possession of federal agencies must be provided to anyone on request unless the information being sought falls within several statutory exemptions: (1) Specifically required by executive order to be kept secret in the interest of the national defense or foreign policy. (2) Related "solely" to agencies' internal personnel rules and practices. (3) Specifically exempted from disclosure by statute. (4) Privileged or confidential trade secrets or financial information. (5) Interagency or intra-agency memoranda or letters that would be unavailable by law to a person in litigation with the agency. (6) Personnel and medical files "the disclosure of which would constitute a clearly unwarranted invasion of personal privacy." (7) Investigatory files compiled for law enforcement purposes except to the extent available by law to private parties. (8) Contained in or related to examination or condition reports of agencies regulating financial institutions. (9) Geological and geophysical information and data, including maps, concerning wells.

The FOIA was opposed by the agencies it affected and was unpopular with the executive branch: Presidents Nixon and Ford did nothing to strengthen the act (Ford even vetoed an attempt to have stiffer disclosure provisions) and President Reagan is not known for his support of the act. Many agencies specialize in foot-dragging and delays (the Federal Bureau of Investigation and the

Central Intelligence Agency are the two worst offenders) and other agencies impose high fees as ways of discouraging requests for information. The FOIA has yet to operate the way Congress envisioned it in 1966.

FREEDOM OF INFORMATION CENTER. This group was established by the School of Journalism, University of Missouri, in 1958. Its major interest and purpose is "to report and comment on actions by government, society, and the communications media that affect the acquisition, presentation, and dissemination of information. Issues of major concern include the evolution of press councils, shield laws, open meetings and open records legislation, and increasing incidence of government invasion of privacy." *Encyclopedia of Associations* (# 12569).

FREEDOM TO READ FOUNDATION. Founded in 1969, this foundation is composed of individuals, associations, corporations, and other organizations concerned with protecting and defending freedom of speech and freedom of press, particularly as these relate to libraries and librarians. The foundation sees as its major purpose: "To promote the recognition and acceptance of libraries as repositories of knowledge and to protect the public right of access to them; to support the right of librarians to make available to the public any creative work legally acquired; to supply legal counsel and other support to librarians and libraries suffering legal injustices by reason of their defense of freedom of speech and freedom of press." *Encyclopedia of Associations* (# 12000).

FROHWERK v. UNITED STATES (1919). Frohwerk and others who were responsible for editing and publishing the newspaper *Missouri Staats Zeitung* were indicted and then convicted for violating the Espionage Act.* The government alleged that several articles that appeared in the newspaper attempted to cause disloyalty, mutiny, and refusal of duty in the military and naval forces of the United States. The court record described some of the articles in the following terms: "There is a remark to the effect that when rulers scheme to use it for their own aggrandizement loyalty serves to perpetuate wrong/The sooner the public wakes up to the fact that we are led and ruled by England, the better; that our sons, our taxes and our sacrifices are only in the interests of England/ There is a sneering contrast between Lord Northcliffe and other Englishmen spending many hundreds of thousands of dollars here to drag us into the war and Count Bernstorff spending a few thousand to maintain peace between his own country and us."

The Supreme Court affirmed the convictions, as they had done with most other prosecutions under the Espionage Act and World War I. The Court opinion contained the following statements in defense of its affirmation: "The First Amendment, while prohibiting legislation against free speech as such, cannot have been, and obviously was not, intended to give immunity for every possible use of language. We venture to believe that neither Hamilton nor Madison, nor any other competent person then or later, ever supposed that to make criminal the counselling of a murder within the jurisdiction of Congress would be an unconstitutional interference with free speech. . . . It may be that all this might be said or written even in time of war in circumstances that would not make it a crime. We do not lose our right to condemn either measures or men because the Country is at war. It does not appear that there was any special effort to reach men who were subject to the draft; and if the evidence should show that the defendant was a poor man, turning out copy for Gleeser, his employer, at less than a day laborer's pay, for Gleeser to use or reject as he saw fit, in a newspaper of small circulation, there would be a natural inclination to test every question of law to be found in the record very thoroughly before upholding the very severe penalty imposed. But we must take the case on the record as it is, and on the record it is impossible to say that it might not have been found that the circulation of the paper was in quarters where a little breath would be enough to kindle a flame and that the fact was known and relied upon by those who sent the paper out. Small compensation would not exonerate the defendant if it were found that he expected the result, even if pay were his chief desire. When we consider that we do not know how strong the Government's evidence may have been we find ourselves unable to say that the articles could not furnish a basis for a conviction." *Frohwerk v. United States*, 249 U.S. 204 (1919).

FULLER v. THE PEOPLE (1879). Fuller was indicted and convicted for violating the Illinois obscenity statute.* Fuller was charged with having in his possession, and showing to certain young ladies, a lead pencil drawing that was characterized as "grossly obscene and indecent." The court ruled that the indictment—stating that he had possession of an obscene drawing without describing the drawing—was sufficient; this is to be compared with more recent decisions (the *Illustrated Report** case is an example) in which the court record reproduces in graphic detail the contents of the alleged obscene material. The full weight of the law fell on Fuller, and as the judge implies, he was lucky that he wasn't executed for having shown an alleged obscene drawing to his girl friend: "Assuming, as the record compels us to, that plaintiff in error is guilty, he has little cause to complain. For such conduct as he is charged with there is no rational excuse, and even the infliction of the extreme penalty of the law would not appear to be too severe punishment for it." *Fuller v. The People*, 92 Ill. 182 (1879).

G

THE GAME OF LOVE. Acting under the authority of the Chicago motion picture censorship* ordinance, the Chicago police commissioner refused to issue an exhibition permit for the film *The Game of Love*. The Times Film Corporation then filed suit in a federal district court, but the court held that the dominant theme of the film was sexuality and thus obscene; a federal court of appeals (*Times Film Corporation v. City of Chicago*, 244 F. 2d 432 [1957] agreed and sustained the police commissioner's refusal to issue the exhibition permit. But in *Times Film Corporation v. City of Chicago*, 355 U.S. 35 (1957), the U.S. Supreme Court, in a per curiam decision, reversed the decision and simply declared that *The Game of Love* was not obscene.

Judge Schnackenberg of the court of appeals described the film thusly: "We do not hesitate to say that the calculated purpose of the producer of this film, and its dominant effect, are substantially to arouse sexual desires. We are of the opinion that the probability of this effect is so great as to outweigh whatever artistic or other merits the film may possess. We think these determinations are supported by the effect which this film would have upon the normal, average person.... The film, as an exhibit in this case, was projected before and viewed by us. We found that, from beginning to end, the thread of the story is super-charged with a current of lewdness generated by a series of illicit sexual intimacies and acts. In the introductory scenes a flying start is made when a 16 year old boy is shown completely nude on a bathing beach in the presence of a group of younger girls. On that plane the narrative proceeds to reveal the seduction of this boy by a physically attractive woman old enough to be his mother. Under the influence of this experience and an arrangement to repeat it, the boy thereupon engages in sexual relations with a girl of his own age. The erotic thread of the story is carried, without deviation toward any wholesome idea, through scene after scene. The narrative is graphically pictured with nothing omitted except those sexual consummations which are plainly suggested but meaningfully omitted and thus, by the very fact of omission, emphasized. The words spoken in French are reproduced in printed English on the lower edge of the moving film. None of it palliates the effect of the scenes portrayed."

THE GARDEN OF EDEN. This 1957 American film (with an undistinguished cast and plot) met with opposition from the city of Chicago (Chicago [IL], Motion Picture Censorship*) and the state of New York (New York, Motion Picture Censorship*) when exhibition permits were denied on grounds that the film was obscene because of the nudity in it.

The film itself was not a classic; de Grazia and Newman (*Banned Films*, pp. 247–248) present a short review: "A young widow leaves the home of her father-in-law, a gruff business tycoon. When her car stalls she is rescued by inhabitants of a nearby nudist camp. Her horror subsides as she beholds the wholesome way of life of the nudists. When her father-in-law arrives, he undergoes the same transformation, and all are happier for their discovery."†

The Board of Regents of the University of the State of New York refused to issue a license to show the film under the following logic: (1) §§ 122 and 124 of the Education Law prohibited the exhibition of "obscene, indecent, or immoral" films; (2) § 1140-b of the New York Penal Law (1935) read: "A person who in any place willfully exposes his private parts in the presence of two or more persons of the opposite sex whose private parts are similarly exposed, or aids or abets any such act . . . is guilty of a misdemeanor"; and therefore, (3) the regents added (1) and (2) and tried to ban a nudist film. But a New York court (*Excelsior Pictures Corporation v. Regents of the University of the State of New York*, 165 N.Y.S. 2d 42 [1957]) ruled that the penal law applied only to public nudity and not to films and that *The Garden of Eden* was not obscene or indecent.

The police commissioner of Chicago refused to issue an exhibition permit on the same grounds—the film was obscene, immoral, and indecent. The film company brought suit in a federal district court (*Excelsior Pictures Corporation v. City of Chicago*, 182 F. Supp. 400 [1960]), and the judge ruled that *The Garden of Eden* was not obscene. Judge Miner's decision is interesting, for it neatly shows the distinction between nudity and obscenity and that nudity per se does not equal obscenity: "The Court has viewed the film in its entirety and finds that the film does, as plaintiff contends, seek to portray nudism as a healthful and happy way of life. The picture does not expose the private parts of the adult characters. Considered as a whole, its 'calculated purpose or dominant effect' is not substantially to arouse sexual desires in 'the normal average person.' It is not 'immoral' or 'obscene' within the meaning of the Chicago ordinance. The Court does not by its ruling purport to encourage the propagandization of nudism in this community. This is not the type of motion picture which the Court, in its personal capacity, would recommend the public to view. But it is not the Court's function to determine legal issues by applying as standards its personal inclinations or its individual proclivities. . . . The mere fact that nudism is not an accepted way of life among the vast majority of persons in the Chicago com-

---

†Reprinted from *Banned Films* with permission of the R. R. Bowker Company. Copyright © 1982 by Edward de Grazia and Roger K. Newman.

munity, or, indeed, among Americans as a whole, cannot and has not been considered by the Court as controlling. . . . This Court further finds that nudity per se is not 'immoral' or 'obscene' within the meaning of the ordinance. There is hardly an art museum or gallery to which one can go where completely nude statues and pictures are not on constant and prominent exhibition. Many popular books and magazines, far too numerous to list, frequently publish human nudity without offending the law. Certainly, if the advocacy, under certain circumstances, of adultery, which is contrary to moral standards and religious precepts, is protected by our Constitution, then the portrayal, by partial nudity, of nudism as a healthy and happy way of life should be accorded like protection. Nudism may be unappealing and unattractive to some people. It may be repulsive and vulgar to others. But that does not brand it as 'obscene' or 'immoral.' It is the conclusion of this Court that, because the motion picture *The Garden of Eden* may not be denied a license on the ground that it is 'obscene' or 'immoral' within the meaning of the Chicago ordinance, the denial of that license by the city authorities on the ground (1) constituted a denial of plaintiff's rights to freedom of speech and press. . . to advocate nudism as a healthful and happy way of life, and (2) represents the application of the said ordinance 'to a picture to which it cannot be applied without invading the area of constitutionally free expression.' ''

Judge Miner did, however, make one last concession to the moral standards of the Chicago community: ''At the Court's suggestion, plaintiff has agreed to limit and restrict the exhibition of the picture to adults only, and not to publicize such exhibition in any manner or form as being authorized by the Court, and it is so ordered.''

GARRISON v. LOUISIANA (1964). Garrison, a Louisiana district attorney, during a dispute with several state court judges, accused them at a press conference of laziness, inefficiency, and obstructing his attempts to enforce the law. A state court then convicted him of violating the Louisiana criminal defamation statute,* and the state supreme court affirmed the conviction. On appeal, the U.S. Supreme Court reversed the conviction, following the doctrine (*New York Times* Rule*) put forth in *New York Times Company v. Sullivan*: The Constitution limits the power of a state to impose sanctions for criticism of the official conduct of public officials to false statements concerning official conduct made with knowledge of their falsity or with reckless disregard of whether they were false or not (malice). In this particular case, Garrison's accusations concerning the judges' official conduct did not become a private defamation because they might also have reflected on the judges' private character.

Justice Black, joined by Justice Douglas, concurred in the reversal of Garrison's conviction but in much stronger terms than the main decision: ''I concur in reversing the conviction of appellant Garrison, based as it is purely on his public discussion and criticism of public officials. I believe that the First Amendment, made applicable to the States by the Fourteenth, protects every person from having a State or the Federal Government fine, imprison, or assess damages against him when he has been guilty of no conduct other than expressing an opinion, even though others may believe that his views are unwholesome, unpatriotic, stupid or dangerous. I believe that the Court is mistaken if it thinks that requiring proof that statements were 'malicious' or 'defamatory' will really create any substantial hurdle to block public officials from punishing those who criticize the way they conduct their office. Indeed, 'malicious,' 'seditious,' and other such evil-sounding words often have been invoked to punish people for expressing their views on public affairs. Fining men or sending them to jail for criticizing public officials not only jeopardizes the free, open public discussion which our Constitution guarantees, but can wholly stifle it. I would hold now and not wait to hold later that under our Constitution there is absolutely no place in this country for the old, discredited English Star Chamber law of seditious criminal libel.'' *Garrison v. Louisiana*, 379 U.S. 64 (1964).

GEORGIA, ABUSIVE LANGUAGE. Georgia Code Ann. § 26-6303 reads ''Any person who shall, without provocation, use to or of another, and in his presence... opprobrious words or abusive language, tending to cause a breach of the peace... shall be guilty of a misdemeanor.'' The Supreme Court, in *Gooding v. Wilson* (1972),* ruled that this statute could not be applied to someone who, to a police officer, used the words, ''White son of a bitch, I'll kill you'' and ''You son of a bitch, I'll choke you to death'' because the statute could be invoked only with ''fighting words.''*

GEORGIA, INSURRECTION. Georgia Code, 1933, §§ 26-901 to 904 provided: ''Insurrection shall consist in any combined resistance to the lawful authority of the State, with the intent to the denial thereof, when the same is manifested or intended to be manifested by acts of violence. Any attempt, by persuasion or otherwise, to induce others to join in any combined resistance to the lawful authority of the State shall constitute an attempt to incite insurrection. Any person convicted of the offense of insurrection, or an attempt to incite insurrection, shall be punished with death; or, if the jury recommend to mercy, confinement in the penitentiary for not less than five nor more than 20 years. If any person shall bring, introduce, print, or circulate... any writing for the purpose of inciting insurrection, riot, conspiracy, or resistance against the lawful authority of the State... [he] shall be punished by confinement in the penitentiary for not less than five nor longer than 20 years.'' The state of Georgia attempted to apply this statute to someone who solicited members for a political party, but the Supreme Court (*Herndon v. Lowry, Sheriff* [1937])* ruled that the statute as applied violated the First Amendment guarantee of free speech.

GEORGIA, OBSCENITY STATUTE. Georgia Code Ann. (1972), §§ 26-2101, 2105, 2011, reads: ''A person commits the offense of distributing obscene materials when he... exhibits or otherwise disseminates to any person any obscene material of any description, knowing the obscene nature thereof....Material is obscene if considered as a whole, applying community standards, its predominant appeal is to prurient interest, that is, a shameful or morbid interest in nudity, sex or excretion, and utterly without redeeming social value and if, in addition, it goes substantially beyond customary limits of candor in describing or representing such matters. It is a crime to exhibit a motion picture portraying acts which would constitute public indecency if performed in a public place. Public indecency: (a) an act of sexual intercourse, (b) a lewd exposure of the sexual organs, (c) a lewd appearance in a state of partial or complete nudity, (d) a lewd caress or indecent fondling of another person [in a public place is a misdemeanor].'' This statute was applied to several films in the state of Georgia; *Carnal Knowledge** was found not to be obscene, but *Deep Throat** was found to be obscene under the statute.

GEORGIA, POSSESSION OF OBSCENE MATERIAL. Georgia Code Ann. (Supp. 1968), § 26-6301, provided: ''Any person who shall knowingly bring or cause to be brought into this State for sale or exhibition, or who shall knowingly sell or offer to sell, or who shall knowingly lend or give away or offer to lend or give away, or who shall knowingly have possession of...any obscene matter shall be guilty of a felony, and, upon conviction thereof, shall be punished by confinement in the penitentiary for not less than one year nor more than five years.'' The U.S. Supreme Court, in the landmark decision of *Stanley v. Georgia* (1969),* ruled that this statute could not be applied to the mere possession of obscene material in the privacy of one's own home. Individuals may not be able to circulate or sell such material, but the state's police power does not extend to the contents of a person's private bookshelf.

GEORGIA, RAPE VICTIMS' PRIVACY. Georgia Code Ann. (1972), § 26-9901, provided: ''It shall be unlawful for any news media or any other person to print and publish, broadcast, televise, or disseminate through any other medium of public dissemination or cause to be printed and published, broadcast, televised, or disseminated in any newspaper, magazine, periodical or other publication published in this State or through any radio or television broadcast originating in the State the name or identity of any female who may have been raped or upon whom an assault with intent to commit rape may have been made. Any person or corporation violating the provisions of this section shall, upon conviction, be punished as for a misdemeanor.'' In *Cox Broadcasting Corporation v. Cohn* (1975),* the Supreme Court ruled that this statute, when applied to a newscast of a rape victim's name (the name was obtained from the court's records open for inspection by anyone), was a violation of freedom of the press.

GERTZ v. ROBERT WELCH, INC. (1974). An article in Robert Welch's magazine, *American Opinion* (the outlet for the views of the John Birch Society), labeled Gertz, an attorney, a ''Leninist'' and a ''Communist-fronter.'' It also implied that Gertz had a criminal record. Gertz then brought suit for libel. The Supreme Court held that a publisher or a broadcaster of defamatory falsehoods about an individual who is neither a public official* nor a public figure* may not claim protection against liability for defamation on the grounds that the defamatory statements concerned an issue of public or general interest. *Gertz v. Robert Welch, Inc.*, 418 U.S. 323 (1974).

GIBONEY v. EMPIRE STORAGE AND ICE COMPANY (1949). A Missouri state court enjoined the officers and members of a labor union of ice peddlers from peacefully picketing the Empire Storage and Ice Company on the grounds that the union's purpose in picketing was to induce the company not to sell ice to non-union peddlers. The court held that the union's activities violated the Missouri restraint of trade* statute.

The U.S. Supreme Court affirmed the decision, holding that the constitutional freedom of speech and press does not immunize speech or writing used as an integral part of conduct in violation of a valid criminal statute. In a rare departure from his usual strong position on the First Amendment, Justice Black delivered the Court's opinion: "It is contended that the injunction against picketing adjacent to Empire's place of business is an unconstitutional abridgment of free speech because the picketers were attempting peacefully to publicize truthful facts about a labor dispute. But the record here does not permit this publicizing to be treated in isolation. . . . The sole immediate object. . . was to compel Empire to agree to stop selling ice to nonunion peddlers. Thus all of appellants' activities. . . constituted a single and integrated course of conduct, which was in violation of Missouri's valid law. In this situation, the injunction did no more than enjoin an offense against Missouri law, a felony. It rarely has been suggested that the constitutional freedom for speech and press extends its immunity to speech or writing used as an integral part of conduct in violation of a valid criminal statute. We reject the contention now." *Giboney v. Empire Storage and Ice Company*, 336 U.S. 490 (1949).

GILBERT v. MINNESOTA (1920). Gilbert was fined $500 and received one year in jail for making the following speech during World War I: "We are going over to Europe to make the world safe for democracy, but I tell you we had better make America safe for democracy first. You say, what is the matter with our democracy. I tell you what is the matter with it: Have you had anything to say as to who should be president? Have you had anything to say as to who should be Governor of this state? Have you had anything to say as to whether we would go into this war? You know you have not. If this is such a great democracy, for Heaven's sake why should we not vote on conscription of men. We were stampeded into this war by newspaper rot to pull England's chestnuts out of the fire for her. I tell you if they conscripted wealth like they have conscripted men, this war would not last over forty-eight hours." The speech was seen, given the war hysteria of the time, as a violation of a Minnesota statute (Minnesota, Discouraging the War Effort*) that made it unlawful to discourage the enlistment of men in the armed forces.

The Supreme Court affirmed Gilbert's conviction, with Justice McKenna delivering the majority opinion: "Gilbert's speech had the purpose to denounce. The Nation was at war with Germany, armies were recruiting, and the speech was the discouragement of that—its purpose was necessarily the discouragement of that. It was not an advocacy of policies or a censure of actions that a citizen had a right to make. The war was flagrant; it had been declared by the power constituted by the Constitution to declare it, and in the manner provided for by the Constitution. It was not declared in aggression, but in defense, in defense of our national honor, in vindication of the 'most sacred rights of our Nation and our people.' This was known to Gilbert for he was informed in affairs and the operations of the Government, and every word that he uttered in denunciation of the war was false, was deliberate misrepresentation of the motives which impelled it, and the objects for which it was prosecuted. He could have had no purpose other than that of which he was charged. It would be a travesty on the constitutional privilege he invokes to assign him its protection."

Justice Brandeis filed an eloquent dissent that, however, did not help Gilbert: "Sections 1 and 2 [of the Minnesota statute] prohibit teaching or advocating by printed matter, writing or word of mouth, that men should not enlist in the military or naval forces of the United States. The prohibition is made to apply whatever the motive, the intention, or the purpose of him who teaches. It applies alike to the preacher in the pulpit, the professor in the university, the speaker at a political meeting, the lecturer at a society or club gathering. Whatever the nature of the meeting and whether it be public or private, the prohibition is absolute, if five persons are assembled. The reason given by the speaker for advising against enlistment is immaterial. Young men considering whether they should enter these services as a means of earning a livelihood or as a career, may not be told that, in the opinion of the speaker, they can serve the country and themselves better by entering the civil service of State or Nation, or by studying for one of the professions. . . . The statute aims to prevent not acts but beliefs. The prohibition imposed by § 3 is even more far-reaching than that provided in §§ 1 and 2. Section 3 makes it punishable to teach in any place a single person that a citizen should not aid in carrying on a war, no matter what the relation of the parties may be. Thus the statute invades the privacy and freedom of the home. Father and mother may not follow the promptings of religious belief . . . [and counsel their children not to enter the army or the navy]." *Gilbert v. Minnesota*, 254 U.S. 325 (1920).

GINSBERG v. NEW YORK (1968). Sam Ginsberg operated a stationery store and a luncheonette in New York, and a sixteen-year-old boy bought a "girlie" magazine from him. Ginsberg was duly charged, tried, and convicted for violating § 484-h of the New York Penal Law (New York, Exposing Minors to Harmful Materials*). This statute made it unlawful to "sell to a minor [under seventeen] any picture which depicts nudity and which is harmful to minors or any magazine which contains such pictures.''

The Supreme Court sustained Ginsberg's conviction, recognizing that the magazines, although not obscene and freely available to adults, could be prohibited to minors on the grounds that minors do not have the capacity to determine what sex material they will read and thus the state can allow a more restricted right of access for minors than it can for adults. Justice Stewart delivered the Court's opinion: "We have no occasion in this case to consider the impact of the guarantees of freedom of expression upon the totality of the relationship of the minor and the State. It is enough for the purposes of this case that we inquire whether it was constitutionally impermissible for New York, insofar as § 484-h does so, to accord minors under 17 a more restricted right than that assured to adults to judge and determine for themselves what sex material they may read or see. We conclude that we cannot say that the statute invades the area of freedom of expression constitutionally secured to minors. . . . A State may permissibly determine that, at least in some precisely delineated areas, a child— like someone in a captive audience—is not possessed of that full capacity for individual choice which is the presupposition of First Amendment guarantees. It is only upon such a premise . . . that a State may deprive children of other rights—the right to marry, for example, or the right to vote—deprivations that would be constitutionally intolerable for adults.''

Justice Fortas dissented from the majority opinion, not on grounds that he supported total access of minors to obscene material (which he did not), but because the majority opinion failed to define the standard of obscenity that was harmful to minors: "In my judgment, the Court cannot properly avoid its fundamental duty to define 'obscenity' for purposes of censorship of material sold to youths. . . . The Court certainly cannot mean that the States and cities and counties and villages have unlimited power to withhold anything and everything that is written or pictorial from younger people. But here it justifies the conviction of Sam Ginsberg because the impact of the Constitution, it says, is variable, and what is not obscene for an adult may be obscene for a child. This it calls 'variable obscenity.' I do not disagree with this, but I insist that to assess the principle—certainly to apply it—the Court must define it. We must know the extent to which literature or pictures may be less offensive than [the Roth Standard*] requires in order to be 'obscene' for purposes of a statute confined to youth.'' *Ginsberg v. New York*, 390 U.S. 629 (1968).

GINZBURG v. UNITED STATES (1966). Ginzburg was convicted of violating the federal obscenity statute, 18 U.S.C. § 1461 (Postal Regulations, Mailing Obscene Material*), for mailing three publications: an expensive hardcover magazine dealing with sex (*EROS*), a sexual newsletter (*Liaison*), and a short book claiming to be a sexual autobiography (*The Housewife's Handbook on Selective Promiscuity*). A federal district court described the material in the following fashion: "EROS is the reverse situation of *Lady Chatterley's Lover*.* There the author used material which, taken out of context, would have been clearly obscene. Nevertheless, the court found no obscenity because of the saving grace of the book as a whole. EROS has no saving grace. The items of possible merit and those items which may be considered innocuous are a mere disguise to avoid the law and in large measure enhance the pruriency of the work. The only overriding theme of EROS is the advocacy of complete sexual expression of whatever sort and manner. The most offensive pornography imaginable . . . has the same dominant effect and purpose. . . . In considering the manner of expression of the idea then, we come to the work itself. . . . For example: 'Bawdry Limericks' consists of the grossest terminology describing unnatural, offensive, disgusting and exaggerated sexual behavior. Also by way of example: the series of pictures, 'Black and White in Color,' constitutes a detailed portrayal of the act of sexual intercourse between a completely nude male and female, leaving nothing to the imagination. 'Liaison' is a newsletter or periodical folder type of publication consisting of commentary from various sources with a general editorial treatment. Specifically it deals with such subjects as 'Slaying the Sex Dragon,' 'Semen in the Diet' and 'Sing a Song of Sex Life.' The material covers the most perverse and offensive human behavior. While the treatment is largely superficial, it is presented entirely without restraint of any kind. According to defendants' own expert, it is entirely without literary merit. We agree. If there is any socially redeeming value in this material it must come from what is advocated or from its entertainment value. There are jokes and rhymes which clearly go beyond contemporary community standards of humor, even in applying liberal night club standards. *The Handbook* requires little discussion. This book is a kind with the above-mentioned admittedly hardcore pornography. It is an explicit description of a woman's sexual experiences from early childhood and thereafter throughout most of her life. It purports to be . . . a factual and highly accurate reporting of actual occurrences. In fact, Mrs. Lillian Maxine Serett, the authoress, stated: 'I have lived every minute of it, or every page of it.' We doubt the accuracy of this book. It also meets the previously mentioned tests of bizarre exaggeration, morbidness and offensiveness. *The Handbook*, standing bare of any socially redeeming value, is a patent offense to the most liberal morality. The descriptions leave nothing to the imagination, and in detail, in a clearly prurient manner offend, degrade and sicken anyone however healthy his mind was before exposure to this material. It is a gross shock to the mind and chore to read. Pruriency and disgust coalesce here creating a perfect example of hardcore pornography.''

The U.S. Supreme Court affirmed Ginzburg's conviction, adding that the manner of advertising and selling the publications was "pandering"*—openly appealing to the customer's erotic interest. The Court's decision was delivered by Justice Brennan: "There was abundant evidence to show that each of the accused publications was originated or sold as stock in trade of the sordid business of pandering—the business of purveying textual or graphic matter openly advertised to appeal to the erotic interest of their customers. EROS early sought mailing privileges from the postmasters of Intercourse and Blue Ball, Pennsylvania. The trial court found the obvious, that these hamlets were chosen only for the value their names would have in furthering petitioners' efforts to sell their publications on the basis of salacious appeal; the facilities of the post offices were inadequate to handle the anticipated volume of mail, and the privileges were denied. Mailing privileges were then obtained from the postmaster of Middlesex, New Jersey. . . . The 'leer of the sensualist' also permeates the advertising for the three publications. . . . We perceive no threat to First Amendment guarantees in thus holding that in close cases evidence of pandering may be probative with respect to the nature of the material in question.''

The decision was a close one, with several dissents. Justice Black: ''A third element which three of my Brethren think is required to establish obscenity is that the material must be 'utterly without redeeming social value.' This element seems to me to be as uncertain, if not even more uncertain, than is the unknown substance of the Milky Way. If we are to have a free society as contemplated by the Bill of Rights, then I find little defense for leaving the liberty of American individuals subject to the judgment of a judge or jury as to whether material that provokes thought or stimulates desire is 'utterly without redeeming social value.' ''

Justice Douglas also filed a strong dissent to Ginzburg's conviction: ''Today's condemnation of the use of sex symbols to sell literature engrafts another exception on First Amendment rights that is as unwarranted as the judge-made exception concerning obscenity. This new exception condemns an advertising technique as old as history. The advertisements of our best magazines are chock-full of thighs, ankles, calves, bosoms, eyes, and hair, to draw the potential buyer's attention to lotions, tires, food, liquor, clothing, autos, and even insurance policies. The sexy advertisement neither adds to nor detracts from the quality of the merchandise being offered for sale. And I do not see how it adds to or detracts one whit from the legality of the book being distributed. . . . This leads me to the conclusion, previously noted, that the First Amendment allows all ideas to be expressed—whether orthodox, popular, offbeat, or repulsive. I do not think it permissible to draw lines between the 'good' and the 'bad' and be true to the constitutional mandate to let all ideas alone. If our Constitution permitted 'reasonable' regulation of freedom of expression, as do the constitutions of some nations, we would be in a field where the legislative and judiciary would have much leeway. But under our charter all regulation or control of expression is barred. Government does not sit to reveal where the 'truth' is. People are left to pick and choose between competing offerings. There is no compulsion to take and read what is repulsive any more than there is to spend one's time poring over government bulletins, political tracts, or theological treatises. The theory is that people are mature enough to pick and choose, to recognize trash when they see it, to be attracted to the literature that satisfies their deepest need, and, hopefully, to move from plateau to plateau and finally reach the world of enduring ideas. I think this is the idea of the Free Society written into our Constitution. We have no business acting as censors or endowing any group with censorship powers. It is shocking to me for us to send to prison anyone for publishing anything, especially tracts so distant from any incitement to action as the ones before us." *Ginzburg v. United States*, 383 U.S. 463 (1966).

GITLOW v. NEW YORK (1925). In 1925, Benjamin Gitlow was convicted of violating a New York statute (New York, Criminal Anarchy*) that made it illegal for anyone to advocate, advise, or teach the duty, necessity, or propriety of overthrowing organized government by force or violence, or to publish anything that advanced that doctrine. Gitlow published his "Left Wing Manifesto"—a rambling tract on the necessity of accomplishing the Communist revolution through the dictatorship of the proletariat and the class struggle. Some excerpts: "Revolutionary Socialism . . . insists that the democratic parliamentary state can never be the basis for the introduction of Socialism; that it is necessary to destroy the parliamentary state, and construct a new state of the organized producers, which will deprive the bourgeoisie of political power, and function as a revolutionary dictatorship of the proletariat. . . . Revolutionary Socialism is alone capable of mobilizing the proletariat for Socialism, for the conquest of the power of the state, by means of revolutionary mass action and proletarian dictatorship. . . . The old order is in decay. Civilization is in collapse. The proletarian revolution and the Communist reconstruction of society—the struggle for these— is now indispensable. This is the message of the Communist International to the workers of the world. The Communist International calls the proletariat of the world to the final struggle."

Although it could find no evidence of any effect whatsoever resulting from the publication and circulation of the manifesto, the Supreme Court sustained Gitlow's conviction because it believed that such utterances and thoughts presented a danger to the security of the nation in the abstract and that a real, immediate danger was not required. Justice Sanford delivered the opinion of the Court, an opinion that brought forth the doctrine of "incorporation"*—that the guarantees contained in the First Amendment were made applicable to the states through the due process clause of the Fourteenth Amendment. The incorporation of free speech, however, did not help Gitlow. Justice Sanford: "That utterances inciting to the overthrow of organized government by unlawful means, present a sufficient danger of substantive evil to bring their punishment within the range of legislative discretion, is clear. Such utterances, by their very nature, involve danger to the public peace and to the security of the State. They threaten breaches of the peace and ultimate revolution. And the immediate danger is none the less real and substantial, because the effect of a given utterance cannot be accurately foreseen. The State cannot reasonably be required to measure the danger from every such utterance in the nice balance of a jeweler's scale. A single revolutionary spark may kindle a fire that, smouldering for a time, may burst into a sweeping and destructive conflagration. It cannot be said that the State is acting arbitrarily or unreasonably when in the exercise of its judgment as to the measures necessary to protect the public peace and safety, it seeks to extinguish the spark without waiting until it has enkindled the flame or blazed into the conflagration. It cannot reasonably be required to defer the adoption of measures for its own peace and safety until the revolutionary utterances lead to actual disturbances of the public peace or imminent and immediate danger of its own destruction; but it may, in the exercise of its judgment, suppress the threatened danger in its incipiency.''

Justice Holmes, joined by Justice Brandeis, dissented, arguing the ''clear and present danger''* test: ''There was no present danger of an attempt to overthrow the government by force on the part of the admittedly small minority who shared the defendant's views. It is said that this Manifesto was more than a theory, that it was an incitement. Every idea is an incitement. It offers itself for belief and if believed it is acted on unless some other belief outweighs it or some failure of energy stifles the movement at its birth. The only difference between the expression of an opinion and an incitement in the narrower sense is the speaker's enthusiasm for the result. Eloquence may set fire to reason. But whatever may be thought of the redundant discourse before us it had no chance of starting a present conflagration. If in the long run the beliefs expressed in proletarian dictatorship are destined to be accepted by the dominant forces of the community, the only meaning of free speech is that they should be given their chance and have their way.'' *Gitlow v. New York*, 268 U.S. 652 (1925).

GLOBE NEWSPAPER COMPANY v. SUPERIOR COURT (1982). The Superior Court of Massachusetts, relying on a statute (Massachusetts, Closed Courtroom*) providing for the exclusion of the general public from trials of specified sexual offenses involving a victim under the age of eighteen, ordered the exclusion of the press and the public from the trial of someone charged with the rape of three minor girls. The *Boston Globe* challenged this exclusion order, but the Massachusetts Supreme Judicial Court held that the statute was valid and that the press and public had to be excluded from such trials. On appeal, the U.S. Supreme Court reversed, holding that the statute violated the First Amendment. The Court noted that criminal trials have historically been open to the press and to the public, and absent a compelling state interest in a case-by-case basis, the sweeping mandatory exclusion denies the right of access. In addition, the Court commented that even though the statute's objective was to protect minor victims of sex crimes from further trauma, the press's full access to the transcript and court personnel means that the statute could not prevent the press from publicizing the substance of testimony or the victim's identity. *Globe Newspaper Company v. Superior Court*, 73 L. Ed. 2d 248 (1982).

GOD'S LITTLE ACRE. The book *God's Little Acre*, by Erskine Caldwell, was the target of two censorship attempts: one in New York in 1933 (*People v. Viking Press*, 264 N.Y.S. 534 [1933]), which failed, and a successful attempt in 1950 in Massachusetts (*Attorney General v. A Book Named God's Little Acre*, 93

N.E. 2d 819 [1950]). The book's plot was described by the court in the Massachusetts case: "We turn to the story itself. It has to do with the life of a poor white farmer and his family on a run down farm in Georgia. The father, Ty Ty Walden, is a pathetic figure with the mentality of a moron. Believing that there is gold on his land, he and two of his sons dig for it incessantly, leaving the raising of cotton to two colored share croppers. Ty Ty, who is pious, dedicates one acre of his land to God and intends to turn over the proceeds of that acre to the church. But he is so busy digging for gold that he never gets around to raising anything on it, and he relocates it from time to time to meet the exigencies of his digging. Ty Ty's sons, daughters, and daughter-in-law become involved in numerous sexual affairs. These lead to quarrels among the brothers, and as the story closes one brother kills another and departs with his shotgun, presumably to kill himself. Ty Ty, who had always tried to keep peace in the family, in despair resumes his digging for gold."

The New York prosecution was instituted by the New York Society for the Suppression of Vice (Comstockery*) through its secretary, John S. Sumner. Viking Press presented to the court several testimonials from eminent literary people as to the book's worth; Sumner dismissed these testimonials with the following comments: "We have seen this attempted before and the question arises as to whether a criminal prosecution is to be determined by interested parties having access to the newspapers and no interest in public welfare or by the Courts existing for that purpose and representing the whole people and not only the literati. These matters must be judged by normal people and not by the abnormal. Conditions would be deplorable if abnormal people were permitted to regulate such matters. Substitute the word 'literati' for 'abnormal people' and we have an exact explanation of the letters, reviews, and other favorable comments presented in behalf of this book and its author."

City Magistrate Greenspan, in dismissing the complaint: "This Court cannot subscribe to Mr. Sumner's opinion of the capacity for fair judgment of these leaders of American literary and educational thought. The court declines to believe that so large and representative a group of people would rally to the support of a book which they did not genuinely believe to be of importance and literary merit. The court is of the opinion, moreover, that this group of people, collectively, has a better capacity to judge the value of a literary production than one [obviously Sumner] who is more apt to search for obscene passages in a book than to regard the book as a whole. . . . In this book, I believe the author has chosen to write what he believes to be the truth about a certain group in American life. To my way of thinking, truth should always be accepted as a justification for literature."

There was another way of thinking, however, seventeen years later, in 1950, in a Massachusetts courtroom. The judge ruled that whatever literary merit the book may have paled in comparison with its tendency to deprave and corrupt its readers by inciting lascivious thoughts or arousing lustful desires, and *God's Little Acre* was seen to be "obscene, indecent, and impure" in Massachusetts.

GOLDWATER v. FEDERAL COMMUNICATIONS COMMISSION (1964). Certain regulations of the Federal Communications Commission (Federal Communications Commission Regulations, Equal Time*) require that a radio or television station that affords time to a candidate for political office must afford "equal time" to the opposing candidate(s). The regulation, however, does not apply to newscasts, news interviews, documentaries, or on-the-spot coverage of news events. Goldwater, the Republican presidential candidate in 1964 against the incumbent President Johnson, believed that the major networks were not affording him equal time on the grounds that their coverage of Johnson's activities didn't come within the exceptions of the equal-time regulations.

A federal district court ruled against Goldwater, and he then appealed to the Supreme Court. The Supreme Court, however, refused to hear the case. Justice Goldberg, joined by Justice Black, registered a dissent to the Court's denial of certiorari: "The statute on its face plainly requires that a licensee who permits any legally qualified candidate for any public office to use his broadcast facilities afford equal opportunities to all other qualified candidates. No exemption is made for a legally qualified candidate who is the incumbent President of the United States. . . . The importance of the question is, I believe, plainly apparent. The statute reflects a deep congressional conviction and policy that in our democratic society all qualified candidates should be given equally free access to broadcasting facilities, regardless of office or financial means, if any candidate is granted free time. This Court, in the recent past, has recognized the importance of making broadcasting facilities available to candidates for office without discrimination. . . . But, since the Court has denied the petition and the application for expedited argument, I am impelled to record this dissent." *Goldwater v. Federal Communications Commission*, 379 U.S. 893 (1964).

GOLDWATER v. GINZBURG (1969). During the 1964 presidential campaign, Ginzburg (the same Ginzburg who was convicted of mailing obscene material and pandering in *Ginzburg v. United States* [1966]*) published in the September–October 1964 issue of his *Fact* magazine an article titled "The Unconscious of a Conservative: A Special Issue on the Mind of Barry Goldwater." Goldwater then brought suit against Ginzburg, alleging that the article and the statements in it "were published and circulated by defendants with actual malice, or with reckless disregard of whether such statements were false or not, and with the deliberate, wilful and malicious purpose and intent to injure plaintiff and to deprive plaintiff of his good name and reputation as a person, a public official and a candidate for office and to bring plaintiff into disrepute and subject him to public scorn, contempt, obloquy and ridicule."

The federal district court ruled for Goldwater; the appeals court agreed; and the Supreme Court (*Ginzburg v. Goldwater*, 396 U.S. 1049 [1970], *cert. denied*) refused to hear the case, thus affirming Goldwater's complaint. The appeals court, mindful of the need for a wide open and robust debate on political issues and candidates, carefully reviewed the record, for Goldwater, as a public figure,* had to show the material was published with malice—knowledge that it was false or with a reckless disregard of whether it was false or not (the *New York Times* Rule*). The court found that Ginzburg did publish the material with reckless disregard (the article questioned Goldwater's sanity) and listed the following points: "(1) The covering letter with which the questionnaire was mailed to the psychiatrists. (2) Ginzburg had information about the 'nervous breakdowns' mentioned in the covering letter from one source only, and did not know whether or not that source had the information from personal knowledge. (3) In showing how the psychiatrists' letters were signed, 'name withheld' was used interchangeably with 'anonymous,' that is, replies which were unsigned were shown as 'name withheld' which might be found to suggest that they had been signed. (4) A letter from the Medical Director of the American Psychiatric Association warned of the invalidity of the *Fact* survey because responses were sought despite the fact that none of those asked to respond had made a 'thorough clinical examination.' Ginzburg read this letter before he published the magazine. The letter was not published with the questionnaire. (5) Ginzburg did not read in their entirety articles from which he took quotes to supply the basis for his own piece. Instead, he read only the parts underscored for him by others. Thus, at times, he would quote one part of an article without quoting another part which might tend to qualify or contradict the part quoted. He omitted contradictory material within the same sentence when quoting from that sentence. (6) There are some statements in Ginzburg's article for which he could not establish a basis on his deposition. (7) There is much to indicate alteration of responses from the psychiatrists. For example: a. a signed letter which was critical of the *Fact* survey was published as 'anonymous'; b. one published 'letter' was in fact a 'distillation' of the original, done by Ginzburg, without so indicating in the magazine; c. there were occasions when two responses were published as one reply; d. in one letter the words were changed and rewritten by Ginzburg; e. on two occasions qualifying paragraphs in a response were omitted when published; and f. Ginzburg testified as to one response that he 'didn't even consider' whether it was true or false, and that all he cared about was printing what the man said." This record convinced the court that Ginzburg employed malice—the reckless disregard of whether something was true or not—and Goldwater was successful in alleging defamation. *Goldwater v. Ginzburg*, 414 F. 2d 324 (1969).

GOODING v. WILSON (1972). Wilson was convicted in a Georgia court on two counts of using opprobrious words and abusive language in violation of a Georgia statute (Georgia, Abusive Language*). The indictment charged that Wilson, without provocation, said to police officers: "White son of a bitch, I'll kill you./You son of a bitch, I'll choke you to death/You son of a bitch, if you ever put your hands on me again, I'll cut you all to pieces." A federal district court found the statute unconstitutional; an appeals court agreed that the conviction should be reversed; and the Supreme Court affirmed the reversal. Citing *Chaplinsky v. New Hampshire*,* the Supreme Court ruled that the statute had to be narrowed by the Georgia courts to apply only to ''fighting words''* that ''by their very utterance . . . tend to incite an immediate breach of the peace.'' Wilson's comments may have been rude, but they were seen not to be fighting words. *Gooding v. Wilson*, 405 U.S. 518 (1972).

GORMLEY v. DIRECTOR, CONNECTICUT STATE DEPARTMENT OF PROBATION (1980). Gormley was convicted for violating a Connecticut telephone harassment statute (Telephone Regulations, State*) that prohibits anyone from making a telephone call in a manner likely to cause annoyance or alarm or with the intent to cause annoyance or alarm. It seems that Gormley had called the director and stated to him that his mother had gone to bed with Gormley's husband, that she had photographs to prove that the director's mother had been in bed with Gormley's husband, and that the director's entire family were a bunch of nuts and were all under psychiatric care. A federal appeals court affirmed Gormley's conviction, and the Supreme Court refused to hear her appeal (449 U.S. 1023 [1981], *cert. denied.*).

Justice White, however, filed a dissent to the denial of certiorari: ''Telephone calls by irate citizens to their Congressmen, by collectors seeking payment of legitimate bills overdue, by customers voicing to a seller dissatisfaction with goods or services purchased, and calls of like tenor, are likely to be annoying, even harassing, to the recipients. Such calls are usually made to influence the person called. No one could seriously question the caller's free speech right under the First Amendment to engage in such telephone conversations. Yet, by prohibiting telephone calls made 'with intent to annoy' and 'in a manner likely to cause annoyance,' the Connecticut statute could be construed as prohibiting the exercise of this free speech. . . . It is no comfort to the citizen telephoning his Congressman or to the defrauded consumer calling the swindler to know that the statute was not intended to apply to their telephone calls if its language plainly does so. The mere existence of a statute prohibiting such obviously lawful exercise of a free speech right has a chilling effect, particularly if enforcement is threatened by the recipient of a call.'' *Gormley v. Director, Connecticut State Department of Probation*, 632 F. 2d 938 (1980).

GRAYNED v. CITY OF ROCKFORD (1972). Grayned was convicted of violating the Rockford, Illinois, anti-picketing ordinance* as well as an anti-noise ordinance for picketing near a school building. The Supreme Court reversed the picketing conviction because the ordinance made an impermissible distinction between the types of picketing that were allowed near school buildings (*Police Department of Chicago v. Mosley* [1972]*) but upheld the anti-noise ordinance as a valid time-place-manner* restriction on expression and First Amendment rights. *Grayned v. City of Rockford*, 408 U.S. 104 (1972).

GREENBELT COOPERATIVE PUBLISHING ASSOCIATION v. BRESLER (1970). Bresler, a prominent real estate developer and Maryland state legislator, brought suit for libel when the Greenbelt Cooperative Publishing Association, in its newspaper, characterized his actions as "blackmail" in his attempts to secure a favorable zoning variance for certain land that he owned. The trial court found for Bresler, but the Supreme Court reversed, holding that the term "blackmail" was nothing more than a vigorous epithet and that it was not used to impute the crime of blackmail to Bresler: "It is simply impossible to believe that a reader who reached the word 'blackmail' in either article would not have understood exactly what was meant: it was Bresler's public and wholly legal negotiating proposals that were being criticized. No reader could have thought that either the speakers at the meetings or the newspaper articles reporting their words were charging Bresler with the commission of a criminal offense. On the contrary, even the most careless reader must have perceived that the word was no more than rhetorical hyperbole, a vigorous epithet used by those who considered Bresler's negotiating position extremely unreasonable. Indeed, the record is completely devoid of evidence that anyone in the city of Greenbelt or anywhere else thought Bresler had been charged with a crime. To permit the infliction of financial liability upon the petitioners for publishing these two news articles would subvert the most fundamental meaning of a free press, protected by the First and Fourteenth Amendments." *Greenbelt Cooperative Publishing Association v. Bresler*, 398 U.S. 6 (1970).

GREER v. SPOCK (1976). Fort Dix, a federal military reservation devoted primarily to basic training for newly inducted army personnel and over which the government exercises exclusive jurisdiction, permits free civilian access to certain unrestricted areas. However, post regulations (Military Regulations, Army*) ban speeches and demonstrations of a partisan political nature and prohibit the distribution of literature without prior approval of the base commander. Pursuant to these regulations, Greer, the commanding officer of Fort Dix, rejected the requests of Benjamin Spock and Julius Hobson (candidates for president and vice-president, respectively, of the People's party) and of Linda Jenness and Andrew Pulley (Socialist Workers party) to distribute campaign literature and hold a political meeting on the post. Other people were barred from reentering the post, for they had previously been evicted for distributing certain literature without prior approval.

Spock et al. claimed that these regulations violated their First Amendment rights, but the Supreme Court did not agree and ruled for the army. The regulations were not seen to be invalid on their face: "Since under the Constitution it is the basic function of a military installation like Fort Dix to train soldiers, not to provide a public forum, and since, as a necessary concomitant to this basic function, a commanding officer has the historically unquestioned power to exclude civilians from the area of his command, any notion that federal military installations, like municipal streets and parks, have traditionally served as a place for free public assembly and communication of thoughts by private citizens is false, and therefore respondents have no generalized constitutional right to make political speeches or distribute leaflets at Fort Dix.''

The Court also ruled that the regulations were not unconstitutionally applied to Spock and the others in this particular situation: ''As to the regulation banning political speeches and demonstrations, there is no claim that the military authorities discriminated in any way among candidates based upon the candidates' supposed political views; on the contrary it appears that Fort Dix has a policy, objectively and evenhandedly applied, of keeping official military activities there wholly free of entanglement with any partisan political campaigns, a policy that the post was constitutionally free to pursue. As to the regulation governing the distribution of literature, a military commander may disapprove only those publications that he clearly perceives endanger the loyalty, discipline, or morale of troops on the base under his command, and, while this regulation might in the future be applied irrationally, invidiously, or arbitrarily, none of the respondents even submitted any material for review, and the noncandidate respondents had been excluded from the post because they had previously distributed literature there without attempting to obtain approval.'' *Greer v. Spock*, 424 U.S. 828 (1976).

GRIFFIN (GA), DISTRIBUTION OF PAMPHLETS. A city ordinance of Griffin, Georgia, read as follows: ''Section 1. That the practice of distributing, either by hand or otherwise, circulars, handbooks, advertising, or literature of any kind, whether said articles are being delivered free, or whether same are being sold, within the limits of the City of Griffin, without first obtaining written permission from the City Manager of the City of Griffin, such practice shall be deemed a nuisance, and punishable as an offense against the City of Griffin. Section 2. The Chief of Police of the City of Griffin and the police force of the City of Griffin are hereby required and directed to suppress the same and to abate any nuisance as is described in the first section of this ordinance.'' The Supreme Court, in *Lovell v. City of Griffin* (1938),* held that this ordinance was an unconstitutional abridgment of the freedom of the press because there were no standards that limited the right of the city manager to refuse the required permission.

GRIMM v. UNITED STATES (1895). This was one of the first cases that reached the Supreme Court that ruled: (1) Mere possession of obscene materials does not constitute an offense (the *Stanley v. Georgia** decision thus had an early precedent). (2) An indictment need not describe precisely the nature of the obscene material (compare the *Illustrated Report** case). (3) It is not entrapment if someone mails obscene materials or information about how to get such material as a response to a request from a government agent or postal inspector. In 1891, Grimm was indicted for violating certain postal regulations (Postal Regulations, Mailing Obscene Material*), specifically for mailing ''obscene, lewd or lascivious'' materials or giving information on how to get such materials. He responded to a request from a postal inspector. The letter written by the postal inspector, mailed from Richmond, Indiana, on July 21, 1890, to St. Louis, and Grimm's reply, written on July 22, follow: "Dear Sir: A friend of mine has just showed me some fancy photographs and advised me that they could be obtained from you. I am on the road all the time, and I am sure many of them could be sold in the territory over which I travel. How many different kinds can you furnish? Send me price list showing your rates by the hundred and dozen. Address me at once . . . and I will send you a trial order. Herman Huntress." Grimm's reply: "Dear Sir: I received your letter this morning [the postal service appears to have been more efficient in 1890—one-day service from Richmond to St. Louis!]. I will let you have them for $2.00 per doz. & $12.50 per 100. I have about 200 negatives of actresses."

Grimm was duly convicted for mailing this letter, and the courts, affirmed by the Supreme Court, determined that "fancy photographs" were the equivalent of obscene photographs. The opinion of the Supreme Court contained the following comments: "A letter, however innocent on its face, intended to convey information in respect of the place or person where or of whom the objectionable matters described in the act could be obtained, is within the statute. . . . When a government detective, suspecting that a person is engaged in a business offensive to good morals, seeks information under an assumed name, directly from him, and that person responding thereto, violates a law of the United States by using the mails to convey such information, he cannot, when indicted for that offence, set up that he would not have violated the law, if the inquiry had not been made of him by the government official." *Grimm v. United States*, 156 U.S. 604 (1895).

GRISWOLD v. CONNECTICUT (1965). A Connecticut statute (Connecticut, Anti-Contraceptive Statute*) made it a crime for any person to use any drug or article designed to prevent conception. Griswold, executive director of the Planned Parenthood League of Connecticut, and the league's medical director, a physician, were convicted as accessories for giving a married couple information on how to prevent conception and for prescribing a contraceptive device for the wife. The conviction was upheld by Connecticut's highest court, but on appeal, the U.S. Supreme Court ruled that the statute invaded the rights guaranteed by the First Amendment. Justice Douglas delivered the opinion of the Court, but the dissents filed by Justices Black and Stewart make for more cogent reading. Justice Black: "These defendants admittedly engaged with others in a planned course of conduct to help people violate the Connecticut law. Merely because some speech was used in carrying on that conduct—just as in ordinary life some speech accompanies most kinds of conduct—we are not in my view justified in holding that the First Amendment forbids the State to punish their conduct. Strongly as I desire to protect all First Amendment freedoms, I am unable to stretch the Amendment so as to afford protection to the conduct of these defendants in violating the Connecticut law. What would be the constitutional fate of the law if hereafter applied to punish nothing but speech is, as I have said, quite another matter.''

Justice Stewart: ''Since 1879 Connecticut has had on its books a law which forbids the use of contraceptives by anyone. I think this is an uncommonly silly law. As a practical matter, the law is obviously unenforceable, except in the oblique context of the present case. As a philosophical matter, I believe the use of contraceptives in the relationship of marriage should be left to personal and private choice, based upon each individual's moral, ethical, and religious beliefs. As a matter of social policy, I think professional counsel about methods of birth control should be available to all, so that each individual's choice can be meaningfully made. But we are not asked in this case to say whether we think this law is unwise, or even asinine. We are asked to hold that it violates the United States Constitution. And that I cannot do.'' *Griswold v. Connecticut*, 381 U.S. 479 (1965).

GROSSJEAN v. AMERICAN PRESS (1936). The state of Louisiana passed an act (Louisiana, Newspaper Tax*) that provided for higher taxes on newspapers that had higher circulation. A publishers' association brought suit to enjoin the applicability of the act, arguing that, among other things, it was an unconstitutional violation of the freedom of the press. The U.S. Supreme Court agreed and affirmed a lower court decision that permanently enjoined enforcement of the act. Justice Sutherland: ''It is not intended by anything we have said to suggest that the owners of newspapers are immune from any of the ordinary forms of taxation for support of the government. But this is not an ordinary form of tax, but one single in kind, with a long history of hostile misuse against the freedom of the press. The predominant purpose of the grant of immunity here invoked was to preserve an untrammeled press as a vital source of public information. The newspapers, magazines and other journals of the country, it is safe to say, have shed and continue to shed, more light on the public and business affairs of the nation than any other instrumentality of publicity; and since informed public opinion is the most potent of all restraints upon misgovernment, the suppression or abridgment of the publicity afforded by a free press cannot be regarded otherwise than with grave concern. The tax here involved is bad not because it takes money from the pockets of the appellees. If that were all, a wholly different question would be presented. It is bad because, in the light of its history and of its present setting, it is seen to be a deliberate and calculated device in the guise of a tax to limit the circulation of information to which the public is entitled in virtue of the constitutional guarantees. A free press stands as one of the great interpreters between the government and the people. To allow it to be fettered is to fetter ourselves. In view of the persistent search for new subjects of taxation, it is not without significance that, with the single exception of the Louisiana statute, so far as we can discover, no state during the one hundred fifty years of our national existence has undertaken to impose a tax like that now in question. The form in which the tax is imposed is in itself suspicious.

It is not measured or limited by the volume of advertisements. It is measured alone by the extent of the circulation of the publication in which the advertisements are carried, with the plain purpose of penalizing the publishers and curtailing the circulation of a selected group of newspapers.'' *Grossjean v. American Press*, 297 U.S. 233 (1936).

H

HAGUE v. CIO (1939). Jersey City, New Jersey, passed a municipal ordinance (Jersey City [NJ], Parade Permits*) that prohibited the distribution of printed matter and the holding without permits of public meetings in streets and other public places. The Congress of Industrial Organizations (CIO) brought suit to enjoin the city from enforcing the ordinances in relation to the CIO's union recruitment activities. The Supreme Court affirmed a lower court's granting of such injunction. The ordinance forbidding public assemblies in the streets or parks without a permit from the director of safety was void on its face because there were no standards employed to reject an application for a permit except the director's opinion that the assembly might lead to a riot or to a disturbance. The ordinance prohibiting the distribution of literature was seen to violate the First Amendment guarantees of the CIO and its agents. *Hague v. CIO*, 307 U.S. 496 (1939).

HAIG v. PHILIP AGEE (1981). Agee, an American citizen and a former employee of the Central Intelligence Agency (CIA), embarked on a campaign "to expose C.I.A. officers and agents and to take the measures necessary to drive them out of the countries where they are operating." He then engaged in certain activities outside the United States that resulted in the identification of alleged undercover CIA agents and intelligence sources located in foreign countries. Because of these activities, Secretary of State Haig revoked Agee's passport, explaining that the revocation was based on a regulation (Passport Act*) that authorized such a revocation when the secretary of state determines that an American citizen's activities abroad "are causing or are likely to cause serious damage to the national security or the foreign policy of the United States."

Agee then filed suit, alleging, among other things, that the passport revocation violated his First Amendment right to criticize government policies. The Supreme Court did not accept Agee's view that the passport revocation was punishment for his speech, but saw it as punishment for his actions. The Court made the following comments: (1) The protection accorded beliefs standing alone is different from the protection accorded conduct. Here, beliefs and speech are only part of Agee's campaign, which presents a serious danger to U.S. officials abroad and to the national security. (2) The revocation of Agee's passport rests in part on the content of his speech: repeated disclosures of intelligence operations and names of intelligence personnel are not protected by the Constitution. (3) To the extent that the revocation of his passport operates to inhibit Agee, it is an inhibition of action, rather than of speech. Restricting Agee's foreign travel, although perhaps not certain to prevent all of Agee's harmful activities, is the only avenue open to the government to limit these activities. Agee is as free to criticize the U.S. government as he was when he held a passport.

Agee would have suffered a great deal more than just a passport revocation if he had engaged in his campaign after the Intelligence Identities Protection Act* was signed into law by President Reagan, in 1982. This act makes it a crime to do what the Court said Agee was still free to do—criticize the government by disclosing the identity of any intelligence operative. *Haig v. Philip Agee*, 453 U.S. 280 (1981).

HAIR. The issue in this case was whether the First Amendment right of free speech was violated when the members of a Chattanooga, Tennessee, municipal board charged with managing a city auditorium refused to issue an exhibition permit for the musical *Hair*. The permit was first denied on grounds that the production would not be "in the best interest of the community" and then on grounds that *Hair* contained obscenity and certain conduct not protected by the First Amendment and thus not entitled to the use of a municipal facility.

The Supreme Court ruled that since certain safeguards were lacking in this prior restraint scheme, the board members' action violated the First Amendment: (1) Denial of use of the municipal facilities for the production was based on the board members' judgment of the musical's content and, as such, constituted a prior restraint. (2) A system of prior restraint "avoids constitutional infirmity only if it takes place under procedural safeguards designed to obviate the dangers of a censorship system: (a) the burden of instituting judicial proceedings, and of proving that the material is unprotected, must rest on the censor; (b) any restraint before judicial review can be imposed only for a specified brief period and only to preserve the status quo; and (c) a prompt judicial determination must be assured."

The Supreme Court's decision did not really inquire into *Hair*'s alleged obscenity; the case was decided on the grounds above. But Justice White filed a stinging dissent, writing that *Hair* was not suitable fare for anyone: "The Court asserts that 'Hair' contains a nude scene and that this is 'the most controversial portion' of the musical. This almost completely ignores the District Court's description of the play as involving not only nudity but repeated 'simulated acts of anal intercourse, frontal intercourse, heterosexual intercourse, homosexual intercourse, and group intercourse.' Given this description of 'Hair,' the First Amendment in my view does not compel municipal authorities to permit production of the play in municipal facilities. Whether or not a production as described by the District Court is obscene and may be forbidden to adult audiences, it is apparent to me that the State of Tennessee could constitutionally forbid exhibition of the musical to children, and that Chattanooga may reserve its auditorium for productions suitable for exhibition to all the citizens of the city, adults and children alike. 'Hair' does not qualify in this respect and . . . it is improvident for the Court to mandate the showing of 'Hair' in the Chattanooga auditorium.''

Justice White then appended to his dissent the district court's description (341 F. Supp. 465, 472–474 [ED Tenn. 1972]) of *Hair*. Excerpts from that description follow: ''The performance then begins to the words and music of the song 'Aquarius,' the melody of which, if not the words, have become nationally, if not internationally, popular, according to the evidence. The theme of the song is the coming of a new age, the age of love, the age of 'Aquarius.' A male character then sings the lyric: SODOMY, FELLATIO, CUNNILINGUS, PEDERASTY—FATHER, WHY DO THESE WORDS SOUND SO NASTY? MASTURBATION CAN BE FUN. JOIN THE HOLY ORGY, KAMA SUTRA, EVERYONE. The first act ends when all performers, male and female, appear nude upon the stage, the nude scene being held without dialogue and without reference to dialogue. Actors simulating police then appear in the audience and announce that they are under arrest for watching this 'lewd, obscene show.' [There are] impersonations of various figures from American history: Lincoln is regaled with the following lyrics: 'I's free now thanks to you, Massa Lincoln, emancipator of the slave, yeah, yeah, yeah! Emanci-mother fucking-pator of the slave, yeah, yeah, yeah!' With Lincoln responding, 'Bang my ass . . . I ain't dying for no white man!' Interspersed throughout the play is such street language as ass, shit, and repeated use of the word fuck. The character Burger performs a full and complete simulation of masturbation while using a red microphone placed in his crotch to simulate his genitals. Repeated acts of taking hold of other actors' genitals occur. While three female actresses sing a song regarding interracial love, three male actors lie on the floor immediately below them repeatedly thrusting their genitals at the singers. The actor Claude pretends to have lost his penis. The action accompanying this line is to search for it in the mouths of other actors and actresses.'' *Southeastern Promotions, Ltd. v. Conrad*, 420 U.S. 546 (1975).

HALTER v. NEBRASKA (1907). This case concerned the constitutionality of a Nebraska statute (Nebraska, Flag Desecration*) that prohibited the desecration of the U.S. flag; among other things, the statute prohibited using the flag in any advertisements. Halter was convicted of selling a bottle of beer on whose label was printed a representation of the U.S. flag.

The Supreme Court, with Justice Harlan delivering the opinion, affirmed the fifty-dollar fine: ''It would seem difficult to hold that the statute infringes any right protected by the Constitution of the United States or that it relates to a subject exclusively committed to the National Government. From the earliest periods in the history of the human race, banners, standards and ensigns have been adopted as symbols of the power and history of the peoples who bore them. It is not then remarkable that the American people, early in their history, prescribed a flag as symbolical of the existence and sovereignty of the Nation. Indeed, it would have been extraordinary if the Government had started this country upon its marvelous career without giving it a flag to be recognized as the emblem of the American Republic. For that flag every true American has not simply an appreciation but a deep affection. No American, nor any foreign born person who enjoys the privileges of American citizenship, ever looks upon it without taking pride in the fact that he lives under this free Government. Hence, it has often occurred that insults to a flag have been the cause of war, and indignities put upon it, in the presence of those who revere it, have often been resented and sometimes punished on the spot. . . . By the statute in question the State has in substance declared that no one . . . shall use the flag for purposes of trade and traffic, a purpose wholly foreign to that for which it was provided by the Nation. Such a use tends to degrade and cheapen the flag in the estimation of the people, as well as to defeat the object of maintaining it as an emblem of National power and National honor. And we cannot hold that any privilege of American citizenship or that any right of personal liberty is violated by a state enactment forbidding the flag to be used as an advertisement on a bottle of beer.'' *Halter v. Nebraska*, 205 U.S. 34 (1907).

HAMMOND v. SOUTH CAROLINA STATE COLLEGE (1967). Hammond, a student at South Carolina State College, was suspended for violating a college rule that prohibited ''parades, celebrations, and demonstrations'' without the prior approval of the college authorities. The suspension came shortly after Hammond received the following letter from the college president: ''You are directed to meet the Faculty Discipline Committee in my office . . . to answer charges that you were in violation of College regulations, specifically #1, under 4, page 49 of the Student Handbook which reads . . . The student body or any part of the student body is not to celebrate, parade, or demonstrate on the campus at any time without the approval of the Office of the President. The Board of Trustees meeting in March of 1960 went on record as disapproving of demonstrations which involve violation of laws or of College regulations, or which disrupt the normal College routine.''

Hammond appealed his suspension to the federal district court, and the court ruled that the regulation was a prior restraint on the right to freedom of speech and freedom of assembly and, as such, was incompatible with the First Amendment and therefore invalid, and that any alleged violation of the regulation could not be employed as a reason to suspend any student. The court's decision, although reinstating Hammond, apparently didn't think much of university students, comparing them to malingerers, fanatics, and rabble-rousers: ''The controversy here revolves around the school rules of deportment and discipline. Their obvious purpose is to protect the authority and administrative responsibility which is imposed on the officers of the institution. Unless the officials have authority to keep order, they have no power to guarantee education. If they cannot preserve order by rule and regulation, and insist on obedience to those rules, they will be helpless in the face of the mob, powerless to command or rebuke the fanatic, the irritant, the malingerer, the rabble rouser. To be sure, this is a tax supported institution, but this does not give license to chaos, or the hope to create chaos. The majority of the taxpayers who established, through representative government, the institution, and all the taxpayers who support this institution, have a vested interest in a peaceful campus, an academic climate of order and culture. The power of the president to oversee, to rule, is an integral part of the mechanism for providing and promoting education at State College. Be that as it may, colleges, like all other institutions, are subject to the Constitution. Academic progress and academic freedom demand their share of Constitutional protection.'' *Hammond v. South Carolina State College*, 272 F. Supp. 947 (1967).

HANDS AROUND. *Hands Around* is the English translation of Schnitzler's classic *Reigen* (*The Ring*). The book is a series of vignettes describing the sexual liaisons of several people: The first is between a prostitute and a soldier, then the soldier and a parlor maid, the parlor maid and a young man, the young man and someone else's wife, the wife and her husband, the husband and a young girl, the girl and a poet, the poet and an actress, the actress and a count, and the last, the count back with the original prostitute.

In 1930, the state of New York (*People v. Pesky*, 243 N.Y.S. 193 [1930]) brought suit, alleging that the book was obscene and thus a violation of § 1141 of the Penal Law (New York, Obscenity Statute*). The judge was appalled by the book and held it to be disgusting, indecent, and obscene: ''There was nothing to it except a description of the licentious. There was no attempt to point to any lesson that might be of value to any one that would read it. It was just a clear attempt to portray filthy ideas, for the book is without a single redeeming feature. As usual it is prefaced by the remark that it will not be appreciated by the Puritan fanatic with his jaundiced inhibitions or the moral ideologist with his heart of leather. This is the usual cry of the libertine who is attempting to justify his own life or writings. Any one who differs with his method of living or writing is Puritanical. With such people clean thinking or clean living is Puritanical. . . . While we appreciate the fact that different people have different standards with reference to such writings and that these standards are often peculiar and difficult to understand, nevertheless people generally and the courts have arrived at what they consider a fair standard by which to judge such books and protect those who need protection. . . . It is very clear that the author of the book now before us for consideration was not thinking of the spiritual, but devoted the whole book to the animal instincts of the human race. His efforts were not an effort in morality, nor an attempt to uplift the mind of the reader, but an attempt to depict, in a manner that might possibly be called clever, adulterous relations, vulgar and disgusting in the extreme. While some people may think this quite smart, a book of this kind, which has nothing to recommend it, and dealing wholly with such details, is properly held to be disgusting, indecent, and obscene.'' The film version of Schnitzler's book, released as *La Ronde*,* also ran into censorship difficulties.

HARISIADES v. SHAUGHNESSY (1952). The Immigration and Nationality Act* authorizes the deportation of a resident alien if the alien ever belonged to the Communist party, even though such membership was terminated before the act was passed. Harisiades was facing deportation under the provisions of the act, and he appealed to the Supreme Court on the grounds that it abridged his freedom of speech in violation of the First Amendment.

The Court did not interpret it that way and affirmed the deportation order. Justice Jackson delivered the opinion of the Court: ''The First Amendment is invoked as a barrier against this enactment. The claim is that in joining an organization advocating overthrow of government by force and violence the alien has merely exercised freedoms of speech, press and assembly which that Amendment guarantees to him. The assumption is that the First Amendment allows Congress to make no distinction between advocating change in the existing order by lawful elective processes and advocating change by force and violence, that freedom for the one includes freedom for the other, and that when teaching of violence is denied so is freedom of speech. Our Constitution sought to leave no excuse for violent attack on the status quo by providing a legal alternative—attack by ballot. To arm all men for orderly change, the Constitution put in their hands a right to influence the electorate by press, speech and assembly. This means freedom to advocate or promote Communism by means of the ballot box, but it does not include the practice or incitement of violence. True, it is often difficult to determine whether ambiguous speech is advocacy of political methods or subtly shades into a methodical but prudent incitement to violence. Communist governments avoid the inquiry by suppressing everything distasteful. Some would have us avoid the difficulty by going to the opposite extreme of permitting incitement to violent overthrow at least unless it seems certain to succeed immediately. We apprehend that the Constitution enjoins upon us the duty, however difficult, of distinguishing between the two. Different formulas have been applied in different situations and the test applicable to the Communist Party has been stated. We think the First Amendment does not prevent the deportation of these aliens.'' *Harisiades v. Shaughnessy*, 342 U.S. 580 (1952).

HARTZEL v. UNITED STATES (1944). Hartzel was a U.S. citizen who served in the armed forces during World War I. He was an economic analyst, and there was no evidence that he was involved in any manner with any foreign or subversive organization. But before the United States entered World War II and during it, Hartzel wrote and circulated several pamphlets that brought him to the attention of the U.S. government. The pamphlets contained scurrilous and vitriolic attacks on the English, the Jews, and President Roosevelt and called for the United States to abandon its allies. Some excerpts follow: From "The British: An Inferior Breed"—"Standing as an outpost to the continent of Europe, they are a parasite on its art, science and civilization. They run at the mouth as well as the bowels." From "The Jew Makes a Sacrifice: The Forthcoming Collapse of America"—"The Jew—oriental hyphenated American, propagand-ist for bloody Joe and the British (Jewish) empire . . . like a snake forced from its nest, the slimy blood lust . . . " From "The Diseased Spinal Cord" (an attack on President Roosevelt, whom Hartzel called "Rosenfeldt")—"Our leader—safe in Washington—escaped the actual horrors of war, but he could not escape the virus of a child's disease. As with syphilis his paralysis is indicative of severe maladjustments within the nation. He reproduces within his body our internal breakdown; he is in fact a degenerate." Hartzel was then indicted and convicted of violating the Espionage Act* of 1917 for attempting to cause insubordination, disloyalty, mutiny, and refusal of duty in the armed forces of the United States.

But on appeal, the Supreme Court reversed the conviction, holding that there was insufficient evidence to convict Hartzel. Justice Murphy delivered the opin-ion of the Court: "There is nothing on the face of the three pamphlets in question to indicate that petitioner intended specifically to cause insubordination, disloy-alty, mutiny or refusal of duty in the military forces or to obstruct the recruiting and enlistment service. No direct or affirmative appeals are made to that effect and no mention is made of military personnel or of persons registered under the Selective Training and Service Act. They contain, instead, vicious and unrea-soning attacks on one of our military allies, flagrant appeals to false and sinister racial theories and gross libels of the President. Few ideas are more odious to the majority of the American people or more destructive of national unity in time of war. But while such iniquitous doctrines may be used under certain circumstances as vehicles for the purposeful undermining of the morale and loyalty of the armed forces and those persons of draft age, they cannot by themselves be taken as proof beyond a reasonable doubt that petitioner had the narrow intent requisite to a violation of this statute." *Hartzel v. United States*, 322 U.S. 680 (1944).

HATCH ACT. The Hatch Act (Title 5 U.S.C. § 7324ff.) delineates the per-missible political activities for federal employees (civil servants; political ap-pointees are not covered by the act). The restrictions were originally seen as a protection for the employee from undue pressure and intimidation from one's supervisor, but lately, several people have seen the act as violating the First Amendment rights of federal employees. The Supreme Court, however, has consistently (but not unanimously; Justice Douglas registered strong dissents) upheld the constitutionality of the restrictions (*Civil Service Commission v. Letter Carriers* [1973]* and *Oklahoma v. United States Civil Service Commission* (1947]*). The general prohibition on federal employees is that they may not take an active part in partisan political activities, except to vote in the election. A federal employee may not be a candidate for nomination or election to a national or state office; become a partisan candidate for nomination or election to public office; campaign for or against a political party or candidate in a partisan election for public office or political party office; serve as an officer of a political party, or as a member of a national, state, or local committee of a political party, or as an officer or member of a committee of a partisan political club, or be a candidate for any of these positions; solicit, receive, collect, handle, disburse, or account for assessments, contributions, or other funds for a partisan political purpose or in connection with a partisan election; sell tickets for or otherwise actively promote such activities as political dinners; take an active part in managing the political campaign of a candidate in a partisan election for public office or political party office; work at the polls on behalf of a partisan candidate or political party by acting as a checker, challenger, or watcher, or in a similar partisan position; distribute campaign material; address a convention, rally, caucus, or similar gathering of a political party in support of or in opposition to a candidate for public office or political party office, or on a partisan political question; endorse or oppose a candidate in a partisan election through a political advertisement, broadcast, campaign literature, or similar material; and finally, a federal employee may not use his or her automobile to drive voters to the polls on behalf of a political party or candidate in a partisan election. Individual states have similar restrictions (state "Hatch Acts") on state employees.

HAVE FIGURE—WILL TRAVEL. In 1964, Fanfare Films was ordered by the Maryland State Board of Censors of Motion Pictures (Maryland, Motion Picture Censorship*) to delete from the film *Have Figure—Will Travel* certain scenes showing girls unclothed while cruising on a boat. The Baltimore City Court affirmed the board's order, and Fanfare Films appealed to a higher Maryland court. The court provided the following description of the film: "*Have Figure—Will Travel* is in form a travelogue portraying the story of three girls, two of whom are confirmed nudists, who take a vacation cruise through the inland waterways from upper New York to Florida on a cabin cruiser belonging to the father of one of the girls. Scenes are shown during stops at New York City and Charleston and at nudist camps in New Jersey and Florida. The third girl becomes a convert to nudism as the trip—and the film—progresses. The Board passed the scenes in the nudist camps, in which there were both unclothed men and women, but it disapproved the scenes of the girls on the boat, unclothed above the waist."

The appeals court reviewed the film and reversed the lower court's ruling; the questioned scenes were not obscene and Fanfare Films had a First Amendment right to exhibit the film uncut. The court's decision contained the board's reasoning for ordering the cut, and the following comments illustrate the absurdity of the Maryland censors: "It is conceded that no sexual activity or awareness was presented and that while on the boat the girls were seen unclothed only by each other. The Chairman of the Board said that the photography was very good, the dialogue was unobjectionable, and the picture had artistic value. The Board took the position that if the picture contained only scenes of nudity within the nudist camps it would have been licensed without deletions, but that while nudity in the camps was not obscene, it was on the boat because in that locale it was not a normal way of life, normal people would not so comport themselves and there was no reason for its portrayal except to arouse sexual desires in the viewers.'' The court ruled that naked people as such were not obscene and reversed the order of the Board. *Fanfare Films, Inc. v. Motion Picture Censor Board of State of Maryland*, 197 A. 2d 839 (1964).

HEALY v. JAMES (1972). James, president of Central Connecticut State College, denied giving the college's stamp of approval for a local chapter of Students for a Democratic Society (SDS) as an officially recognized campus organization. A federal district court and an appeals court affirmed James' refusal. The appeals court (445 F. 2d 1122 [1971] ruled that "where plaintiffs at an administrative hearing on an application requesting official campus recognition of a local chapter of the national SDS organization, which had engaged in campus violence and disruption, failed to submit a copy of their charter or bylaws, failed candidly to clarify the conflict between the name of their chapter and a disclaimer of being under the dictates of the national organization, failed candidly to respond to inquiries whether they would resort to violence . . . students had no constitutional or other right to official college approval of the organization." The court added: "Plaintiffs as individuals have not been denied their rights, on or off campus, to speak, to assemble, to petition or to demonstrate. Nor have they been prevented from organizing off campus any group, club, chapter or other collective activity."

The Supreme Court, however, did not see it the same way. The Court reversed the decision, saying that the burden of proof was on the college to justify its nonrecognition of the group rather than on the SDS to prove its entitlement to recognition, and further, the SDS's First Amendment rights were violated when the college assumed the special relationship between the local chapter and the national organization. *Healy v. James*, 408 U.S. 169 (1972).

HEFFRON v. INTERNATIONAL SOCIETY FOR KRISHNA CONSCIOUSNESS (1981). A Minnesota Agricultural Society state fair rule* required any person, group, or firm who wanted to sell, exhibit, or distribute printed or written material within the state fair's grounds to do so only from an assigned, fixed location. The International Society for Krishna Consciousness (ISKCON) then asserted that the rule violated the First Amendment by suppressing the practice of Sankirtan, a religious ritual that requires the society's members to go into public places to distribute and sell religious literature and to solicit donations in support of the Krishna religion. A state trial court upheld the constitutionality of the rule, but the Supreme Court of Minnesota reversed, holding that ISKCON's right to free speech was violated by the rule. On appeal, the U.S. Supreme Court reversed the Minnesota ruling and held that the rule did not violate the First Amendment.

The Court was not unanimous on the various questions. Justice White delivered the majority opinion: (1) The rule allocated space to exhibitors on a straightforward, nondiscriminatory first come, first served basis. (2) The rule served the significant governmental interest of maintaining the orderly movement of the crowd given the large number of exhibitors and people attending the fair. (3) ISKCON was not prevented from conducting any activity outside the fairgrounds; it was not prevented from mingling with the crowd to present its views orally and was not denied a fixed location to distribute literature and solicit funds. The Court saw this case as a valid time-place-manner* restriction on First Amendment guarantees. Justices Brennan, Marshall, Stevens, and Blackmun concurred in the view that the rule was constitutional as applied to the sale of literature and the solicitation of funds but dissented regarding distribution of literature; these four thought that the rule restricting the location of distributing literature unduly restrained the First Amendment rights of the society. *Heffron v. International Society for Krishna Consciousness*, 452 U.S. 640 (1981).

HELLENIC SUN. Title 19 U.S.C. § 1305 (Tariff Act* of 1930), prohibits the importation into the United States of any obscene matter and permits U.S. Customs to seize what they consider to be obscene. The government then must appeal to a federal district court for a judicial ruling on the material's obscenity. If the court so rules, the material is destroyed. This case concerned the magazine *Hellenic Sun*, a magazine that both a district court and an appeals court ruled was patently offensive, without redeeming social value, appealed exclusively to a clearly defined deviant group (male homosexuals), and was thus clearly obscene under the statute. The court records contained a description of the magazine: "The magazine . . . is a collection of photographs of undressed men. Some are in color. There is one of a group of boys. They are posed in the out-of-doors, but the generally languid models are not engaged in outdoor activity. In the composition of the photographs, the genitals of the models are made the focal points of the pictures. The camera's interest is languished upon the penis, and, if the general pose of each model be languid, the penis in some of the pictures appears not in complete repose. The pictures have no apparent artistic value. They have no semblance of the qualities of Michelangelo's David. Raw in the extreme, and with no redeeming attribute, the normal male, if Dr. Kinsey will permit us to retain a belief there is such a thing, can view them only with revulsion. The late Dr. Manfred A. Guttmacher, the well-known psychiatrist of Baltimore, was a witness for the government. He testified that the pictures would have a prurient appeal for a large proportion of male homosexuals, particularly juvenile males with homosexual tendencies. The one picture of the boys would have a prurient appeal for paedophiles. Adolescent girls would find them frightening as well as shocking, but with some exceptions, mature women would find little stimulation in such material. . . . The copies . . . cost the importer about 24 cents apiece and are sold for $5.00. It is impossible to believe that anyone would pay more than a few cents for the text, let alone $5.00." *United States v. Magazine Entitled "Hellenic Sun,"* 373 F. 2d 635 (1967).

HERNDON v. LOWRY, SHERIFF (1937). A Georgia statute (Georgia, Insurrection*) prohibited any attempt to incite insurrection or to induce others to join in any attempt to resist the authority of the state. Herndon was convicted in the Georgia courts for violating this statute when he solicited members for a political party that the state viewed as believing in the violent overthrow of the government. The Georgia Supreme Court commented: "Force must have been contemplated but . . . the statute does not include either its occurrence or its imminence as an ingredient of the particular offense charged. Nor would it be necessary to guilt that the alleged offender should have intended that an insurrection should follow instantly or at any given time, but it would be sufficient that he intended it to happen at any time, as a result of his influence, by those whom he sought to incite."

On appeal, the U.S. Supreme Court reversed the conviction on the grounds that the statute violated Herndon's right of free speech: "The power of a state to abridge freedom of speech and of assembly is the exception rather than the rule and the penalizing even of utterances of a defined character must find its justification in a reasonable apprehension of danger to organized government. The judgment of the legislature is not unfettered. The limitation upon individual liberty must have appropriate relation to the safety of the state. Legislation which goes beyond this need violates the principle of the Constitution. If, therefore, a state statute penalizes innocent participation in a meeting held with an innocent purpose merely because the meeting was held under the auspices of an organization membership in which, or the advocacy of whose principles, is also denounced as criminal, the law, so construed and applied, goes beyond the power to restrict abuses of freedom of speech and arbitrarily denies that freedom." *Herndon v. Lowry, Sheriff*, 301 U.S. 242 (1937).

HESS v. INDIANA (1973). Hess was arrested during an anti-war demonstration on a college campus for violating the Indiana disorderly conduct* statute. He was convicted for the court found that his statements during the demonstration were "intended to incite further lawless action on the part of the crowd in the vicinity and [were] likely to produce such action."

The Supreme Court reversed the conviction, saying that Hess' statements did not fall into any of the categories that could be punished and that there was no evidence that imminent disorder was likely to take place. The Court's opinion: "The sheriff heard Hess utter the word 'fuck' in what he later described as a loud voice and immediately arrested him on the disorderly conduct charge. It was later stipulated that what appellant had said was 'We'll take the fucking street later,' or 'We'll take the fucking street again.' Two witnesses . . . indicated that Hess did not appear to be exhorting the crowd to go back into the street, that he was facing the crowd and not the street when he uttered the statement, that his statement did not appear to be addressed to any particular person or group, and that his tone, although loud, was no louder than that of the other people in the area. Indiana's disorderly conduct statute was applied in this case to punish only spoken words. It hardly needs repeating that the constitutional guarantees of freedom of speech forbid the States to punish the use of words or language not within 'narrowly limited classes of speech.' The words here did not fall within any of these 'limited classes.' In the first place, it is clear that the Indiana court specifically abjured any suggestion that Hess' words could be punished as obscene under *Roth v. United States.** Indeed, after *Cohen v. California,** such a contention with regard to the language at issue would not be tenable. By the same token, any suggestion that Hess' speech amounted to 'fighting words'* (*Chaplinsky v. New Hampshire**) could not withstand scrutiny. Even if under other circumstances this language could be regarded as a personal insult, the evidence is undisputed that Hess' statement was not directed to any person or group in particular. Although the sheriff testified that he was offended by the language, he also stated that he did not interpret the expression as being directed personally at him.'' *Hess v. Indiana*, 414 U.S. 105 (1973).

HICKLIN RULE. The Hicklin Rule—a test of obscenity—was announced in 1868 in Great Britain by Lord Chief Justice Cockburn. In dealing with a pamphlet entitled *The Confessional Unmasked*, Cockburn announced, in *Regina v. Hicklin* (L.R. 3 Q.B. 360 [1868]): ''The test of obscenity is this, whether the tendency of the matter charged as obscenity is to deprave and corrupt those whose minds are open to such immoral influences and into whose hands a publication of this sort may fall.'' This guide became the standard for all obscenity cases in Great Britain and in the United States. The Hicklin Rule basically declared a publication to be obscene if isolated passages—not the work taken as a whole—could corrupt the most susceptible person.

The Hicklin Rule was applied in the United States until 1934, when, in *United States v. One Book Entitled Ulysses* (72 F. 2d 705 [1934]) (*Ulysses**), Judge Woolsey ruled that obscenity is to be determined by the effect of a book read in its entirety on a person with average sex instincts. Woolsey's general standard (Ulysses Standard*) has since been refined by the Roth*/Memoirs*/Miller* standards, and few people have mourned the passing of the Hicklin Rule. One of the most trenchant comments on the rule was given by Judge Curtis Bok: ''Strictly applied, this rule renders any book unsafe, since a moron could pervert to some sexual fantasy to which his mind is open the listings of a seed catalogue.'' See Robert W. Haney, *Comstockery in America* (1960).

HIGHWAY BEAUTIFICATION ACT. The federal Highway Beautification Act of 1965, Public Law 89-285, 79 Stat. 1028, as amended, 23 U.S.C. § 131, requires that states eliminate billboards from areas adjacent to certain highways constructed with federal funds. The federal government also prohibits billboards on federal lands. Three states have enacted statewide bans on billboards: Maine, Vermont, and Hawaii. The Maine statute (Maine, Traveler Information Services Act*) was seen to be a violation of the First Amendment guarantees of free

speech and press in *John Donnelly & Sons v. Campbell* (1980).* The city of
San Diego attempted to restrict billboards, but this, too, was seen to be a violation
of the First Amendment (*Metromedia v. City of San Diego* [1981]*).

HOLLYWOOD PEEP SHOW. John Scope, a theater owner, was convicted in
a Delaware court in 1951 for violating the Delaware obscenity statute.* He
exhibited what was described as a "lewd, obscene, and indecent" film to an
audience that, for the most part, were teenagers. The film was *Hollywood Peep
Show*, described by the court as "no more than a complete movie of a low grade
burlesque. The so-called dances were accompanied by highly suggestive motions
of the body known as 'bumps' and 'grinds.' All the dancers were in a semi-
nude state and some of the dances, being strip-tease acts, ended with the female
performer in a completely naked condition except for the proverbial fig leaf.
Interwoven into this dreary scene was the usual low and suggestive comedy
dialogue of the alleged comedians."

The government called in a psychiatrist as an expert witness, a Dr. Tarumianz,
who proceeded to expound on the deleterious effect the film would have on the
minds and passions of anyone unfortunate enough to view it: "From my past
experience, I have found that such films are not only detrimental to the youth,
but detrimental to any human being who has normal endowments and is not
particularly psychopathically inclined. It creates a various deviation of thinking
and emotional instability in regard to sex problems. A happily married individual
who is considered a mature adult individual, seeing such films, becomes seriously
concerned with whether he is obtaining the necessary gratification of his sex
desires from his normal and normally endowed and inclined wife. It may deviate
him in accepting that there is something which arouses him to become interested
in an abnormal type of sex satisfaction which he had perhaps from this picture.
So that it is unquestionably seriously detrimental to the adults. As to the juveniles,
it is my sincere opinion that we consider very seriously the normal development
of our youth who eventually have to become the backbone of this country and
civilization." Civilization was indeed protected from the bumps and grinds, and
Scope was convicted. *State of Delaware v. Scope*, 86 A. 2d 154 (1952).

**HOUCHINS, SHERIFF OF THE COUNTY OF ALAMEDA, CALIFOR-
NIA v. KQED, INC. (1978).** Broadcasting company KQED had been refused
permission to inspect and take photographs of a section of a county jail in which
conditions were alleged to have been responsible for prisoners' problems. The
sheriff then announced a program of regular monthly tours open to the public,
including media reporters, of certain parts of the jail. Cameras or tape recorders
were not allowed on the tours, nor were interviews with inmates, but anyone,
including reporters, who knew a prisoner at the jail could visit him at the regular
visiting times. KQED brought suit, alleging a violation of the freedom of the
press. A federal district court (affirmed by an appeals court) agreed and enjoined
the sheriff from denying KQED news personnel and other media representatives

reasonable access to the jail, from preventing their using photographic or sound equipment, and from not allowing them to interview the inmates.

The sheriff appealed, and the Supreme Court reversed the lower courts' decision: (1) The First Amendment does not provide a right of access to government information or sources of information within the government's control, and the news media have no constitutional right of access to the county jail, over and above that of other people, to interview inmates and make sound recordings, films, and photographs for publication and broadcasting by newspapers, radio, and television. (2) The public importance of conditions in penal facilities and the media's role in providing information afford no basis for reading into the Constitution a right of the public or the media to enter those institutions, gather information, and take pictures for broadcast purposes. Previous cases concerned the freedom of the press to communicate information already obtained, but the Constitution does not compel the government to provide the press with information. *Houchins, Sheriff of the County of Alameda, California v. KQED, Inc.* (1978).

HUGHES v. SUPERIOR COURT (1950). Hughes and others were involved in picketing some grocery stores, demanding that the stores hire sufficient black clerks to represent the approximate proportion of black to white customers, about 50 percent. A California state court enjoined the picketing. When it continued, Hughes was fined and sentenced to a jail term for contempt of the court's order. Hughes appealed, but the Supreme Court ruled that the conviction did not violate his right of freedom of speech. Justice Frankfurter delivered the Court's opinion: "To deny to California the right to ban picketing in the circumstances of this case would mean that there could be no prohibition of the pressure of picketing to secure proportional employment on ancestral grounds of Hungarians in Cleveland, of Poles in Buffalo, of Mexicans in San Antonio, of Germans in Milwaukee, of Portuguese in New Bedford, of the numerous minority groups in New York, and so on through the whole gamut of racial and religious concentrations in various cities. States may well believe that such constitutional sheltering would inevitably encourage use of picketing to compel employment on the basis of racial discrimination. In disallowing such picketing States may act under the belief that otherwise community tensions and conflicts would be exacerbated. The differences in cultural traditions instead of adding flavor and variety to our common citizenry might well be hardened into hostilities by leave of law. The Constitution does not demand that the element of communication in picketing prevail over the mischief furthered by its use in these situations." *Hughes v. Superior Court*, 339 U.S. 460 (1950).

HUTCHINSON v. PROXMIRE (1979). Senator William Proxmire is known for many things, including his "Golden Fleece of the Month Award." This "award" publicizes what Proxmire thinks is wasteful spending by certain governmental agencies. One such award was given to a federal agency that funded

Professor Ronald Hutchinson's research on monkeys. Most of Hutchinson's research dealt with the study of emotional behavior, and he was seeking an empirical measure of aggression, concentrating on the behavior of monkeys. Both the National Aeronautics and Space Agency (NASA) and the navy were interested in the research, for they saw a potential relationship between it and the problems associated with people being confined in close quarters for extended periods (space capsules and undersea exploration). Hutchinson received approximately $500,000 from the National Science Foundation, NASA, and the Office of Naval Research.

Proxmire then bestowed the award, with appropriate explanatory comments. The comments were made on the floor of the Senate, in a newsletter to his constituents, in telephone calls, and on a television interview program. Hutchinson then brought suit against Proxmire, alleging that the senator's comments damaged his professional and academic reputation and were defamatory. Proxmire countered with the speech and debate clause (protecting him from prosecution for whatever he might have said) and said that "malice" had to be shown, since Hutchinson was a public figure. Some of the comments made by Proxmire were as follows: "The funding of this nonsense makes me almost angry enough to scream and kick or even clench my jaw. It seems to me it is outrageous. Dr. Hutchinson's studies should make the taxpayers as well as his monkeys grind their teeth. In fact, the good doctor has made a fortune from his monkeys and in the process made a monkey out of the American taxpayer. It is time for the Federal Government to get out of this 'monkey business.' In view of the transparent worthlessness of Hutchinson's study of jaw-grinding and biting by angry or hard-drinking monkeys, it is time we put a stop to the bite Hutchinson and the bureaucrats who fund him have been taking out of the taxpayer."

The Supreme Court had a mixed opinion. It ruled that Proxmire was indeed protected by the speech and debate clause and thus his speech on the Senate floor was protected; but the Court ruled that this protection did not extend to the newsletter and press release and thus Proxmire could be held liable for defamatory statements originally made in the Senate chamber. Additionally, the Court ruled that Hutchinson was not a "public figure" and the *New York Times* Rule* regarding "malice" did not apply. Justice Brennan dissented from this view: "I disagree with the Court's conclusion that Senator Proxmire's newsletters and press releases fall outside the protection of the speech-or-debate immunity. In my view, public criticism by legislators of unnecessary governmental expenditures, whatever its form, is a legislative act shielded by the Speech or Debate Clause [and the First Amendment]." *Hutchinson v. Proxmire*, 443 U.S. 111 (1979).

HYLAND v. PROCUNIER (1970). Hyland, a parolee from a California prison, was required, as a condition of his parole, to obtain prior permission from his parole officer before giving any public speech. Such permission was refused two times. Hyland then brought suit to prevent the California authorities from limiting his right to free speech. A federal district court agreed that the condition imposed on Hyland was an unconstitutional prior restraint of his First Amendment rights: "Defendants confine their argument for the most part to allegations that the plaintiff on many occasions has been allowed to speak and otherwise publish his views without restraint. This, of course, is beside the point. Not only have there been at least two occasions when an attempt was made to bar plaintiff from speaking, but the State also gives no indications that it will not continue to require advance permission for all speaking engagements. If the past is any guide, such permission-seeking procedures will inevitably involve a scrutiny by the parole officers concerned of the proposed content of petitioner's proposed speeches. The Court, making use of a sadly overworked phrase, finds that this would have an unwarranted chilling effect on the exercise by plaintiff of his undisputed rights." *Hyland v. Procunier*, 311 F. Supp. 749 (1970).

HYNES v. MAYOR OF ORADELL (1976). This case concerned whether a municipal ordinance (Oradell [NJ], Door-to-Door Canvassing*) that required advance notice to be given to the local police department before charitable or political canvassing could begin violated the guarantee of freedom of speech. The Supreme Court held that in this specific situation, such an ordinance did violate the First Amendment. The Court said that, although there is no absolute right under the Constitution to enter on the private premises of another person and knock on a door for any purpose, and although the police power permits reasonable regulation for public safety, the Oradell ordinance was invalid because of its vagueness: "The coverage of the ordinance is unclear—it does not explain 'recognized charitable cause' and the ordinance does not sufficiently specify what those within its reach must do in order to comply" [the applicant is not told what to put in the "notice" to the police nor what the police would consider sufficient "identification"]. *Hynes v. Mayor of Oradell*, 425 U.S. 610 (1976).

I

I AM CURIOUS—YELLOW. U.S. Customs regulations (Tariff Act*) allow the Customs Service to seize material thought to be obscene. Then a judicial determination is made as to the material's obscenity. If the court process judges the material as obscene, the Customs Service has the right to destroy the material. The Swedish film *I Am Curious—Yellow* was seized by Customs as obscene, and a federal district court jury agreed that the film was obscene (the film's dominant theme, taken as a whole, appealed to the prurient interest and it was utterly without redeeming social value). But on appeal, Judge Hays of an appeals court ruled that although the film contained sexual content presented with greater explicitness than had been seen in any other film produced for general viewing, it could not be classified as obscene because it was not utterly without redeeming social value (*United States v. A Motion Picture Entitled I Am Curious—Yellow*, 404 F. 2d 196 [1968]).

The film was duly distributed and shown and harassed by local authorities, notwithstanding the appeals court decision that the film was not obscene. Between 1968 and 1971, the film was banned and found obscene in Alabama (*Grove Press v. Bailey*, 318 F. Supp. 244 [1970]), Phoenix, California, Colorado, Georgia, Kansas City, Baltimore, Boston, Michigan, Missouri (*Hoffman v. Dickinson*, 468 S.W. 2d 27 [1971]), New Mexico, Ohio (*Grove Press v. Flask*, 326 F. Supp. 574 [1970]), Spokane, and Virginia. But the same film was also seen not to be obscene in other areas (*Lordi v. United Artists Theatres* [New Jersey], 259 A. 2d 734 [1969]).

I Am Curious—Yellow finally reached the Supreme Court in 1971 (*Grove Press v. Maryland State Board of Censors*, 401 U.S. 480 [1971]), and the Court, by a 4 to 4 per curiam decision with Justice Douglas not participating, affirmed a lower court's ruling (*Wagonheim v. Maryland*, 258 A. 2d 240 [1969]) that the film was obscene. But this "final" judicial determination of the film's obscenity didn't prevent its exhibition—it was shown in more than 125 places in the United States.

The film itself, along with *Deep Throat*,* received an immense amount of publicity and is now considered to be one of the classic X-rated films. The film was produced in Sweden in 1967, directed by Vilgot Sjoman (*491**), and starred

Lena Nyman, Borje Ahlstedt, and Peter Lindgren. It was reviewed or discussed in such publications as *Variety*, *Box Office*, *New York Times*, *Washington Post*, *New Republic*, *Holiday*, *Newsweek*, *London Financial Times*, *Time*, *Saturday Review*, *Life*, *Cosmopolitan*, and *Harper's Bazaar*. De Grazia and Newman (*Banned Films*, p. 298) present the "plot": "Lena, an aspiring young actress making a movie for director Vilgot Sjoman while being his lover, is intensely and provocatively inquisitive, demanding and implementing new solutions to the social, political, and sexual problems that trouble her and Swedish society in the 1960s. She demonstrates against the Vietnam War outside the American embassy and interviews Stockholm citizens, union members, and returning tourists, insisting upon answers that tend to accuse the persons asked. She imagines a national policy of nonviolence, 'talks' to civil rights leader Martin Luther King, Jr., and desperately fantasizes about her unhappy relations with a married automobile salesman who is untroubled by politics. They play, fight, and make love, often in odd and amusing public circumstances."†

It was this lovemaking in odd and amusing public circumstances that upset the censors. The following description was provided by the Maryland attorney general in his brief in *Wagonheim v. Maryland*: "(1) Lena's singing 'In Rio de Janeiro you can fuck for free'; (2) the display of erotic Indian sculpture depicting a man with his hand on a woman's vagina; (3) the discussion between Lena and another girl about different methods of masturbation; (4) Lena's dialogue, 'Are you that fucking stupid?'; (5) detailed love making scene in Lena's room showing both parties completely naked, exposing the male genital area, showing attempted intercourse standing against a wall and also a scene of Borje caressing the girl's breasts with his tongue; (6) scene depicting sexual intercourse between Borje and Lena on the palace balustrade in which, although the parties are clothed, the act of intercourse is vividly displayed; (7) scenes of nudity at the retreat and scene depicting Lena looking at a sex manual showing various unusual positions for sexual intercourse; (8) scene at the retreat showing Borje throwing Lena to the ground and committing an act of cunnilingus, followed by a scene depicting the parties completely nude with Lena kissing Borje's penis as he caresses her vagina; (9) a discussion regarding sex which 'makes them both horny'; (10) scene depicting intercourse in the water; (11) scene depicting sexual intercourse in a tree; (12) scene showing fully the naked bodies of the two lying on the floor engaged in either sodomy or sexual intercourse with the man behind the woman; (13) a scene in which the nude Borje chases the nude Lena from one room to another, throws her to the floor and mounts her in a position of sexual intercourse; (14) a fantasy scene in which Lena shoots Borje and castrates him with a knife; (15) Lena's dialogue: 'He's a big fucking shit and I'll kill him when I get hold of him. I'll cut off his cock'; and (16) nudity at the clinic with again emphasis on the genital area of the male and female."

†Reprinted from *Banned Films* with permission of the R. R. Bowker Company. Copyright © 1982 by Edward de Grazia and Roger K. Newman.

IF I DIE. In 1936, John S. Sumner, representing the New York Society for the Suppression of Vice (Comstockery*), brought suit against the Gotham Book Mart (*People on Complaint of Savery v. Gotham Book Mart, Inc.*, 285 N.Y.S. 563 [1936]) for an alleged violation of the New York Obscenity Statute.* It appears that Sumner did not like André Gide's autobiography, *If I Die.* Prosecuting for the people, Sumner did not charge that the entire book was obscene but directed his attack at seventy-six pages (about 20 percent of the book) and, more specifically, against certain paragraphs contained in twenty-two of those pages. Sumner based his argument on the Hicklin Rule*—the offending paragraphs in a book could be taken from their context and the book judged by them alone, and that the test of obscenity was whether the tendency of these passages in themselves was "to deprave the minds of those open to such influences and into whose hands a publication of this character might come." Unfortunately for Sumner and the New York Society for the Suppression of Vice, the Hicklin Rule had already been discredited as a test for obscenity, and the New York City magistrate who heard the case, Nathan D. Perlman, approached the obscenity question on the basis of the Ulysses Standard,* laid down by Justice Woolsey in *United States v. One Book Entitled Ulysses* (*Ulysses**). The Ulysses Standard did not dwell on isolated passages of a book, but rather considered the entire book.

Perlman dismissed the complaint, ruling that Gide's *If I Die* was not obscene. Some of Perlman's comments follow: "I have read the book in question carefully. The author is described in *The Columbia Encyclopedia* (1935) as 'one of the most distinguished of contemporary novelists and a leader of French liberal thought.' The London Royal Society of Literature, desiring a French member to replace Anatole France, unanimously elected Gide. . . . The book contains a few paragraphs dealing with isolated instances of inversion, which, taken by themselves, are undoubtedly vulgar and indecent. The author himself states they are ugly. They are, however, subordinate to, although forming an essential part of, the main theme. The greater portion of the book, however, is devoted to a straight-forward and sincere narrative of his early years. The book essentially is an interpretive autobiography. It explains why he acted and not so much how he acted. Gide does not extoll his temporary departure from virtue; he does not deride virtue. . . . André Gide is considered a great author; he is therefore entitled to be heard; for the whole value of personal testimony lies in the quality of the witness. There may be an evil side to many great lives; the vices of a vital nature must not be left out in any estimate of that nature's development. If we eliminate the pages complained of, we would have a distorted and untruthful picture of our subject. If Gide, in unveiling the darker corners of his life, is moved by sincerity, by the deep-rooted desire to appear as he really is, an entire creature, then it is as an entire creature we must study him, omitting nothing."

ILLINOIS, GROUP LIBEL. Section 224a of the Illinois Criminal Code, Illinois Rev. Stat., 1949, c. 38, Div. 1, § 471, provided: "It shall be unlawful for any person, firm or corporation to manufacture, sell, or offer for sale, advertise or publish, present or exhibit in any public place in this state any lithograph, moving picture, play, drama or sketch, which publication or exhibition portrays depravity, criminality, unchastity, or lack of virtue of a class of citizens, or any race, color, creed or religion which said publication or exhibition exposes the citizens of any race, color, creed or religion to contempt, derision, or obloquy or which is productive of breach of the peace or riots." This statute was not seen to be an unconstitutional restriction of free press when, in *Beauharnais v. Illinois* (1952),* a fine of $200 was levied against Beauharnais for circulating anti-black tracts.

ILLINOIS, MILITARY PARADES. Article XI of the Military Code of Illinois, Act of May 28, 1879, Laws of 1879: "§ 5. It shall not be lawful for any body of men whatever, other than the regular organized volunteer militia of this State, and the troops of the United States, to associate themselves together as a military company or organization, or to drill or parade with arms in any city, or town, of this State, without the license of the Governor thereof, which license may at any time be revoked. . . . § 6. Whoever offends . . . shall be punished by a fine not exceeding the sum of ten dollars ($10), or by imprisonment in the common jail for a term not exceeding six months, or both." The requirement of having a license from the governor before any such parade was seen to be within the state's general powers and thus not a prior restraint in *Presser v. Illinois* (1886).*

ILLINOIS, OBSCENITY STATUTE. Section 223 of the Illinois Criminal Code was adopted by an act of the General Assembly, approved March 27, 1874, and provided: "Whoever . . . shall have in his possession, with or without intent to sell or give away, any obscene and indecent . . . drawing . . . or shall draw and expose any such article, shall be confined in the county jail not more than six months, or be fined not less than $100 nor more than $1,000." The full weight of this statute was applied to someone (*Fuller v. The People* [1879])* who showed an "indecent" drawing to his girl friend.

ILLINOIS, STATUTE ON PICKETING. Illinois Rev. Stat., ch. 38, § 21.1-2 (1977), provided: "It is unlawful to picket before or about the residence or dwelling of any person, except when the residence or dwelling is used as a place of business. However, this Article does not apply to a person peacefully picketing his own residence or dwelling and does not prohibit the peaceful picketing of a place of employment involved in a labor dispute or the place of holding a meeting or assembly on premises commonly used to discuss subjects of general public interest." This statute was declared to be unconstitutional by the Supreme Court (*Carey v. Brown* [1980]*) because it distinguished between labor picketing (allowed) and other types of picketing (not allowed); thus it was the content of the message rather than the conduct itself that the statute attempted to control.

ILLUSTRATED REPORT. Various people were convicted in a federal district court of violating 18 U.S.C. § 1461 (Postal Regulations, Mailing Obscene Material*). An advertisement brochure was mailed to about 55,000 persons, trying to get them to buy a copy of the *Illustrated Report*, an illustrated version of the final report issued by the Commission on Obscenity and Pornography.* One side of the advertising brochure contained a collage of photographs from the *Illustrated Report* and the other side contained ordering information. The U.S. Supreme Court, in *Hamling v. United States* (418 U.S. 87 [1974]), affirmed the lower court's decision that the brochure was obscene and thus a violation of § 1461: "Since evidence of pandering can be relevant in determining obscenity, as long as the proper constitutional definition of obscenity is applied, it was not improper for the jury to consider whether the brochure had been pandered by looking to the manner of its distribution and editorial intent."

Justices Brennan and Douglas filed dissents, however. Justice Brennan: "At least in the absence of distribution to juveniles or obtrusive exposure to unconsenting adults, the First and Fourteenth Amendments prohibit the State and Federal Governments from attempting wholly to suppress sexually oriented materials on the basis of their allegedly 'obscene' contents." Justice Douglas: "What petitioners did was to supply the Report [the official Report of the President's Commission on Obscenity and Pornography] with a glossary—not in dictionary terms but visually. Every item in the glossary depicted explicit sexual material within the meaning of that term as used in the Report. . . . If officials may constitutionally report on obscenity, I see nothing in the First Amendment that allows us to bar the use of a glossary factually to illustrate what the [U.S. Government] Report discusses."

This case is also noted for illustrating a change in the Court's thinking: In many prior decisions, both the indictment and the court decision would refer to the material as "obscene" or "indecent" and would not describe the material. The Court felt that "good taste" prevented them from describing the material, for it would "debase" the court record. This view is no longer in vogue; the court records now contain a graphic description of the material. If, in this particular case, Hamling was convicted of using the mails for his brochure, a strong argument could be made that the U.S. Supreme Court also violated § 1461 for having its printed opinion sent through the mails.

The Court described the advertising brochure in the following terms (no photographs were included, however): "The folder opens to a full page splash of pictures portraying heterosexual and homosexual intercourse, sodomy and a variety of deviate sexual acts. Specifically, a group picture of nine persons, one male engaged in masturbation, a female masturbating two males, two couples engaged in intercourse in reverse fashion while a female participant engages in fellatio of a male; a second group picture of six persons, two males masturbating, two fellatrices practicing the act, each bearing a clear depiction of ejaculated seminal fluid on their faces; two persons with the female engaged in the act of fellatio and the male in female masturbation by hand; two separate pictures of males engaged in cunnilinction; a film strip of six frames depicting lesbian love scenes including a cunnilinguist in action and female masturbation with another's hand and a vibrator, and two frames, one depicting a woman mouthing the penis of a horse, and a second poising the same for entrance into her vagina.''

IMAGES. The magazine *Images* was a chartered and recognized student publication at the University of Mississippi. First published in 1969, it came out at irregular intervals and was designed for presentation of student-written and student-edited literary compositions. The university's administration took offense at the content of one of the issues and attempted to censor it; the students brought suit. An appeals court, in *Bazaar v. Fortune* (476 F. 2d 570 [1973]), ruled that although the university is not required to have the university's English department give the students advice, the university did not have the right to censor the contents of the magazine. In a rehearing (489 F. 2d 225 [1973]), the appeals court ruled that the university could place a stamp on the cover of the magazine to the effect that "This is not an official publication of the University." The appeals court said that the real question was not one of censorship, but between the right to publish *Images* with or without official university sponsorship. The university administration was not satisfied with the compromise reached by the appeals court and appealed to the Supreme Court (*Bazaar v. Fortune*, 416 U.S. 995 [1974]).

The Supreme Court, however, denied certiorari and refused to hear the case, thus leaving intact the appeals court ruling. *Images* could be published, but the university could disclaim all responsibility for it. Chief Justice Burger filed a brief opinion concurring in the denial of certiorari: "The University is not required to continue to make available to respondents, at public expense, facilities of the University for the production of any future publication. Those attending a state university have a right to be free from official censorship in their speech and writings, but this does not require the University to commit its faculty or financial resources to any activity which it considers to be of substandard or marginal quality."

The particular offense that *Images* gave to the administration of the university was described by the appeals court as follows: "It is necessary to have a clear grasp on the nature of the stories, their characters, and the manner in which the language found objectionable by the University is used. The objectionable portions consist of what are commonly known as 'four-letter words,' often colloquially referred to as 'obscenities.' They include use of that 'four-letter word' [fuck] generally felt to be the most offensive in polite conversation. While the University does not specify which words it most objects to, we assume that this epithet and its derivatives [mother fucker] are high on the list. We feel that it is imperative, however, to stress the manner in which these words are used and the alleged literary justification for their use. The protagonist of each story is a black male growing up in and confronted by a basically white society. Each of the two 'heroes' is suggestive of a latter-day Holden Caulfield, struggling to find himself in the world. As what could be termed a natural and necessary phase of character development, the 'heroes' of these stories occasionally talk and think in a vernacular which is definitely not suited for parlor conversation. It must be realized that these characters are young blacks who often express themselves by using somewhat crude epithets of the street. The language, while admittedly unacceptable in some quarters, is readily recognized as common-place in various strata of society, both black and white. The tendency to use such language would seem more prevalent among young males in less-favored social groups of all races. In short, it could be well considered strained and artificial for these characters to speak and think in proper prep school diction. While some may feel that they are used a bit too often, this is a difficult matter to judge and rests largely with individual taste. Certainly, it seems an unsuitable standard for governmental censorship.''

IMMIGRATION AND NATIONALITY ACT, VISA REGULATIONS. Certain sections of the Immigration and Nationality Act of 1952, 66 Stat. 182, 8 U.S.C. § 1182, provide that certain aliens could be ineligible to receive visas and could be excluded from the United States unless the attorney general, in his discretion, on recommendation by the secretary of state, or a consular officer, waives inadmissibility and approves temporary admission. The relevant provisions of the statute are "Section 212(a). Except as otherwise provided in this Act, the following classes of aliens shall be ineligible to receive visas and shall be excluded from admission into the United States: (28) Aliens who are, or at any time have been, members of any of the following classes: (D) Aliens not within any of the other provisions of this paragraph who advocate the economic, international, and governmental doctrines of world communism or the establishment in the United States of a totalitarian dictatorship; (G) Aliens who write or publish . . . (v) the economic, international, and governmental doctrines of world communism or the establishment in the United States of a totalitarian dictatorship; (3) Except as provided in this subsection, an alien (A) who is applying for a nonimmigrant visa and is known or believed by the consular officer to be ineligible for such a visa under one or more of the paragraphs enumerated in subsection (a) . . . may, after approval by the Attorney General of a recommendation by the Secretary of State or by the consular officer that the alien be admitted temporarily despite his inadmissibility, be granted such a visa and may be admitted into the United States temporarily as a nonimmigrant in the discretion of the Attorney General.''

The Supreme Court, in *Kleindienst v. Mandel* (1972),* ruled that these regulations were not a violation of freedom of speech guaranteed by the First Amendment. The regulations have been used frequently by the U.S. government to prevent ''undesirable'' people from visiting and lecturing in the United States. The following is a partial listing of some of the people who have been affected by this statute: Nobel Prize–winner Gabriel Garcia Márquez, a Colombian—and a critic of U.S. foreign policy—had his visa applications denied on a routine basis from 1963 to 1971. In 1971, he finally received a restricted visa in order to accept an honorary degree awarded him by Columbia University. Márquez has refused subsequent restricted visas because they come with a condition attached—an FBI agent must accompany him during his travels! Dario Fo, an Italian playwright (*Accidental Death of an Anarchist*), was denied a visa to attend an arts festival in New York sponsored by the Italian government and New York University. Carlos Fuentes, a Mexican novelist and former ambassador to France, was refused a visa when NBC, in 1961, invited him to participate in a debate on Latin-American affairs. He was admitted in 1964, when his novel *The Death of Artemio Cruz* was published, but the visa was valid for only five days and he was restricted to Manhattan. Other prominent people who have been barred entry include English novelist Graham Greene, novelist Iris Murdoch, Italian novelist Alberto Moravia, French writers Michel Foucault and Regis Debray (Debray has been an adviser to French President François Mitterrand), film stars Yves Montand and Simone Signoret, Hortensia Allende (widow of the late Chilean president), Tomas Borge (Nicaraguan interior minister), and Nino Pasti (a former NATO general and a member of the Italian Senate, who opposed the stationing of Pershing and cruise missiles in Europe). The Reagan administration attempted to tighten up this process even further; in addition to the "national security" justification for denial of a visa, the government wanted to add "foreign policy factors" as a reason to deny entry. This move was countered by Representative Barney Frank, a Democrat from Massachusetts. Frank introduced a bill that would limit the exclusion of people to those "believed likely to engage in espionage or sabotage, or to endanger public safety or national security, or to act to oppose or overthrow the government by force or violence, or who belong to terrorist organizations." If Frank's bill passes, the administration could no longer base the denial of visas on the applicant's politics or lack of support for U.S. foreign policy.

INCITEMENT. It is generally accepted that the government has the authority to punish someone who incites or induces another person to commit a criminal act, just as it has the authority to punish the doer of the act itself. Some early cases (*Schenck v. United States**) ruled that the act sought need not be immediate. Schenck was convicted of attempting to incite insubordination in the armed services and to obstruct the country's recruiting efforts in time of war. The Supreme Court rejected a challenge based on a violation of free speech: "When a nation is at war, many things that might be said in time of peace are such a hindrance to its effort that their utterance will not be endured." But later cases (*Yates v. United States**) have ruled that the incitement or inducement of others to commit criminal acts cannot be mere "advocacy"* of such action but must represent an immediate, imminent, and clear and present inducement to such acts.

INCORPORATION. This theory says that the Bill of Rights is applicable to the states through the due process clause of the Fourteenth Amendment. The

U.S. Constitution prior to 1868, when the Fourteenth Amendment was adopted, did not protect the right of free speech or press against state action and the Bill of Rights restrained only the federal government. Until 1868, the various rights were safeguarded solely by the constitutions of the various states. Although these rights were not totally unprotected, there were many instances in which certain state regulations were left intact but would not have been if they had been applied by the federal government. The U.S. Supreme Court, starting in 1925 (*Gitlow v. New York**), has slowly implemented the incorporation theory and now the Court has moved close to total incorporation; most of the guarantees contained in the Bill of Rights are now applicable to the states through the due process clause of the Fourteenth Amendment. Four rights, however, have not yet been incorporated: The Supreme Court has ruled that the right to a grand jury hearing and the right to a jury trial are not "fundamental"; it has yet to rule on the right to keep and bear arms and the right to refuse to quarter soldiers. *Annotation: Incorporation*, 23 L. Ed. 2d 985.

INDIANA, DISORDERLY CONDUCT. Indiana Code 35-27-2-1 (1971), Indiana Ann. Stat. § 10–1510 (Supp. 1972): "Whoever shall act in a loud, boisterous or disorderly manner so as to disturb the peace and quiet of any neighborhood or family, by loud or unusual noise, or by tumultuous or offensive behavior, threatening, traducing, quarreling, challenging to fight or fighting, shall be deemed guilty of disorderly conduct, and upon conviction, shall be fined in any sum not exceeding five hundred dollars ($500) to which may be added imprisonment for not to exceed one hundred eighty (180) days." This statute was seen to be unconstitutional on its face because of vagueness as well as how applied to someone who, during a street demonstration, yelled, "Let's take the fucking street" (*Hess v. Indiana* [1973]*).

INDIANA, LOYALTY OATH. Indiana Ann. Stat. § 29–3812 (1969) provided in part: "No political party or organization shall be recognized and given a place on or have the names of its candidates printed on the ballot used at any election which advocates the overthrow, by force or violence, of the local, state or national government, or which advocates, or carries on, a program of sedition or of treason, and which is affiliated or cooperates with or has any relation with any foreign government, or any political party or group of individuals of any foreign government. . . . No existing or newly-organized political party or organization shall be permitted on or to have the names of its candidates printed on the ballot used at any election until it has filed an affidavit, by its officers, under oath, that it does not advocate the overthrow of . . . the government." The Supreme Court, in *Communist Party of Indiana v. Whitcomb* (1974),* ruled that such a loyalty oath violated the free speech guarantee of the First Amendment.

IN RE PRIMUS (1978). Edna Primus, a cooperating attorney with the South Carolina American Civil Liberties Union (ACLU), informed a woman by letter that free legal assistance was available from the ACLU. After hearings by the Disciplinary Board of the South Carolina Supreme Court, Primus received a public reprimand for "soliciting" a client (South Carolina, Bar Association Disciplinary Rules*). The Supreme Court reversed the reprimand: "Solicitation of prospective litigants by nonprofit organizations that engage in litigation as 'a form of political expression' and 'political association' constitutes expressive and associational conduct entitled to First Amendment protection." *In Re Primus*, 436 U.S. 412 (1978).

IN RE RAPIER (1892). Rapier was arrested and indicted for mailing a newspaper containing an advertisement for the Louisiana Lottery, a violation of the act of September 19, 1890—the Anti-Lottery Act (Postal Regulations, Lotteries*). This act prohibited the use of the U.S. mail for any publication containing lottery ads. Lotteries at that time were seen to be a moral outrage. The assistant U.S. attorney general, arguing the case for the government, equated a lottery with a dram shop, leading to unimaginable behavior. Rapier argued that the prohibition was a form of censorship—that a newspaper's contents would determine whether it could go through the mail. The Supreme Court did not agree with Rapier: Congress has the authority to establish the postal system and thus can determine what could be sent through the mails; Congress can thus refuse to allow the mail facilities to be used to distribute material dealing with what is seen to debase public morality (lotteries). But the distribution of the banned information cannot be prevented by means other than the mails: "The denial of the mails is no abridgment of the freedom of the press. All other channels are left open; channels of commerce, railroads and newspaper trains. The circulation of newspapers is not prohibited, but the government declines itself to become an agent in the circulation of printed matter which it regards as injurious to the people." *In Re Rapier*, 143 U.S. 110 (1892).

IN RE WORTHINGTON (1894). This case pitted Anthony Comstock (Comstockery*) of the New York Society for the Suppression of Vice against the receiver of the assets of the Worthington Company. It appears that the receiver had some books and wished to sell them; Comstock wanted them destroyed on grounds of obscenity—Comstock lost. The books in question were rare and costly editions of Payne's *Arabian Nights*, Fielding's novel *Tom Jones*, the works of Rabelais, Ovid's *Art of Love*, the *Decameron* of Boccaccio, the *Heptameron* of Queen Margaret of Navarre, the *Confessions* of Jean-Jacques Rousseau, *Tales from the Arabic*, and *Aladdin*.

Judge O'Brien of the Supreme Court for New York County anticipated the demise of the Hicklin Rule* and stated the Ulysses Standard* even before the *Ulysses* case: "It is very difficult to see upon what theory these world-renowned classics can be regarded as specimens of that pornographic literature which it is the office of the Society for the Suppression of Vice to suppress. . . . The works under consideration . . . have so long held a supreme rank in literature that it would be absurd to call them now foul and unclean. A seeker after the sensual and degrading parts of a narrative may find in all these works, as in those of other great authors, something to satisfy his pruriency. But to condemn a standard literary work because of a few of its episodes, would compel the exclusion from circulation of a very large proportion of the works of fiction of the most famous writers of the English language. They rank with the highest literature, and would not be bought nor appreciated by the class of people from whom unclean publications ought to be withheld. They are not corrupting in their influence upon the young, for they are not likely to reach them." *In Re Worthington*, 30 N.Y.S. 361 (1894).

INTELLIGENCE IDENTITIES PROTECTION ACT (1982). After being passed by an overwhelming margin in both the House and the Senate, President Reagan signed this act into law on June 29, 1982. This act makes it a crime to publish any information that identifies an individual as a covert agent of the Central Intelligence Agency (CIA) or the Federal Bureau of Investigation, even if the information is unclassified, is a matter of public record, or is derived from public sources. The text of the act, 96 Stat. 122, reads as follows: "Whoever, in the course of a pattern of activities intended to identify and expose covert agents and with reason to believe that such activities would impair or impede the foreign intelligence activities of the United States, discloses any information that identifies an individual as a covert agent to any individual not authorized to receive classified information, knowing that the information disclosed so identifies such individual and that the United States is taking affirmative measures to conceal such individual's intelligence relationship to the United States, shall be fined not more than $15,000 or imprisoned not more than three years, or both." This act, if in effect at the time of *Haig v. Philip Agee*,* would have meant that Agee would have received a much sterner sentence than mere revocation of his passport for identifying certain covert CIA agents.

INTERSTATE COMMERCE REGULATIONS, TRANSPORTING OB-SCENE MATERIAL. Title 18 U.S.C. § 1465 provides: "Whoever knowingly transports in interstate or foreign commerce for the purpose of sale or distribution any obscene, lewd, lascivious, or filthy book, pamphlet, picture, film, paper, letter, writing, print, silhouette, drawing, figure, image, cast, phonograph recording, electrical transcription or other article capable of producing sound or any other matter of indecent or immoral character, shall be fined not more than $5,000 or imprisoned not more than five years, or both." This statute has been applied to many people, and the courts have consistently ruled it to be constitutional (*United States v. Orito* [1973]*).

IOWA, TEACHING IN A FOREIGN LANGUAGE. Chapter 198 of the Iowa Laws (1919) provided: "Section 1. That the medium of instruction in all secular subjects taught in all of the schools, public and private, within the State of Iowa, shall be the English language, and the use of any language other than English in secular subjects in said schools is hereby prohibited, provided, however, that nothing herein shall prohibit the teaching and studying of foreign languages as such as a part of the regular school course in any such school, in all courses above the eighth grade. Section 2. That any person violating any of the provisions of this act shall be deemed guilty of a misdemeanor, and upon conviction shall be fined not less than $25.00 nor more than $100.00.'' This ban on teaching in a foreign language was seen to be unconstitutional by the Supreme Court in *Bartels v. Iowa* (1923).*

IRVINGTON (NJ), DISTRIBUTION OF LITERATURE. The following ordinance was judged to be a violation of free speech by the Supreme Court in *Schneider v. State* (1939)*: ''No person except as in this ordinance provided shall canvass, solicit, distribute circulars, or other matter, or call from house to house in the Town of Irvington without first having reported to and received a written permit from the Chief of Police or the officer in charge of Police Headquarters. The permit to canvass shall specify the number of hours or days it will be in effect; that the canvasser must make an application giving his name, address, age, height, weight, place of birth, whether or not previously arrested or convicted of crime, by whom employed, address of employer, clothing worn, and description of project for which he is canvassing; that each applicant shall be fingerprinted and photographed; that the Chief of Police shall refuse a permit in all cases where the application, or further investigation made at the officer's discretion, shows that the canvasser is not of good character or is canvassing for a project not free from fraud; that canvassing may only be done between 9 A.M. and 5 P.M.; that the canvasser must furnish a photograph of himself which is to be attached to the permit; that the permittee must exhibit the permit to any police officer or other person upon request, must be courteous to all persons in canvassing, must not importune or annoy the town's inhabitants or conduct himself in an unlawful manner and must, at the expiration of the permit, surrender it at police headquarters.''

J

JACKSONVILLE (FL), NUDITY IN DRIVE-INS. A Jacksonville city ordinance (330.313, "Drive-In Theaters, Films Visible From Public Streets or Public Places," adopted January 14, 1972) provided: "It shall be unlawful and it is hereby declared a public nuisance for any ticket seller, ticket taker, usher, motion picture projection machine operator, manager, owner, or any other person connected with or employed by any drive-in theater in the City to exhibit, or aid or assist in exhibiting any motion picture, slide, or other exhibit in which the human male or female bare buttocks, human female bare breasts, or human bare pubic areas are shown, if such motion picture, slide, or other exhibit is visible from any public street or public place. Violation of this section shall be punishable as a Class C offense." The city applied this ordinance to the manager of a drive-in when the film *Class of '74** was shown, but the Supreme Court, in *Erznoznik v. Jacksonville* (442 U.S. 205 [1975]), ruled that the ordinance, even though aimed at the protection of minors, was too broad. The Court remarked that the ordinance would have prohibited the showing of a baby's bare buttocks, a newsreel shot of nude war victims, or perhaps a documentary of a culture in which nudity was *de rigueur*. The Court also stated that nudity per se is not synonymous with obscenity.

JAMISON v. TEXAS (1943). A Dallas municipal ordinance (Dallas [TX], Distribution and Scattering of Handbills*) prohibited the distribution of handbills on the public streets. Jamison, a member of the Jehovah's Witnesses, was convicted in a Dallas court for violating the ordinance (the handbills invited the purchase of books for the improved understanding of religion and promoted the raising of funds for religious purposes).

On appeal, the Supreme Court reversed the conviction. Justice Black: "We think the judgment below must be reversed because the Dallas ordinance denies to the appellant the freedom of press . . . guaranteed to her by the First and Fourteenth Amendments of the Federal Constitution. The city contends that its power over its streets is not limited to the making of reasonable regulations for the control of traffic and the maintenance of order, but that it has the power absolutely to prohibit the use of the streets for the communication of ideas. It relies primarily on *Davis v. Massachusetts*.* This same argument, made in reliance upon the same decision, has been directly rejected by this Court (*Hague v. CIO**). Of course, states may provide for control of travel on their streets in order to insure the safety and convenience of the traveling public. They may punish conduct on the streets which is in violation of a valid law. But one who is rightfully on a street which the state has left open to the public carries with him there as elsewhere the constitutional right to express his views in an orderly fashion. This right extends to the communication of ideas by handbills and literature as well as by the spoken word. Here, the ordinance as construed and applied, prohibits the dissemination of information by handbills. As such, it cannot be sustained. The right to distribute handbills concerning religious subjects on the streets may not be prohibited at all times, at all places, and under all circumstances. . . . The city contends, however, that in the instant case the prohibition is permissible because the handbills, although they were distributed for the unquestioned purpose of furthering religious activity, contained an invitation to contribute to the support of that activity by purchasing books related to the work of the group. The mere presence of an advertisement of a religious work on a handbill of the sort distributed here may not subject the distribution of the handbill to prohibition.'' *Jamison v. Texas*, 318 U.S. 413 (1943).

JEANNETTE (PA), SOLICITING LICENSE. The city of Jeannette, Pennsylvania, had an ordinance, passed in the first decade of the twentieth century, that provided: ''That all persons canvassing for or soliciting within said Borough, orders for goods, paintings, pictures, wares, or merchandise of any kind, or persons delivering such articles under orders so obtained or solicited, shall be required to procure from the Burgess a license to transact said business and shall pay to the Treasurer of said Borough therefore the following sums according to the time for which said license shall be granted. For one day $1.50, for one week seven dollars ($7.00), for two weeks twelve dollars ($12.00), for three weeks twenty dollars ($20.00), provided that the provisions of this ordinance shall not apply to persons selling by sample to manufacturers or licensed merchants or dealers doing business in said Borough of Jeannette.'' This ordinance was seen to be an invalid restriction on speech and press by the Supreme Court in *Murdock v. Pennsylvania* (1943).*

JERSEY CITY (NJ), PARADE PERMIT. The following ordinance of Jersey City was held to be an unconstitutional restriction on the right of free speech because of its vagueness and lack of standards by the Supreme Court in *Hague v. CIO* (1939)*: ''The Board of Commissioners of Jersey City Do Ordain: 1. From and after the passage of this ordinance, no public parades or public assembly in or upon the public streets, highways, public parks or public buildings of Jersey City shall take place or be conducted until a permit shall be obtained from the Director of Public Safety. 2. The Director of Public Safety is hereby authorized and empowered to grant permits for parades and public assembly, upon application made to him at least three days prior to the proposed parade or public assembly. 3. The Director of Public Safety is hereby authorized to refuse to issue said permit when, after investigation of all of the facts and circumstances pertinent to said application, he believes it to be proper to refuse the issuance thereof; provided, however, that said permit shall only be refused for the purpose of preventing riots, disturbances or disorderly assemblage. 4. Any person or persons violating any of the provisions of this ordinance shall upon conviction before a police magistrate of the City of Jersey City be punished by a fine not exceeding two hundred dollars or imprisonment in the Hudson County jail for a period not exceeding ninety days or both.''

JOBIN v. ARIZONA (1942). The city of Casa Grande, Arizona, had an ordinance (Casa Grande [AZ], Book Sellers' License*) that made it a misdemeanor for any person to carry on any occupation or business without first obtaining a license. Transient merchants, peddlers, and street vendors were listed as subject to a quarterly license fee of twenty-five dollars, payable in advance. Jobin, a transient bookseller, was tried and convicted in a county court for having attempted to carry on a business without the license. The Supreme Court sustained the conviction, and the decision is contained in *Jones v. Opelika* (1942).* But in a rehearing one year later, in 1943, the Court vacated the judgment and reversed Jobin's conviction, citing their decisions in *Largent v. Texas* (1943)* and *Jamison v. Texas* (1943).* *Jobin v. Arizona*, 316 U.S. 584 (1942).

JOHN DONNELLY & SONS v. CAMPBELL (1980). The state of Maine (Maine, Traveler Information Services Act*) passed a wide-ranging statute that was intended to abolish billboards from its public highways and to reduce the number, size, and contents of all other signs viewable by travelers on any public road in the state. The legislature gave three justifications for the statute's prohibitions: (1) the protection of the state's landscape, a natural resource; (2) the enhancement of the tourist industry; and (3) the public interest in highway safety. The state listed its general policy and purposes buttressing the act: ''To promote the public health, safety, economic development and other aspects of the general welfare, it is in the public interest to provide tourists and travelers with information and guidance concerning public accommodations, facilities, commercial services and other businesses, and points of scenic, cultural, historic, educational, recreational and religious interest. To provide this information and guidance, it is the policy of the State and the purpose of this chapter to: 1. Official information centers; signs. Establish and maintain official information centers and a system of official business directional signs; 2. Information publications. Provide official directories, guidebooks, maps and other tourist and traveler information publications; 3. Control outdoor advertising. Prohibit and control the indiscriminate use of outdoor advertising; and 4. Protection of scenic beauty. Enhance and protect the natural scenic beauty of the State.''

John Donnelly & Sons, the largest billboard advertiser in the state, brought suit, challenging the goal of prohibiting outdoor advertising on the grounds that it was a violation of the First Amendment guarantee of free speech and press. A federal district court dismissed the complaint, but an appeals court ruled that the Maine act violated the First Amendment. The Supreme Court (453 U.S. 916 [1981]) affirmed without opinion the appeals court's ruling. A concurring opinion in the appeals court was delivered by Justice Pettine: "If any one, consistent thread runs through First Amendment jurisprudence, surely it must be the recognition that the preservation of free expression is neither easy nor comfortable. It often requires of us that we tolerate things we would rather not see and endure things that we would rather not hear. It requires that we accept a less-than-perfect world—a world that is not as quiet [*Saia v. New York** and loudspeakers], as neat [*Schneider v. New York** and the distribution of literature], as refined [*Cohen v. California** and "Fuck the Draft"], or even, I believe, as scenic [this case] as we might like." *John Donnelly & Sons v. Campbell*, 639 F. 2d 6 (1980).

JOINT ANTI-FASCIST REFUGEE COMMITTEE v. McGRATH (1951).

U.S. Attorney General McGrath designated the Joint Anti-Fascist Refugee Committee as a "Communist" or "Communist-front" organization in a list given to the Loyalty Review Board* for its use in connection with the determination of disloyalty of government employees. The committee then brought suit, alleging that the board's dissemination of the list to all government departments hampered their activities and that the original classification by the attorney general violated their First Amendment rights. A federal district court and then an appeals court dismissed the complaint, but the Supreme Court ordered the district court to give the committee a full hearing on the complaint. Justice Burton delivered the majority opinion, but the comments of Justice Black in a concurring opinion are more relevant: "(1) I agree with Mr. Justice Burton that petitioners have standing to sue for the reason among others that they have a right to conduct their admittedly legitimate political, charitable and business operations free from unjustified governmental defamation. Otherwise, executive officers could act lawlessly with impunity. And, assuming that the President may constitutionally authorize the promulgation of the Attorney General's list, I further agree with Mr. Justice Burton that this Court should not attribute to the President a purpose to vest in a cabinet officer the power to destroy political, social, religious or business organizations by arbitrary fiat and thus the methods employed by the Attorney General exceed his authority under Executive Order No. 9835. (2) . . . (3) More fundamentally, however, in my judgment the executive has no constitutional authority, with or without a hearing, officially to prepare and publish the lists challenged by the petitioners. In the first place, the system adopted effectively punishes many organizations and their members merely because of their political beliefs and utterances, and to this extent smacks of a most evil type of censorship. This cannot be reconciled with the First Amendment as I interpret it."

Justice Reed filed a strong dissent, believing that no abridgment of the First

Amendment was involved: "Petitioners assert their inclusion on the disloyal list has abridged their freedom of speech, since listeners or readers are more difficult to obtain for their speeches and publications, and parties interested in their work are more hesitant to become associates. The Refugee Committee brief adds that thought is also abridged. A concurring opinion accepts these arguments to the point of concluding that the publication of the lists with or without a hearing violates the First Amendment. This Court, throughout the years, has maintained the protection of the First Amendment as a major safeguard to the maintenance of a free republic. This Nation has never suffered from an enforced conformity of expression or a limitation of criticism. But neither are we compelled to endure espionage and sedition. Wide as are the freedoms of the First Amendment, this Court has never hesitated to deny the individual's right to use the privileges for the overturn of law and order. Reasonable restraints for the fair protection of the Government against incitement to sedition cannot properly be said to be undemocratic or contrary to the guarantees of free speech. Otherwise the guarantees of civil rights would be a mockery. Even when this Court spoke out most strongly against previous restraints, it was careful to recognize that the security of the community life may be protected against incitements to acts of violence and the overthrow by force of orderly government. Recognizing that the designation, rightly or wrongly, of petitioner organizations as communist impairs their ability to carry forward successfully whatever legitimate objects they seek to accomplish, we do not accept their argument that such interference is an abridgment of First Amendment guarantees. They are in the position of every proponent of unpopular views. Heresy induces strong expressions of opposition. So long as petitioners are permitted to voice their political ideas, free from suggestions for the opportune use of force to accomplish their social and economic aims, it is hard to understand how any advocate of freedom of expression can assert that their right has been unconstitutionally abridged. As nothing in the orders or regulations concerning this list limits the teachings or support of these organizations, we do not believe that any right of theirs under the First Amendment is abridged by publication of the list." *Joint Anti-Fascist Refugee Committee v. McGrath*, 341 U.S. 123 (1951).

JONES v. NORTH CAROLINA PRISONERS' LABOR UNION (1977). A certain North Carolina Department of Corrections regulation* prohibited the delivery of packets of union publications that had been mailed in bulk to several inmates for later redistribution among other prisoners. The prisoners' labor union brought suit, claiming that its First Amendment rights were violated. A district court agreed, but on appeal, the Supreme Court found no First Amendment violation: "(a) The fact of confinement and the needs of the penal institution impose limitations on constitutional rights; (b) First Amendment rights are barely implicated, mail rights themselves not being involved but only the cost savings through bulk mailings; and (c) The prison does not constitute a public forum." *Jones v. North Carolina Prisoners' Labor Union*, 433 U.S. 119 (1977).

JONES v. OPELIKA (1942). The city of Opelika, Alabama, had an ordinance (Opelika [AL], Book Sellers' License*) that required a license and the payment of a fee for the privilege of doing business in the city. This requirement extended to the business of selling books and pamphlets on the street or door to door. The license fee for book agents (Bibles excepted) was ten dollars per year and five dollars for transient dealers. Jones was convicted of selling books without a license.

The Supreme Court upheld the conviction, although not without a vigorous dissent. Justice Reed delivered the majority opinion: "To subject any religious or didactic group to a reasonable fee for their money-making activities does not require a finding that the licensed acts are purely commercial. It is enough that money is earned by the sale of articles. A book agent cannot escape a license requirement by a plea that it is a tax on knowledge. It would hardly be contended that the publication of newspapers is not subject to the usual governmental fiscal exactions or the obligations placed by statutes on other business. The Constitution draws no line between a payment from gross receipts or a net income tax and a suitable calculated occupational license. . . . When proponents of religious or social theories use the ordinary commercial methods of sales of articles to raise propaganda funds, it is a natural and proper exercise of the power of the State to charge reasonable fees for the privilege of canvassing. Careful as we may and should be to protect the freedoms safeguarded by the Bill of Rights, it is difficult to see in such enactments a shadow of prohibition of the exercise of religion or of abridgment of the freedom of speech or the press. It is prohibition and unjustifiable abridgment which are interdicted, not taxation. Nor do we believe it can be fairly said that because such proper charges may be expanded into unjustifiable abridgments they are therefore invalid on their face. . . . It may well be that the wisdom of American communities will persuade them to permit the poor and weak to draw support from the petty sales of religious books without contributing anything for the privilege of using the streets and conveniences of the municipality. Such an exemption, however, would be a voluntary, not a constitutionally enforced, contribution."

Justice Murphy filed a vigorous dissent, a dissent that one year later became majority opinion, for in a 1943 rehearing, the Court vacated this decision and reversed the conviction, citing *Largent v. Texas* (1943)* and *Jamison v. Texas* (1943).* Justice Murphy: "It matters not that petitioners asked contributions for their literature. Freedom of speech and freedom of the press cannot and must not mean freedom only for those who can distribute their broadsides without charge. There may be others with messages more vital but purses less full, who must seek some reimbursement for their outlay or else forgo passing on their ideas. The pamphlet, an historic weapon against oppression, is today the convenient vehicle of those with limited resources because newspaper space and radio time are expensive and the cost of establishing such enterprises great. If freedom of speech and freedom of the press are to have any concrete meaning, people seeking to distribute information and opinion, to the end only that others shall have the benefit thereof, should not be taxed for circulating such matter. . . . Taxes such as the instant ones violate petitioners' right to freedom of speech and freedom of the press, protected against state invasion by the Fourteenth Amendment." *Jones v. Opelika*, 316 U.S. 584 (1942).

JONES v. STATE BOARD OF EDUCATION OF TENNESSEE (1970).

Jones was suspended as a student from Tennessee A. & I. University in 1967 after a hearing. Jones claimed that he had been suspended solely because he distributed some leaflets that urged a boycott of fall registration. The Supreme Court refused to hear the case, saying that the evidence showed that Jones had lied during his hearing and that fact sufficiently "clouded the record"; the Court would not hear his charges of First Amendment violations. Justice Douglas, with whom Justice Brennan concurred, filed a dissenting opinion: "[Jones] . . . was dismissed from the school on charges preferred by a Faculty Advisory Committee and heard by it. One of the charges read as follows: 'You are charged with distributing literature and soliciting students, all of which was designed to boycott the registration at the University.' Our failure to reverse is a serious setback for First Amendment rights in a troubled field. The leaflet now censored may be ill-tempered and in bad taste. But we recognized in *Terminiello v. Chicago** that even strongly abusive utterances or publications, not merely polished and urbane pronouncements of dignified people, enjoy First Amendment rights. This does not mean that free speech can be used with impunity as an excuse to break up classrooms, to destroy the quiet and decorum of convocations, or to bar the constitutional privileges of others to meet together in matters of common concern. But the campus, where this leaflet was distributed, is a fitting place for the dissemination of a wide spectrum of ideas. Moreover, it is far too late to suggest that since attendance at a state university is a 'privilege,' not a 'right,' there are no constitutional barriers to summary withdrawal of the 'privilege.' . . . The circulation did not disrupt a classroom or any other university function. It would seem, therefore, that it is immune from punishment, censorship, and any form of retaliatory action. . . . The suspension of petitioner was based in part on distributing the literature and in part on the committee's conclusion that, when petitioner at the hearing denied that he 'passed out such literature,' he 'did not tell the truth.' But lying to school authorities was no part of the charges leveled against petitioner. If he is to be expelled for lying, he is entitled to notice and opportunity to be heard on that charge." *Jones v. State Board of Education of Tennessee*, 397 U.S. 31 (1970).

J-R DISTRIBUTORS, INC. v. WASHINGTON (1974).

J-R Distributors was convicted in a Washington state court for violating the state's obscenity statute (sale of obscene material). One of the allegedly obscene materials was a publication entitled "Sex Between Humans and Animals." The Supreme Court refused to hear an appeal, and thus the conviction was sustained. In denying certiorari, Justice White commented: "I do not construe the First Amendment as preventing the States from prohibiting the distribution of a publication whose dominant theme is represented by repeated photographs of men and women performing sex acts with a variety of animals.'' *J-R Distributors, Inc. v. Washington*, 418 U.S. 949 (1974), *cert. denied*.

JUDICIAL CONFERENCE OF THE UNITED STATES, ORDER NO. 381. Misc. Order No. 381 (December 17, 1965), subscribed by each judge of the Northern District of Texas, provides: "Standing Order. The Judicial Conference of the United States having adopted the following resolution: Resolved, That the Judicial Conference of the United States condemns the taking of photographs in the courtrooms or its environs in connection with any judicial proceeding, and the broadcasting of judicial proceedings by radio, television, or other means, and considers such practices to be inconsistent with fair judicial procedure and that they ought not be permitted in any federal court; and the 'environs' of the courtroom having been generally interpreted to include all areas upon the same floor of the building upon which the courtrooms are located. It is ordered that the taking of photographs or broadcasting or televising in connection with any judicial proceeding on or from the same floor of the building on which courtrooms are located is forbidden." This order was sustained in a contempt of court citation against a reporter who took photographs on the same floor as a courtroom (*Seymour v. United States* [1967]).*

K

KANSAS, CRIMINAL SYNDICALISM ACT. The relevant portions of this act are as follows: "Section 1. 'Criminal Syndicalism' is hereby defined to be the doctrine which advocates crime, physical violence, arson, destruction of property, sabotage, or other unlawful acts or methods, as a means of accomplishing or effecting industrial or political revolution, or for profit. . . . Section 3. Any person who, by word of mouth, or writing, advocates, affirmatively suggests or teaches the duty, necessity, propriety, or expediency of crime, criminal syndicalism, or sabotage . . . is guilty of a felony." The Supreme Court, in *Fiske v. State of Kansas* (1927),* overturned a conviction under this act.

KANSAS, MOTION PICTURE CENSORSHIP. The Supreme Court, in upholding the constitutionality of the Kansas motion picture censorship statute in *Mutual Film Corporation v. Kansas* (1915),* described the act as follows: "It is entitled 'An Act regulating the exhibiting or using of moving picture films or reels; providing and regulating the examination and approval of moving picture films and reels, and fixing penalties for the violation of this act, and making an appropriation for clerical help to carry this act into effect.' The following are its provisions: On or after April 1, 1913, it shall be unlawful to exhibit or use any moving picture film or reel unless the same shall have been examined and approved by the Superintendent of Public Instruction. Films used in institutions of learning are exempt from the provisions of the act. It is made the duty of such officer to examine the films or reels intended for exhibition and approve such as he shall find to be moral and instructive and to withhold his approval from such as tend to debase or corrupt the morals. He is given the power and authority to supervise and regulate the display of all moving picture films or reels in all places of amusement or elsewhere within the State, to inquire and investigate, and to have displayed for his benefit to aid him in his investigation, those which are intended to be displayed, and shall approve such as shall be moral and proper and disapprove such as are sacrilegious, obscene, indecent or immoral, or such as tend to corrupt the morals." This act was one of the first state schemes to censor motion pictures (Film Censorship*), and it set the tone and nature—films that were seen to be immoral or tending to corrupt or deprave the viewer—for decades of prior restraint. The courts, however, slowly came around to the view that motion pictures were a form of expression protected by the First Amendment, and censorship schemes such as the one in Kansas were eventually declared unconstitutional in 1955 (*The Moon Is Blue**).

KAPLAN v. CALIFORNIA (1974). Kaplan, owner of the Peek-A-Boo Bookstore in Los Angeles, was convicted by a jury of violating the California obscenity statute* for selling a book entitled *Suite 69*. The Supreme Court refused to hear Kaplan's appeal, thus affirming his conviction, but offered a side comment: "Obscene material in book form is not entitled to First Amendment protection merely because it has no pictorial content. A state may control commerce in such a book, even distribution to consenting adults, to avoid the deleterious consequences it can reasonably conclude (conclusive proof is not required) result from the continuing circulation of obscene literature." *Kaplan v. California*, 419 U.S. 915 (1974), *cert. denied*.

KASPER v. BRITTAIN (1957). Kasper was involved in an anti–school desegregation movement. A federal district court judge issued a restraining order prohibiting Kasper and others from hindering, obstructing, or in any way interfering with the carrying out of the court's desegregation order. Kasper refused and made a speech inciting other people to disobey the order. The district court found him guilty of criminal contempt and an appeals court affirmed the conviction. The appeals court, in affirming the conviction, made the following comments: "The right to speak is not absolute and may be regulated to accomplish other legitimate objectives of government. The First Amendment does not confer the right to persuade others to violate the law. The speech here enjoined was clearly calculated to cause a violation of law and speech of that character is not within the protection of the First Amendment. [The speech] . . . was not a mere exposition of ideas. It was advocacy of immediate action to accomplish an illegal result, sought to be avoided by the restraining order. The clear and present danger* test is here met by the mob violence that followed the urgings of the appellant. Danger that calls for the presence of the State Patrol and the National Guard, with the use of bayonets and tear gas, is, we think, within the narrowest limits of the concept and cries aloud for such court action as was here taken." *Kasper v. Brittain*, 245 F. 2d 92 (1957).

KATZEV v. COUNTY OF LOS ANGELES (1959). The county of Los Angeles passed an ordinance (Los Angeles County [CA], Crime Comic Books*) that had as its objective the prohibition of comic books that portrayed its characters engaged in crime. At the trial of Katzev, who sold such a comic book, the California judge found three reasons why the ordinance was a blatant form of censorship and an unconstitutional abridgment of speech and press: (1) "The ordinance is an unjustifiable abridgment of freedom of the press, because distribution of such crime comic books is protected by the state and federal Constitutions, and no showing has been made of a clear and present danger of a substantive evil justifying suppression of the constitutional guarantee.'' (2) ''Because it applies to publications that have no relationship to juvenile delinquency, the ordinance is too broad. The ordinance makes it a crime to circulate any comic books which contain fictional, nonreligious accounts of crime. . . . Crime [is defined] by listing specific crimes . . . and includes acts by animals or imaginary beings which if performed by humans would constitute one of the crimes named. The ordinance does not require that the drawings be lewd or depict brutality, sadism, gore or horror; nor does the ordinance limit its application to accounts of crime which glorify the crime or the criminal, make crime attractive or depict in detail the manner in which crimes are committed. The ordinance brings within its scope such publications as 'New Funnies' (town attacked by bandits in Woody Woodpecker story); 'Bugs Bunny' (Bugs steals diamonds); and 'Classic Comics' (*Treasure Island*). Conversely, it is quite obvious that many crime, horror, or sex comic books containing the features most objectionable may continue unaffected by the ordinance because they are not fictional.'' (3) ''The ordinance denies distributors equal protection of the laws, since it establishes arbitrary and unreasonable exemptions. Sections 3c and 3d of the ordinance exempt from the ban many comic books dealing solely with luridly depicted tales of violence and crime, because the stories are true or drawn from religious writings. Section 3b grants exemption to comic strips in newspapers, although these comic strips may not vary one iota from those appearing in the comic book media. . . . No valid reason has been presented why comic books dealing in a disgustingly detailed way with the exploits of Murder, Incorporated, John Dillinger, or Jesse James will have any less harmful effect on children than Popeye, Tom Mix, or fictionalized accounts of the activities of law enforcement officials like G-Men. . . . Section 4c of the ordinance says that a crime comic includes depiction of 'acts by human beings, and further includes acts by animals or any non-human, part human, or imaginary beings, which if performed by a human would constitute any of the crimes named.' . . . The problem thus arises, when does an animal commit a crime on a human? If the ordinance is taken literally this 'as if' test would make an 'account of crime' out of a person's losing an arm to a shark, since if the shark were human its act would constitute cannibalism or mayhem, or to a dog's eating some food found on a person's porch, since if the dog were human its act would constitute theft [or to Bugs Bunny 'stealing' a carrot from Elmer Fudd's garden].'' *Katzev v. County of Los Angeles*, 341 P. 2d 310 (1959).

KENTUCKY, CORRUPT PRACTICES ACT. Kentucky Revised Statutes, § 121.055 (1982), provided the following: ''Candidates prohibited from making expenditure, loan, promise, agreement, or contract as to action when elected, in consideration for vote.—No candidate for nomination or election to any state, county, city or district office shall expend, pay, promise, loan or become pecuniarily liable in any way for money or other thing of value, either directly or indirectly, to any person in consideration of the vote or financial or moral support of that person. No such candidate shall promise, agree or make a contract with any person to vote for or support any particular individual, thing or measure, in consideration for the vote or the financial or moral support of that person in any election, primary or nominating convention, and no person shall demand that any candidate make such a promise, agreement or contract.'' The Supreme Court, in *Brown v. Hartlage* (1982),* decided that this act could not be used to convict a candidate for public office who promised the voters that he would reduce his salary—and thus save the taxpayers some money—if elected.

KENTUCKY, OBSCENITY STATUTE. Kentucky Revised Statutes, § 436.101 (1973), reads in part: ''Obscene matter, distribution, penalties, destruction. (1) As used in this section: (a) 'Distribute' means to transfer possession of, whether with or without consideration. (b) 'Matter' means any book, magazine, newspaper, or other printed or written material or any picture, drawing, photograph, motion picture, or other pictorial representation of any statue or other figure, or any recording, transcription or mechanical, chemical or electrical reproduction or any other articles, equipment, machines or materials. (c) 'Obscene' means that to the average person, applying contemporary standards, the predominant appeal of the matter, taken as a whole, is to prurient interest, a shameful or morbid interest in nudity, sex, or excretion, which goes substantially beyond customary limits of candor in description or representation of such matters.'' This statute was involved with the attempt by the state of Kentucky to censor the motion picture film *Cindy and Donna** in 1973.

KEYISHIAN v. BOARD OF REGENTS (1967). The New York Civil Service Law,* supplemented by the New York Education Law* and the so-called New York Feinberg Law,* made any person ineligible for employment in any New York public school if the person was a member of any organization advocating the overthrow of the government by force, violence, or any unlawful means. The constitutionality of these regulations was upheld by the Supreme Court in 1952 (*Adler v. Board of Education**) but faced the same questions again in this particular case. Keyishian, a faculty member at the State University of New York, and others were threatened with termination when they refused to sign an oath attesting that they did not belong to any association that advocated the overthrow of the government (the Communist party).

The Supreme Court saw that the decision reached in the *Adler* case was not controlling and found that the Feinberg Law was unconstitutional: ''The essentiality of freedom in the community of American universities is almost self-evident. No one should underestimate the vital role in a democracy that is played by those who guide and train our youth. To impose any strait jacket upon the intellectual leaders in our colleges and universities would imperil the future of our Nation. No field of education is so thoroughly comprehended by man that new discoveries cannot yet be made. Particularly is that true in the social sciences, where few, if any, principles are accepted as absolutes. Scholarship cannot flourish in an atmosphere of suspicion and distrust. Teachers and students must always remain free to inquire, to study and to evaluate, to gain new maturity and understanding; otherwise our civilization will stagnate and die.''

Justice Clark was not pleased with the majority opinion and filed a vigorous dissent: ''The majority says that the Feinberg Law is bad because it has an 'overbroad sweep.' I regret to say . . . that the majority has by its broadside swept away one of our most precious rights, namely, the right of self-preservation. Our public educational system is the genius of our democracy. The minds of our youths are developed there and the character of that development will determine the future of our land. Indeed, our very existence depends upon it. The issue here is a very narrow one. It is not freedom of speech, freedom of thought, freedom of press, freedom of assembly, or of association, even in the Communist Party. It is simply this: May the State provide that one who, after a hearing with full judicial review, is found to have wilfully and deliberately advocated, advised, or taught that our Government should be overthrown by force or violence or other unlawful means; or to have wilfully and deliberately printed, published, etc., any book or paper that so advocated *and to have personally* advocated such doctrine himself; or to have wilfully and deliberately become a member of an organization that advocates such doctrine, is prima facie disqualified from teaching in its university? My answer, in keeping with all of our cases up until today, is 'Yes'!'' *Keyishian v. Board of Regents*, 385 U.S. 589 (1967).

K. GORDON MURRAY PRODUCTIONS, INC. v. FLOYD (1962).

This case concerned the validity of the Atlanta, Georgia, film censorship* statute. K. Gordon Murray Productions sought to enjoin the censorship of an unnamed film, saying that the city censor announced that she would not approve the film and thus the exhibitors would not contract out for the picture. The Georgia judge remarked that the Atlanta ordinance was not unconstitutional under the U.S. Constitution, but rather, Atlanta's censorship scheme was unconstitutional as a prior restraint under the Georgia Constitution. The court cited a section from the Georgia Constitution—''No law shall ever be passed to curtail, or restrain the liberty of speech, or of the press; any person may speak, write and publish his sentiments, on all subjects''—and found that Atlanta's prior restraint was irreconcilable with the Georgia Constitution.

The court concluded its opinion with a personal view of obscene films, written by Chief Justice Duckworth of the Georgia Supreme Court: ''The far reaching effect of this decision does not escape our notice or concern. As individual citizens we hate to see the youth of this State, who will govern the State in the future, subjected to all the evil influence that obscene pictures might exert upon them. But as trusted judges we have no alternative to saying, thus sayeth the Constitution, and we cheerfully obey. It would seem that legislative wisdom could devise a law containing no censorship that would conform to the Constitution as we have construed it and at the same time afford a large degree of protection against obscene pictures. A severe penalty for exhibiting an obscene picture with a provision that if it had been voluntarily submitted to a board created by the law for making such voluntary inspections, and had been judged not to be obscene by that board the courts should give serious consideration of this demonstrated lack of intent when imposing sentence, might be within the bounds of constitutionally permissible legislation." *K. Gordon Murray Productions, Inc. v. Floyd*, 125 S.E. 2d 207 (1962).

KIM YOUNG v. CALIFORNIA (1939). Young was convicted in a Los Angeles court of violating an ordinance (Los Angeles [CA], Distribution of Handbills*) that prohibited distribution of handbills on the grounds that such indiscriminate distribution on a public sidewalk would result in littering. The particular handbill being distributed contained a notice for a meeting to be held by the "Friends Lincoln Brigade" at which speakers were to discuss the Spanish Civil War. The U.S. Supreme Court reversed the conviction, holding the city ordinance to be unconstitutional. The full decision is contained in *Schneider v. State* (1939).* *Kim Young v. California*, 308 U.S. 147 (1939).   ·

KISSINGER v. REPORTERS COMMITTEE FOR FREEDOM OF THE PRESS (1980). The Freedom of Information Act (FOIA)* permits federal district courts to enjoin a governmental agency from "withholding agency records and to order the production of any agency records improperly withheld." When Henry Kissinger served as an assistant to the president for national security affairs (1969–1975) and as secretary of state (1973–1975), his telephone conversations were monitored and summaries or verbatim transcripts were prepared. Kissinger later donated the notes to the Library of Congress with the condition of restricting for a specified period public access to the notes.

Three requests were subsequently filed under the FOIA for the notes: (1) William Safire, the columnist; (2) the Military Audit Project; and (3) the Reporters Committee for Freedom of the Press. The requests were not honored, and the case finally reached the Supreme Court. The Court held: (1) The request by Safire for Kissinger's notes made while he was an assistant to the president need not be granted. The documents were not "agency records" within the meaning of the act, since the office of the president is not included in the category "Executive Office." (2) Although the notes made by Kissinger while he was secretary of state were "agency documents" within the FOIA, and although they should not have been given to the Library of Congress (the Library of Congress does not fall under the category "Executive Office"), the agency that received the request—the State Department—did not withhold the documents because they no longer had possession of them. The Court added that it had no authority to order the Library of Congress to produce the records or to return them to the State Department. *Kissinger v. Reporters Committee for Freedom of the Press*, 445 U.S. 136 (1980).

KLEINDIENST v. MANDEL (1972). Mandel, a Belgian journalist and a Marxian theoretician, was invited to a series of conferences in the United States. He was found ineligible for an entry visa (Immigration and Nationality Act, Visa Regulations*) because it was determined that he advocated and published on the "economic, international, and governmental doctrines of world communism." The attorney general declined to waive ineligibility, as he had the power to do under the act, and the Supreme Court held that the act and the attorney general's actions under it were constitutional: "In the exercise of Congress' plenary power to exclude aliens or prescribe the conditions for their entry into this country, Congress in §§ 212(a)(28) of the Act has delegated conditional exercise of this power to the Executive Branch. When, as in this case, the Attorney General decides for a legitimate and bona fide reason not to waive the statutory exclusion of an alien, courts will not look behind his decision or weigh it against the First Amendment interests of those who would personally communicate with the alien."

Justice Douglas, in a stinging dissent that illustrated the absurdity of the entire process, made the following comments: "Can the Attorney General under the broad discretion entrusted in him decide: that one who maintains that the earth is round can be excluded?; that no one who believes in the Darwinian theory shall be admitted?; that those who promote a Rule of Law to settle international differences rather than a Rule of Force may be barred?; that a genetic biologist who lectures on the way to create life by one sex alone is beyond the pale?; that an exponent of plate tectonics can be barred?; that one should be excluded who taught that Jesus when he arose from the sepulcher, went east (not up) and became a teacher at Hemis Monastery in the Himalayas? I put the issue that bluntly because national security is not involved. Nor is the infiltration of saboteurs [or dope pushers or carriers of plague]. . . . Thought control is not within the competence of any branch of government." *Kleindienst v. Mandel*, 408 U.S. 753 (1972).

KNOWLEDGE TAXES. There have been several cases in which the Supreme Court has ruled that fees or taxes levied on the rights guaranteed by the First Amendment could be seen as "taxes on knowledge" and, as such, violate the freedoms of press and speech. The following comments are by Justice Sutherland (*Grossjean v. American Press**): "A determination of the question whether the tax is valid in respect of the point now under review, requires an examination of the history and circumstances which antedated and attended the adoption of the abridgment clause of the First Amendment. . . . The history is a long one; but for present purposes it may be greatly abbreviated. For more than a century prior to the adoption of the amendment—and, indeed for many years thereafter—history discloses a persistent effort on the part of the British government to prevent or abridge the free expression of any opinion which seemed to criticize or exhibit in an unfavorable light, however truly, the agencies and operations of the government. The struggle between the proponents of measures to that end and those who asserted the right of free expression was continuous and unceasing. As early as 1644, John Milton, in an 'Appeal for the Liberty of Unlicensed Printing,' assailed an act of Parliament which had just been passed providing for censorship of the press previous to publication. He vigorously defended the right of every man to make public his honest views 'without previous censure'; and declared the impossibility of finding any man base enough to accept the office of censor and at the same time good enough to be allowed to perform its duties. (Collett, *History of the Taxes on Knowledge*, vol. I, pp. 4–6). The act expired by its own terms in 1695. It was never renewed; and the liberty of the press thus became (as pointed out by Wickwar, *The Struggle for the Freedom of the Press*, p. 15) merely 'a right or liberty to publish *without* a license what formerly could be published only *with* one.' But mere exemption from previous censorship was soon recognized as too narrow a view of the liberty of the press. In 1712, in response to a message from Queen Anne (Hansard's *Parliamentary History of England*, vol. 6, p. 1063), Parliament imposed a tax upon all newspapers and upon advertisements (Collett, vol. I, pp. 8–10). That the main purpose of these taxes was to suppress the publication of comments and criticisms objectionable to the Crown does not admit of doubt (Stewart, 'Lennox and the Taxes on Knowledge,' 15 *Scottish Historical Review*, 322–327).

"There followed more than a century of resistance to, and evasion of, the taxes, and of agitation for their repeal. In the article last referred to (p. 326), which was written in 1918, it was pointed out that these taxes constituted one of the factors that aroused the American colonists to protest against taxation for the purpose of the home government; and that the revolution really began when, in 1765, that government sent stamps for newspaper duties to the American colonies. Those duties were quite commonly characterized as 'taxes on knowledge,' a phrase used for the purpose of describing the effect of the exactions and at the same time condemning them. That the taxes had, and were intended to have, the effect of curtailing the circulation of newspapers, and particularly the cheaper ones whose readers were generally found among the masses of the people, went almost without question, even on the part of those who defended the act. May (*Constitutional History of England*, 7th ed., vol. 2, p. 245), after discussing the control by 'previous censure,' says: '. . . a new restraint was devised in the form of a stamp duty on newspapers and advertisements,—avowedly for the purpose of repressing libels. This policy, being found effectual in limiting the circulation of cheap papers, was improved upon in the two following reigns, and continued in high esteem until our own time.' Collett (vol. I, p. 14) says, 'Any man who carried on printing or publishing for a livelihood was actually at the mercy of the Commissioners of Stamps, when they chose to exert their powers.'

"Citations of similar import might be multiplied many times; but the foregoing is enough to demonstrate beyond peradventure that in the adoption of the English newspaper stamp tax and the tax on advertisements, revenue was of subordinate concern; and that the dominant and controlling aim was to prevent, or curtail the opportunity for, the acquisition of knowledge by the people in respect of their governmental affairs. It is idle to suppose that so many of the best men in England would for a century of time have waged, as they did, stubborn and often precarious warfare against these taxes if a mere matter of taxation had been involved. The aim of the struggle was not to relieve taxpayers from a burden, but to establish and preserve the right of the English people to full information in respect of the doings or misdoings of their government. Upon the correctness of this conclusion the very characterization of the exactions as 'taxes on knowledge' sheds a flood of corroborative light. In 1785, only four years before Congress had proposed the First Amendment, the Massachusetts legislature, following the English example, imposed a stamp tax on all newspapers and magazines. The following year an advertisement tax was imposed. Both taxes met with such violent opposition that the former was repealed in 1786, and the latter in 1788 (Duniway, *Freedom of the Press in Massachusetts*, pp. 136–137). The framers of the First Amendment were familiar with the English struggle, which then had continued for nearly eighty years and was destined to go on for another sixty-five years, at the end of which time it culminated in a lasting abandonment of the obnoxious taxes. The framers were likewise familiar with the then recent Massachusetts episode; and while that occurrence did much to bring about the adoption of the amendment, the predominant influence must have come from the English experience. It is impossible to concede that by the words 'freedom of the press' the framers of the amendment intended to adopt merely the narrow view then reflected by the law of England that such freedom consisted only in immunity from previous censorship; for this abuse had then permanently disappeared from English practice . . .

"In the light of all that has now been said, it is evident that the restricted rules of the English law in respect of the freedom of the press in force when the Constitution was adopted were never accepted by the American colonists, and that by the First Amendment it was meant to preclude the national government, and by the Fourteenth Amendment to preclude the states, from adopting any form of previous restraint upon printed publications, or their circulation, including that which had theretofore been effected by these two well-known and odious methods."

KOIS v. WISCONSIN (1972). Kois was convicted of violating Wisconsin's obscenity statute (prohibiting the dissemination of lewd, obscene, or indecent material) and was sentenced to two years in jail and a $2,000 fine. Kois was the publisher of an "underground" newspaper and published a certain issue that contained, on an inside page, two pictures of a nude man and woman embracing in a sitting position. Accompanying these pictures was a poem, "Sex Poem," that was a play-by-play account of the poet's recollection of sexual intercourse.

The Supreme Court of Wisconsin upheld the conviction, but on appeal, the U.S. Supreme Court reversed: (1) In the context in which the photographs appeared in the newspaper, they were rationally related to an article that itself was entitled to First Amendment protection. (2) Although the poet's reach exceeded his grasp, the poem does have some of the earmarks of an attempt at serious art and thus is entitled to First Amendment protection. Justice Douglas hurled a parting shot at the Wisconsin authorities: "In this case, the vague umbrella of obscenity laws was used in an attempt to run a radical newspaper out of business." *Kois v. Wisconsin*, 408 U.S. 229 (1972).

KONIGSBERG v. STATE BAR OF CALIFORNIA (1957). In 1954, the Committee of Bar Examiners of California refused to certify Konigsberg to practice law, even though he passed the bar examination, on the grounds that he had failed to prove (1) that he was of good moral character and (2) that he did not advocate the forcible overthrow of the government (California, State Bar Code*).

The California Supreme Court refused to order the bar examiners to certify him, but Konigsberg found relief from the U.S. Supreme Court. Justice Black delivered the opinion of the Court: "In 1950 Konigsberg wrote a series of editorials for a local newspaper. In these editorials he severely criticized, among other things, this country's participation in the Korean War, the actions and policies of the leaders of the major political parties, the influence of 'big business' in American life, racial discrimination, and this Court's decisions. When read in the light of the ordinary give-and-take of political controversy the editorials Konigsberg wrote are not unusually extreme and fairly interpreted only say that certain officials were performing their duties in a manner that, in the opinion of the writer, was injurious to the public. We do not believe that an inference of bad moral character can rationally be drawn from these editorials. Because of the very nature of our democracy such expressions of political views must be permitted. Citizens have a right under our constitutional system to criticize government officials and agencies. Courts are not, and should not be, immune to such criticism. Government censorship can no more be reconciled with our national constitutional standard of freedom of speech and press when done in the guise of determining 'moral character,' than if it should be attempted directly." *Konigsberg v. State Bar of California*, 353 U.S. 252 (1957).

KOVACS v. COOPER (1949). A city ordinance (Trenton [NJ], Sound Trucks*) forbade the use or operation on the public streets of a sound truck or of any instrument that emitted "loud and raucous noises" and was attached to any vehicle. Kovacs was found guilty of violating this ordinance, and the Supreme Court ruled that the ordinance did not infringe on the right of free speech. Justice Reed delivered the majority opinion: "City streets are recognized as a normal place for the exchange of ideas by speech or paper. But this does not mean the freedom is beyond all control. We think it is a permissible exercise of legislative discretion to bar sound trucks with broadcasts of public interest, amplified to a loud and raucous volume, from the public ways of municipalities. . . . There is no restriction upon the communication of ideas or discussion of issues by the human voice, by newspapers, by pamphlets, by dodgers. We think that the need for reasonable protection in the homes or business houses from the distracting noises of vehicles equipped with such sound amplifying devices justifies the ordinance.''

Justice Rutledge dissented from the majority opinion: ''For myself, I have no doubt of state power to regulate their abuse in reasonable accommodation, by narrowly drawn statutes, to other interests concerned in use of the streets and in freedom from public nuisance. But that the First Amendment limited its protections of speech to the natural range of the human voice as it existed in 1790 would be, for me, like saying that the commerce power remains limited to navigation by sail and travel by the use of horses and oxen in accordance with the principal modes of carrying on commerce in 1789. The Constitution was not drawn with any such limited vision of time, space and mechanics. It is one thing to hold that the states may regulate the use of sound trucks by appropriately limited measures [*Saia v. New York**]. It is entirely another to say their use can be forbidden altogether.'' *Kovacs v. Cooper*, 336 U.S. 77 (1949).

KUNZ v. NEW YORK (1951). A city ordinance (New York City [NY], Use of Streets*) required the granting of a permit before the streets could be used for religious meetings and also allowed the permit to be withdrawn by the police commissioner if the commissioner had ''good reason'' to revoke the permit. Kunz was convicted of holding a religious meeting on the street after his permit was revoked.

The Supreme Court reversed the conviction, ruling that the New York City ordinance was an invalid prior restraint. Chief Justice Vinson delivered the majority opinion: ''We are here concerned only with the propriety of the action of the police commissioner in refusing to issue that permit. Disapproval of the 1948 permit application by the police commissioner was justified by the New York court on the grounds that a permit had previously been revoked 'for good reasons.' It is noteworthy that there is no mention in the ordinance of reasons for which such a permit application can be refused. This interpretation allows the police commissioner, an administrative official, to exercise discretion in denying subsequent permit applications on the basis of his interpretation, at that time, of what is deemed to be conduct condemned by the ordinance. We have here, then, an ordinance which gives an administrative official discretionary power to control in advance the right of citizens to speak on religious matters on the streets of New York. As such, the ordinance is clearly invalid as a prior restraint on the exercise of First Amendment rights.''

In a stinging dissent, Justice Jackson discussed some of the ''good reasons'' involved in denying Kunz a speaking permit: ''At these meetings, Kunz preached, among many other things of like tenor, that 'The Catholic Church makes merchandise out of souls,' that Catholicism is 'a religion of the devil,' and that the Pope is 'the anti-Christ.' The Jews he denounced as 'Christ-killers,' and said of them, 'All the garbage that didn't believe in Christ should have been burnt in the incinerators. It's a shame they all weren't.' These utterances, as one might expect, stirred strife and threatened violence. Testifying in his own behalf, Kunz stated that he 'became acquainted with' one of the complaining witnesses, whom he thought to be a Jew, 'when he happened to sock one of my Christian boys in the puss.' . . . The Court today initiates the doctrine that language such as this, in the environment of the street meeting, is immune from prior municipal control. We would have a very different question if New York had presumed to say that Kunz could not speak his piece in his own pulpit or hall. But it has undertaken to restrain him only if he chooses to speak at street meetings. There is a world of difference. The street preacher takes advantage of people's presence on the streets to impose his message upon what, in a sense, is a captive audience. A meeting on private property is made up of an audience that has volunteered to listen. The question, therefore, is not whether New York could, if it tried, silence Kunz, but whether it must place its streets at his service to hurl insults at the passer-by. . . . 'Fighting words,' when thrown at Catholics and Jews who are rightfully on the streets of New York, are statements that 'The Pope is the anti-Christ' and the Jews are 'Christ-killers.' These terse epithets come down to our generation weighted with hatreds accumulated through centuries of bloodshed. They are recognized words of art in the profession of defamation. They are not the kind of insult that men bandy and laugh off when the spirits are high and the flagons are low. They are not in that class of epithets whose literal sting will be drawn if the speaker smiles when he uses them. They are always, and in every context, insults which do not spring from reason and can be answered by none. Their historical associations with violence are well understood, both by those who hurl and those who are struck by these missiles. Jews, many of whose families perished in extermination furnaces of Dachau and Auschwitz, are more than tolerant if they pass off lightly the suggestion that unbelievers in Christ should all have been burned. . . . In this case the Court does not justify, excuse, or deny the inciting and provocative character of the language, and it does not, and on this record could not, deny that when Kunz speaks he poses a 'clear and present' danger to peace and order. Why, then, does New York have to put up with it?'' *Kunz v. New York*, 340 U.S. 290 (1951).

L

LADY CHATTERLEY'S LOVER. Now a classic, this book, by D. H. Lawrence, and the film version, were subject to several censorship attempts on grounds of its alleged obscenity and its alleged advocacy of adultery. In 1944, the state of New York, represented by John S. Sumner of the New York Society for the Suppression of Vice (Comstockery*), brought suit against Dial Press (*People on Complaint of Sumner v. Dial Press, Inc.* (48 N.Y.S. 2d 480 [1944]) for publishing and having in its possession with intent to sell a book that was alleged to be obscene, a violation of the New York Penal Code, § 1141 (New York, Obscenity Statute*). Even though the Ulysses Standard* (the test of obscenity was to evaluate the dominant theme of the entire book) had been announced several years previously, the city magistrate hearing the case still operated under the Hicklin Rule* (isolated passages could render the entire work obscene). Magistrate Keutgen apparently did not like the book: "The defendant demanded a hearing in this court. At the hearing, it was proved by sufficient evidence that the defendant had a considerable number of copies of the book in its possession with intent to sell and the defendant admitted that it published this book. A copy of the book was received in evidence. The author's central theme and the dominant effect of the whole book is that it is dangerous to the physical and mental health of a young woman to remain continent [citations to ten pages are given] and that the most important thing in her life, more important than any rule of law or morals, is the gratification of her sexual desire [a citation to two pages and one paragraph]. The book is clearly obscene and the defendant will be held for the Court of Special Sessions."

The New York decision, however, was not the last with *Lady Chatterley's Lover*. In 1960, Grove Press discovered that the postmaster general had ruled that the book was obscene and thus non-mailable under the federal obscenity statute, 18 U.S.C. § 1461 (Postal Regulations, Mailing Obscene Material*). A federal district court did not agree with the postmaster general, and on appeal, an appeals court affirmed the decision, ruling that the book was not obscene (*Grove Press, Inc. v. Christenberry*, 276 F. 2d 433 [1960]). Judge Clark delivered the opinion of the appeals court: "D. H. Lawrence completed the third manuscript version of his novel *Lady Chatterley's Lover* in Italy in 1928, and it was then published in Florence for private distribution. It is this version which has now been published by the plaintiff Grove Press, Inc., in a sumptuous edition selling for $6.00, with a prefatory letter of commendation by Archibald MacLeish, poet, playwright, and Boylston Professor of Rhetoric and Oratory at Harvard University, and with an extensive Introduction and a concluding Bibliographical Note by Mark Schorer, Professor of English Literature at the University of California and a Lawrence scholar. . . . The Postmaster General wrote a substantial decision, of which these are salient paragraphs: 'The contemporary community standards are not such that this book should be allowed to be transmitted in the mails. The book is replete with descriptions in minute detail of sexual acts engaged in or discussed by the book's principal characters. These descriptions utilize filthy, offensive, and degrading words and terms. Any literary merit the book may have is far outweighed by the pornographic and smutty passages and words, so that the book, taken as a whole, is an obscene and filthy work.' ''

Judge Clark, after giving a synopsis of the plot, simply stated: ''Examined with care and 'considered as a whole,' the predominant appeal of *Lady Chatterley's Lover* in our judgment is demonstrably not to prurient interest as thus defined.'' Judge Clark reproduced Professor Schorer's summary as contained in the Introduction: ''Constance Chatterley, the frustrated wife of an aristocratic mine owner who has been wounded in the war and left paralyzed and impotent, is drawn to his game-keeper, the misanthropic son of a miner, becomes pregnant by him, and hopes at the end of the book to be able to divorce her husband and leave her class for a life with the other man.'' Obviously displaying more talent for literary criticism than did Magistrate Keutgen, Judge Clark also commented that ''of course the story is a small part of the work. Actually the book is a polemic against three things which Lawrence hated: the crass industrialization of the English Midlands, the British caste system, and inhibited sex relations between man and woman.''

The film version was produced in France in 1957 and released under the title of *L'Amant de Lady Chatterley*. It was directed by Marc Allegret, starred Danielle Darrieux and Erno Crisa, was reviewed in the *New York Herald-Tribune* and *New York Times*, and was banned in New York in 1957. The film was banned by the New York Board of Regents, not because it was judged to be obscene, but because the New York Education Law (New York, Motion Picture Censorship*) required the denial of an exhibition permit ''if a motion picture's subject matter is adultery presented as being right and desirable for certain people under certain circumstances.''

The distributor of the film, Kingsley International Pictures Corporation, appealed the decision of the regents not to issue a license, and the case reached the Supreme Court in 1959 (*Kingsley International Pictures Corp. v. Regents of the University of the State of New York*, 360 U.S. 684 [1959]). The Supreme Court ruled that New York could not prevent the showing of *L'Amant de Lady Chatterley*: ''What New York has done, therefore, is to prevent the exhibition of a motion picture because that picture advocates an idea—that adultery under certain circumstances may be proper behavior. Yet the First Amendment's basic guarantee is freedom to advocate ideas. The State, quite simply, has thus struck at the very heart of constitutionally protected liberty. It is contended that the State's action was justified because the motion picture attractively portrays a relationship which is contrary to the moral standards, the religious precepts, and the legal code of its citizenry. This argument misconceives what it is that the Constitution protects. Its guarantee is not confined to the expression of ideas that are conventional or shared by a majority. It protects advocacy of the opinion that adultery may sometimes be proper, no less than advocacy of socialism or the single tax. And in the realm of ideas it protects expression which is eloquent no less than that which is unconvincing.''

It is instructive to present the remarks of Justices Black and Frankfurter, comments that were offered in separate concurring opinions. Justice Black: ''I concur in the Court's opinion and judgment but add a few words because of concurring opinions by several Justices who rely on their appraisal of the movie *Lady Chatterley's Lover* for holding that New York cannot constitutionally bar it. Unlike them, I have not seen the picture. My view is that stated by Mr. Justice Douglas, that prior censorship of moving pictures like prior censorship of newspapers and books violates the First and Fourteenth Amendments. If despite the Constitution, however, this Nation is to embark on the dangerous road of censorship, my belief is that this Court is about the most inappropriate Supreme Board of Censors that could be found. So far as I know, judges possess no special expertise providing exceptional competency to set standards and to supervise the private morals of the Nation. In addition, the Justices of this Court seem especially unsuited to make the kind of value judgments as to what movies are good or bad for local communities which the concurring opinions appear to require. We are told that the only way we can decide whether a State or municipality can constitutionally bar movies is for this Court to view and appraise each movie on a case-by-case basis. Under these circumstances, every member of the Court must exercise his own judgment as to how bad a picture is, a judgment which is ultimately based at least in large part on his own standard of what is immoral. The end result of such decisions seems to me to be a purely personal determination by individual Justices as to whether a particular picture viewed is too bad to allow it to be seen by the public. Such an individualized determination cannot be guided by reasonably fixed and certain standards. Accordingly, neither States nor moving picture makers can possibly know in advance, with any fair degree of certainty, what can or cannot be done in the field of movie making and exhibiting. This uncertainty cannot easily be reconciled with the rule of law which our Constitution envisages.''

Justice Frankfurter: ''As one whose taste in art and literature hardly qualifies him for the *avant-garde*, I am more than surprised, after viewing the picture, that the New York authorities should have banned *Lady Chatterley's Lover*. To assume that this motion picture would have offended Victorian moral sensibilities is to rely only on the stuffiest of Victorian conventions. Whatever one's personal preferences may be about such matters, the refusal to license the exhibition of this picture . . . can only mean that [the Education Law] forbids the public showing of any film that deals with adultery except by way of sermonizing condemnation or depicts any physical manifestation of an illicit amorous relation. . . . I have no choice but to agree with this Court's judgment in holding that the State exceeded the bounds of free expression protected by the 'liberty' of the Fourteenth Amendment.''

LAMONT v. POSTMASTER GENERAL (1965). Certain regulations (Postal Regulations, Communist Political Propaganda*) required the postmaster general to detain and deliver only on the addressee's request, unsealed foreign mailings that the postmaster general classified as ''communist political propaganda.'' Under the procedure, the post office sent a card to the individual to be checked and returned if the addressee wanted the material. The card stated that if it were not returned within twenty days, the post office would assume that the addressee did not want the publication or any similar one in the future. In this case, the addressee received a card saying that the post office was ''holding'' a copy of the *Peking Review*, and Lamont brought suit to enjoin the enforcement of the regulations.

The Supreme Court held that the regulations were unconstitutional, since they imposed on the addressee an obligation that amounted to a limitation of his rights under the First Amendment. Justice Douglas delivered the opinion of the Court: ''We conclude that the Act is unconstitutional because it requires an official act (returning the reply card) as a limitation on the unfettered exercise of the addressee's First Amendment rights. As stated by Mr. Justice Holmes in *Milwaukee Pub. Co. v. Burleson*: 'The United States may give up the Post Office when it sees fit, but while it carries it on the use of the mails is almost as much a part of free speech as the right to use our tongues.' Here the Congress—expressly restrained by the First Amendment from 'abridging' freedom of speech and of press—is the actor. The Act sets administrative officials astride the flow of mail to inspect it, appraise it, write the addressee about it, and await a response before dispatching the mail. . . . The addressee carries an affirmative obligation which we do not think the Government may impose on him. This requirement is almost certain to have a deterrent effect, especially as respects those who have sensitive positions. Their livelihood may be dependent on a security clearance. Public officials, like schoolteachers who have no tenure, might think they would invite disaster if they read what the Federal Government says contains the seeds of treason. Apart from them, any addressee is likely to feel some inhibition in sending for literature which federal officials have condemned as 'communist political propaganda.' The regime of this Act is at war with the 'uninhibited, robust, and wide-open' debate and discussion that are contemplated by the First Amendment.'' *Lamont v. Postmaster General*, 381 U.S. 301 (1965).

LANDMARK COMMUNICATIONS, INC. v. VIRGINIA (1978). A Virginia statute (Virginia, Confidentiality Rule*) made it a crime to divulge information regarding proceedings before a state judicial review commission authorized to hear complaints about judges' disability or misconduct. For printing in its newspaper an article accurately reporting on a pending inquiry by the commission and identifying the judge whose conduct was under scrutiny, the publisher was convicted of violating the statute.

On appeal, the Supreme Court reversed the conviction: (1) The First Amendment does not permit the criminal punishment of third persons who are strangers to proceedings before such a commission for divulging or publishing truthful information regarding confidential proceedings of the commission. (2) A major purpose of the First Amendment is to protect the free discussion of governmental affairs and injury to the reputation of judges or the institutional reputation of courts is not sufficient to justify ''repressing speech that would otherwise be free.''

Justice Stewart added these comments: ''I find nothing in the Constitution to prevent Virginia from punishing those who violate this confidentiality. But in this case Virginia has extended its law to punish a newspaper, and it cannot constitutionally do so. If the constitutional protection of a free press means anything, it means that government cannot take it upon itself to decide what a newspaper may or may not publish. Though government may deny access to information and punish its theft [the publisher in this case did not 'steal' the information—it was 'leaked' to the newspaper], government may not prohibit or punish the publication of that information once it falls into the hands of the press, unless the need for secrecy is manifestly overwhelming . . . national defense [and intelligence operations are] the most obvious justification for government restrictions on publication. Even then, distinctions must be drawn between prior restraints* and subsequent penalties.'' *Landmark Communications, Inc. v. Virginia*, 435 U.S. 829 (1978).

LARGENT v. TEXAS (1943). A municipal ordinance (Paris [TX], Handbill Distribution*) prohibited the distribution of religious publications except with a permit from the city. The issuing officer had wide discretion as to whether to grant or to refuse the permit, and the permit could be revoked at any time for any reason. The Supreme Court found this process to be a violation of the First Amendment. Justice Reed: ''Upon the merits, this appeal is governed by recent decisions of this Court involving ordinances which leave the granting or withholding of permits for the distribution of religious publications in the discretion of municipal officers. It is unnecessary to determine whether the distributions of the publications in question are sales or contributions. The mayor issues a permit only if after thorough investigation he 'deems it proper or advisable.' Dissemination of ideas depends upon the approval of the distributor by the official. This is administrative censorship in an extreme form. It abridges the freedom of religion, of the press and of speech guaranteed by the Fourteenth Amendment.'' *Largent v. Texas*, 318 U.S. 418 (1943).

LA RONDE. *La Ronde* is the film version of Schnitzler's classic *Reigen* (*The Ring*; published in English as *Hands Around**). The plot is a series of vignettes recounting the sexual activities of several people: The first is between a prostitute and a soldier, then the soldier and a parlor maid, the parlor maid and a young man, the young man and someone else's wife, the wife and her husband, the husband and a young girl, the girl and a poet, the poet and an actress, the actress and a count, and the last, the count back with the original prostitute. The book was described in the following terms by the judge in *People v. Pesky* 243 N.Y.S. 193 (1930) (*Hands Around*): "While some people may think this quite smart, a book of this kind, which has nothing to recommend it, and dealing wholly with such [sexual] details, is properly held to be disgusting, indecent, and obscene."

The film version ran into the same reception in *Commercial Pictures Corp. v. Board of Regents of the University of the State of New York* (113 N.E. 2d 502 [1953]). The New York Board of Regents, acting under the New York Education Law (New York, Motion Picture Censorship*), banned the film in 1953 on the grounds that it would "tend to corrupt the morals" of anyone unfortunate enough to view the film.

A New York Appellate Division court affirmed the regents' decision, Judge Froessel delivering the majority opinion: "Of course it is true that the State may not impose upon its inhabitants the moral code of saints, but, if it is to survive, it must be free to take such reasonable and appropriate measures as may be deemed necessary to preserve the institution of marriage and the home, and the health and welfare of its inhabitants. History bears witness to the fate of peoples who have become indifferent to the vice of indiscriminate sexual immorality— a most serious threat to the family, the home and the State. An attempt to combat such threat is embodied in the sections of the Education Law here challenged. It should not be thwarted by any doctrinaire approach to the problems of free speech raised thereby. That a motion picture which panders to base human emotions is a breeding ground for sensuality, depravity, licentiousness and sexual immorality can hardly be doubted. That these vices represent a 'clear and present danger' to the body social seems manifestly clear. The danger to youth is self-evident. And so adults, who may react with limited concern to a portrayal of larceny, will tend to react quite differently to a presentation wholly devoted to promiscuity, seductively portrayed in such a manner as to invite concupiscence and condone its promiscuous satisfaction, with its evil social consequences. A single motion picture may be seen simultaneously in theatres throughout the State. May nothing be done to prevent countless individuals from being exposed to its vicious effects? To us the answer seems obvious, especially in the light of recent technical developments which render the problem more acute than ever. Now we have commercially feasible three dimensional projection, some forms of which are said to bring the audience 'right into the picture.' There can be no doubt that attempts will be made to bring the audience right into the bedchamber if it be held that the State is impotent to apply preventative measures." The specter of three-dimensional sex and the imminent collapse of society was apparently too much for Judge Froessel, and his opinion clearly shows the attitude of the pro-censorship position.

There was, however, a dissenting opinion by Judge Dye: "According to the record, the picture *La Ronde* since its admission through Customs [Tariff Act*] without objection, has been exhibited throughout the United States in cities and towns in [seventeen states]. Nowhere has the showing of *La Ronde* been banned except in New York . . . indicating that in a large segment of society the picture is not offensive. On the contrary, we are told that the showing elsewhere has been well received and has elicited favorable acclaim by the premier dramatic critics of eminent publications. In addition, it has been shown in the principal cities of most foreign countries and has received special recognition for merit from several motion picture academies as, for instance, in Cuba as the best film of 1951, by the British Film Academy in London as the best film from any source, British or foreign, and in 1952, a nomination for an award at the Hollywood Academy."

Commercial Pictures appealed Judge Froessel's decision to the Supreme Court, and the Court, in *Commercial Pictures v. Board of Regents* (346 U.S. 587 [1954]), reversed the New York ban. The Court, in a per curiam decision, citing *The Miracle** decision of 1952, stated that censorship could not be applied just because the film was alleged to have been "immoral."

LATUKO. This film was made in Africa in 1950 under the direction of Edward M. Queeny, a trustee of the American Museum of Natural History, during an official museum expedition into the Anglo-Egyptian Sudan in Africa. The film, an educational documentary, was described as "an authentic photographic record of the life, customs and ceremonies of the Latuko tribe, reported with absolute fidelity, depicting in documentary form the actual day-to-day living of the tribe." The Latuko people, however, didn't wear clothes in their native environment. The thought of a film showing nudity upset Keenan, the public safety officer of Newark, New Jersey, and he prohibited the museum from showing the film in Newark.

The museum then appealed Keenan's decision (*American Museum of Natural History v. Keenan*, 89 A. 2d 98 [1952]) and asked the court to restrain the city from interfering with the exhibition of *Latuko* and to have the city return the confiscated film (Keenan was so upset that he impounded the film). The court, Judge Freund delivering the opinion, granted the museum's requests: "From my viewing of the film . . . there is nothing suggestive, obscene, indecent, malicious or immoral in the showing of the Latuko aborigines in their normal living state. While it is true that the men have been photographed naked and the women naked above the waist, the exposure of their bodies is not indecent; it is simply their normal way of living. They are not shown in any attitude or function to which exception might justifiably be taken. In my opinion, only a narrow or unhealthy mind [Keenan?] could find any depravity in the film. The nakedness of the natives is such an inconsequential factor in what is an absorbing and instructive documentation that the plaintiffs should be protected. . . . The defendants have no authority to interfere with the presentation of the film or to confiscate it.''

LEGION OF DECENCY. The Legion of Decency, a Roman Catholic organization, was established in April 1934 by the Episcopal Committee on Motion Pictures with the goal to improve the moral quality of films. De Grazia and Newman (*Banned Films*, pp. 40–60) present the entire story of the Legion's censorship of motion pictures, and they comment (p. 42) that Catholics were expected to promise to refrain from viewing all ''objectionable'' movies or patronizing any theater that showed such movies. The ''pledge'' read as follows: ''I wish to join the Legion of Decency, which condemns vile and unwholesome moving pictures. I unite with all who protest against them as a grave menace to youth, to home life, to country, and to religion. . . . Considering these evils, I hereby promise to remain away from all motion pictures except those which do not offend decency and Christian morality. I promise further to secure as many members as possible for the Legion of Decency. I make this protest in a spirit of self-respect, and with the conviction that the American public does not demand filthy pictures, but clean entertainment and educational features.''†

De Grazia and Newman continue and write that approximately 10 million Catholics signed this oath, pledging themselves to ''rid the country of its greatest menace—the salacious motion picture.''† At the urging of local bishops, protestors threatened offending exhibitors with public demonstrations (*The Miracle**), and ''communicants were told that attendance at such a movie would constitute a venial sin.''†

The Legion of Decency evolved a rating system that has been revised from time to time. Haney (*Comstockery in America*, pp. 109–131) writes that the 1957 rating system contained six categories: A-1 (morally sound for most people); A-2 (unobjectionable for adolescents and adults); A-3 (unobjectionable only for adults); B (morally objectionable in part for adults, adolescents, and children [Haney, pp. 118–119, comments that ''some Catholics might be able to attend these films without harm; but even for these people, repeated exposure could be dangerous and should be avoided'' and cites a Legion of Decency publication: ''Out of desire to do the better thing, a loyal member of the Legion of Decency will generally prefer to avoid B pictures altogether. Unless he has some real necessity for going, he will not want to give his patronage to producers and distributors who are dragging down the nation's moral standards'']); C (condemned for all—C films are ''so bad that the average person seeing them would rarely escape a severe temptation to sin''); and the last classification, one that

---

†Reprinted from *Banned Films* with permission of the R. R. Bowker Company. Copyright © 1982 by Edward de Grazia and Roger K. Newman.

was rarely used, is described by Haney as identifying films that, "while not morally offensive, require some analysis and explanation as a protection to the uninformed against wrong interpretations and false conclusions." The film *Martin Luther* was placed in this last category. Here are some sample classifications: A-1 (morally unobjectionable for all audiences)—*The Old Man and the Sea, No Time for Sergeants, Bridge on the River Kwai*; A-2 (morally unobjectionable for adults and adolescents but not for children)—*Hatfull of Rain, Witness for the Prosecution, The Return of Dracula*; A-3 (morally unobjectionable for adults but not for adolescents and children)—*South Pacific, Cat on a Hot Tin Roof, Desire Under the Elms*; B (morally objectionable in part for all audiences)—*A Farewell to Arms, God's Little Acre,* * *The Sun Also Rises*; and C (condemned)— *The Game of Love,* * *She Should'a Said No!,* * *And God Created Woman.*

The Legion of Decency has since changed its name to the National Catholic Office for Motion Pictures. Its current rating system is similar to the one described above. Its ratings are publicized and distributed through diocesan newspapers and Catholic journals and publications.

LEHMAN v. CITY OF SHAKER HEIGHTS (1974). Harry J. Lehman, a candidate for Ohio state representative, was refused available advertising space on cars of the Shaker Heights, Ohio, rapid transit system. The refusal of space was based on a municipal policy of not allowing any political advertising but permitting other types of public transit advertising. Lehman then brought suit, challenging the constitutionality of this policy, but the Supreme Court found no violation of Lehman's right of free speech: Car card space on a city transit system is not a First Amendment forum. The decision to limit transit advertisements to innocuous and less controversial commercial and service-oriented advertising— thus minimizing chances of abuse, appearances of political favoritism, and the risk of imposing on a captive audience—is within the city's discretion and involves no First or Fourteenth Amendment violation.

In a uncharacteristic departure from strong and traditional support of the freedoms of speech and press, Justice Douglas agreed with this decision: "Lehman is free to express his views to a willing audience but has no constitutional right to force his message upon a captive audience which uses public transportation not as a place for discussion, but only as a means of transport." *Lehman v. City of Shaker Heights*, 418 U.S. 298 (1974).

LES AMANTS. This film, produced in France in 1958 and directed by Louis Malle, starred Jeanne Moreau and Alain Ainy and was awarded second prize at the 1959 Venice Film Festival; it was also banned in the cities of Cleveland, Dayton, Chicago, Boston, Providence, Portland, and Memphis and in the states of New York, Virginia, and Maryland. The plot is summarized by de Grazia and Newman (*Banned Films*, pp. 263–264): "This film was adapted from the nineteenth-century novel *Point de Lendemain* by Dominique Vivant. Jeanne Tournier, a 30-year-old woman living in the French city of Lyon, is trapped in an unhappy marriage. Neglected by her busy husband, who is a publisher, she is encouraged by her friend Maggy to have an affair in Paris. But the lover, a man-about-town named Raoul, offers Jeanne no real escape from her loneliness. When her husband becomes suspicious, he invites Maggy and Raoul for a week-end visit. Jeanne's car breaks down on the way from Paris, and she accepts a ride from a young archaeologist, Bernard, who expresses contempt for the society in which she moves. Jeanne's husband invites Bernard to spend the night and after an unpleasant dinner, all but Bernard retire. Jeanne cannot sleep and goes for a moonlight walk on the grounds. She meets Bernard and they become lovers. The next morning Jeanne is unable to return to her former life and unwilling to relinquish her newly found happiness. She rejects her family, her home, and her friends, and leaves with Bernard to face an uncertain future.''†

This film was involved in several court cases, most notably in Chicago (*Zenith International Film Corporation v. City of Chicago*, 291 F. 2d 785 [1961]), which involved the Chicago, Illinois, motion picture censorship* scheme, and in Ohio (*Jacobellis v. Ohio*, 378 U.S. 184 [1964]), which involved the Ohio obscene material* statute. In the Ohio case, Jacobellis, a manager of a motion picture theater, was convicted for possessing and exhibiting an obscene film (*Les Amants*). On appeal, the Supreme Court reversed the conviction, ruling that the film was not obscene under the Roth Standard.*

The decision really had less to do with the film itself and was concerned more with the evolving view of obscenity and the role, if any, the Supreme Court would play in such cases. Justice Brennan: ''Motion pictures are within the ambit of the constitutional guarantees of freedom of speech and of the press. But in *Roth v. United States*,* we held that obscenity is not subject to those guarantees. Application of an obscenity law to suppress a motion picture thus requires ascertainment of the 'dim and uncertain line' that often separates obscenity from constitutionally protected expression. It has been suggested that this is a task in which our Court need not involve itself. We are told that the determination whether a particular motion picture, book, or other work of expression is obscene can be treated as a purely factual judgment on which a jury's verdict is all but conclusive, or that in any event the decision can be left essentially to state and lower federal courts, with this Court exercising only a limited review such as that needed to determine whether the ruling below is supported by 'sufficient evidence.' This suggestion is appealing, since it would lift from our shoulders a difficult, recurring, and unpleasant task. But we cannot accept it. . . . The Court has explicitly refused to tolerate a result whereby 'the constitutional limits of free expression in the Nation would vary with state lines'; we see even less justification for allowing such limits to vary with town or county lines. We thus

†Reprinted from *Banned Films* with permission of the R. R. Bowker Company. Copyright © 1982 by Edward de Grazia and Roger K. Newman.

reaffirm the position taken in *Roth* to the effect that the constitutional status of an allegedly obscene work must be determined on the basis of a national standard. It is, after all, a national Constitution we are expounding.''

LEWIS v. CITY OF NEW ORLEANS (1974). A city ordinance (New Orleans [LA], Cursing Police*) made it unlawful to curse or to use opprobrious language toward a police officer. Lewis was convicted under this ordinance for saying, ''You god damn mother fucker police.'' The Louisiana Supreme Court upheld the conviction, but the U.S. Supreme Court reversed on the grounds of over-breadth*: The ordinance sweeps within its ambit protected expression as well. The Court noted that the ordinance plainly had a broader sweep than the constitutional definition of ''fighting words''* as being words that by their very utterance inflict injury or tend to incite an immediate breach of the peace (*Chaplinsky v. New Hampshire**). The ordinance, by also prohibiting ''opprobrious'' language—words conveying or intended to convey disgrace—was an invalid restriction on the right of free speech. *Lewis v. City of New Orleans*, 415 U.S. 130 (1974).

LILES v. OREGON (1976). Liles and others were convicted of selling obscene motion picture films in violation of the Oregon obscenity statute. The Supreme Court refused to grant certiorari and thus the conviction stood. But Justice Brennan, joined by Justices Stewart and Marshall, filed a brief dissent to the refusal to grant certiorari. Brennan's comments show that even with decision after decision by the Supreme Court in obscenity cases and the attempt to formulate some general standards (Roth*/Memoirs*/Miller*), some judges insist on applying their own particular (and often peculiar) standards. The standard used in this case was the trial judge's mother's sensibilities. Justice Brennan: ''I note that this case particularly exemplifies the difficulty and arbitrariness inherent in any attempt to articulate a standard of obscenity. I need only quote the standard applied by the judge before whom petitioners' case was tried: 'Well, what is patently offensive? And, frankly, I had to kind of apply my own standard, which, I believe, corresponds with the standards of the community. And the standard probably, simply stated and boiled down, is the same one which was taught to me by my mother from the day I was a small child. If there was something of which I would not want her to know, then don't do it. Pretty simple. Applying that standard I would think that I wouldn't get any quarrel out of anyone in this room, that they wouldn't want their mothers sitting next to them while they looked at either one of these movies. They are patently offensive.' '' It would appear that Alexander Portnoy is alive and well! *Liles v. Oregon*, 425 U.S. 963 (1976), *cert. denied*.

LINMARK ASSOCIATES, INC. v. TOWNSHIP OF WILLINGBORO (1977). The township of Willingboro, New Jersey, enacted an ordinance that prohibited the posting of real estate ''For Sale'' and ''Sold'' signs on residential property for the purpose of stemming what the township perceived as the flight of white homeowners from a racially integrated community. The Supreme Court held the ordinance to be a violation of the First Amendment as a form of censorship over the content of a message: (1) The ordinance cannot be sustained on the grounds that it restricts only one method of communication while leaving ample alternative communication channels open. The alternatives (newspaper ads and listings) involve more cost and may be less effective. The ordinance is not concerned with the time-place-manner* of the speech but prohibits certain kinds of signs based on their content because the township fears the effect of the message—those receiving the information might act on it. (2) Although the asserted goal of promoting stable integrated housing is important, the ordinance cannot be upheld on the grounds that it promotes an important governmental objective—the objective can be attained by other means—and even if it couldn't, the township cannot achieve its objective by restricting the free flow of truthful commercial information. *Linmark Associates, Inc. v. Township of Willingboro*, 431 U.S. 85 (1977).

LIQUOR. The preferred position of the rights guaranteed by the First Amendment appears to have been lost when in conflict with the Twenty-first Amendment (giving to the states broad authority to regulate alcoholic beverages). In two cases (*California v. LaRue* [1972]* and *New York State Liquor Authority v. Dennis Bellanca* [1981]*), the Supreme Court ruled (although with some vigorous dissent) that the Twenty-first Amendment allows a state to prohibit certain kinds of activities that would normally be protected by the First Amendment in places serving alcoholic beverages. The state can prohibit, for example, lewd or naked entertainment in places in which liquor is served, even though the entertainment is not obscene. Seen as a valid time-place-manner* restriction, activities that could freely be done in a theater or in a film may be prohibited in a bar or nightclub.

LOCKPORT (NY), SOUND TRUCKS. The following Lockport city ordinance was declared unconstitutional as a prior restraint by the Supreme Court in *Saia v. New York* (1948)*: "It shall be unlawful for any person to maintain and operate in any building, or on any premises or on any automobile, motor truck or other motor vehicle, any radio device, mechanical device, or loud speaker or any device of any kind whereby the sound therefrom is cast directly upon the streets and public places and where such device is maintained for advertising purposes or for the purpose of attracting the attention of the passing public, or which is so placed and operated that the sounds coming therefrom can be heard to the annoyance or inconvenience of travelers upon any street or public places or of persons in neighboring premises. Exception. Public dissemination, through radio loudspeakers, of items of news and matters of public concern and athletic activities shall not be deemed a violation of this section provided that the same be done under permission obtained from the Chief of Police." The flaw of this ordinance was the exception: One had to receive prior permission from the chief of police, but there were no standards to limit the chief's discretion to issue or refuse the permit.

LOS ANGELES (CA), ANONYMOUS HANDBILLS. Municipal Code of the City of Los Angeles, § 28.06, read as follows: "No person shall distribute any handbill in any place under any circumstances, which does not have printed on the cover, or the face thereof, the name and address of the following: (a) The person who printed, wrote, compiled or manufactured the same; (b) The person who caused the same to be distributed; provided, however, that in the case of a fictitious person or club, in addition to such fictitious name, the true names and addresses of the owners, managers, or agents of the person sponsoring said handbill shall also appear thereon." This prohibition against anonymous handbills was seen to be a violation of the right to free speech and press by the Supreme Court in *Talley v. California* (1960).*

LOS ANGELES (CA), DISTRIBUTION OF HANDBILLS. The Municipal Code (1936) of the City of Los Angeles, § § 28.00 and 28.01, provided: " 'Handbill' shall mean any handbill, dodger, commercial advertising circular, folder, booklet, letter, card, pamphlet, sheet, poster, sticker, banner, notice or other written, printed or painted matter calculated to attract attention of the public. No person shall distribute any handbill to or among pedestrians along or upon any street, sidewalk or park, or to passengers on any street car, or throw, place or attach any handbill in, to, or upon any automobile or other vehicle." This sweeping ban on the distribution of literature was seen to be an unconstitutional restriction on First Amendment rights in *Kim Young v. California* (1939).*

LOS ANGELES (CA), POSSESSION OF OBSCENE MATTER. The Municipal Code of the City of Los Angeles, § 41.01.1, provided: "It shall be unlawful for any person to have in his possession any obscene or indecent writing, book, pamphlet, picture, photograph, drawing, figure, motion picture film, phonograph recording, wire recording or transcription of any kind in any of the following places: 1. In any school, school-grounds, public park or playground or in any public place, grounds, street or way within 300 yards of any school, park or playground; 2. In any place of business where ice cream, soft drinks, candy, food, school supplies, magazines, books, pamphlets, papers, pictures or postcards are sold or kept for sale; 3. In any toilet or restroom open to the public; 4. In any poolroom or billiard parlor, or in any place where alcoholic liquor is sold or offered for sale to the public; 5. In any place where phonograph records, photographs, motion pictures, or transcriptions of any kind are made, used, maintained, sold or exhibited." This ordinance was judged to be unconstitutional by the Supreme Court in *Smith v. California* (1959),* for it made booksellers liable for the contents of the books in the store; the Court ruled that the booksellers, therefore, would have to censor each book offered for sale in order to escape punishment. The Court did not wish to see that type of informal censorship scheme.

LOS ANGELES COUNTY (CA), CRIME COMIC BOOKS. In ordinance No. 6633, the county of Los Angeles prohibited the sale and circulation of crime comic books to children under the age of eighteen years. The salient parts of the ordinance follow: "Many children have been incited to attempt crimes as a consequence of looking at crime comic books. There is a clear and present danger that the continued sale and circulation of crime comic books will incite such children to commit crimes and inculcate a preference in the minds of many of the children to participate in crime. Every person is guilty of a misdemeanor who sells or circulates a crime comic book to any child under the age of eighteen years. This ordinance shall not apply to (a) Those accounts of crime which are part of the general dissemination of news; (b) Those accounts of crime which appear in a newspaper of general circulation; (c) Those accounts which delineate occurrences actually set forth in the sacred scriptures of any religion. Crime: The commission or attempted commission of an act of arson, burglary, kidnapping, mayhem, murder, rape, robbery, theft, trainwrecking, or voluntary manslaughter; or the commission of an act of assault with caustic chemicals or assault with a deadly weapon. As the term 'crime' is used, it includes but is not limited to, acts by human beings, and further includes acts by animals or any nonhuman, part human, or imaginary beings, which if performed by a human would constitute any of the crimes named. Every violation of this ordinance shall be punishable by imprisonment in the county jail for not more than six months or by a fine of not more than $500, or by both."

A California court, in *Katzev v. County of Los Angeles* (1959),* declared this absurd ordinance to be an unconstitutional restriction of the right of free press for several reasons, one such reason being the clause that an act performed by a cartoon character, if performed by a human, would constitute a crime. Under this definition, Bugs Bunny, if he took a carrot from Elmer Fudd's garden, would have committed "theft" and the person who sold that particular issue of the comic book would be guilty; likewise, when Bluto dragged Olive Oyl away from Popeye, he would be guilty of "kidnapping" and the seller of the comic book could have received six months or a $500 fine or both.

LOUISIANA, BREACH OF THE PEACE. Louisiana Revised Stat., § 14:103.1 (Cum. Supp. 1962), the breach of the peace statute, reads: "Whoever with intent to provoke a breach of the peace, or under circumstances such that a breach of the peace may be occasioned thereby . . . crowds or congregates with others . . . in or upon a public street or public highway, or upon a public sidewalk, or any other public place or building . . . and who fails or refuses to disperse and move on . . . when ordered to do so by any law enforcement officer of any municipality, or parish, in which such act or acts are committed, or by any law enforcement officer of the State of Louisiana, or any other authorized person...shall be guilty of disturbing the peace." The Supreme Court, in *Cox v. Louisiana* (1965),* reversed a conviction under this statute, holding that the state of Louisiana applied it to Cox not for disturbing the peace, but for holding a demonstration protesting segregation.

LOUISIANA, COURTHOUSE PICKETING. Louisiana Revised Stat., § 14:401 (Cum. Supp. 1962), reads: "Whoever, with the intent of interfering with, obstructing, or impeding the administration of justice, or with the intent of influencing any judge, juror, witness, or court officer, in the discharge of his duty pickets or parades in or near a building housing a court of the State of Louisiana...shall be fined not more than five thousand dollars or imprisoned not more than one year, or both." The Supreme Court, in *Cox v. Louisiana* (1965),* reversed a conviction under this statute, holding that the state of Louisiana applied it to Cox not for courthouse picketing, but for holding a demonstration to protest segregation in Louisiana.

LOUISIANA, CRIMINAL DEFAMATION STATUTE. Louisiana Revised Stat., 1950, Title 14, reads: "Defamation is the malicious publication or expression in any manner, to anyone other than the party defamed, of anything which tends: (1) To expose any person to hatred, contempt, or ridicule, or to deprive him of the benefit of public confidence or social intercourse; or (2) To expose the memory of one deceased to hatred, contempt, or ridicule; or (3) To injure any person, corporation, or association of persons in his or their business or occupation. Whoever commits the crime of defamation shall be fined not more than three thousand dollars, or imprisoned for not more than one year, or both." The Supreme Court, in *Garrison v. Louisiana* (1964),* reversed Garrison's conviction under this statute, holding that Garrison's criticism of certain state judges was protected by the First Amendment guarantee of free speech.

LOUISIANA, NEWSPAPER TAX. Section 1 of the Act of the Legislature of Louisiana, known as Act No. 23, passed July 12, 1934, read as follows: "That every person, firm, association, or corporation, domestic or foreign, engaged in the business of selling, or making any charge for, advertising or for advertisements, whether printed or published, or to be printed or published, in any newspaper, magazine, periodical or publication whatever having a circulation of more than 20,000 copies per week, or displayed and exhibited, or to be displayed and exhibited by means of moving pictures, in the State of Louisiana, shall, in addition to all other taxes and licenses levied and assessed in this State, pay a license tax for the privilege of engaging in such business in this State of two per cent (2%) of the gross receipts of such business." The Supreme Court, in *Grossjean v. American Press* (1936),* found that this tax, based on the circulation figures of the publication, was an odious form of the long-discredited knowledge taxes* and held the act to be a violation of the First Amendment.

LOUISIANA, OBSTRUCTING PUBLIC PASSAGES. Louisiana Revised Stat., § 14:100.1 (Cum. Supp. 1962), reads: "No person shall wilfully obstruct the free, convenient, and normal use of any public sidewalk, street, highway, bridge, alley, road, or other passageway, or the entrance, corridor or passage of any public building, structure, watercraft or ferry, by impeding, hindering, stifling, retarding or restraining traffic or passage thereon or therein. Providing however nothing herein contained shall apply to a bona fide legitimate labor organization or to any of its legal activities such as picketing, lawful assembly or concerted activity in the interest of its members for the purpose of accomplishing or securing more favorable wage standards, hours of employment and working conditions." The Supreme Court, in *Cox v. Louisiana* (1965),* reversed a conviction under this statute, holding that it was applied to Cox not for obstructing public passages, but for holding a demonstration protesting segregation in Louisiana.

LOUISIANA, SUBVERSIVE ACTIVITIES AND COMMUNIST CONTROL LAW. The state of Louisiana attempted to apply the statutes below to several individuals, but the Supreme Court, in *Dombrowski v. Pfister* (1965),* issued a rare order that prevented (enjoined) the state from prosecuting Dombrowski. The relevant portions of the statute: "It shall be a felony for any person knowingly and wilfully to assist in the formation or participate in the management or to contribute to the support of any subversive organization or foreign subversive organization knowing said organization to be a subversive organization or a foreign subversive organization. 'Subversive organization' means any organization which engages in or advocates, abets, advises, or teaches . . . activities intended to overthrow, destroy . . . the constitutional form of the government of the state of Louisiana, or of any political subdivision thereof by revolution, force, violence or other unlawful means . . . and to establish in place thereof any form of government not responsible to the people of the state of Louisiana. . . . 'Communist Front Organization' shall . . . include any communist action organization, communist front organization, communist infiltrated organization or communist controlled organization and the fact that an organization has been officially cited or identified by the Attorney General of the United States, the Subversive Activities Control Board of the United States or any committee or subcommittee of the United States Congress as a communist organization . . . shall be considered as presumptive evidence of the factual status of any such organization."

LOVELL v. CITY OF GRIFFIN (1938). The city of Griffin passed a municipal ordinance (Griffin [GA], Distribution of Pamphlets*) that required permission from the city manager before distributing any pamphlets, leaflets, or circulars within the city. Lovell, a Jehovah's Witness, was sentenced to fifty days in jail for distributing without such permission copies of the *Kingdom of Jehovah* and the *Golden Age*.

The Supreme Court, Chief Justice Hughes delivering the Court's opinion, held that such an ordinance struck at the very foundation of the freedom of the press by subjecting it to prior licensing and censorship. Chief Justice Hughes: ''The ordinance is comprehensive with respect to the method of distribution. It covers every sort of circulation 'either by hand or otherwise.' There is thus no restriction in its application with respect to time or place. It is not limited to ways which might be regarded as inconsistent with the maintenance of public order or as involving disorderly conduct, the molestation of the inhabitants, or the misuse or littering of the streets. The ordinance prohibits the distribution of literature of any kind at any time, at any place, and in any manner without a permit from the City Manager. We think that the ordinance is invalid on its face. Whatever the motive which induced its adoption, its character is such that it strikes at the very foundation of the freedom of the press by subjecting it to license and censorship. The struggle for the freedom of the press was primarily directed against the power of the licensor. It was against that power that John Milton directed his assault by his 'Appeal for the Liberty of Unlicensed Printing.' And the liberty of the press became initially a right to publish 'without a license what formerly could be published only with one.' While this freedom from previous restraint upon publication cannot be regarded as exhausting the guaranty of liberty, the prevention of that restraint was a leading purpose in the adoption of the constitutional provision. Legislation of the type of the ordinance in question would restore the system of license and censorship in its baldest form. The liberty of the press is not confined to newspapers and periodicals. It necessarily embraces pamphlets and leaflets. These indeed have been historic weapons in the defense of liberty, as the pamphlets of Thomas Paine and others in our own history abundantly attest. The press in its historic connotation comprehends every sort of publication which affords a vehicle of information and opinion. The ordinance cannot be saved because it relates to distribution and not to publication. 'Liberty of circulating is as essential to that freedom as liberty of publishing; indeed, without the circulation, the publication would be of little value.' As the ordinance is void on its face, it was not necessary for appellant to seek a permit under it.'' *Lovell v. City of Griffin*, 303 U.S. 444 (1938).

LOYALTY REVIEW BOARD, SUBVERSIVE ORGANIZATIONS. Part III, § 3, of Executive Order No. 9835, issued by President Truman, March 21, 1947, reads: ''The Loyalty Review Board shall currently be furnished by the Department of Justice the name of each foreign or domestic organization, association, movement, group, or combination of persons which the Attorney General, after appropriate investigation and determination, designates as totalitarian, fascist, communist or subversive, or as having adopted a policy of advocating or approving the commission of acts of force or violence to deny others their rights under the Constitution of the United States, or as seeking to alter the form of government of the United States by unconstitutional means. The Loyalty Review Board shall disseminate such information to all departments and agencies.'' The Supreme Court, in *Joint Anti-Fascist Refugee Committee v. McGrath* (1951),* ruled that the Loyalty Board had to at least hold a hearing before distributing the attorney general's list.

LUCAS v. ARKANSAS (1974). At midnight, a North Little Rock policeman on routine patrol drove through a parking lot adjacent to a motel and restaurant. He heard loud language and thought a fight was in progress. He rolled down the window and heard, ''Well, there goes the big, bad mother fucking cops.'' He ignored this and slowly drove on. The language grew louder and he pulled over. Someone said, ''Look at the chicken shit mother fucker hide over there behind that sign.'' He drove back and someone then said, ''Now the sorry son-of-a-bitch is going to come back over here.'' The police officer then arrested Lucas and others, and they were duly convicted, for a breach of the peace, in violation of an Arkansas statute (Arkansas, Insulting Language*).

In affirming the conviction, the Supreme Court of Arkansas (494 S.W. 2d 705 [1973]) commented that ''perhaps a well-trained police officer, by virtue of his training and the nature of his profession, should be conditioned, or even immune to some extent, to uncomplimentary remarks from that segment of society that recognizes no bounds in the exercise of the constitutional right to free speech; but no person, whether in police uniform or not, should be expected or required to sacrifice all his own rights to human dignity and self-respect to the perverted idea that such language . . . is protected by the First Amendment to the Constitution. We conclude that the 'freedom of speech' contemplated by the First Amendment . . . [does not include the right to call a police officer a mother fucker].'' The Supreme Court, however, apparently thought otherwise and vacated the judgment, remanding the case back to Arkansas for further consideration in light of *Lewis v. City of New Orleans* (1974).* *Lucas v. Arkansas*, 416 U.S. 919 (1974).

LUROS v. UNITED STATES (1968). Luros was convicted by a jury in a federal district court in Iowa of violating Title 18 U.S.C. § 1461 (Postal Regulations, Mailing Obscene Material*). Luros appealed, and the appeals court, Judge Lay delivering the opinion, reversed the conviction. Judge Lay: ''The government's argument can be summarized as follows: that appellant Luros and his corporations publish nudist magazines simply to make money; that many of the nudist models, although signing complete 'releases' for the photographs, nevertheless did not contemplate national publication; that paid professional models, who were not nudists, posed for the magazines; that the magazines falsely represent that the models are nudists; that the magazines pictured 'staged' scenes outside nudist camps depicting activities such as cooking, boating, hiking, etc., which nudists do not normally do in the nude; that appellant Luros continually sought legal advice as to whether his magazines were 'defensible'; that appellant Luros instructed his editors that they could now use photographs showing the male genitalia in the foreground; that appellant Luros bought a nudist camp for the sole purpose of taking pictures; that their own editors described the magazines as 'crap plus one' and that 'zetz' was required to make them sell. In summary, the government urges appellants' sale of the nudist material is nothing more than 'commercial exploitation on the basis of prurient appeal.' The basic fallacy of this argument, in the context of the nudist publications involved, is the false premise that 'commercial exploitation of nudism' is equated with prurience. The different pictures taken and published show both men and women, as well as children, in various poses and activities. We would agree that young female models or subjects dominate most pictures. Yet there is no magazine in evidence where men and women are shown embracing or in any alleged provocative or suggestive pose that smacks of a prurient appeal.

This brings us to the so-called lesbian books. We would agree that these books constitute undoubted trash and have little if any literary value or social importance. They are written, as one author testified, with one purpose in mind—to sell! They produce high profit for appellants and can be described as distasteful, cheap and tawdry. Yet these facts alone do not constitute a crime. Many well-intentioned citizens become disgusted or offended with the freedom by which purveyors of trash place their publications in the mail. But within the juridical balance is the basic concern over governmental interference into free channels of expression. It is far better there be a tight rein on authoritarian suppression, notwithstanding a conflict with some individuals' tastes or customary limits of candor, than that we live in a stifled community of self-censorship where men must feel apprehension over expression of an unpopular idea or theme. Still within our human possession is the free will to make an independent choice of values and to teach our children to do the same. Paternalistic censorship by government must continue to limit that choice only in the most extreme of circumstances.'' *Luros v. United States*, 389 F. 2d 200 (1968).

LUST JOB. A publisher, Books, Inc., was convicted of violating Title 18 U.S.C. § 1462 (Interstate Commerce Regulations, Transporting Obscene Material*) for transporting copies of a book entitled *Lust Job*, described by the appeals court as devoted exclusively to sexual adventures of its principal characters and that described not only sexual intercourse, but also sodomy and other perversions, and that did not have literary merit, and was utterly without redeeming social value. The book was further described in the appeals court record (358 F. 2d 935 [1966]) in the following terms: "On the front cover of the book is an unclothed woman, her back toward the reader. She is seated on the floor, her back and buttocks showing, her head tilted backwards and her arms clasping below the knees the trousers of a clothed man. The title *Lust Job* is printed so that it crosses the woman's back. Above the woman's head and across the man's trousers are the words 'He climbed to the top on a ladder of sin.' '' The publisher appealed to the Supreme Court (*Books, Inc. v. United States* 388 U.S. 449 [1967]), and without a written opinion, the Court reversed the conviction and held that *Lust Job* was not obscene.

M

M. This 1952 American film was directed by Joseph Losey and starred David Wayne, Howard da Silva, and Raymond Burr; it was also banned in Ohio in 1952. The plot (de Grazia and Newman, *Banned Films*, p. 235) is as follows: "This film is a remake of the 1932 German film by Fritz Lang and Thea von Harbon. It is the case history of a psychopathic killer who murders little girls and then steals their shoes. In the face of an overwhelming public outcry, the police begin to round up the entire underworld, which, in order to protect its own interests, also hunts for the killer. The dual chase for the killer comes to a climax when the psychopath is finally trapped and must plead his case before both the underworld and the police."†

The Ohio Board of Censors refused to issue an exhibition license for *M* for the following reasons: "(1) There is a conviction that the effect of this picture on unstable persons of any age level could lead to a serious increase in immorality and crime; (2) Presentation of actions and emotions of child killer emphasizing complete perversion without serving any valid educational purpose. Treatment of perversion creates sympathy rather than a constructive plan for dealing with perversion; and (3) The motion picture is filled with brutal crime. Two cold blooded murders are presented, another implied and a third attempted. A schizophrenic killer is treated with sympathy and an underworld boss is depicted as vastly more efficient than the police. Twice, the methods for abducting children on the streets are elaborated." The Board of Censors based their decision on the Ohio motion picture censorship* statute, which required the board to license only those films that were, in its judgment, of a moral, educational, or amusing and harmless character.

The Ohio censorship act was previously upheld as constitutional by the Supreme Court in *Mutual Film Corporation v. Industrial Commission of Ohio* (1915),* in which Justice McKenna said: "Films of a 'moral, educational, or amusing and harmless character shall be passed and approved,' are the words

---

†Reprinted from *Banned Films* with permission of the R. R. Bowker Company. Copyright © 1982 by Edward de Grazia and Roger K. Newman.

of the statute. No exhibition, therefore, or 'campaign' of complainant will be prevented if its pictures have those qualities. Therefore, however missionary of opinion films are or may become, however educational or entertaining, there is no impediment to their value or effect in the Ohio statute. But they may be used for evil, and against that possibility the statute was enacted. Their power of amusement, and, it may be, education, the audiences they assemble, not of women alone nor of men alone, but together, not of adults only, but of children, make them the more insidious in corruption by a pretense of worthy purpose or if they should degenerate from worthy purpose. Indeed, we may go beyond that possibility. They take their attraction from the general interest, eager and whole-some it may be, in their subjects, but a prurient interest may be excited and appealed to. Besides, there are some things which should not have pictorial representation in public places and to all audiences. And not only the state of Ohio, but other states, have considered it to be in the interest of the public morals and welfare to supervise moving picture exhibitions. We would have to shut our eyes to the facts of the world to regard the precaution unreasonable or the legislation to effect it a mere wanton interference with personal liberty. . . . It cannot be put out of view that the exhibition of moving pictures is a business, pure and simple, originated and conducted for profit, like other spectacles, not to be regarded, nor intended to be regarded by the Ohio Constitution, we think, as part of the press of the country, or as organs of public opinion. They are mere representations of events, of ideas and sentiments published and known; vivid, useful, and entertaining, no doubt, but, as we have said, capable of evil, having power for it, the greater because of their attractiveness and manner of exhibition. It was this capability and power that induced the state of Ohio to require censorship before exhibition.''

The distributor of *M*, Superior Films, appealed the Board of Censors' decision, but the Ohio Supreme Court (*Superior Films v. Department of Education of Ohio, Division of Film Censorship*, 112 N.E. 2d 311 [1953]) sustained the refusal to issue an exhibition permit. Judge Hart of the Ohio Supreme Court: "As we view it, the United States Supreme Court has not *ipso facto* taken away all community control of moving pictures by censorship, and this court will not do so under the claim of complete unconstitutionality of censorship laws.''

Superior Films then appealed to the Supreme Court (346 U.S. 587 [1954]), and the Court reversed the decision banning the exhibition of *M*. Justice Douglas, in a concurring opinion joined by Justice Black, offered some comments not on *M* itself, but on the entire question of the relationship of films to the freedom of expression (Film Censorship*). Justice Douglas: "The argument of Ohio that the government may establish censorship over moving pictures is one I cannot accept. In 1925 Minnesota passed a law aimed at suppressing before publication any 'malicious, scandalous and defamatory newspaper.' The Court, speaking through Chief Justice Hughes, struck down that law as violating the Fourteenth Amendment, which has made the First Amendment applicable to the States (*Near v. Minnesota ex rel. Olson**). The 'chief purpose' of the constitutional guaranty of liberty of the press, said the Court, was 'to prevent previous restraints upon publication.' The history of censorship is so well known it need not be summarized here. Certainly a system, still in force in some nations, which required a newspaper to submit to a board its news items, editorials, and cartoons before it published them could not be sustained. Nor could book publishers be required to submit their novels, poems, and tracts to censors for clearance before publication. Any such scheme of censorship would be in irreconcilable conflict with the language and purpose of the First Amendment. Nor is it conceivable to me that producers of plays for the legitimate theatre or for television could be required to submit their manuscripts to censors on pain of penalty for producing them without approval. Certainly the spoken word is as freely protected against prior restraints as that which is written. The freedom of the platform which it espouses carries with it freedom of the stage. The same result in the case of motion pictures necessarily follows as a consequence of our holding in [*The Miracle** case] that motion pictures are 'within the free speech and free press guaranty of the First and Fourteenth Amendments.' Motion pictures are of course a different medium of expression than the public speech, the radio, the stage, the novel, or the magazine. But the First Amendment draws no distinction between the various methods of communicating ideas. On occasion one may be more powerful or effective than another. The movie, like the public speech, radio, or television, is transitory—here now and gone in an instant. The novel, the short story, the poem in printed form are permanently at hand to reenact the drama or to retell the story over and again. Which medium will give the most excitement and have the most enduring effect will vary with the theme and the actors. It is not for the censor to determine in any case. The First and the Fourteenth Amendments say that Congress and the States shall make 'no law' which abridges freedom of speech or of the press. In order to sanction a system of censorship I would have to say that 'no law' does not mean what it says, that 'no' law is qualified to mean 'some' laws. I cannot take that step. In this Nation every writer, actor, or producer, no matter what medium of expression he may use, should be freed from the censor.''

McCORMICK (SC), LICENSE TAX ON BOOK AGENTS. A McCormick city ordinance provided: "The following license on business, occupation and professions to be paid by the person or persons carrying on or engaged in such business, occupation or professions within the corporate limits of the Town of McCormick, South Carolina: Agents selling books, per day $1.00, per year $15.00." The Supreme Court, in *Follett v. Town of McCormick* (1944),* held that the ordinance was an invalid restriction of the right of a free press when applied to a Jehovah's Witness distributing pamphlets and asking for contributions in return.

McGEHEE v. CASEY (1983). In 1952, when he joined the Central Intelligence Agency (CIA), Ralph W. McGehee signed a secrecy agreement (Central Intelligence Agency, Secrecy Agreements*/Publishing Agreements* and Classified Information*) promising not to divulge classified information obtained by virtue of his employment unless specifically authorized in writing to do so by the CIA. On March 20, 1981, McGehee submitted an article to the CIA for pre-publication review. The article asserted that the CIA had mounted a campaign of deceit to convince the world that the "revolt of the poor natives against a ruthless U.S.-backed oligarchy" in El Salvador was really "a Soviet, Cuban, Bulgarian, Vietnamese, PLO, Ethiopian, Nicaraguan, International Terrorism challenge to the United States." To lend plausibility to his assertion, McGehee's article proceeded "to review a few examples of . . . CIA disinformation programs" in Iran, Viet Nam, Chile, and Indonesia. On March 24, the CIA notified McGehee that portions of his article contained "secret" information and, accordingly, withheld permission to publish those portions. McGehee's article, with the censored portions deleted, was then published in *The Nation* ("The C.I.A. and the White Paper on El Salvador," April 11, 1981, pp. 423ff.), but then McGehee brought suit against the CIA, challenging the constitutionality of the CIA's classification and censorship scheme, and the propriety under that scheme of classifying portions of his article "secret."

A federal district court rejected McGehee's arguments, and an appeals court affirmed. Judge Wald delivered the opinion of the appeals court: "(1) C.I.A. censorship of 'secret' information contained in former agent's writings and obtained by former agent during course of C.I.A. employment, did not violate First Amendment, inasmuch as government has substantial interest in assuring secrecy in conduct of foreign intelligence operations and criteria for what constitutes 'secret' information are neither overbroad nor excessively vague, and (2) C.I.A. properly classified as 'secret' the censored portions of the subject article."

Judge Wald, however, was not entirely satisfied with her own opinion, and she appended some additional remarks to the court record: "I write separately to stress, however, that neither the agency's nor our analysis takes account of any separate public right to know critical albeit classified facts about the activities of our intelligence agencies. It would of course be extremely difficult for judges to 'balance' the public's right to know against an acknowledged national security risk, and I do not believe we are currently authorized to do so. However, it seems important in view of recent revelations about past indiscretions in the name of national security, for some governmental institution, if not the classification system itself, to conduct such a balance. As Emerson explained, 'history . . . give[s] value to the present hour and its duty.' By not weighing the value to the public of knowing about particularly relevant episodes in the intelligence agencies' history, we may undermine the public's ability to assess the government's performance of its duty. Economic and criminal sanctions against agents who violate the preclearance and agency classification scheme are justifiable. But with no mechanism in the system for balancing the public's right to know with possible risks to security, those sanctions can also result in the permanent loss of information critical to public debate. Our decision today, reflecting current restraints on our authority, cannot and does not fill the public's need for such a balance." *McGehee v. Casey*, 718 F. 2d 1137 (1983).

MAINE, TRAVELER INFORMATION SERVICES ACT. This act, better titled as an Act to Eliminate Billboards, was passed by the Maine legislature in order to protect and enhance the scenic beauty of the state. Some companies involved with billboard advertising brought suit, however, alleging that the act violated their right of free speech and press. An appeals court (*John Donnelly & Sons v. Campbell* [1980*]) agreed and held the following act (23 M.R.S.A. §§ 1901–1913) to be a violation of the First Amendment: " 'Sign' means any structure, display, logo, device or representation which is designed or used to advertise or call attention to any thing, person, business, activity or place and is visible from any public way. It does not include the flag, pennant or insignia of any nation, state or town. Whenever dimensions of a sign are specified they shall include frames. No person may erect or maintain signs visible to the traveling public from a public way except as provided in this chapter. The following signs may be erected and maintained without license or permit under this chapter as follows: A. Signs of a duly constituted government; B. Signs located on or in the rolling stock of common carriers, except those which are determined by the commissioner to be circumventing the intent of this chapter; C. Signs on registered and inspected motor vehicles, except those which are determined by the commissioner to be circumventing the intent of this chapter; D. Signs, with an area of not more than 260 square inches, identifying stops or fare zone limits of motor buses; E. Signs showing the place and time of service or meetings of churches and civic organizations in the municipality or township. Each church or civic organization may erect no more than 4 signs. No sign shall exceed in size 24 inches by 30 inches; F. Signs to be maintained for not more than 3 weeks announcing an auction, public supper, lawn sale, campaign, drive or other like event of a public, civic, philanthropic or religious organization, provided these signs are located within the municipality or township where the activity is located. The date of this event is to be conspicuously posted on each sign; G. Memorial signs or tablets; H. Signs erected by fairs and expositions within the county where the activity is located. These signs may be erected and maintained for 3 weeks before the event. The date of the event is to be conspicuously posted on each sign. I. Signs erected for an election, primary or referendum. These signs shall be erected no sooner than 3 weeks before the date of the election, primary or referendum and shall be removed no later than one week after that date; and J. Signs erected outside the public right-of-way by nonprofit historical and cultural institutions. Each institution, who has certified its nonprofit status with the commissioner, may erect no more than 2 signs with a surface area not to exceed 50 square feet per sign."

MALICE. Malice, in libel and slander, involves an evil intent or motive arising from spite or ill will; personal hatred or ill will; or recklessness or a willful and wanton disregard of the rights and interests of the person defamed. In a libel case, it consists in intentionally publishing, without justifiable cause, any written or printed matter that is injurious to the character of another. Malice may be defined as acting in bad faith and with knowledge of the falsity of the statements. In the context of a libel suit brought by a public figure* or by a public official,* the *New York Times* Rule* (*New York Times Company v. Sullivan* [1964])* defines malice as publishing the false information knowing it to be false or with a reckless disregard of whether it is true or false.

MANUAL/GRECIAN GUILD PICTORIAL/TRIM. After an administrative hearing, the judicial officer of the Post Office Department issued a ruling that barred the use of the mails for several magazines (*Manual, Grecian Guild Pictorial*, and *Trim*) under Title 18 U.S.C. § 1461 (Postal Regulations, Mailing Oscene Material*). The judicial officer found that the magazines, consisting largely of photographs of nude men, (1) were composed primarily, if not exclusively, for homosexuals and had no literary, scientific, or other merit; (2) would appeal to the "prurient interest" of such sexual deviates but would not have any interest for sexually normal individuals; (3) are read almost entirely by homosexuals and possibly a few adolescent males; and (4) would not ordinarily be bought by normal male adults.

The court records contain the following description of the magazines: "The magazines contained little textual material, with pictures of male models dominating almost every page. . . . The typical page consisted of a photograph, with the name of the model and the photographer and occasional references to the model's age (usually under 26), color of eyes, physical dimensions and occupation. The magazines contained little, either in text or pictures, that could be considered as relating in any way to weight lifting, muscle building or physical culture. . . . Many of the photographs were of nude male models, usually posed with some object in front of their genitals; a number were of nude or partially nude males with emphasis on their bare buttocks. Although none of the pictures directly exposed the model's genitals, some showed his pubic hair and others suggested what appeared to be a semi-erect penis; others showed male models reclining with their legs (and sometimes their arms as well) spread wide apart. Many of the pictures showed models wearing only loin cloths, 'V gowns,' or posing straps; some showed the model apparently removing his clothing. Two of the magazines had pictures of pairs of models posed together suggestively. Each of the magazines contained photographs of models with swords or other long pointed objects. The magazines also contained photographs of virtually nude models wearing only shoes, boots, helmets or leather jackets. There were also pictures of models posed with chains or of one model beating another while a third held his face in his hands as if weeping."

A federal district court found for the post office and judged the magazines obscene; an appeals court affirmed this decision; the Supreme Court (*Manual Enterprises v. Day*, 370 U.S. 478 [1962]) reversed, holding the magazines not to be obscene. The majority decision could not agree on a single reason for the reversal, but the following comments by Justice Harlan are instructive: "We find lacking in these magazines an element which, no less than 'prurient interest,' is essential to a valid determination of obscenity under § 1461. . . . These magazines cannot be deemed so offensive on their face as to affront current community standards of decency—a quality that we shall hereafter refer to as 'patent offensiveness' or 'indecency.' The words of § 1461, 'obscene, lewd, lascivious, indecent, filthy or vile,' connote something that is portrayed in a manner so offensive as to make it unacceptable under current community mores. While in common usage the words have different shades of meaning, the statute since its inception has always been taken as aimed at obnoxiously debasing portrayals of sex. . . . We cannot accept in full the Government's description of these magazines which tends to emphasize and in some respects overdraw certain features in several of the photographs, at the expense of what the magazines fairly taken as a whole depict. Our own independent examination of the magazines leads us to conclude that the most that can be said of them is that they are dismally unpleasant, uncouth, and tawdry. But this is not enough to make them 'obscene.' Divorced from their 'prurient interest' appeal to the unfortunate persons whose patronage they were aimed at capturing (a separate issue), these portrayals of the male nude cannot fairly be regarded as more objectionable than many portrayals of the female nude that society tolerates. Of course not every portrayal of male or female nudity is obscene. Were we to hold that these magazines, although they do not transcend the prevailing bounds of decency, may be denied access to the mails by such undifferentiated legislation as that before us, we would be ignoring the admonition that 'the door . . . into this area [the First Amendment] cannot be left ajar; it must be kept tightly closed and opened only the slightest crack necessary to prevent encroachment upon more important interests.' We conclude that the administrative ruling respecting nonmailability is improvident insofar as it depends on a determination that these magazines are obscene."

Justice Clark thought the majority opinion was improvident, and he lashed out at his colleagues in a dissenting opinion: "While those in the majority like ancient Gaul are split into three parts, the ultimate holding of the Court today, despite the clear congressional mandate found in § 1461, requires the United States Post Office to be the world's largest disseminator of smut and Grand Informer of the names and places where obscene material may be obtained."

THE MAN WITH THE GOLDEN ARM. This 1956 American film, produced and directed by Otto Preminger and starring Frank Sinatra and Kim Novak, was censored in Maryland (Maryland, Motion Picture Censorship*) in 1956. The following description of the film is from de Grazia and Newman, *Banned Films* (pp. 248–249): "This film was adapted from Nelson Algren's novel of the same title. It describes the plight of Frankie Machine, a professional card dealer in the slums of Chicago. Frankie, a man with a golden arm who can instinctively control a card game, returns to Chicago after drying out in a federal narcotics hospital. His attempt at a fresh start is foiled by a gambler who makes him deal cards again and by a dope peddler who coaxes him back onto narcotics. He finally succeeds in kicking his habit when his would-be girl friend locks him in her room to dry out. He then discovers that he is wanted for a murder he did not commit, and that his crippled wife has been maintaining her invalidism to keep him from leaving her. After his wife accidentally reveals to him her power to walk, she flees from Frankie and commits suicide. Frankie is exonerated from all criminal charges and begins a new life with the girl who helped him kick his habit.''†

The Maryland State Board of Censors, relying on the statute authorizing the censorship of motion pictures that tend to debase or corrupt morals or incite to crimes, ordered the deletion of a two-minute scene from the film before it would grant an exhibition permit. The State Board of Censors also relied on the fact that the film did not receive the seal of approval of the Motion Picture Association of America.* It was not surprising that *The Man with the Golden Arm* did not receive the ''seal''—the Motion Picture Production Code at that time disapproved of any film that portrayed drug addiction, and United Artists had resigned from the association because it did not agree with the association's taboo against films dealing with narcotics.

The court records contain the following description of the offending scene: ''This scene, which runs less than two minutes, shows Frankie Machine, a young Chicago tough, played by Frank Sinatra, taking a narcotic after six months in the United States Public Health Service Hospital for Drug Addicts at Lexington, Kentucky. Ostensibly he was cured, but all the pressures were there waiting for him. The scene shows him rolling up his sleeve, and tying a necktie around the upper arm, while a dope 'pusher' prepares the drug for injection. While the particular kind of narcotic is not named, the picture shows the powdered narcotic, the liquid solution, the spoon, and the hypodermic needle. The 'pusher' takes the filled needle and advances toward Frankie. The actual injection is not shown, but the viewer sees the needle being removed from the arm. Just before the needle is pulled out, Frankie indicates by a facial twitch that he felt a slight pain from the injection. Complete relaxation follows.''

On January 12, 1956, C. Morton Goldstein, chairman of the State Board of Censors, issued the following order to United Artists, an order that had to be obeyed before the Board would issue an exhibition license: ''Following Frankie entering Louie's room and removing his coat, eliminate all views from the point where Frankie is shown rolling up his sleeve down to the point immediately preceding his reclining on couch.'' United Artists took exception to this order and appealed the board's decision to the Baltimore City Court, which affirmed

---

†Reprinted from *Banned Films* with permission of the R. R. Bowker Company. Copyright © 1982 by Edward de Grazia and Roger K. Newman.

the board's order. United Artists then appealed to the Maryland Court of Appeals (*United Artists Corporation v. Maryland State Board of Censors*, 124 A. 2d 292 [1956]), which reversed the board's order. Judge Delaplaine held that the censored part of the film did not violate the statute: The statute authorizing the censorship of motion pictures that tend to debase or corrupt morals or incite to crimes and providing that a film would be considered as tending to incite to crime if the film advocated or taught the use of, or methods of use, of narcotics, did not prohibit the showing of a film that merely explained, without advocating, the use of such drugs. The state of Maryland was the only locality that attempted to censor this film: It was exhibited across the United States and western Europe without problems and even won a scientific and cultural award in The Netherlands.

MARRIED LOVE. U.S. Customs regulations (Tariff Act*) permit the Customs Service to seize what it considers "obscene" matter and then resort to a federal district court for a judicial determination as to the matter's obscenity. If the court judges the material obscene, then Customs can destroy the material.

This particular case concerned the seizure and eventual judicial determination of a book entitled *Married Love* in 1931 before Judge Woolsey, the same judge who enunciated the Ulysses Standard* as a test of obscenity. Judge Woolsey: "*Married Love* is a considered attempt to explain to married people how their mutual sex life may be made happier. To one who had read Havelock Ellis, as I have, the subject matter of Dr. Stope's book is not wholly new, but it emphasizes the woman's side of sex questions. It makes also some apparently justified criticisms of the inopportune exercise by the man in the marriage relation in what are often referred to as his conjugal or marital rights, and it pleads with seriousness, and not without some eloquence, for a better understanding by husbands of the physical and emotional side of the sex life of their wives. I do not find anything exceptionable anywhere in the book, and I cannot imagine a normal mind to which this book would seem to be obscene or immoral within the proper definition of these words or whose sex impulses would be stirred by reading it. Whether or not the book is scientific in some of its theses is unimportant. It is informative and instructive, and I think that any married folk who read it cannot fail to be benefited by its counsels of perfection and its frank discussion of the frequent difficulties which necessarily arise in the more intimate aspects of married life. . . . The book before me has as its whole thesis the strengthening of the centripetal forces in marriage, and instead of being inhospitably received, it should, I think, be welcomed within our borders." *United States v. One Obscene Book Entitled Married Love*, 48 F. 2d 821 (1931).

MARSH v. ALABAMA (1946). Marsh, a Jehovah's Witness, entered a company town in Alabama that required a permit from the town's management before allowing the distribution of literature in the town's streets (the property of the corporation). She stood near the post office and started to distribute religious literature to the residents of Chickasaw. The corporation owning Chickasaw had signs posted to the effect "This Is Private Property, And Without Written Permission, No Street, Or House Vendor, Agent Or Solicitation Of Any Kind Will Be Permitted," and Marsh was told that she would not receive a permit. She was duly arrested and convicted of distributing the literature without the permit.

The Supreme Court reversed the conviction, seeing no difference between a company town, although private property, and a public town. Justice Black delivered the Court's opinion: (1) "A state cannot, consistently with the freedom of religion and the press guaranteed by the First and Fourteenth Amendments, impose criminal punishment on a person for distributing religious literature on the sidewalk of a company-owned town contrary to regulations of the town's management, where the town and its shopping district are freely accessible to and freely used by the public in general, even though the punishment is attempted under a state statute making it a crime for anyone to enter or remain on the premises of another after having been warned not to do so." (2) "Whether a corporation or a municipality owns or possesses a town, the public in either case has an identical interest in the functioning of the community in such manner that the channels of communication remain free." (3) "People living in company-owned towns are free citizens of their State and country, just as residents of municipalities; and there is no more reason for depriving them of the liberties guaranteed by the First and Fourteenth Amendments than there is for curtailing those freedoms with respect to any other citizen." *Marsh v. Alabama*, 326 U.S. 501 (1946).

MARTIN v. CITY OF STRUTHERS (1943). A municipal ordinance (Struthers [OH], Distribution of Handbills*) prohibited any person from knocking on doors, ringing doorbells, or otherwise summoning to the door the occupants of any residence for the purpose of distributing handbills or circulars. Martin was convicted under this statute of distributing advertisements for a religious meeting.

The Supreme Court, Justice Black delivering the opinion, reversed the conviction, holding the ordinance to be a denial of freedom of speech and press. Justice Black: "For centuries it has been a common practice in this and other countries for persons not specifically invited to go from home to home and knock on doors or ring doorbells to communicate ideas to the occupants or to invite them to political, religious, or other kinds of public meetings. Whether such visiting shall be permitted has in general been deemed to depend upon the will of the individual master of each household, and not upon the determination of the community. In the instant case, the City of Struthers has attempted to make this decision for all its inhabitants. . . . We are faced in the instant case with the necessity of weighing the conflicting interests of the appellant in the civil rights she claims, as well as the right of the individual householder to determine whether she is willing to receive her message, against the interest of the community which by this ordinance offers to protect the interests of all of its citizens, whether particular citizens want that protection or not. The ordinance does not control anything but the distribution of literature, and in that respect it substitutes the judgment of the community for the judgment of the individual householder. . . . For this reason . . . we conclude that the ordinance is invalid because it is in conflict with the freedom of speech and press.''

Justice Reed, joined by Justices Roberts and Jackson, dissented: ''The First Amendment does not compel a pedestrian to pause on the street to listen to the argument supporting another's views of religion or politics. Once the door is opened, the visitor may not insert a foot and insist on a hearing. He certainly may not enter the home. To knock or ring, however, comes close to such invasions. To prohibit such a call leaves open distribution of the notice on the street or at the home without signal to announce its deposit. Such assurance of privacy falls far short of an abridgment of freedom of the press. The ordinance seems a fair adjustment of the privilege of distributors and the rights of house-holders.'' *Martin v. City of Struthers*, 319 U.S. 141 (1943).

MARTIN v. STATE OF GEORGIA (1928). As the court record relates, a police officer was called to a certain place in Macon, Georgia, and ''when he arrived there, he saw Mrs. N. R. Martin and the other accused persons lying on a bank on the side of Ocmulgee street, where they could have been seen by more than one person. Mrs. Martin had her dress up and was exposing her private parts, and the others had their dresses up, exposing their limbs, and the defendant [Mr. N. R. Martin] was standing over them with a kodak, taking a picture of the females. The officer arrested the defendant and . . . had the film developed and . . . they were reproductions of the private parts of Mrs. Martin and the naked limbs of the other females.''

Martin was duly convicted of participating in an act of public indecency, and Judge Luke thought this behavior to be ''shockingly obscene'' and tending to ''debauch the morals.'' As Judge Luke commented: ''What is decent and what is indecent are determined by the sensibilities and moral standards of a people, as evolved from generation to generation along with their civilization. When, by general consensus of the people and practical unanimity of public opinion, an act tending to debauch the morals is understood to be offensive to the common instincts of decency if done under particular circumstances, that act when so done is, in contemplation of law, a notorious act of indecency.'' The court record contains no information why the Martins were taking the photographs in public on a street corner rather than in the privacy of their own home. *Martin v. State of Georgia*, 144 S.E. 36 (1928).

MARYLAND, MOTION PICTURE CENSORSHIP. In 1916, the Maryland legislature passed an act that provided that the Maryland State Board of Censors shall consist of three members, appointed by the governor with the advice and consent of the Maryland Senate. The original act directed that the board ''shall approve such films, reels or views which are moral and proper, and shall dis-approve such as are sacrilegious, obscene, indecent, or immoral, or such as tend, in the judgment of the Board, to debase or corrupt morals'' (Laws of 1916, Chapter 209).

In 1955, the legislature amended the statute by striking out the word ''sacrilegious'' and by stating more specifically what types of films the board must disapprove. The new law, Laws 1955, ch. 201, Code Supp. 1955, Article 66A, § 6, provides as follows: ''(a) The Board shall examine or supervise the examination of all films or views to be exhibited or used in the State of Maryland and shall approve and license such films or views which are moral and proper, and shall disapprove such as are obscene, or such as tend, in the judgment of the Board, to debase or corrupt morals or incite to crimes. All films exclusively portraying current events or pictorial news of the day, commonly called news reels, may be exhibited without examination and no license or fees shall be required therefor. (b) For the purposes of this Article, a motion picture film or view shall be considered to be obscene if, when considered as a whole, its calculated purpose or dominant effect is substantially to arouse sexual desires, and if the probability of this effect is so great as to outweigh whatever other merits the film may possess. (c) For the purposes of this Article, a motion picture film or view shall be considered to be of such character that its exhibition would tend to debase or corrupt morals if it portrays acts of sexual immorality, lust or lewdness, or if it expressly or impliedly presents such acts as desirable, acceptable or proper patterns of behavior. (d) For the purposes of this Article, a motion picture film or view shall be considered of such a character that its exhibition would tend to incite to crime if the theme or the manner of its presentation presents the commission of criminal acts or contempt for law as constituting profitable, desirable, acceptable, respectable or commonly accepted behavior, or if it advocates or teaches the use of, or the methods of use of, narcotics or habit-forming drugs.''

The 1955 act also gave any person or corporation submitting a film to the board for examination the right to take an appeal first to the Baltimore City Court and then to the Court of Appeals of Maryland. The first appeal that reached the appeals court concerned *The Man with the Golden Arm.**

MARYLAND, SALE OF OBJECTIONABLE MATERIAL TO MINORS.
Article 27 of the Maryland Code, as amended in 1959, § 421, ''Sale of Certain Publications to Minors Prohibited,'' read as follows: ''(a) It shall be unlawful and an offense for any person operating any newsstand, book store, drug store, market, or other mercantile establishment to wilfully sell or distribute to any child below the age of eighteen years, or permit the perusal of by any such child, or have in his possession with intent to sell, distribute or otherwise offer for sale or distribution to any such child, any book, pamphlet, magazine or other printed paper principally composed of pictures and specifically including but not limited to comic books, devoted to the publication and exploitation of actual or fictional deeds of violent bloodshed, lust or immorality, or which, for a child below the age of eighteen years, are obscene, lewd, lascivious, filthy, indecent

or disgusting and so presented as reasonably to tend to incite a child below the age of eighteen years to violence or depraved or immoral acts against the person. . . . (d) It shall be unlawful . . . to exhibit upon any public street or highway or in any other place within view of children below the age of eighteen years passing upon any such street or highway any book, pamphlet, magazine or other printed paper, prohibited and made unlawful by subsection (a) of this section.''

This statute was held to be unconstitutional by the Maryland Court of Appeals because of vagueness, particularly the section making it unlawful to exhibit any such publication where children might see it; the court ruled that this was an invalid restriction on the rights of adults to view books that they had a right to read. The Supreme Court, in *Police Commissioner v. Siegel Enterprises, Inc.* (364 U.S. 909 [1960]), refused to grant certiorari and thus upheld the Maryland decision as to the invalidity of the statute.

MASSACHUSETTS, CHILD LABOR LAWS. Chapter 149, General Laws of Massachusetts, §§ 69, 80, and 81, provided: "No boy under twelve and no girl under eighteen shall sell, expose or offer for sale any newspapers, magazines, periodicals or other articles of merchandise of any description, or exercise the trade of bootblack or scavenger, or any other trade, in any street or public place." § 69. "Whoever furnishes or sells to any minor any article of any description with the knowledge that the minor intends to sell such article . . . shall be punished by a fine of not less than ten nor more than two hundred dollars or by imprisonment for not more than two months, or both." § 80. "Any parent, guardian, or custodian having a minor under his control who compels or permits such minor to work in violation . . . shall for a first offense be punished by a fine of not less than two nor more than ten dollars or by imprisonment for not more than five days, or both." § 81.

These provisions were upheld by the Supreme Court, in *Prince v. Massachusetts* (1944),* as not being a violation of the right to free press by ruling that the child labor laws took precedence over the right of a minor to distribute religious literature in the streets.

MASSACHUSETTS, CLOSED COURTROOM. Massachusetts General Laws, Chapter 278, § 16A, provided in part: "At the trial of a complaint or indictment for rape, incest, carnal abuse or other crime involving sex, where a minor under eighteen years of age is the person upon, with or against the crime is alleged to have been committed . . . the presiding justice shall exclude the general public from the court room, admitting only such persons as may have a direct interest in the case." This sweeping exclusion of the general public, which includes the news media, was seen to be an invalid abridgment on the right to a free press by the Supreme Court, in *Globe Newspaper Company v. Superior Court* (1982).*

MASSACHUSETTS, CORPORATE POLITICAL CONTRIBUTIONS. Massachusetts General Laws Ann., Chapter 55, § 8 (West Supp. 1977), prohibited certain corporations from making contributions or expenditures relating to certain referendum issues: "No corporation carrying on the business of a bank, trust, surety, indemnity, safe deposit, insurance, railroad, street railway, telegraph, telephone, gas, electric light, heat, power, canal, aqueduct, water company . . . shall directly or indirectly give, pay, expend or contribute . . . any money or other valuable thing for the purpose of . . . influencing or affecting the vote on any question submitted to the voters, other than one materially affecting any of the property, business or assets of the corporation. No question submitted to the voters solely concerning the taxation of the income, property or transactions of individuals shall be deemed materially to affect the property, business or assets of the corporation. . . . Any corporation violating any provision of this section shall be punished by a fine of not more than fifty thousand dollars and any officer, director or agent of the corporation violating any provision thereof or authorizing such violation . . . shall be punished by a fine of not more than ten thousand dollars or by imprisonment for not more than one year, or both."

The Supreme Court, in *First National Bank of Boston v. Francis X. Bellotti* (1978),* ruled that this statute was an unconstitutional muzzle on the right of corporations to enter the public debate, for as the Court noted, it is the content of the message that is important, not its source.

MASSACHUSETTS, FLAG DESECRATION. Massachusetts General Laws Ann., Chapter 264, § 5: "Whoever publicly mutilates, tramples upon, defaces or treats contemptuously the flag of the United States or of Massachusetts, whether such flag is public or private property, or whoever displays such flag or any representation thereof upon which are words, figures, advertisements or designs . . . shall be punished by a fine of not less than ten nor more than one hundred dollars or by imprisonment for not more than one year, or both." The term "treats contemptuously" was at issue in *Smith v. Goguen* (1974),* when Goguen was convicted— the only case in Massachusetts involving this statute— of wearing a pair of trousers with a small American flag sewed to the seat of the pants. The Supreme Court reversed Goguen's conviction, holding that the Massachusetts statute was too vague and overbroad.

MASSACHUSETTS, OBSCENITY STATUTE. Massachusetts General Laws, Chapter 272, § 28A, provides: "Whoever imports, prints, publishes, sells or distributes a pamphlet, ballad, printed paper, phonographic record, or other thing which is obscene, indecent or impure, or an obscene, indecent or impure print, picture, figure, image or description, or buys, procures, receives or has in his possession any such pamphlet . . . for the purpose of sale, exhibition, loan or circulation, shall be punished."

MASSACHUSETTS, SUNDAY EXHIBITIONS/ENTERTAINMENT. Massachusetts General Laws, Chapter 136, § 4, provided: "The mayor of a city may, upon written application describing the proposed entertainment, grant, upon such terms or conditions as . . . [he] may prescribe, a license to hold on the Lord's Day a public entertainment, in keeping with the character of the day and not inconsistent with its due observance . . . provided that no such license shall . . . have effect unless the proposed entertainment shall . . . have been approved in writing by the Commissioner of Public Safety as being in keeping with the character of the day [with a $500 fine for each violation].''

The Supreme Judicial Court of Massachusetts, in *Brattle Films v. Commissioner of Public Safety* (1955),* held that this statute was a violation of the First Amendment, for it imposed a prior restraint on any activity that was to be offered on a Sunday.

MEDIA COALITION. Founded in 1973, the coalition is an association of publishers, booksellers, periodical distributors, and college bookstores. It defines its objectives in the *Encyclopedia of Associations* (# 12001): ''Serves as a nationwide clearinghouse on obscenity legislation at the state levels, analyzes the legality of bills and their projected effects on the media industry, and monitors their progress through the legislative process. It initiates citizen lobbying activities in the state legislatures and uses the media and direct contact with politicians and other civic leaders to inform the public about the dangers of censorship.''

MEMOIRS OF A WOMAN OF PLEASURE/FANNY HILL. This classic by John Cleland, first published around 1749, has endured to the present day despite periodic efforts to suppress it. In *Commonwealth of Massachusetts v. Holmes* (17 Mass. 335 [1821]), one of the earliest recorded U.S. obscenity cases, the book was judged to be ''lewd and wicked.'' Holmes was indicted—and duly convicted—for ''being a scandalous and evil-disposed person, and contriving, devising and intending, the morals of youth and of other good citizens of said commonwealth to debauch and corrupt, and to raise and create in their minds inordinate and lustful desires, with force and arms, at, &c., on, &c., knowingly, unlawfully, wickedly, maliciously, and scandalously, did utter, publish and deliver to A.B. a certain lewd, wicked, scandalous, infamous and obscene printed book, entitled, &c., which said printed book is so lewd, wicked and obscene, that the same would be offensive to the Court here, and improper to be placed upon the records thereof.''

Some 142 years later, a New York court (*Larkin v. G. P. Putnam's Sons*, 243 N.Y.S. 2d 145 [1963]) declared the book to be obscene and restrained Putnam's from selling or distributing it. The long history of attempts to censor the book came to a climax in 1966, however. In 1963, the book was again published in the United States. The court records show that an unusually large number of orders were placed by universities and libraries and that the Library of Congress requested the right to translate *Memoirs* into Braille. But the attorney general of Massachusetts brought suit, charging the book to be obscene, and thus ensuring that the citizens of Massachusetts might be spared the necessity of determining for themselves whether or not to read it. The Massachusetts trial court did indeed find the book to be obscene, and the Massachusetts Supreme Judicial Court affirmed that decision (206 N.E. 2d 403).

At the time of the Massachusetts case, the test or standard for obscenity was the Roth Standard*: "Whether to the average person, applying contemporary community standards, the dominant theme of the material taken as a whole appeals to prurient interest." Subsequent decisions refined this standard to read: "Three elements must coalesce: it must be established that (a) the dominant theme of the material taken as a whole appeals to a prurient interest in sex; (b) the material is patently offensive because it affronts contemporary community standards relating to the description or representation of sexual matters; and (c) the material is utterly without redeeming social value."

The Massachusetts Supreme Judicial Court found that *Memoirs* satisfied the prurient appeal and patent offensiveness criteria but, and this was central to the subsequent Supreme Court decision, misinterpreted the social value criterion. The Massachusetts court found that the prurient appeal and patent offensiveness "outweighed" whatever value the book may have had and felt that such a book did not have to be "unqualifiedly worthless" before it could be deemed obscene: "It remains to consider whether the book can be said to be 'utterly without social importance.' We are mindful that there was expert testimony, much of which was strained, to the effect that *Memoirs* is a structural novel with literary merit; that the book displays a skill in characterization and a gift of comedy; that it plays a part in the history of the development of the English novel; and that it contains a moral, namely, that sex with love is superior to sex in a brothel. But the fact that the testimony may indicate this book has some minimal literary value does not mean it is of any social importance. We do not interpret the 'social importance' test as requiring that a book which appeals to prurient interest and is patently offensive must be unqualifiedly worthless before it can be deemed obscene."

The case reached the Supreme Court in 1966 (*Memoirs v. Massachusetts*, 383 U.S. 413 [1966]), and the Court reversed the Massachusetts obscenity ruling. The majority could not agree on a single decision—some ruled that the book wasn't obscene; others (Justice Douglas in particular) wrote that the First Amendment forbids censorship of expression of ideas, obscene or not, not linked with illegal action—but the result was that *Memoirs* was held not to be obscene. The major reason for the decision was that the Court held that a book had to be "utterly" without social value and no matter the degree of prurient appeal or patent offensiveness; the presence of any social value would thus protect the book.

Justice Douglas, however, went further than his colleagues and argued that there is no societal interest that justifies establishing a censorship scheme over speech and the press. Justice Douglas: "The censor is always quick to justify his function in terms that are protective of society. But the First Amendment, written in terms that are absolute, deprives the States of any power to pass on the value, the propriety, or the morality of a particular expression. Perhaps the most frequently assigned justification for censorship is the belief that erotica produce antisocial sexual conduct. But that relationship has yet to be proven. Indeed, if one were to make judgments on the basis of speculation, one might guess that literature of the most pornographic sort would, in many cases, provide a substitute—not a stimulus—for antisocial sexual conduct. As I read the First Amendment, judges cannot gear the literary diet of an entire nation to whatever tepid stuff is incapable of triggering the most demented mind. The First Amendment demands more than a horrible example or two of the perpetrator of a crime of sexual violence, in whose pocket is found a pornographic book, before it allows the Nation to be saddled with a regime of censorship.''

Justice Clark seemed overwhelmed by the book and filed a dissenting opinion: ''It is with regret that I write this dissenting opinion. However, the public should know of the continuous flow of pornographic material reaching this Court and the increasing problem States have in controlling it. *Memoirs of a Woman of Pleasure*, the book involved here, is typical. I have 'stomached' past cases for almost ten years without much outcry. Though I am not known to be a purist— or a shrinking violet—this book is too much even for me. It is important that the Court has refused to declare it obscene and thus affords it further circulation. In order to give my remarks the proper setting I have been obliged to portray the book's contents, which causes me embarrassment. However, quotations from typical episodes would so debase our Reports that I will not follow that course. . . . *Memoirs* is nothing more than a series of minutely and vividly described sexual episodes. The book starts with Fanny Hill, a young 15-year-old girl, arriving in London to seek household work. She goes to an employment office where through happenstance she meets the mistress of a bawdy house. This takes ten pages. The remaining 200 pages of the book detail her initiation into various sexual experiences, from a lesbian encounter with a sister prostitute to all sorts and types of sexual debauchery in bawdy houses and as the mistress of a variety of men. This is presented to the reader through an uninterrupted succession of descriptions by Fanny, either as an observer or participant, of sexual adventures so vile that one of the male expert witnesses in the case was hesitant to repeat any one of them in the courtroom. These scenes run the gamut of possible sexual experience such as lesbianism, female masturbation, homosexuality between young boys, the destruction of a maidenhead with consequent gory descriptions, the seduction of a young virgin boy, the flagellation of male by female, and vice versa, followed by fervid sexual engagement, and other abhorrent acts, including over two dozen separate bizarre descriptions of different sexual intercourses between male and female characters. In one sequence four girls in a bawdy house are required in the presence of one another to relate the lurid details of their loss of virginity and their glorification of it. This is followed the same evening by 'publick trials' in which each of the four girls engages in sexual intercourse with a different man while the others witness, with Fanny giving a detailed description of the movement and reaction of each couple. In each of the sexual scenes the exposed bodies of the participants are described in minute and individual detail. The pubic hair is often used as a background to the most vivid and precise descriptions of the response, condition, size, shape, and color of the sexual organs before, during and after orgasms. There are some short transitory passages between the various sexual episodes, but for the most part they only set the scene and identify the participants for the next orgy, or make smutty reference and comparison to past episodes. . . . My study of *Memoirs* leads me to think that it has no conceivable 'social importance.' The author's obsession with sex, his minute descriptions of phalli, and his repetitious accounts of bawdy sexual experiences and deviant sexual behavior indicate the book was designed solely to appeal to prurient interests. . . . To say that Fanny is an 'intellectual' is an insult to those who travel under that tag.''

MEMOIRS OF HECATE COUNTY. In 1946, a collection of short stories by Edmund Wilson, *Memoirs of Hecate County*, was published. *Memoirs* is composed of six related stories about the lives of some upper-class residents of a fictional New York City suburban community. One of the stories, "The Princess with the Golden Hair," provoked some controversy, particularly since it described in some literary detail, as only Edmund Wilson could do, certain sexual activities and sexual intercourse. The reviews were mixed: "Wilson's name will attract some readers to a book that will enhance neither his reputation nor his publishers. . . . This isn't even good erotica" (*Kirkus*, January 15, 1946, p. 21); "This is a good, distinguished book" (Ralph Bates, *New York Times*, March 31, 1946, p. 7). Harrison Smith, writing in the *Saturday Review of Literature* (March 23, 1946, p. 27), commented: "A great deal of what is fine and accurate writing and observation in *Memoirs of Hecate County* may be swept away in the mind of future readers by the notoriety that these scenes will evoke. We have managed to keep at bay the literary censors and the keyhole peepers who insist that books shall not be printed that their little Lucy should not read. It would be unfortunate and ironic if our foremost literary critic should rouse those dogs to bay at literature again. . . . There are embedded [in 'The Princess with the Golden Hair'] some of the most frankly erotic passages that can be found in the modern writing that need not be sold under the counter."

Unfortunately, the dogs were unleashed again and *Memoirs of Hecate County* was forced under the counter. The oldest dog of all, the Anthony Comstock–founded New York Society for the Suppression of Vice (Comstockery*)—since renamed the New York Society for the Improvement of Morals—began to bark and this time it had a bite! Wilson's publisher, Doubleday and Co., was convicted in a New York court (*People v. Doubleday*, 77 N.E. 2d 6 [1947]) of violating § 1141 of the New York Penal Code (New York, Obscenity Statute*). The New York court did not present a full written opinion; it simply held that the book was obscene and that the conviction did not violate the First Amendment.

Doubleday appealed to the Supreme Court (*Doubleday and Co. v. New York*, 335 U.S. 848 [1948] but was not able to get the New York ruling reversed. Justice Frankfurter did not participate in this case, and the Supreme Court, in a

4 to 4 per curiam decision (there was no written opinion), simply said that the book was obscene and thus affirmed the ruling of the lower court that *Memoirs of Hecate County*, especially "The Princess with the Golden Hair," was obscene under the New York statute.

MEMOIRS STANDARD. The subject of obscenity* has produced a variety of views among the members of the U.S. Supreme Court. The 1957 Roth Standard* (*Roth v. United States**) stated the test to be "whether to the average person,* applying contemporary community standards,* the dominant theme of the material taken as a whole appeals to prurient interest."* The Roth Standard was refined in 1966 in *Memoirs v. Massachusetts*, which created the Memoirs Standard: "Three elements must coalesce: it must be established that (a) the dominant theme of the material taken as a whole appeals to prurient interest in sex; (b) the material is patently offensive because it affronts contemporary community standards relating to the description or representation of sexual matters; and (c) the material is utterly without redeeming social value." Each of the three criteria is to be applied independently; the social value of a book, for example, cannot be weighed against or canceled out by its prurient appeal or patent offensiveness.

The Memoirs Standard itself was refined in 1973 (*Miller v. California**), and the resulting Miller Standard* is the current standard or test of obscenity. The Miller Standard deleted the "utterly without redeeming social value" criterion of *Memoirs* and substituted "whether the work, taken as a whole, lacks serious literary, artistic, political, or scientific value."

METROMEDIA v. CITY OF SAN DIEGO (1981). The city of San Diego enacted an ordinance (San Diego [CA], Outdoor Advertising Displays*) that imposed a substantial prohibition on the erection of outdoor advertising displays (billboards) within the city. Some companies that were engaged in the business of outdoor advertising in San Diego brought suit, contending that the ordinance abridged their First Amendment right and was a form of government censorship. Although unable to agree on a single majority decision, the Supreme Court agreed with Metromedia and held the ordinance to be a violation of the First Amendment: (1) The ordinance reached too far into the realms of protected speech by distinguishing, through the use of its statutory exceptions, in several ways between permissible and impermissible signs at a particular location by reference to their content. (2) Although a city can ban billboards, it has to be related to a legitimate governmental interest (traffic safety, for example), and this particular ordinance did not meet any acceptable governmental interest. A related case concerned an attempt by the state of Maine to ban billboards throughout the state, but that statute, too, was seen to be a violation of the First Amendment, in *John Donnelly & Sons v. Campbell* (1980).* *Metromedia v. City of San Diego*, 453 U.S. 490 (1981).

MEYER v. NEBRASKA (1923). A Nebraska state law (Nebraska, Teaching Foreign Languages*) prohibited the teaching in any private, denominational, parochial, or public school in the state, any modern language other than English to any child who had not yet passed the eighth grade. The statute was applied to convict Meyer who taught reading in German to a ten-year-old child in a parochial school.

The Supreme Court reversed the conviction: "It is said that the purpose of the legislation was to promote civic development by inhibiting training and education of the immature in foreign tongues and ideals before they could learn English and acquire American ideals; and 'that the English language should be and become the mother tongue of all children reared in this State.' It is also affirmed that the foreign born population is very large, that certain communities commonly use foreign words, follow foreign leaders, move in a foreign atmosphere, and that the children are thereby hindered from becoming citizens of the most useful type and the public safety is imperiled. That the State may do much, go very far, indeed, in order to improve the quality of its citizens, physically, mentally and morally, is clear; but the individual has certain fundamental rights which must be respected. The protection of the Constitution extends to all, those who speak other languages as well as to those born with English on the tongue. Perhaps it would be highly advantageous if all had ready understanding of our ordinary speech, but this cannot be coerced by methods which conflict with the Constitution—a desirable end cannot be promoted by prohibited means. . . . The power of the State to compel attendance at some school and to make reasonable regulations for all schools, including a requirement that they shall give instructions in English, is not questioned. Nor has challenge been made of the State's power to prescribe a curriculum for insitutions which it supports. . . . [But] no emergency has arisen which renders knowledge by a child of some language other than English so clearly harmful as to justify its inhibition with the consequent infringement of rights long freely enjoyed. We are constrained to conclude that the statute as applied is arbitrary and without reasonable relation to any end within the competency of the State."

Justice Holmes, joined by Justice Sutherland, dissented: "It is with hesitation and unwillingness that I differ from my brethren with regard to a law like this but I cannot bring my mind to believe that in some circumstances, and circumstances existing it is said in Nebraska, the statute might not be regarded as a reasonable or even necessary method of reaching the desired result. The part of the act with which we are concerned deals with the teaching of young children. Youth is the time when familiarity with a language is established and if there are sections in the State where a child would hear only Polish or French or German spoken at home I am not prepared to say that it is unreasonable to provide that in his early years he shall hear and speak only English at school." *Meyer v. Nebraska*, 262 U.S. 390 (1923).

MIAMI (FL), SALE OF OBSCENE MATERIAL. Section 38 of Chapter 43 of the Miami Code provides that it shall be unlawful for any person to commit an act that is recognized by the laws of the state as a misdemeanor. Under c. 61-7, Laws 1961, Florida Stat. § 847.011 (1)(a), it is a misdemeanor to have in one's "possession, custody, or control with intent to sell . . . any obscene, lewd, lascivious, filthy, indecent [or] immoral . . . figure [or] image." Chapter 61-7, Laws 1961, Florida Stat. § 847.011(10), has this test for obscenity: "Whether to the average person, applying contemporary community standards, the dominant theme of the material taken as a whole appeals to prurient interest." This statute was invoked to convict a Miami resident who had attempted to sell some statues (*Fort v. City of Miami* [1967].*

MIAMI HERALD PUBLISHING CO. v. TORNILLO (1974). The *Miami Herald* was found guilty of violating a Florida statute (Florida, Right of Reply*) when it refused a political candidate (Tornillo) equal space in the newspaper to answer criticism and attacks on his record made by the newspaper. The Supreme Court reversed the conviction, holding that the statute violated the First Amendment's guarantee of a free press by mandating what a newspaper had to publish: (1) Governmental compulsion on a newspaper to publish that which "reason" tells it should not is unconstitutional. (2) The statute operates as a command by a state in the same sense as a statute or regulation forbidding the publication of specified matter. (3) The statute exacts a penalty on the basis of the content of a newspaper by imposing additional printing, composing, and materials cost and by taking up space that could be devoted to other material the newspaper may have preferred to print. (4) Even if a newspaper would face no additional costs to comply with the statute and would not be forced to forgo publication of news or opinion by the inclusion of a reply, the statute still fails to clear the First Amendment's barriers because of its intrusion into the function of editors in choosing what material goes into a newspaper and deciding on the size and content of the paper and the treatment of public issues and officials. *Miami Herald Publishing Co. v. Tornillo*, 418 U.S. 241 (1974).

MICHIGAN, PROTECTION OF MINORS. The Michigan Penal Code, § 343, provided: "Any person who shall import, print, publish, sell, possess with the intent to sell . . . any book, magazine, newspaper, print, picture, drawing, photograph, publication or other thing . . . or obscene, immoral, lewd or lascivious prints, pictures, figures or descriptions, tending to incite minors to violent or depraved or immoral acts, manifestly tending to the corruption of the morals of youth, or shall introduce into any family, school or place of education . . . any such book . . . shall be guilty of a misdemeanor." This statute was declared to be unconstitutional in *Butler v. Michigan* (1957),* for as the Court noted, the impact of the statute would be to reduce the adult population of Michigan to reading only what is fit for children.

MILITARY REGULATIONS, ACCESS TO MILITARY BASES. Title 18 U.S.C. § 1382 provides that "whoever reenters or is found within [a military] reservation . . . after having been removed therefrom or ordered not to reenter by any officer or person in command or charge thereof—Shall be fined not more than $500 or imprisoned not more than six months, or both.'' This statute has been applied several times to prevent individuals from circulating petitions or distributing literature within the confines of military bases. *Flower v. United States* (1972).*

MILITARY REGULATIONS, AIR FORCE. Certain air force regulations recognize that air force personnel have the right to petition members of Congress and other public officials (Air Force Reg. 30-1 [9] [1971]; Military Regulations, Petitioning Congress*). The regulations, however, prohibit ''the public solicitation or collection of signatures on a petition by any person within an Air Force facility or by a member when in uniform or when in a foreign country . . . unless first authorized by the appropriate commander'' (Air Force Reg. 30-1 [19] [b] [1977]).

Certain regulations (Air Force Reg. 35-15 [3] [a] [1970]) also provide: ''(1) No member of the Air Force will distribute or post any printed or written material other than publications of an official governmental agency or base regulated activity within any Air Force installation without permission of the commander or his designee. A copy of the material with a proposed plan or method of distribution or posting will be submitted when permission is requested. Distribution of publications and other materials through the United States mail or through official outlets, such as military libraries and exchanges, may not be prohibited under this regulation. (2) When prior approval for distribution or posting is required, the commander will determine if a clear danger to the loyalty, discipline, or morale of members of the Armed Forces, or material interference with the accomplishment of a military mission, would result. If such a determination is made, distribution or posting will be prohibited. . . . (3) Mere possession of materials unauthorized for distribution or posting may not be prohibited unless otherwise unlawful. However, such material may be impounded if a member of the Armed Forces distributes or posts or attempts to distribute or post such material within the installation. Impounded materials will be returned to the owner when departing the installation unless determined to be evidence of a crime. (4) Distribution or posting may not be prohibited solely on the ground that the material is critical of Government policies or officials. (5) In general, installation commanders should encourage and promote the availability to service personnel of books, periodicals, and other material which present a wide range of viewpoints on public issues.''

Although a blatant prior restraint (the base commander's permission is required) on the distribution of literature, the Supreme Court has held (*Brown, Secretary of Defense v. Glines* [1980]*) these regulations to be valid in pursuit of higher governmental interests—the maintenance of loyalty, discipline, and morale within the armed forces.

MILITARY REGULATIONS, ARMY. In 1976, Benjamin Spock, then a candidate for president, attempted to hold a campaign rally and distribute some campaign literature within the confines of Fort Dix, in New Jersey. Spock encountered an emphatic refusal of the base commander to allow him to campaign on the base, and the Supreme Court, in *Greer v. Spock* (1976),* again relying on the governmental interest of protecting the loyalty, discipline, and morale of armed services personnel, upheld the use of prior restraints within the military.

The following recitation of some army regulations comes from the court record in *Greer v. Spock*. Civilian speakers have occasionally been invited to the base (Fort Dix) to address military personnel. The subjects of their talks have ranged from business management to drug abuse. Visiting clergymen have, by invitation, participated in religious services at the base chapel. Theatrical exhibitions and musical productions have also been presented on the base. Speeches and demonstrations of a partisan political nature, however, are banned by Fort Dix Reg. 210-26 (1968), which provides that "demonstrations, picketing, sit-ins, protest marches, political speeches and similar activities are prohibited and will not be conducted on the Fort Dix Military Reservation." The regulation has been rigidly enforced: No political campaign speech has ever been given at Fort Dix.

Restrictions are also placed on other types of expressive activity. Fort Dix Reg. 210-27 (1970) provides that "the distribution or posting of any publication, including newspapers, magazines, handbills, flyers, circulars, pamphlets or other writings, issued, published or otherwise prepared by any person, persons, agency or agencies . . . is prohibited on the Fort Dix Military Reservation without prior written approval of the Adjutant General, this headquarters." This regulation does not permit the Fort Dix authorities to prohibit the distribution of conventional political campaign literature. The post regulation was issued in conformity with Army Reg. 210-10, ¶5-5 (c) (1970), which states that permission to distribute a publication may be withheld only when "it appears that the dissemination of [the] publication presents a clear danger to the loyalty, discipline, or morale of troops at [the] installation." The army regulation further provides that if a base commander decides to withhold permission to distribute a publication, he shall "inform the next major commander and Headquarters, Department of the Army . . . and request . . . approval to prohibit the distribution of that publication or the particular issue thereof." ¶5-5 (d). The base commander may delay distribution of the publication in question pending approval or disapproval of his request by army headquarters.

A Department of the Army letter dated June 23, 1969, entitled "Guidance on Dissent" ¶5 (a)(3), gives as examples of materials that a commander need not allow to be distributed "publications which are obscene or otherwise unlawful (e.g., counseling disloyalty, mutiny, or refusal of duty)." Commercial magazines and newspapers distributed through regular outlets, such as post exchange newsstands, need not be approved before distribution. Army Reg. 210–10, ¶¶ 5-5 (c) and (d), does provide that a commander may delay, and the Department of the Army may prohibit, the distribution of particular issues of such publications through official outlets. The substantive standards for such restrictions are the same as those applicable to publications distributed other than through official outlets. Army Reg. 210-10, ¶ 5-5 (e). This provision, allowing commanders to halt the distribution of particular issues of publications through regular outlets, appears to be inconsistent with Department of Defense Directive 1325.6, ¶ III (a)(1) (1969), which provides that "a Commander is not authorized to prohibit the distribution of a specific issue of a publication through official outlets such as post exchanges and military libraries."

There are several other restrictions placed on military personnel, some of which do not apply to civilians: Members of the armed forces may not be polled by any person or political party to determine their choice among candidates for elective office (18 U.S.C. § 596); it is unlawful to solicit political contributions in any fort or arsenal (18 U.S.C. § 603); candidates for federal office are prohibited from soliciting contributions from military personnel (18 U.S.C. § 602); and no commissioned or non-commissioned officer in the armed forces may attempt to influence any member of the armed forces to vote for any particular candidate (50 U.S.C. § 1475).

MILITARY REGULATIONS, NAVY AND MARINE CORPS. The U.S. Navy and the U.S. Marine Corps have regulations similar to those of the U.S. Air Force and the U.S. Army that require a commander's prior approval before certain First Amendment rights can be exercised by navy and Marine Corps personnel. These regulations were seen as necessary to maintain the loyalty, discipline, and morale of the troops by the Supreme Court in *Secretary of the Navy v. Huff* (1980).* The listing of certain navy and Marine Corps regulations are contained in the court records for the *Huff* case. Fleet Marine Force Pacific Order 5370.3, ¶ 3 (b) (1974): "No Fleet Marine Force, Pacific or Marine Corps Bases, Pacific, personnel will originate, sign, distribute, or promulgate petitions, publications, including pamphlets, newspapers, magazines, handbills, flyers, or other printed or written material, on board any ship, craft, aircraft, or in any vehicle of the Department of the Navy, or any military installation on duty or in uniform, or anywhere within a foreign country irrespective of uniform or duty status, unless prior command approval is obtained." Other regulations, although different in geographic scope, use substantially the identical language: Pacific Fleet Instruction 5440.3C, § 2604.2(2) (1974); First Marine Aircraft Wing Order 5370.1B, ¶ 5 (a)(2) (1974); and Iwakuni Marine Corps Air Station Order 5370.3A, ¶ (a)(2) (1973). Each regulation directs a commander to "control or prohibit" the circulation of written materials that, in his judgment, would: "(1) Materially interfere with the safety, operation, command, or control of his unit or the assigned duties of particular members of the command; or (2) Present a clear danger to the loyalty, discipline, morale, or safety to personnel of his command; or (3) Involve distribution of material or the rendering of advice or counsel that causes, attempts to cause, or advocates, insubordination, disloyalty, mutiny, refusal of duty, solicits desertion, discloses classified information, or contains obscene or pornographic matter; or (4) Involve the planning or perpetration of an unlawful act or acts.'' Fleet Marine Force Pacific Order 5370.3, ¶ 4(a) (1974).

MILITARY REGULATIONS, PETITIONING CONGRESS. Although just about every conceivable activity within the First Amendment guarantees of free speech and free press within the military requires the prior approval of the individual's commanding officer, there is one outlet that is free from such prior restraint—an individual letter or petition to a member of Congress. Title 10 U.S.C. § 1034 provides: ''No person may restrict any member of an armed force in communicating with a member of Congress, unless the communication is unlawful or violates a regulation necessary to the security of the United States.'' Congress enacted § 1034 to ensure that an individual member of the armed forces could write to his elected representatives without sending the communication through official channels, and this has been seen not to endanger a commander's ability to preserve loyalty, discipline, and morale among his troops.

MILITARY REGULATIONS, UNIFORM CODE OF MILITARY JUSTICE. The Uniform Code of Military Justice (UCMJ) contains several regulations that, if they were to be applied to the civilian world, would be a blatant violation of the First Amendment guarantees of free speech and free press. But as the Supreme Court has ruled several times, as well as various military courts-martial and tribunals, the individual in the armed forces loses some of his rights and is open to prior restraints, censorship, and vague and loosely worded prohibitions. Article 88 of the UCMJ provides: ''Any commissioned officer who uses contemptuous words against the President . . . shall be punished as a court-martial may direct'' (*United States v. Howe* [1965]*); Article 133: ''Any commissioned officer, cadet, or midshipman who is convicted of conduct unbecoming an officer and a gentleman shall be punished as a court-martial may direct'' (*Parker v. Levy* [1974]*); Article 134: ''Though not specifically mentioned in this chapter, all disorders and neglects to the prejudice of good order and discipline in the armed forces, all conduct of a nature to bring discredit upon the armed forces . . . shall be punished at the discretion of [a] court'' (*United States v. Jewson,* * *United States v. Priest,* * *United States v. Gray**).

MILITARY REGULATIONS, WEARING UNIFORMS—MILITARY PERSONNEL. Paragraph 1-10, Air Force Manual 35-10C, dated 11 May 1967, states: ''When Wear of the Uniform is Prohibited. Air Force members will not wear the uniform: a. At any meeting or demonstration that is a function of, or sponsored by any organization, association, movement, group, or combination of persons that: (1) The Attorney General of the United States has designated as totalitarian, Fascist, Communist, or subversive. (2) Advocates or approves the commission of acts of force or violence to deny others their rights under the Constitution of the United States. (3) Seeks to alter the form of the United States

Government by unconstitutional means. b. During or in connection with the furtherance of private employment or commercial interests when an inference of official sponsorship for the activity or interest would be drawn. c. Under circumstances which would bring discredit upon the Armed Forces. d. Under such other circumstances as may be specified and published by the Secretary of the Air Force.'' This prohibition against wearing the uniform at meetings of unpopular causes was upheld in *United States v. Toomey*** and *United States v. Locks.***

MILITARY REGULATIONS, WEARING UNIFORMS—NON-MILITARY PERSONNEL.

Title 18 U.S.C. § 702 reads: ''Whoever, in any place within the jurisdiction of the United States or in the Canal Zone, without authority, wears the uniform or a distinctive part thereof or anything similar to a distinctive part of the uniform of any of the armed forces of the United States, Public Health Service or any auxiliary of such, shall be fined not more than $250 or imprisoned not more than six months, or both.'' But Title 10 U.S.C. § 772(f) provides: ''When wearing by persons not on active duty authorized— While portraying a member of the Army, Navy, Air Force, or Marine Corps, an actor, in a theatrical or motion-picture production may wear the uniform of that armed force if the portrayal does not tend to discredit that armed force.'' This last section (§ 772-f), allowing the wearing of a uniform by an actor only if the play or drama presents the armed forces in a favorable light, was seen to be an invalid censorship scheme by the Supreme Court in *Schacht v. United States* (1970).*

MILK WAGON DRIVERS UNION v. MEADOWMOOR DAIRIES (1941).

This case concerned the question whether a state could prevent acts of peaceful picketing by a labor union in a labor dispute if the acts were accompanied by violent conduct. The state of Illinois attempted such, and the Supreme Court saw no violation of the right of free speech. Justice Frankfurter delivered the opinion of the Court: ''The Constitution is invoked to deny Illinois the power to authorize its courts to prevent the continuance and recurrence of flagrant violence . . . [but] peaceful picketing is the workingman's means of communication. It must never be forgotten, however, that the Bill of Rights was the child of the Enlightenment. Back of the guarantee of free speech lay faith in the power of an appeal to reason by all the peaceful means for gaining access to the mind. It was in order to avert force and explosions due to restrictions upon rational modes of communication that the guarantee of free speech was given a generous scope. But utterance in a context of violence can lose its significance as an appeal to reason and become part of an instrument of force. Such utterance was not meant to be sheltered by the Constitution. A final word. Freedom of speech and freedom of the press cannot be too often invoked as basic to our scheme of society. But these liberties will not be advanced or even maintained by denying to the states with all their resources, including the instrumentality of their courts, the power to deal with coercion due to extensive violence.''

Justice Black, joined by Justice Douglas, dissented: ''In my belief the opinion just announced gives approval to an injunction which seriously infringes upon the constitutional rights of freedom of speech and the press. To such a result I cannot agree.'' *Milk Wagon Drivers Union v. Meadowmoor Dairies*, 312 U.S. 287 (1941).

MILLER STANDARD. The subject of obscenity* has produced a variety of views among the members of the U.S. Supreme Court. The 1957 Roth Standard* (*Roth v. United States**) stated the test to be ''whether to the average person,* applying contemporary community standards,* the dominant theme of the material taken as a whole appeals to prurient interest.''* The Roth Standard was refined in 1966 in *Memoirs v. Massachusetts*, which created the Memoirs Standard*: ''It must be established that (a) the dominant theme of the material taken as a whole appeals to a prurient interest in sex; (b) the material is patently offensive* because it affronts contemporary community standards; and (c) the material is utterly without redeeming social value.'' The Memoirs Standard itself was refined in 1973 (*Miller v. California**), and the resulting Miller Standard is the current test or measure of obscenity: ''The basic guidelines must be: (a) whether the average person, applying contemporary community standards, would find that the work, taken as a whole, appeals to the prurient interest; (b) whether the work depicts or describes, in a patently offensive way, sexual conduct specifically defined by the applicable state law; and (c) whether the work, taken as a whole, lacks serious literary, artistic, political, or scientific value.'' The Miller Standard thus rejected the ''utterly without redeeming social value'' element of *Memoirs* and substituted ''lacks serious literary, artistic, political, or scientific value.'' Each of the elements must be applied independently; the value of a book, for example, cannot be weighed against or canceled out by its prurient appeal or offensiveness. The Miller Standard also allows the jury to measure prurient appeal and patent offensiveness by the standard that prevails in the local or regional forum community and it need not employ a ''national community'' standard. The vast majority of the states have either legislatively adopted or judicially incorporated the Miller test as the measure of obscenity.

MILLER v. CALIFORNIA (1973). Miller was convicted by a California court of violating § 311.2 of the California Penal Code (California, Obscenity Statute*). The conviction was for mailing unsolicited sexually explicit material (advertising brochures for a film [*Marital Intercourse*] and for four books (*Intercourse, Man—Woman, Sex Orgies Illustrated*, and *An Illustrated History of Pornography*]). The U.S. Supreme Court upheld the conviction and in so doing refined the Memoirs Standard* obscenity test and developed the Miller Standard.* The Court ruled: (1) Obscene material is *not* protected by the First Amendment (*Roth v. United States**). A work may be subject to state regulation if that work, taken as a whole, appeals to the prurient interest in sex; portrays in a patently offensive way, sexual conduct specifically defined by the applicable state law; and taken as a whole, does not have serious literary, artistic, political, or scientific value. (2) The basic guidelines must be (a) whether "the average person, applying contemporary community standards, would find that the work, taken as a whole, appeals to the prurient interest; (b) whether the work depicts or describes, in a patently offensive way, sexual conduct specifically defined by the applicable state law; and (c) whether the work, taken as a whole, lacks serious literary, artistic, political, or scientific value." (3) The test of *"utterly* without redeeming social value" (*Memoirs*) is rejected. (4) The jury may measure prurient appeal and patent offensiveness by the standard that prevails in the forum community and need not employ a "national standard." *Miller v. California,* 413 U.S. 15 (1973).

MILLS v. ALABAMA (1966). Mills, a Birmingham, Alabama, newspaper editor, was arrested for violating a state statute (Alabama, Corrupt Practices Act*) that prohibited any electioneering or soliciting of votes on election day for or against any proposition or candidate involved in the election. Mills wrote and published on election day a newspaper editorial that supported the adoption of a mayor-council form of municipal government. The Alabama Supreme Court ruled that the statute was constitutional, and since Mills admitted that he published the article, his conviction in Alabama was all but assured.

Mills appealed to the Supreme Court before his trial, however, and the Supreme Court held the statute to be a flagrant type of governmental censorship over free speech and free press, thus obviating a trial. Justice Black delivered the opinion of the Court: "We now come to the merits. The First Amendment, which applies to the States through the Fourteenth, prohibits laws 'abridging the freedom of speech, or of the press.' The question here is whether it abridges freedom of the press for a State to punish a newspaper editor for doing no more than publishing an editorial on election day urging people to vote a particular way in the election. We should point out at once that this question in no way involves the extent of a State's power to regulate conduct in and around the polls in order to maintain peace, order and decorum there. The sole reason for the charge that Mills violated the law is that he wrote and published an editorial on election day urging Birmingham voters to cast their votes in favor of changing their form of government. Whatever differences may exist about interpretations of the First Amendment, there is practically universal agreement that a major purpose of that Amendment was to protect the free discussion of governmental affairs. This of course includes discussions of candidates, structures and forms of government, the manner in which government is operated or should be operated, and all such matters relating to political processes. The Constitution specifically selected the press, which includes not only newspapers, books, and magazines, but also humble leaflets and circulars (*Lovell v. City of Griffin**) to play an important role in the discussion of public affairs. Thus the press serves and was designed to serve as a powerful antidote to any abuses of power by governmental officials and as a constitutionally chosen means for keeping officials elected by the people responsible to all the people whom they were selected to serve. Suppression of the right of the press to praise or criticize governmental agents and to clamor and contend for or against change, which is all that this editorial did, muzzles one of the very agencies the Framers of our Constitution thoughtfully and deliberately selected to improve our society and keep it free. The Alabama Corrupt Practices Act by providing criminal penalties for publishing editorials such as the one here silences the press at a time when it can be most effective. It is difficult to conceive of a more obvious and flagrant abridgment of the constitutionally guaranteed freedom of the press." *Mills v. Alabama*, 284 U.S. 214 (1966).

MILWAUKEE (WI), DISTRIBUTION OF LITERATURE. A Milwaukee ordinance provided: "It is hereby made unlawful for any person to throw paper or to circulate or distribute any circular, handbills, cards, posters, dodgers, or other printed or advertising matter in or upon any sidewalk, street, alley, wharf, boat landing, dock or other public place, park or ground within the City of Milwaukee." The Supreme Court, in *Snyder v. Milwaukee* (1939),* held that the anti-littering ("throw") portion of this ordinance was a legitimate regulation in pursuit of a governmental interest but that the ban on the circulation or distribution of literature was a violation of the right of free speech and press.

MINERSVILLE SCHOOL DISTRICT v. GOBITIS (1940). A West Virginia regulation required that all students in the state's public schools participate in a daily ceremony of saluting the flag while reciting the Pledge of Allegiance. Any student who refused to participate could be expelled from the school. Although this case is really a freedom of religion case—the recalcitrant pupils were Jehovah's Witnesses who had the conscientious belief that obeisance to the flag is forbidden by the Bible—it can also be seen as a governmental censorship case. Censorship can be seen as a two-sided coin: The first side presents the government in a position of preventing or punishing what people think or say or write; the other side is represented by the government forcing people to think or say or write that which the individual does not believe.

The Supreme Court saw no problems in 1940 with the idea of forcing children to say publicly things in which they did not believe. Justice Frankfurter delivered the opinion of the Court: "The wisdom of training children in patriotic impulses by those compulsions which necessarily pervade so much of the educational process is not for our independent judgment. Even were we convinced of the folly of such a measure, such belief would be no proof of its unconstitutionality. For ourselves, we might be tempted to say that the deepest patriotism is best engendered by giving unfettered scope to the most crochety beliefs. Perhaps it is best, even from the standpoint of those interests which ordinances like the one under review seek to promote, to give to the least popular sect leave from conformities like those here in issue. But the courtroom is not an arena for debating issues of educational policy. It is not our province to choose among competing considerations in the subtle process of securing effective loyalty to the traditional ideas of democracy, while respecting at the same time individual idiosyncracies among a people so diversified in racial origins and religious allegiances. So to hold would in effect make us the school board for the country. That authority has not been given to this Court, nor should we assume it.'' This doctrine was short-lived, for only three years later, in 1943 (*West Virginia State Board of Education v. Barnette**), the Court did exercise some independent judgment and overturned the *Gobitis* decision. *Minersville School District v. Gobitis*, 310 U.S. 586 (1940).

MINNEAPOLIS STAR AND TRIBUNE CO. v. MINNESOTA COMMIS-SIONER OF REVENUE (1983). The state of Minnesota imposed a ''use tax'' (Minnesota, Use Tax on Ink and Paper*) on newspapers and periodical publications on the cost of the ink and paper used to produce the publication. The publications were exempt from the state's general sales and use tax and also exempted from the tax was the first $100,000 worth of ink and paper used in any year. The *Minneapolis Star and Tribune* Co. then brought suit, claiming a refund for the use taxes it had paid in previous years and also claiming that the tax violated the guarantee of the freedom of the press in the First Amendment.

The Minnesota Supreme Court upheld the tax, but the U.S. Supreme Court ruled that the use tax violated the First Amendment: ''(1) By creating the special use tax, without parallel in the state's tax scheme, Minnesota had singled out the press for special treatment. When a state so singles out the press, the political constraints that prevent a legislature from imposing crippling taxes of general applicability are weakened, and the threat of burdensome taxes becomes acute. That the threat can operate as effectively as a censor to check critical comment by the press, thus undercutting the basic assumption of our political system that the press will often serve as an important restraint on government. Moreover, differential treatment, unless justified by some special characteristic of the press, suggests that the goal of the regulation is not unrelated to suppression of expression, and such goal is presumptively unconstitutional. Differential treatment of the press, then, places such a burden on the interests protected by the First Amendment that such treatment cannot be countenanced unless the State asserts a counterbalancing interest of compelling importance that it cannot achieve without differential taxation; (2) Minnesota has offered no adequate justification for the special treatment of newspapers. Its interest in raising revenue, standing alone, cannot justify such treatment, for the alternative means of taxing business generally is clearly available. And the State has offered no explanation of why it chose to use a substitute for the sales tax rather than the sales tax itself. A rule that would automatically allow the State to single out the press for a different method of taxation as long as the effective burden is no different from that on other taxpayers or, as Minnesota asserts here, is lighter than that on other businesses, is to be avoided. The possibility of error inherent in such a rule poses too great a threat to concerns at the heart of the First Amendment; and (3) Minnesota's ink and paper tax violates the First Amendment not only because it singles out the press, but also because it targets a small group of newspapers. The effect of the $100,000 exemption is that only a handful of publishers in the State pay any tax at all, and even fewer pay any significant amount of tax. To recognize a power in the State not only to single out the press but also to tailor the tax so that it singles out a few members of the press presents such a potential for abuse that no interest suggested by Minnesota can justify the scheme.'' *Minneapolis Star and Tribune Co. v. Minnesota Commissioner of Revenue*, 75 L. Ed. 2d 295 (1983).

MINNESOTA, AGRICULTURAL SOCIETY STATE FAIR RULE. Rule 6.05 (in part) of the Agricultural Society reads: ''Sale or distribution of any merchandise, including printed or written material except under license issued by the Society from a duly licensed location [at the State Fair] . . . shall be a misdemeanor.'' Although there was a difference of opinion within the Supreme Court over this regulation, the Agricultural Society's State Fair Rule was upheld as a valid time-place-manner* restriction on the distribution of literature and the right of free speech in *Heffron v. International Society for Krishna Consciousness* (1981).*

MINNESOTA, DISCOURAGING THE WAR EFFORT. A Minnesota statute (Chapter 463 of the Laws of Minnesota, approved April 20, 1917) made it unlawful ''to interfere with or discourage the enlistment of men in the military or naval forces of the United States or of the State of Minnesota.'' Sections 2 and 3 read as follows: ''Speaking by word of mouth against enlistment unlawful.—It shall be unlawful for any person in any public place, or at any meeting where more than five persons are assembled, to advocate or teach by word of mouth or otherwise that men should not enlist in the military or naval forces of the United States or the State of Minnesota. Teaching or advocating by written or printed matters against enlistment unlawful.—It shall be unlawful for any person to teach or advocate by any written or printed matter whatsoever, or by oral speech, that the citizens of this state should not aid or assist the United States in prosecuting or carrying on war with the public enemies of the United States.'' This prohibition against anti-war sentiments was seen to be constitutional by the Supreme Court in *Gilbert v. Minnesota* (1920).*

MINNESOTA, MALICIOUS AND SCANDALOUS PUBLICATIONS. This statute (Chapter 285 of the Session Laws of Minnesota for 1925, Minnesota Stat., 1927, § 10123-1 to § 10123-3) was seen to be an unconstitutional prior restraint on the press by the Supreme Court in the landmark decision of *Near v. Minnesota ex rel. Olson* (1931).* The following description of the act is from the court records in the *Near* decision: ''Section 1. Any person who, as an individual, or as a member or employee of a firm, or association or organization, or as an officer, director, member or employee of a corporation, shall be engaged in the business of regularly or customarily producing, publishing or circulating, having in possession, selling or giving away (a) an obscene, lewd and lascivious newspaper, magazine, or other periodical, or (b) a malicious, scandalous and defamatory newspaper, magazine or other periodical, is guilty of a nuisance, and all persons guilty of such nuisance may be enjoined, as hereinafter provided.'' Section 2 provides that ''whenever any such nuisance is committed or exists, the County Attorney of any county where any such periodical is published or circulated, or, in case of his failure or refusal to proceed upon written request in good faith of a reputable citizen, the Attorney General, or upon like failure or refusal of the latter, any citizen of the county, may maintain an action in the district court of the county . . . in the name of the State to enjoin perpetually the persons committing or maintaining any such nuisance from further committing or maintaining it. Upon such evidence as the court shall deem sufficient, a temporary injunction may be granted. . . . The court is empowered, as in other cases of contempt, to punish disobedience to a temporary or permanent injunction by a fine of not more than $1,000 or by imprisonment in the county jail for not more than twelve months.''

MINNESOTA, USE TAX ON INK AND PAPER. Since 1967, Minnesota has imposed a sales tax on most sales of goods for a price in excess of a nominal sum (Act of June 1, 1967, ch. 32, Art. XIII, § 2, 1967 Minn. Laws Sp. Session 2143, 2179, codified at Minn. Stat. § 297A.02 [1982]). In general, the tax applies only to retail sales. An exemption for industrial and agricultural users shields from the tax the sales of components to be used in the production of goods that will themselves be sold at retail.

As part of this general system of taxation and in support of the sales tax, Minnesota also enacted a tax on the ''privilege of using, storing or consuming in Minnesota tangible personal property.'' This use tax applies to any non-exempt tangible personal property unless the sales tax was paid on the sales price (Minn. Stat. § 297A.14 [1982]). Like the classic use tax, this use tax protects the state's sales tax by eliminating the residents' incentive to travel to states with lower sales taxes to buy goods rather than buying them in Minnesota (§§ 297A.14, 297A.24). A provision of this tax scheme levied the use tax on newspapers' and periodicals' use of paper and ink in excess of $100,000 each year. The *Minneapolis Star and Tribune* filed suit, claiming a refund for its back use taxes and also claiming that the use tax on ink and paper was an unconstitutional abridgment of the freedom of the press. The U.S. Supreme Court agreed and, in *Minneapolis Star and Tribune Co. v. Minnesota Commissioner of Revenue* (1983),* held that the ink and paper use tax unfairly singled out the press.

THE MIRACLE. The motion picture *The Miracle* was at the center of a swirling controversy in the early 1950s. The resulting Supreme Court decision (*Joseph*

Burstyn, Inc. v. Wilson, 343 U.S. 495 [1952]) was a landmark decision, for it established the general principle that films were a form of expressive communication and, as such, were protected by the First Amendment.

The story of the film is summarized by de Grazia and Newman (*Banned Films*, p. 231): "This film, based on an original story by Federico Fellini, tells the tale of a simple peasant woman who, plied with wine and in a transport of religious emotion, permits a bearded stranger, whom she takes to be St. Joseph, to seduce her. She becomes pregnant and supposes she has conceived immaculately, miraculously. Her fellow villagers scorn and ridicule her, clamping a wash basin on her head for a halo. She waits alone for the birth of her child, which she delivers in an empty church."† The film—only forty minutes long—was produced in 1948 in Italy by Roberto Rossellini and starred Anna Magnani (as the demented goatherd) and Federico Fellini; it was also banned in the state of New York because it was judged to be "sacrilegious."

The Supreme Court records contain a rather lengthy discussion of this film, and the following comments are from that record. The film was first exhibited at the Venice Film Festival in August 1948, and according to an affidavit from the director of the festival, the film would have been barred if it had been "blasphemous." In October 1948, a month after the Rome premiere of *The Miracle*, the Vatican's censorship agency, the Catholic Cinematographic Centre, declared that the picture "constitutes in effect an abominable profanation from religious and moral viewpoints." By the Lateran agreements and the Italian Constitution, the Italian government was bound to bar whatever may offend the Catholic religion. But the Catholic Cinematographic Centre did not invoke any governmental sanction provided. The Italian government's censorship agency gave the film a regular clearance. The film was then freely shown throughout Italy, but the Italian movie critics were divided in their opinion.

In 1949, the film was brought into the United States without any problems from the Customs Service (the Tariff Act* authorizes Customs to seize any obscene or immoral film), and on March 2, 1949, *The Miracle* was licensed for exhibition in New York state (New York, Motion Picture Censorship*). A second license was issued in November 1950 by the Motion Picture Division of the New York State Education Department. The division was directed by statute (New York, Education Law [§ 122]) to "issue a license . . . unless [a] film or a part thereof is obscene, indecent, immoral, inhuman, sacrilegious, or is of such a character that its exhibition would tend to corrupt morals or incite to crime." The film opened in Manhattan on December 12, 1950, and the New York critics, on the whole, praised the film, but even those who panned it did not suggest that it was sacrilegious. *The Miracle*, however, was promptly attacked as "a sacrilegious and blasphemous mockery of Christian religious truth" by the Le-

---

†Reprinted from *Banned Films* with permission of the R. R. Bowker Company. Copyright © 1982 by Edward de Grazia and Roger K. Newman.

gion of Decency,* a private Catholic organization dedicated to rid the motion picture industry of filth, corruption, and immorality. Shortly thereafter, on December 23, Edward T. McCaffrey, commissioner of licenses for New York City, declared the film "officially and personally blasphemous" and ordered it withdrawn at the risk of the exhibiting theater losing its license. The film was restored for exhibition a week later, when the distributor of the film went to court (*Joseph Burstyn, Inc. v. McCaffrey*, 101 N.Y.S. 2d 892), and the New York Supreme Court ruled that the city license commissioner had exceeded his authority in that he was without powers of movie censorship.

The Roman Catholic Church's hierarchy then entered the fray. On January 7, 1951, Francis Cardinal Spellman condemned the picture and called on "all right thinking citizens" to unite to tighten up censorship laws. The cardinal termed *The Miracle* "a vile and harmful picture/a despicable affront to every Christian/ we believe in miracles/This picture ridicules that belief/a vicious insult to Italian womanhood/we, as the guardians of the moral law, must summon you and all people with a sense of decency to refrain from seeing it and supporting the venal purveyors of such pictures."

The right-thinking people did more than stay away; the theater was picketed several times (one such demonstration had more than 1,000 persons) and there were even two bomb threats that forced the theater's evacuation. During this period, the New York State Board of Regents, the parent of the Education Department, received "hundreds" of letters and telegrams protesting the exhibition of *The Miracle*. The Board of Regents then held a new hearing. On February 16, 1951, the regents, after viewing the film, determined that it was indeed "sacrilegious" and for that reason ordered the commissioner of education to rescind the exhibition license. The commissioner complied immediately with the order, and the case eventually reached the Supreme Court.

The Supreme Court issued a threefold decision: (1) Motion pictures are included within the free speech and free press guarantees of the First Amendment. (2) The New York Education Law, which prohibited the showing of any motion picture without a license, was void as a prior restraint on this freedom of speech and the press. (3) Even if *The Miracle* were "sacrilegious"—a conclusion not accepted by the Court—a censor could not bar such a film on that ground. Justice Clark delivered the opinion of the Court: "It is further urged that motion pictures possess a greater capacity for evil, particularly among the youth of a community, than other modes of expression. Even if one were to accept this hypothesis, it does not follow that motion pictures should be disqualified from First Amendment protection. If there be capacity for evil it may be relevant in determining the permissible scope of community control, but it does not authorize substantially unbridled censorship such as we have here. . . . We conclude that expression by means of motion pictures is included within the free speech and free press guaranty of the First and Fourteenth Amendments. To the extent that language in the opinion in *Mutual Film Corporation v. Industrial Commission of Ohio* (1915),* is out of harmony with the views here set forth, we no longer adhere to it. [The *Mutual* decision held that films were not a form of expression but only a commercial enterprise and thus open to any sort of regulation the government wished to impose.] . . . The statute involved here does not seek to punish, as a past offense, speech or writing falling within the permissible scope of subsequent punishment. On the contrary, New York requires that permission to communicate ideas be obtained in advance from state officials who judge the content of the words and pictures sought to be communicated. This Court recognized many years ago that such a previous restraint is a form of infringement upon freedom of expression to be especially . . . [avoided]. New York's highest court says there is 'nothing mysterious' about the statutory provision applied in this case: 'It is simply this: that no religion, as that word is understood by the ordinary, reasonable person, shall be treated with contempt, mockery, scorn and ridicule.' This is far from the kind of narrow exception to freedom of expression which a state may carve out to satisfy the adverse demands of other interests of society. In seeking to apply the broad and all-inclusive definition of 'sacrilegious' given by the New York courts, the censor is set adrift upon a boundless sea amid a myriad of conflicting currents of religious views, with no charts but those provided by the most vocal and powerful orthodoxies. New York cannot vest such unlimited restraining control over motion pictures in a censor. Under such a standard the most careful and tolerant censor would find it virtually impossible to avoid favoring one religion over another, and he would be subject to an inevitable tendency to ban the expression of unpopular sentiments sacred to a religious minority. Application of the 'sacrilegious' test, in these or other respects, might raise substantial questions under the First Amendment's guaranty of separate church and state with freedom of worship for all. However, from the standpoint of freedom of speech and the press, it is enough to point out that the state has no legitimate interest in protecting any or all religions from views distasteful to them which is sufficient to justify prior restraints upon the expression of those views. It is not the business of government in our nation to suppress real or imagined attacks upon a particular religious doctrine, whether they appear in publications, speeches, or motion pictures.''

MISHKIN v. NEW YORK (1966). Mishkin was convicted (and received a three-year sentence) by a New York court of violating § 1141 of the New York Penal Code (New York, Obscenity Statute*). Mishkin's specific crime was that he published, hired others to prepare, and possessed with the intent to sell, obscene books. There were some fifty books involved, and the Supreme Court records, as presented by Justice Brennan, describe the books as follows: ''They portray sexuality in many guises. Some depict relatively normal heterosexual relations, but more depict such deviations as sado-masochism, fetishism, and homosexuality. Many have covers with drawings of scantily clad women being whipped, beaten, tortured, or abused. Many, if not most, are photo-offsets of typewritten books written and illustrated by authors and artists according to detailed instructions given by [Mishkin]. Typical of [the] instructions was that related by one author who testified that [Mishkin] insisted that the books be 'full of sex scenes and lesbian scenes/the sex had to be very strong, it had to be rough, it had to be clearly spelled out/I had to write sex very bluntly, make the sex scenes very strong/the sex scenes had to be unusual sex scenes between men and women, and women and women, and men and men/he wanted scenes in which women were making love with women/lesbian scenes/sex in an abnormal and irregular fashion/deal very graphically with the darkening of the flesh under flagellation.' All the books were cheaply prepared paperbound 'pulps' with imprinted sales prices that were several thousand percent above costs.''

It serves no useful purpose to list all fifty books; the following is a representative sample of the titles: *Mistress of Leather, The Whipping Chorus Girls, Bound in Rubber, Return Visit to Fetterland, So Firm and Fully Packed, Swish Bottom, The Strap Returns*, and last but not least, *Stud Broad*. The Supreme Court affirmed Mishkin's three-year prison sentence, and Justice Brennan, in a rather uncharacteristic pro-censorship position, delivered the opinion of the Court: ''Appellant was not prosecuted for anything he said or believed, but for what he did, for his dominant role in several enterprises engaged in producing and selling allegedly obscene books. . . . The First Amendment prohibits criminal prosecution for the publication and dissemination of allegedly obscene books that do not satisfy the *Roth* definition of obscenity [Roth Standard*]. States are free to adopt other definitions of obscenity only to the extent that those adopted stay within the bounds set up by the constitutional criteria of the *Roth* definition, which restrict the regulation of the publication and sale of books to that traditionally and universally tolerated in our society. The New York courts have interpreted obscenity in § 1141 to cover only so-called 'hard-core pornography.' Since that definition of obscenity is more stringent than the *Roth* definition, the judgment that the constitutional criteria are satisfied is implicit in the application of § 1141. Indeed, appellant's sole contention regarding the nature of the material is that some of the books involved in this prosecution, those depicting various deviant sexual practices, such as flagellation, fetishism, and lesbianism, do not satisfy the prurient-appeal interest of the 'average person' in sex, that 'instead of stimulating the erotic, they disgust and sicken.' We reject this argument as being founded on an unrealistic interpretation of the prurient-appeal requirement.''

Justice Black dissented from the opinion: ''I have [not] read the alleged obscene matter. This is because I believe . . . that this Court is without constitutional power to censor speech or press regardless of the particular subject discussed. . . . I would reverse this conviction. . . . Censorship methods, no matter how laudably motivated, cannot in my judgment protect our cherished First Amendment freedoms from the destructive aggressions of both state and national government.'' *Mishkin v. New York*, 383 U.S. 502 (1966).

MISSOURI, RESTRAINT OF TRADE. Missouri Revised Stat. Ann., §§ 8301 and 8305 (1939), read as follows: ''Any person who shall create, enter into, become a member of or participate in any pool, trust, agreement, combination, confederation or understanding with any person or persons in restraint of trade or competition in the importation, transportation, manufacture, purchase or sale of any product or commodity in this state, or any article or thing bought or sold whatsoever, shall be deemed and adjudged guilty of a conspiracy in restraint of trade, and shall be punished. . . . [Anyone violating the above section] shall be adjudged guilty of a felony, and upon conviction thereof shall be punished by imprisonment in the penitentiary not exceeding five years, or by imprisonment in the county jail not exceeding one year, or by a fine of not less than five hundred dollars nor more than five thousand dollars, or by both such fine and imprisonment.'' This statute was involved in a case in which a labor union, during a labor dispute, was found guilty of restraint of trade; the U.S. Supreme Court, in *Giboney v. Empire Storage and Ice Company* (1949),* held that the union's right of free speech was not violated by the Missouri statute.

MISSOURI, SUPREME COURT REGULATIONS ON ADVERTISING.
Rule 4 of the Missouri Supreme Court, regulating advertising by lawyers, stated that a lawyer may include ten categories of information in a published advertisement: name, address, and telephone number; areas of practice; date and place of birth; schools attended; foreign language ability; office hours; fee for an initial consultation; availability of a schedule of fees; credit arrangements; and the fixed fee to be charged for certain "routine" legal services. Although the rule did not state explicitly that these ten categories of information were the only information that would be permitted, that was the interpretation given the rule by the Missouri Supreme Court. An addendum to the rule specifies two ways in which areas of practice may be listed in an advertisement, under one of which the lawyer may use one or more of a list of twenty-three areas of practice but could not deviate from the precise wording stated in the rule to describe these areas. In addition, the rule permitted a lawyer to send professional announcement cards announcing a change of address or firm name, or similar matters, but only to "lawyers, clients, former clients, personal friends, and relatives." This detailed restriction on attorney advertising was seen to be an invalid use of state power and was a violation of the attorney's right of free press. The Court, in *Re R.M.J.* (1982),* ruled that absent proof that a particular advertisement was false or misleading, an attorney was free to advertise as he saw fit.

MISSOURI, UNIVERSITY BOARD OF CURATORS, BUILDING USE.
The Board of Curators, University of Missouri, in 1972 adopted certain regulations that prohibited the use of university buildings or grounds "for purposes of religious worship or religious teaching." The relevant portions of the regulations read as follows: "No University buildings or grounds (except chapels as herein provided) may be used for purposes of religious worship or religious teaching by either student or nonstudent groups. . . . The general prohibition against use of University buildings and grounds for religious worship or religious teaching is a policy required, in the opinion of The Board of Curators, by the

Constitution and laws of the State and is not open to any other construction. No regulations shall be interpreted to forbid the offering of prayer or other appropriate recognition of religion at public functions held in University facilities'' (4.0314.0107). ''Regular chapels established on University grounds may be used for religious services but not for regular recurring services of any groups. Special rules and procedures shall be established for each such chapel by the Chancellor. It is specifically directed that no advantage shall be given to any religious group'' (4.0314.0108).

A group of students at the University of Missouri at Kansas City brought suit, challenging these regulations, and in *Widmar v. Vincent* (1981),* the Supreme Court held that the curators' regulations were an unconstitutional abridgment of the freedom of speech because the university based its policy on the content of such speech.

MLLE DE MAUPIN. On November 17, 1917, in New York City, one Halsey sold to John S. Sumner of the New York Society for the Suppression of Vice (Comstockery*) a copy of Théophile Gautier's novel *Mademoiselle de Maupin* (originally published in 1835). Sumner didn't like the book—certain passages were deemed obscene. He then brought a charge against Halsey for violating § 1141 of the New York Penal Code (New York, Obscenity Statute*). The examining magistrate found that the book was not obscene and released Halsey; Halsey then filed suit against the society to recover damages for malicious prosecution (*Halsey v. New York Society for the Suppression of Vice*, 136 N.E. 219 [1922]). The court ruled, after examining the book, that no probable cause existed for Sumner to charge Halsey and that the society was liable for damages. The court record contains a review of the book by Judge Andrews, and his comments follow: ''Théophile Gautier is conceded to be among the greatest French writers of the nineteenth century. *Mademoiselle de Maupin* is a book of over 400 pages. The moment it was issued it excited the criticism of many, but not all, of the great Frenchmen of the day. It has since become a part of French literature. No review of French writers of the last 100 years fails to comment upon it. With the author's felicitous style, it contains passages of purity and beauty. It seems to be largely a protest against what the author, we believe mistakenly, regards as the prudery of newspaper criticism. It contains many paragraphs, however, which, taken by themselves, are undoubtedly vulgar and indecent. No work may be judged from a selection of such paragraphs alone. Printed by themselves they might, as a matter of law, come within the prohibition of the statute. So might a similar selection from Aristophanes or Chaucer or Boccaccio, or even from the Bible. The book, however, must be considered broadly, as a whole. . . . We have quoted estimates of the book as showing the manners in which it affects different minds. The conflict among the members of this court itself [a dissenting opinion by Judge Crane follows] points a finger at the dangers of a censorship entrusted to men of one profession. Far better than we is a jury drawn from those of varied experiences fitted to say whether the defendant had reasonable ground to believe that a book such as this was obscene or indecent. Here is the work of a great author, written in admirable style, which has become a part of classical literature. We may take judicial notice that it has been widely sold, separately and as a part of every collection of the works of Gautier. It has excited admiration as well as opposition. We know that a book merely obscene soon dies. Many a Roman poet wrote a *Metamorphoses*. Ovid survives. So this book also has lived for a hundred years.''

There was some dissent to this opinion. Judge Crane thought that Gautier was a degenerate, that *Mademoiselle de Maupin* was unfit for human consumption, and that Sumner most definitely had ''probable cause'' to haul Halsey to court. Judge Crane: ''When the people of France and Gautier's time condemned his book as being vicious and unfit for general perusal, are we going to say that the defendant in this case did not have probable cause to believe the same thing when the translation was published in America by a publisher who was ashamed to put his name to it? Many things have moved in the past century, and with the teachings of church, synagogue, and college, we, at least, have the right to expect that the general tone of morality in America in 1922 is equal to that of France in 1835. It may be true that Gautier's style is fascinating and his imagination rich, but neither style, imagination, nor learning can create a privileged class, or permit obscenity because it is dressed up in a fashion difficult to imitate or acquire. American literature has been fairly clean. That the policy of this state to keep it so is indicated by § 1141 of the Penal Law. The Legislature has declared in this section that no obscene, lewd, lascivious, or disgusting books shall be sold. Language could not be plainer. If the things said by Gautier in this book . . . were stated openly and frankly in the language of the street, there would be no doubt in the minds of anybody, I take it, that the work would be lewd, vicious, and indecent. The fact that the disgusting details are served up in a polished style, with exquisite settings and perfumed words, makes it all the more dangerous and insidious, and none the less obscene and lascivious. Gautier may have a reputation as a writer, but this reputation does not create a license for the American market. Oscar Wilde had a great reputation for style, but went to jail just the same. Literary ability is no excuse for degeneracy.''

MOM AND DAD. Keenan, the public safety director of Newark, New Jersey, attempted to censor, in 1948, a motion picture entitled *Mom and Dad*. The film described and illustrated the conception and delivery of an infant, both in a normal manner and by cesarean operation; it also depicted the ravages of venereal diseases. Keenan did not want the film to be exhibited by the usual theaters open to the general public; he insisted that it be exhibited only under ''educational, medical, or social welfare supervision.'' The distributors of the film then brought suit, and the judge, Judge Freund, was the same one who had ordered Keenan to permit the showing of the film *Latuko** (Keenan didn't like this film either because it was a documentary account of an African tribe that didn't wear any clothes). Judge Freund, in *Hygienic Productions v. Keenan* (62 A. 2d 150

[1948]), stated: "The Court has not viewed the film and does not make any comment on its merits or demerits, nor on its educational value . . . [but] (1) The censoring of motion pictures or any accompanying lecture or auspices under which it is presented is not within the province of the Court; (2) If presentation of a motion picture film would not be objectionable if conducted under non-commercial auspices, the showing of such a film under commercial auspices would not authorize the city authorities to revoke a theater license; and (3) Where affidavits submitted by the city and its Director of Public Safety showed that the motion picture film proposed to be presented by plaintiffs was not immoral or obscene and that the sole basis for objection to the exhibition of the film was that it was being exhibited under commercial auspices, rather than under educational, medical, or social welfare supervision, the city and its Director of Public Safety had no authority to interfere with the presentation of . . . [*Mom and Dad*]."

MONFRED v. STATE OF MARYLAND (1961). Monfred was convicted in a Baltimore court of violating Maryland Code, Article 27, § 418-a (Maryland, Obscenity Statute*), which made it a misdemeanor for any person to knowingly sell any lewd, obscene, or indecent book, magazine, drawing, or photograph. Monfred was found guilty in Baltimore under seven separate counts—one count was for selling a set of photographs and the remaining six were for selling issues of specific magazines.

Monfred then appealed, and the Court of Appeals of Maryland reversed two of the convictions but affirmed the remaining five. As the court decided, the set of photographs—a sequential "strip-tease" containing semi-nudity—"might be offensive or repulsive to the normal person but are not obscene." The magazine *Black Garter* was also found not to be obscene—"scantily dressed females, obviously intended to arouse sex appeal, innocuous text but not obscene." Monfred had less success with counts three through seven—the magazines *Candid*,* *Consort*, *Sextet*, *Cloud 9*, and *Torrid*: "When the pictures and the text are considered as a whole, they are obscene; semi-nude women with 'come hither' expressions and poses; suggestive sex stories so placed that a reader if he needs visual aid in following the story has only to glance at the opposite page for additional stimulation; they are calculated to excite lustful thoughts in the mind of the reader." *Monfred v. State of Maryland*, 173 A. 2d 173 (1961).

MONITOR PATRIOT CO. v. ROY (1971). Just before the 1960 New Hampshire Democratic primary election, the newspaper *Monitor Patriot* published a column characterizing senatorial candidate Alphonse Roy as a "former small-time bootlegger." Roy, who was not elected, sued the newspaper and the distributor of the column for libel. Roy won his suit—and $20,000—and the New Hampshire Supreme Court affirmed the judgment; the U.S. Supreme Court reversed: (1) Publications concerning candidates for public office must be accorded at least as much protection under the First Amendment as those concerning occupants of public office; (2) A charge of criminal conduct, no matter how remote in time or place, can never be irrelevant to an official's or candidate's fitness for office; and (3) The rule (*New York Times* Rule*) in *New York Times Company v. Sullivan** applies here—no damages can be awarded unless it is proven that the offending statement was made with actual malice (knowing falsehood or a reckless disregard of whether the statement was false or not).

Justices Black and Douglas concurred in the decision, but for them, the *New York Times* Rule represented an unwarranted restriction on the right of free press: "It is time for this Court to abandon *New York Times Company v. Sullivan* and adopt the rule to the effect that the First Amendment was intended to leave the press free from the harassment of libel judgments." *Monitor Patriot Co. v. Roy*, 401 U.S. 265 (1971).

THE MOON IS BLUE. Produced and directed by Otto Preminger, this 1953 American film, adapted from F. Hugh Herbert's play of the same title, starred William Holden, David Niven, and Maggie McNamara; it was also censored (banned) in Milwaukee, Jersey City, Ohio, Maryland, and Kansas. It was the Kansas censorship attempt that reached the Supreme Court in 1955 (*Holmby Productions v. Vaughn*, 350 U.S. 870 [1955]). Pursuant to certain regulations (Kansas, Motion Picture Censorship*), the Kansas State Board of Review refused to issue an exhibition permit for the following reasons: "Sex theme throughout, too frank bedroom dialogue: many sexy words; both dialogue and action have sex as their theme." The board had a rehearing and again disapproved the film: "The Board has found [the] film to be obscene, indecent and immoral, or such as tend to debase or corrupt morals."

A Kansas trial court disagreed with this ruling and ordered the issuance of the permit; on appeal, the Kansas Supreme Court reversed the trial court's ruling and reinstated the order of the Kansas State Board of Review. But in a per curiam decision, the U.S. Supreme Court reversed the Kansas Supreme Court's decision—it cited the previous cases of *The Miracle,** *M,** and *La Ronde**— and held that the words "obscene, indecent, or immoral, or such as tend to debase or corrupt morals" were too vague and indeterminate to support a motion picture licensing and censorship statute.

The film itself, however, was not among Otto Preminger's best. As summarized by de Grazia and Newman (*Banned Films*, p. 240), the film "begins with a chance meeting between boy [William Holden] and girl [Maggie McNamara] in the Empire State Building. He invites her to his apartment for dinner, but she does not know that the boy is engaged to another girl who lives with her family on the floor above. The boy's father-in-law-to-be [David Niven] learns of this dinner date and 'comes down to do the outraged parent act but . . . stays on and makes his own pass at the girl in the most unfatherly fashion and with the easy confidence of a veteran in polite amour.' The young woman is startlingly frank and curious concerning sexual matters, despite her obvious innocence.''†

MORALITY IN MEDIA. Founded in 1962 and formerly called Operation Yorkville, this group has about 50,000 members and is concerned with the availability and distribution of pornographic material to children. According to its objectives, the group seeks ''to educate and alert parents and community leaders to the problem of, the scale of and the danger in the distribution of obscene material; to encourage communities to express themselves in a unified, organized way to legitimate media requesting responsibility and to law enforcement officials urging vigorous enforcement of obscenity law; to work for media based on the principles of love, truth, taste. A major project of the organization is the National Obscenity Law Center, a clearinghouse of legal information on obscenity cases and materials for prosecutors, other members of the bar and other interested persons.'' *Encyclopedia of Associations* (# 13090). Morality in Media's major publications are *Morality in Media Newsletter* (monthly) and *Obscenity Law Bulletin* (bimonthly).

MORAL MAJORITY. Founded in 1979 by the Rev. Jerry Falwell, the Moral Majority describes itself as a ''political movement dedicated to convincing morally conservative Americans that it is their duty to register and vote for candidates who agree with their moral principles. Was organized in response to developments such as the legalization of abortion, the spread of pornography and agitation for homosexual rights—developments which the movement feels indicate that the United States is experiencing a 'terrible moral decline.' The group does not specifically endorse candidates by name, but strives through letters, leaflets, and mass rallies to make clear where candidates stand relative to issues important to the organization.'' *Encyclopedia of Associations* (# 12176). Moral Majority claims membership of some 72,000 ministers and some 4 million lay persons, with chapters in all fifty states. Moral Majority, although not directly involved as an organization in censorship, encourages its members to oppose that which is felt to be immoral; in many respects it is a modern-day version of the New York Society for the Suppression of Vice (Comstockery*).

MOTION PICTURE ASSOCIATION OF AMERICA. Founded in 1922, the Motion Picture Association of America (MPAA) is the professional organization of the principal producers and distributors of motion pictures in the United States. The MPAA, through its production code and rating classifications, sets the tone and nature for the film industry throughout the nation. The story of the MPAA

†Reprinted from *Banned Films* with permission of the R. R. Bowker Company. Copyright © 1982 by Edward de Grazia and Roger K. Newman.

and its code is too lengthy to reproduce here; de Grazia and Newman (*Banned Films*, 1982) present the entire story—only some brief extracts are presented here. De Grazia and Newman (pp. 34–35) write that the rating code "was destined to represent the American movie industry's 'official' morality for nearly 40 years. It entailed an industry-wide non-governmental form of censorship no less effective for being 'private' and no less moralistic for being 'secular.' The Code imposed the judgments and tastes of the handful of individuals who came to administer it. If it was administered by those persons independently of state and municipal governmental censors as well as of the Catholic church [Legion of Decency*], it usually involved a collaboration with these institutions. It successfully constrained creative freedom of the movies until several factors began coalescing after World War II to break its grip on the industry."†

A neat description of the MPAA and its code for most of its existence was given by Judge Musmanno of the Pennsylvania Supreme Court (*William Goldman Theatres, Inc. v. Dana**): "The motion picture industry, made up of responsible companies which have, over the years, earned the respect and the admiration of the American public, is aware of the need for decency on the screen. These companies have of their own volition agreed upon a Production Code which contains such excellent precepts as the following: 'Motion picture producers recognize the high trust and confidence which have been placed in them by the people of the world and which have made motion pictures a universal form of entertainment.' 'They recognize their responsibility to the public because of this trust and because entertainment and art are important influences in the life of a nation.' 'Hence though regarding motion pictures primarily as entertainment without any explicit purposes of teaching or propaganda, they know that the motion picture within its own field of entertainment may be directly responsible for spiritual or moral progress, for higher types of social life, and for much correct thinking.' 'So correct entertainment raises the whole standard of a nation. Wrong entertainment lowers the whole living conditions and moral ideals of a race.' " This emphasis on moral progress and correct thinking underpinned the original code and three basic principles governed: (1) No picture shall be produced which will lower the moral standards of those who see it. Hence the sympathy of the audience shall never be thrown to the side of crime, wrong-doing, evil, or sin. (2) Correct standards of life, subject only to the requirements of drama and entertainment, shall be presented. (3) Law, natural or human, shall not be ridiculed, nor shall sympathy be created for its violation.

There were many specific subjects or themes that were seen as unfit material for inclusion in films (de Grazia and Newman, p. 34): violations of the law (murder, methods of crime, illegal drug traffic, use of liquor), sex (adultery and illicit sex, scenes of passion, seduction, rape, sex perversion, white slavery,

†Reprinted from *Banned Films* with permission of the R. R. Bowker Company. Copyright © 1982 by Edward de Grazia and Roger K. Newman.

miscegenation, sex hygiene, actual childbirth, children's sex organs), vulgarity, obscenity, profanity, certain dress (nudity, undressing scenes, indecent or undue exposure), ridicule of religion and clergy, and repellent subjects (hangings, electrocutions, the third degree, brutality, branding, cruelty, surgical operations, birth control, and abortion). But as the years passed, several producers and production companies chaffed at the code and began to offer films that fell beyond the guidelines (one such example was *The Man with the Golden Arm**). With films no longer directed at "moral progress" and "correct thinking," and with a growing concern that films were corrupting the morals of youth, state after state and city after city began to develop motion picture classification/ review/censor boards. These boards (the *Viva Maria** case in Dallas is but one example) began to devise guidelines to determine a picture's suitability for children and to prevent young people from seeing a film judged unsuitable. To head off what would obviously be conflicting standards, the MPAA, under the leadership of Jack Valenti, established its own age-classification scheme. Under this new system, all films produced or distributed by MPAA members (and therefore most movies shown in the United States) must be submitted to the MPAA's Code and Rating Administration. The resulting ratings are G—suggested for general audiences, including children of all ages; PG—parental guidance suggested, as some material may not be suitable for pre-teenagers; R—restricted, persons under seventeen are not admitted unless accompanied by parent or adult guardian; and X—persons under seventeen not admitted (X-rated films are sexually explicit). Other than the Tariff Act* (U.S. Customs can prevent the importation of "obscene" films into the country) and a handful of municipal schemes protecting minors (Dallas and Chicago, for example), the MPAA's rating code is the only such categorization scheme in operation.

MOUNT EPHRAIM (NJ), NUDE DANCING. The town of Mount Ephraim, in an attempt to ban nude dancing in one of the town's bookstores, passed a zoning regulation (§ 99-15B) that, by listing the approved types of businesses permitted in a certain area, prevented any establishment from offering live entertainment. The approved businesses were as follows: "Offices and banks; taverns; restaurants and luncheonettes for sit-down dinners only and with no drive-in facilities; automobile sales; retail stores, such as but not limited to food, wearing apparel, millinery, fabrics, hardware, lumber, jewelry, paint, wallpaper, appliances, flowers, gifts, books, stationery, pharmacy, liquors, cleaners, novelties, hobbies and toys; repair shops for shoes, jewels, clothes and appliances; barbershops and beauty salons; cleaners and laundries; pet stores; and nurseries."

This zoning ordinance was eventually held to be an invalid restriction on the First Amendment's guarantee of free speech by the Supreme Court in *Schad v. Borough of Mount Ephraim* (1981).* The Court found that the ordinance was being selectively enforced against nude dancing—there were other establishments within the commercial zone that offered live entertainment—and it was of the opinion that nude dancing was a form of symbolic non-obscene speech protected by the First Amendment.

MOUNT VERNON (NY), NEWSPAPER LICENSING AND PROHIBIT-ING SALE OF NEWSPAPERS. The mayor and aldermen of the town of Mount Vernon, New York, did not like the newspapers *New York American* and *New York Evening Journal*. So in 1918, the town passed an ordinance prohibiting the sale of those newspapers in the town until World War I was over; the court invalidated the ordinance. The town tried again, passing an ordinance requiring a newspaper to have a distribution license (and such licenses would not be granted to the offending newspapers); the court (*Star Co. v. Brush* [1918]*) invalidated the licensing ordinance as well. The ordinances read as follows: Ordinance of 14 May, 1918, § 2: "It shall be unlawful after the date when this ordinance takes effect, and until the end of the present war, within the City of Mount Vernon, for any person, firm, corporation or association to print, publish, circulate, sell or distribute . . . certain newspapers . . . which have heretofore been known and designated as the *New York American* and *New York Evening Journal*."

Licensing Ordinance: "It shall be unlawful within the City of Mt. Vernon for any person, firm, corporation or association to sell, circulate or distribute . . . any newspaper or publication without first having obtained a license therefor. . . . All licenses issued under this ordinance may be revoked by the common council at any time without notice to the holder thereof. A license granted hereunder shall include the bona fide employees of any such person, firm, corporation or association to whom such a license has been issued, provided the holder of such license shall have registered such employee with the chief of police. Any such employee not registered shall be deemed a person without a license for the purpose of this ordinance, and it shall be the duty of the holder of a license to register such employee as herein provided with the chief of police within twenty-four hours after the employment of such employee. No person of bad repute shall be employed to sell or distribute newspapers or other publications by the holder of such a license. The holder of such a license shall forthwith discharge such employee from such service when notified by the chief of police that such employee is a person of bad repute. Any conviction for a criminal offense or violation of a city ordinance, or having led a life of apparent idleness for a period of three months, may be sufficient to constitute such a person of bad repute within the meaning of this ordinance. The holder of such license shall obtain and furnish to the chief of police, promptly upon request therefor, any desired information concerning any employee." As noted, these absurd ordinances were ruled to be invalid.

MURDOCK v. PENNSYLVANIA (1943). The town of Jeannette, Pennsylvania, had a municipal ordinance (Jeannette [PA], Soliciting License*) that required religious colporteurs to pay a license tax as a condition to the pursuit of their activities of distributing certain religious publications (and soliciting contributions). Murdock, a Jehovah's Witness, was convicted under this ordinance.

The Supreme Court, however, reversed the conviction: (1) A state may not impose a charge for the enjoyment of a right protected by the First Amendment.

(2) It is immaterial that the ordinance was not discriminatory (it also applied to peddlers of wares and merchandise) because the liberties guaranteed by the First Amendment are in a "preferred position." Justice Douglas delivered the opinion of the Court: "The mere fact that the religious literature is 'sold' by itinerant preachers rather than 'donated' does not transform evangelism into a commercial enterprise. If it did, then the passing of the collection plate in church would make the church service a commercial project. The constitutional rights of those spreading their religious beliefs through the spoken and printed word are not to be gauged by standards governing retailers or wholesalers of books. The right to use the press for expressing one's views is not to be measured by the protection afforded commercial handbills. It should be remembered that the pamphlets of Thomas Paine were not distributed free of charge. It is plain that a religious organization needs funds to remain a going concern. But an itinerant evangelist, however misguided or intolerant he may be, does not become a mere book agent by selling the Bible or religious tracts to help defray his expenses or to sustain him. Freedom of speech, freedom of the press, freedom of religion are available to all, not merely to those who can pay their own way. . . . It is a distortion of the facts of record to describe their activities as the occupation of selling books and pamphlets. . . . The taxes imposed by this ordinance can hardly help but be as severe and telling in their impact on the freedom of the press and religion as the 'taxes on knowledge' [Knowledge Taxes*] at which the First Amendment was partly aimed. They may indeed operate even more subtly. Itinerant evangelists moving throughout a state or from state to state would feel immediately the cumulative effect of such ordinances as they become fashionable. The way of the religious dissenter has long been hard. But if the formula of this type of ordinance is approved, a new device for the suppression of religious minorities will have been found. This method of disseminating religious beliefs can be crushed and closed out by the sheer weight of the toll or tribute which is exacted town by town, village by village. The spread of religious ideas through personal visitations by the literature ministry of numerous religious groups would be stopped. The fact that the ordinance is 'nondiscriminatory' is immaterial. The protection afforded by the First Amendment is not so restricted. A license tax certainly does not acquire constitutional validity because it classifies the privileges protected by the First Amendment along with the wares and merchandise of hucksters and peddlers and treats them all alike. Such equality does not save the ordinance. Freedom of press, freedom of speech, freedom of religion are in a preferred position." *Murdock v. Pennsylvania*, 319 U.S. 105 (1943).

MUTUAL FILM CORPORATION v. INDUSTRIAL COMMISSION OF OHIO (1915). In 1913, Ohio passed a statute (Ohio, Motion Picture Censorship*) that created a Board of Censors that had to approve, in advance, any motion picture before it could be exhibited anywhere in the state. The exhibitor had to pay a fee for the examination of the film and could be fined if any film were shown without the prior approval and the exhibition license of the Board of Censors. The statute said that only films of "moral, educational or amusing and harmless character" would be approved by the board. This was at the beginning of the motion picture industry in the United States—the Court even explained what motion pictures were. The Supreme Court, in 1915, upheld the constitutionality of the Ohio statute. The Court, viewing films to be a commercial enterprise totally devoid of any speech or press elements, saw absolutely no violation of the freedom of speech or of press by the Ohio statute.

This 1915 decision set the stage for decades and decades of government control, harassment, and censorship of films (Film Censorship*) throughout the country (see de Grazia and Newman, *Banned Films*). It was not until 1952 that the Supreme Court overruled the *Mutual* decision, stating, in *The Miracle** case, that films were a form of speech and press fully protected as other forms of expression by the First Amendment. Justice McKenna delivered the Court's 1915 opinion: "Films of a 'moral, educational or amusing and harmless character shall be passed and approved' are the words of the statute. No exhibition, therefore, or 'campaign' of complainant will be prevented if its pictures have those qualities. Therefore, however missionary of opinion films are or may become, however educational or entertaining, there is no impediment to their value or effect in the Ohio statute. But they may be used for evil, and against that possibility that statute was enacted. Their power of amusement and, it may be, education, the audiences they assemble, not of women alone nor of men alone, but together, not of adults only, but of children, make them the more insidious in corruption by a pretense of worthy purpose or if they should degenerate from worthy purpose. Indeed, we may go beyond that possibility. They take their attraction from the general interest, eager and wholesome it may be, in their subjects, but a prurient interest may be excited and appealed to. Besides, there are some things which should not have pictorial representation in public places and to all audiences. And not only the State of Ohio but other States have considered it to be in the interest of the public morals and welfare to supervise moving picture exhibitions. We would have to shut our eyes to the facts of the world to regard the precaution unreasonable or the legislation to effect it a mere wanton interference with personal liberty. . . . We need not pause to dilate upon the freedom of opinion and its expression, and whether by speech, writing or printing. They are too certain to need discussion—of such conceded value as to need no supporting praise. . . . Are moving pictures within the principle, as it is contended they are? . . . The first impulse of the mind is to reject the contention. We immediately feel that the argument is wrong or strained which extends the guaranties of free opinion and speech to [moving pictures]. It cannot be put out of view that the exhibition of moving pictures is a business, pure and simple, originated and conducted for profit, like other spectacles, not to be regarded as part of the press of the country, or as organs of public opinion." *Mutual Film Corporation v. Industrial Commission of Ohio*, 236 U.S. 230 (1915).

MUTUAL FILM CORPORATION v. KANSAS (1915). This case was similar to (and decided along with) *Mutual Film Corporation v. Industrial Commission*

*of Ohio** and dealt with the constitutionality of a Kansas statute (Kansas, Motion
Picture Censorship*) that established a censorship scheme over films. The Court
relied on the same reasoning as the Ohio case and upheld the constitutionality
of the Kansas censorship statute. Justice McKenna: ''Both statutes [Ohio and
Kansas] are valid exercises of the police power of the States and are not amenable
to the objections urged against them—that is, [they] do not interfere with interstate commerce nor abridge the liberty of opinion; nor are they delegations of
legislative power to administrative officers.'' *Mutual Film Corporation v. Kansas*, 236 U.S. 248 (1915).

N

NAKED AMAZON. The opposition that this film aroused in 1957 is but another example of the censorship that was prevalent in the not-so-distant past. The views of Anthony Comstock and the various societies to suppress vice (Comstockery*) and to protect the morals of other people may have had their origins in the Puritan perception of the world but have far outlived the Puritans.

The Maryland State Board of Censors (Maryland, Motion Picture Censorship*) ordered some scenes deleted from *Naked Amazon* before it would issue an exhibition permit. The board felt that the offending scenes—showing bodies below the waist of the Camayura Indians, who lived without clothes in the Amazon jungles in Brazil—made the film obscene. The chairman of the Board of Censors testified that the deletions were ordered under certain sections of the censorship statute that required the disapproval of any film that "arouses sexual desires, and if the probability of this effect is so great as to outweigh whatever other merits the film may possess." He stated that it was the considered judgment of the board that "the showing of nudity, of nude people, in a pseudodocumentary, which this officially is, is calculated to arouse sexual desires of substantial numbers of people." He also pointed out that the Maryland law did not provide for banning a film to certain categories or groups of people. If it were passed by the board, it would then be available to all who had the desire and opportunity to see it. He said the board felt that the public would find the film shocking and tending to arouse sexual desires "certainly in irresponsible numbers of people." The chairman said the board's interpretation of the statute was that possible obscenity was not to be weighed with the artistic or other merits of the film as a whole, but rather that particular views were to be considered, and the obscenity of those views was to be weighed against the artistic or other merits of the same views. He testified that the board read the statute in the light of "pornographic" being synonymous with "obscene" and acted on that reading.

The film's production company, Times Film Corporation, appealed the board's order to the Baltimore City Court, and Judge Byrnes reversed the board. Judge Byrnes, who saw the whole film once and the deleted parts twice, noted that the film, as presented to the board, had been prepared so that close-ups of the natives showing their bodies below the waist had been omitted and found that "the producers were unsuccessful in their efforts to attribute a pornographic theme to the movie," and therefore, it did not come under the ban of the statute. Judge Byrnes continued: "The Board was of the opinion that showing of the uncensored film might have an undesirable effect on 'segments of our population.' As this Court does not believe that such reasoning comes within the restrictions contained in Article 66A, it must order the restoration of the eliminated scenes."

The Board of Censors was not content, however, knowing that people might see naked Amazon Indians in a documentary, and filed an appeal with the Maryland Court of Appeals (*Maryland State Board of Motion Pictures Censors v. Times Film Corporation*, 129 A. 2d 833 [1957]). The appeals court, Judge Hammond delivering the opinion, said that only narrow or unhealthy minds could find any depravity in the film, and it affirmed the Baltimore court's order to restore the deleted scenes. Judge Hammond: "We think the Board's basis of decision and its findings were predicated not only on the unsound legal ground remarked on by Judge Byrnes, but on another false premise. . . . The Board acted on the assumption that a scene could be eliminated because its possible obscenity outweighed any of its merits, considering that scene alone. It did not weigh the scenes it found objectionable in relation to the picture as a whole to determine whether overall worth more than counter-balanced possible obscene or pornographic bits or sequences."

Judge Hammond continued and equated the mentality of the board to another unhealthy mind—that of the commissioner of public safety in Newark, New Jersey (Keenan), who attempted to censor certain scenes from the film *Latuko*** because some African natives were photographed without clothes. He cited the remarks of the judge in the *Latuko* case; it is obvious that these remarks were directed at the Maryland State Board of Censors: "From my viewing of the film, the proofs and argument, I wholeheartedly agree with the plaintiffs' contention that 'there is nothing suggestive, obscene, indecent, malicious or immoral in the showing of the Latuko aborigines in their normal living state.' While it is true that the men have been photographed naked and the women naked above the waist, the exposure of their bodies is not indecent; it is simply their normal way of living. They are not shown in any attitude or function to which exception might justifiably be taken. In my opinion, only a narrow or unhealthy mind could find any depravity in the film."

The following description of *Naked Amazon* is from Judge Hammond: "One Zygmunt Sulistrowski, who is described as an 'explorer and photographer, and a man of adventure,' headed an expedition to the Matto Grosso region of the Brazilian jungles, financed in part by the American Museum of Natural History. The expedition took motion pictures in color, some of which form a part of the picture *Naked Amazon* which is largely a factual showing of the lives of the natives of the jungles of Brazil. After scenes depicting pre-lenten festivities in Rio de Janeiro including dances which the narrator describes as 'exotic, voluptuous and sensuous,' but which the Board did not find objectionable, the expedition group is shown proceeding by boat up the Amazon River. During this river trip, against a scenic background of the Brazilian jungle, a few nonfactual or staged scenes appear. The voyage through the primeval beauty of the jungle— the camera was focused on wild animals, fish, birds, butterflies, and sundry flora and fauna—is sought to be made dramatic by suggesting the struggle of the group against the natural dangers of the country by scenes such as those of a man struggling with what is represented to be a dangerous boa constrictor. When the group makes contact with the Camayura Indians the scenes are entirely genuine and documentary. The Indians are aborigines who are said to bring to mind pictures of prehistoric man. Their physical structure and features are ugly and primitive compared with the current concept of physical attractiveness. They were described by one reviewer as particularly 'homely and unprepossessing.' They are shown in their daily activities with the narrative discussion pointing out their unusual customs and rituals. When presented to the Maryland Board for censorship, the film already had been edited, as a prerequisite to approval by both the motion picture industry censorship body and the New York State Censors so that, as Judge Byrnes noted, 'intimate parts of the body cannot be seen.' None of the scenes portray any action which is even suggestive of sexual activity. The natives are quite unaware that they are without clothing and the narration accompanying the scenes in no manner suggests that they are sexually excited, or exciting, rather, the photography and narration dwell on their unusual customs and rituals, which seemingly give the appearance of rather childlike games.''

NAKED LUNCH. In 1959, Grove Press published *Naked Lunch* by William S. Burroughs. Burroughs was, at the time, an ex-patriate American author living in Paris, and the book described the hallucinations of a drug addict (Burroughs was an addict at the time). The reviews of the book were mixed. Eric Moon, writing in the *Library Journal* (December 1, 1962), commented: ''Mary McCarthy and Norman Mailer . . . told an astounded audience that the outstanding contemporary American writer was . . . William Burroughs. This is a unique book by an incredibly talented writer but . . . I don't share the extravagant opinions of McCarthy and Mailer.'' John Wain, writing in the *New Republic* (December 1, 1962), thought both the book and Burroughs were trash: ''A book like *Naked Lunch* requires far less talent in the writer and . . . less intelligence in the reader than the humblest magazine story. From the literary point of view, it is the merest trash, not worth a second glance. What is worth a glance, however, is the respectful attitude that some well-known writers have shown towards it. The only writer of any talent of whom Burroughs occasionally manages to remind one is the Marquis de Sade.''

The attorney general of Massachusetts also thought *Naked Lunch* to be trash and was able to convince Judge Hudson; the latter declared the book to be obscene. But an appeal was taken to the Massachusetts Supreme Judicial Court (*Attorney General v. A Book Named Naked Lunch*, 218 N.E. 2d 571 [1966]), where the book, although not totally free from judicial harassment, was at least declared not to be obscene in violation of the law (Massachusetts, Obscenity Statute*). The Supreme Judicial Court, taking note that the book was "grossly offensive" and that Burroughs himself described it as "brutal, obscene and disgusting," nonetheless also took note that there were many reviews and articles in literary and other magazines discussing the book. These reviews showed that a "substantial and intelligent group" in the community believed that the book was of some literary significance, and the record did not show that Grove Press had commercially exploited the book for the sake of prurient appeal (read "pandering"*). The court concluded that *Naked Lunch* was not utterly without redeeming social value (Memoirs Standard*) and thus the book was not obscene. But *Naked Lunch* was not totally absolved; the court left open further prosecution if "any persons have been or are advertising or distributing this book in this Commonwealth in a manner to exploit it for the sake of its possible prurient appeal."

THE NAKED TRUTH. This 1924 American silent film was the object of two attempts at censorship: one (unsuccessful) in New Jersey in 1926 and one (successful) in New York in 1928. De Grazia and Newman (*Banned Films*, p. 204) describe the film: "Clean-living young lawyer Bob, who has had good sex education, marries. Another youth becomes infected with venereal disease because his father allowed him to 'have a fling.' He refuses legitimate treatment, but accepts treatment from a quack doctor. His pending marriage is stopped by a legitimate doctor. A third young man does have venereal disease, consults a quack doctor, and marries. The disease eventually affects his brain and he kills his wife. Lawyer Bob gets him off by pleading insanity. The film 'shows a male and a female in the nude, and, among other things, the progress of different venereal diseases and the effects thereof.' "†

The Newark, New Jersey, attempt to ban *The Naked Truth*, according to the court records (*Public Welfare Pictures Corp. v. Brennan*, 134 A. 868 [1926]), was as follows. Before the date of the first public exhibition, a private view was had, attended by Dr. Charles V. Craster, chief of the Board of Health of Newark; Justina T. Ellar and Robert Lawrence of the Newark Police Department (these two being known as the Board of Censors and appointed by William J. Brennan, head of the department of Public Safety of Newark); and a number of women invited by the Board of Censors and Brennan. Craster saw nothing objectionable in the film. The Board of Censors thought it objectionable unless presented in a YMCA, a school building, or a church. What the invited women thought of the film does not appear in the records. Commissioner Brennan then caused a notice to be given to the Public Welfare Pictures Corporation, saying that the

†Reprinted from *Banned Films* with permission of the R. R. Bowker Company. Copyright © 1982 by Edward de Grazia and Roger K. Newman.

presentation of the film was prohibited, that if presented he would prevent the production by force, would revoke the theater license, and arrest all those connected with the exhibition. The corporation then went to Commissioner Brennan and offered to exhibit the film to him (he had not yet viewed it), and if he decided it was objectionable, it would not be exhibited. Commissioner Brennan said that he would not view the film, that Ellar and Lawrence were the people in his department to whom he confided the censorship of films, and that he would stand behind their judgment. The corporation then filed suit, asking for an injunction to restrain the commissioner and the city from interfering with the film's exhibition. Neither the city nor Commissioner Brennan filed any answering affidavits.

The Court of Chancery granted the injunction, thus permitting *The Naked Truth* to be exhibited in Newark. Vice Chancellor Church delivered the opinion: "The question here is not, Has the Legislature the right to say by statute that a municipality may, in the exercise of its police power, control theaters and moving picture shows and decide what are and what are not proper exhibitions? It is, Has the Legislature done this? . . . If the Legislature had clothed the municipality of the City of Newark with the right to censor plays, it might or might not be legal. But, certainly, by no stretch of the imagination can it be held that the director of public safety of a municipality can delegate to a policeman or a policewoman or a voluntary committee of women or to all combined the authority to say whether a certain play should or should not be produced. . . . No one is more anxious than I to see that the city of Newark is and remains a clean city, and no one is more opposed to indecent exhibitions than I. However, I cannot set up my personal opinion in the matter and I must decide this motion according to the law which seems to me to govern and according to the decisions heretofore rendered by this court. I wish to be distinctly understood that I am expressing no opinion as to the morality of this production. I have not seen it."

There is an interesting footnote to this case, a relationship or influence that went far beyond Newark, New Jersey, and *The Naked Truth*. As de Grazia and Newman comment (*Banned Films*, p. 205): "William J. Brennan, the Newark Director of Public Safety, was the father of U.S. Supreme Court Justice William J. Brennan, Jr., the single most influential figure in modern obscenity law. 'It is difficult to assess exactly how important [the senior Brennan's position] was in influencing the younger Brennan,' a commentator has written, 'but it was probably the most single important factor in shaping Brennan, Jr.'s life.' David S. Jobrack, 'Mr. Justice Brennan . . . the Man and the Judge,' 2 *New Jersey St. B.J.* 241 (1959)."†

The New York attempt to censor *The Naked Truth* in 1928 was more successful. The New York censorship board refused to issue an exhibition permit

---

†Reprinted from *Banned Films* with permission of the R. R. Bowker Company. Copyright © 1982 by Edward de Grazia and Roger K. Newman.

after viewing the film. The New York State Supreme Court (*Public Welfare Pictures Corporation v. Lord*, 230 N.Y.S. 137 [1928]) held—without viewing the film for itself—that the New York law did not require a court to review the censor's decision to deny a license if the refusal was not based on arbitrary or bad-faith reasons.

NATIONAL ASSOCIATION FOR THE ADVANCEMENT OF COLORED PEOPLE v. BUTTON (1963). The National Association for the Advancement of Colored People (NAACP) sued in a federal district court to enjoin enforcement of a Virginia statute (Virginia, Legal Ethics*) that, in the section defining and punishing malpractice by attorneys, broadened the definition of solicitation of legal business to include acceptance of employment or compensation from any person or organization not a party to a judicial proceeding and having no pecuniary right or liability in it. The Virginia statute also made it an offense for any such person or organization to solicit business for any attorney. Taken on its face, the statute would put the NAACP (and other like organizations, such as the American Civil Liberties Union) out of business in the state, for the NAACP's major purpose was use of the judicial process to eliminate racial segregation and discrimination.

The Virginia courts, ranging from the trial court to the Virginia Supreme Court of Appeals, held the statute to be both constitutional and applicable to the NAACP; the U.S. Supreme Court found otherwise, ruling that it was unconstitutional, and enjoined the state of Virginia from applying the statute to the NAACP. A rather lengthy decision is summarized here: (1) The activities of the NAACP, its affiliates, and legal staff are modes of expression and association protected by the First and Fourteenth Amendments, which Virginia may not prohibit under its power to regulate the legal profession. (2) Although the NAACP is a corporation, it may still assert its right and that of its members and lawyers to associate for the purpose of assisting those who seek legal redress for infringement of their constitutionally guaranteed rights. (3) Abstract discussion is not the only species of communication that the Constitution protects; the First Amendment also protects vigorous advocacy, certainly of lawful ends, against governmental intrusion. (4) In the context of the NAACP's objectives, litigation is not a means of resolving private differences; it is a form of political expression and a means for achieving the lawful objectives of equality of treatment by all governments—federal, state, and local—for the members of the black community. (5) In order to find constitutional protection for the kind of cooperative, organizational activity pursued by the NAACP, it is not necessary to subsume such activity under a narrow, literal conception of freedom of speech, petition, or assembly, for there is no longer any doubt that the First Amendment protects certain forms of orderly group activity. (6) As construed by the Virginia courts, a person who, under the statute, advises another that his legal rights have been infringed and refers him to a particular attorney or group of attorneys for assistance has committed a crime and this presents the gravest danger of smothering all discussion looking to the eventual institution of litigation on behalf of the rights of blacks. (7) It is no answer to the constitutional claims asserted by the Virginia courts to say that the purpose of the statute was merely to ensure high professional standards and not to curtail freedom of expression, for a state may not, under the guise of prohibiting professional misconduct, ignore constitutional rights. *National Association for the Advancement of Colored People v. Button*, 371 U.S. 415 (1963).

NATIONAL COALITION AGAINST CENSORSHIP. This umbrella-type organization is concerned with preserving freedom of thought, inquiry, and expression in contemporary America. It was established in 1974, and among its forty or so constituent groups can be found the American Library Association, the National Association of College Bookstores, the Association of American Publishers, the American Society of Journalists and Authors, the Authors League of America, and the American Association of University Professors.

According to its objectives, the National Coalition holds "that freedom of communication is the indispensable condition of a healthy democracy and that censorship constitutes an unacceptable dictatorship over our minds, and a dangerous opening to religious, political, artistic, and intellectual repression. Helps its participating organizations to educate their own members about the dangers of censorship and how to oppose it. Carries out educational work through the mass media and the general public. [The National Coalition posts lists of banned books in bookstores, recruits authors of banned books to speak to community groups, supports lawsuits against book banning, and offers anti-censorship films to television stations.] Conducts meetings for discussion and debate of First Amendment issues. Maintains the National Information Clearinghouse on Book-banning Litigation in Public Schools which provides information to attorneys, the press, and organizations. Encourages involvement of national organizations in cases, coordinates amicus briefs and other activities. Maintains a library of extensive literature on First Amendment issues." *Encyclopedia of Associations* (# 12002).

The coalition's major publications are *Censorship News* (quarterly) and *Report on Book Censorship Litigation in Public Schools* (also quarterly). As reported in the *New York Times Book Review* (October 23, 1983, p. 47), one *Report* (June 1982 to June 1983) contained a listing of some seventy-five books that were challenged in schools and libraries. The list included Judy Blume's *Are You There God? It's Me Margaret*, challenged in the school system of Fond du Lac, Wisconsin, for being "sexually offensive and amoral"; Doris Day's *Doris Day: Her Own Story*, removed from two Anniston, Alabama, high school libraries because of the "shocking" contents "in light of Miss Day's All-American image" but later reinstated on a restricted basis; Judith Guest's *Ordinary People*, challenged at the Merrimack, New Hampshire, high school after a parent found the novel "obscene and depressing"; Arthur Miller's play *The Crucible*, challenged at Cumberland Valley High School in Harrisburg, Pennsylvania, because it contained "sick words from the mouths of demon-possessed people"; Studs Terkel's *Working*, challenged in senior vocational English school in Girard, Pennsylvania, because some parents and students considered the book's language "obscene"; and Kurt Vonnegut's *Slaughterhouse-Five*, challenged in Lakeland, Florida, and in many other cities, too, because of "explicit sexual scenes, violence and obscene language."

NATIONAL COMMITTEE FOR SEXUAL CIVIL LIBERTIES. Founded in 1970, this organization describes itself as composed of "lawyers and scholars in government, sociology, religion, anthropology and history and with experience in civil liberties. Works for dismantling the entire structure of criminality and discrimination surrounding private sexual conduct between consenting adults, including repeal of all adultery, fornication and sodomy laws to the extent that they punish such conduct; and for the removal of all discriminatory practices based on sexual orientation. Also seeks repeal of laws punishing distribution, importation or sale of pornographic material to adults." *Encyclopedia of Associations* (# 12053).The committee's publication is the *Sexual Law Reporter* (quarterly).

NATIONAL FEDERATION FOR DECENCY. Founded in 1977 and based in Tupelo, Mississippi, this organization reports that it "promotes the biblical ethic of decency in American society with a primary emphasis on television. Urges viewers to write letters to networks and sponsors, protesting shows seen to promote violence, immorality, profanity and vulgarity, encouraging the airing of programs which are clean, constructive, wholesome and family oriented. Compiles statistics on televisions sex, profanity and beverage use." *Encyclopedia of Associations* (# 11968).

NATIONAL FOUNDATION v. FORT WORTH (1970). A Fort Worth municipal ordinance (Forth Worth [TX], Charitable Soliciting*) prohibited any organization from soliciting charitable contributions within the city if the cost of such solicitation exceeded 20 percent of the amount collected. The ordinance also permitted any organization seeking a permit to solicit to request a waiver from the 20 percent rule if they could prove the excess costs were not "unreasonable." The National Foundation, whose costs did exceed the 20 percent level, was denied a solicitation permit, and the city did not waive the requirement. The foundation then brought suit, arguing that the right to disseminate information publicly about a charitable organization and to solicit funds publicly is a right of free speech and press protected under the First Amendment against prior restraint by municipal censorship. A federal appeals court (415 F. 2d 41 [1969]) held, however, that the ordinance limiting the cost of solicitation within the city to 20 percent was a valid and constitutional exercise of the city's police power, and that the grounds on which a waiver could be granted were not arbitrary or vague. The foundation then appealed to the Supreme Court, but the Court declined to review the case, thus letting stand the appeals court's ruling. *National Foundation v. Fort Worth*, 396 U.S. 1040 (1970), *cert. denied*.

NATIONAL LABOR RELATIONS BOARD v. ROBBINS TIRE AND RUBBER CO. (1978). The Freedom of Information Act* permits governmental agencies to withhold (exemption 7–A) material "of investigatory records compiled for law enforcement purposes, but only to the extent that the protection of such records . . . would interfere with enforcement proceedings." This case resulted in the decision that the National Labor Relations Board did not have to disclose witnesses' statements that were gathered during an investigation that led to the filing of an unfair labor practice. *National Labor Relations Board v. Robbins Tire and Rubber Co.*, 437 U.S. 214 (1978).

NATIONAL LABOR RELATIONS BOARD v. VIRGINIA ELECTRIC AND POWER CO. (1941). The National Labor Relations Board (NLRB), during a labor-management dispute, concluded that the various bulletins and speeches of company officials were an unfair labor practice, for the bulletins and speeches "interfered with, restrained, and coerced its employees." The Supreme Court, recognizing that certain utterances could be seen as coercive and thus an unfair labor practice, sent the case back to the NLRB, for the Court felt that the board looked at the specific utterances only in isolation, rather than evaluating the whole course of conduct by the company in the dispute. Justice Murphy presented the justification for this ruling: "Upon the basis of these findings and the entire record in the case, the Board concluded that the Company had committed unfair labor practices. . . . Its order directed the Company to cease and desist from its unfair labor practices and from giving effect to its contract with the Independent, to withdraw recognition from and disestablish that organization, to reinstate with back pay the four wrongfully discharged employees, to reimburse each of its employees who was a member of the Independent in the amount of the dues and assessments checked off his wages by the Company on behalf of the Independent, and to post appropriate notices. . . . The Company strongly urges that such a finding is repugnant to the First Amendment. Neither the Act nor the Board's order here enjoins the employer from expressing its view on labor policies or problems, nor is a penalty imposed upon it because of any utterances which it has made. The sanctions of the Act are imposed not in punishment of the employer but for the protection of the employees. The employer in this case is as free now as ever to take any side it may choose on this controversial issue. But, certainly, conduct, though evidenced in part by speech, may amount, in connection with other circumstances, to coercion within the meaning of the Act. If the total activities of an employer restrain or coerce his employees in their free choice, then those employees are entitled to the protection of the Act. And in determining whether a course of conduct amounts to restraint or coercion, pressure exerted vocally by the employer may no more be disregarded than pressure

exerted in other ways. For 'Slight suggestions as to the employer's choice between unions may have telling effect among men who know the consequences
of incurring that employer's strong displeasure.' " *National Labor Relations
Board v. Virginia Electric and Power Co*, 314 U.S. 468 (1941).

NATIONAL ORGANIZATION FOR DECENT LITERATURE. The National Organization for Decent Literature (NODL), a Roman Catholic organization, was formed in 1938 by an Episcopal committee appointed by the Roman
Catholic hierarchy in the United States to "devise a plan for organizing a sys-
tematic campaign in all dioceses of the United States against the publication and
sale of lewd magazine and brochure literature." As Lockhart and McClure
("Literature, Law, Obscenity and the Constitution," 38 *Minnesota Law Review*,
pp. 304ff.) write, the NODL's activities included the following: "1. The arousal
of public opinion against 'objectionable' magazines, comics, and paper-bound
books; 2. More rigorous enforcement of existing laws governing obscene literature; 3. Promotion of new and more strict legislation to suppress such literature;
4. Preparation of monthly lists of magazines, comics, and paper-bound books
disapproved by the Organization; and 5. Visitation of newsstands and drug stores
to secure the removal of blacklisted literature. Because of its extensive local
organization in Roman Catholic dioceses, the NODL soon became a powerful
and effective instrument for the accomplishment of its goal."

The original standards established by the NODL to rid the United States of
"objectionable" literature were the following (Lockhart and McClure, p. 305):
"(a) Those which glorify crime and the criminal; (b) Those whose contents are
largely 'sexy'; (c) Those whose illustrations and pictures border on the indecent
[all these terms were not defined]; (d) Those which make a habit of carrying
articles on 'illicit love'; and (e) Those which carry disreputable advertising."
The NODL knew how the political process worked and used the sytem to the
utmost; Lockhart and McClure comment that "within less than a year after its
organization, when about half the Roman Catholic dioceses of the country had
been covered by organized campaigns, the magazine publishers 'one by one,
began to ask for interviews with the National Committee and offered to agree
to almost anything which might lead to the elimination of their particular periodicals from the NODL blacklist.' "

In some communities, the local organization of the NODL issued "certificates" to cooperating dealers for displaying the following notice: "This store
has satisfactorily complied with the request of the Committee [the local committee
of the NODL] to remove all publications listed as 'OBJECTIONABLE' by the
National Organization of Decent Literature from its racks during the above
month." Lockhart and McClure continue and write that the NODL blacklists
were the most elaborate of all the blacklists. Writing in 1954, they comment
that, at one time or another, the following books were placed on the NODL's
list of "objectionable" material: Mickey Spillane's *The Big Kill, I, the Jury,
One Lonely Night,* and *Vengeance Is Mine*; several books by James M. Cain

(*Love's Lovely Counterfeit, Mildred Pierce, Past All Dishonor,* and *The Postman Always Rings Twice*); several books by Erskine Caldwell (*Episode in Palmetto, God's Little Acre,** and *Tobacco Road*); nine novels by James T. Farrell; Pierre Louys' *Aphrodite* and *Collected Works*; W. Somerset Maugham's *Fools and Their Folly* and *The Painted Veil* (this is only a partial list); John O'Hara's *Appointment in Samarra* and *Butterfield Eight*; and Emile Zola's *Nana, Piping Hot,* and *Theresa.* Lockhart and McClure list some of the other books that the NODL found "objectionable": Nelson Algren's *The Man with the Golden Arm;**; Niven Busch's *Duel in the Sun*; C. S. Forester's *The African Queen*; Ernest Hemingway's classic *A Farewell to Arms*; D. H. Lawrence's *Lady Chatterley's Lover** and *Love Among the Haystacks*; James A. Michener's *Tales of the South Pacific*; Christopher Morley's *Kitty Foyle*; Irwin Shaw's *The Young Lions* (one of the best books dealing with World War II); and, not surprisingly, Boccaccio's *Decameron* and Flaubert's *Madame Bovary.* The NODL is now defunct and no longer exists as a formal organization. The NODL's basic philosophy, however, is still present in U.S. society, for much of the NODL's view of life and literature has been absorbed by Citizens for Decency Through Law.* This latter group has no connection or ties with the Roman Catholic hierarchy in the United States, and although many of its members are Catholic (as well as other religions), it is not a Catholic organization.

NATIONAL ORGANIZATION FOR WOMEN. Founded in 1966 and having for its first president Betty Friedan, author of the best-seller *The Feminine Mystique*, the National Organization for Women (NOW) has groups in all fifty states, with an approximate membership of 260,000. The bottom line for NOW is women's rights and full equality for women in U.S. society. According to NOW, the organization: "acts to end prejudice and discrimination against women in government, industry, the professions, the churches, the political parties, the judiciary, the labor unions, education, science, medicine, law, religion, and every other field of importance in American society. The group supports passage of the Equal Rights Amendment, enforcement of federal legislation prohibiting discrimination on the basis of sex, social innovations to enable women to work while rearing a family, and reexamination of laws and mores governing marriage and divorce. NOW promotes its views through various action techniques such as research, litigation and political action." *Encyclopedia of Associations* (# 13428). One such "action technique" employed in pursuit of their objectives has been the monitoring of various textbooks to ensure that they are non-discriminatory toward women. Even though directed at admirable ends, this monitoring—and the resulting demands for change—is clearly a form of censorship.

NATIVE SON. This 1951 American film was directed by Pierre Chenal and was adapted from the novel by Richard Wright, who played a leading role in the film; it was also banned in Ohio in 1953 (Ohio, Motion Picture Censorship*). The Ohio Motion Picture Censorship Board refused on several occasions to issue an exhibition permit for *Native Son* on the grounds that the film "contributes to racial misunderstanding, presenting situations undesirable to the mutual interests of both races . . . undermining confidence that justice can be carried out . . . and presenting racial frictions at a time when all groups should be united against everything that is subversive." The Ohio Supreme Court upheld the board's decision, saying that even though a film could not be banned on grounds of it being "sacrilegious" (*The Miracle** decision), states still had the power to refuse to issue exhibition permits to films seen to "contribute to immorality or to crime" (*Classic Pictures v. Hissong*, 112 N.E.2d 311 [1953]).

Classic Pictures, in its brief to the Ohio Supreme Court, described *Native Son* as follows: "The action of the story takes place in Chicago, and part of the picture was filmed there. The role of the central character, Bigger Thomas, an embittered young negro, is acted by Richard Wright, the author of the book. Bigger accidentally kills a white girl, Mary Dalton, and after disposing of her body, attempts to extort money from her parents by means of a ransom note. After the murder is discovered, Bigger goes into hiding with his sweetheart, Bessie Mears, and immediately before his capture, murders Bessie in the mistaken belief that she betrayed him. The picture ends with a scene between Bigger and his lawyer, in which it is made clear that Bigger will be electrocuted for his crimes." Classic Pictures then appealed to the Supreme Court, and the case of *Native Son* was decided along with *M,** another film banned by the censors in Ohio (*Superior Films v. Department of Education of Ohio*, 346 U.S. 587 [1954]).

The Supreme Court reversed the decisions banning *Native Son* and ordered the issuance of an exhibition license. Justice Douglas, in a concurring opinion, joined by Justice Black, offered some comments not on *Native Son* itself, but on the entire question of the relationship of films to the freedom of expression (Film Censorship*). Justice Douglas: "The argument of Ohio that the government may establish censorship over moving pictures is one I cannot accept. In 1925 Minnesota passed a law aimed at suppressing before publication any 'malicious, scandalous and defamatory newspaper.' The Court, speaking through Chief Justice Hughes, struck down that law as violating the Fourteenth Amendment, which has made the First Amendment applicable to the States (*Near v. Minnesota ex rel. Olson**). The 'chief purpose' of the constitutional guaranty of liberty of the press, said the Court, was 'to prevent previous restraints upon publication.' The history of censorship is so well known that it need not be summarized here. Certainly a system, still in force in some nations, which required a newspaper to submit to a board its news items, editorials, and cartoons before it published them could not be sustained. Nor could book publishers be required to submit their novels, poems, and tracts to censors for clearance before publication. Any such scheme of censorship would be in irreconcilable conflict with the language and purpose of the First Amendment. Nor is it conceivable to me that producers of plays for the legitimate theatre or for television could be required to submit their manuscripts to censors on pain of penalty for producing them without approval. Certainly the spoken word is as freely protected against prior restraints as that which is written. The freedom of the platform which it espouses carries with it freedom of the stage. The same result in the case of motion pictures necessarily follows as a consequence of our holding in [*The Miracle** case] that motion pictures are 'within the free speech and free press guaranty of the First and Fourteenth Amendments.' Motion pictures are of course a different medium of expression than the public speech, the radio, the stage, the novel, or the magazine. But the First Amendment draws no distinction between the various methods of communicating ideas. On occasion one may be more powerful or effective than another. The movie, like the public speech, radio, or television, is transitory—here now and gone in an instant. The novel, the short story, the poem in printed form are permanently at hand to reenact the drama or to retell the story over and again. Which medium will give the most excitement and have the most enduring effect will vary with the theme and the actors. It is not for the censor to determine in any case. The First and Fourteenth Amendments say that Congress and the States shall make 'no law' which abridges freedom of speech or of the press. In order to sanction a system of censorship I would have to say that 'no law' does not mean what it says, that 'no law' is qualified to mean 'some' laws. I cannot take that step. In this Nation every writer, actor, or producer, no matter what medium of expression he may use, should be freed from the censor.''

NEAR v. MINNESOTA EX REL. OLSON (1931). A Minnesota statute (Minnesota, Malicious and Scandalous Publications*) declared that one who engaged ''in the business of regularly and customarily publishing a malicious, scandalous and defamatory newspaper, magazine, or other periodical'' would be guilty of a nuisance, and that subsequent publications could be enjoined or prevented from being published. Disobedience to the injunction was punishable as a contempt of court. The statute, in one of the landmark decisions of the Supreme Court, was held to be a prior restraint on the freedom of the press and, as such, was therefore unconstitutional as a violation of the First Amendment.

As is unfortunately true with many other ground-breaking Supreme Court decisions, good law evolves from some pretty nasty people: The publisher of the paper (*The Saturday Press*) in this case, one Near, was an anti-Semite, whose articles were in fact malicious, defamatory, slanderous, ugly, and mean-spirited. The articles that appeared in *The Saturday Press*, as summarized by the court records, charged in substance that a Jewish gangster was in control of gambling, bootlegging, and racketeering in Minneapolis, and that the law enforcement officers, in league with the criminals, were not performing their duties. Following are a few extracts from Near's articles: ''There have been too many men in this city and especially those in official life, who HAVE been taking orders and suggestions from JEW GANGSTERS, therefore we HAVE Jew gangsters, practically ruling Minneapolis/Practically every vendor of vile hooch, every owner of a moonshine still, every snake-faced gangster and embryonic yegg in the

Twin Cities is a JEW/It is Jew, Jew, Jew, as long as one cares to comb over the records/ I am launching no attack against the Jewish people AS A RACE. I am merely calling attention to a FACT. And if the people of that race and faith wish to rid themselves of the odium and stigma THE RODENTS OF THEIR OWN RACE HAVE BROUGHT UPON THEM, they need only to step to the front and help the decent citizens of Minneapolis to rid the city of these criminal Jews/I have withdrawn all allegiance to anything with a hook nose that eats herring. I have adopted the sparrow as my national bird until the . . . K.K.K. hammers the eagle's beak out straight.''

Minnesota felt that such writings were malicious, scandalous, and defamatory; Near was enjoined from future publication and was cited for contempt when he disobeyed the order. The Supreme Court ruled that the statute was an unconstitutional prior restraint on the First Amendment right of a free press. Chief Justice Hughes delivered the opinion of the Court: ''If we cut through mere details of procedure, the operation and effect of the statute in substance is that public authorities may bring the owner or publisher of a newspaper or periodical before a judge upon a charge of conducting a business of publishing scandalous and defamatory matter and unless the owner or publisher is able and disposed to bring competent evidence to satisfy the judge that the charges are true and are published with good motives and for justifiable ends, his newspaper or periodical is suppressed and further publication is made punishable as a contempt. This is of the essence of censorship. The question is whether a statute authorizing such proceedings in restraint of publication is consistent with the conception of the liberty of the press as historically conceived and guaranteed. In determining the extent of the constitutional protection, it has been generally, if not universally, considered that it is the chief purpose of the guaranty to prevent previous restraints upon publication.

''The struggle in England, directed against the legislative power of the licensor, resulted in renunciation of the censorship of the press. The liberty deemed to be established was thus described by Blackstone: 'The liberty of the press is indeed essential to the nature of a free state; but this consists in laying no *previous* restraints upon publications, and not in freedom from censure for criminal matter when published. Every freeman has an undoubted right to lay what sentiments he pleases before the public; to forbid this, is to destroy the freedom of the press; but if he publishes what is improper, mischievous or illegal, he must take the consequence of his own temerity.' The distinction was early pointed out between the extent of the freedom with respect to censorship under our constitutional system and that enjoyed in England. Here, as Madison said, 'the great and essential rights of the people are secured against legislative as well as against executive ambition. They are secured, not by laws paramount to prerogative, but by constitutions paramount to laws. This security of the freedom of the press requires that it should be exempt not only from previous restraint by the Executive, as in Great Britain, but from legislative restraint also.' . . .

''In the present case, we have no occasion to inquire as to the permissible scope of subsequent punishment. For whatever wrong [Near] has committed or may commit, by his publications, the State appropriately affords both public and private redress by its libel laws. As has been noted, the statute in question does not deal with punishments; it provides for no punishment, except in case of contempt for violation of the court's order, but for suppression and injunction, that is, for restraint upon publication. The objection has also been made that the principle as to immunity from previous restraint is stated too broadly, if every such restraint is deemed to be prohibited. That is undoubtedly true; the protection even as to previous restraint is not absolutely unlimited. But the limitation has been recognized only in exceptional cases: 'When a nation is at war many things that might be said in time of peace are such a hindrance to its effort that their utterance will not be endured so long as men fight and that no Court could regard them as protected by any constitutional right' (*Schenck v. United States**). No one would question but that a government might prevent actual obstruction to its recruiting service or the publication of the sailing date of transports or the number and location of troops. On similar grounds, the primary requirements of decency may be enforced against obscene publications. The security of the community life may be protected against incitements to acts of violence and the overthrow by force of orderly government. The constitutional guaranty of free speech does not 'protect a man from an injunction against uttering words that may have all the effect of force.' These limitations are not applicable here. Nor are we now concerned with questions as to the extent of authority to prevent publications in order to protect private rights according to the principles governing the exercise of the jurisdiction of courts of equity. The exceptional nature of its limitations places in a strong light the general conception that liberty of the press, historically considered and taken up by the Federal Constitution, has meant, principally although not exclusively, immunity from previous restraints or censorship." *Near v. Minnesota ex rel. Olson*, 283 U.S. 697 (1931).

NEBRASKA, FLAG DESECRATION. On July 3, 1903, the state of Nebraska approved "An Act to prevent and punish the desecration of the flag of the United States" (1 Cobbey's Ann. Stat. Neb. 1903, c. 139). The following section (§ 2375g) was upheld as constitutional by the Supreme Court in 1907 (*Halter v. Nebraska**), when someone used a representation of the flag on a beer bottle label: "Any person who in any manner . . . [exhibits] any article or substance, being an article of merchandise, or a receptacle of merchandise, upon which shall have been printed, painted, attached or otherwise placed, a representation of any such flag . . . to advertise, call attention to, decorate, mark, or distinguish, the article, or substance on which so placed, or who shall publicly mutilate, deface, defile, or defy, trample upon or cast contempt, either by words, or act, upon any such flag . . . shall be deemed guilty of a misdemeanor, and shall be punished by a fine not exceeding one hundred dollars, or by imprisonment for not more than thirty days, or both in the discretion of the court."

NEBRASKA PRESS ASSOCIATION v. STUART (1976). A Nebraska state trial judge, in anticipation of a trial for a multiple murder that had attracted widespread news coverage, restrained newspapers, broadcasters, journalists, news media associations, and national newswire services from publishing or broadcasting accounts of any confessions or admissions made by the accused to law enforcement officers or to third parties and other facts strongly implicative of the accused's guilt.

The Nebraska Press Association appealed to the Supreme Court, arguing that such a blanket prior restraint was governmental censorship at its extreme, and that the order violated the right of a free press; the Supreme Court agreed with the association's arguments. The Court held: (1) While the guarantees of freedom of expression are not an absolute prohibition under all circumstances, the barriers to prior restraint remain high and the presumption against its use continues intact. Although it is unnecessary to establish a priority between First Amendment rights and the Sixth Amendment rights to a fair trial under all circumstances, as the authors of the Bill of Rights themselves declined to do, the protection against prior restraint should have particular force as applied to reporting of criminal proceedings. (2) The heavy burden imposed as a condition to securing a prior restraint was not met in this particular case for (a) The trial judge was justified in concluding that there would be intense pre-trial publicity, but his conclusion as to the impact of such publicity on prospective jurors was, of necessity, speculative, dealing as he was with factors unknown and unknowable; (b) It is not clear that the prior restraint on publication would have effectively protected the accused's rights; and (c) To the extent that the order prohibited the reporting of evidence adduced at the open preliminary hearing to determine whether the accused should be bound over for trial, it violated the settled principle that "there is nothing that proscribes the press from reporting events that transpire in the courtroom," and the portion of the order restraining publication of other facts "strongly implicative" of the accused is too vague and too broad to survive the scrutiny given to restraints on First Amendment rights. *Nebraska Press Association v. Stuart*, 427 U.S. 539 (1976).

NEBRASKA, TEACHING FOREIGN LANGUAGES. On May 25, 1920, while an instructor in Zion Parochial School (Hamilton County), one Meyer taught the subject of reading in the German language to one Raymond Parpart, a ten-year-old child, who had not yet attained and successfully passed the eighth grade. Meyer was then duly convicted of violating "An Act relating to the teaching of foreign languages in the State of Nebraska," approved April 9, 1919 (Laws 1919, c. 249): "No person, individually or as a teacher, shall, in any private, denominational, parochial or public school, teach any subject to any person in any language other than the English language. Languages, other than the English language, may be taught as languages only after a pupil shall have attained and successfully passed the eighth grade as evidenced by a certificate of graduation issued by the county superintendent of the county in which the child resides. Any person who violates any of the provisions of this act shall be deemed guilty of a misdemeanor and upon conviction, shall be subject to a fine of not less than $25.00, nor more than $100 or be confined in the county jail for any period not exceeding thirty days for each offense. Whereas, an emergency exists, this act shall be in force from and after its passage and approval.'' The Supreme Court, in *Meyer v. Nebraska* (1923),* declared this act to be a violation of the freedom of speech.

NEW AMERICAN LIBRARY OF WORLD LITERATURE, INC. v. AL-LEN (1953). As the court records relate, early in 1953 the chief of police of Youngstown, Ohio, a certain Allen, inaugurated ''a campaign against the sale of lewd and indecent literature.'' Chief Allen based his campaign on an ordinance (Youngstown [OH], Obscene Literature*) that defined the sale or distribution of obscene or immoral books as a misdemeanor. Continuing with the court records, on January 5, 1953, Chief Allen wrote a letter to one Bernard Bloch in which he commented on the discussions between them since 1948 and Bloch's expressed willingness to remove ''objectionable literature and pictures.'' Reference was also made in this letter to Bloch's agreement to ''permit us to act as censors but only to a degree.'' The letter also contained the following: ''These books include almost all of the so-called paper-backed 'pocket-book' type of magazine, which as a matter of policy, glorify and dwell upon immorality. Admittedly, there are some few which are not in this category, yet so few are they in number that their publication would seem to be a subterfuge designed to whitewash the great bulk of these publications. . . . Such periodicals must be removed, and failure to act in this matter will result in arrest and prosecution, under the law, and final disposition by the court.''

Bloch requested Allen to specify the titles that the chief considered to be obscene. Allen, assisted by members of his vice squad, then examined the books, but only a few were read in their entirety by the vice squad. Allen stated that, in forming his opinion, he was influenced by the illustrations on the covers of the books and by the content of the ''advertising blurbs,'' and that blasphemy and detailed description of sexual acts—and violation of the second commandment—were among the standards employed to determine whether a book was obscene under the ordinance. Allen and his vice squad compiled a list of some 108 books and thirty-three magazines (the court record does not identify these). On January 15, 1953, he forwarded this list to Bloch, together with a letter requesting that the publications be removed from the newsstands.

The New American Library of World Literature, one of the offending publishers, then brought suit in a federal district court, seeking to recover damages and to enjoin Allen from suppressing its books. Judge McNamee issued such an injunction, ruling that the chief of police had no authority to have engaged in such censorship activity. Judge McNamee: ''The defendant was without authority to censor books. Such a drastic power can be vested in a police officer only by a valid express legislative grant. As Chief of Police it was defendant's duty to examine the suspected publications to determine whether there was probable cause for prosecution. He was without authority to determine with finality whether the books were obscene or immoral in violation of the ordinance. In the event prosecutions were undertaken, the burden would rest upon city officials to establish by proof beyond a reasonable doubt every element of the offense, including the obscene or immoral nature of the books. Until a court of competent jurisdiction adjudged a book to be obscene or immoral, there would exist no warrant in law for its suppression. Not only did the defendant exceed his lawful powers in suppressing the publications, but the methods he employed in censoring the books were arbitrary and unreasonable. This is not to impugn the defendant's sincerity of purpose or his praise-worthy ambition to suppress lewd and indecent literature. But a Chief of Police, like all other public officials, must act within the scope of his express and implied powers under the law. So important is the principle it expresses that it never becomes trite to say 'Ours is a government of laws and not of men.' It is the duty of courts to protect the integrity of this principle. The judicial office has no higher function to serve than the restraint of official arbitrariness. Arbitrary power inspired by good motives, no less than that animated by evil intent, is an attack upon the supremacy of the law. It is of the utmost importance to prevent the distribution of all forms of lewd and indecent literature with its demoralizing effect upon the young. It is vital in the interest of public morality that the laws against obscenity be vigorously enforced. But if a free society is to endure, its primary obligation is to protect its 'government of laws' from all intrusions of arbitrary power.'' *New American Library of World Literature, Inc. v. Allen*, 114 F. Supp. 823 (1953).

NEW HAMPSHIRE, LICENSE PLATES. Since 1969, the state of New Hampshire has required that non-commercial vehicles bear license plates embossed with the state motto. Many other states also have a motto or some descriptive phrase (''Land of Lincoln'' in Illinois, for example) on their automobile license plates. In New Hampshire, the motto is ''Live Free or Die.'' (New Hampshire Rev. Stat Ann. § 263:1, Supp. 1975). Another New Hampshire statute (New Hampshire Rev. Stat. Ann. § 262:27-c, Supp. 1975) makes it a misdemeanor ''knowingly [to obscure] . . . the figures or letters on any numbr plate''; the term ''letters'' in this section has been interpreted by New Hampshire's supreme court to include the state motto. Most people didn't give this a second thought until a Jehovah's Witness refused to ride around in public with the motto displayed on his car; he claimed that it was an affront to his religious beliefs. The Supreme Court, in *Wooley v. Maynard* (1977),* ruled that persons need not have to display a governmental message on their property if they were offended by it, for this was a form of censorship, not as an example of the state preventing someone from saying or writing what that person believes to be true, but as an example of the state forcing a person to advocate something that the person believes to be false.

NEW HAMPSHIRE, LICENSING OF PARADES. New Hampshire, Public Laws, Chapter 145, § 2, reads: ''No theatrical or dramatic representation shall be performed or exhibited, and no parade or procession upon any public street or way, and no open-air public meeting upon any ground abutting thereon, shall be permitted, unless a special license therefor shall first be obtained from the selectmen of the town, or from a licensing committee for cities hereinafter provided for.'' The provisions (§§ 3, 4, and 5) are as follows: ''Licensing Board. Any city may create a licensing board to consist of the person who is the active head of the police department, the mayor of such city and one other person who shall be appointed by the city government, which board shall have delegated powers to investigate and decide the question of granting licenses under this chapter, and it may grant revocable blanket licenses to fraternal and other like organizations, to theatres and to undertakers. Licenses: Fees. Every such special license shall be in writing, and shall specify the day and hour of the permit to perform or exhibit or of such parade, procession or open-air public meeting. Every licensee shall pay in advance for such license, for the use of the city or town, a sum not more than three hundred dollars for each day such licensee shall perform or exhibit, or such parade, procession or open-air public meeting shall take place; but the fee for a license to exhibit in any hall shall not exceed fifty dollars. Penalty. If any person shall violate the provisions of the preceding sections he shall be fined not more than five hundred dollars; and it shall be the duty of the selectmen to prosecute for every violation of this chapter.'' Although an obvious prior restraint, the Supreme Court, in *Cox v. New Hampshire* (1941),* ruled that this requirement of a parade license was a valid time-place-manner* restriction.

NEW HAMPSHIRE, OFFENSIVE CONDUCT. New Hampshire Public Laws, Chapter 378, § 2, reads as follows: ''No person shall address any offensive, derisive or annoying word to any other person who is lawfully in any street or other public place, nor call him by any offensive or derisive name, nor make any noise or exclamation in his presence and hearing with intent to deride, offend or annoy him, or to prevent him from pursuing his lawful business or occupation.'' This statute formed the backdrop to the landmark decision of *Chaplinsky v. New Hampshire* (1942),* in which the Supreme Court enunciated the doctrine of ''fighting words''*—words which, when addressed to any individual are likely to lead to an immediate breach of the peace. Chaplinsky called some municipal officers ''god damn Fascists,'' and the Court upheld his conviction under the New Hampshire statute.

NEW HAMPSHIRE, SUBVERSIVE ACTIVITIES. Originally passed in 1951, the New Hampshire Subversive Activities Act was a comprehensive scheme of regulation of alleged subversive activities. There was a section defining criminal conduct in the nature of sedition. ''Subversive organizations'' were declared unlawful and ordered dissolved. ''Subversive persons'' were made ineligible for employment by the state government. Included in the disability were those employed as teachers or in other capacities by any public educational institution. A loyalty program was instituted to eliminate "subversive persons" among government personnel. All present employees, as well as candidates for elective office in the future, were required to make sworn statements that they were not "subversive persons."

The following definition (§ 1 of the Subversive Activities Act, New Hampshire Rev. Stat., 1955, c. 588, §§ 1–16) was used for subversive person: " 'Subversive person' means any person who commits, attempts to commit, or aids in the commission, or advocates, abets, advises or teaches, by any means any person to commit, attempt to commit, or aid in the commission of any act intended to overthrow, destroy or alter, or to assist in the overthrow, destruction or alteration of, the constitutional form of the government of the United States, or of the state of New Hampshire, or any political subdivision of either of them, by force, or violence; or who is a member of a subversive organization or a foreign subversive organization." This was at the height of the cold war and the McCarthy witch-hunts, and the Supreme Court, in *Uphaus v. Wyman*,* upheld the constitutionality of the above description of a "subversive person."

Based on the above statute, the New Hampshire legislature, in 1953, adopted a "Joint Resolution Relating to the Investigation of Subversive Activities" (New Hampshire Public Laws, 1953, Chapter 307). It was resolved "that the attorney general is hereby authorized and directed to make full and complete investigation with respect to violations of the Subversive Activities Act of 1951 and to determine whether subversive persons as defined in said act are presently located within this state. The attorney general is authorized to act upon his own motion and upon such information as in his judgment may be reasonable or reliable. . . . The attorney general is directed to proceed with criminal prosecutions under the subversive activities act whenever evidence presented to him in the course of the investigation indicates violations thereof."

This was construed by the New Hampshire courts to constitute the attorney general as a one-man investigation committee. The attorney general did indeed scour the state to see if subversive people were in New Hampshire, but with one such investigation (*Sweezy v. New Hampshire**), in 1957, the Supreme Court ruled that the plaintiff's constitutional rights were violated by the methods of the investigation.

NEW JERSEY, GROUP LIBEL. The following New Jersey statutes were declared to be an invalid prior restraint on the right of free speech by a New Jersey court, in *State v. Klapprott* (1941)*: "Any person who shall, in the presence of two or more persons, in any language, make or utter any speech, statement or declaration, which in any way incites, counsels, promotes, or advocates hatred, abuse, violence or hostility against any group or groups of persons residing or being in this state by reason of race, color, religion or manner of worship, shall be guilty of a misdemeanor." (R.S. 2:157B-5, N.J.S.A. 2:157B-

5.) "Any owner, lessee, manager, agent or other person who shall knowingly let or hire out, or permit the use of any building, structure, auditorium, hall or room, or any part thereof, whether licensed or not, to or for the use of any organization, association, society, order, club, group or meeting of three or more persons where it is proposed or intended to hold any meeting or assembly of three or more persons whereat provision or provisions of sections 2:157B-2 to 2:157B-5 of this titles are to be violated, shall be guilty of a misdemeanor; and any person or persons who shall knowingly hire any such building, structure, auditorium, hall, or room, or any part thereof, for the purpose of using or permitting the same to be used by others for the purpose of violating any provision or provisions of said sections . . . shall be guilty of a misdemeanor."

NEW ORLEANS (LA), CURSING POLICE. New Orleans Ordinance 823, M.C.S. § 49–7, read as follows: "It shall be unlawful and a breach of the peace for any person wantonly to curse or revile or to use obscene or opprobrious language toward or with reference to any member of the city police while in the actual performance of his duty." The Supreme Court, in *Lewis v. City of New Orleans* (1974),* held that this ordinance could not be used to convict someone who called a police officer a "mother fucker" because (1) the term "mother fucker" is not obscene and (2) even if "mother fucker" were opprobrious, such language is protected speech under the First Amendment.

NEW YORK, ADVERTISING CONTRACEPTIVES. Section 6811(8) of the New York Education Law made it a crime (1) for any person to sell or distribute any contraceptive of any kind to a minor under the age of sixteen years; (2) for anyone other than a licensed pharmacist to distribute contraceptives to persons sixteen or over; and (3) for anyone, including licensed pharmacists, to advertise or display contraceptives: "It shall be a class A misdemeanor for . . . any person to sell or distribute any instrument or article, or any recipe, drug or medicine for the prevention of conception to a minor under the age of sixteen years; the sale or distribution of such to a person other than a minor under the age of sixteen years is authorized only by a licensed pharmacist but the advertisement or display of said articles within or without the premises of such pharmacy, is hereby prohibited. . . . This article shall not be construed to affect or prevent . . . any physician . . . who is not the owner of a pharmacy, or registered store, or who is not in the employ of such owner, from supplying his patients with such drugs as the physician . . . deems proper in connection with his practice." This ban on the display and advertising of contraceptives was seen as an invalid restriction of the right of commercial speech by the Supreme Court in *Carey v. Population Services International* (1977).*

NEW YORK, ALCOHOLIC BEVERAGE CONTROL LAW. The following statute (§ 106, subd. 6-a, New York State Liquor Authority) was seen by the Supreme Court (*New York State Liquor Authority v. Dennis Bellanca* [1981]*) to be a valid restriction on what might be protected symbolic speech if performed in a different setting: "No retail licensee for on premises consumption shall suffer or permit any person to appear on licensed premises in such manner or attire as to expose to view any portion of the pubic area, anus, vulva, or genitals, or any simulation thereof, nor shall suffer or permit any female to appear on licensed premises in such manner or attire as to expose any portion of the breast below the top of the areola, or any simulation thereof." The Court reasoned that the Twenty-first Amendment (giving to the states the right to regulate the consumption of alcoholic beverages) took precedence over the First Amendment's protection of certain types of behavior.

NEW YORK, BREACH OF THE PEACE. Section 722 of the Penal Law of New York reads: "Any person who with intent to provoke a breach of the peace, or whereby a breach of the peace may be occasioned, commits any of the following acts shall be deemed to have committed the offense of disorderly conduct: 1. Uses offensive, disorderly, threatening, abusive or insulting language, conduct or behavior; 2. Acts in such a manner as to annoy, disturb, interfere with, obstruct, or be offensive to others; 3. Congregates with others on a public street and refuses to move on when ordered by the police." This statute was employed to convict someone who gave a speech on a street corner in Syracuse, New York, where some of the people hearing the speech did not like what they heard and threatened to haul the speaker off the platform; the Supreme Court affirmed the conviction in 1951 (*Feiner v. New York**).

NEW YORK CITY (NY), ADVERTISING ON VEHICLES. Section 124 of the Traffic Regulations of the City of New York provides: "No person shall operate, or cause to be operated, in or upon any street an advertising vehicle; provided that nothing herein contained shall prevent the putting of business notices upon business delivery vehicles, so long as such vehicles are engaged in the usual business or regular work of the owner and not used merely or mainly for advertising." In other words, a vehicle could carry an ad for its own business but not for any other type of business. This regulation was promulgated by the police commissioner pursuant to the power granted the police department under § 435 of the New York City charter, which provides as follows: "The police department and force shall have the power and it shall be their duty to . . . regulate, direct, control and restrict the movement of vehicular and pedestrian traffic for the facilitation of traffic and the convenience of the public as well as the proper protection of human life and health. . . . The Commissioner shall make such rules and regulations for the conduct of pedestrian and vehicular traffic in the use of the public streets, squares and avenues as he may deem necessary." Although an obvious restriction of the right of free speech based on the content of the message (a truck could carry a sign for its own moving business but not for, say, a commercial product), the Supreme Court ruled that such a regulation was a valid exercise of the police power to regulate the "health and safety" of the population (*Railway Express Agency v. New York* [1949]*).

NEW YORK CITY (NY), DISTRIBUTION OF COMMERCIAL MATERIAL. Section 318 of the Sanitary Code of New York City provided as follows: "Handbills, cards and circulars.—No person shall throw, cast or distribute, or cause to permit to be thrown, cast or distributed, any handbill, circular, card, booklet, placard or other advertising matter whatsoever in or upon any street or public place, or in a front yard or court yard, or in any stoop, or in the vestibule of any hall of any building, or in a letterbox therein; provided that nothing herein contained shall be deemed to prohibit or otherwise regulate the delivery of any such matter by the United States postal service, or prohibit the distribution of sample copies of newspapers regularly sold by the copy or by annual subscription. This section is not intended to prevent the lawful distribution of anything other than commercial and business advertising matter." This restriction on the distribution of advertisements and commercial matter was not seen by the Supreme Court (*Valentine v. Chrestensen**), in 1942, to be a violation of the First Amendment, for it was felt at that time, that commercial speech had less protection than non-commercial speech. In addition, the Court ruled that the addition of a public service message on a commercial handbill would not transform the handbill into a "non-commercial" circular free of the distribution restrictions.

NEW YORK CITY (NY), USE OF STREETS. Section 435-7.0 of Chapter 18 of the Administrative Code of the City of New York read as follows: "a. Public worship.—It shall be unlawful for any person to be concerned or instrumental in collecting or promoting any assemblage of persons for public worship or exhortation, or to ridicule or denounce any form of religious belief, service or reverence, or to preach or expound atheism or agnosticism, or under any pretense therefor, in any street. A clergyman or minister of any denomination, however, or any person responsible to or regularly associated with any church or incorporated missionary society, or any lay-preacher, or lay-reader may conduct religious services, or any authorized representative of a duly incorporated organization devoted to the advancement of the principles of atheism or agnosticism may preach or expound such cause, in any public place or places specified in a permit therefor which may be granted and issued by the police commissioner. This section shall not be construed to prevent any congregation of the Baptist denomination from assembling in a proper place for the purpose of performing the rites of baptism, according to the ceremonies of that church. b. Interference with street services.—It shall be unlawful for any person to disturb, molest or interrupt any clergyman, minister, missionary, lay-preacher or lay-reader, who shall be conducting religious services by authority of a permit, issued hereunder, or any minister or people who shall be performing the rite of baptism as permitted herein, nor shall any person commit any riot or disorder in any such assembly.

c. Violations.—Any person who shall violate any provision of this section, upon conviction thereof, shall be punished by a fine of not more than twenty-five dollars, or imprisonment for thirty days, or both.'' The requirement of having a permit issued by the police commissioner before using the streets for such purposes—and having the permit revoked at any time for any reason—led the Supreme Court to rule this regulation to be an invalid prior restraint (*Kunz v. New York* [1951]*).

NEW YORK, CIVIL RIGHTS LAW. The New York Civil Rights Law and, specifically, the right of privacy, was involved in the case of *Time, Inc. v. Hill* (1967),* in which *Life* magazine was charged with violating the privacy rights of someone (*Life* was alleged to have falsely reported that a new play portrayed the experience of a certain real-life family). *Life* contended that the application of the law was a violation of the constitutional protections of speech and press.

The text of the New York Civil Rights Law, §§ 50–51, is as follows: ''A person, firm or corporation that uses for advertising purposes, or for the purposes of trade, the name, portrait or picture of any living person without first obtaining the written consent of such person, or if a minor of his or her parent or guardian, is guilty of a misdemeanor. Any person whose name, portrait or picture is used within this state for advertising purposes or for the purposes of trade without the written consent first obtained as above provided may maintain an equitable action in the supreme court of this state against the person, firm or corporation so using his name, portrait or picture, to prevent and restrain the use thereof; and may also sue and recover damages for any injuries sustained by reason of such use and if the defendant shall have knowingly used such person's name, portrait or picture in such a manner as is forbidden or declared to be unlawful by the last section, the jury, in its discretion, may award exemplary damages.''

NEW YORK, CIVIL SERVICE LAW. The New York Civil Service Law, implemented by the New York Education Law* and the so-called New York Feinberg Law,* dealt with the eligibility of those people who could be public employees (including public school teachers and university professors) in the state of New York. These laws were upheld as being a valid exercise of a state's power to regulate public employment in 1952, in *Adler v. Board of Education,** but the Supreme Court, in 1967 (*Keyishian v. Board of Regents**), ruled that the regulations were vague, guilty of overbreadth,* and an unconstitutional restraint on First Amendment rights.

The relevant sections of the Civil Service Law provided: ''§ 105. Subversive activities; disqualification. 1. Ineligibility of persons advocating overthrow of government by force or unlawful means. No person shall be appointed to any office or position in the service of the state or of any civil division thereof, nor shall any person employed in any such office or position be continued in such employment, nor shall any person be employed in the public service as super-intendent, principal or teacher in a public school or academy or in a state college or any other state educational institution who: (a) by word of mouth or writing wilfully and deliberately advocates, advises or teaches the doctrine that the government of the United States or of any state or of any political subdivision thereof should be overthrown or overturned by force, violence or any unlawful means; or (b) prints, publishes, edits, issues or sells any book, paper, document or written or printed matter in any form containing or advocating the doctrine . . . or (c) organizes or helps to organize or becomes a member of any society or group of persons which teaches or advocates . . . [the doctrine]. For the purposes of this section, membership in the communist party of the United States of America or the communist party of the state of New York shall constitute prima facie evidence of disqualification for appointment to or retention in any office or position in the service of the state or of any city or civil division thereof. . . . 3. Removal for treasonable or seditious acts or utterances. A person in the civil service of the state or of any civil division thereof shall be removable therefrom for the utterance of any treasonable or seditious word or words or the doing of any treasonable or seditious act or acts while holding such position. . . . A seditious word or act shall mean 'criminal anarchy' as defined in the penal law'' [Penal Law, § 160: ''Criminal anarchy is the doctrine that organized government should be overthrown by force or violence, or by assassination of the head or of any of the executive officials of government, or by any unlawful means. The advocacy of such doctrine either by word of mouth or writing is a felony.''].

NEW YORK, CRIME STORIES. Subsection 2 of § 1141 of the New York Penal Law provided: ''A person . . . who . . . prints, utters, publishes, sells, lends, gives away, distributes or shows, or has in his possession with intent to sell, lend, give away, distribute or show, or otherwise offers for sale, loan, gift or distribution, any book, pamphlet, magazine, newspaper or other printed paper devoted to the publication, and principally made up of criminal news, police reports, or accounts of criminal deeds, or pictures, or stories of deeds of bloodshed, lust or crime . . . is guilty of a misdemeanor.'' This blatant form of censorship over a certain type of publication—crime stories—was ruled to be a violation of the First Amendment guarantee of free press by the Supreme Court in 1948, in *Winters v. New York.** The Court decision also noted that approximately twenty other states had similar legislation, some of the statutes dating back to the 1880s, which, by extension, were also ruled unconstitutional by the *Winters* decision.

NEW YORK, CRIMINAL ANARCHY. Originally enacted in 1902 (Laws of 1902, Ch. 371), this statute was employed to convict Benjamin Gitlow for advocating criminal anarchy (*Gitlow v. New York**) in 1925. At that time, it was codified as §§ 160–161, New York Penal Laws, 1909, Ch. 40: ''Criminal anarchy defined. Criminal anarchy is the doctrine that organized government should be overthrown by force or violence, or by assassination of the executive head or of any of the executive officials of government, or by any unlawful means. The advocacy of such doctrine either by word of mouth or writing is a felony. Advocacy of criminal anarchy. Any person who: 1. By word of mouth or writing advocates, advises or teaches the duty, necessity or propriety of overthrowing or overturning organized government by force or violence, or by assassination of the executive head or of any of the executive officials of government, or by any unlawful means; or, 2. Prints, publishes, edits, issues or knowingly circulates, sells, distributes or publicly displays any book, paper, document, or written or printed matter in any form, containing or advocating, advising or teaching the doctrine that organized government should be overthrown by force, violence or any unlawful means . . . is guilty of a felony and punishable by imprisonment or fine, or both.''

NEW YORK, EDUCATION LAW. The New York Education Law, implemented by the New York Civil Service Law* and the so-called New York Feinberg Law,* dealt with the eligibility of those people who could be public employees (including public school teachers and university professors) in the state of New York. The laws were upheld in 1952 as a valid exercise of a state's power to regulate public employment (*Adler v. Board of Education**), but in 1967, the Supreme Court ruled in *Keyishian v. Board of Regents** that the regulations were too vague, guilty of overbreadth,* and an unconstitutional restraint on First Amendment rights. The relevant section of the Education Law (§ 3021. Removal of Superintendents, Teachers and Employees for Treasonable or Seditious Acts or Utterances) provided: ''A person employed as superintendent of schools, teacher or employee in the public schools, in any city or school district of the state, shall be removed from such position for the utterance of any treasonable or seditious word or words or the doing of any treasonable or seditious act or acts while holding such position.''

NEW YORKER STAATS-ZEITUNG v. NOLAN (1918). During the anti-German hysteria generated by World War I, Nolan, the mayor of North Bergen, New Jersey, along with the town council, passed a resolution that forbade the circulation and distribution in the town of the *New Yorker Staats-Zeitung*, a newspaper printed in the German language. Town officials claimed that such a resolution was valid because some citizens might have resorted to violence over resentment in seeing a German-language newspaper in the streets, and in addition, the regulation was a valid war measure.

   The newspaper then brought suit in a New Jersey court, requesting the court to prevent the town from enforcing the regulation. The court, Judge Lane delivering the opinion, granted the injunction. Judge Lane: ''The respondents insist that the municipality had power to pass the resolution because of what is called its 'police power.' It is said that the circulation of the newspapers in the German language may lead to riot in the township, and for that reason the township may, to prevent riot, forbid their circulation. I think to state the proposition is almost to demonstrate its absurdity. If the township may prevent the circulation of a newspaper for no reason other than that some of its inhabitants may violently disagree with it, and resent its circulation by resorting to physical violence, there is no limit to what may be prohibited. The residence in the township of a person obnoxious to the vast majority of its inhabitants may be prevented. The carrying on of a perfectly legitimate business may be prevented because, to stop it, inhabitants objecting to it, may resort to violence. . . .

There can be no justification for the passage of the resolution as a war measure. That is a matter to be dealt with by the national authorities, and not by the local authorities. In the instant case, the national authorities have granted a permit to complainant to publish its newspapers in the German language. The government might have, under recent legislation, suppressed the publication entirely. It might have granted a permit which would require the submission of the articles to be published to censorship. It might have, as it did, granted a permit to publish whatever the publishers thought proper without censorship. The papers published carry at their head the words: 'Published and distributed under Permit No. 7, authorized by the Act of October 6th, 1917, on file at the Post Office, New York, New York, by order of the President. A. S. Burleson, Postmaster General.' The government sends to the newspaper copy to be published. The government undoubtedly desires to reach a very large number of individuals of German extraction, who cannot understand English, through the medium of these newspapers so that they may be advised as to the purpose of this country in the present war and so that they may be acquainted with the situation as it develops from day to day. There can be no question, in my mind, but that this is a wise thing to do. It is the only method of approach that can be at all efficacious. There are thousands of Germans in this country, many of them in North Bergen, who cannot understand English. Anything which will prevent the development of a national menace is justifiable. There is nothing more dangerous than a person left in ignorance of current events. We are confronted with a fact, not a theory. You cannot communicate with a person in a language he cannot understand. The resolution, in question, as appears from its context, was adopted at the request of the National Security League. That League seems to have taken direct issue with the administration as to the advisability of the circulation of any newspapers in the German language.

I am quite convinced that the reason actuating the passage of this resolution was not any real fear on the part of the municipal officers that there would be any disorder, but simply the request of the League, and a desire to go as far as they could in order to demonstrate their patriotism. My view is that the resolution, far from being in line with the war purposes of the government, is directly opposed to them.'' *New Yorker Staats-Zeitung v. Nolan*, 105 A. 72 (1918).

NEW YORK, EXPOSING MINORS TO HARMFUL MATERIALS. New York Penal Law, § 484-h, as enacted by L. 1965. c. 327, Exposing Minors to Harmful Materials, provides: ''1. Definitions. As used in this section: (a) 'Minor'

means any person under the age of seventeen years. (b) 'Nudity' means the showing of the human male or female genitals, pubic area or buttocks with less than a full opaque covering, or the showing of the female breast with less than a fully opaque covering of any portion thereof below the top of the nipple, or the depiction of covered male genitals in a discernibly turgid state. (c) 'Sexual conduct' means acts of masturbation, homosexuality, sexual intercourse, or physical contact with a person's clothed or unclothed genitals, pubic area, buttocks, or, if such person be a female, breast. (d) 'Sexual excitement' means the condition of human male or female genitals when in a state of sexual stimulation or arousal. (e) 'Sado-masochistic abuse' means flagellation or torture by or upon a person clad in undergarments, a mask or bizarre costume, or the condition of being fettered, bound or otherwise physically restrained on the part of one so clothed. (f) 'Harmful to minors' means that quality of any description or representation, in whatever form, of nudity, sexual conduct, sexual excitement, or sado-masochistic abuse, when it: (i) predominantly appeals to the prurient, shameful or morbid interest of minors, and (ii) is patently offensive to prevailing standards in the adult community as a whole with respect to what is suitable material for minors, and (iii) is utterly without redeeming social importance for minors. (g) 'Knowingly' means having general knowledge of, or reason to know, or a belief or ground for belief which warrants further inspection of inquiry or both: (i) the character and content of any material described herein which is reasonably susceptible of examination by the defendant, and (ii) the age of the minor, provided however, that an honest mistake shall constitute an excuse from liability hereunder if the defendant made a reasonable bona fide attempt to ascertain the true age of such minor. 2. It shall be unlawful for any person knowingly to sell or loan for monetary consideration to a minor: (a) any picture, photograph, drawing, sculpture, motion picture film, or similar visual representation or image of a person or portion of the human body which depicts nudity, sexual conduct or sado-masochistic abuse and which is harmful to minors, or (b) any book, picture, magazine, printed matter however reproduced, or sound recording which contains any matter enumerated in paragraph (a) of subdivision two hereof, or explicit and detailed verbal descriptions or narrative accounts of sexual excitement, sexual conduct or sado-masochistic abuse and which, taken as a whole, is harmful to minors. 3. It shall be unlawful for any person knowingly to exhibit for a monetary consideration to a minor or knowingly to sell to a minor an admission ticket or pass or knowingly to admit a minor for a monetary consideration to premises whereon there is exhibited, a motion picture, show or other presentation which, in whole or in part, depicts nudity, sexual conduct or sado-masochistic abuse and which is harmful to minors. 4. A violation of any provision hereof shall constitute a misdemeanor." A New York City luncheonette operator was convicted under this statute of selling a "girlie" magazine to a minor (*Ginsberg v. New York* [1968]*).

NEW YORK, FEINBERG LAW. The New York Feinberg Law, implemented by the New York Education Law* and the New York Civil Service Law,* dealt with the eligibility of those people who could be public employees (including public school teachers and university professors) in the state of New York. These laws were upheld in 1952 (*Adler v. Board of Education**) as a valid exercise of a state's power to regulate public employment, but in 1967, the Supreme Court (*Keyishian v. Board of Regents**) ruled that the regulations were too vague, guilty of overbreadth,* and an unconstitutional restraint on First Amendment rights. The relevant section (§ 3022 of the Education Law, Elimination of Subversive Persons from the Public School System) provided: "The Board of Regents shall adopt, promulgate, and enforce rules and regulations for the disqualification or removal of superintendents of schools, teachers or employees in the public schools in any city or school district of the state and the faculty members and all other personnel and employees of any college or other institution of higher education owned and operated by the state or any subdivision thereof who . . . [are subversive, evidenced by advocacy of the overthrow of the government by force]."

NEW YORK, FLAG DISRESPECT. New York Penal Law, § 1425, subd. 16, par. d, made it a misdemeanor to "publicly mutilate, deface, defile, or defy, trample upon, or cast contempt upon either by words or act [any flag of the United States]." When someone was convicted of violating this statute by burning a flag in public while saying, "We don't need no god-damn flag," in a protest against the shooting of James Meredith, the Supreme Court (*Street v. New York* [1969]*) ruled that the application of the New York flag disrespect statute was unconstitutional because it was impossible to determine whether Street was convicted for burning the flag (conduct that may in certain circumstances be prohibited) or for casting "contempt" on the flag by saying certain things (speech that is protected by the First Amendment).

NEW YORK, MINORS AND SEXUAL PERFORMANCES. Article 263 of the New York Penal Law, §263.05, criminalizes as a Class C felony the use of a child in a sexual performance: "A person is guilty of the use of a child in a sexual performance if knowing the character and content thereof he employs, authorizes or induces a child less than sixteen years of age to engage in a sexual performance or being a parent, legal guardian or custodian of such child, he consents to the participation by such child in a sexual performance." A "sexual performance" is defined as "any performance or part thereof which includes sexual conduct by a child less than sixteen years of age" (§ 263.1). "Sexual conduct" is in turn defined in § 263.3: " 'Sexual conduct' means actual or simulated sexual intercourse, deviate sexual intercourse, sexual bestiality, masturbation, sado-masochistic abuse, or lewd exhibition of the genitals." A performance is defined as "any play, motion picture, photograph or dance or any other visual presentation exhibited before an audience" (§ 263.4). Section 263.15, defining a Class D felony, reads: "A person is guilty of promoting a sexual performance by a child when, knowing the character and content thereof, he produces, directs or promotes any performance which includes sexual conduct by a child less than sixteen years of age.'' The word ''promote'' is defined: '' 'Promote' means to procure, manufacture, issue, sell, give, provide, lend, mail, deliver, transfer, transmute, publish, distribute, circulate, disseminate, present, exhibit or advertise, or to offer or agree to do the same.''

This anti-child pornography statute was upheld by the Supreme Court in *New York v. Ferber* (1982),* when the Court affirmed a conviction against Ferber for showing a movie depicting two young boys masturbating. The film itself was not seen as obscene for adults, but the Court made the distinction between what was obscene if children were the participants compared with if adults were the leading actors.

NEW YORK, MOTION PICTURE CENSORSHIP. The New York Education Law (McKinney's N.Y. Laws, 1953, §§ 122, 122-a, 129) made it unlawful ''to exhibit or to sell, lease or lend for exhibition at any place of amusement for pay or in connection with any business in the State of New York, any motion picture film or reel . . . unless there is at the time in full force and effect a valid license or permit therefor of the education department.'' The law provided that a license shall be issued ''unless such film or a part thereof is obscene, indecent, immoral, inhuman, sacrilegious, or is of such character that its exhibition would tend to corrupt morals or incite to crime.''

The term ''immoral'' and the phrase ''of such a character that its exhibition would tend to corrupt morals'' denoted a motion picture film or part thereof, ''the dominant purpose or effect of which is erotic or pornographic; or which portrays acts of sexual immorality, perversion, or lewdness, or which expressly or impliedly presents such acts as desirable, acceptable or proper patterns of behavior.'' This motion picture censorship scheme (Film Censorship*) was part and parcel of the censorship of the motion picture industry until the Supreme Court ruled that films were a form of expression protected by the First Amendment (*The Miracle** case), and the courts slowly whittled away at the ground on which the state of New York could censor motion pictures (*Lady Chatterley's Lover*,* for example, was banned because it presented adultery in a favorable light, and *The Miracle* was banned because it was thought to be ''sacrilegious'').

NEW YORK, OBSCENITY STATUTE. Section 1141 of the New York Penal Law provides: ''A person who . . . has in his possession with intent to sell, lend, distribute . . . any obscene, lewd, lascivious, filthy, indecent, sadistic, masochistic or disgusting book . . . or who prints, utters, publishes, or in any manner manufactures, or prepares any such book . . . or who . . . in any manner, hires, employs, uses or permits any person to do or assist in doing any act or thing mentioned in this section, or any of them, is guilty of a misdemeanor. . . . The possession by any person of six or more identical or similar articles coming within the provisions of subdivision one of this section is presumptive evidence of a violation of this section. The publication for sale of any book, magazine or pamphlet designed, composed or illustrated as a whole to appeal to and commercially exploit prurient interest by combining covers, pictures, drawings, illustrations, caricatures, cartoons, words, stories and advertisements or any combination or combinations thereof devoted to the description, portrayal or deliberate suggestion of illicit sex, including adultery, prostitution, fornication, sexual crime and sexual perversion or to the exploitation of sex and nudity by the presentation of nude or partially nude female figures, posed, photographed or otherwise presented in a manner calculated to provoke or incite prurient interest, or any combination or combinations thereof, shall be a violation of this section.''

Section 235.05 of the Penal Law (Supp. 1973–1974) considers any material or performance to be obscene if ''(a) considered as a whole, its predominant appeal is to prurient, shameful or morbid interest in nudity, sex, excretion, sadism or masochism, and (b) it goes substantially beyond customary limits of candor in describing or representing such matters, and (c) it is utterly without redeeming social value. Predominant appeal shall be judged with reference to ordinary adults unless it appears from the character of the material or the circumstances of its dissemination to be designed for children or other specifically susceptible audience.''

NEW YORK, PUBLIC SERVICE COMMISSION, ADVERTISING REGULATION. In December 1973, the New York Public Service Commission ordered all electric utilities in New York State to cease all advertising that ''promot[ed] the use of electricity.'' The order was based on the commission's finding that ''the interconnected utility system in New York State does not have sufficient fuel stocks or sources of supply to continue furnishing all customer demands for the 1973–1974 winter.'' Three years later, in 1976, when the fuel shortage had eased, the commission requested comments from the public on its proposal to continue the ban on promotional advertising. After reviewing the public comments, the commission extended the prohibition in a policy statement issued on February 25, 1977. The policy statement divided advertising expenses ''into two broad categories: promotional—advertising intended to stimulate the purchase of utility services—and institutional and informational, a broad category inclusive of all advertising not clearly intended to promote sales.'' The commission declared all promotional advertising contrary to the national policy of conserving energy. This ban on promotional commercial advertising was seen to be a violation of the First Amendment's guarantee of free speech and free press by the Supreme Court in *Central Hudson Gas and Electric Corporation v. Public Service Commission of New York* (1980).*

NEW YORK, PUBLIC SERVICE COMMISSION, INSERT BAN. The ban on inserts to public utilities bills was considered by the Supreme Court in *Consolidated Edison Company v. Public Service Commission of New York* (1980),* and the Court ruled that a corporation had a First Amendment right to include such inserts with their bills. In January 1976, the Consolidated Edison Company of New York placed written material entitled "Independence Is Still a Goal, and Nuclear Power Is Needed To Win the Battle" in its billing envelopes sent to its customers. The insert stated Consolidated Edison's views on "the benefits of nuclear power," saying that they "far outweigh any potential risk" and that nuclear power plants are safe, economical, and clean. The utility also contended that increased use of nuclear energy would further U.S. independence from foreign energy sources. In March 1976, the National Resources Defense Council, Inc. (NRDC), requested Consolidated Edison to enclose a rebuttal prepared by NRDC in the next month's billing envelopes. When Consolidated Edison refused, NRDC asked the Public Service Commission of the state of New York to open Consolidated Edison's billing envelopes to contrasting views on controversial issues of public importance. On February 17, 1977, the commission denied NRDC's request but prohibited "utilities from using bill inserts to discuss political matters, including the desirability of future development of nuclear power." The commission explained its decision in a Statement of Policy on Advertising and Promotional Practices of Public Utilities, issued on February 25, 1977. The commission concluded that Consolidated Edison customers who receive bills containing inserts are a captive audience of diverse views who should not be subjected to the utility's beliefs. Accordingly, the commission barred utility companies from including bill inserts that express "their opinions or viewpoints on controversial issues of public policy." The commission did not, however, bar utilities from sending bill inserts discussing topics that are not "controversial issues of public policy."

NEW YORK, SALE OF OBSCENE MATERIAL TO MINORS. Section 484 of the New York Penal Law prohibited the dissemination to minors (under eighteen years old) of materials seen to be "obscene" for minors but not obscene for adults. Section 484-i divided the material into three subdivisions: (1) photographs, drawings and motion pictures depicting specified parts of the body or acts; (2) a combination of such photographs, drawings or motion pictures "depicted or shown in such a posture or way that the viewer's attention or concentration is primarily focused on . . . described parts of the body," and (3) books, magazines, phonograph records or similar sound reproductions containing "details, descriptions or narrative accounts of specified sex acts." The definition of "obscenity" was virtually the same for each subdivision; to be "obscene," the material must be "posed or presented in such a manner as to exploit lust for commercial gain and . . . which would appeal to the lust of persons under the age of eighteen years or to their curiosity as to sex or to the anatomical differences between the sexes." It was this last phrase—"curiosity as to sex or to the anatomical differences between the sexes"—that led the courts to rule the statute to be unconstitutional (*Candid,* Rabeck v. New York,* People v. Bookcase, Inc.**): In addition to outlawing "girlie" magazines, the statute would also prohibit, for example, constitutionally protected sex education material, and thus the statute was overbroad (Overbreadth*).

NEW YORK, SEIZURE OF OBSCENE MATERIAL. Section 22-a of the New York Code of Criminal Procedure (L. 1941, c. 925), as amended in 1954 (L. 1954, c. 702), authorizes the chief executive or legal officer of a municipality to invoke a limited injunctive remedy, under closely defined procedural safeguards, against the sale and distribution of written and printed matter found after a trial to be obscene, and to obtain an order for the seizure of the condemned publications. The Supreme Court, in *Kingsley Books v. Brown* ("Nights of Horror"*) upheld the constitutionality of the statute, for it was determined that it was not a prior restraint*; seizure of the materials could take place only after a judicial determination of the material's obscenity.

NEW YORK STATE LIQUOR AUTHORITY v. DENNIS BELLANCA (1981). The owners of several nightclubs, bars, restaurants, and watering places who had been offering their customers topless dancing as a form of entertainment, challenged a New York statute (New York, Alcoholic Beverage Control Law*) that prohibited nude dancing in establishments licensed by the state to sell liquor. The New York Supreme Court ruled that the statute was unconstitutional. The Court of Appeals of New York affirmed the decision, holding that topless dancing was a form of protected expression under the First Amendment, and that the state of New York had not demonstrated an overriding need for prohibiting the bars from presenting non-obscene topless dancing to willing and consenting customers.

On appeal, the U.S. Supreme Court reversed the New York decisions, holding that the statute did not violate the First Amendment. The statute was within the state's power under the Twenty-first Amendment, which, in this case, took precedence over the First Amendment, and any "expressive or communicative value" of topless dancing was "overcome" by the state's power to regulate the circumstances under which alcoholic beverages were sold. This was a per curiam decision, and the following remarks represent the views of Chief Justice Burger and Justices Stewart, White, Blackmun, Powell, and Rehnquist: "It is . . . well established that a State has broad power under the Twenty-first Amendment to regulate the times, places, and circumstances under which liquor may be sold. In *California v. LaRue*,* we upheld the facial constitutionality of a statute prohibiting acts of 'gross sexuality,' including the display of the genitals and live or filmed performances of sexual acts, in establishments licensed by the State to serve liquor. Although we recognized that not all of the prohibited acts would be found obscene and were therefore entitled to some measure of First Amendment protection, we reasoned that the statute was within the State's broad power under the Twenty-first Amendment to regulate the sale of liquor. . . . Those findings exist in this case. The purposes of the statute have been set forth in an accompanying legislative memorandum, New York State Legislative Annual 150 (1977): 'Nudity is the kind of conduct that is a proper subject for legislative action as well as regulation by the State Liquor Authority as a phase of liquor licensing. It has long been held that sexual acts and performances may constitute disorderly behavior within the meaning of the Alcoholic Beverage Control Law. Common sense indicates that any form of nudity coupled with alcohol in a public place begets undesirable behavior. This legislation prohibiting nudity in public will once and for all, outlaw conduct which is now quite out of hand.' In short, the elected representatives of the State of New York have chosen to avoid the disturbances associated with mixing alcohol and nude dancing by means of a reasonable restriction upon establishments which sell liquor for on-premises consumption. Given the 'added presumption in favor of the validity of the state regulation' . . . we cannot agree with the New York Court of Appeals that the statute violates the United States Constitution. Whatever artistic or communicative value may attach to topless dancing is overcome by the State's exercise of its broad powers under the Twenty-first Amendment. Although some may quarrel with the wisdom of such legislation and may consider topless dancing a harmless diversion, the Twenty-first Amendment makes that a policy for the state legislature, not the courts.''

Justice Stevens dissented, arguing that the Twenty-first Amendment does not take precedence over the First Amendment, and that non-obscene topless dancing is a form of symbolic speech that should be protected, regardless of the presence of alcoholic beverages. *New York State Liquor Authority v. Dennis Bellanca*, 452 U.S. 714 (1981).

NEW YORK TIMES **COMPANY v. SULLIVAN (1964).** L. B. Sullivan, one of the three elected commissioners of the city of Montgomery, Alabama, testified that he was commissioner of public affairs, supervising the Police Department, Fire Department, Cemetery Department, and Department of Scales. On March 29, 1960, the *New York Times* carried a paid, full-page advertisement dealing with the city of Montgomery's official behavior actions regarding civil rights. The ad was paid for by a group of Alabama clergymen, all of whom were black. The advertisement included statements, some of which were eventually proven to be false, about police action directed against students who participated in a civil rights movement. Sullivan then brought suit in an Alabama court against the *New York Times*, claiming that the statements in the ad referred to him because he was in charge of the Police Department and that the statements libeled him. The black clergymen were also named in the libel suit. A jury in the Circuit Court of Montgomery County awarded Sullivan $500,000—the full amount claimed as damages—and the Supreme Court of Alabama affirmed the decision; the Supreme Court reversed.

This case saw the creation of the *New York Times* Rule*: The constitutional guarantees of a free press and free speech require a public official* such as Sullivan who sues for defamation to prove malice on the part of the defendant. Malice in this context is the publishing of the material knowing it to be false or with a reckless disregard of whether it is true or false. Justice Brennan delivered the opinion in this landmark case: ''The second contention is that the constitutional guarantees of freedom of speech and of the press are inapplicable here, at least so far as the *Times* is concerned, because the allegedly libelous statements were published as part of a paid 'commercial' advertisement. . . . The publication here was not a 'commercial' advertisement in the sense in which the word was used in *Valentine v. Chrestensen.** It communicated information, expressed opinion, recited grievances, protested claimed abuses, and sought financial support on behalf of a movement whose existence and objectives are matters of the highest public interest and concern [the National Association for the Advancement of Colored People]. That the *Times* was paid for publishing the advertisement is as immaterial in this connection as is the fact that newspapers and books are sold. Any other conclusion would discourage newspapers from carrying 'editorial advertisements' of this type, and so might shut off an important outlet for the promulgation of information and ideas by persons who do not themselves have access to publishing facilities—who wish to exercise their freedom of speech even though they are not members of the press. The effect would be to shackle the First Amendment in its attempt to secure 'the widest possible dissemination of information from diverse and antagonistic sources.' To avoid placing such a handicap upon the freedoms of expression, we hold that if the allegedly libelous statements would otherwise be constitutionally protected from the present judgment, they do not forfeit that protection because they were published in the form of a paid advertisement.''

Justice Brennan continued and said that the evidence did not support the finding that the statements were made with actual malice, even though they might have been false or contained defamatory content, and concluded with what has been known as the *New York Times* Rule:* ''The constitutional guarantees require, we think, a federal rule that prohibits a public official from recovering damages for a defamatory falsehood relating to his official conduct unless he proves that the statement was made with 'actual malice'—that is, with knowledge that it was false or with reckless disregard of whether it was false or not.'' *New York Times Company v. Sullivan*, 376 U.S. 254 (1964).

NEW YORK TIMES **RULE.** This rule, stated in *New York Times Company v. Sullivan*,* held that the constitutional guarantees of a free press and free speech require a public official* who sues for defamation to prove malice on the part of the defendant. Malice in this context is the publishing of the material knowing it to be false or with a reckless disregard of whether it is true or false. The law with respect to defamation of public officials and public figures* was much simpler before the 1964 decision—libelous utterances were not protected by the First Amendment. In several decisions subsequent to 1964, the Supreme Court has interpreted, extended, and clarified the rule that the freedoms of speech and of the press prevent public officials or public figures from receiving damages unless actual malice is proven. The rationale for the Court's position started from the initial premise of the profound national commitment to the principle that debate on public issues should be uninhibited, robust, and wide open. Because the threat of defamation suits possesses a great potential for intrusion into the zone of protected public speech, the Court declared that the traditional principles of defamation law were incompatible with the First Amendment. The *New York Times* Rule maximizes public debate through minimizing the incentives for self-censorship presented by the threat of defamation suits. Annotation: *New York Times Rule*, 61 L. Ed. 2d 975.

NEW YORK v. FERBER (1982). A New York statute (New York, Minors and Sexual Performances*) prohibits anyone from promoting a sexual perform- ance by a child under the age of sixteen or from distributing or exhibiting material that depicts such a performance. The statute does not make a distinction between obscene performances and non-obscene performances. The statute defines "sex- ual performance" as any performance that includes "sexual conduct" by a child, and "sexual conduct" is defined as "actual or simulated sexual intercourse, deviate sexual intercourse, sexual bestiality, masturbation, sado-masochistic abuse, or lewd exhibition of the genitals."

The proprietor of a Manhattan bookstore, one Ferber, was convicted under this statute in the Supreme Court, New York County, of "promoting a sexual performance of a child under 16 years old"—Ferber sold films that depicted young boys (under sixteen) masturbating. The Appellate Division of the New York Supreme Court affirmed Ferber's conviction, but the New York Court of Appeals reversed, holding the statute to be a violation of the First Amendment because of overbreadth*: Because the statute did not make a distinction between obscene and non-obscene sexual conduct (*all* such conduct was prohibited), the statute swept into its ambit activity that is protected by the First Amendment.

The U.S. Supreme Court reversed this decision, holding that the statute did not violate the First Amendment. There were several different opinions filed in this case, although the thread of general agreement was that states could prohibit certain types of activity involving children notwithstanding the fact that the activity in question is not seen as obscene under any of the tests or standards for obscenity. Justice White delivered the opinion of the Court, joined by Chief Justice Burger and Justices Powell, Rehnquist, and O'Connor: The states are entitled to greater leeway in the regulation of pornographic depictions of children for the following reasons: (1) The legislative judgment that the use of children as subjects of pornographic materials is harmful to the physiological, emotional, and mental health of the child, easily passes muster under the First Amendment. (2) The Miller Standard* for determining what is legally obscene is not a sat- isfactory solution to the child pornography problem. (3) The advertising and selling of child pornography provides an economic motive for and thus is an integral part of the production of such materials, an activity that is illegal through- out the United States. (4) The value of permitting live performances and pho- tographic reproductions of children engaged in lewd exhibitions is modest at best. (5) The determination that child pornography is a category of material outside the protection of the First Amendment is not in conflict with any previous decision of the Supreme Court. *New York v. Ferber*, 73 L. Ed. 2d 1113 (1982).

NICHOLS v. MASSACHUSETTS (1939). Nichols and others were distributing leaflets to passersby in a street in Worcester, Massachusetts. The leaflets contained an announcement about a meeting to be held protesting the administration of the state unemployment insurance system. Although some of the recipients of the leaflets tossed them on the ground, with the result that the sidewalk was littered, Nichols and his group did not scatter any of the leaflets about. Nichols was duly arrested and charged with a Worcester city ordinance: "No person shall distribute in, or place upon any street or way, any placard, handbill, flyer, poster, advertisement or paper of any description." The Superior Court of Worcester County convicted Nichols, and the Supreme Judicial Court of Massachusetts affirmed: "[The ordinance] . . . interferes in no way with the publication of anything in the city of Worcester, except only that it excludes the public streets and ways from the places available for free distribution. It leaves open for such distribution all other places in the city, public and private." The U.S. Supreme Court found this ordinance to be an invalid restriction on the First Amendment guarantees of freedom of speech and of the press; the reasoning is contained in the companion case of *Schneider v. State.* Nichols v. Massachusetts*, 308 U.S. 147 (1939).

NIEMOTKO v. MARYLAND (1951). Niemotko, a Jehovah's Witness, applied to a Maryland town's city council for a permit to use a city park for Bible talks. The permits were denied, according to the court records, for no apparent reason except the council's dislike for the Jehovah's Witnesses and disagreement with their views. Niemotko held his meeting anyhow and was then arrested—and convicted—for disorderly conduct, although no disorderly conduct had taken place.

The Supreme Court reversed the convictions. Chief Justice Vinson delivered the opinion of the Court: "The convictions cannot stand. At the time of the arrest of each of the appellants, there was no evidence of disorder, threats of violence or riot. There was no indication that the appellants conducted themselves in a manner which could be considered as detrimental to the public peace or order. On the contrary, there was positive testimony by the police that each of the appellants had conducted himself in a manner beyond reproach. It is quite apparent that any disorderly conduct which the jury found must have been based on the fact that appellants were using the park without a permit, although there is no statute or ordinance prohibiting or regulating the use of the park without a permit. . . . Rarely has any case been before this Court which shows so clearly an unwarranted discrimination in a refusal to issue such a license. It is true that the City Council held a hearing at which it considered the application. But we have searched the record in vain to discover any valid basis for the refusal. In fact, the Mayor testified that the permit would probably have been granted if, at the hearing, the applicants had not started to 'berate' the Park Commissioner for his refusal to issue the permit. The only questions asked of the Witnesses at the hearing pertained to their alleged refusal to salute the flag, their views of the Bible, and other issues irrelevant to unencumbered use of the public parks. The conclusion is unescapable that the use of the park was denied because of the City Council's dislike for or disagreement with the Witnesses or their views. The right to equal protection of the laws, in the exercise of those freedoms of speech and religion protected by the First and Fourteenth Amendments, has a firmer foundation than the whims or personal opinions of a local governing body.''

Justice Frankfurter filed a concurring opinion, an opinion that briefly reviews some of the reasons (absent in this case) a state can rely on to regulate the freedom of speech. Justice Frankfurter: ''(1) What is the interest deemed to require the regulation of speech? The State cannot of course forbid public proselyting or religious argument merely because public officials disapprove the speaker's views. It must act in patent good faith to maintain the public peace, to assure the availability of the streets for their primary purposes of passenger and vehicular traffic, or for equally indispensable ends of modern community life. (2) What is the method used to achieve such ends as a consequence of which public speech is constrained or barred? A licensing standard which gives an official authority to censor the content of a speech differs *toto coelo* from one limited by its terms, or by nondiscriminatory practice, to considerations of public safety and the like. Again, a sanction applied after the event assures consideration of the particular circumstances of a situation. The net of control must not be cast too broadly. (3) What mode of speech is regulated? A sound truck may be found to affect the public peace as normal speech does not. A man who is calling names or using the kind of language which would reasonably stir another to violence does not have the same claim to protection as one whose speech is an appeal to reason. (4) Where does the speaking which is regulated take place? Not only the general classification—streets, parks, private buildings—are relevant. The location and size of a park; its customary use for the recreational, esthetic and contemplative needs of a community; the facilities, other than a park or street corner, readily available in a community for airing views, all are pertinent considerations in assessing the limitations the Fourteenth Amendment puts on State power in a particular situation." *Niemotko v. Maryland*, 340 U.S. 268 (1951).

"NIGHTS OF HORROR." A New York statute (New York, Seizure of Obscene Material*) permits, after a judicial determination of a matter's obscenity, enjoining further distribution of the material and allows the ordering of the material's destruction. The statute was employed against a series of books ("Nights of Horror"). The Supreme Court ruled that the statute was not a prior restraint and that the provision in the statute allowing for the seizure and destruction of already determined obscene material is a legal remedy long sanctioned in the Anglo-American tradition of jurisprudence.

There were really two separate court cases here: The first (*Burke v. Kingsley Books, Inc.*, 142 N.Y.S. 2d 735 [1955]) determined that the "Nights of Horror" books were obscene under the statute (New York, Obscenity Statute*) and issued the search and destroy order; the second (*Kingsley Books v. Brown*, 354 U.S. 436 [1957]) was the Supreme Court decision upholding the order to destroy the books. Judge Levy of the New York court described the "Nights of Horror" in the following terms: "In determining what is obscene in any particular case, 'the law will not hold the crowd to the morality of saints and seers.' Neither will the law honor the views of the bestial and the debased. Nor should it be governed by the morals of the prude on the one hand or of the perverted on the other. 'All that we can say is that the line will be higher than the lowest level of moral principle and practice, and lower than the highest.' Sex relationships can be and normally are beautiful, profound, inspiring and healthy. And some of the finest literature of all time—of fact and fancy, lasting and cherished through the ages—has presented and discussed, analyzed and novelized the concept of sex. Not so the present publications.

"If ever there could be found appropriate applicability for [the statute], this case emerges as the perfect example of what the Legislature has sought to curb. Judge Learned Hand felt that the word 'obscene' should 'be allowed to indicate the present critical point in the compromise between candor and shame.' No such problem is here presented; for 'Nights of Horror' will be found resting at the foot of the scale, clearly marked 'shame.' No matter how strict the test or how broad the criteria, these volumes will readily measure up and even surpass the most generous standard. The booklets in evidence offer naught but glorified concepts of lustful and vicious concupiscence, and by their tenor deride love and virtue, invite crime and voluptuousness, and excite lecherous desires. There is no true dissemination of lawful ideas—rather there is a direct incitement to sex crimes and the sordid excitement of brutality. These booklets are sold indiscriminately to all who may wish to purchase them—men and women, adults and youths. . . . These booklets are not sex literature, as such, but pornography, unadulterated by plot, moral or writing style. That there is no attempt to achieve any literary standard is obvious. Each issue is a paper-covered booklet of from 70 to 96 pages, with a suggestive sex drawing on the front cover under the caption 'Nights of Horror.' The price varies from $1.98 to $3.00 per issue. The volumes are replete with misspelled words, typographical errors, faulty grammar, misplaced pages and generally poor workmanship. While these factors do not, of course, classify the issues as pornographic, they are somewhat helpful in ascertaining whether there truly exists a genuine literary intent.

" 'Nights of Horror' makes but one 'contribution' to literature. It serves as a glossary of terms describing the private parts of the human body (notably the female breast, buttocks and vagina), the emotions sensed in illicit sexual climax and various forms of sadistic, masochistic and sexual perversion. The volumes before me are not a description of a period of history or the people or characters of an earlier time and of their conduct and habits of life. They are not a relating of folk tales or stories of primitive people living in isolated regions. They do not purport to depict the lives and customs of those who are here now or are expected to inhabit this land or this earth in the time to come. 'Nights of Horror' is no haphazard title. Perverted sexual acts and macabre tortures of the human body are repeatedly depicted. The books contain numbers of acts of male torturing female and some vice versa—by most ingenious means. These gruesome acts included such horrors as cauterizing a woman's breast with a hot iron, placing hot coals against a woman's breast, tearing breasts off, placing hot irons against a female's armpits, pulling off a girl's fingernails with white-hot pincers, completely singeing away the body hairs, working a female's skin away from her flesh with a knife, gouging and burning eyes out of their sockets, ringing the nipples of the breast with needles. Hanging by the thumbs, hair pulling, skin burning, putting on bone-compressing iron boots, were usual. The torture rack abounded. Self-torture was frequent. Sucking a victim's blood was pictured; and so was pouring molten lead into a girl's mouth and ears; and putting honey on a girl's breasts, vagina and buttocks—and then putting hundreds of great red ants on the honey. Sodomy, rape, lesbianism, seduction prevail. Youngsters disrobing in the presence and to the detailed recorded delight of elderly males was described. Incidental training of the teen-ager to narcotic addiction and sexual perversion was part of the activities engaged in. The volumes expressed a philosophy of man's omnipotent physical power over the female. . . .

"While it appears, as a study of earlier cases will indicate, that some courts have held a publication obscene on the basis of selected passages [Hicklin Rule*], each volume here was read (a distasteful task, it turned out to be—to say the least) to determine whether, taken as a whole, it was obscene within the proscription of the statute. . . . Suffice it to say at this point that there is not a single 'story' which is not 'obscene, lewd, lascivious, filthy, indecent or disgusting.' More often than not these adjectives must be used in combination . . . the whole here is 'emetic.' The authors have left nothing to fantasy or to the unimaginative mind. The volumes are vividly detailed and illustrated. The many drawings that embellish these stories are obviously intended to arouse unnatural desire and vicious acts. Violence—criminal, sexual—degradation and perversion are the sole keynote. Sadism and masochism are pictured as appropriate characteristics of human nature and pleasure. In short, the volumes of 'Nights of Horror' are obscene and constitute pornography—'dirt for dirt's sake.' 'Nights of Horror' does not deserve to be listed among the missing when the next edition of *Banned Books* is published."

As noted, the Supreme Court, Justice Frankfurter speaking for the majority, ruled that New York could go on a search and destroy mission with "Nights of Horror," and the material's obscenity was not an issue with the Supreme Court. This was not a unanimous decision, however; Justice Douglas, joined by Justices Black and Brennan, dissented: "There are two reasons why I think this restraining order should be dissolved. First, the provision for an injunction *pendente lite* gives the State the paralyzing power of a censor. A decree can issue *ex parte*— without a hearing and without any ruling or finding on the issue of obscenity. This provision is defended on the ground that it is only a little encroachment, that a hearing must be promptly given and a finding of obscenity promptly made. But every publisher knows what awful effect a decree issued in secret can have. We tread here on First Amendment grounds. And nothing is more devastating to the rights that it guarantees than the power to restrain publication before even a hearing is held. This is prior restraint and censorship at its worst. Second, the procedure for restraining by equity decree the distribution of all the condemned literature does violence to the First Amendment. The judge or jury which finds the publisher guilty in New York City acts on evidence that may be quite different from evidence before the judge or jury that finds the publisher not guilty in Rochester. In New York City the publisher may have been selling his tracts to juveniles, while in Rochester he may have sold to professional people. The nature of the group among whom the tracts are distributed may have an important bearing on the issue of guilt in any obscenity prosecution. Yet the present statute makes one criminal conviction conclusive and authorizes a state-wide decree that subjects the distributor to the contempt power. I think every publication is a separate offense which entitles the accused to a separate trial. Juries or judges may differ in their opinions, community by community, case by case. The publisher is entitled to that leeway under our constitutional system. One is entitled to defend every utterance on its merits and not to suffer today for what he uttered yesterday. Free speech is not to be regulated like diseased cattle and impure butter. The audience (in this case the judge or the jury) that hissed yesterday may applaud today, even for the same performance. The regime approved by the Court goes far toward making the censor supreme. It also substitutes punishment by contempt for punishment by jury trial. In both respects it transgresses constitutional guarantees.''

NIGHTSTAND BOOKS. A Kansas obscenity statute authorized the seizure of allegedly obscene material before a judicial determination as to the legal obscenity of the material. An attorney general obtained a warrant from a local judge after the judge perused seven books; the warrant authorized the seizure of 1,715 copies of thirty-one separate titles (many of which the judge had not seen before the issuance of the warrant). A hearing was held about seven weeks after the seizure, and the court ruled that all thirty-one titles were obscene and were to be destroyed.

The Kansas Supreme Court affirmed the lower court's order, but the U.S. Supreme Court (*A Quantity of Books v. Kansas*, 378 U.S. 205 [1964]) reversed. The majority opinion, delivered by Justice Brennan, did not consider whether the titles were obscene or not. Rather, the Court concluded that the entire process— issuing and executing the warrant of seizure *before* a judicial hearing on the question of obscenity—was unconstitutional as a prior restraint. The books themselves would never make the best-seller lists. Published under the series ''Nightstand Books,'' they all seem to have the same plot. A few titles will suffice: *Born for Sin, No Longer a Virgin, Flesh Is My Undoing, Orgy Town, Lesbian Love, Lust Hungry*, and *The Wife-Swappers*. Each of the books contains 192 pages, and the covers portray a highly sexual suggestive picture with blurbs of what is inside (''Her Body Was the Ticket to a Shame Career'').

NON-MAILABLE MATTER. Title 18 U.S.C. § 1461 (Postal Regulations, Mailing Obscene Material*) and its predecessor statutes describe in some detail what material cannot be sent through the U.S. mail. In general, § 1461 provides that there should not be carried in the U.S. mail any "obscene, lewd, lascivious, filthy book, pamphlet, picture, print, or other publication of a vulgar or indecent character" or "any letter upon the envelope of which, or postal card upon which scurrilous epithets may have been written or printed, or disloyal devices printed or engraved." The penalty for the first offense is not more than $5,000 or not more than five years or both; for each subsequent offense, $10,000 or 10 years or both. In addition, advertisements that of and by themselves do not fall under any of the above categories are prohibited under the same terms if they contain information on where and how to obtain any "obscene" or "filthy" or "vulgar" material. The various material coming under this regulation—books, films, photographs, pamphlets, magazines, drawings, records, tapes—must first be adjudged obscene by the judicial process before the penalty can be invoked; the Postal Service itself cannot make the sole determination as to the obscenity of something in the mail.

NORTH CAROLINA, DEPARTMENT OF CORRECTIONS REGULATION. The North Carolina Prisoners' Labor Union was incorporated in 1974 with a stated goal of the "promotion of charitable labor union purposes" and the formation of a "prisoners' labor union at every prison and jail in North Carolina to seek through collective bargaining . . . to improve working conditions." It also proposed to work toward the alteration or elimination of practices and policies of the Department of Corrections that it did not approve of, and to serve as a vehicle for the presentation and resolution of inmate grievances. By early 1975, the union had attracted some 2,000 inmate "members" in forty prison units throughout North Carolina. The state of North Carolina, unhappy with these developments, set out to prevent the inmates from forming or operating a union. The state allowed individual "belief" in the union, but it prohibited inmate solicitation of other inmates and meetings between members of the union and prevented bulk mailings of union information from outside sources. The North Carolina Department of Corrections issued a regulation on March 26, 1975, and such activity was prohibited. The Supreme Court, in *Jones v. North Carolina Prisoners' Labor Union*,* ruled that although inmates do not lose all First Amendment rights while in jail, the right to union activities was not among those they retained and the North Carolina regulation did not violate the inmates' right of free speech.

NORTHERN v. NELSON (1970). Harry X. Northern, an inmate in San Quentin State Prison, in California, filed suit in a federal district court against Louis S. Nelson, the warden of San Quentin. As the record relates, the following represents the charges that Northern made and the district court's decision on each of the charges: (1) He had not been allowed to receive on a regular basis the newspaper *Muhammad Speaks*—he is to be allowed to receive at his expense on a regular basis the newspaper *Muhammad Speaks* unless it can be demonstrated clearly that a specific issue will substantially disrupt prison discipline. (2) Eleven of the thirteen prison facilities listed do not have copies of the book entitled *The Holy Quran* by Usef Ali—the facilities shall make available to inmates requesting it and in accordance with Department of Corrections and institutional library rules, which are uniformly applicable to all inmates, at least one copy of the book entitled *The Holy Quran* by Usef Ali. (3) There are no provisions for payment by state authorities of a Muslim minister at a rate comparable to that which is paid to chaplains of the Catholic, Jewish, and Protestant faiths—a Muslim minister, when available and otherwise authorized to perform religious services pursuant to and in accordance with Department of Corrections and institutional rules, shall be paid by the prison authorities at an hourly rate comparable to that which is paid to chaplains of the Catholic, Jewish, and Protestant faiths. (4) That reasonable access to copies of *Muhammad Speaks* and *The Holy Quran* are necessary for the effective exercise of the Muslim religion—the prison facilities that have made available Muslim literature in addition to *Muhammad Speaks* and *The Holy Quran* shall not interpret this order to mean that such additional literature should be discarded. *Northern v. Nelson*, 315 F. Supp. 687 (1970).

NORTH HEMPSTEAD (NY), ORDINANCE ON TOPLESS DANCING.

On July 17, 1973, the town of North Hempstead, New York, enacted Local Law No. 1-1973, an ordinance making it unlawful for bar owners and others to permit waitresses, barmaids, and entertainers to appear in their establishments with breasts uncovered or so thinly draped as to appear uncovered. The Supreme Court, in *Doran v. Salem Inn*,* ruled that the ordinance was unconstitutional because of overbreadth*; the ordinance was written to prohibit bare breasts in "any public place" within the town, and if the *Ballet Africain* came to town, its dancers would be in violation of the ordinance.

NORTON v. DISCIPLINE COMMITTEE OF EAST TENNESSEE STATE UNIVERSITY (1969).

Norton and others, students at East Tennessee State University, were suspended from the university for distributing literature on campus. The literature urged students to stand up and fight and called the university administrators "despots" and "problem children." A federal district court held that the literature was not protected by the First Amendment, and a court of appeals affirmed the suspension: "The language, referring to their fellow students, 'Have they seized buildings and raised havoc until they got what they were entitled to like other American students,' was obviously intended to call their attention to campus disturbances around the country, and would include such universities as Columbia, Berkeley, Harvard, Cornell, Ohio State and Kent State. The students were urged to 'stand up and fight' and to 'assault the bastions of administrative tyranny.' This was an open exhortation to the students to engage

in disorderly and destructive activities. The University administration was referred to with an obscenity and called 'despots.' This vicious attack on the
administration was calculated to subject it to ridicule and contempt, and to
damage the reputation of the University. The reference to 'chastity belts' for
girls is a crude, vulgar remark offensive to women students and beyond the
dignity of most college students to make. It is not required that the college
authorities delay action against the inciters until after the riot has started and
buildings have been taken over and damaged. The college authorities had the
right to nip such action in the bud and prevent it in its inception. This is authorized
even in criminal cases.''

   The suspension was affirmed, but there was one dissent from Judge Celebrezze:
''The majority apparently relies upon three grounds: First, that there was sufficient evidence that the distribution of leaflets by the students would probably
lead to an eruption or riot on campus that the University was justified in disci-
plining these students with indefinite suspension. Second, that there was sufficient
evidence that the distribution of the leaflets by the students would create a
substantial and material interference with the normal activities of East Tennessee
State University that the University was justified. . . . Third, that the University
had inherent authority to discipline by suspending indefinitely those students
who engage in peacefully handing out leaflets containing false and inflammatory
statements. I believe that the pamphleteering in the instant case was protected
First Amendment activity. Therefore, I dissent on all three grounds.'' *Norton
v. Discipline Committee of East Tennessee State University*, 419 F. 2d 195
(1969). The U.S. Supreme Court refused to hear Norton's appeal (399 U.S. 906
[1970]), *cert. denied*.

NORWELL v. CITY OF CINCINNATI (1973). Norwell was arrested, tried,
convicted, and fined ten dollars for violating a Cincinnati statute (Cincinnati
[OH], Annoying Behavior*). It appears that Norwell may have had one too many
in one of the local watering holes and ''annoyed'' a police officer who stopped
him on the street. Officer Johnson testified that he arrested Norwell for ''being
loud and boisterous'' and because ''he was annoying me.'' The Supreme Court
reversed the ten dollar fine: ''Upon this record, we are convinced that [Norwell]
was arrested and convicted merely because he verbally and negatively protested
Officer Johnson's treatment of him. Surely, one is not to be punished for non-
provocatively voicing his objection to what he obviously felt was a highly questionable detention by a police officer. Regardless of what the motivation may
have been behind the expression in this case, it is clear that there was no abusive
language or fighting words.* If there had, we would have a different case.''
Norwell v. City of Cincinnati, 414 U.S. 14 (1973).

NOVEMBER. In 1935, John S. Sumner, secretary of the Anthony Comstock-
inspired New York Society for the Suppression of Vice (Comstockery*), brought
suit to have a New York court declare that a novel by Gustave Flaubert, *No-*

vember, was obscene (New York, Obscenity Statute*). Flaubert wrote the novel before he was twenty, but it was not published during his lifetime because it was considered too "revealing." It was originally published in France in 1914; the first English edition appeared in 1932. The *Saturday Review of Literature* (February 6, 1932) described it as follows: "A great deal of *November* is both beautiful and moving. . . . It is anything but mere sordid realism, though that is most certainly involved in it. It deals with the sick fever period of the youthful imagination." The *New Republic* (April 13, 1932) wrote: "As Flaubert's first novel, *November* has an importance which it would not otherwise have. For, in spite of the unusual and beautifully told story of Marie, with whom the hero has his first love affair, the novel is so soaked in the ennui of the Romantic era, so permeated with the wish to be any other where, that it grows wearisome; and its content seems only a pleasant reflection of the style of the period."

The judge dismissed Sumner's complaint (*People on Complaint of Sumner v. Miller*, 279 N.Y.S. 583 [1935]), ruling that *November* was not obscene: "The criterion of decency is fixed by time, place, geography, and all the elements that make for a constantly changing world. . . . Although § 1141 of the Penal Law has been on our statute books since 1884, the test that the book is required to meet is the measure of public opinion in the city of New York in the year 1935. . . . To change standards of morals is the task of school and church; the task of the judge is to record the tides of public opinion, not to emulate King Canute in an effort to turn back the tide." *November* was seen not to be obscene, given the state of public opinion and the standards of decency in New York in 1935.

NUDISM IN MODERN LIFE. U.S. Customs regulations (Tariff Act*) permit the seizure of material that Customs deems to be obscene. After seizure, there is to be a hearing in the federal district court for a judicial determination of the material's obscenity. If the material is judged to be obscene, it can be destroyed; if it is not obscene, Customs must release the material. In this particular case, copies of the book *Nudism in Modern Life* were seized but the court ruled that the book was not obscene (*Parmelee v. United States*, 113 F. 2d 729 [1940]). The court records provide the following description of *Nudism in Modern Life*: "On argument, it was conceded by the government that the text of the books and most of the photographs are unobjectionable. All that remains in dispute, therefore, is whether the books are objectionable, within the meaning of the statute, because of the presence therein of three or four photographs in which appear full front views of nude female figures, and two photographs in which nude male and female figures appear together. The photographs complained of are uncolored and apparently unretouched and are approximately 2 1/4 by 3 1/4 inches in size. The human figures which appear therein are approximately 1 1/2 inches in height."

Although the judge equated nudity with cancer, leprosy, and syphilis, the book was found not to be obscene: "Nudity in art has long been recognized as the reverse of obscene. Art galleries and art catalogues contain many nudes, ancient and modern. Even such a conservative source book as *Encyclopaedia Britannica*, contains nudes, full front view, male and female, and nude males and females pictured together and in physical contact. The use of nude figures and photographs in medical treatises and textbooks is also commonly practiced today. It was conceded on argument that this, also, constitutes an exception to the earlier prohibition. But this was not always true. In the earlier periods of medical history, censorship of scientific investigation was so restrictive that anatomical drawings alleged to represent the human body were made from studies of animals or upon a basis of pure hypothesis. Later, as indicated by such cases as *Regina v. Hicklin* (1868) (Hicklin Rule*) and *People v. Muller* (1884), the old censorship was relaxed to permit the use of such figures and photographs, provided the textbooks and treatises in which they appeared were restricted to use among practitioners and students. No reasonable person at the present time would suggest even that limitation upon the circulation and use of medical texts, treatises and journals. In many homes such books can be found today; in fact standard dictionaries, generally, contain anatomical illustrations. It is apparent, therefore, that civilization has advanced far enough, at last, to permit picturization of the human body for scientific and educational purposes. That fact is decisive of the present case. The picturization here challenged has been used in the libeled book to accompany an honest, sincere, scientific and educational study and exposition of a sociological phenomenon and is, in our opinion, clearly permitted by present-day concepts of propriety. There is, perhaps, as great or greater need for freedom of scientific research and exposition in this field as in any other. And, at this point, it may be well to repeat that the question is not whether nudity in practice is justifiable or desirable. All would agree that cancer, leprosy, and syphilis are highly undesirable; still, it is recognized, generally, by normal, intelligent persons, that there is a need for scientific study, exposition and picturization of their manifestations.''

O

___

OBSCENITY. The concept of obscenity has produced a variety of views from the Supreme Court, and there has been some difficulty in arriving at a unanimous and permanent definition of the term. It has been far easier for the Court to decide what obscenity is not than to decide what it is (e.g., sex and obscenity are not synonymous, nor is nudity alone synonymous with obscenity). But the Supreme Court has long recognized that the line between obscenity and constitutionally protected speech and press and conduct is uncertain and vague, and most obscenity decisions have been made on a case-by-case basis rather than applying a general standard. The following represents a brief overview of the changing views and definitions of obscenity: the "standards" of Hicklin,* Ulysses,* Roth,* Memoirs,* and Miller.*

The "Hicklin Rule" was announced in 1868, in Great Britain, by Lord Chief Justice Cockburn. In dealing with a pamphlet entitled *The Confessional Unmasked*, Cockburn announced in *Regina v. Hicklin* (L.R. 3 Q.B. 360 [1868]): "The test of obscenity is this, whether the tendency of the matter charged as obscenity is to deprave and corrupt those whose minds are open to such immoral influences and into whose hands a publication of this sort may fall." This guide then became the standard for practically all obscenity cases in Great Britain and the United States. The Hicklin Rule basically declared a publication to be obscene if isolated passages (not the work taken as a whole) could "corrupt" the most susceptible person who might read it. One of the most trenchant comments on the rule was given by Judge Curtis Bok: "Strictly applied, this rule renders any book unsafe, since a moron could pervert to some sexual fantasy to which his mind is open the listings of a seed catalogue."

The Hicklin Rule was in effect until 1934, when, in *United States v. One Book Entitled Ulysses (Ulysses*)*, Judge Woolsey formulated the "Ulysses" standard. Reacting against the Hicklin Rule, Woolsey ruled that obscenity was to be determined by the effect of a book read in its entirety on a person with average sex instincts: "We think the same immunity should apply to literature as to science, where the presentation, when viewed objectively, is sincere, and the erotic matter is not introduced to promote lust and does not furnish the dominant note of the publication. The question in each case is whether a publication taken as a whole has a libidinous effect.'' This standard has not been overruled; it has been refined, expanded, and made more precise by the subsequent decisions in *Roth, Memoirs,* and *Miller.*

The Roth test (*Roth v. United States* [1957]*) stated the standard to be ''whether to the average person,* applying contemporary community standards,* the dominant theme of the material taken as a whole appeals to prurient interest.* The Roth standard was refined in 1966, in *Memoirs v. Massachusetts (Memoirs of a Woman of Pleasure*),* which created the Memoirs standard: ''Three elements must coalesce: it must be established that (a) the dominant theme of the material taken as a whole appeals to prurient interest in sex; (b) the material is patently offensive because it affronts contemporary community standards relating to the description or representation of sexual matters; and (c) the material is utterly without redeeming social value.'' Under the *Memoirs* standard, each of the three criteria is to be applied independently; the social value of a book, for example, cannot be weighed against or canceled out by its prurient appeal or patent offensiveness.

The Memoirs test or standard itself was refined in 1973 (*Miller v. California*), and the resulting Miller standard is the current view or test of obscenity: ''The basic guidelines must be: (a) whether the average person, applying contemporary community standards, would find that the work, taken as a whole, appeals to the prurient interest; (b) whether the work depicts or describes, in a patently offensive way, sexual conduct specifically defined by the applicable state law; and (c) whether the work, taken as a whole, lacks serious literary, artistic, political, or scientific value.'' The Miller standard thus rejected the ''utterly without redeeming social value'' element of the Memoirs standard and substituted ''lacks serious literary, artistic, political, or scientific value.'' Each of the elements under Miller is to be applied independently; if a publication is seen to have ''serious value,'' it is protected regardless of its prurient appeal or patent offensiveness. The Miller standard also allows the jury to measure prurient appeal and patent offensiveness by the standard that prevails in the local forum community; the jury need not employ a national standard (the same book could be judged obscene by the contemporary community standard in, say, Maine but seen as not obscene by the standards prevailing in New York City). These tests or standards, however, did not (and do not) receive unanimous support from the Supreme Court. Several justices, most notably Justices Brennan, Stewart, Marshall, and Douglas, have expressed misgivings and reservations over prosecutions for obscenity and have generally expressed the view that the proper test or standard should be that ''the First and Fourteenth Amendments prohibit the state and federal governments from attempting, at least in the absence of distribution to juveniles or obtrusive exposure to unconsenting adults, to suppress sexually oriented materials on the basis of their allegedly 'obscene' contents.''

OCALA STAR-BANNER COMPANY v. DAMRON (1971).

The *Ocala Star-Banner* printed a story about Damron (then a mayor and a candidate for county tax assessor in Citrus County, Florida) that he previously had been charged with perjury in a federal district court. The story was false; it was Damron's brother who had been charged and not the candidate Damron. Damron the candidate sued for libel and won a $22,000 judgment against the newspaper, but the Supreme Court reversed the award. The Court considered two questions: Were charges of criminal conduct relevant to a candidate's fitness for office? and, Was malice involved? The Court concluded that a charge of criminal conduct (in this case, perjury) against a public official or a candidate for public office, no matter how remote in time or place, is always relevant to his fitness for office, and damages cannot be awarded unless malice was shown (the *New York Times* Rule*). In this particular case, even though the story was false, the newspaper did not exhibit reckless disregard for the truth (the reporter merely confused the two brothers). *Ocala Star-Banner Co. v. Damron*, 401 U.S. 295 (1971).

OHIO, BAR ASSOCIATION DISCIPLINARY RULES. The Ohio Code of Professional Responsibility, promulgated by the Supreme Court of Ohio, contains the following provisions: DR 2-103(A) of the Ohio Code (1970)—"A lawyer shall not recommend employment, as a private practitioner, of himself, his partner, or associate to a non-lawyer who has not sought his advice regarding employment of a lawyer"; and DR-104(A)—"A lawyer who has given unsolicited advice to a layman that he should obtain counsel or take legal action shall not accept employment resulting from that advice, except that: (1) a lawyer may accept employment by a close friend, relative, former client (if the advice is germane to the former employment), or one whom the lawyer reasonably believes to be a client." The Supreme Court found that these regulations were not a violation of free speech rights of an Ohio attorney who was found to have violated these disciplinary rules. *Ohralik v. Ohio State Bar Association* (1978).*

OHIO, CAMPAIGN EXPENSE REPORTING LAW. Ohio Revised Code Ann., §§ 3517.01 and 3517.11(A), provided, in part: "(A) Every campaign committee, political committee, and political party which made or received a contribution or made an expenditure in connection with the nomination or election of any candidate at any election held in this state shall file, on a form prescribed under this section, a full, true, and itemized statement, made under penalty of election falsification, setting forth in detail . . . the following information: (a) The month, date, and year of the contribution; (b) The full name and address of each person from whom contributions are received; (c) A description of the contribution received, if other than money; (d) The value in dollars and cents of the contribution; (e) All contributions and expenditures shall be itemized separately regardless of the amount except a receipt of a contribution from a person in the sum of twenty-five dollars or less at one social or fund-raising activity. . . . (5) A statement of expenditures which shall include: (a) The month, day, and year of expenditure; (b) The full name and address of each person to whom the expenditure was made; (c) The object or purpose for which the expenditure was made; (d) The amount of each expenditure. . . . All such statements shall be open to public inspection." This campaign contribution and expenditure reporting law was seen to be a violation of free speech in *Brown v. Socialist Workers '74 Campaign Committee* (1982),* for the Supreme Court judged that the regulations, rather than serving a legitimate state interest, were used to harass the unpopular Socialist Workers party.

OHIO, CRIMINAL SYNDICALISM. Ohio Revised Code Ann., § 2923.13, made it a crime to "advocate the duty, necessity, or propriety of crime, sabotage, violence, or unlawful methods of terrorism as a means of accomplishing industrial or political reform and/or to voluntarily assemble with any society, group, or assemblage of persons formed to teach or advocate the doctrines of criminal syndicalism." The Supreme Court, in *Brandenburg v. Ohio* (1969),* reversed a conviction under this statute (and, by so doing, overruled *Whitney v. California**) by holding that advocacy was protected by the Constitution: The freedoms of speech and press do not permit a state to forbid advocacy of the use of force or of law violation except when such advocacy is directed to inciting or producing imminent lawless action and is likely to incite or produce such action.

OHIO, MOTION PICTURE CENSORSHIP. On April 16, 1913, the Ohio General Assembly passed an act setting up a prior censorship scheme for films shown in the state. Section 3 of the act made it the duty of the Board of Censors to examine and censor motion picture films to be exhibited and displayed publicly in the state; the films were required to be exhibited to the board before they could be delivered to the exhibitor. Section 4 provided the guidelines for which films would receive the censors' approval: "Only such films as are in the judgment and discretion of the board of censors of a moral, educational or amusing and harmless character shall be passed and approved by such board." Section 5 of the act allowed the Ohio board to work in conjunction with censor boards of other states as a censor congress, and the actions of such congress in approving or rejecting films was to be considered as the action of the board itself. This act was one of the first state attempts at censorship of motion pictures (Film Censorship*), and the Supreme Court, in *Mutual Film Corporation v. Industrial Commission of Ohio* (1915),* saw no problems with forbidding films that were not judged "harmless" or "educational." The Court did not see films as a form of speech—they were a business, pure and simple—and this 1915 decision opened the way to decades of governmental censorship of films for just about any reason the censor cared to offer. The Industrial Commission of Ohio's censorship of films is no longer in operation.

OHIO, OBSCENE MATERIAL. Ohio Revised Code (1963 Supp.), § 2905.34, Selling, Exhibiting, and Possessing Obscene Literature or Drugs, for Criminal Purposes, provided: "No person shall knowingly sell, lend, give away, exhibit, or offer to sell, lend, give away, or exhibit, or publish or offer to publish or have in his possession or under his control an obscene, lewd, or lascivious book, magazine, pamphlet, paper, writing, advertisement, circular, print, picture, photograph, motion picture film, or book, pamphlet, paper, magazine not wholly obscene but containing lewd or lascivious articles, advertisements, photographs, or drawing, representation, figure, image, cast, instrument, or article of an indecent or immoral nature, or a drug, medicine, article, or thing intended for the prevention of conception or for causing an abortion, or advertise any of them for sale, or write, print, or cause to be written or printed a card, book, pamphlet, advertisement, or notice giving information when, where, how, of whom, or by what means any of such articles or things can be purchased or obtained, or manufacture, draw, print, or make such articles or things, or sell, give away, or show to a minor, a book, pamphlet, magazine, newspaper, story paper, or other paper devoted to the publication, or principally made up, of criminal news, police reports, or accounts of criminal deeds, lust, or crime, or exhibit upon a street or highway or in a place which may be within the view of a minor, any of such books, papers, magazines, or pictures. Whoever violates this section shall be fined not less than two hundred nor more than two thousand dollars or imprisoned not less than one nor more than seven years, or both.'' This all-encompassing and sweeping prohibition was seen to violate the rights of free speech and press by the Supreme Court in *Les Amants** (*Jacobellis v. Ohio* [1964]).

OHIO, TEACHING IN A FOREIGN LANGUAGE. On June 5, 1919, the Ohio General Assembly passed an act that mandated the use of English in the schools of the state and also prohibited the teaching of German to any student below the eighth grade. Section 7762–1: ''That all subjects and branches taught in the elementary schools of the State of Ohio below the eighth grade shall be taught in the English language only. . . . Provided, that the German language shall not be taught below the eighth grade in any of the elementary schools of the state.'' Section 7762–3: ''Any person or persons violating the provisions of this act shall be guilty of a misdemeanor and shall be fined in any sum not less than twenty-five dollars nor more than one hundred dollars, and each separate day in which such act shall be violated shall constitute a separate offense.'' This anti-German statute was seen to be a violation of the right of free speech by the Supreme Court in *Bohning v. Ohio* (1923).*

OHRALIK v. OHIO STATE BAR ASSOCIATION (1978). Albert Ohralik, an Ohio lawyer, visited an automobile accident victim in her hospital room and solicited a contingency-fee arrangement to represent her. The Disciplinary Board of the Ohio Supreme Court found that this in-person solicitation violated certain disciplinary rules (Ohio, Bar Association Disciplinary Rules*) and recommended a public sanction.

The Ohio Supreme Court increased the penalty to indefinite suspension, and the U.S. Supreme Court upheld the suspension—the bar association, with state authorization, may discipline a lawyer for soliciting clients in person and Ohralik's First Amendment rights were not violated. Justice Marshall delivered the opinion of the Court: (1) A lawyer's solicitation of business through direct, in-person communication with the prospective clients has long been viewed as inconsistent with the profession's idea of the attorney-client relationship and as posing a significant potential for harm to the prospective client. (2) The state does not lose its power to regulate commercial activity deemed harmful to the public simply because speech is a component of that activity. (3) A lawyer's procurement of remunerative employment is only marginally affected with First Amendment concerns. Although entitled to some constitutional protection, the conduct is subject to regulation in furtherance of important state interests. (4) In addition to its general interest in protecting consumers and regulating commercial transactions, the state bears a special responsibility for maintaining standards among members of the licensed professions. Protection of the public from those aspects of solicitation that involve fraud, undue influence, intimidation, overreaching, and other forms of "vexatious conduct" is a legitimate and important state interest. Justice Marshall concluded by saying that "the circumstances in which Ohralik initially approached his two clients provide classic examples of 'ambulance chasing,' fraught with obvious potential for misrepresentation and overreaching." *Ohralik v. Ohio State Bar Association*, 436 U.S. 447 (1978).

OKLAHOMA PUBLISHING CO. v. DISTRICT COURT (1977). This case concerned the question whether a judge could prevent the news media from publishing identifying information about a minor involved in the judicial process. An Oklahoma state court issued a pre-trial restraining order enjoining the news media from publishing the name or photograph of an eleven-year-old boy involved with a murder charge. The U.S. Supreme Court ruled that such an order violated the First Amendment's freedom of the press and constituted prior censorship over what could or could not be printed in a newspaper: A state court cannot prohibit the publication of widely disseminated information obtained at court proceedings that were open to the public. *Oklahoma Publishing Co. v. District Court*, 430 U.S. 308 (1977).

OKLAHOMA, STATE HATCH ACT. Oklahoma's Merit System of Personnel Administration Act of 1959, Oklahoma Stat. Ann., Title 74, Section 818, was patterned after the federal Hatch Act*; the other forty-nine states have similar provisions relating to certain proscribed activities of state employees, particularly political activities. The relevant sections of this act are as follows: (6) "No employee in the classified service, and no member of the Personnel Board shall, directly or indirectly, solicit, receive, or in any manner be concerned in soliciting or receiving any assessment, subscription or contribution for any political organization, candidacy or other political purpose; and no state officer or state employee in the unclassified service shall solicit or receive any such assessment, subscription or contribution from an employee in the classified service''; and (7) "No employee in the classified service shall be a member of any national, state or local committee of a political party, or an officer or member of a committee of a partisan political club, or a candidate for nomination or election to any paid public office, or shall take part in the management or affairs of any political party or in any political campaign, except to exercise his right as a citizen privately to express his opinion and to cast his vote." This obvious restraint on the First Amendment rights of civil service employees was seen not to be a violation of free speech or press in *Broaderick v. Oklahoma* (1973).*

OKLAHOMA v. UNITED STATES CIVIL SERVICE COMMISSION (1974). A member of the Oklahoma State Highway Commission, whose principal employment was in connection with an activity financed in part by loans and grants from a federal agency, served at the same time as chairman of the Democratic State Central Committee. During his service on the highway commission, there was no general election in the state, but he worked with the governor concerning a dinner sponsored by the committee to raise funds for political purposes, called the meeting to order, and introduced the toastmaster. Citing certain sections of the Hatch Act,* the U.S. Civil Service Commission determined that these activities constituted taking an "active part in political management or in political campaigns," and that this warranted his removal from office. The U.S. Supreme Court agreed, Justice Reed writing: (1) The Hatch Act is not unconstitutional even though it restrains the employee's freedom of expression in political matters (*United Public Workers v. Mitchell* [1947]*); and (2) The Civil Service Commission's determination that the highway commissioner's acts constituted a violation of the Hatch Act was in accordance with law and was not arbitrary, unreasonable, or an abuse of discretion. *Oklahoma v. United States Civil Service Commission*, 330 U.S. 127 (1947).

OLD DOMINION BRANCH NO. 496, NATIONAL ASSOCIATION OF LETTER CARRIERS, AFL-CIO v. AUSTIN (1974). This case involved three state (Virginia) libel judgments imposing liability of $165,000 on a labor union as a result of statements ("scabs" and "traitors") contained in a union newsletter during an organizational drive. The question was whether these libel judgments could be squared with the freedom of speech in labor disputes guaranteed under certain federal regulations. The Supreme Court reversed the libel judgments, basing its decision on Section 8(c) of the National Labor Relations Act ["The expressing of any views, argument, or opinion, or the dissemination thereof . . . shall not constitute or be evidence of an unfair labor practice . . . if such expression contains no threat or reprisal or force or promise of benefit"]: Federal labor laws favor uninhibited, robust, and wide open debate in labor disputes, and a union cannot be found guilty of libel for using the words "scab" and "traitor." *Old Dominion Branch No. 496, National Association of Letter Carriers, AFL-CIO v. Austin*, 418 U.S. 264 (1974).

ONE. Title 18 U.S.C. § 1461 (Postal Regulations, Mailing Obscene Material*) prohibits the use of the mails to send "obscene" matter. The magazine *One* was judged to be obscene by a federal district court, and the ruling was upheld by an appeals court (*One, Inc. v. Olesen*, 241 F. 2d 777 [1957]).

Justice Ross of the court of appeals held that the magazine, purportedly published for the purpose of dealing with homosexuality from a scientific, historical, and critical point of view, contained articles that were nothing more than cheap pornography calculated to promote lesbianism and other forms of homosexuality. Judge Ross described a specific issue in the following terms: "The article 'Sappho Remembered' is the story of a lesbian's influence on a young girl only twenty years of age but 'actually nearer sixteen in many essential ways of maturity,' in her struggle to choose between a life with the lesbian, or a normal married life with her childhood sweetheart. The lesbian's affair with her room-mate while in college, resulting in the lesbian's expulsion from college, is recounted to bring in the jealousy angle. The climax is reached when the young girl gives up her chance for a normal married life to live with the lesbian. The article is nothing more than cheap pornography calculated to promote lesbianism. It falls far short of dealing with homosexuality from the scientific, historical and critical point of view. The poem 'Lord Samuel and Lord Montagu' is about the alleged homosexual activities of Lord Montagu and other British Peers and contains a warning to all males to avoid the public toilets while Lord Samuel is 'sniffing round the drains' of Piccadilly. The stories 'All This and Heaven Too,' and 'Not Til the End,' are similar to the story 'Sappho Remembered,' except that they relate to the activities of the homosexuals rather than lesbians."

The publisher of the magazine appealed this decision, and the Supreme Court (*One, Incorporated v. Olesen*, 355 U.S. 371 [1958]) reversed the ruling that *One* was not mailable. This last decision was per curiam, with no written opinion.

OPELIKA (AL), BOOK SELLERS' LICENSE. The town of Opelika passed the following ordinance: "It shall be unlawful for any person . . . to engage in any of the businesses or vocations for which a license may be required without first having procured a license therefor, and any violation hereof shall constitute a criminal offense, and shall be punishable by fine and by imprisonment." The businesses and vocations, with the license fee for each, were as follows: "Book Agents (Bibles excepted)—$10.00; Transient or itinerant agents selling rugs, antiques, goods, wares, merchandise or taking orders for same—$25.00; Peddlers, or itinerant dealers, distributors or salesmen not otherwise included in this schedule—$75.00; Transient agents or dealers or distributors of books—$5.00; and Transient dealers—$25.00." The ordinance also included the statement: "All licenses, permits, or other grants to carry on any business, trade, vocation, or professions for which a charge is made by the City shall be subject to revocation in the discretion of the City Commission, with or without notice to the licensee." This ordinance was held to be constitutional and thus not an abridgment on the right of free press by the Supreme Court in *Jones v. Opelika* (1942),* but one year later, in a rehearing, the Court reversed itself by citing *Largent v. Texas* (1943)* and *Jamison v. Texas* (1943).*

ORADELL (NJ), DOOR-TO-DOOR CANVASSING. Ordinance Number 598A of the Borough of Oradell read: "Any person desiring to canvass, solicit or call from house to house in the Borough for a recognized charitable cause, or any person desiring to canvass, solicit or call from house to house for a Federal, State, County or municipal political campaign or cause, shall be required to notify the Police Department, in writing, for identification only." The Supreme Court, citing the vagueness of this ordinance, held that it was a violation of the First Amendment in *Hynes v. Mayor of Oradell* (1976).*

OREGON, CRIMINAL SYNDICALISM. Oregon Code, 1930, §§ 14-3110-3112 as amended by chapter 459, Oregon Laws (1933), provided: "Criminal syndicalism is hereby defined to be the doctrine which advocates crime, physical violence, sabotage, or any unlawful acts or methods as a means of accomplishing or effecting industrial or political change or revolution. Sabotage is hereby defined to be intentional and unlawful damage, injury or destruction of real or personal property. Any person who, by word of mouth or writing, advocates or teaches the doctrine of criminal syndicalism or sabotage . . . or who shall organize or help to organize . . . any society . . . which teaches or advocates the doctrine . . . is guilty of a felony and, upon conviction thereof, shall be punished by imprisonment in the state penitentiary for a term of not less than one year nor more than ten years, or by a fine of not more than $1,000, or by both." The Supreme Court, in *De Jonge v. Oregon* (1937),* ruled that this Oregon statute could not be applied to someone who organized a meeting held under the auspices of an organization that might have advocated the doctrine of criminal syndicalism.

OREGON, DENTISTS ADVERTISING. The Supreme Court, in *Semler v. Oregon State Board of Dental Examiners* (1935),* held that an Oregon statute (Oregon Laws, Chapter 166 [1933]) prohibiting dentists from advertising was not a violation of the First Amendment. The statute prohibited "advertising professional superiority or the performance of professional services in a superior manner; advertising prices for professional service; advertising by means of large display, glaring light signs, or containing as a part thereof the representation of a tooth, teeth, bridge work or any portion of the human head; employing or making use of advertising solicitors or free publicity press agents; or advertising any free dental work, or free examination; or advertising to guarantee any dental service, or to perform any dental operation painlessly." These restrictions are no longer in place.

ORGANIZATION FOR A BETTER AUSTIN v. KEEFE (1971). Keefe, a real estate broker, was accused of "blockbusting" and "panic peddling" by a group of people who were from a racially integrated community and who wanted to stabilize the community. The organization distributed leaflets peacefully and did not disrupt traffic. Keefe sought an injunction, and the Circuit Court of Cook County, Illinois, granted an injunction against the distribution of pamphlets, leaflets, or literature of any kind anywhere in Keefe's residential suburb. An Illinois appeals court affirmed, holding that the organization's activities in the suburb were coercive, and that the right of free speech was not involved. On appeal, the Supreme Court reversed and lifted the injunction: The injunction, operating not to redress alleged private wrongs, but to suppress, on the basis of previous publications, distribution of literature of any kind in the suburb, was unconstitutional as a prior restraint* on the defendants' First Amendment rights. *Organization for a Better Austin v. Keefe*, 402 U.S. 415 (1971).

OVERBREADTH. The doctrine of overbreadth is of recent origin. It is a doctrine applied by the Supreme Court that requires that a particular statute or ordinance be invalidated if it is fairly capable of being applied to punish people for constitutionally protected speech or conduct. A law is void on its face if it "does not aim specifically at evils within the allowable area of [government] control, but . . . sweeps within its ambit other activities that constitute an exercise of protected expressive or associational rights" (*Thornhill v. Alabama* [1940]*). Overbreadth is applied only when the protected activity is a significant part of the law's target and there exists no satisfactory way of severing the law's constitutional applications from its unconstitutional applications. The application of the overbreadth doctrine has been held by the Supreme Court to be limited to freedoms guaranteed by the Bill of Rights. The following are some areas in which the doctrine of overbreadth was applicable: abusive language, breach of the peace, annoying conduct, distribution of literature, licensing, loyalty oaths, military laws, obscenity, picketing, prison regulations, and public employment. *Black's Law Dictionary; Annotation: Overbreadth*, 45 L. Ed. 2d 725.

P

PACKER CORPORATION v. UTAH (1932). A Utah statute (Utah, Tobacco Advertisements on Billboards*) prohibited the advertising of cigarettes and other tobacco products on billboards, street car signs, and placards, but the statute did not apply to advertisements in newspapers and periodicals. The Packer Corporation was prosecuted under this statute for displaying a large poster advertising Chesterfield cigarettes on a billboard it owned that was located in Salt Lake City.

The Supreme Court affirmed the conviction, Justice Brandeis delivering the Court's opinion: "Moreover, as the state court has shown, there is a difference which justifies the classification between display advertising and that in periodicals and newspapers: 'Billboards, street car signs, and placards and such are in a class by themselves. They are wholly intrastate, and the restrictions apply without discrimination to all in the same class. Advertisements of this sort are constantly before the eyes of observers on the streets and in street cars to be seen without the exercise of choice or volition on their part. Other forms of advertising are ordinarily seen as a matter of choice on the part of the observer. The young people as well as the adults have the message of the billboard thrust upon them by all the arts and devices that skill can produce. In the case of newspapers and magazines, there must be some seeking by the one who is to see and read the advertisement. The radio can be turned off, but not so the billboard or street car placard. These distinctions clearly place this kind of advertisement in a position to be classified so that regulations or prohibitions may be imposed upon all within the class. This is impossible with respect to newspapers and magazines.' The legislature may recognize degrees of evil and adapt its legislation accordingly." *Packer Corporation v. Utah*, 285 U.S. 105 (1932).

PANDERING. Although not included as an element in the definition of obscenity,* including the tests or standards laid down by the Supreme Court in the *Roth*/*Memoirs*/*Miller* cases, a publication which in and of itself may not be obscene, may nevertheless be judged obscene in a close case if "pandering" (the particular circumstances of production, sale, and publicity of the material) is present.

Pandering figured most prominently in the case of *Ginzburg v. United States**: ''The accused publications were originated or sold as stock in trade of the sordid business of pandering—the business of purveying textual or graphic matter openly advertised to appeal to the erotic interest of their customers.'' One of Ginzburg's publications was the magazine *EROS*, and Ginzburg sought mailing privileges from the postmasters of Intercourse and Blue Ball, Pennsylvania (*EROS* was finally mailed from Middlesex, New Jersey). The trial court found the obvious, that ''these hamlets were chosen only for the value their names would have in furthering [Ginzburg's] efforts to sell their publications on the basis of salacious appeal. The 'leer of the sensualist' also permeates the advertising. . . . We perceive no threat to First Amendment guarantees in thus holding that in close cases evidence of pandering may be probative with respect to the nature of the material in question and thus satisfy the Roth test.'' Some justices, however—Justice Douglas in particular—felt that the tone or nature of the advertising could not transform a non-obscene publication into an obscene one and that reliance on ''pandering'' was a threat to First Amendment guarantees.

PAPISH v. BOARD OF CURATORS OF THE UNIVERSITY OF MISSOURI (1973). Papish, a graduate student at the University of Missouri, was expelled from the institution for distributing on campus a newspaper ''containing forms of indecent speech'' (i.e., ''mother fucker'') in violation of a bylaw of the university's Board of Curators. Papish appealed her expulsion through the courts, and in 1973, the Supreme Court ruled that her expulsion was an impermissible violation of her First Amendment speech rights, since ''the mere dissemination of ideas on a state university campus cannot be proscribed in the name of 'conventions of decency.' '' The Supreme Court remanded the case back to the district court, instructing that court to order the university to restore to Papish any course credits she earned for the semester in question and, unless she were to be barred from reinstatement for valid academic reasons, to reinstate her as a student. *Papish v. Board of Curators of the University of Missouri*, 410 U.S. 667 (1973).

PARENTS' ALLIANCE TO PROTECT OUR CHILDREN. Founded in 1979, the alliance is a pro-life, pro-family organization. It describes itself as seeking to ''protect children from what the Alliance calls manipulation in education and politics which leads to secular humanism which recognizes no higher authority than man himself. Provides information and opinions on children's welfare and protection, and on parents' rights, through: publishing newsletters and educational material; sponsoring seminars; and conducting research and studies on children, parents, and the secular and religious life in the traditional family. Specific areas of interest include: sex education; abortion; population control; child abuse; curricula in both public and private schools; religious education; secular humanism; and legislation affecting family issues.'' *Encyclopedia of Associations* (# 12181).

PARIS ADULT THEATRE I v. SLATON, DISTRICT ATTORNEY (1973).

Slaton, a district attorney in Georgia, sued the Paris Adult Theatre under a Georgia law (Georgia, Obscenity Statute*) to enjoin the continuing exhibition by the theatre of two films alleged to be obscene (*Magic Mirror* and *It All Comes Out in the End*). The correct judicial procedure was employed, and there was no prior restraint over the showing of the films. The Georgia trial court viewed the films and then dismissed Slaton's complaint, ruling that the display of the films in commercial theaters to consenting adult audiences (reasonable precautions were taken to exclude minors from seeing the films) was constitutionally permissible. But the Georgia Supreme Court reversed that decision, holding that the films constituted "hard core" pornography not within the protection of the First Amendment.

On appeal, the Supreme Court remanded the case back to the Georgia courts in order to evaluate the films' obscenity in terms of the Miller Standard.* The Supreme Court ruled that not all conduct involving "consenting adults" had a claim to constitutional protection: (1) States have a legitimate interest in regulating commerce in obscene material and its exhibition in places of public accommodation, including "adult" theaters. (2) There is a proper state concern with safeguarding against crime and the other arguably ill effects of obscenity by prohibiting the public or commercial exhibition of obscene material. Although conclusive proof is lacking, the states may reasonably determine that a nexus does or might exist between anti-social behavior and obscene material, just as states have acted on unprovable assumptions in other areas of public control. (3) Although states are free to adopt a laissez-faire policy toward commercialized obscenity, they are not constitutionally obliged to do so. (4) Exhibition of obscene material in places of public accommodation is not protected by any constitutional doctrine of privacy. A commercial theater cannot be equated with a private home (*Stanley v. Georgia*), nor can the privacy of the home be equated with a "zone of privacy" that follows a consumer of obscene materials wherever he goes. (5) Preventing the unlimited display of obscene material is not thought control. (6) Not all conduct directly involving consenting adults only has a claim to constitutional protection. The Georgia courts found the films to be obscene at the retrial, and the Supreme Court (*Paris Adult Theatre I v. Slaton*, 418 U.S. 939 [1974], *cert. denied*) refused to hear a new appeal, thus affirming the decision that *Magic Mirror* and *It All Comes Out in the End* were obscene. *Paris Adult Theatre I v. Slaton District Attorney*, 413 U.S. 49 (1973).

PARIS (TX), HANDBILL DISTRIBUTION.

The town of Paris, Texas, passed the following ordinance (Ordinance No. 612): "From and after the passage of this ordinance it shall be unlawful for any person, firm or corporation to solicit orders for books, wares, merchandise, or any household article of any description whatsoever within the residence portion of the City of Paris, or to sell books, wares, merchandise, or any household article within the residence district of the City of Paris, or to canvass, take census without first filing an application in writing with the Mayor and obtaining a permit, which said application shall state the character of the goods, wares, or merchandise intended to be sold or the nature of the canvass to be made, or the census to be taken, and by what authority. The application shall also state the name of the party desiring the permit, his permanent street address and number while in the city and if after investigation the Mayor deems it proper or advisable he may issue a written permit to said person for the purpose of soliciting.'' The phrase ''the Mayor deems it proper or advisable'' was fatal for this ordinance; the Supreme Court (*Largent v. Texas* [1943]*) ruled that this was a form of prior restraint and gave too much discretion to the mayor whether to issue or not to issue the permit.

PARKER V. LEVY (1974). Article 133 of the Uniform Code of Military Justice punishes a commissioned officer for ''conduct unbecoming an officer and a gentleman''; Article 134 of the code punishes any person subject to the Uniform Code of Military Justice for ''all disorders and neglect to the prejudice of good order and discipline in the armed forces'' (Military Regulations, Uniform Code of Military Justice*). Levy, an army physician assigned to a hospital, was convicted by a general court-martial of violating Articles 133 and 134. Levy had made public statements urging black enlisted men to refuse to obey orders to go to Viet Nam and referring to special forces personnel as ''liars and thieves,'' ''killers of peasants,'' and ''murderers of women and children.'' Levy was dismissed from the army, forfeited all pay and allowances, and received a three-year jail term at hard labor.

Holding that the right to free speech was much more limited in the armed forces, the U.S. Supreme Court affirmed the decision of the court-martial: Articles 133 and 134 do not violate the First Amendment, and although military personnel do enjoy some First Amendment protection, the fundamental necessity for obedience and the consequent necessity for discipline may render permissible within the military that which would be constitutionally impermissible outside it. Justice Rehnquist delivered the Court's opinion: ''While the members of the military are not excluded from the protection granted by the First Amendment, the different character of the military community and of the military mission requires a different application of those protections. The fundamental necessity for obedience, and the consequent necessity for imposition of discipline may render permissible within the military that which would be constitutionally impermissible outside it. . . . The United States Court of Military Appeals [*United States v. Priest**] has sensibly expounded the reason for this different application of First Amendment doctrines: 'In the armed forces some restrictions exist for reasons that have no counterpart in the civilian community. Disrespectful and contemptuous speech, even advocacy of violent change, is tolerable in the civilian community, for it does not directly affect the capacity of the Government to discharge its responsibilities unless it both is directed to inciting imminent lawless action and is likely to produce such action (*Brandenburg v. Ohio**). In military life, however, other considerations must be weighed. The armed forces depend on a command structure that at times must commit men to combat, not only hazarding their lives but ultimately involving the security of the Nation itself. Speech that is protected in the civilian population may nonetheless undermine the effectiveness of response to command. If it does, it is constitutionally unprotected.' ''

This blatant muzzling of Levy's unpopular remarks was not accepted by the entire Supreme Court, however. Justice Stewart, joined by Justices Douglas and Brennan, dissented from the majority opinion: ''Articles 133 and 134 are in practice as well as theory 'catch-alls' designed to allow prosecutions for practically any conduct that may offend the sensibilities of a military commander. Article 133 has been recently employed to punish such widely disparate conduct as dishonorable failure to repay debts, selling whiskey at an unconscionable price to an enlisted man, cheating at cards, having an extramarital affair, and for showing an allegedly obscene photograph to a friend in a private home. Article 134 has been given an even wider sweep, having been applied to sexual acts with a chicken, window peeping in a trailer park, and cheating while calling bingo numbers. . . . [W]e deal here with criminal statutes. And I cannot believe that such meaningless statutes as these can be used to send men to prison under a constitution that guarantees due process of law.'' *Parker v. Levy*, 417 U.S. 733 (1974).

PASSPORT ACT. The Passport Act of 1926 (22 U.S.C. §211a [1976 ed., Supp. III]) reads in part: ''The Secretary of State may grant and issue passports, and cause passports to be granted, issued, and verified in foreign countries by diplomatic representatives of the United States . . . under such rules as the President shall designate and prescribe for and on behalf of the United States, and no other person shall grant, issue, or verify such passports.'' The Passport Act does not in so many words confer on the secretary of state the power to revoke a passport, nor does it expressly authorize the secretary to deny a passport application. However, there is no statute that expressly limits the secretary's power to do so, and the courts have usually accepted the view that the secretary of state can deny or revoke a passport for reasons not specified in the statutes. For example, the Supreme Court (*Kent v. Dulles*, 357 U.S. 116 [1958]) recognized congressional acquiescence in executive policies of refusing passports to applicants ''participating in illegal conduct, trying to escape the toils of the law, promoting passport frauds, or otherwise engaging in conduct which would violate the laws of the United States.'' This power of the secretary of state to revoke passports came into play when Alexander Haig revoked the passport of Philip Agee (*Haig v. Philip Agee**) in 1981, in retribution for Agee's disclosing the names of covert Central Intelligence Agency operatives; the Supreme Court upheld the revocation.

PATENT OFFENSIVENESS. The concept ''patent offensiveness'' or ''patently offensive'' is one of the elements used in the definition of obscenity* as laid down by the Supreme Court in *Miller v. California.** It appears that the term ''hard-core pornography'' has been equated with patently offensive sexual conduct. The *Miller* decision ruled that prohibiting hard-core sexual conduct does not repress the free and robust exchange of ideas, and that the regulation of patently offensive hard-core materials is permissible: ''We [the Supreme Court's majority opinion in the *Miller* case] emphasize that it is not our function to propose regulatory schemes for the States. That must await their concrete legislative efforts. It is possible, however, to give a few plain examples of what a state statute could define for regulation . . . (a) patently offensive representations or descriptions of ultimate sexual acts, normal or perverted, actual or simulated; (b) patently offensive representations or descriptions of masturbation, excretory functions, and lewd exhibition of the genitals. At a minimum, prurient, patently offensive depiction or description of sexual conduct must have serious literary, artistic, political, or scientific value to merit First Amendment protection.''

PATTERSON v. COLORADO (1907). Patterson was convicted of contempt of court for the publication of certain articles and a cartoon that, it was charged, reflected on the motives and conduct of the Supreme Court of Colorado in cases still pending and that were intended to embarrass the court in the impartial administration of justice. Patterson claimed that he published the articles in the pursuit of a public duty and that he was prepared to prove the truth of the publications.

Patterson's claims were rejected, and the U.S. Supreme Court affirmed his conviction. Justice Holmes delivered the opinion of the Court: ''The defense upon which [Patterson] most relies is raised by the allegation that the articles complained of are true and the claim of the right to prove the truth. . . . We leave undecided the question whether there is to be found in the Fourteenth Amendment a prohibition similar to that in the First. But even if we were to assume that freedom of speech and freedom of the press were protected from abridgment on the part not only of the United States but also of the States [Incorporation*], still we should be far from the conclusion that [Patterson] would have us reach. In the first place, the main purpose of such constitutional provisions is 'to prevent all such *previous restraints* upon publications as had been practiced by other governments,' and they do not prevent the subsequent punishment of such as may be deemed contrary to the public welfare. The preliminary freedom extends as well to the false as to the true; the subsequent punishment may extend as well to the true as to the false. That was the law of criminal libel apart from statute in most cases, if not in all. In the next place, the rule applied to criminal libels applies yet more clearly to contempts. A publication likely to reach the eyes of a jury, declaring a witness in a pending case a perjurer, would be none the less a contempt that it was true. It would tend to obstruct the administration of justice, because even a correct conclusion is not to be reached or helped in that way, if our system of trials is to be maintained. The theory of our system is that the conclusions to be reached in a case will be induced only by evidence and argument in open court, and not by any outside influence, whether of private talk or public print.''

Justice Harlan dissented from this decision, and his rather lengthy comments are quite significant. Eighteen years before the *Gitlow v. New York** decision, he argued for the applicability of the First Amendment to the states through the Fourteenth Amendment (the theory of incorporation). Justice Harlan: ''Now, the Fourteenth Amendment declares, in express words, that 'no State shall make or enforce any law which shall abridge the privileges or immunities of citizens of the United States.' As the First Amendment guaranteed the rights of free speech and of a free press against hostile action by the United States, it would seem clear that when the Fourteenth Amendment prohibited the States from impairing or abridging the privileges of citizens of the United States it necessarily prohibited the States from impairing or abridging the constitutional rights of such citizens to free speech and a free press. But the court announces that it leaves undecided the specific question whether there is to be found in the Fourteenth Amendment a prohibition as to the rights of free speech and a free press similar to that in the First. It yet proceeds to say that the main purpose of such constitutional provisions was to prevent all such *previous* restraints upon publications as had been practiced by other governments, but not to prevent the subsequent punishment of such as may be deemed contrary to the public welfare. I cannot assent to that view, if it be meant that the legislature may impair or abridge the rights of a free press and of free speech whenever it thinks that the public welfare requires that to be done. The public welfare cannot override constitutional privileges, and if the rights of free speech and of a free press are, in their essence, attributes of national citizenship, as I think they are, then neither Congress nor any State since the adoption of the Fourteenth Amendment can, by legislative enactments or by judicial action, impair or abridge them. In my judgment the action of the court below was in violation of the rights of free speech and a free press as guaranteed by the Constitution. I go further and hold that the privileges of free speech and of a free press, belonging to every citizen of the United States, constitute essential parts of every man's liberty, and are protected against violation by that clause of the Fourteenth Amendment forbidding a State to deprive any person of his liberty without due process of law. It is, I think, impossible to conceive of liberty, as secured by the Constitution against hostile action, whether by the Nation or by the States, which does not embrace the right to enjoy free speech and the right to have a free press.'' *Patterson v. Colorado*, 205 U.S. 454 (1907).

PAWTUCKET (RI), PUBLIC SPEECHES IN PARKS. The city of Pawtucket, Rhode Island, had an ordinance that read as follows: ''No person shall address any political or religious meeting in any public park; but this section shall not be construed to prohibit any political or religious club or society from visiting any public park in a body, provided that no public address shall be made under the auspices of such club or society in such park.'' The ordinance was held to be a violation of the First Amendment by the Supreme Court in 1953 (*Fowler v. Rhode Island**), when the Court found that the city of Pawtucket would allow religious services to be held in public parks by practically all denominations—calling the sermon a sermon and not a "public address"—but prohibiting the Jehovah's Witnesses from doing the same; the city called their sermons a "public address."

PAYNE v. WHITMORE (1971). This case concerned certain regulations within the San Mateo County, California, jail that prohibited the inmates in the main jail and in the medium security facility from receiving any newspaper or magazine through the mail or from any other source within or without the jail. Although the right to receive books, newspapers, and periodicals is guaranteed to convicted felons in the California state prison system (California Penal Code, § 2600-4), no such right is expressly extended to those at San Mateo who are jailed either for misdemeanor violations or for their inability to make bail pending trial. A group of inmates challenged this prohibition in a federal district court. The county of San Mateo argued that the standard of § 2600-4 does not mandate the same for San Mateo, and in addition, even if there were a First Amendment right to receive newspapers and magazines while in jail, the county was justified in denying that right because of four overriding considerations: "(1) Such materials would be used by certain inmates to start fires; (2) Such materials might also be used to plug toilets and drains in the jail facility; (3) Inmates would quarrel over each other's newspapers and magazines; and (4) It would be costly for jail personnel to process inmate subscriptions."

The district court, Judge Wollenberg delivering the opinion, found that this regulation was not reasonable and that it was not a valid time-place-manner* restriction on First Amendment rights. Judge Wollenberg: "That the right to receive newspapers and magazines is part of the First Amendment is beyond question. Whether couched in terms of the rights explicitly listed in the first ten amendments, or in terms of equal protection, or in terms of constitutional reasonability [previous cases] are united on one point: prison rules must bear a reasonable relationship to valid prison goals, and rules which infringe upon particularly important rights will require a proportionately stronger justification. The explanations offered by defendants for their total and absolute prohibition of protected literature are stated in over-inclusive terms and without consideration of reasonable rules concerning 'time, place and manner.' Jail cells are already filled with an abundance of materials quite suitable for fire starting and drain clogging; yet no one suggests that cells ought to be stripped of bedding, clothing, toilet paper, writing materials, and so on. Nearly all inmates have personal property; occasionally this might cause disputes, but this problem seems susceptible of control by less stringent measures than an absolute bar enforced against possession of such property. Finally, funds for purchase of newspapers and magazines can be managed in the same way such funds are disbursed for purchases of candy, cigarettes, and other commissary items."

Judge Wollenberg, however, left the door open for future censorship over the type of reading material the inmates may receive: "Nothing in this opinion should be read to prevent the defendants from promulgating reasonable time, place, and manner restrictions on the receipt and use of reading materials in the San Mateo County Jail. Defendants may also take reasonable steps to prevent receipt of obscene materials, or reading matter which might pose an imminent threat to jail security." *Payne v. Whitmore*, 325 F. Supp. 1191 (1971).

PEACHTREE NEWS CO., INC. v. UNITED STATES (1974). The Peachtree News Company was convicted in a federal district court on twelve counts of using a common carrier to transport obscene materials in violation of 18 U.S.C. § 1462 (Interstate Commerce Regulations, Transporting Obscene Material*). The federal district court employed the Miller Standard* and found that all twelve magazines, each taken as a whole, "lacked serious literary, artistic, political or scientific value." The appeals court, however, ruled that the standard to be applied should have been the Memoirs Standard*—the work, taken as a whole, is "utterly without redeeming social value" and that six of the twelve magazines were thus protected under the Memoirs test. The six magazines that were found to be obscene were *Duo, Domino, Love Knot, Wanton, My Boys*, and *In & Its Nice*; the six that were found to have some redeeming social value were *Boys and Their Male Lovers, Girlfriends, Pussy Willow, Arcadia, Teenage Jaybirds*, and *Cloud 9*. The Supreme Court refused to hear an appeal by Peachtree News. *Peachtree News Co., Inc. v. United States*, 418 U.S. 932 (1974), *cert. denied*.

PECK v. TRIBUNE COMPANY (1909). This case concerned a published advertisement for a brand of whiskey, accompanied by a picture of a woman and certain statements by the woman attesting to the quality of the whiskey; the problem was that the photograph was of another person who did not make the published statements and who did not give any testimonial for the whiskey. The Supreme Court ruled that such a publication was a libel, even if it were the result of an honest mistake by the publisher. The Court opinion stated that "it seems to us impossible to say that the obvious tendency of what is imputed to the plaintiff by this advertisement is not seriously to hurt her standing with a considerable and respectable class in the community. Therefore it was the plaintiff's right to prove her case and go to the jury, and the defendant would have got all that it could ask if it had been permitted to persuade them, if it could, to take a contrary view." *Peck v. Tribune Company*, 214 U.S. 185 (1909).

PELL v. PROCUNIER (1974). Four California prison inmates and three professional journalists brought this suit, challenging the constitutionality of a regulation (California, Prison Regulations*) as a violation of the First Amendment. The regulation, § 415.071 of the California Department of Corrections Manual, provided that "press and other media interviews with specific individual inmates will not be permitted." The regulation was issued after a violent prison episode that the penal authorities attributed, at least in part, to the former policy of free, face-to-face prisoner-press interviews, which had resulted in a relatively small number of inmates gaining disproportionate notoriety and influence among their fellow inmates.

The Supreme Court upheld the constitutionality of the regulation: "(1) In light of the alternative channels of communication that are open to the inmates, § 415.071 does not constitute a violation of their rights of free speech. A. A prison inmate retains those First Amendment rights that are not inconsistent with his status as a prisoner or with the legitimate penological objectives of the corrections system, and here the restrictions on inmates' free speech rights must be balanced against the State's legitimate interest in confining prisoners to deter crime, to protect society by quarantining criminal offenders for a period during which rehabilitative procedures can be applied, and to maintain the internal security of penal institutions; B. Alternative means of communication remain open to the inmates: they can correspond by mail with persons (including media representatives); they have rights of visitation with family, clergy, attorneys, and friends of prior acquaintance; and they have unrestricted opportunity to communicate with the press or public through their prison visitors; and (2) The rights of the media are not infringed by § 415.071, which does not deny the press access to information available to the general public. Newsmen, under California policy, are free to visit both maximum security and minimum security sections of California penal institutions and to speak with inmates whom they may encounter, and (unlike members of the general public) are also free to interview inmates selected at random. The First Amendment does not guarantee the press a constitutional right of special access to information not available to the public generally." *Pell v. Procunier*, 417 U.S. 817 (1974).

P.E.N. AMERICAN CENTER. Founded in 1921, PEN is the autonomous American center of an international organization that has as its objective "to promote and maintain friendship and intellectual cooperation between men of letters in all countries in the interests of literature, freedom of expression and international goodwill. P.E.N. stands for the principle of unhampered transmission of thought within each nation and between all nations and members pledge themselves to oppose any form of suppression of freedom of expression in the country and community to which they belong. The acronym PEN stands for poets, playwrights, editors, essayists, and novelists. Membership is open by invitation to qualified writers, editors, and translators. Approximately 80 such autonomous centers in 60 countries are associated with the international organization." *Encyclopedia of Associations* (# 8881).

PENNEKAMP v. FLORIDA (1946). Pennekamp, associate editor of the *Miami Herald*, was responsible for the publication of two editorials and a cartoon criticizing certain actions previously taken by a Florida court as being too favorable to criminals and gambling establishments. This resulted in Pennekamp's being cited for contempt. The Florida Supreme Court affirmed the conviction on the grounds that the publications in question reflected on and impugned the integrity of the court, tended to create a distrust for the court, willfully withheld and suppressed the truth, and tended to obstruct the fair and impartial administration of justice in pending cases. Pennekamp argued that the publications were legitimate criticism and comment, protected by the First Amendment's guarantee of a free press, and that the publications created no clear and present danger to the administration of justice.

The Supreme Court reversed the conviction, seeing that there was no clear and present danger: That a judge may be influenced by a desire to placate the accusing newspaper to retain public esteem and secure reelection at the cost of unfair rulings against an accused is too remote a possibility to be considered a clear and present danger to the administration of justice. Justice Reed delivered the opinion of the Court: "Whether the threat to the impartial and orderly administration of justice must be a clear and present or a grave and immediate danger, a real and substantial threat, one which is close and direct or one which disturbs the court's sense of fairness depends upon a choice of words. Under any one of the phrases, reviewing courts are brought in cases of this type to appraise the comment on a balance between the desirability of free discussion and the necessity for fair adjudication, free from interruption of its processes. Free discussion of the problems of society is a cardinal principle of Americanism—a principle which all are zealous to preserve. Discussion that follows the termination of a case may be inadequate to emphasize the danger to public welfare of supposedly wrongful judicial conduct. It does not follow that public comment of every character upon pending trials or legal proceedings may be as free as a similar comment after complete disposal of the litigation. Between the extremes there are areas of discussion which an understanding writer will appraise in the light of the effect on himself and of the public of creating a clear and present danger to fair and orderly judicial administration. Courts must have power to protect the interests of prisoners and litigants before them from unseemly efforts to pervert judicial action. In the borderline instances where it is difficult to say upon which side the alleged offense falls, we think the specific freedom of public comment should weigh heavily against a possible tendency to influence pending cases. Freedom of discussion should be given the widest range compatible with the essential requirement of the fair and orderly administration of justice."

Justice Murphy filed a concurring opinion: "Were we to sanction the judgment rendered by the court below we would be approving, in effect, an unwarranted restriction upon the freedom of the press. That freedom covers something more than the right to approve and condone insofar as the judiciary and the judicial process are concerned. It also includes the right to criticize and disparage, even though the terms be vitriolic, scurrilous or erroneous. To talk of a clear and present danger arising out of such criticism is idle unless the criticism makes it impossible in a very real sense for a court to carry on the administration of justice. That situation is not even remotely present in this case. Judges should be foremost in their vigilance to protect the freedom of others to rebuke and castigate the bench and in their refusal to be influenced by unfair or misinformed censure. Otherwise freedom may rest upon the precarious base of judicial sensitiveness and caprice. And a chain reaction may be set up, resulting in countless restrictions and limitations upon liberty.'' *Pennekamp v. Florida*, 328 U.S. 331 (1946).

PENNSYLVANIA, MOTION PICTURE CONTROL ACT. The censorship of motion picture films in the state of Pennsylvania goes back almost to the beginning of the industry (Film Censorship*). The film censorship scheme was originally enacted in 1915, giving to a Board of Censors the right to examine every film before issuing an exhibition permit. The board was mandated to approve only those films that were ''moral and proper'' and to disapprove those that were ''sacrilegious, obscene, indecent, immoral, or tend to debase or corrupt morals.''

The act was amended several times; the 1959 version is what follows. The 1959 Pennsylvania Motion Picture Control Act required any person intending to exhibit a film in the state to register with the Board of Censors within forty-eight hours before the first showing. The board could request for examination a copy of the film, and the exhibitor had to pay for such an examination. If a majority of the board thought that the film was ''obscene,'' the film could be disapproved or be listed as ''unsuitable for children.'' A child was defined as anyone under seventeen years, and a film was obscene ''if to the average person applying contemporary community standards its dominant theme, taken as a whole, appeals to prurient interest.'' A film was ''unsuitable for children'' if it were obscene or ''incites to crime.'' Incites to crime was defined as that ''which represents or portrays as acceptable conduct or as conduct worthy of emulation the commission of any crime, or the manifesting of contempt for law.''

Section 13 of the 1959 act made the violation of any provision of the act a criminal offense subject to a fine of from $400 to $1,000 or a prison sentence not exceeding six months or both. Section 14 provided that the act ''does not apply to any sale, lease, loan, exhibition or use of films, reels or views for purely educational, charitable, fraternal, family or religious purpose by any religious association, fraternal society, family, library, museum, public school or private school, or industrial, business, institutional, advertising or training films, or films concerned exclusively with the advancement of law, medicine and other professions: Provided, That any such film is not exhibited or to be exhibited in theatres or in public places of entertainment commonly used as such.''

The Pennsylvania Motion Picture Control Act, and the censorship scheme it established, was held to be an unconstitutional prior restraint on the right of free speech and of a free press by a Pennsylvania court in 1961, in *William Goldman Theatres, Inc. v. Dana.**

PENNSYLVANIA, SEDITION ACT. Pennsylvania Penal Code § 207, "Sedition Act," read as follows: "The word 'sedition,' as used in this section, shall mean: Any writing, publication, printing, cut, cartoon, utterance, or conduct, either individually or in connection or combination with any other person, the intent of which is: (a) To make or cause to be made any outbreak or demonstration of violence against this State or against the United States. (b) To encourage any person to take any measures or engage in any conduct with a view of overthrowing or destroying or attempting to overthrow or destroy, by any force or show or threat of force, the Government of this State or of the United States. (c) To incite or encourage any person to commit any overt act with a view to bringing the Government of this State or the United States into hatred or contempt. (d) To incite any person or persons to do or attempt to do personal injury or harm to any officer of this State or of the United States, or to damage or destroy any public property or the property of any public official because of his official position. . . . Sedition shall be a felony. Whoever is guilty of sedition shall, upon conviction thereof, be sentenced to pay a fine not exceeding ten thousand dollars ($10,000), or to undergo imprisonment not exceeding twenty (20) years, or both." The Supreme Court, in *Pennsylvania v. Nelson* (1956),* held this act to be unenforceable, not because it was unconstitutional on its face ($10,000 or twenty years or both for bringing the government into "hatred" or "contempt"), but because the federal Smith Act* superseded the Pennsylvania act.

PENNSYLVANIA v. NELSON (1956). Nelson, an acknowledged member of the Communist party, was convicted in a Pennsylvania court of a violation of the Pennsylvania Sedition Act* and received a sentence of twenty years in prison, a fine of $10,000, and court costs of $13,000. A state appeals court affirmed the conviction, but the Supreme Court of Pennsylvania reversed. That court decided the case on the narrow issue of supersession of the state law by the federal Smith Act* (it ignored several serious trial errors and conduct of the trial judge infringing on Nelson's right to due process of law). The Pennsylvania Supreme Court stated: "And, while the Pennsylvania statute proscribes sedition against either the Government of the United States or the Government of Pennsylvania, it is only alleged sedition against the United States with which the instant case is concerned. Out of all the voluminous testimony, we have not found, nor has anyone pointed to, a single word indicating a seditious act or even utterance directed against the Government of Pennsylvania."

The government of Pennsylvania was not happy with this decision and appealed to the U.S. Supreme Court. The Supreme Court agreed with the Pennsylvania decision: The federal Smith Act of 1940, as amended in 1948, which prohibits the knowing advocacy of the overthrow of the government of the United States by force and violence, supersedes the enforceability of the Pennsylvania Sedition Act, which proscribed the same conduct. *Pennsylvania v. Nelson*, 350 U.S. 497 (1956).

THE PENTAGON PAPERS. *The Pentagon Papers* concerned the now-famous attempt of the U.S. government, during the Nixon administration, to prevent the *New York Times* and the *Washington Post* from publishing the contents of a classified study formally entitled *History of United States Decision-Making Process on Viet Nam Policy*, but commonly referred to as *The Pentagon Papers*. The study contained the Pentagon's view of three decades of U.S. involvement in Viet Nam. One weakness of the *Papers* was that it came from only one source—the Pentagon—and did not contain other views from other agencies. The *Papers* did not contain any "secret" documents (Classified Information*), although the government alleged that its publication would "harm the national interest." The *New York Times* published extracts on June 13, 14, and 15, 1971, but was then interrupted by a restraining order by a federal appeals court; publication was resumed on July 1 through July 5, 1971. The *Washington Post* was similarly attacked by the government.

On June 30, 1971, the Supreme Court, in the two companion cases (*New York Times v. United States* and *United States v. Washington Post*, 403 U.S. 713 [1971]), ruled that the government had not justified its attempt at prior restraint, and the newspapers were then free to continue to publish as they saw fit. The Court's decision was a three-paragraph per curiam decision; several justices, however, added their own concurring opinions. Justice Black, joined by Justice Douglas, made the following comments: "I believe that every moment's continuance of the injunctions against these newspapers amounts to a flagrant, indefensible, and continuing violation of the First Amendment. In my view it is unfortunate that some of my Brethren are apparently willing to hold that the publication of news may sometimes be enjoined. Such a holding would make a shambles of the First Amendment. Our Government was launched in 1789 with the adoption of the Constitution. The Bill of Rights, including the First Amendment, followed in 1791. Now, for the first time in the 182 years since the founding of the Republic, the federal courts are asked to hold that the First Amendment does not mean what it says, but rather means that the Government can halt the publication of current news of vital importance to the people of this country. In seeking injunctions against these newspapers and in its presentation to the Court, the Executive Branch seems to have forgotten the essential purpose and history of the First Amendment.

"When the Constitution was adopted, many people strongly opposed it because the document contained no Bill of Rights to safeguard certain basic freedoms. They especially feared that the new powers granted to a central government might be interpreted to permit the government to curtail freedom of religion, press, assembly, and speech. In response to an overwhelming public clamor, James Madison offered a series of amendments to satisfy citizens that these great liberties would remain safe and beyond the power of government to abridge. ... The amendments were offered to *curtail* and *restrict* the general powers granted to the Executive, Legislative, and Judicial Branches two years before in the original Constitution. The Bill of Rights changed the original Constitution into a new charter under which no branch of government could abridge the people's freedoms of press, speech, religion, and assembly. Yet the Solicitor General argues and some members of the Court appear to agree that the general powers of the Government adopted in the original Constitution should be interpreted to limit and restrict the specific and emphatic guarantees of the Bill of Rights adopted later. I can imagine no greater perversion of history. Madison and the other Framers of the First Amendment, able men that they were, wrote in language they earnestly believed could never be misunderstood: 'Congress shall make no law . . . abridging the freedom . . . of the press.'

''Both the history and language of the First Amendment support the view that the press must be left free to publish news, whatever the source, without censorship, injunctions, or prior restraints. In the First Amendment the Founding Fathers gave the free press the protection it must have to fulfill its essential role in our democracy. The press was to serve the governed, not the governors. The Government's power to censor the press was abolished so that it could bare the secrets of government and inform the people. Only a free and unrestrained press can effectively expose deception in government. And paramount among the responsibilities of a free press is the duty to prevent any part of the government from deceiving the people and sending them off to distant lands to die of foreign fevers and foreign shot and shell. In my view, far from deserving condemnation for their courageous reporting, the *New York Times*, the *Washington Post*, and other newspapers should be commended for serving the purpose that the Founding Fathers saw so clearly. In revealing the workings of government that led to the Vietnam war, the newspapers nobly did precisely that which the Founders hoped and trusted they would do.

''The Government's case here is based on premises entirely different from those that guided the Framers of the First Amendment. The Solicitor General has carefully and emphatically stated: 'Now, Mr. Justice [Black], your construction of . . . [the First Amendment] is well known, and I certainly respect it. You say that no law means no law, and that should be obvious. I can only say, Mr. Justice, that to me it is equally obvious that ''no law'' does not mean ''no law,'' and I would seek to persuade the Court that that is true. . . . There are other parts of the Constitution that grant powers and responsibilities to the Executive, and . . . the First Amendment was not intended to make it impossible for the Executive to function or to protect the security of the United States.' And the Government argues in its brief that in spite of the First Amendment, 'the authority of the Executive Department to protect the nation against publication of information whose disclosure would endanger the national security stems from two interrelated sources: the constitutional power of the President over the conduct of foreign affairs and his authority as Commander-in-Chief.' In other words, we are asked to hold that despite the First Amendment's emphatic command, the Executive Branch, the Congress, and the Judiciary can make laws enjoining publication of current news and abridging freedom of the press in the name of 'national security.' The Government does not even attempt to rely on any act of Congress.

Instead it makes the bold and dangerously far-reaching contention that the courts should take it upon themselves to 'make' a law abridging freedom of the press in the name of equity, presidential power and national security, even when the representatives of the people in Congress have adhered to the command of the First Amendment and refused to make such a law.

"To find that the President has 'inherent power' to halt the publication of news by resort to the courts would wipe out the First Amendment and destroy the fundamental liberty and security of the very people the Government hopes to make 'secure.' No one can read the history of the adoption of the First Amendment without being convinced beyond any doubt that it was injunctions like those sought here that Madison and his collaborators intended to outlaw in this Nation for all time. The word 'security' is a broad, vague generality whose contours should not be invoked to abrogate the fundamental law embodied in the First Amendment. The guarding of military and diplomatic secrets at the expense of informed representative government provides no real security for our Republic. The Framers of the First Amendment, fully aware of both the need to defend a new nation and the abuses of the English and Colonial governments, sought to give this new society strength and security by providing that freedom of speech, press, religion, and assembly should not be abridged."

Justice Brennan also filed a concurring opinion, but he was less sanguine about the absoluteness of the First Amendment. Justice Brennan: "The error that has pervaded these cases from the outset was the granting of any injunctive relief whatsoever, interim or otherwise. The entire thrust of the Government's claim throughout these cases has been that publication of the material sought to be enjoined 'could,' or 'might,' or 'may' prejudice the national interest in various ways. But the First Amendment tolerates absolutely no prior judicial restraints of the press predicated upon surmise or conjecture that untoward consequences may result. Our cases, it is true, have indicated that there is a single, extremely narrow class of cases in which the First Amendment's ban on prior judicial restraint may be overridden. Our cases have thus far indicated that such cases may arise only when the Nation 'is at war' (*Schenck v. United States**), during which times 'no one would question but that a government might prevent actual obstruction to its recruiting service or the publication of the sailing dates of transports or the number and location of troops' (*Near v. Minnesota ex rel. Olson**). Even if the present world situation were assumed to be tantamount to a time of war, or if the power of presently available armaments would justify even in peacetime the suppression of information that would set in motion a nuclear holocaust, in neither of these actions has the Government presented or even alleged that publication of items from or based upon the material at issue would cause the happening of an event of that nature. The chief purpose of the First Amendment's guaranty is to prevent previous restraints upon publication. Thus, only governmental allegation and proof that publication must inevitably, directly, and immediately cause the occurrence of an event kindred to imperiling the safety of a transport already at sea can support even the issuance of an interim restraining order. . . . Unless and until the Government has clearly made out its case, the First Amendment commands that no injunction may issue."

PEOPLE FOR THE AMERICAN WAY. Founded in 1980 by television producer Norman Lear (*All in the Family*) and currently chaired by John H. Buchanan, a former Republican congressman from Alabama, People for the American Way is a national organization seeking to counteract censorship of books and television programs. It views the Moral Majority* and the Eagle Forum* as its main opposition. The organization describes itself as: "Religious, business, media and labor figures committed to reaffirming the traditional American values of pluralism, diversity, and freedom of expression and religion. Does not engage in political or lobbying activity. People for the American Way was developed out of concern that an anti-democratic and divisive climate was being created by groups that sought to use religion and religious symbols for political purposes. Seeks to help Americans maintain their belief in self; to reaffirm that in this society the individual still matters; that to improve the quality of life [one] must strengthen the common cords that unite us as humans and as citizens. Engaged in a mass media campaign to create a positive climate of tolerance and respect for diverse peoples, religions, and values. Maintains speakers bureau; conducts research programs. Distributes educational materials, leaflets and brochures." *Encyclopedia of Associations* (# 12057). People for the American Way was the catalyst for the 1984 decision by the Texas State Textbook Committee* not to require biology textbooks to have a disclaimer to the effect that evolution was only one of several theories as to the origins of man.

PEOPLE ON COMPLAINT OF ARCURI v. FINKELSTEIN (1952). Finkelstein ran a neighborhood candy store and luncheonette in a section of Brooklyn, New York. He was charged with and duly convicted of a violation of the New York Obscenity Statute.* Finkelstein was convicted of selling to high school students pictures showing females in stages of undress reaching nudity and magazines containing pictures of nude and semi-nude females, even though the picture sets were accompanied by a brochure explaining their artistic worth and the magazines were purported to teach photography. City Magistrate Malbin thought that this was an abomination, and even though his reasoning had been discredited years earlier, he employed the Hicklin Rule* (the "obscenity" of any material can be judged by the effects of isolated passages on the most susceptible mind) in deciding that Finkelstein should be held for trial in Special Sessions. City Magistrate Malbin: "Let us look at this case with a realistic approach. Here is a small neighborhood store serving the families of the area. It caters to high school children who come in, observe these pictures, purchase them and [what is the abomination] seek dark corners and privacy to snicker over its contents and pass the pictures around among their friends. This is a condition we may not be able to cure, but when the opportunity arises to alleviate it, it should not be allowed to pass. . . . An important but not the sole test to be applied in determining whether a book offends the law against obscene publications is, does the matter charged as obscene tend to deprave or corrupt those whose minds are open to immoral influences and who might come in contact with it, ever bearing in mind the consideration that the statute looks to the protection not of the mature and the intelligent, with minds strengthened to withstand the influence of the prohibited data, but of the young and immature, the ignorant and sensually inclined [i.e., high school students]. The nude pictures of female figures were on display open to view to the young and impressionable, particularly to those the statute was expressly designed to protect. The inclusion of the brochure is a transparent device and a subterfuge which cannot change or disguise the true nature and purpose of the materials. Pictures are obscene which tend to stir sexual impulses or to lead to sexually impure thoughts.'' *People on Complaint of Arcuri v. Finkelstein*, 114 N.Y.S. 2d 810 (1952).

PEOPLE v. BIRCH (1963). This case concerned an attempt by the state of New York to have the courts declare certain books obscene as a violation of § 1141 of the New York Penal Code (New York, Obscenity Statute*) and to have the books' authors declared criminals. The specific books and authors were *Sex Kitten* (Greg Caldwell), *Clipjoint Cutie* (Monte Steele), *The Wild Ones* (Nell Holland), *The Hottest Party in Town* (Sam Hudson), *Passion Pit* (David Spencer), *Bedroom at the Top* (Bruce Rald), and *Butch* and *College for Sinners* (Andrew Shaw).

In a wide-ranging decision, Judge Shapiro demolished the state's argument: (1) The effect of books on children and their reactions are not legally valid tests to determine what constitutes illegal pornography. (2) Poorly written books, which were mostly lurid descriptions of sexual activities in socially acceptable language, were not obscene or hard-core pornography within the meaning of the statute dealing with obscene prints and articles as constitutionally construed in the light of the free press guarantee of the First Amendment. (3) If obscenity is to be suppressed, the question of whether a particular work is obscene involves not an issue of fact, but a question of constitutional judgment of the most sensitive and delicate kind. (4) The fact that the literary value of certain books alleged to be obscene may be nil does not mean that the books may therefore be suppressed or that their authors or distributors are criminals. (5) The basic question in determining whether the books were obscene was whether the books went beyond the present critical point in compromise between candor and shame at which the community has arrived, and a community cannot, when liability of speech and press are at issue, condemn that which it generally tolerates. (6) The fact that adulterous or other sexually immoral relationships are portrayed approvingly in a book cannot serve as a reason for declaring the book obscene without running afoul of the First Amendment, since the Constitution protects advocacy of opinion that adultery may sometimes be proper (*Lady Chatterley's Lover**), no less than advocacy of socialism or the single tax. (7) The failure of these authors to achieve literary recognition does not make their works more objectionable, legally or morally, than the works of writers who merit or who have received high acclaim of the critics for their literary style and grace. (8) Certain words that supposedly are not used in polite society and that are denoted as "four-letter words," do not in and of themselves make for obscenity. (9) Undue legal restraint on writings alleged to be obscene must be guarded against, since the exercise of censorship tends to feed on itself and to extend into and encroach on areas of personal liberties, which are at the very foundation of a free society. *People v. Birch*, 243 N.Y.S. 2d 525 (1963).

PEOPLE v. BOOKCASE, INC. (1964). This case concerned § 484-h of the New York Penal Code (New York, Sale of Obscene Material to Minors*) when the defendant was convicted in the Criminal Court of New York City of having sold a copy of John Cleland's *Memoirs of a Woman of Pleasure** (*Fanny Hill*) to a minor under eighteen years of age. The case did not concern itself with whether or not *Fanny Hill* was obscene; the issue was that § 484-h, besides prohibiting the sale of obscene material, made it a crime to sell material to minors if the material was principally devoted to "subjects of illicit sex or sexual immorality"—a description par excellence of *Memoirs*.

The New York Court of Appeals reversed the conviction, however, holding that the statute was too vague and that it would prohibit the circulation to minors of all publications dealing with illicit sex or sexual immorality regardless of the manner in which the subject was presented. Judge Van Voorhis delivered the opinion of the New York Court of Appeals: "The quality of the printed or pictorial material which is forbidden by the portion of the statutory enactment which is now before us is, consequently, not to be judged by whether it tends to incite minors or adults to immoral acts, or by whether it is in its nature obscene in the eyes of minors or of adults, but whether the Legislature can constitutionally prevent the sale to minors of this age material which deals mainly with illicit sex or sexual immorality. The purpose and the only object of this clause in the statute . . . was to prevent or limit publications or pictures coming before the eyes of the young which are principally based upon the theme of sexual conduct that is contrary to the mores of society. The statute does not distinguish between material regarded as obscene for teenagers but unobjectionable to adults; it sets no variable standards of what constitutes obscenity according to the age or other type of group at which the material in question is principally aimed, nor does this clause in the statute render it necessary to conviction that the material dealing with illicit sex or sexual immorality shall have been presented in a salacious manner. A statute could hardly be drawn which would permit exhibition of intimate sexual details of married life, for example, and at the same time exclude similar presentations where the participants are not married [to each other]. On the contrary, the only construction of which this statutory language is susceptible is that the subject of illicit sex or sexual immorality is not to be brought before the young by pictures or writings—scientific, fictional . . . sociological discussion, moralizing, or otherwise. The Oedipus legend in classic Greek drama would be forbidden because it is principally devoted to incest, the Tristan and Isolde legend and Hawthorne's *Scarlet Letter* would be illicit reading for the young because it is principally made up of adultery. Bernard Shaw's *Mrs. Warren's Profession* would be outlawed for obvious reasons, as well as all writings dealing with homosexuality. Such a list could be extended almost indefinitely. It is not suggested that these or other parallel works of literature are likely to be offered for sale at the same newsstands where the type of comic books are purchased which was the main reason for the adoption of this legislation, but the constitutionality of a statute governing publications is to be tested by what can be done under it and not by the particular violation which is charged with having occurred [Overbreadth*]. It seems to us that this statute is drawn so broadly as to render criminal sales or other exhibition to the young of pictures and publications of all kinds which are principally devoted to these subjects, in however serious or dignified a manner, and, in our view, it is so broad and so obscure in its coverage as to abridge the constitutionally protected freedom of speech and of the press as well as the due process clauses in the Federal and State Constitutions." *People v. Bookcase, Inc.*, 201 N.E. 2d 14 (1964).

PEOPLE v. BRUCE (1964). Comedian Lenny Bruce was convicted in the Municipal Court of Chicago for giving an "obscene" performance in a Chicago nightclub. The court record described his act as follows: "The performance here consisted of a 55-minute monologue upon numerous socially controversial subjects interspersed with such unrelated topics as the meeting of a psychotic rapist and a nymphomaniac who have both escaped from their respective institutions, defendant's intimacies with three married women, and a supposed conversation with a gas station attendant in a rest room which concludes with the suggestion that the defendant and the attendant both put on contraceptives and take a picture. The testimony was that defendant also made motions indicating masturbation and accompanied these with vulgar comments, and that persons leaving the audience were subjected to revolting questions and suggestions."

Bruce appealed his conviction, and the Supreme Court of Illinois reversed, saying the performance was not obscene: "The entire performance was originally held by us to be characterized by its continual reference, by words and acts, to sexual intercourse or sexual organs in terms which ordinary adult individuals find thoroughly disgusting and revolting as well as patently offensive; that, as is evident from these brief summaries, it went beyond customary limits of candor, a fact which becomes even more apparent when the entire monologue is considered. Our original opinion recognized defendant's right to satirize society's attitudes on contemporary social problems and to express his ideas, however bizarre, as long as the method used in doing so was not so objectionable as to render the entire performance obscene. Affirmance of the conviction was predicated upon the rule . . . that the obscene portions of the material must be balanced against its affirmative values to determine which predominates. We rejected defendant's argument that *Roth v. United States** struck down this balancing test and held that material, no matter how objectionable the method of its presentation, was constitutionally privileged unless it was utterly without redeeming social importance. It is apparent from the opinions of a majority of the [Supreme Court] in *Jacobellis v. Ohio* (*Les Amants**) that the 'balancing test' rule . . . is no longer a constitutionally accepted method of determining whether material is obscene, and it is there made clear that material having *any* social importance is constitutionally protected. While we would not have thought that constitutional guarantees necessitate the subjection of society to the gradual deterioration of its moral fabric which this type of presentation promotes, we must concede that some of its topics commented on by defendant are of social importance. Under *Jacobellis* the entire performance is thereby immunized, and we are constrained to hold that the judgment of the circuit court of Cook County must be reversed and defendant discharged.'' *People v. Bruce*, 202 N.E. 2d 497 (1964).

PERRY EDUCATION ASSOCIATION v. PERRY LOCAL EDUCATORS' ASSOCIATION (1983). Under a collective bargaining agreement signed by the Board of Education of Perry Township, Indiana, and the Perry Educational Association (PEA), PEA was named as the exclusive bargaining representative for the school district's teachers. The agreement also gave PEA sole and exclusive access to the inter-school mail system and the teachers' mailboxes within each school; rival unions, such as the Perry Local Educators' Association (PLEA), were denied access to the mail system and the mailboxes. PLEA then brought suit, charging that the school district, by giving only one union access to the mails, violated the First Amendment rights of those unions not granted such access.

In a close decision (5 to 4), the U.S. Supreme Court ruled that the First Amendment was not violated by the preferential access to the inter-school mail system granted to PEA. Justice White delivered the majority opinion: (1) With respect to public property that is not by tradition or government designation a forum for public communication (Public Forum/Public Place*), a state may reserve the use of the property for its intended purposes, communicative or otherwise, as long as a regulation on speech is reasonable and not an effort to suppress expression merely because public officials oppose the speaker's view. The school mail facilities were not a "limited public forum" merely because the system had been opened for periodic use by civic and church organizations, or because PLEA was allowed to use the facilities (for the distribution of material without postage; the mailboxes were open to any stamped matter) on an equal footing with PEA before PEA's certification as the teachers' exclusive bargaining representative; and (2) The differential access is consistent with the school district's legitimate interest in preserving the property for the use to which it was lawfully dedicated. The use of the facilities enables PEA to perform its obligations as exclusive representative of *all* the teachers in the district; PLEA does not have any official responsibility in connection with the school district and thus need not be entitled to the same rights of access to the mailboxes.

There was a strong dissent from the minority, Justice Brennan speaking for those who viewed this as a violation of the First Amendment. Justice Brennan: "In order to secure the First Amendment's guarantee of freedom of speech and to prevent distortions of the 'marketplace of ideas,' governments generally are prohibited from discriminating among viewpoints on issues within the realm of protected speech. In this case the board has infringed [PLEA's] First Amendment rights by granting exclusive access to an effective channel of communication to [PEA] and denying such access to [PLEA]. In view of [PEA's] failure to establish even a substantial state interest that is advanced by the exclusive access policy, the policy must be held to be constitutionally infirm." *Perry Education Association v. Perry Local Educators' Association*, 74 L. Ed. 2d 794 (1983).

PHILADELPHIA (PA), STATE OF EMERGENCY. The city of Philadelphia had passed an ordinance (10-819) that authorized the mayor to declare a state of emergency. The relevant sections of the ordinance read as follows (§ 10-819, State of Emergency): "The Mayor of the City of Philadelphia is authorized, if he finds that the City or any part thereof is suffering, or is in imminent danger of suffering civil disturbance, disorder, riot or other occurrence which will seriously and substantially endanger the health, safety and property of the citizens, to declare a STATE OF EMERGENCY and take the following specified measures throughout the City or any part thereof: (a) Prohibit or limit the number of persons who may gather or congregate upon the public highways or public sidewalks or in any outdoor place, except persons who are awaiting transportation, engaging in recreational activities at a usual and customary place, or peacefully entering or leaving a building."

Pursuant to this ordinance, the mayor, on the day after the assassination of Martin Luther King, Jr., issued a proclamation that was in effect from 9:00 P.M., April 5, 1968, until 6:00 A.M., April 10, 1968. The proclamation, in part, read: "WHEREAS, Widespread public disorder has erupted in cities throughout the nation, resulting in numerous deaths, personal injuries and extensive damage to property; and, WHEREAS, There exists a threat of public disorder in the City of Philadelphia, particularly as a result of meetings and gatherings in public places; and WHEREAS, The City has made and continues to make substantial efforts to prevent disorders but it is deemed that the threat to the City warrants additional action to protect the health, safety, and property of the citizens of Philadelphia. Now, This Fifth day of April, 1968, pursuant to the powers vested in me under Section 4-100 of the Philadelphia Home Rule Charter, and Chapter 10-800 of the Philadelphia Code, I hereby declare a limited State of Emergency in the City of Philadelphia. All persons in groups of twelve (12) or more are hereby prohibited from gathering or congregating upon public highways or public sidewalks, or in any other outdoor place, except persons who are awaiting transportation, engaging in recreational activities at a usual and customary place, or peaceably entering or leaving buildings.''

This state of emergency was employed to convict several people (*Commonwealth of Pennsylvania v. Stotland**) who argued that their First Amendment right of free speech was violated by the proclamation; a Pennsylvania court (the Supreme Court refused to hear the appeal) ruled that the restrictions were a valid time-place-manner* restraint on the freedom of speech.

PICKERING v. BOARD OF EDUCATION (1968). A local Board of Education in Illinois fired Pickering, a teacher, for writing and publishing in a newspaper a letter criticizing the board's allocation of school funds between educational and athletic programs and the board's and school superintendent's methods of informing (or lack thereof) the school district's taxpayers of the "real" reasons additional tax revenues were being sought for the schools. At a hearing, the school board charged that Pickering made numerous false statements in the letter and that the publication of the letter "unjustifiably impugned" the board and the school administration.

The Illinois courts, all concluding that the publication was indeed "detrimental to the best interests of the schools," upheld Pickering's dismissal; the Supreme Court reversed on the grounds that Pickering's right of free speech was violated. Justice Douglas delivered the opinion of the Court: "To the extent that the Illinois Supreme Court's opinion may be read to suggest that teachers may constitutionally be compelled to relinquish the First Amendment rights they would otherwise enjoy as citizens to comment on matters of public interest in connection with the operation of the public schools in which they work, it proceeds on a premise that has been unequivocally rejected . . . [by this] Court. . . . Accordingly, to the extent that the Board's position here can be taken to suggest that even comments on matters of public concern that are substantially correct [as were portions of Pickering's letter] may furnish grounds for dismissal if they are sufficiently critical in tone, we unequivocally reject it. We next consider the statements in [the] letter which we agree to be false. The Board's original charges included allegations that the publication of the letter damaged the professional reputations of the Board and the superintendent and would foment controversy and conflict among the Board, teachers, administrators, and the residents of the district. However, no evidence to support these allegations was introduced at the hearing. So far as the record reveals, Pickering's letter was greeted by everyone but its main target, the Board, with massive apathy and total disbelief. The only way in which the Board could conclude, absent any evidence of the actual effect of the letter, that the statements contained therein were *per se* detrimental to the interest of the schools was to equate the Board members' own interests with that of the schools. . . . Debate is vital to informed decision-making by the electorate. Teachers are, as a class, the members of a community most likely to have informed and definite opinions as to how funds allotted to the operation of the schools should be spent. Accordingly, it is essential that they be able to speak out freely on such questions without fear of retaliatory dismissal.'' *Pickering v. Board of Education*, 391 U.S. 563 (1968).

PIERCE v. UNITED STATES (1920). Pierce and others were convicted of violating the Espionage Act*—they published and circulated a pamphlet (''The Price We Pay'') that was characterized by the government as ''attempting to cause insubordination and disloyalty and refusal of duty in the military and naval forces'' and containing ''false statements with intent to interfere with the operation and success of those forces in the war with Germany.'' As political polemics go these days, ''The Price We Pay'' was a rather tame document issued by the national office of the Socialist party, in Chicago. Its general tone was a protest against U.S. involvement in World War I, along with some anti-war statements in general and that with the coming of socialism, the world would be a better place.

The Supreme Court did not like the anti-war Socialists in the early years (*Debs v. United States**), and the court record reproduced some statements from ''The Price We Pay'' that the Court viewed as 'sensational': ''Conscription is upon us; the draft law is a fact!/Into your homes the recruiting officers are coming. They will take your sons of military age and impress them into the army./Stand them up in long rows, break them into squads and platoons, teach them to deploy and wheel;/Guns will be put into their hands; they will be taught not to think, only to obey without questioning./Then they will be shipped thru the submarine zone by the hundreds of thousands to the bloody quagmire of Europe./Into that seething, heaving swamp of torn flesh and floating entrails they will be plunged, in regiments, divisions and armies, screaming as they go./Agonies of torture will rend their flesh from their sinews, will crack their bones and dissolve their lungs; every pang will be multiplied in its passage to you.''

The Supreme Court did not like such language when the order of the day was to support the war effort; Pierce's conviction was affirmed—not on the grounds that the war effort was impaired, but because Pierce hoped or intended that the effort would suffer: '' 'The Price We Pay' . . . was intended, as the jury found, to interfere with the conscription and recruitment services; to cause men eligible for the service to evade the draft; to bring home to them, and especially to their parents, sisters, wives, and sweethearts, a sense of impending personal loss, calculated to discourage the young men from entering the service.''

The affirmation of the conviction was not unanimous, however; Justices Brandeis and Holmes dissented on the grounds that no ''clear and present danger'' existed: ''A verdict should have been directed for the defendants on these counts because the leaflet was not distributed under such circumstances, nor was it of such a nature, as to create a clear and present danger of causing either insubordination, disloyalty, mutiny or refusal of duty in the military or naval forces. The leaflet contains lurid and perhaps exaggerated pictures of the horrors of war. Its arguments as to the causes of this war may appear to us shallow and grossly unfair. The remedy proposed [Socialism] may seem to us worse than the evil which, it is argued, will be thereby removed. But the leaflet, far from counselling disobedience to law, points to the hopelessness of protest, under the existing system, pictures the irresistible power of the military arm of the Government, and indicates that acquiescence is a necessity. . . . The fundamental right of free men to strive for better conditions through new legislation and new institutions will not be preserved, if efforts to secure it by argument to fellow citizens may be construed as criminal incitement to disobey the existing law—merely, because the argument presented seems to those exercising judicial power to be unfair in its portrayal of existing evils, mistaken in its assumptions, unsound in reasoning or intemperate in language. No objections more serious than these can . . . be made to the arguments presented in 'The Price We Pay.' " *Pierce v. United States*, 252 U.S. 239 (1920).

PINKUS, dba ROSSLYN NEWS CO. v. UNITED STATES (1978). Pinkus was convicted of violating 18 U.S.C. § 1461 (Postal Regulations, Mailing Obscene Material*) for mailing certain materials and advertising brochures that were eventually judged to be obscene. He appealed his conviction to the Supreme Court, challenging that the trial court judge's instructions to the jury on the question of obscenity were improper because the instructions included (1) children within the definition of the "community" by whose standards obscenity was to be judged; (2) "sensitive" persons; (3) members of deviant sexual groups could be considered in determining whether the materials appealed to the prurient interest; and (4) that "pandering"* (commercial exploitation of erotica solely for the sake of their prurient interest) could be considered in the definition of obscenity.

The Supreme Court held that (2), (3), and (4)—sensitive persons, deviant sexual groups, and pandering—could be considered, but children cannot be included as part of the "community." The Court ruled that a jury, striving to define such a community—the "average person" by whose standards obscenity is to be judged—might very well reach a much lower "average" when children are part of the equation than it would if it restricted its consideration to the effect of allegedly obscene materials on adults. *Pinkus, dba Rosslyn News Co. v. United States*, 436 U.S. 293 (1978).

PINKY. This 1949 American film was produced by Darryl F. Zanuck, directed by Elia Kazan, and starred Ethel Barrymore, Ethel Waters, and William Lundigan; it was also banned in 1952 in Marshall, Texas. The exhibitor of the film, Gelling, was convicted under an ordinance of the city of Marshall for exhibiting the film after being denied permission to do so by the local Board of Censors. The city ordinance allowed the Board of Censors to deny permission for the showing of a motion picture that, in the opinion of the board, is "of such character as to be prejudicial to the best interests of the people of said City," and made the showing of a film without having the board's permission a misdemeanor.

The film is described by de Grazia and Newman (*Banned Films*, pp. 238–239): "The film is based on the novel of the same title by Cid Ricketts Summer. Pinky is a light-skinned young black nurse who visits her grandmother's home in the South after 12 years away in Boston. Her grandmother tells Pinky that she must nurse the owner of the plantation, Miss Em, because years ago Miss Em had nursed the grandmother. Although Pinky would rather leave and marry her fiance, a white Boston doctor, she complies with her grandmother's wishes and stays. While in the South, she is labeled a black and suffers from racist slurs and threats. Before dying, Miss Em changes her will so that she can leave the plantation to Pinky. Pinky comes to realize that she must not seek to escape her color by fleeing to Boston and marrying, but instead stay and open a nursing home for the blacks who live on the estate."†

Gelling's conviction was affirmed by the Court of Criminal Appeals of Texas. The decision rendered by the court, Judge Beauchamp, needs no additional explanation except to note that censors are not the only people who take it on themselves to judge what is right and proper for other people—there have been (and still are) many judges whose views approximate those of Anthony Comstock (Comstockery*). Judge Beauchamp of the Court of Criminal Appeals of Texas: "We cannot concede that the motion picture industry has emerged from the business of amusement and become propagators of ideas entitling it to freedom of speech. If in fact circumstances have developed surrounding the industry whereby television can bring to the youth of our cities, and even of rural areas, matters which are improper and even though magazines of a type are circulated through the U.S. Mails which present ideas derogatory to the proper development of good citizens, yet we cannot concede that this has divested the municipal authorities of a right to regulate such subjects. If some are exposed to evil, if evil it be, there is within such fact no argument that other and all evil should be strown in the path of our youth. The desire of a great industry to reap greater fruits from its operations should not be indulged at the expense of Christian character, upon which America must rely for its future existence. Every boy and every girl reaching manhood or womanhood is, to an extent, the product of the community from which he comes. If the citizens of that community are divested of all power to surround them with wholesome entertainment and character building education, then their product will go forth weak indeed. If the community surrenders its power voluntarily, if the state does, then we may expect our Federal Government to move into fields with which it should not be encumbered and in which it cannot best serve. Our loyalty to our government is based on an appreciation for its efficiency. We cherish the history of a Federal Government which has been based on a constitution as solid as the rocks and whose constancy is not shifted by the changing winds. It is the duty of this court, and

†Reprinted from *Banned Films* with permission of the R. R. Bowker Company. Copyright © 1982 by Edward de Grazia and Roger K. Newman.

of all courts, to follow the mandates and stay within the powers of our constitutional provisions. This is fundamental.''

The Supreme Court dismissed both Judge Beauchamp's appeal to save Christianity from the evils of films and Gelling's conviction (*Gelling v. Texas*, 343 U.S. 960 [1952]). In a concurring opinion, Justice Douglas commented: ''The evil of prior restraint, condemned by *Near v. Minnesota, ex rel. Olson** in the case of newspapers and by [*The Miracle** case] in the case of motion pictures, is present here in flagrant form. If a board of censors can tell the American people what is in their best interests to see or to read or to hear, then thought is regimented, authority is substituted for liberty, and the great purpose of the First Amendment to keep uncontrolled the freedom of expression defeated.''

PITTSBURGH (PA), NEWSPAPER ADVERTISEMENTS. Acting on a recommendation of the Pittsburgh Commission on Human Relations, the city passed an ordinance proscribing discrimination in employment on the basis of race, color, religion, ancestry, national origin, place of birth, or sex. In relevant part, § 8 of the ordinance declared it to be an unlawful employment practice, ''except where based upon a bona fide occupational exemption certified by the Commission'' for ''(a) Any employer to refuse to hire any person or otherwise discriminate against any person with respect to hiring . . . because of . . . sex. (e) Any 'employer,' employment agency or labor organization to publish or circulate, or cause to be published or circulated, any notice or advertisement relating to 'employment' or membership which indicates any discrimination because of . . . sex. (j) Any person, whether or not an employer, employment agency or labor organization, to aid . . . in the doing of any act declared to be an unlawful employment practice by this ordinance.'' The Supreme Court, in *Pittsburgh Press Co. v. Pittsburgh Commission on Human Relations* (1973),* ruled that the regulation over the content of the help-wanted ads was ''incidental to and coextensive with'' the regulation of employment discrimination, and thus the ordinance was not a prior restraint over the content of what a newspaper could or could not publish.

***PITTSBURGH PRESS* CO. v. PITTSBURGH COMMISSION ON HUMAN RELATIONS (1973).** Following a recommendation of the Pittsburgh Commission on Human Relations, the city passed an ordinance (Pittsburgh [PA], Newspaper Advertisements*) that prohibited newspapers from carrying help-wanted ads in sex-designated columns except when the employer or advertiser received an exemption to list them on the basis of sex. The Supreme Court upheld the ordinance as not violating the newspaper's First Amendment protections: The regulation of the want ads was ''incidental to and coextensive with'' the regulation of employment discrimination and the ordinance was not a prior restraint. Justice Powell: ''We emphasize that nothing in our holding allows government at any level to forbid the *Pittsburgh Press* to publish and distribute ads commenting on the Ordinance, the enforcement practices of the Commission, or the propriety of sex preferences in employment. . . . We reaffirm unequivocally the protection afforded to editorial judgment and to the free expression of views on these and other issues, however controversial. We hold only that the Ordinance does not infringe the First Amendment rights of the *Pittsburgh Press." Pittsburgh Press Co. v. Pittsburgh Commission on Human Relations*, 413 U.S. 376 (1973).

PLUMMER v. CITY OF COLUMBUS, OHIO (1973). According to the court records, Plummer was a Columbus taxi driver. He had a female fare in his cab who had requested to be taken to a certain address. When Plummer passed the address, the fare complained and—according to the statement of the trial court— Plummer's response was "a series of absolutely vulgar, suggestive and abhorrent sexually-oriented statements." Plummer was charged with and duly convicted (the conviction was affirmed by the Ohio courts, including the Ohio Supreme Court) of violating § 2327.03 of the Columbus City Code ("No person shall abuse another by using menacing, insulting, slanderous, or profane language").

The Supreme Court reversed Plummer's conviction and held that the Columbus ordinance was unconstitutional because of overbreadth.* The Court's opinion, in part, read as follows: "Section 2327.03 punishes only spoken words and, as construed by the Ohio courts, is facially unconstitutional because not limited in application 'to punish only unprotected speech' but is 'susceptible of application to protected expression.' In that circumstance, the Ohio Supreme Court erred when it found no constitutional infirmity in the holding . . . that the ordinance might constitutionally reach appellant's conduct because 'the words as used by [Plummer] are in the nature of fighting words and thereby fall within that limit of conduct proscribed by the ordinance.' [But] although the ordinance may be neither vague, overbroad, nor otherwise invalid as applied to the conduct charged against a particular defendant, he is permitted to raise its vagueness or unconstitutional overbreadth as applied to others. And if the law is found deficient in one of these respects, it may not be applied to him either, until and unless a satisfactory limiting construction is placed on the ordinance. The ordinance, in effect, is stricken down on its face." *Plummer v. City of Columbus, Ohio*, 414 U.S. 2 (1973).

POHL v. OHIO (1923). An Ohio statute (Ohio, Teaching in a Foreign Language*) prohibited teaching in a language other than English in any school in the state. Relying on its decision in *Meyer v. Nebraska* (1923),* the Supreme Court ruled that the Ohio statute was a violation of the First Amendment. *Pohl v. Ohio*, 262 U.S. 404 (1923).

POLICE DEPARTMENT OF CHICAGO v. MOSLEY (1972). This suit was brought by Earl Mosley, a federal postal employee, who for several months before the enactment of a city of Chicago anti-picketing ordinance (Chicago [IL], Ordinance on Picketing*), picketed a Chicago high school with a sign that read "Jones High School practices black discrimination. Jones High School has a black quota.'' After the ordinance passed, Mosley was told by the police that he would be arrested if he continued to picket the school. The Supreme Court ruled that the ordinance in question was unconstitutional because it made an impermissible distinction between labor picketing (this was permitted at a school) and other peaceful picketing (not permitted near schools): ''The central problem with Chicago's ordinance is that it describes permissible picketing in terms of its subject matter. Peaceful picketing on the subject of a school's labor-management dispute is permitted, but all other peaceful picketing is prohibited. The operative distinction is the message on a picket sign. But, above all else, the First Amendment means that government has no power to restrict expression because of its message, its ideas, its subject matter, or its content.'' *Police Department of Chicago v. Mosley*, 408 U.S. 92 (1972). The city of Rockford, Illinois, enacted a similar ordinance prohibiting non-labor picketing at schools, but that, too, was seen to be unconstitutional in *Grayned v. City of Rockford* (1972).*

POLITICAL ACTIVITY, CAMPAIGN EXPENDITURES. The Supreme Court has determined, in *Buckley v. Valeo*,* that limitations on campaign expenditures by individuals and groups, or expenditures by an individual candidate from his personal funds, impermissibly violate the First Amendment right of free expression. These limitations, contained in the Federal Election Campaign Act of 1971,* could not be sustained on the basis of the alleged governmental interests in preventing corruption and the appearance of corruption, or in equalizing the relative ability of individuals and groups to influence the outcome of elections. Annotation: *Right of Association—Political Parties*, 67 L. Ed. 2d 859; Annotation: *State Regulation of the Giving or Making of Political Contributions and Expenditures by Private Individuals*, 94 A.L.R. 3d. 944.

POLITICAL ACTIVITY, FINANCIAL CONTRIBUTIONS. The Supreme Court has determined, in *Buckley v. Valeo*,* that legislation limiting individual contributions to candidates in federal election campaigns does not violate the First Amendment. The Federal Election Campaign Act of 1971,* imposing certain limitations, was not seen as violating the First Amendment, since the Court ruled that the act's primary purpose of limiting the actuality and appearance of corruption was sufficient to justify the limited effect on such First Amendment freedoms caused by the contribution ceiling; and the act's contribution limitations in themselves did not undermine to any material degree the potential for robust and effective discussion of candidates and campaign issues by individual citizens, associations, the institutional press, candidates, and political parties. The Court also ruled, in *California Medical Association v. Federal Election Commission*,* that a provision of the 1971 act prohibiting individuals and unincorporated associations from contributing more than $5,000 per calendar year to any multicandidate political committee did not violate the First Amendment. Annotation:

Right of Association—Political Parties, 67 L. Ed. 2d 859; Annotation: *State Regulation of the Giving or Making of Political Contributions and Expenditures by Private Individuals*, 94 A.L.R. 3d. 944.

POLITICAL ACTIVITY, FINANCIAL REPORTING AND DISCLO-SURE. The Supreme Court has determined, in *Buckley v. Valeo*,* that the reporting and disclosure provisions of the Federal Election Campaign Act of 1971* (names and addresses of people contributing more than ten dollars) are not overbroad and thus not a violation of the First Amendment. The Court ruled that any serious infringement of First Amendment rights was highly speculative, and that the harm generally alleged was outweighed by the substantial govern-mental interests in informing the public as to the sources of campaign monies in order to aid voters in evaluating candidates, deterring corruption and the appearance of corruption, and gathering data to detect violations of the act's contribution limitations. Annotation: *Right of Association—Political Parties*, 67 L. Ed. 2d 859.

POLITICAL ACTIVITY, GOVERNMENT EMPLOYEES. The Supreme Court has upheld certain government legislation and action (Hatch Act*) to curtail certain partisan political activity by government employees. Emphasizing that the right to participate in political activities are not absolute, the Court, in *Civil Service Commission v. Letter Carriers*,* stated that the danger to "fair and effective government" posed by partisan political conduct on the part of federal employees charged with administering the law, was a sufficiently important concern to justify broad restrictions on the employees' rights of partisan political association and of free speech. The Court found it a legitimate goal of Congress to avoid the appearance of improper influence in order to maintain confidence in the system of representative government. The Court also upheld, against a challenge of overbreadth,* a state statute patterned after the Hatch Act that imposed significant restrictions on the partisan political activity of state public employees (*Broaderick v. Oklahoma**). Annotation: *Right of Association—Po-litical Parties*, 67 L. Ed. 2d 859.

POLLARD v. LYON (1875). As the court record relates, the defendant, one Mr. Lyon, was sued for slander by Mrs. Pollard when Lyon charged her with fornication: "I saw her in bed with Captain Denty" and "I looked over the transom-light and saw Mrs. Pollard in bed with Captain Denty." The trial court, finding no slander, ruled for Lyon; the Supreme Court affirmed. Justice Clifford delivered the opinion of the Court in one of the earliest slander cases: "Different definitions of slander are given . . . but it will be sufficient to say that oral slander, as a cause of action, may be divided into five classes: (1) Words falsely spoken of a person which impute to the party the commission of some criminal offense involving moral turpitude, for which the party, if the charge is true, may be indicted and punished; (2) Words falsely spoken of a person which impute that the party is infected with some contagious disease, where, if the charge is true, it would exclude the party from society; (3) Defamatory words falsely spoken of a person, which impute to the party unfitness to perform the duties of an office or employment of profit, or the want of integrity in the discharge of the duties of such an office or employment; (4) Defamatory words falsely spoken of a party which prejudice such party in his or her profession or trade; or (5) Defamatory words falsely spoken of a person, which, though not in themselves actionable, occasion the party special damages.''

Pollard lost her suit because (1) it was not sufficient to allege that she had suffered some damage and injury to her name and fame—she had to prove a precise loss or injury; and (2) the charge that Lyon made did not impute any criminal act, infectious disease, unfitness for office or did not prejudice her profession (i.e., fornicating with Captain Denty may not have been nice for the married Mrs. Pollard to do, but there was nothing wrong with Lyon telling everyone about it). *Pollard v. Lyon*, 91 U.S. 225 (1875).

PORTSMOUTH (NH), MEETING LICENSE. The following ordinance was seen to be a valid time-place-manner* restriction on the First Amendment by the Supreme Court (*Poulos v. New Hampshire**) in 1953, because the Court found the authorities exercised no discretion in issuing the required license: ''No theatrical or dramatic representation shall be performed or exhibited and no parade or procession upon any public street or way, and no open air public meeting upon any ground abutting thereon shall be permitted unless a license therefor shall first be obtained from the City Council. Every such license shall be in writing and shall specify the day and hour of the permit to perform or exhibit, or of such parade, procession or open air public meeting. The fee for such license shall not be more than Three Hundred Dollars for each day such licensee shall perform or exhibit or such parade, procession, or open air public meeting shall take place, but the fee for a license to exhibit in any hall shall not exceed Fifty Dollars. Any person who violates . . . this Article shall be fined Twenty Dollars.''

POSTAL REGULATIONS, ADVERTISING CONTRACEPTIVES. Title 39 U.S.C. § 3001(e)(2), ''Mailing Unsolicited Ads for Contraceptives,'' states that ''any unsolicited advertisement of matter which is designed, adapted, or intended for preventing conception is nonmailable matter, shall not be carried or delivered by mail, and shall be disposed of as the Postal Service directs.'' Any violation of this statute is punishable by a fine of not more than $5,000 or imprisonment for not longer than five years or both for the first offense and a fine of not more than $10,000 or imprisonment for not longer than ten years or both for each subsequent offense. In *Bolger v. Youngs Drug Products Corporation* (1983),* the Supreme Court ruled that this statute was unconstitutional, for it restrained the free flow of truthful commercial information.

POSTAL REGULATIONS, COMMUNIST POLITICAL PROPAGANDA.

Section 305 (a) of the Postal Service and Federal Employees Salary Act of 1962 (39 U.S.C. § 4008-a) provided, in part: "Mail matter, except sealed letters, which originates or which is printed or otherwise prepared in a foreign country and which is determined by the Secretary of the Treasury pursuant to rules and regulations to be promulgated by him to be 'communist political propaganda,' shall be detained by the Postmaster General upon its arrival for delivery in the United States, or upon its subsequent deposit in the United States domestic mails, and the addressee shall be notified that such matter has been received and will be delivered only upon the addressee's request, except that such detention shall not be required in the case of any matter which is furnished pursuant to subscription or which is otherwise ascertained by the Postmaster General to be desired by the addressee."

The statute goes on to define "communist political propaganda" in the same terms as § 1 (j) of the Foreign Agents Registration Act of 1938 (22 U.S.C. § 611 [j]): "The term 'political propaganda' includes any oral, visual, graphic, written, pictorial, or other communication or expression by any person (1) which is reasonably adapted to, or which the person disseminating the same believes will, or which he intends to, prevail upon, indoctrinate, convert, induce, or in any other way influence a recipient or any section of the public within the United States with reference to the political or public interests, policies, or relations of a government of a foreign country or a foreign political party or with reference to the foreign policies of the United States or to promote in the United States racial, religious, or social dissensions, or (2) which advocates, advises, instigates, or promotes any racial, social, political, or religious disorder, civil riot, or other conflict involving the use of force or violence in any other American republic or the overthrow of any government or political subdivision of any other American republic by any means involving the use of force or violence."

The statute contains an exemption from its provisions for mail addressed to governmental agencies and educational institutions, or their officials, and for mail sent pursuant to a reciprocal cultural international agreement. To implement the statute, the Post Office maintained about eleven screening points through which was routed all unsealed mail from the designated foreign countries. At these points the non-exempt mail was examined by Customs authorities. When it was determined that a piece of mail was "communist political propaganda," the addressee was mailed a notice identifying the mail being detained and advising that it would be destroyed unless the addressee requested delivery by returning an attached reply card within twenty days. The Supreme Court did not like this governmental censorship scheme. In *Lamont v. Postmaster General,* the Court ruled the entire process was unconstitutional, for it required the individual addressee to perform a positive act—return the attached reply card—before he could exercise his First Amendment rights. In addition, the Court felt that the government had no business knowing what Americans cared to read in publications originating the specified countries.

POSTAL REGULATIONS, LOTTERIES. Section 3894 of the Revised Statutes, as amended by the act of September 19, 1890 (26 Stat. 465, c. 908), generally known as the Anti-Lottery Act, provided: "No letter, postal-card or circular concerning any lottery, so-called gift-concert, or other similar enterprise offering prizes dependent upon lot or chance, or concerning schemes devised for the purpose of obtaining money or property under false pretences, and no list of the drawings at any lottery or similar scheme, and no lottery ticket or part thereof, and no check, draft, bill, money, postal-note or money order for the purchase of any ticket, tickets or part thereof, or of any share or any chance in any such lottery or gift enterprise, shall be carried in the mail or delivered at or through any post office or branch thereof, or by any letter-carrier; nor shall any newspaper, circular, pamphlet or publication of any kind containing any advertisement [for the above] . . . be carried in the mail or delivered by any postmaster or letter-carrier. . . . [Any person] on conviction shall be punished by a fine of not more than five hundred dollars, or by imprisonment for not more than one year, or by both such fine and imprisonment for each offence."

The Supreme Court (*In Re Rapier**), in 1892, ruled that this prohibition against sending newspapers that contained lottery advertisements through the mail was not a violation of the freedom of the press—newspapers could carry such ads but had to circulate by means other than the mail.

POSTAL REGULATIONS, MAILING OBSCENE MATERIAL. Originally passed in 1865, this statute has been responsible for practically all the federal convictions for obscenity. The statute does not make obscenity a federal crime, but rather, it makes using the mails to send obscene (and other) matter illegal. The statute is now located at Title 18 U.S.C. § 1461 and reads as follows: "Every obscene, lewd, lascivious, indecent, filthy or vile article, matter, thing, device, or substance; and Every article or thing designed, adapted, or intended for producing abortion, or for any indecent or immoral use ["preventing conception" was originally included in the indecent and immoral use category]; and Every article, instrument, substance, drug, medicine, or thing which is advertised or described in a manner calculated to lead another to use or apply it for producing abortion, or for any indecent or immoral purpose; and Every written or printed card, letter, circular, book, pamphlet, advertisement, or notice of any kind giving information, directly or indirectly, where, or how, or from whom, or by what means any of such mentioned matters, articles, or things may be obtained or made, or where or by whom any act or operation of any kind for the procuring or producing of abortion will be done or performed, or how or by what means abortion may be produced, whether sealed or unsealed . . . is declared to be nonmailable matter and shall not be conveyed in the mails or delivered from any post office or by any letter carrier. Whoever knowingly uses the mails for the mailing . . . of anything declared . . . to be nonmailable . . . shall be fined not more than $5,000 or imprisoned not more than five years, or both, for the first such offense, and shall be fined not more than $10,000 or imprisoned not more than ten years, or both, for each such offense thereafter.''

The history of federal legislation and activity in the obscenity area is fascinating, and the following comments were made by Justice Douglas in *Manual Enterprises v. Day* (1962) [*Manual/Grecian Guild Pictorial/Trim**]: "Prior to the Tariff Act of 1842, which forbade the importation of 'indecent and obscene' pictorial matter and authorized such matter's confiscation, Congress did not act in this area and the only noncriminal procedure authorized against obscene material before 1865 was a judicial proceeding for imported materials' forfeiture (*United States v. Three Cases of Toys*, 28 Fed. Cas. 112, No. 16,499). In fact, Congress had rejected in 1836 a request by President Jackson for legislation aimed at suppressing the distribution by mail of 'incendiary' abolitionist literature. In 1865, Congress passed the first Postal Act touching upon the mailing of obscene matter, making it a crime to deposit an 'obscene book . . . or other publication of a vulgar and indecent character' in the mails. The reenactment of the 1865 Act in the codification of the postal laws in 1873 (the Comstock Act [comstockery*]) did not change the several adjectives describing the objectionable material. The Comstock Act added the descriptive terms 'lewd' and 'lascivious' so that the proscription then included any 'obscene, lewd, or lascivious book . . . or other publication of an indecent character.' In 1909, the phrase 'and every filthy' as well as the word 'vile' were included in the provisions of the Comstock Act.''

POSTAL REGULATIONS, SECOND CLASS MAIL. Congress has made obscene material non-mailable (Postal Regulations, Mailing Obscene Material*) and has applied criminal sanctions for the enforcement of that policy. Congress has also divided mailable matter into four classes, periodical publications constituting the second-class category (§ 7 of the Classification Act of 1879, 20 Stat. 358, 43 Stat. 1067, 39 U.S.C. § 221): "That mailable matter of the second class shall embrace all newspapers and other periodical publications which are issued at stated intervals."

Four conditions are specified on which a publication shall be admitted to second class. The first three conditions simply define what a newspaper or periodical is; it was the fourth condition that a postmaster attempted to use in a censorship scheme. The fourth condition provided: "Except as otherwise provided by law, the conditions upon which a publication shall be admitted to the second class are as follows: . . . Fourth. It must be originated and published for the dissemination of information of a public character, or devoted to literature, the sciences, arts, or some special industry, and having a legitimate list of subscribers. Nothing herein contained shall be so construed as to admit to the second-class rate regular publications designed primarily for advertising purposes, or for free circulation, or for circulation at nominal rates."

In 1946, the postmaster general attempted to exclude *Esquire* magazine from the second-class category, not because it was obscene (which it was not), but because the postmaster general thought the magazine's contents did not contain "information of a public character" and it was not devoted to "literature." The Supreme Court, in *Hanegan v. Esquire (Esquire*)*, refused to allow the postmaster general to employ his own personal views as to what is or what is not eligible for the second-class category.

POSTAL REGULATIONS, UNLAWFUL MAIL. Title 39 U.S.C. § 4006 provided, in part: "Upon evidence satisfactory to the Postmaster General that a person is obtaining or attempting to obtain remittances of money or property of any kind through the mail for an obscene . . . matter . . . or is depositing or causing to be deposited in the United States mail information as to where, how, or from whom the same may be obtained, the Postmaster General may—(1) direct postmasters at the office at which registered letters or other letters or mail arrive, addressed to such a person or to his representative, to return the registered letters by mail to the sender marked 'Unlawful'; and (2) forbid the payment by a postmaster to such a person or his representative of any money order or postal note drawn to the order of either and provide for the return to the remitters of the sums named in the money orders or postal notes."

Title 39 U.S.C. § 4007 provided, in part: "In preparation for or during the pendency of proceedings under [§ 4006] of this title, the United States District Court in the district in which the defendant receives his mail shall, upon application therefor by the Postmaster General and upon a showing of probable cause to believe the statute is being violated, enter a temporary restraining order and preliminary injunction . . . directing the detention of the defendant's incoming mail by the postmaster pending the conclusion of the statutory proceedings and any appeal therefrom." The Supreme Court, in *Blount v. Rizzi* (1971),* ruled that this entire scheme was vague, a prior restraint, and an invalid administrative censorship scheme.

POSTAL REGULATIONS, UNWANTED MAIL. Title III of the Postal Revenue and Federal Salary Act of 1967, 81 Stat. 645, 39 U.S.C. § 4009 (1964 ed., Supp. IV), allows an individual to insulate himself from mail that he "in his sole discretion believes to be erotically arousing or sexually provocative." The section is entitled "Prohibition of Pandering Advertisements" and is the result of congressional concern over the use of the U.S. mails to transmit such advertisements. The Congress, before enacting the statute, listed the reasons such a regulation was necessary. Section 14 of Public Law 91-375 (Congressional Findings): "The Congress finds—(1) that the United States mails are being used for the indiscriminate dissemination of advertising matter so designed and so presented as to exploit sexual sensationalism for commercial gain; (2) that such matter is profoundly shocking and offensive to many persons who receive it, unsolicited, through the mails; (3) that such use of the mails constitutes a serious threat to the dignity and sanctity of the American home and subjects many persons to an unconscionable and unwarranted intrusion upon their fundamental personal right to privacy; (4) that such use of the mail reduces the ability of responsible parents to protect their minor children from exposure to material which they as parents believe to be harmful to the normal and healthy ethical, mental, and social development of their children; and (5) that the traffic in such offensive advertisements is so large that individual citizens will be helpless to protect their privacy or their families without stronger and more effective Federal controls over the mailing of such matter. On the basis of such findings, the Congress determines that it is contrary to the public policy of the United States for the facilities and services of the United States Postal Service to be used for the distribution of such materials to persons who do not want their privacy invaded in this manner or to persons who wish to protect their minor children from exposure to such material.''

The resulting statute, its constitutionality upheld by the Supreme Court in 1970, in *Rowan v. United States Post Office Department*,* reads as follows: ''(a) Whoever for himself, or by his agents or assigns, mails or causes to be mailed any pandering advertisement which offers for sale matter which the addressee in his sole discretion believes to be erotically arousing or sexually provocative shall be subject to an order of the Postal Service to refrain from further mailings of such materials to designated addresses thereof. . . . (c) The order of the Postal Service shall expressly prohibit the sender and his agents or assigns from making any further mailings to the designated addresses. . . . (e) Failure to observe such order may be punishable by the court as contempt thereof. . . . (g) Upon request of any addressee, the order of the Postal Service shall include the names of any of his minor children who have not attained their nineteenth birthday, and who reside with the addressee.''

POSTAL REGULATIONS, USE OF LETTER BOXES. In the 1981 case of *United States Postal Service v. Council of Greenburgh Civic Associations*,* the Supreme Court ruled that as long as Congress maintained the postal service, it could determine what could be placed in individual letter boxes, and thus the following statute (18 U.S.C. § 1725) was upheld: ''Whoever knowingly and willfully deposits any mailable matter such as statements of accounts, circulars, sale bills, or other like matter, on which no postage has been paid, in any letter box established, approved, or accepted by the Postal Service, for the receipt or delivery of mail matter on any mail route with intent to avoid payment of lawful postage thereon, shall for each such offense be fined not more than $300.'' The impact of this statute is twofold: (1) Although it does not hamper the distribution of material to private homes—the flyer can be pushed under the door or stuck someplace—the distribution to large apartment buildings is hampered because the letter box is often the only receptacle available; and (2) this statute would appear not to prohibit the distribution in letter boxes without proper postage of obscene material, since obscene matter is ''unmailable.''

POULOS v. NEW HAMPSHIRE (1953). A city ordinance (Portsmouth [NH], Meeting License*) prohibited the holding of a religious meeting in a public park without a license. The New Hampshire Supreme Court construed the ordinance as leaving to the licensing officials no discretion as to the granting of licenses, no power to discriminate, and no control over speech, and as merely a time-place-manner* ordinance for the comfort and convenience of the city. The U.S. Supreme Court affirmed that the licensing ordinance did not violate the First Amendment. Justice Reed delivered the opinion of the Court: "The principles of the First Amendment are not to be treated as a promise that everyone with opinions or beliefs to express may gather around him at any public place and at any time a group for discussion or instruction. It is a *non sequitur* to say that First Amendment rights may not be regulated because they hold a preferred position* in the hierarchy of the constitutional guarantees of the incidents of freedom. This Court has never so held and indeed has definitely indicated the contrary. It has indicated approval of reasonable nondiscriminatory regulation by governmental authority that preserves peace, order and tranquillity without deprivation of the First Amendment guarantees of free speech, press and the exercise of religion. . . . New Hampshire's determination that the ordinance is valid and that the Council could be compelled to issue the requested license on demand brings us face to face with another constitutional problem. May this man be convicted for holding a religious meeting without a license when the permit required by a valid enactment has been wrongfully refused by the municipality? It must be admitted that judicial correction of arbitrary refusal by administrators to perform official duties under valid laws is exulcerating and costly. But to allow applicants to proceed without the required permits to run businesses, erect structures, purchase firearms, transport or store explosives or inflammatory products, hold public meetings without prior public safety arrangements or take other unauthorized action is apt to cause breaches of the peace or create public dangers. The valid requirements of license are for the good of the applicants and the public. . . . Delay is unfortunate, but the expense and annoyance of litigation is a price citizens must pay for life in an orderly society where the rights of the First Amendment have a real and abiding meaning."

   Justice Douglas, in a dissenting opinion, thought something more than some "expense and annoyance" was involved. Justice Douglas: "A legislature that undertakes to license or censor the right of free speech is imposing a prior restraint, odious in our history. The Constitution commands that government keep its hands off the exercise of First Amendment rights. No matter what the legislature may say, a man has the right to make his speech, print his handbill, compose his newspaper, and deliver his sermon without asking anyone's permission. The contrary suggestion is abhorrent to our traditions. If the citizen can flout the legislature when it undertakes to tamper with his First Amendment rights, I fail to see why he may not flout the official or agency who administers a licensing law designed to regulate the exercise of the right of free speech. . . . There is no free speech in the sense of the Constitution when permission must be obtained from an official before a speech can be made. That is a previous restraint condemned by history and at war with the First Amendment. The nature of the particular official who has the power to grant or deny the authority does not matter. Those who wrote the First Amendment conceived of the right to free speech as wholly independent of the prior restraint of anyone." *Poulos v. New Hampshire*, 345 U.S. 395 (1953).

PREFERRED POSITION. The freedoms of speech and press guaranteed by the First Amendment are not absolute in the sense that anyone can speak or publish whatever one wants, at any time, at any place, and under any circumstances. The First Amendment does not protect every utterance, and certain forms of speech and publication can be punished for their impact on an individual or on the society in general. It is the now-classic dictum: "The most stringent protection of free speech would not protect a man in falsely shouting 'Fire!' in a crowded theater." But the Supreme Court has been wary of such restrictions on speech and press, for it has elevated the First Amendment rights to a "preferred position"—any law restricting speech or the press is suspect by definition, and the Court will scrutinize carefully the law's constitutionality. As the Court stated in *Schneider v. State**: "In every case, therefore, where legislative abridgment of the rights [freedom of speech and of the press] is asserted, the courts should be astute to examine the effect of the challenged legislation. Mere legislative preferences or beliefs respecting matters of public convenience may well support regulation directed at other personal activities, but be insufficient to justify such as diminishes the exercise of rights so vital to the maintenance of democratic institutions. And so, as cases arise, the delicate and difficult task falls upon the courts to weigh the circumstances and to appraise the substantiality of the reasons advanced in support of the regulation of the free enjoyment of the rights."

PREPARING FOR MARRIAGE. In 1945, the postmaster general, pursuant to 18 U.S.C. § 1461 (Postal Regulations, Mailing Obscene Material*) attempted to prohibit from the mails a pamphlet entitled *Preparing for Marriage*. A federal district court granted the author and publisher (Popenhoe) of the pamphlet a judgment preventing Postmaster General Walker from refusing to carry the pamphlet; the postmaster general still didn't like the ideas contained in the publication and he appealed to an appeals court. The appeals court dismissed the claim that *Preparing for Marriage* was obscene and ordered the postmaster general to carry it in the mails. The pamphlet was described by the appeals court thusly: "The pamphlet contains detailed information and advice regarding the physical and emotional aspects of marriage. Appellees have devoted serious study to the subject. The language of their pamphlet is plain but decent. Its obvious purpose is to educate, and so to benefit, persons who are about to marry. Its premises are that marriage should be made as happy, and as permanent as possible; that too many marriages are unhappy and too many end in divorce; that some sorts of sexual behavior are more conducive than others to happiness and permanence in marriage; that there is a body of knowledge on this subject which is not instinctive and should be made available to those who need it; and that pamphlets can aid in the diffusion of this knowledge." *Walker v. Popenhoe*, 149 F. 2d 511 (1945).

PRESS-ENTERPRISE COMPANY v. SUPERIOR COURT OF CALIFORNIA, RIVERSIDE COUNTY (1984). Before the *voir dire* examination of prospective jurors began at a trial for the rape and murder of a teenage girl, the *Press-Enterprise* requested that the process be open to the press and public. The state of California opposed the motion, arguing that if the press were present, juror responses would lack the candor necessary to assure a fair trial. The trial judge agreed, and all but three days of the more than six weeks of *voir dire* was closed to the press and the public. The trial judge refused to release the *voir dire* transcript after the jury was empaneled; he also refused to release it after the trial was over on the grounds that the jurors' right to privacy would be violated. The *Press-Enterprise* then brought suit, seeking an order that would release the transcript.

The U.S. Supreme Court ruled that the guarantees of open public proceedings in criminal trials include the *voir dire* proceedings. Chief Justice Burger delivered the opinion of the Court: (1) The historical evidence reveals that the process of jury selection has been a public process with exceptions only for good cause. The openness of jury selection in England carried over to colonial America, and public jury selection was the common practice in the United States when the Constitution was adopted. (2) Openness enhances both the basic fairness of the criminal trial and the appearance of fairness so essential to public confidence in the criminal justice system. Public proceedings vindicate the concerns of the victims and the community in knowing that offenders are being brought to account for their criminal conduct by jurors fairly and openly selected. Closed proceedings, although not absolutely precluded, must be rare and only for cause shown that outweighs the value of openness. (3) The presumption of openness has not been rebutted in this case. There were no findings to support the trial court's conclusion that an open proceeding would threaten the defendant's right to a fair trial and the prospective jurors' interests in privacy. *Press-Enterprise Company v. Superior Court of California, Riverside County*, 78 L. Ed. 2d 629 (1984).

PRESSER v. ILLINOIS (1886). An Illinois statute (Illinois, Military Parades*) prohibited any group of people from parading in public in any city as a military organization or with arms unless the group had a permit to parade from the governor. Presser was convicted of violating the statute.

The Supreme Court affirmed the conviction, saying that a state had the power to regulate such activity. Justice Woods delivered the opinion of the Court: "The right voluntarily to associate together as a military company or organization, or to drill or parade with arms, without, and independent of, an act of Congress or law of the State authorizing the same, is not an attribute of national citizenship. Military organization and military drill and parade under arms are subjects especially under the control of the government of every country. They cannot be claimed as a right independent of law. Under our political system they are subject to the regulation and control of the State and Federal governments, acting in due regard to their respective prerogatives and powers. The Constitution and laws of the United States will be searched in vain for any support to the view that these rights are privileges and immunities of citizens of the United States independent of some specific legislation on the subject. It cannot be successfully questioned that the State governments, unless restrained by their own Constitutions, have the power to regulate or prohibit associations and meetings of the people, except in the case of peaceable assemblies to perform the duties or exercise the privileges of citizens of the United States; and have also the power to control and regulate the organization, drilling and parading of military bodies or associations, except when such bodies or associations are authorized by the militia laws of the United States. The exercise of this power by the States is necessary to the public peace, safety and good order. To deny the power would be to deny the right of the State to disperse assemblages organized for sedition and treason, and the right to suppress armed mobs bent on riot and rapine." *Presser v. Illinois*, 116 U.S. 252 (1886).

PRINCE v. MASSACHUSETTS (1944). A state statute (Massachusetts, Child Labor Laws*) provided that no minor (boys under twelve or girls under eighteen) could sell newspapers or other articles in the public streets and also made it unlawful for any adult to permit a minor to sell or distribute the publications. Prince, a Jehovah's Witness, was convicted under this statute. Prince and a minor were distributing religious publications, but the Supreme Court, Justice Rutledge delivering the majority opinion, felt that the state's power to regulate the activities of children took precedence over any alleged First Amendment claim to freedom of speech and of the press. Justice Rutledge: "Parents may be free to become martyrs themselves. But it does not follow they are free, in identical circumstances, to make martyrs of their children before they have reached the age of full and legal discretion when they can make that choice for themselves. Massachusetts has determined that an absolute prohibition, though one limited to streets and public places and to the incidental uses proscribed, is necessary to accomplish its legitimate objectives. Its power to attain them is broad enough to reach these peripheral instances in which the parent's supervision may reduce but cannot eliminate entirely the ill effects of the prohibited conduct. We think that with reference to the public proclaiming of religion, upon the streets and in other similar public places, the power of the state to control the conduct of children reaches beyond the scope of its authority over adults, as is true in the case of other freedoms, and the rightful boundary of its power has not been crossed in this case." *Prince v. Massachusetts*, 321 U.S. 158 (1944).

PRIOR RESTRAINT. The term "prior restraint" or "previous restraint" refers to any act of a governmental body or administrative agency or official to prevent or restrain the exercise of free speech or free press *prior* to any judicial determination, with all the guarantees of due process of law, that the speech or publication is unprotected speech* (obscenity,* for example). The Supreme Court has generally, but not always, held that prior restraints violate the First Amendment because the government cannot regulate in advance what may be said or published (*Near v. Minnesota ex rel. Olson**). Prior restraint does not apply if there has already been a judicial determination that the material is unprotected; if a certain publication is judged to be obscene by a court, authorities then have the power to restrain its publication. In a few areas, however, prior restraint is permitted, areas in which the Court feels that any punishment after the fact would not be sufficient to atone for the harm done by the publication: military information in times of war (the classic ''sailing dates of troop ships''); the dissemination of political campaign information on military bases (*Greer v. Spock**) in order to protect the morale, loyalty, and fighting discipline of the troops; certain forms of obscenity; and the writings of current and former Central Intelligence Agency agents about their employment, especially when there is an agreement requiring pre-publication review (*Snepp v. United States** and *McGehee v. Casey**). One of the most famous attempts by the U.S. government to apply a prior restraint—an attempt that the Supreme Court refused to allow—was with the publication by the *New York Times* and the *Washington Post* of *The Pentagon Papers.**

PRISON REGULATIONS, FEDERAL. Paragraph 4b (6) of Policy Statement 1220.1A of the Federal Bureau of Prisons reads as follows: ''Press representatives will not be permitted to interview individual inmates. This rule shall apply even where the inmate requests or seeks an interview. However, conversation may be permitted with inmates whose identity is not to be made public, if it is limited to the discussion of institutional facilities, programs and activities.'' This regulation was not seen as a violation of the freedom of the press in *Saxbe v. Washington Post,** for the Supreme Court ruled that the news media have no special access to government information and that a prison is not a public forum* or a public place.

PRIVACY. The concept of privacy in relation to obscene material is limited. Only the possession of obscene material in the privacy of one's own home is protected by the First Amendment. *Stanley v. Georgia** ruled that the government cannot determine what an individual may have, or may not have, on the bookshelves in his own home. The First Amendment guarantees each individual the right to possess in the privacy of his own home whatever information desired regardless of the material's obscenity, appeal to the prurient interest, or lack of redeeming social value. The *Stanley* decision reiterated the view that a man's home is his castle and the government cannot regulate the types of books or films in the house. But this is the limit to such privacy—''the zone of privacy'' around the individual in the home does not extend beyond the front door. Although an individual has the right to possess obscene materials in the home, other individuals do *not* have the absolute right to deliver, sell, produce, or mail such material (*United States v. Reidel**); obscene films may be prohibited from being shown in theaters, even if admission is limited to consenting adults (*Paris Adult Theatre I v. Slaton, District Attorney**); the individual may be prosecuted for transporting such material across state lines, even if the material is in the trunk of his private automobile or in the moving van with the rest of his private possessions (*United States v. Orito**); and the importation of such material can be prevented (*United States v. Thirty-Seven Photographs**).

PROCUNIER v. MARTINEZ (1974). A California Department of Corrections regulation (California, Prison Director's Rules on Correspondence*) prohibited inmate correspondence that "unduly complained, magnified grievances, expressed inflammatory political, racial, religious or other views or beliefs, or contained matter deemed defamatory or otherwise inappropriate." A federal district court held this regulation to be an unconstitutional restriction on the First Amendment rights of inmates and an unacceptable censorship scheme over the contents of the inmates' letters; the Supreme Court affirmed the district court's ruling: (1) The censorship of direct personal correspondence involves incidental restrictions on the right to free speech of both prisoners and their correspondents, and it is justified if the following criteria are met: (a) it must further one or more of the important and substantial governmental interests of security, order, and the rehabilitation of inmates, and (b) it must be no greater than is necessary to further the legitimate governmental interest involved. (2) Under this standard the invalidation of the mail censorship regulations by the district court was correct and the decision to censor or withhold delivery of a particular letter must be accompanied by minimum procedural safeguards against arbitrariness or error. *Procunier v. Martinez*, 416 U.S. 396 (1974).

PRUNEYARD SHOPPING CENTER v. ROBINS (1980). Soon after Robins and others began soliciting signatures from passersby for a petition in opposition to a certain United Nations resolution, a security guard of the Pruneyard Shopping Center, a privately owned area in which the soliciting was done, told them they would have to leave because the shopping center prohibited anyone from engaging in any "expressive" activity that was not directly related to the center's commercial activity. The California Supreme Court, reversing the trial court decision that Robins was not entitled to exercise First Amendment rights on private property without the consent of the owner, ruled that the California Constitution protects speech and petitioning, even on private property, and the result did not infringe on the center's property rights.

The Supreme Court agreed, Justice White delivering the Court's opinion: "The question here is whether the Federal Constitution forbids a State to implement its own free-speech guarantee by requiring owners of shopping centers to permit entry on their property for the purpose of communicating with the public about subjects having no connection with the shopping centers' business. The Supreme Court of California held that in the circumstances of this case the federally protected property rights of appellants were not infringed. The state court recognized, however, that reasonable time and place limitations could be imposed and that it was dealing with the public or common areas in a large shopping center and not with an individual retail establishment within or without the shopping center or with the property or privacy rights of a homeowner. On the facts before it, 'a handful of additional orderly persons soliciting signatures and distributing handbills . . . would not markedly dilute defendant's property rights.' " *Pruneyard Shopping Center v. Robins*, 447 U.S. 74 (1980).

PRURIENT INTEREST. The concept of prurient interest is used as an element in the definition of obscenity,* including the tests or standards laid down by the Supreme Court in the Roth*/Memoirs*/Miller* cases. The term "prurient interest" has been defined by the Supreme Court thusly: "Obscene material is material which deals with sex in a manner appealing to prurient interest; i.e., material having a tendency to excite lustful thoughts." Other words that are similar in meaning are "lewd" and "lascivious."

PUBLIC FIGURE. The *New York Times* Rule* has been extended by the Supreme Court in cases subsequent to *New York Times Company v. Sullivan* (1964)* to cover "public figures" as well as "public officials."* The Court has defined the term to include any person having some special prominence in the affairs of society, or the resolution of public questions, either by having achieved such pervasive fame or notoriety that he becomes a public figure for all purposes and in all contexts, or by voluntarily injecting himself or being drawn into a particular public controversy and thereby becoming a public figure for a limited range of issues. But the media cannot, by virtue of the attention they give to a private person, create a "public figure" and then claim the protection of the *New York Times* Rule. The term public figure in defamation actions includes artists, athletes, business people, dilettantes, and anyone who is famous or infamous because of who he is or what he has done. Public figures in libel actions are those who have assumed roles of special prominence in society; commonly, those classed as public figures have thrust themselves to the forefront of particular public controversies in order to influence resolution of the issues involved. Annotation: *New York Times Rule*, 61 L. Ed 2d 975.

PUBLIC FORUM/PUBLIC PLACE. The concept of a "public forum" or "public place" is essential to an understanding of the First Amendment, since the right to a free press and to free speech almost by definition includes the right to express one's views in public places. This right is not absolute, however, and there are many valid time-place-manner* restrictions on public First Amendment activities. In general, peaceful presence for the exercise of First Amendment rights in a place open to the public cannot be made a crime. But the fact that property is publicly owned does not necessarily turn it into a public forum—military bases, jails, courthouses, transit system cars are not totally open to free speech and free press. But most other public areas—parks, streets, sidewalks, libraries, stores, theaters, and the area around public buildings—are public places and as such, in the absence of valid time, place, and manner restrictions, are open to individuals to pursue their First Amendment rights. The doorbells of private homes are seen to be public forums for political, charitable, or religious solicitations but not for purely commercial solicitations.

PUBLIC INTEREST, CONVENIENCE, AND NECESSITY. Owing to the scarcity of spectrum space, broadcast operation requires a license from the Federal Communications Commission (FCC). The FCC's authority to issue (or deny) these three-year renewable licenses to broadcasters, and its authority to issue rules and regulations governing the use of the licenses, are governed by the Communications Act's "public interest, convenience, and necessity" standard. The public interest standard is as vague a term as obscenity,* and the FCC and the courts have had more success in determining what is *not* in the public interest, convenience, and necessity than in determining what is within the standard. Broadcast of "indecent" but not obscene material during hours when children are likely to be present is not in the public interest ("Filthy Words"*); refusal to furnish reply time (Right of Reply/Equal Time*) to an individual attacked on a broadcast is not in the public interest (*Red Lion Broadcasting Company v. Federal Communications Commission**); forcing broadcasters to air paid editorial advertisements is not in the public interest (*Columbia Broadcasting System v. Democratic National Committee*); the refusal to permit reasonable access (Reasonable Access Rule*) to legally qualified candidates for federal elective office is also not in the public interest (*Columbia Broadcasting System v. Federal Communications Commission*). Annotation: *Broadcast Regulation*, 69 L. Ed. 2d 1110.

PUBLIC OFFICIAL. The Supreme Court, in *New York Times Company v. Sullivan* (1964)* and in subsequent cases, has clarified the definition of the term "public official" under the *New York Times* Rule.* The Court held that the concept relates to one in the hierarchy of government having, or appearing to have, substantial responsibility for or control over the conduct of governmental affairs such that his position invites public scrutiny. The Court has yet to make a definitive list, but not all governmental employees are public officials. The Court has indicated that, in appropriate circumstances, the concept may relate to a former official or an official in charge of a group that has been defamed, but it does not relate to a de facto public official having no real involvement in governmental affairs. Candidates for elective office at any level of government are under the *New York Times* Rule, regardless of whether they are categorized as public officials or public figures.*

PUBLISHER-ONLY RULE. The U.S. Bureau of Prisons has a regulation that allows inmates to receive hardcover books only from publishers, book clubs, or bookstores directly. The regulation was promulgated by fears that contraband would be smuggled into the prisons if the books came from family and friends, and the bureau regarded hardcover books as a "dangerous source of risk to institutional security." The regulation (43 Fed. Reg. 30576 [1978], 28 CFR § 540.71, "Incoming Publications") also authorizes the warden of each prison to inspect the incoming publications and censor those he determines to be detrimental to the security, good order, or discipline of the institution.

The regulation was upheld as a reasonable restriction on inmates' First Amendment rights by the Supreme Court in *Bell, Attorney General v. Wolfish.** The rule reads as follows: § 540.70: "(a) The Bureau of Prisons permits an inmate to subscribe to or to receive publications without prior approval and has established procedures to determine if an incoming publication is detrimental to the security, discipline, or good order of the institution or if it might facilitate criminal activity." §540.71: (a) An inmate may receive hardcover publications only from the publisher, from a book club, or from a book store. An inmate may receive softcover material (for example, paperback books, newspapers, magazines) from any source. The Warden may have all incoming publications inspected for contraband. (b) The Warden may reject a publication only if it is determined detrimental to the security, good order, or discipline of the institution or if it might facilitate criminal activity. The Warden may not reject a publication solely because its content is religious, philosophical, political, social or sexual, or because its content is unpopular or repugnant. Publications which may be rejected by a Warden include but are not limited to publications which meet one of the following criteria: (1) It depicts or describes procedures for the construction or use of weapons, ammunition, bombs or incendiary devices; (2) It depicts, encourages, or describes methods of escape from correctional facilities, or contains blueprints, drawings or similar descriptions of Bureau of Prisons institutions; (3) It depicts or describes procedures for the brewing of alcoholic beverages, or the manufacture of drugs; (4) It is written in code; (5) It depicts, describes or encourages activities which may lead to the use of physical violence or group disruption; (6) It encourages or instructs in the commission of criminal activity; (7) It is sexually explicit material which by its nature or content poses a threat to the security, good order, or discipline of the institution, or facilitates criminal activity. (c) The Warden may not establish an excluded list of publications. This means the Warden shall review the individual publication prior to the rejection of that publication. Rejection of several issues of a subscription publication is not sufficient reason to reject the subscription in its entirety."

PUGSLEY v. SELLMEYER (1923). This case is an excellent example of the absurd rules and regulations that have been passed over the years and the extent to which the court system is bogged down dealing with the strange varieties of such regulations. Miss Pearl Pugsley was expelled from high school by the principal because she violated a regulation established by the local school board—she came to school one day with makeup on her face! She challenged the regulation in court, but the judges, feeling that respect for constituted authority was absolutely necessary in developing citizenship, ruled that cosmetics, women, and education do not mix. The court's opinion: "Courts have other and more important functions to perform than that of hearing the complaints of disaffected pupils of the public schools against rules and regulations promulgated by the school boards for the government of the schools. The courts have this right of review, for the reasonableness of such rules, when the question is presented. But, in so doing, it will be kept in mind that the directors are elected by the patrons of the schools over which they preside, and the election occurs annually. These directors are in close and intimate touch with the affairs of their respective districts, and know the conditions with which they have to deal. It will be remembered also that respect for constituted authority and obedience thereto is an essential lesson to qualify one for the duties of citizenship, and that the schoolroom is an appropriate place to teach that lesson: so that the courts hesitate to substitute their will and judgment for that of the school boards which are delegated by law as the agencies to prescribe rules for the government of the public schools of the state, which are supported at the public expense."

There was a glimmer of rationality, however; Judge Hart filed a dissenting opinion that could be applied to a whole litany of rules and regulations. Judge Hart: "Miss Pearl Pugsley was eighteen years old on the 15th of August, 1922. I think that a rule forbidding a girl of her age from putting talcum powder on her face is so far unreasonable and beyond the exercise of discretion that the court should say that the board of directors acted without authority in making and enforcing it. 'Useless laws diminish the authority of necessary ones.' The tone of the majority opinion exemplifies the wisdom of this old proverb." *Pugsley v. Sellmeyer*, 250 S.W. 538 (1923).

R

RABECK v. NEW YORK (1968). Rabeck was convicted in a New York court of violating § 484-i of the New York Penal Law (New York, Sale of Obscene Material to Minors*) for selling "girlie" magazines to a minor under eighteen years of age. Among the things prohibited by the statute was the sale of "magazines which would appeal to the lust of persons under the age of eighteen years or to their curiosity as to sex or to the anatomical differences between the sexes." The Supreme Court found this section to be unconstitutionally vague, and Rabeck's conviction was reversed. The prohibition against information that would appeal to a minor's "curiosity as to sex or to the anatomical differences between the sexes" would prohibit, among other things, such protected publications that are used in sex education classes. *Rabeck v. New York*, 391 U.S. 462 (1968).

RAILWAY EXPRESS AGENCY v. NEW YORK (1949). A New York City traffic regulation (New York City [NY], Advertisements on Vehicles*) prohibited any vehicle from carrying advertisements on it except advertisements of the products or services of the owner of the vehicle. In other words, a moving van could carry an ad for the moving company itself but not, say, for beer or other products. The Railway Express Agency (REA) operated many trucks on the New York streets, and the company sold space on the exterior of the trucks for advertising goods and services other than for REA itself. REA was duly convicted in a New York court of violating the regulation. The actual advertisements for which REA was convicted consisted of posters from three by seven feet to four by ten feet portraying Camel Cigarettes, Ringling Brothers and Barnum & Bailey Circus, radio station WOR, Prince Albert Smoking Tobacco, and a recruitment poster for the U.S. Navy.

The REA appealed to the Supreme Court, arguing that the claims of the state that the regulation was related to the legitimate state interest of traffic control were false in that it was not the fact that ads were being carried, but rather that the content of the ads determined whether one was guilty or innocent under the statute. The ad for the U.S. Navy was a violation; an ad for REA itself would be exempt. The Supreme Court did not agree with the REA's argument and affirmed the conviction, Justice Douglas delivering the Court's opinion: (1) It is not the function of the Court to rule on the soundness or wisdom of the regulation. (2) The Court could not say that the regulation had no relation to the traffic problem of New York City. (3) The Court could not say that the exemption of vehicles having advertisements of products sold by the owner rendered the regulation unconstitutional as a denial of the equal protection of the laws. (4) The Court could not say that the forbidden advertising had less incidence on traffic than that which was exempted. (5) The regulation was not rendered invalid by the fact that it did not extend to what were probably even greater distractions affecting traffic safety, such as the displays at Times Square. (6) When there is no conflicting federal legislation, the Court will allow local authorities great leeway in the areas of traffic control and the use of highways.

Justice Douglas offered this comment: "We would be trespassing on one of the most intensely local and specialized of all municipal problems if we held that this regulation had no relation to the traffic problem of New York City. It is the judgment of the local authorities that it does have such a relation. And nothing has been advanced which shows that to be palpably false." *Railway Express Agency v. New York*, 336 U.S. 106 (1949).

RATCHFORD, PRESIDENT, UNIVERSITY OF MISSOURI v. GAY LIB (1978). The University of Missouri refused to grant official recognition to a student organization—Gay Lib—on the grounds that the organization would result in the commission of felonious acts of sodomy in violation of Missouri law. (Missouri Ann. Stat. § 563.230 provides: "Every person who shall be convicted for the detestable and abominable crime against nature, committed with mankind or with beast, with the sexual organs or with the mouth, shall be punished by imprisonment in the penitentiary not less than two years.") Gay Lib countered that it would not incite anyone to break the law, but that the organization's basic purpose was to provide a forum for discussion about homosexuality.

A U.S. district court ruled that the school officials were justified in not granting recognition, but an appeals court reversed that decision, holding that Gay Lib's First Amendment rights were violated by the university. Judge Lay delivered the majority opinion: "In the present case, none of the purposes or aims of Gay Lib evidences advocacy of present violations of state law or of university rules or regulations. . . . It is of no moment, in First Amendment jurisprudence, that ideas advocated by an association may to some or most of us be abhorrent, even sickening. The stifling of advocacy is even more abhorrent, even more sickening. It rings the death knell of a free society. Once used to stifle 'the thought that we hate,' in Holmes' phrase, it can stifle the ideas we love. It signals a lack of faith in people, in its supposition that they are unable to choose in the market place of ideas. . . . It is difficult to singularly ascribe evil connotations to the group simply because they are homosexuals. An interesting fact is that not all members of the group are homosexuals. . . . Finally, such an approach smacks of penalizing persons for their status rather than their conduct, which is constitutionally impermissible.''

This decision in the appeals court was not unanimous, however; Judge Regan dissented: ''Here, the officials' denial of recognition to Gay Lib was not based on 'mere disagreement' with the group's 'philosophy.' State University officials have a responsibility not only to taxpayers but to *all* students on campus, and that responsibility encompasses a right to protect latent or potential homosexuals from becoming overt homosexual students. In carrying out these responsibilities, they were aware that unlike recognition of political associations, whether of the right, center or left, an organization dedicated to the furtherance and advancement of homosexuality would, in any realistic sense, certainly so to impressionistic students, imply approval not only of the organization per se but of homosexuality and the normality of such conduct, and thus adversely affect potential homosexual students. In my opinion, the University was entitled to protect itself and the other students on campus, in this small way, against abnormality, illness and compulsive conduct of the kind here described in the evidence.'' *Gay Lib v. Ratchford*, 558 F. 2d 848 (1977).

The University of Missouri was not pleased with this decision, and they attempted to bring an appeal to the U.S. Supreme Court; the Supreme Court refused to hear the case by denying certiorari and thus let stand the appeals court ruling that the university had to grant official recognition to Gay Lib. But Chief Justice Burger and Justices Rehnquist and Blackmun dissented from the denial of certiorari—these three would have heard the case—and the following comments are taken from Justice Rehnquist's dissent (by the tenor of Rehnquist's remarks, it is obvious that he would have supported the university): ''The sharp split amongst the judges who considered this case below demonstrates that our past precedents do not conclusively address the issues central to this dispute. In the same manner that we expect considered and deliberate treatment of cases by these courts, we have a concomitant responsibility to aid them where confusion or uncertainty in the law prevails. By refusing to grant certiorari in this case, we ignore our function and responsibility in the framework of the federal court system and place added burdens on other courts in that system. Writ large, the issue posed in this case is the extent to which a self-governing democracy, having made certain acts criminal, may prevent or discourage individuals from engaging in speech or conduct which encourages others to violate those laws. . . . [This case] goes on to the heart of the inevitable clash between the authority of a State to prevent the subversion of the lawful rules of conduct which it has enacted pursuant to its police power and the right of individuals under the First and Fourteenth Amendments who disagree with various of those rules to urge that they be changed through democratic processes. The University in this case did not ban the discussion in the classroom, or out of it, of the wisdom of repealing sodomy statutes. The State did not proscribe membership in organizations devoted to advancing 'gay liberation.' The University merely refused to recognize an organization whose activities were found to be likely to incite a violation of a valid state criminal statute. . . . Expert psychological testimony established the fact that the meeting together of individuals who consider themselves homosexual in an officially recognized university organization can have a distinctly different effect from the mere advocacy of repeal of the State's sodomy statute. As the University has recognized, this danger may be particularly acute in the university setting where many students are still coping with the sexual problems which accompany late adolescence and early adulthood." *Ratchford, President, University of Missouri v. Gay Lib*, 434 U.S. 1080 (1978), *cert. denied.*

REASONABLE ACCESS RULE. The "reasonable access rule" of the Communications Act (§ 312 [a] [7]) provides that the Federal Communications Commission is authorized to revoke a broadcaster's license for willful or repeated failure to grant legally qualified candidates for federal elective office "reasonable access" to the licensee's broadcast facilities or to permit the purchase of reasonable amounts of broadcast time. In *Columbia Broadcasting System v. Federal Communications Commission*, the Supreme Court ruled that the refusal of the three major television networks to make available reasonable access to a presidential campaign committee violated the reasonable access rule and dismissed the networks' argument that the rule, by unduly circumscribing their editorial discretion as to what should or should not be broadcast, violated the First Amendment. The Court stated: "The right of access to the media under § 312 (1) (7), as defined by the Federal Communications Commission and applied here, does not violate the First Amendment rights of broadcasters by unduly circumscribing their editorial discretion, but instead properly balances the First Amendment rights of federal candidates, the public, and broadcasters. Although the broadcasting industry is entitled under the First Amendment to exercise 'the widest journalistic freedom consistent with its public duties [*Columbia Broadcasting System v. Democratic National Committee*], it is the right of the viewers and listeners, not the right of the broadcasters, which is paramount' [*Red Lion Broadcasting Co. v. Federal Communications Commission**]. Section 312 (a)(7), which creates only a *limited* right of access to the media, makes a significant contribution to freedom of expression by enhancing the ability of candidates to present, and the public to receive, information necessary for the effective operation of the democratic process." Annotation: *Broadcast Regulation*, 69 L. Ed. 2d 1110.

REDEEMING SOCIAL VALUE. The concept of "redeeming social value" as one of the elements in the definition of obscenity* was first stated in *Roth v. United States*,* which created the Roth Standard,* under the words "redeeming social importance." In *Memoirs v. Massachusetts* (*Memoirs of a Woman of Pleasure/Fanny Hill**), the case that established the Memoirs Standard,* the Supreme Court used the term "redeeming social value," and although the Court never precisely defined the term, a book had to be "*utterly* without redeeming social value" (unqualifiedly worthless) before it could be judged obscene. But in *Miller v. California*,* the Court revised this element: "The *Memoirs* plurality produced a drastically altered test that called on the prosecution to prove a negative, i.e., that the material was *utterly* without redeeming social value'—a burden virtually impossible to discharge under our criminal standards of proof. Such consideration caused Mr. Justice Harlan to wonder if the *utterly* without redeeming social value' test had any meaning at all.'' The Court in *Miller* then rejected the test of ''utterly without redeeming social value'' and substituted the Miller Standard*: ''whether the work, taken as a whole, lacks serious literary, artistic, political, or scientific value.''

RED LION BROADCASTING CO. v. FEDERAL COMMUNICATIONS COMMISSION (1969). The Red Lion Broadcasting Company was licensed to operate a Pennsylvania radio station, WGCB. On November 27, 1964, WGCB carried a fifteen-minute broadcast by the Reverend Billy James Hargis as part of a ''Christian Crusade'' series. A book by Fred J. Cook entitled *Goldwater—Extremist on the Right* was discussed by Hargis, who said that Cook had been fired by a newspaper for making false charges against city officials; that Cook had then worked for a Communist-affiliated publication; that he had defended Alger Hiss and attacked J. Edgar Hoover and the Central Intelligence Agency; and that he had now written a book ''to smear and destroy Barry Goldwater.'' When Cook heard of the broadcast, he asked WGCB for some broadcast time to rebut Hargis' charges—the request was made pursuant to the Federal Communications Commission's (FCC's) ''fairness doctrine''*—but the radio station refused. The fairness doctrine required that broadcasters air public issues and that each side of those issues be given ''fair'' coverage. The FCC ordered WGCB to send a transcript of the broadcast to Cook and to provide him with reply time, whether or not Cook would pay for it.

The Supreme Court upheld the FCC's order and thus upheld the fairness doctrine: (1) The history of the fairness doctrine and of related legislation shows that the FCC's action did not exceed its authority, and in adopting the regulations the FCC was only implementing congressional policy; (2) The fairness doctrine began shortly after the Federal Radio Commission was established to allocate frequencies among competing applicants in the public interest, and there is an affirmative obligation on the part of the broadcaster to see that both sides of certain issues are presented; (3) The FCC's mandate to see that broadcasters operate in the public interest, convenience, and necessity* supports the application of the fairness doctrine; (4) The fairness doctrine in general and its specific application to WGCB in this case do not violate the First Amendment protection against an abridgment of speech or of the press; (5) The First Amendment is relevant to broadcasting, but it is the right of the viewing and listening public, not the right of the broadcasters, that is paramount; and (6) The First Amendment does not protect private censorship by broadcasters who are licensed by the government to use a scarce resource that is denied to others.

The opinion of the Supreme Court contained these comments: ''The broadcasters challenge the fairness doctrine and its specific manifestations in the personal attack and political editorial rules on conventional First Amendment grounds, alleging that the rules abridge their freedom of speech and press. Their contention is that the First Amendment protects their desire to use their allotted frequencies continuously to broadcast whatever they choose, and to exclude whomever they choose from ever using that frequency. No man may be prevented from saying or publishing what he thinks, or from refusing in his speech or other utterances to give equal weight to the views of his opponents. This right, they say, applies equally to broadcasters. By the same token, as far as the First Amendment is concerned those who are licensed stand no better than those to whom licenses are refused. A license permits broadcasting, but the licensee has no constitutional right to be the one who holds the license or to monopolize a radio frequency to the exclusion of his fellow citizens. There is nothing in the First Amendment which prevents the Government from requiring a licensee to share his frequency with others and to conduct himself as a proxy or fiduciary with obligations to present those views and voices which are representative of his community and which would otherwise, by necessity, be barred from the airwaves. This is not to say that the First Amendment is irrelevant to public broadcasting. On the contrary, it has a major role to play as the Congress itself recognized in § 326, which forbids F.C.C. interference with 'the right of free speech by means of radio communication.' Because of the scarcity of radio frequencies, the Government is permitted to put restraints on licensees in favor of others whose views should be expressed on this unique medium. But the people as a whole retain their interest in free speech by radio and their collective right to have the medium function consistently with the ends and purposes of the First Amendment. It is the right of the viewers and listeners, not the right of the broadcasters, which is paramount. It is the purpose of the First Amendment to preserve an uninhibited marketplace of ideas in which truth will ultimately prevail, rather than to countenance monopolization of that market, whether it be by the Government itself or a private licensee. . . . It is the right of the public to receive suitable access to social, political, esthetic, moral, and other ideas and experiences which is crucial here. That right may not constitutionally be abridged either by Congress or by the F.C.C. [or by the broadcaster].'' *Red Lion Broadcasting Co. v. Federal Communications Commission*, 395 U.S. 367 (1969).

REDRUP v. NEW YORK (1967). This case was decided along with two others: *Austin v. Kentucky* and *Gent v. Arkansas*. Redrup was a clerk at a New York City newsstand. A plainclothes patrolman approached the newsstand, saw two paperback books on a rack—*Lust Pool* and *Shame Agent*—and asked for them by name. Redrup handed him the books and collected the price of $1.65. As a result of this transaction, Redrup was convicted in the New York courts for violating § 1141 of the New York Penal Law (New York, Obscenity Statute*). Austin owned and operated a retail bookstore and newsstand in Paducah, Kentucky. A woman resident of Paducah purchased two magazines from a salesgirl in Austin's store after asking for them by name—*High Heels* and *Spree*. As a result of this transaction, Austin was convicted in the Kentucky courts of violating the Kentucky obscenity statute. In the case involving *Gent*, the prosecuting attorney of a judicial district in Arkansas brought a proceeding under an Arkansas statute to have certain issues of various magazines declared obscene, to prevent their distribution, and to order their surrender and destruction. The order was granted against *Gent, Swank, Bachelor, Modern Man, Cavalcade, Gentleman, Ace*, and *Sir*.   In a rather short and unsigned *per curiam* decision, the Supreme Court reversed all the convictions, holding that the distribution of these publications was protected by the First Amendment from governmental suppression. The reversals were ordered with the following comments: ''Two members of the Court [Justices Douglas and Black] have consistently adhered to the view that a State is utterly without power to suppress, control, or punish the distribution of any writing or pictures upon the ground of their 'obscenity.' A third [Justice Brennan] has held to the opinion that a State's power in this area is narrowly limited to a distinct and clearly identifiable class or material [exposure to minors or unconsenting adults]. Others have subscribed to a not dissimilar standard, holding that a State may not constitutionally inhibit the distribution of literary material as obscene unless '(a) the dominant theme of the material taken as a whole appeals to a prurient interest in sex; (b) the material is patently offensive because it affronts contemporary community standards relating to the description or representation of sexual matters; and (c) the material is utterly without redeeming social value' [Memoirs Standard*], emphasizing that the 'three elements must coalesce,' and that no such material can 'be proscribed unless it is found to be *utterly* without redeeming social value.' . . . Whichever of these constitutional views is brought to bear upon the cases before us, it is clear that the judgments cannot stand. Accordingly, the judgment in each case is reversed.'' *Redrup v. New York*, 386 U.S. 767 (1967).

REPORTERS COMMITTEE FOR FREEDOM OF THE PRESS. Founded in 1970 and now with approximately 6,800 members, this organization professes that it is ''devoted to protecting the freedom of information rights of the working press of all media, and upholding the First Amendment. Conducts studies on the impact of subpoenas for reporters' notes and testimony upon journalists' ability to gather news from confidential sources; and examines efforts to close criminal justice proceedings to the public and press. Has acted as plaintiff or friend-of-court in most major lawsuits since 1972 affecting the First Amendment rights of working news reporters and editors. Provides free legal advice to reporters whose First Amendment rights are infringed upon by subpoenas or other legal pressures.'' *Encyclopedia of Associations* (# 13107). Its publications are *News Media Update* (biweekly) and *News/Media and the Law* (quarterly).

RE R.M.J. (1982). A practicing Missouri attorney was charged in the Missouri Supreme Court with violating some rules of behavior that regulated advertising by attorneys (Missouri, Supreme Court Regulation on Advertising*). The attorney had published advertisements that listed both areas of practice and courts in which he was admitted to practice in language other than that specified in the regulation. In addition, the attorney had sent announcement cards about his practice to people other than those permitted by the regulation. The attorney argued that these restrictions on advertising were unconstitutional under the First Amendment.

The Supreme Court agreed, Justice Powell delivering the opinion for a unanimous Court: (1) Although the states retain the ability to regulate commercial speech, such as lawyer advertising, that is inherently misleading, false, or fraudulent, the First Amendment requires that the states do so "with care" and in a manner no more extensive than reasonably necessary to achieve a substantial governmental interest. (2) Because the listing published by the attorney—"real estate" instead of "property law," and "contracts and securities," which were not in the approved list—has not been shown to be misleading, prohibiting such listing is an invalid restriction on free speech. (3) The information identifying the attorney as licensed to practice in Illinois and Missouri is true and highly relevant to prospective clients, and there is nothing misleading about this information. (4) The state cannot justify the restriction of the potential audience that can receive the mailed announcements, especially when the content of the mailed cards was not misleading, false, or fraudulent. *Re R.M.J.*, 455 U.S. 191 (1982).

REVENGE AT DAYBREAK. This film was produced in France in 1964 under the title *Desperate Decision* and was released in the United States in 1964 as *Revenge at Daybreak*. The film was directed by Yves Allegret and starred Danielle Delorme and Henry Vidal; it was also banned in Maryland (Maryland, Motion Picture Censorship*) in 1964. De Grazia and Newman (*Banned Films*, p. 277) present a summary of the plot: "The film was adapted from a novel by Catherine Beauchamp. It is set in Dublin at the time of the Anglo-Irish struggle, in 1916, when the Republicans were resisting the Free State movement with guerilla warfare. It is a melodrama of the vengeance taken by a young convent girl for the death of her brother, whom a Republican gang leader brutally executed for informing on their activities. In her search for his murderer, the young girl meets and falls in love with the gang leader, not knowing of his responsibility for her brother's gruesome death. Once she learns of this, she becomes crazed and takes revenge by murdering him."†

An exhibitor of the film, one Freedman, was convicted of exhibiting the film without first having submitted it to the Maryland Board of Censors for review and approval; Freedman argued that such a scheme violated freedom of speech. The Maryland Board of Censors testified that the film contained no material

†Reprinted from *Banned Films* with permission of the R. R. Bowker Company. Copyright © 1982 by Edward de Grazia and Roger K. Newman.

whatsoever that might have led to a refusal of the exhibition permit and that *Revenge at Daybreak* would have received the license if submitted.

The Maryland courts affirmed Freedman's conviction, but the U.S. Supreme Court, in *Freedman v. Maryland*, 380 U.S. 51 (1965), reversed. The reversal was *not* on the grounds that the Maryland censorship scheme represented an unconstitutional prior restraint on the freedoms of speech and of the press (the Court did not invalidate the general requirement of prior submission), but rather that the specific procedure employed by the Maryland Board of Censors was such a prior restraint. In effect, the Court would allow a board of censors to approve in advance the exhibition of films but only if the process afforded adequate procedural safeguards. The Court issued a three-pronged process: (1) The censor must have the burden of instituting judicial proceedings. (2) Any restraint prior to judicial review can be imposed only briefly in order to preserve the status quo. (3) A prompt judicial determination of obscenity must be assured.

As the opinion of the Court relates: "Applying the settled rule of our cases, we hold that a noncriminal process which requires the prior submission of a film to a censor avoids constitutional infirmity only if it takes place under procedural safeguards designed to obviate the dangers of a censorship system. First, the burden of proving that the film is unprotected expression must rest on the censor. Second, while the State may require advance submission of all films, in order to proceed effectively to bar all showings of unprotected films, the requirement cannot be administered in a manner which would lend an effect of finality to the censor's determination whether a film constitutes protected expression. The teaching of our cases is that, because only a judicial determination in an adversary proceeding ensures the necessary sensitivity to freedom of expression, only a procedure requiring a judicial determination suffices to impose a valid final restraint. To this end, the exhibitor must be assured that a censor will, within a specified brief period, either issue a license or go to court to restrain showing of the film. Any restraint imposed in advance of a final judicial determination on the merits must similarly be limited to the preservation of the status quo for the shortest fixed period compatible with sound judicial resolution. Moreover, we are well aware that, even after expiration of a temporary restraint, an administrative refusal to license, signifying the censor's view that the film is unprotected, may have a discouraging effect on the exhibitor. Therefore, the procedure must also assure a prompt final judicial decision, to minimize the deterrent effect of an interim and possibly erroneous denial of a license. . . . [It is] apparent that the Maryland procedural scheme does not satisfy these criteria."

Justice Douglas, joined by Justice Black, concurred in the decision but for reasons that went far beyond the Court's insistence on procedural safeguards. Justice Douglas: "On several occasions I have indicated my view that movies are entitled to the same degree and kind of protection under the First Amendment as other forms of expression. . . . I do not believe any form of censorship—no matter how speedy or prolonged it may be—is permissible. If censors are banned from the publishing business, from the pulpit, from the public platform—as they are—they should be banned from the theatre. . . . Any authority to obtain a temporary injunction gives the State 'the paralyzing power of a censor.' . . . I would put an end to all forms and types of censorship and give full literal meaning to the command of the First Amendment.''

RHODE ISLAND, COMMISSION ON YOUTH MORALITY. In 1956, the Rhode Island legislature created the Rhode Island Commission to Encourage Morality in Youth, whose mandate was to clean up the thoughts of the state's teenagers and to make sure that none of them had any "impure" impulses (Resolution No. 73 H 1000, R.I. Acts and Resolves, January Session 1956, 1102–1103). The original mandate of the commission—nine people appointed by the governor—was superseded in part by Resolution No. 95 S 444, R.I. Acts and Resolves, January Session 1959, 880, which read as follows: "It shall be the duty of said Commission to educate the public concerning any book, picture, pamphlet, ballad, printed paper or other thing containing obscene, indecent or impure language . . . and to investigate and recommend the prosecution of all violations of said sections, and it shall be the further duty of said Commission to combat juvenile delinquency and encourage morality in youth by (a) investigating situations which may cause, be responsible for or give rise to undesirable behavior of juveniles, (b) educate the public as to these causes and (c) recommend legislation, prosecution and/or treatment which would ameliorate or eliminate said causes.''

A modern-day reincarnation of Anthony Comstock's New York Society for the Suppression of Vice (Comstockery*), the Rhode Island Commission to Encourage Morality in Youth issued a report (January 1960) warning that Western civilization was about to disappear because Rhode Island teenagers were not being supervised when they went to drive-in movies on dates. Be that as it may, the Supreme Court, in *Bantam Books, Inc. v. Sullivan* (1963),* ruled that the entire enterprise was an administrative censorship scheme and thus violated the guarantees of the First Amendment.

RICHMOND NEWSPAPERS, INC. v. VIRGINIA (1980). This case involved a complaint from a Virginia newspaper that a Virginia trial court judge, during a murder trial, had the trial continue "with the press and public excluded." The Virginia Supreme Court affirmed the exclusion order, but the U.S. Supreme Court reversed. The Court held that, absent an overriding and compelling reason for exclusion in a criminal case, the First Amendment guarantees to the press and to the public the right to attend such trials: (1) The historical evidence of the evolution of the criminal trial in Anglo-American justice demonstrates conclusively that at the time this nation's organic laws were adopted, criminal trials both here and in England had long been presumptively open, thus giving the assurance that the proceedings were conducted fairly to all concerned and discouraging perjury, the misconduct of participants, or decisions based on secret bias or partiality. (2) The freedoms of speech, press, and assembly, expressly guaranteed by the First Amendment, share a common core purpose of assuring freedom of communication on matters relating to the functioning of government. In guaranteeing freedoms such as those of speech and press, the First Amendment can be read as protecting the right of everyone to attend trials so as to give meaning to those explicit guarantees; the First Amendment right to receive information and ideas means, in the context of trials, that the guarantees of speech and press, standing alone, prohibit government from summarily closing courtroom doors that had long been open to the public at the time the First Amendment was adopted. (3) Even though the Constitution contains no provision that by its terms guarantees to the public the right to attend criminal trials, various fundamental rights, not expressly guaranteed, have been recognized as indispensable to the enjoyment of enumerated rights. The right to attend criminal trials is implicit in the guarantees of the First Amendment; without the freedom to attend such trials, which people have exercised for centuries, important aspects of freedom of speech and of the press could be eviscerated. *Richmond Newspapers, Inc. v. Virginia*, 448 U.S. 555 (1980).

RIGHT OF REPLY/EQUAL TIME. The "right of reply/equal time" doctrine as defined by the Federal Communications Commission (FCC) and the Supreme Court is related to—but conceptually different from—the Federal Communications Commission Regulations Fairness Doctrine.* "Pointing out the different impact of the fairness doctrine and the F.C.C. personal attack and political editorial regulations, the [Supreme] Court stated [*Red Lion Broadcasting Co. v. Federal Communications Commission**] that when a personal attack has been made on a figure involved in a public issue, the individual attacked must be offered an opportunity to respond. Likewise, where one candidate is endorsed in a political editorial, the other candidates must themselves be offered reply time to use personally or through a spokesperson. These obligations differ from the general fairness requirement that issues be presented, and presented with coverage of competing views, in that the broadcaster does not have the option of presenting the attack himself or choosing the third party to represent that side. But insofar as there is an obligation of the broadcaster to see that both sides are presented, and insofar as that is an affirmative obligation, the personal attack doctrine and regulations do not differ [much] from the fairness doctrine. The simple fact that the attacked persons or unendorsed candidates may respond themselves or through agents is not a critical distinction, in the Court's view." Annotation: *Broadcast Regulation*, 69 L. Ed. 2d 1125.

But this "right of reply" doctrine does not apply to newspapers or other publications. A Florida statute (Florida, Right of Reply*) that required newspapers to print a reply to its editorials by political candidates criticized in the editorials was held to be invalid under the First Amendment: Government cannot tell a newspaper what to print just as it cannot tell a newspaper what not to print. *Miami Herald Publishing Company v. Tornillo.**

ROCKFORD (IL), ANTI-PICKETING ORDINANCE. The following ordinance of the city of Rockford (c. 28, § 19.2[a]) was seen to be an unconstitutional restriction on freedom of speech by the Supreme Court in *Grayned v. City of Rockford**: "No person, while on public or private grounds adjacent to any building in which a school or any class thereof is in session, shall willfully make or assist in the making of any noise or diversion which disturbs or tends to disturb the peace or good order of such school session or class thereof. . . . ''

ROSEN v. UNITED STATES (1896). Rosen was indicted and duly convicted of violating Section 3893 of the Revised Statutes (Postal Regulations, Mailing Obscene Material*). The case really was not concerned with obscenity/censorship/freedom of the press, but with the validity of the indictment that was issued against Rosen. The indictment said only that the material Rosen mailed was "obscene" and did not contain a precise description.

The Supreme Court affirmed the conviction, saying that "obscene" matter was not proper to be spread on the pages of the court record—it would debase the court—and the reader thus must accept the court's determination that the material was, in fact, obscene. The only descriptive information about what Rosen was sending through the mail—copies of a publication entitled *Broadway*—was as follows: "The paper, *Broadway*, referred to in the indictment, was produced in evidence, first, by the United States, and afterwards by the accused. The copy read in evidence by the government was the one which, it was admitted at the trial, the defendant had caused to be deposited in the mail. The pictures of females appearing in that copy were, by direction of the defendant, partially covered with lamp black that could be easily erased with a piece of bread. The object of sending them out in that condition was, of course, to excite a curiosity to know what was thus concealed. The accused read in evidence a copy that he characterized as a 'clean' one, and in which the pictures of females, in different attitudes of indecency, were not obscured by lamp black.''

The nature of the indictment should be compared with the *Illustrated Report** case (and others), in which the court records and decisions contain explicit descriptions of the material's obscenity so as, perhaps, to make the court's decision "nonmailable" to the same extent as was the original publication. But in 1896, the courts were quite squeamish and prudish and did not want to "debase" the record. *Rosen v. United States* 161 U.S. 29 (1896).

ROTH STANDARD. The subject of obscenity* has produced a variety of views among the members of the U.S. Supreme Court. The 1957 Roth Standard or test (*Roth v. United States**) stated the standard to be "whether to the average person,* applying contemporary community standards,* the dominant theme of the material taken as a whole appeals to prurient interest''* The Roth Standard was refined in 1966, in *Memoirs v. Massachusetts* (*Memoirs of a Woman of Pleasure/Fanny Hill**), which created the Memoirs Standard*: "It must be established that (a) the dominant theme of the material taken as a whole appeals to a prurient interest in sex; (b) the material is patently offensive* because it affronts contemporary community standards; and (c) the material is utterly without redeeming social value.''* The Memoirs Standard was itself refined in 1973 (*Miller v. California**), and the resulting Miller Standard* is the current standard or test of obscenity. The Miller Standard deleted the ''utterly without redeeming social value'' criterion of Memoirs and substituted ''whether the work, taken as a whole, lacks serious literary, artistic, political, or scientific value.'' To be judged obscene, a work has to meet all the stated requirements of the standard; each of the elements must independently be satisfied before the material can be held obscene.

ROTH v. UNITED STATES (1957). Roth conducted a business in New York that published and sold books, photographs, and magazines. He used circulars and flyers and advertising matter to solicit sales. He was convicted in a federal district court of using the U.S. mails to mail obscene material (Postal Regulations, Mailing Obscene Material*), and his conviction was affirmed by a court of appeals. In a landmark decision, the Supreme Court affirmed the conviction. This particular case was doubly important for it established (1) the Roth Standard* to judge obscenity, and more important, (2) the Court ruled that obscenity is not within the area of constitutionally protected freedom of speech or press— that obscene speech is ''unprotected speech.''*

In a rare and uncharacteristic departure from his previous views on obscenity and the freedoms of speech and of the press, Justice Brennan delivered the majority opinion of the Court. The Roth Standard is explained elsewhere; Brennan's remarks concern the view that obscene speech is unprotected speech. Justice Brennan: ''The dispositive question is whether obscenity is utterance within the area of protected speech and press. Although this is the first time the question has been squarely presented to the Court, either under the First Amendment or under the Fourteenth Amendment, expressions found in numerous opinions indicate that this Court has always assumed that obscenity is not protected by the freedoms of speech and press. . . . The guaranties of freedom of expression in effect in 10 of the 14 States which by 1792 had ratified the Constitution, gave no absolute protection for every utterance. Thirteen of the 14 States provided for the prosecution of libel, and all of the States made either blasphemy or profanity, or both, statutory crimes. As early as 1712, Massachusetts made it criminal to publish 'any filthy, obscene, or profane song, pamphlet, libel or mock sermon' in imitation or mimicking of religious services. (Acts and Laws of the Province of Massachusetts Bay, c. CV, § 8 [1712], Massachusetts Bay Colony Charters & Laws 399 [1814]). Thus, profanity and obscenity were related offenses. In light of this history, it is apparent that the unconditional phrasing of the First Amendment was not intended to protect every utterance. The phrasing did not prevent this Court from concluding that libelous utterances are not within the area of constitutionally protected speech (*Beauharnais v. Illinois**). At the time of the adoption of the First Amendment, obscenity was not as fully de-

veloped as libel law, but there is sufficiently contemporaneous evidence to show
that obscenity, too, was outside the protection intended for speech and press.
. . . The protection given speech and press was fashioned to assure unfettered
interchange of ideas for the bringing about of political and social changes desired
by the people. This objective was made explicit as early as 1774 in a letter of
the Continental Congress to the inhabitants of Quebec: 'The last right we shall
mention, regards the freedom of the press. The importance of this consists,
besides the advancement of truth, science, morality, and arts in general, in its
diffusion of liberal sentiments on the administration of Government, its ready
communication of thoughts between subjects, and its consequential promotion
of union among them, whereby oppressive officers are shamed or intimidated,
into more honourable and just modes of conducting affairs.' 1 *Journals* of the
Continental Congress 108 (1774). All ideas having even the slightest redeeming
social importance—unorthodox ideas, controversial ideas, even ideas hateful to
the prevailing climate of opinion—have the full protection of the guaranties,
unless excludable because they encroach upon the limited area of more important
interests. But implicit in the history of the First Amendment is the rejection of
obscenity as utterly without redeeming social importance . . . [and, as such, is
unprotected speech].''

This decision also created the Roth Standard—material is obscene if, to the
average person applying contemporary community standards, the dominant theme
of the material taken as a whole appeals to the prurient interest. Justice Douglas,
joined by Justice Black, filed a dissenting opinion, arguing against the Roth
Standard and against the view that obscenity is unprotected speech. Justice
Douglas: ''When we sustain these convictions, we make the legality of a publication turn on the purity of thought which a book or tract instills in the mind
of the reader. I do not think we can approve that standard and be faithful to the
command of the First Amendment, which by its terms is a restraint on Congress
and which by the Fourteenth is a restraint on the States. In the *Roth* case the
trial judge charged the jury that the statutory words 'obscene, lewd and lascivious'
describe 'that form of immorality which has relation to sexual impurity and has
a tendency to excite lustful thoughts.' He stated that the term 'filthy' in the
statute pertains 'to that sort of treatment of sexual matters in such a vulgar and
indecent way, so that it tends to arouse a feeling of disgust and revulsion.' He
went on to say that the material 'must be calculated to corrupt and debauch the
minds and morals' of 'the average person in the community,' not those of any
particular class. 'You judge the circulars, pictures and publications which have
been put in evidence by present-day standards of the community. You may ask
yourselves does it offend the common conscience of the community by present-
day standards.' . . . By these standards punishment is inflicted for thoughts provoked, not for overt acts nor antisocial conduct. This test cannot be squared with
our decisions under the First Amendment. Even the ill-starred *Dennis* case conceded that speech to be punishable must have some relation to action which
would be penalized by government. (*Dennis v. United States**). The tests by

which these convictions were obtained require only the arousing of sexual thoughts. Yet the arousing of sexual thoughts and desires happens every day in normal life in dozens of ways. Nearly 30 years ago a questionnaire was sent to college and normal school woman graduates that asked what things were most stimulating sexually. Of 409 replies, 9 said 'music'; 18 said 'pictures'; 29 said 'dancing'; 40 said 'drama'; 95 said 'books'; and 218 said 'man' (Alpert, 'Judicial Censorship of Obscene Literature,' 52 *Harvard Law Review* 40). Any test that turns on what is offensive to the community's standards is too loose, too capricious, too destructive of freedom of expression to be squared with the First Amendment. Under that test, juries can censor, suppress, and punish what they don't like, provided the matter relates to 'sexual impurity' or has a tendency 'to excite lustful thoughts.' This is community censorship in one of its worst forms. It creates a regime where in the battle between the literati and the Philistines, the Philistines are certain to win. If experience in this field teaches anything, it is that 'censorship of obscenity has almost always been both irrational and indiscriminate.' The test adopted here accentuates that trend. I assume there is nothing in the Constitution which forbids Congress from using its power over the mails to proscribe *conduct* on the grounds of good morals. No one would suggest that the First Amendment permits nudity in public places, adultery, and other phases of sexual misconduct. I can understand (and at times even sympathize) with programs of civic groups and church groups to protect and defend the existing moral standards of the community. I can understand the motives of the Anthony Comstocks who would impose Victorian standards on the community [Comstockery*]. When speech alone is involved, I do not think that government, consistently with the First Amendment, can become the sponsor of any of these movements. I do not think that government can throw its weight behind one school or another. The test of obscenity the Court endorses today gives the censor free rein over a vast domain. To allow the State to step in and punish mere speech or publication that the judge or the jury thinks has an *undesirable* impact on thoughts but that is not shown to be a part of unlawful action is drastically to curtail the First Amendment. I would give the broad sweep of the First Amendment full support. I have the same confidence in the ability of our people to reject noxious literature as I have in their capacity to sort out the true from the false in theology, economics, politics, or any other field." *Roth v. United States*, 354 U.S. 476 (1957).

ROWAN v. UNITED STATES POST OFFICE DEPARTMENT (1970).

Rowan operated a mail order business and brought suit to enjoin the enforcement of 39 U.S.C. § 4009 (Postal Regulations, Unwanted Mail*), which permitted an individual addressee, if he receives any advertisements for material that he considers to be a "pandering" advertisement ("erotically arousing" or "sexually provocative"), to inform the postmaster general. The postmaster general then would issue an order to the sender to stop mailing such material to the complaining addressee, and a violation of the "cease and desist" order could result in a conviction for contempt of court.

The Supreme Court held that § 4009 was not unconstitutional on the grounds that the sender does not have a constitutional right to send unwanted material into someone's home, and that the mailer's right to communicate stops at the mailbox of an unreceptive addressee. The Supreme Court's decision contained the following comments: "The essence of [Rowan's] argument is that the statute violates their constitutional right to communicate. One sentence in [Rowan's] brief perhaps characterizes their entire position: 'The freedom to communicate orally and by the written word and, indeed, in every manner whatsoever is imperative to a free and sane society.' . . . Weighing the highly important right to communicate, but without trying to determine where it fits into constitutional imperatives, against the very basic right to be free from sights, sounds, and tangible matter we do not want, it seems to us that a mailer's right to communicate must stop at the mailbox of an unreceptive addressee. The court has traditionally respected the right of a householder to bar, by order or notice, solicitors, hawkers, and peddlers from his property. In this case the mailer's right to communicate is circumscribed only by an affirmative act of the addressee giving notice that he wishes no further mailings from that mailer. To hold less would tend to license a form of trespass and would make hardly more sense than to say that a radio or television viewer may not twist the dial to cut off an offensive or boring communication and thus bar its entering his home. Nothing in this Constitution compels us to listen to or view any unwanted communication, whatever its merit; we see no basis for according the printed word or pictures a different or more preferred status because they are sent by mail. The ancient concept that 'a man's home is his castle' into which 'not even the king may enter' has lost none of its vitality, and none of the recognized exceptions includes any right to communicate offensively with another. . . . In effect, Congress has erected a wall—or more accurately permits a citizen to erect a wall—that no advertiser can penetrate without his acquiescence. The continuing operative effect of a mailing ban once imposed presents no constitutional obstacles; the citizen cannot be put to the burden of determining on repeated occasions whether the offending mailer has altered its material so as to make it acceptable. Nor should the householder have to risk that offensive material come into the hands of his children before it can be stopped. We therefore categorically reject the argument that a vendor has a right under the Constitution or otherwise to send unwanted material into the home of another. If this prohibition operates to impede the flow of even valid ideas, the answer is that no one has a right to press even 'good' ideas on an unwilling recipient. That we are often 'captives' outside the sanctuary of the home and subject to objectionable speech and other sound does not mean we must be captives everywhere. The asserted right of a mailer, we repeat, stops at the outer boundary of every person's domain." *Rowan v. United States Post Office Department*, 397 U.S. 728 (1970).

S

SAIA v. NEW YORK (1948). A city ordinance (Lockport [NY], Sound Trucks*) prohibited the use of sound amplification devices (sound trucks) in public places except with the prior permission of the chief of police. Saia was a minister of the Jehovah's Witnesses, and pursuant to the city ordinance, he obtained permission from the chief of police to use sound equipment to amplify lectures on religious subjects. He gave his talks at a fixed place in a public park on Sundays. He applied for another permit when the original one expired, but the chief of police refused, saying that complaints had been made. Saia nonetheless used his equipment without the permit and was tried in police court. Some witnesses testified that they were annoyed by the sound but not by the content of the talks; others were not disturbed by either. Saia received a fine and a jail sentence; the conviction was affirmed by the New York state courts.

The Supreme Court reversed, holding the ordinance to be a prior restraint* on the right of free speech in violation of the First Amendment. Justice Black delivered the opinion of the Court: "We hold that § 3 of this ordinance is unconstitutional on its face, for it establishes a previous restraint on the right of free speech in violation of the First Amendment which is protected by the Fourteenth Amendment against state action [Incorporation*]. To use a loud-speaker or amplifier one has to get a permit from the Chief of Police. There are no standards prescribed for the exercise of his discretion. The statute is not narrowly drawn to regulate the hours or places of use of loud-speakers, or the volume of sound (the decibels) to which they must be adjusted. . . . The present ordinance would be a dangerous weapon if it were allowed to get a hold on our public life. Noise can be regulated by regulating decibels. The hours and place of public discussion can be controlled. But to allow the police to bar the use of loud-speakers because their use can be abused is like barring radio receivers because they too make a noise. The police need not be given the power to deny a man the use of his radio to protect a neighbor against sleepless nights. The same is true here. Any abuses which loud-speakers create can be controlled by narrowly drawn statutes. When a city allows an official to ban them in his uncontrolled discretion, it sanctions a device for suppression of free communication of ideas. In this case a permit is denied because some persons were said to have found the sound annoying. In the next one a permit may be denied because some people find the ideas annoying. Annoyance at ideas can be cloaked in annoyance at sound. The power of censorship inherent in this type of ordinance reveals its vice. Courts must balance the various community interests in passing on the constitutionality of local regulations of the character involved here. But in that process they should be mindful to keep the freedoms of the First Amendment in a preferred position.

Justice Frankfurter dissented from the majority's reasoning: "I cannot say that it was beyond constitutional limits to refuse a license to [Saia] for the time and place requested. The State was entitled to authorize the local authorities of Lockport to determine that the well-being of those of its inhabitants who sought quiet and other pleasures that a park affords, outweighed [Saia's] right to force his message upon them. Nor did it exceed the bounds of reason for the chief of police to base his decision refusing a license upon the fact that the manner in which the license had been used in the past was destructive of the enjoyment of the park by those for whom it was maintained. That people complained about an annoyance would seem to be a pretty solid basis in experience for not sanctioning its continuance. . . . It is not unconstitutional for a State to vest in a public official the determination of what is in effect a nuisance merely because such authority may be outrageously misused by trying to stifle the expression of some undesired opinion under the meretricious cloak of a nuisance. Judicial remedies are available for such abuse of authority, and courts, including this Court, exist to enforce such remedies." *Saia v. New York*, 334 U.S. 558 (1948).

ST. AMANT v. THOMPSON (1968).

ST. AMANT v. THOMPSON (1968). St. Amant made a televised political speech during which he read questions that he had previously put to a union member (one Albin), and Albin's answers; the answers falsely charged Thompson, a public official,* with criminal conduct. Thompson then sued St. Amant for defamation and was awarded damages by the trial judge. The trial judge denied a motion for a new trial after having considered *New York Times Company v. Sullivan*,* decided after the trial. An appeals court reversed the trial court's decision, ruling that St. Amant had not acted with actual malice within the meaning of the *New York Times* Rule,* that is, with knowledge that the statements were false or with reckless disregard of whether they were false or not.

The state Supreme Court reversed this decision, reinstating the trial court's ruling that St. Amant was guilty. The state Supreme Court ruled: (1) There had been sufficient evidence that St. Amant had acted in "reckless disregard" of the truth in that he had no personal knowledge of Thompson's activities. (2) St. Amant had relied solely on Albin's statements, although there was no evidence as to Albin's veracity. (3) St. Amant failed to verify the information offered by Albin with others who might have known the facts. (4) St. Amant did not consider whether the statements were defamatory. (5) St. Amant was wrong in believing that he had no responsibility for the broadcast because he was merely quoting Albin.

The U.S. Supreme Court reversed this decision, holding that St. Amant's conduct did not fall beyond the protection created by the *New York Times* Rule: (1) The people's stake in the conduct of public officials is so great that neither the defense of truth nor the standard of ordinary care would adequately implement First Amendment policies. (2) In order that it can be found that a defendant, within the meaning of the *New York Times* Rule, acted in "reckless disregard" of whether a defamatory statement that he made about a public official is false or not, there must be sufficient evidence to permit the conclusion that the defendant had serious doubts as to the truth of his publication. (3) The evidence in this case is not sufficient to permit the conclusion that St. Amant acted in reckless disregard of whether the statements about Thompson were false or not. *St. Amant v. Thompson*, 390 U.S. 727 (1968).

ST. LOUIS (MO), INDECENT BEHAVIOR. Section 38, Chapter 46, Revised Code of St. Louis, provides in part that any person who shall "permit to be exhibited or performed, upon premises under his management or control, any indecent, immoral or lewd play or other representation shall be deemed guilty of a misdemeanor." Section 37 provides that any person who shall appear in a public place "in a state of nudity or in a dress not belonging to his or her sex or in an indecent or lewd dress, or shall make an indecent exposure of his or her person, or be guilty of an indecent or lewd act of behavior shall be guilty of a misdemeanor." These sections were used to convict Mikes and Elliott, of "permitting to be exhibited," and Ware, of "exhibiting," an indecent and lewd act in St. Louis (*City of St. Louis v. Mikes**) in 1963. It appears that Ware staged a burlesque act in a St. Louis nightclub.

SAN DIEGO (CA), OUTDOOR ADVERTISING DISPLAYS. San Diego Ordinance No. 10795 (New Series), enacted March 14, 1972, prohibited the following signs: (1) any sign identifying a use, facility, or service that is not located on the premises; (2) any sign identifying a product that is not produced, sold, or manufactured on the premises; (3) any sign that advertises or otherwise directs attention to a product, service or activity, event, person, institution, or business that may or may not be identified by a brand name and that occurs or is generally conducted, sold, manufactured, produced, or offered elsewhere than on the premises where such sign is located. This almost total ban on billboards was seen to be an unconstitutional restriction of the rights of free speech and press by the Supreme Court in *Metromedia v. City of San Diego*.*

SAXBE v. *WASHINGTON POST* (1974). The *Washington Post* initiated this suit to challenge the constitutionality of § 4b(6) of Policy Statement 1220.1A of the Federal Bureau of Prisons (Prison Regulations, Federal*). Paragraph 4b(6) provided that press representatives would no longer be permitted to interview individual inmates, even in situations in which the inmate requested or sought an interview, although the press was permitted to have conversations with inmates

whose identity was not to be made public and if the conversations were limited
to the discussion of institutional facilities, programs, and activities. The Supreme
Court held that the policy statement did not violate the First Amendment rights
of either the inmates or the press: ¶ 4b(6) does not deny the press access to
sources of information available to members of the general public but is merely
a particularized application of the general rule that nobody may enter a prison
and designate an inmate whom he would like to visit unless the prospective
visitor is a lawyer, a member of the clergy, a relative, or a friend of the inmate.
Saxbe v. Washington Post, 417 U.S. 843 (1974).

SCHACHT v. UNITED STATES (1970). Schacht, a civilian, participated in
a skit performed several times in front of an armed forces induction center in
Houston, Texas. The skit demonstrated obvious opposition to the U.S. involvement in Viet Nam. The skit was described in the following terms: "The skit
was composed of three people. There was Schacht who was dressed in a uniform
and cap. A second person was wearing 'military colored' coveralls. The third
person was outfitted in typical Viet Cong apparel. The first two men carried
water pistols. One of them would yell, 'Be an able American,' and then they
would shoot the Viet Cong with their pistols. The pistols expelled a red liquid
which, when it struck the victim, created the impression that he was bleeding.
Once the victim fell down the other two would walk up to him and exclaim,
'My God, this is a pregnant woman.' Without noticeable variation this skit was
reenacted several times during the morning of the demonstration.''

Schacht was duly arrested, tried, and convicted of two violations: (1) The
wearing of military uniforms by civilians in unauthorized situations is criminal
(18 U.S.C. § 702), for although the statute allows the wearing of uniforms by
an actor in a theatrical or motion picture production, the government didn't think
the skit was a "theatrical" production; and 2. Even if the skit were a "theatrical"
production, 10 U.S.C. § 772 (f) allows the wearing of a uniform only "if the
portrayal does not tend to discredit that armed force" (Military Regulations,
Wearing Uniforms—Non-Military Personnel*).

The U.S. Supreme Court reversed the convictions, holding that § 772 (f) was
a blatant form of government censorship. Justice Black delivered the opinion of
the Court: "Our previous cases would seem to make it clear that 18 U.S.C. §
702, making it an offense to wear our military uniforms without authority is,
standing alone, a valid statute on its face. But the general prohibition of § 702
cannot always stand alone in view of 10 U.S.C. § 772, which authorizes the
wearing of military uniforms under certain conditions and circumstances including the circumstance of an actor portraying a member of the armed services
in a 'theatrical production' (§ 772-f). The Government's argument in this case
seems to imply that somehow what these amateur actors did in Houston should
not be treated as a 'theatrical production' within the meaning of § 772 (f). We
are unable to follow such a suggestion. Certainly theatrical productions need not
always be performed in buildings or even on a defined area such as a conventional

stage. Nor need they be performed by professional actors or be heavily financed
or elaborately produced. Since time immemorial, outdoor theatrical performances, often performed by amateurs, have played an important part in the entertainment and the education of the people of the world. Here, the record shows
without dispute the preparation and repeated presentation by amateur actors of
a short play designed to create in the audience an understanding of and opposition
to our participation in the Viet Nam war. It may be that the performances were
crude and amateurish and perhaps unappealing, but the same thing can be said
about many theatrical performances. We cannot believe that when Congress
wrote out a special exemption for theatrical productions it intended to protect
only a narrow and limited category of professionally produced plays. Of course,
we need not decide here all the questions concerning what is and what is not
within the scope of § 772 (f). We need only find, as we emphatically do, that
the street skit in which Schacht participated was a 'theatrical production' within
the meaning of that section.

"This brings us to [Schacht's] complaint that giving force and effect to the
last clause of § 772 (f) would impose an unconstitutional restraint on his right
of free speech. We agree. This clause on its face simply restricts § 772(f)'s
authorization to those dramatic performances that do not 'tend to discredit' the
military, but, when this restriction is read together with 18 U.S.C. § 702, it
becomes clear that Congress has in effect made it a crime for an actor wearing
a military uniform to say things during his performance critical of the conduct
or policies of the Armed Forces. An actor, like everyone else in our country,
enjoys a constitutional right to freedom of speech, including the right openly to
criticize the Government during a dramatic performance. The last clause of §
772 (f) denies this constitutional right to an actor who is wearing a military
uniform by making it a crime for him to say things that tend to bring the military
into discredit and disrepute. In the present case Schacht was free to participate
in any skit at the demonstration that praised the Army, but under the final clause
of § 772 (f) he could be convicted of a federal offense if his portrayal attacked
the Army instead of praising it.

"In light of our earlier finding that the skit in which Schacht participated was
a 'theatrical production' within the meaning of § 772 (f), it follows that his
conviction can be sustained only if he can be punished for speaking out against
the role of our Army and our country in Vietnam. Clearly punishment for this
reason would be an unconstitutional abridgment of freedom of speech [but only
for civilians; military personnel have received harsh sentences for speaking out
against the Viet Nam War; some illustrative cases are *United States v. Locks*,*
United States v. Priest,* and *United States v. Toomey**]. The final clause of
§ 772 (f), which leaves Americans free to praise the war in Vietnam but can
send persons like Schacht to prison for opposing it, cannot survive in a country
which has the First Amendment. To preserve the constitutionality of § 772 (f)
that final clause [tend to discredit the military] must be stricken from the section."
Schacht v. United States, 398 U.S. 58 (1970).

SCHAD v. BOROUGH OF MOUNT EPHRAIM (1981). After an adult bookstore located in the commercial zone of the borough of Mount Ephraim, New Jersey, introduced a coin-operated mechanism that permitted customers to watch a live dancer—usually nude females—performing behind a glass panel (the customer would deposit the money, the cover would rise, and he could watch for a few minutes; some similar establishments in New York's Time Square area would, on payment of an additional sum to the dancer, have the glass panel open to enable physical contact between the dancer and the customer), complaints were filed against the bookstore's operators, charging that the exhibition of live dancing violated the borough's zoning ordinance (Mount Ephraim, Nude Dancing*), which governed uses permitted in a commercial zone. The bookstore operators were found guilty, and the New Jersey courts, although recognizing that live nude dancing was protected by the First Amendment, ruled that the First Amendment guarantees did not apply in this circumstance.

On appeal, the U.S. Supreme Court reversed, holding that the attempt to ban nude dancing was a violation of the First Amendment. Justice White delivered the opinion of the Court: (1) The borough's contention that permitting live entertainment would conflict with its plan to create a commercial area catering to the "immediate needs" of its residents was patently insufficient. (2) The borough presented no evidence in support of its argument that it may selectively exclude commercial live entertainment from permitted commercial uses because such entertainment poses problems of a unique nature, especially when the ordinance was not narrowly drawn to respond to such distinctive problems and it was not clear that a more selective approach would fail to address such problems. (3) The borough, in attempting to establish that the ordinance was a reasonable time-place-manner* restriction, did not identify the municipal interests making it reasonable to exclude all commercial live entertainment but to allow a variety of other commercial uses in the borough, and did not present evidence establishing that live entertainment was incompatible with the uses presently permitted by the borough. (4) The borough was not able to avail itself of the argument that the zoning restriction was permissible because live entertainment in general and nude dancing in particular were amply available in close-by areas outside the borough's limits.

Chief Justice Burger, joined by Justice Rehnquist, apparently did not like nude dancing and dissented from the majority opinion: The ordinance was valid as applied to ban nude dancing—opposed to "traditional" live entertainment—because a community of people are, within limits, masters of their own environment and should have the right to ban an activity incompatible with a quiet residential atmosphere. *Schad v. Borough of Mount Ephraim*, 452 U.S. 61 (1981).

SCHAEFFER v. UNITED STATES (1920). Schaeffer and others were convicted and sentenced to a penitentiary for printing seventeen articles in a German-language newspaper, published in Philadelphia, between June and September

1917. The convictions were based on the violation of § 3, Title 1 of the June 15, 1917 act (Espionage Act*).

The U.S. Supreme Court reversed the convictions of Peter Schaeffer and Paul Vogel (the Court could find no evidence that these two men were responsible for the publications) but affirmed the convictions of Louis Werner, Martin Darkow, and Herman Lemke. Schaeffer and the others were prosecuted under the Espionage Act for willfully making and conveying false reports and statements with "intent to promote the success of Germany and to obstruct the recruiting and enlistment service of the United States to the injury of the United States" in the war with Germany. It appears that their newspaper took news dispatches from other papers and republished them with omissions, additions, and changes. The Court held: (1) The falsity of the publications depended on the fact of the alterations and the resulting tendency of the articles was to weaken zeal and patriotism and thus hamper the United States in raising armies and conducting the war. (2) The constitutional provision protecting speech and press does not protect criminal abuse of these rights.

Justice McKenna minced no words in the majority decision that held the First Amendment did not apply to someone who attempted to weaken the morale of the army. Justice McKenna: "But simple as the law [Espionage Act] is, perilous to the country as disobedience to it was, offenders developed and when it was exerted against them challenged it as a violation of the right of free speech assured by the Constitution of the United States. A curious spectacle was presented: that great ordinance of government and orderly liberty was invoked to justify the activities of anarchy or of the enemies of the United States, and by a strange perversion of its precepts, it was adduced against itself. In other words and explicitly, though it empowered Congress to declare war and war is waged with armies, their formation (recruiting or enlisting) could be prevented or impeded, and the morale of the armies when formed could be weakened or debased by question or calumny of the motives of authority, and this could not be made a crime—that it was an impregnable attribute of free speech upon which no curb could be put. Verdicts and judgments of conviction were the reply to the challenge and when they were brought here (*Schenck v. United States,* *Frohwerk v. United States,* *Debs v. United States,* *Abrams v. United States*) our response to it was unhesitating and direct. We did more than reject the contention; we forestalled all shades of repetition of it."

The Court's opinion was not unanimous, however; Justices Brandeis, Holmes, and Clarke filed dissents. Justice Brandeis' dissent contained some of the articles and statements that formed the basis of the convictions: "The army of ten million and the hundred thousand airships which were to annihilate Germany, have proved to be American boasts, which will not stand washing. It is worthy of note how much the Yankees can yell their throats out without spraining their mouths. This is in accord with their spiritual quality."

Justice Brandeis, joined by Justice Holmes: "The jury which found men guilty for publishing news items or editorials like those here in question must have supposed it to be within their province to condemn men not merely for disloyal acts but for a disloyal heart; provided only that the disloyal heart was evidenced by some utterance. To prosecute men for such publications reminds of the days when men were hanged for constructive treason. And, indeed, the jury may well have believed from the charge that the Espionage Act had in effect restored the crime of constructive treason. To hold that . . . such impotent expressions of editorial opinion . . . can afford the basis even of a prosecution will doubtless discourage criticism of the policies of the Government. To hold that such publications can be suppressed as false reports, subjects to new perils the constitutional liberty of the press, already seriously curtailed in practice under powers assumed to have been conferred upon the postal authorities. Nor will this grave danger end with the passing of the war. The constitutional right of free speech has been declared to be the same in peace and in war. In peace, too, men may differ widely as to what loyalty to our country demands; and an intolerant majority, swayed by passion or by fear, may be prone in the future, as it has often been in the past, to stamp as disloyal opinions with which it disagrees. Convictions such as these, besides abridging freedom of speech, threaten freedom of thought and of belief.''

Justice Clarke, feeling the convictions were due to the anti-German war hysteria, also filed a dissent. Justice Clarke: ''I cannot see, as my associates seem to see, that the disposition of this case involves a great peril either to the maintenance of law and order and governmental authority on the one hand, or to the freedom of the press on the other. To me it seems simply a case of flagrant mistrial, likely to result in disgrace and great injustice, probably in life imprisonment for two old men, because this Court hesitates to exercise the power, which it undoubtedly possesses, to correct, in this calmer time, errors of law which would not have been committed but for the stress and strain of feeling prevailing in the early months of the late deplorable war.'' *Schaeffer v. United States*, 251 U.S. 466 (1920).

SCHAUMBURG (IL), ORDINANCE ON SOLICITING. The Village of Schaumburg Code, Article III, Chapter 22, §§ 22.19—22.24, required a permit before the town would allow charitable solicitations. The permit applications required, among other things, ''satisfactory proof that at least seventy-five per cent of the proceeds of such solicitations will be used directly for the charitable purpose of the organization.'' In determining whether an organization satisfied the 75 percent requirement, the ordinance provided ''the following items shall not be deemed to be used for the charitable purposes of the organization, to wit: (1) Salaries or commissions paid to solicitors; (2) Administrative expenses of the organization, including, but not limited to, salaries, attorney's fees, rents, telephone, advertising expenses, contributions to other organizations and persons, except as a charitable contribution and related expenses incurred as administrative or overhead items.'' This 75 percent requirement was seen to be an invalid restriction on the right of free speech by the Supreme Court in *Village of Schaumburg v. Citizens for a Better Environment.**

SCHENCK v. UNITED STATES (1919). Schenck and others were convicted of mailing printed circulars in a conspiracy to obstruct the recruiting and enlistment service of the U.S. military forces, a violation of the Espionage Act* of 1917. The Supreme Court affirmed the convictions in the case, now famous for it was here that the "clear and present danger"* doctrine was enunciated: Words that, ordinarily and in many places, would be within the freedom of speech protected by the First Amendment, may become subject to prohibition when of such a nature and used in such circumstances as to create a clear and present danger that they will bring about the substantive evils that Congress has a right to prevent; the character of every act depends on the circumstances in which it is done.

Justice Holmes spoke for the Court: "The document in question upon its first printed side recited the first section of the Thirteenth Amendment, said that the idea embodied in it was violated by the Conscription Act and that a conscript is little better than a convict. In impassioned language it intimated that conscription was despotism in its worst form and a monstrous wrong against humanity in the interest of Wall Street's chosen few. It said 'Do not submit to intimidation,' but in form at least confined itself to peaceful measures such as a petition for the repeal of the act. The other and later printed side of the sheet was headed 'Assert Your Rights.' It stated reasons for alleging that anyone violated the Constitution when he refused to recognize 'your right to assert your opposition to the draft,' and went on 'If you do not assert and support your rights, you are helping to deny or disparage rights which it is the solemn duty of all citizens and residents of the United States to retain.' It described the arguments on the other side as coming from cunning politicians and a mercenary capitalist press, and even silent consent to the conscription law as helping to support an infamous conspiracy. It denied the power to send our citizens away to foreign shores to shoot up the people of other lands, and added that words could not express the condemnation such cold-blooded ruthlessness deserves, winding up 'You must do your share to maintain, support and uphold the rights of the people of this country.' Of course the document would not have been sent unless it had been intended to have some effect, and we do not see what effect it could be expected to have upon persons subject to the draft except to influence them to obstruct the carrying of it out. The defendants do not deny that the jury might find against them on this point. But it is said, suppose that that was the tendency of this circular, it is protected by the First Amendment to the Constitution.... We admit that in many places and in ordinary times the defendants in saying all that was said in the circular would have been within their constitutional rights. But the character of every act depends upon the circumstances in which it is done. The most stringent protection of free speech would not protect a man in falsely shouting fire in a theatre and causing a panic. ... The question in every case is whether the words used are used in such circumstances and are of such a nature as to create a clear and present danger that they will bring about the substantive evils that Congress has a right to prevent. It is a question of proximity and degree. When a nation is at war many things that might be said in time of peace are such a hindrance to its effort that their utterance will not be endured so long as men fight and that no Court could regard them as protected by any constitutional right. It seems to be admitted that if an actual obstruction of the recruiting service were proved, liability for words that produced that effect might be enforced. The statute of 1917 in § 4 punishes conspiracies to obstruct as well as actual obstruction. If the act (speaking or circulating a paper), its tendency and the intent with which it is done are the same, we perceive no ground for saying that success alone warrants making the act a crime.'' *Schenck v. United States*, 249 U.S. 47 (1919).

SCHNEIDER v. STATE (1939). A municipal ordinance (Irvington [NJ], Distribution of Literature*) prohibiting the distribution of literature within the town unless licensed in advance by the police, after an inquiry and investigation, was seen to be a censorship scheme as applied to Schneider. Schneider went from house to house distributing religious literature and soliciting contributions.

The Supreme Court wrote: ''Pamphlets have proved most effective instruments in the dissemination of opinion. And perhaps the most effective way of bringing them to the notice of individuals is their distribution at the homes of the people. On this method of communication the ordinance imposes censorship, abuse of which engendered the struggle in England which eventuated in the establishment of the doctrine of the freedom of the press embodied in our Constitution. To require a censorship through license which makes impossible the free and un-hampered distribution of pamphlets strikes at the very heart of the constitutional guarantees. Conceding that fraudulent appeals may be made in the name of charity and religion, we hold a municipality cannot, for this reason, require all who wish to disseminate ideas to present them first to police authorities for their consideration and approval, with a discretion in the police to say some ideas may, while others may not, be carried to the homes of citizens; some persons may, while others may not, disseminate information from house to house. Frauds may be denounced as offenses and punished by law. Trespasses may similarly be forbidden. If it is said that these means are less efficient and convenient than bestowal of power on police authorities to decide what information may be disseminated from house to house, and who may impart the information, the answer is that considerations of this sort do not empower a municipality to abridge freedom of speech and press. . . . We are not to be taken as holding that commercial soliciting and canvassing may not be subjected to such regulation as the ordinance requires. Nor do we hold that the town may not fix reasonable hours when canvassing may be done by persons having such objects as [Schneider]. Doubtless there are other features of such activities which may be regulated in the public interest without prior licensing or other invasion of constitutional liberty. We do hold, however, that the ordinance in question, as applied to [Schneider's] conduct, is void, and she cannot be punished for acting without a permit.'' *Schneider v. State*, 308 U.S. 147 (1939).

SCHOLARS AND CITIZENS FOR FREEDOM OF INFORMATION.
Scholars and Citizens for Freedom of Information is composed of those in the
academic community who support the Freedom of Information Act (FOIA).*
The group describes as its objective: "To support the Freedom of Information
Act in maintaining and protecting the nation's records and in guaranteeing public
access to them; to promote a greater understanding of the F.O.I.A. as a key
research tool and as a protective instrument for the vital interests of a democratic
society. Monitors legislative and executive efforts to bypass, reduce, or revoke
the F.O.I.A. and organizes opposition to such maneuvers; raises funds and
attempts to establish channels of communication among professional organizations and between scholars and the public." *Encyclopedia of Associations* (#
12579). This group had its origins in Historians for Freedom of Information
(founded in 1978).

SCOPES v. STATE (1927). John T. Scopes was convicted in Tennessee of a
violation of Chapter 27 of the Acts of 1925 (Tennessee, Anti-Evolution Act*),
for "that he did teach in the public schools of Rhea county a certain theory that
denied the story of the divine creation of man, as taught in the Bible, and did
teach instead thereof that man had descended from a lower order of animals."
After a verdict of guilty by the jury, the trial judge imposed a fine of one hundred
dollars.

Scopes appealed his conviction to the Tennessee Supreme Court. Chief Justice
Green of the Tennessee Supreme Court delivered the court's opinion: "It is
contended that the statute violates section 8 of article 1 of the Tennessee Constitution. . . . We think there is little merit in this contention. [Scopes] was a
teacher in the public schools of Rhea county. He was an employee of the state
of Tennessee or of a municipal agency of the state. He was under contract with
the state to work in an institution of the state. He had no right or privilege to
serve the state except upon such terms as the state prescribed. His liberty, his
privilege, his immunity to teach and proclaim the theory of evolution elsewhere
. . . [remained unhampered]. The relevant portion of section 12 of article 11 of
the [Tennessee] Constitution is in these words: 'It shall be the duty of the General
Assembly in all future periods of this government, to cherish literature and
science.' The argument is that the theory of the descent of man from a lower
order of animals is now established by the preponderance of scientific thought
and that the prohibition of the teaching of such theory is a violation of the
legislative duty to cherish science. While this clause of the Constitution has been
mentioned in several of our cases, these references have been casual, and no act
of the Legislature has ever been held inoperative by reason of such provision.
. . . If the Legislature thinks that, by reason of popular prejudice, the cause of
education and the study of science generally will be promoted by forbidding the
teaching of evolution in the schools of the state, we can conceive of no ground
to justify the court's interference. The courts cannot sit in judgment on such acts
of the Legislature or its agents and determine whether or not the omission or

addition of a particular course of study tends 'to cherish science.' The last serious criticism made of the act is that it contravenes the provision of section 3 of article 1 of the [Tennessee] Constitution, 'that no preference shall ever be given, by law, to any religious establishment or mode of worship.' . . . We are not able to see how the prohibition of teaching the theory that man has descended from a lower order of animals gives preference to any religious establishment or mode of worship. So far as we know, there is no religious establishment or organized body that has in its creed or confession of faith any article denying or affirming such a theory. So far as we know, the denial or affirmation of such a theory does not enter into any recognized mode of worship. Since this cause has been pending in this court, we have been favored, in addition to briefs of counsel and various *amici curiae*, with a multitude [an understatement] of resolutions, addresses, and communications from scientific bodies, religious factions, and individuals giving us the benefit of their views upon the theory of evolution. Examination of these contributions indicates that Protestants, Catholics, and Jews are divided among themselves in their beliefs, and that there is no unanimity among the members of any religious establishment as to this subject. Belief or unbelief in the theory of evolution is no more a characteristic of any religious establishment or mode of worship than is belief or unbelief in the wisdom of the prohibition laws. It would appear that members of the same churches quite generally disagree as to these things. [In a concurring opinion, Judge Chambliss did, however, refer to the defense contention that Tennessee's anti-evolution law gave a 'preference' to 'religious establishments that have as one of their tenets or dogmas the instantaneous creation of man.'] Furthermore, chapter 277 of the Acts of 1925 *requires* the teaching of nothing. It only *forbids* the teaching of the evolution of man from a lower order of animals. . . . As the law thus stands, while the theory of evolution of man may not be taught in the schools of the state, nothing contrary to that theory is required to be taught. . . . Our school authorities are therefore quite free to determine how they shall act in this state of the law. Those in charge of the educational affairs of the state are men and women of discernment and culture. If they believe that the teaching of the [theory of evolution is not to be performed in Tennessee, this court will accept their judgment].''

The Anti-Evolution Act was declared valid, but the court reversed Scopes' conviction on the grounds that the jury and not the trial judge should have assessed the one-hundred-dollar fine. Judge Green concluded by saying that, since Scopes ''was no longer in the service of the state, we see nothing to be gained by prolonging the life of this bizarre case. On the contrary, we think the peace and dignity of the state . . . would be the better conserved by the entry of a *nolle prosequi* herein.'' Thus ended the bizarre case of John Scopes and the ''monkey trial.''

But the anti-evolution philosophy lived (and lives) on. Mississippi (Code Ann. §§ 6798, 6799 [1942]) and Arkansas (Stat. Ann. §§ 80-1627, 80-1628 [1928]) passed similar legislation, and the Arkansas anti-evolution statute was on the books until 1968, when, in *Epperson v. Arkansas*,* the Supreme Court ruled it unconstitutional. Oklahoma enacted an anti-evolution law, but it was repealed in 1926. The Florida and Texas legislatures adopted resolutions against teaching the doctrine of evolution. In all, between 1921 and 1929, bills to this effect were introduced in some twenty states. Clarence Darrow, who was Scopes' defense counsel, pointed out in his 1932 autobiography (*The Story of My Life*, p. 247) that states with anti-evolution laws did not insist on the fundamentalist sectarian theory in all respects: "I understand that the States of Tennessee and Mississippi both continue to teach that the earth is round and that the revolution on its axis brings the day and night, in spite of all opposition." The Tennessee statute was not repealed until 1967, and it was not until 1984 that Texas no longer required textbook publishers to place a disclaimer in books to the effect that evolution was only a "theory" (Texas, State Textbook Committee*). *Scopes v. State*, 289 S.W. 363 (1927).

SCREW. The New York Court of Appeals, in *Buckley v. New York* (307 N.E. 2d 805 [1973]), found the magazine *Screw* to be obscene and thus in violation of the New York Penal Code (New York, Obscenity Statute*). The U.S. Supreme Court affirmed this finding by refusing to hear an appeal (418 U.S. 944 [1974], *cert. denied*). The New York court described *Screw* in the following terms: "The magazine *Screw* is clearly obscene by any standard. The issues in evidence are crammed with photographs of naked men and women engaging in homosexual and heterosexual acts, in many instances with genitals prominently and lewdly displayed. Drawings and cartoons are also explicit, exaggerating sexual activity to preposterous degrees. Book and movie reviews are confined only to those works which deal with sex, the worth of a movie being measured by the degree of male erection it is likely to induce. The advertising is no less egregious. The issues contain display ads for what used to be called stag films; sex paraphernalia such as dildoes are prominently illustrated in detail; and personal ads soliciting male and female participation in sex acts of every conceivable sort are written quite unambiguously. Many of the articles are totally sex oriented and are written in the most graphic terms. The use of all the most abominable dirty words is prevalent both in headlines and text. Indeed, it is hard to conceive of how a publication could reach any further lows in attempts to appeal to prurient interests."

SECRETARY OF THE NAVY v. HUFF (1980). Certain military regulations (Military Regulations, Navy and Marine Corps*) require military personnel on an overseas base to obtain command approval before circulating petitions on the base. Huff circulated such petitions without the required prior approval and was subject to disciplinary proceedings. The Supreme Court ruled, as they also did in *Brown, Secretary of Defense v. Glines*,* that these regulations do not violate the First Amendment: "They [the regulations] protect a substantial Government interest unrelated to the suppression of free expression—the interest in maintaining the respect for duty and discipline so vital to military effectiveness—and restrict speech no more than is reasonably necessary to protect such interest. Since a military commander is charged with maintaining morale, discipline, and readiness, he must have authority over the distribution of materials that could affect adversely these essential attributes of an effective military force. . . . Such regulations do not violate 10 U.S.C. § 1034 (Military Regulations, Petitioning Congress*), which proscribes unwarranted restrictions on a serviceman's right to communicate with a member of Congress. As § 1034's legislative history makes clear, Congress enacted the statute to ensure that an individual member of the Armed Services could write to his elected representatives without sending his communication through official channels, and not to protect the circulation of collective petitions within a military base. Permitting an individual serviceman to submit a petition directly to any member of Congress serves § 1034's legislative purpose without unnecessarily endangering a commander's ability to preserve morale and good order among his troops." *Secretary of the Navy v. Huff*, 444 U.S. 348 (1980).

SEDITION. The Smith Act* (Title 18 U.S.C. § 2385), enacted in 1940 and amended in 1948, made it unlawful for any person (1) "to knowingly or willfully advocate, abet, advise, or teach the duty, necessity, desirability, or propriety of overthrowing or destroying any government in the United States by force or violence"; (2) "to print, publish, edit, issue, circulate, sell, distribute, or publicly display any written or printed matter advocating, advising, or teaching the duty, necessity, desirability, or propriety of overthrowing or destroying any government in the United States by force or violence"; (3) "to organize or help to organize any society, group or assembly of persons who teach . . . or to be or become a member of . . . any group." The penalty imposed for a violation of the Smith Act was $10,000 or ten years in prison or both.

The validity and constitutionality of the Smith Act was upheld in 1951, in *Dennis v. United States**—the Supreme Court ruled that since Congress had the authority to protect the government from violent overthrow, it could then legitimately limit speech and press activities directed at inciting such a result. But in a later decision, in 1957 (*Yates v. United States**), the Supreme Court refined the advocacy section of the Smith Act: The Smith Act does *not* prohibit "mere advocacy" or teaching of any prohibited activities as an abstract principle or doctrine, even if the advocacy or teaching is done with an "evil intent" and with the "hope" that a violent overthrow of the government might eventually occur. The urging of *action*—direct, immediate, imminent, clear and present danger action—can be punished; advocating or teaching the necessity or goodness of such action now falls within the area of "protected speech."

SEDITION ACT, 1798. This infamous act was passed on July 14, 1798, Fifth Congress, Session II (Ch. 74, 1798). The act had only a three-year life as contained in the legislation, and it did, in fact, expire on March 3, 1801. The United States was well rid of the Sedition Act when it expired. Chapter LXXIV was entitled "An Act in addition to the act, entitled 'An Act for the punishment of certain crimes against the United States' " and the text, in part, of the Sedition Act read as follows: Section 1. "That, if any persons shall unlawfully combine or conspire together, with intent to oppose any measure or measures of the government of the United States, which are or shall be directed by proper authority, or to impede the operation of any law of the United States, or to intimidate or prevent any person holding a place or office in or under the government of the United States, from undertaking, performing or executing his trust or duty; and if any person or persons, with intent as aforesaid, shall counsel, advise or attempt to procure any insurrection, riot, unlawful assembly, or combination, whether such conspiracy, threatening, counsel, advice, or attempt shall have the proposed effect or not, he or they shall be deemed guilty of a high misdemeanor, and on conviction, before any court of the United States having jurisdiction thereof, shall be punished by a fine not exceeding five thousand dollars [an *extraordinary* amount in 1798], and by imprisonment during a term not less than six months nor exceeding five years; and further, at the discretion of the court may be holden to find sureties for his good behaviour in such sum, and for such time, as the said court may direct." Section 2. "That if any person shall write, print, utter or publish, or shall cause or procure to be written, printed, uttered or published, or shall knowingly and willingly assist or aid in writing, printing, uttering or publishing any false, scandalous and malicious writing or writings against the government of the United States, of either house of the Congress of the United States, or the President of the United States, with intent to defame the said government, or either house of the said Congress, or the said President, or to bring them, or either of them, into contempt or disrepute; or to excite against them, or either or any of them, the hatred of the good people of the United States, or to stir up sedition within the United States, or to excite any unlawful combinations therein, for opposing or resisting any law of the United States, or any act of the President of the United States, done in pursuance of any such law, or of the powers in him vested by the constitution of the United States, or to resist, oppose, or defeat any such law or act, or to aid, encourage or abet any hostile designs of any foreign nation against the United States, their people or government, then such person, being thereof convicted before any court of the United States having jurisdiction thereof, shall be punished by a fine not exceeding two thousand dollars, and by imprisonment not exceeding two years."

Several parts of Section 2 need to be emphasized: A person was liable for two years and $2,000 for "publishing any false, scandalous and malicious writing" against the government or the president or for bringing the government or the president into "contempt or disrepute" or exciting the "hatred of the good people" against the government or the president—all this in face of the First Amendment, which commands Congress to pass no law abridging the freedoms of speech or press! John Adams, who was president at the time (1797–1801), was a Federalist; Federalist rivals were the Jeffersonian Republicans, who attacked, in their press and in speech, Adams, his policies, and the Federalists. Congress at the time was dominated by the Federalists and wanted to put an end to the Jeffersonian broadsides; the Sedition Act made it a crime to "oppose" the government in either print or speech.

John C. Miller (*Crisis in Freedom: The Alien and Sedition Acts*, pp. 74–75) writes that the "Federalists thought that the existing common law of seditious libel wouldn't support prosecutions so its authority had to be affirmed by a specific statute" and that the Sedition Act "was an implied acknowledgment by the Federalists that force and coercion rather than reason and argument were to be the ultimate arbiters of political controversy in the United States. Differences of opinion were to be erased and the American mind was to be forced into an intellectual strait jacket."

Some twenty-five people (mostly Jeffersonian Republican newspaper editors) were arrested under the act and ten were ultimately convicted by the Federalist courts. John Daly Burk was arrested in July 1798 on a warrant signed by President Adams for the crime of seditious libel (Adams did not appreciate Burk's comments in his New York newspaper, *Time Piece*). The U.S. government wanted to deport Burk but decided that a fine would be better (he wouldn't pay the fine if he was deported). Burk fled to Virginia, a state that gave refuge to fugitives from the Sedition Act. A Republican Jeffersonian member of Congress from Vermont, Matthew Lyon, was found guilty under the act and received four months in jail and a $1,000 fine. Lyon was convicted of writing certain articles in the *Vermont Journal* and of publishing a letter in which the author "urged Congress to commit President Adams to the madhouse." Luther Baldwin received a $100 fine for stating, while inebriated, to a drinking companion who said, "There goes the President . . . and they are firing at his . . . " the following reply: "I don't care if they fired thro' his . . . " David Brown received eighteen months in jail and a $450 fine for stating, "Peace and retirement to the President; long live the Vice President and the minority." Anthony Haswell received two months and a fine of $200 for publishing an ad in the *Vermont Gazette* that solicited contributions to pay off Matthew Lyon's fine. In 1800, Charles Holt, editor of the New Haven *Bee*, received six months in jail and a $200 fine for being "a wicked, malicious, seditious and ill-disposed person."

When Jefferson took office as president, he pardoned all those still serving terms under the act, declaring (Miller, p. 231) that he considered the law "to be a nullity as absolute and as palpable as if Congress had ordered us to fall down and worship a golden image." The Sedition Act expired on March 3, 1801; the United States was well rid of it.

SEMLER v. OREGON STATE BOARD OF DENTAL EXAMINERS (1935).

An Oregon statute (Oregon, Dentists Advertising*) prohibited dentists, on penalty of license revocation, from engaging in certain types of advertising (professional superiority, fees, free examinations, painless dentistry, guaranteed work, etc.). Semler, a dentist, brought suit to enjoin the enforcement of the statute, but the Supreme Court refused to issue the order. The Court ruled that even though Semler's ads were not false, misleading, or fraudulent, the state was free to regulate such commercial speech because such ads "tend to lower the standards of the profession and demoralize it."

Such a restriction on commercial speech and advertising by the professions is today inapplicable, but in 1935, the dominant view was that commercial speech was outside the First Amendment and that the states could regulate such speech as they saw fit. Chief Justice Hughes delivered the opinion of the Court: "The state court defined the policy of the statute. The court said that while, in itself, there was nothing harmful in merely advertising prices for dental work or in displaying glaring signs illustrating teeth and bridge work, it could not be doubted that practitioners who were not willing to abide by the ethics of their profession often resorted to such advertising methods 'to lure the credulous and ignorant members of the public to their offices for the purpose of fleecing them.' The legislature was aiming at 'bait advertising.' 'Inducing patronage,' said the court, 'by representations of painless dentistry, professional superiority, free examinations, and guaranteed dental work' was, as a general rule, 'the practice of the charlatan and the quack to entice the public.' We do not doubt the authority of the State to estimate the baleful effect of such methods and to put a stop to them. The legislature was not dealing with traders in commodities, but with the vital interest of public health, and with a profession treating bodily ills and demanding different standards of conduct from those which are traditional in the competition of the market place. The community is concerned with the maintenance of professional standards which will ensure not only competency in individual practitioners, but protection against those who would prey upon a public peculiarly susceptible to imposition through alluring promises of physical relief. And the community is concerned in providing safeguards not only against deception, but against practices which would tend to demoralize the profession by forcing its members into an unseemly rivalry which would enlarge the opportunities of the least scrupulous. What is generally called the 'ethics' of the profession is but the consensus of expert opinion as to the necessity of such standards. It is no answer to say, as regards [Semler's] claim of right to advertise his 'professional superiority' or his 'performance of professional services in a superior manner,' that he is telling the truth. In framing its policy the legislature was not bound to provide for determinations of the relative proficiency of particular practitioners. The legislature was entitled to consider the general effects of the practices which it described, and if these effects were injurious in facilitating unwarranted and misleading claims, to counteract them by a general rule, even though in particular instances there might be no actual deception or misstatement." *Semler v. Oregon State Board of Dental Examiners*, 294 U.S. 608 (1935).

THE SEX ADDICTS. *The Sex Addicts* never made the best-seller list, but that is beside the point; the court record described the book in the following terms:

"The book is entitled *The Sex Addicts* and tells of a vacation cruise to tropical islands during which the hero and his cabin-mate engage in a series of sexual exploits with various girls they meet aboard the ship. The hero has sexual intercourse with several female acquaintances in succession. He finally finds himself falling in love with one of two sisters, with whom he and his roommate had had a 'four-way affair' in the girls' cabin, including an exchange of partners [the court record does not specify the direction of the "exchange"; one can only assume it was heterosexual]. The roommate is portrayed as a man obsessed with the urge to make new conquests who cannot be satisfied with the same girl more than once. The hero was left with the two sisters, and before ending up with the girl of his choice he has relations with both. The book contains the suggestion that the roommate, with his compulsive urge to move from one conquest to another, is mentally ill and ought to see an analyst."

In 1966, Charles Kimmel, in a Cook County, Illinois, court, was found guilty of selling an obscene book (*The Sex Addicts*) in violation of the Illinois obscenity statute and was fined $2,000 and placed on probation for three years. He appealed his conviction to the Illinois Supreme Court (*People v. Kimmel*, 220 N.E. 2d 203 [1966]), and the court reversed the conviction: "We think the material in [this case], under the constitution as construed by the United States Supreme Court, can hardly be denied protection. True, the cover of this paperback is rather blatant in suggesting illicit sexual conduct, as are the title and descriptive remarks. And the contents consist principally of a more or less continuous account of sexual engagements and the preliminaries. But there is little violence and no . . . descriptions of perverted behavior. The acts of intercourse are not described in detail, so as to exceed the limits of contemporary candor in such matters, nor do we find repulsive and disgusting language."

SEX SIDE OF LIFE. As the court record relates, in 1930, Dennett, the defendant in this bizarre case, was the mother of two boys. When the boys reached the ages of eleven and fourteen, Dennett concluded that she ought to teach them about sex. After examining about sixty publications on the subject, Dennett concluded that they were inadequate and unsatisfactory; she then wrote and published her own pamphlet, entitled *Sex Side of Life*. She was duly indicted, tried, and convicted in a federal district court of violating Title 18 U.S.C. § 1461 (Postal Regulations, Mailing Obscene Material*)—the government proved without doubt that Dennett mailed a copy of her pamphlet to one C. A. Miles, a married woman in Grottoes, Virginia. Even though the pamphlet was intended to aid parents in the sex education of their children, and even though it was distributed only to parents and social agencies, the trial judge ruled that these facts were not relevant.

The trial judge instructed the jury that the motive of Dennett in mailing the pamphlet was immaterial, that it was for the jury "to determine whether it was obscene, lewd, or lascivious within the meaning of the statute," and that the test (the Hicklin Rule*) was "whether its language has a tendency to deprave and corrupt the morals of those whose minds are open to such things and into whose hands it may fall; arousing and implanting in such minds lewd and obscene thought or desires.'' The trial judge also charged the jury that "even if the matter sought to be shown in the pamphlet complained of were true, that fact would be immaterial, if the statements of such facts were calculated to deprave the morals of the readers by inciting sexual desires and libidinous thoughts." The jury found Dennett guilty as charged and fined her $300 (quite a large sum in 1930).

Dennett's conviction was reversed by an appeals court (*United States v. Dennett*, 39 F. 2d 564 [1930]). The appeals court described the *Sex Side of Life* in the following terms: "The pamphlet . . . purported to give accurate information concerning the sex side of life and the functions of the sex organs. The pamphlet then proceeded to explain sex life in detail, both physically and emotionally, and it described the sex organs and their operation and the way children are begotten. It negatived the idea that sex impulse was base passion and treated it as normal and its satisfaction as great and justifiable joy when accompanied by love between two human beings. It warned against perversion, venereal disease, and prostitution, and argued for continence and healthy mindedness and against promiscuous sex relations.''

In reversing Dennett's conviction for sending through the mail what the government prosecutors (and the jury at the district court level) claimed to be obscene and lewd, the appeals court rejected the Hicklin Rule and held that a little sex education for adolescents might not be a bad thing: "It may be assumed that any article dealing with the sex side of life and explaining the functions of the sex organs is capable in some circumstances of arousing lust. The sex impulses are present in every one, and without doubt cause much of the weal and woe of human kind. But it can hardly be said that, because of the risk of arousing sex impulses, there should be no instruction of the young in sex matters, and that the risk of imparting instruction outweighs the disadvantages of leaving them to grope about in mystery and morbid curiosity and of requiring them to secure such information, as they may be able to obtain, from ill-informed and often foul-mouthed companions, rather than from intelligent and high-minded sources. It may be argued that suggestion plays a large part in such matters, and that on the whole the less sex questions are dwelt upon the better. But it by no means follows that such a desideratum is attained by leaving adolescents in a state of inevitable curiosity, satisfied only by the casual gossip of ignorant playmates. The old theory that information about sex matters should be left to chance has greatly changed, and, while there is still a difference of opinion as to just the kind of instruction which ought to be given, it is commonly thought in these days that much was lacking in the old mystery and reticence. This is evident from the current literature on the subject, particularly such pamphlets as *Sex Education*, issued by the Treasury Department, United States Public Health Service in 1927. The statute [§ 1461] we have to construe was never thought to bar from the mails everything which *might* stimulate sex impulses. If so, much chaste poetry and fiction, as well as many useful medical works, would be under the ban.''

SEYMOUR v. UNITED STATES (1967). On March 11, 1966, Seymour, a television news photographer, took television photographs of a defendant and his attorney in a hallway outside a courtroom as the defendant was being led from the courtroom after some proceedings. Seymour was then found guilty, and fined $25, of criminal contempt for violating a standing order (Miscellaneous Order 281) of the court (Judicial Conference of the United States*) that prohibited the taking of photographs in connection with any judicial proceeding on or from the same floor of the building on which courtrooms are located. A court of appeals affirmed the contempt citation, Judge Thornberry ruling that enforcement of the order ''did not represent an unconstitutional prior restraint upon liberty of the press, but was within the ambit of permissible maintenance of judicial decorum and represented a reasonable implementation of the mandate to preserve a fair trial.'' *Seymour v. United States,* 373 F. 2d 629 (1967).

SHASTA COUNTY (CA), ORDINANCE ON PICKETING. The following ordinance was declared to be unconstitutional by the Supreme Court in 1940, in *Carlson v. California**: ''It shall be unlawful for any person, in or upon any public street, highway, sidewalk, alley or other public place in the County of Shasta, State of California, to loiter in front of, or in the vicinity of, or to picket in front of, or in the vicinity of, or to carry, show or display any banner, transparency, badge or sign in front of, or in the vicinity of, any works, or factory, or any place of business or employment, for the purpose of inducing or influencing, or attempting to induce or influence, any person to refrain from entering any such works, or factory, or place of business, or employment, or for the purpose of inducing or influencing, or attempting to induce or influence, any person to refrain from purchasing or using any goods, wares, merchandise, or other articles, manufactured, made or kept for sale therein, or for the purpose of inducing or influencing, or attempting to induce or influence, any person to refrain from doing or performing any service or labor in any works, factory, place of business or employment, or for the purpose of intimidating, threatening or coercing, or attempting to intimidate, threaten or coerce any person who is performing, seeking or obtaining service or labor in any such works, factory, place of business or employment.''

SHEPPARD v. MAXWELL (1966). Dr. Sam Sheppard's wife was bludgeoned to death at their home in a suburb of Cleveland, Ohio, on July 4, 1954. The police suspected the husband from the beginning: He was arrested on July 30; he was indicted August 17; the trial began October 18; he was convicted on December 21.

The following description of the events is taken from the court records: ''During the entire pretrial period virulent and incriminating publicity about [Sheppard] and the murder made the case notorious, and the news media frequently aired charges and countercharges besides those for which [Sheppard] was tried. Three months before trial he was examined for more than five hours without counsel in a televised three-day inquest conducted before an audience of several hundred spectators in a gymnasium. Over three weeks before trial the newspapers published the names and addresses of prospective jurors causing them to receive letters and telephone calls about the case. The trial began two weeks before a hotly contested election at which the chief prosecutor and the trial judge were candidates for judgeships. Newsmen were allowed to take over almost the entire small courtroom, hounding [Sheppard] and most of the participants. Twenty reporters were assigned seats by the court within the bar and in close proximity to the jury and counsel, precluding privacy between [Sheppard] and his counsel. The movement of the reporters in the courtroom caused frequent confusion and disrupted the trial; and in the corridors and elsewhere they were allowed free rein by the trial judge. A broadcasting station was assigned space next to the jury room. Before the jurors began deliberations they were not sequestered and had access to all news media though the court made 'suggestions' and 'requests' that the jurors not expose themselves to comment about the case. Though they were sequestered during the five days and four nights of their deliberations, the jurors were allowed to make inadequately supervised telephone calls during that period. Pervasive publicity was given to the case throughout the trial, much of it involving incriminating matter not introduced at the trial, and the jurors were thrust into the role of celebrities. At least some of the publicity deluge reached the jurors. At the very inception of the proceedings and later, the trial judge announced that neither he nor anyone else could restrict the prejudicial news accounts. Despite his awareness of the excessive pretrial publicity, the trial judge failed to take effective measures against the massive publicity which continued throughout the trial or to take adequate steps to control the conduct of the trial.''

Sheppard eventually filed a writ, claiming that he did not receive a fair trial. A federal district court agreed but was reversed by an appeals court; the U.S. Supreme Court ruled that the massive, pervasive, and prejudicial publicity prevented Sheppard from receiving a fair trial, and the Court remanded the case back to the district court with instructions to release Sheppard unless he was tried again within a reasonable time. Sheppard was eventually released from prison. In attempting to balance the First Amendment's guarantee of a free press with the right of a fair trial, the Supreme Court made the following comments: "The principle that justice cannot survive behind walls of silence has long been reflected in the Anglo-American distrust for secret trials. A responsible press has always been regarded as the handmaiden of effective judicial administration, especially in the criminal field. Its function in this regard is documented by an impressive record of service over several centuries. The press does not simply publish information about trials but guards against the miscarriage of justice by subjecting the police, prosecutors, and judicial processes to extensive public scrutiny and criticism. This Court has, therefore, been unwilling to place any direct limitations on the freedom traditionally exercised by the news media for what transpires in the court room is public property. We have consistently required that the press have a free hand, even though we sometimes deplored its sensationalism. But the Court has also pointed out that legal trials are not like elections, to be won through the use of the meeting-hall, the radio, and the newspaper. . . . We [previously] set aside a federal conviction where the jurors were exposed through news accounts to information that was not admitted at trial. We held that the prejudice from such material may indeed be greater than when it is part of the prosecution's evidence for it is then not tempered by protective procedures. . . . With his life at stake, it is not requiring too much that petitioner be tired in an atmosphere undisturbed by so huge a wave of public passion." *Sheppard v. Maxwell*, 384 U.S. 333 (1966).

SHE SHOULD'A SAID NO! On March 20, 1950, the Pennsylvania State Board of Censors (Pennsylvania, Motion Picture Control Act*) viewed a film entitled *Wild Weed* and rejected it as being "immoral, indecent, not proper, and tending to corrupt and debase morals." The film was resubmitted on January 24, 1951, with the title changed to *Devil's Weed*. It was again rejected for the identical reasons. The owner of the film tried again, retitling it *She Should'a Said No!*, but the Board of Censors again refused to issue an exhibition permit.

The film presented the story of a dope peddler and how he enticed people to use marijuana. There were several scenes in particular that the Board of Censors thought were immoral, indecent, and tending to corrupt morals: (1) The scene of two teenage couples in an open roadster on a hill overlooking Hollywood and being under the influence of the drug; each boy having a girl in his arms and smoking a marijuana cigarette depicts depravity and indecency. (2) The scene showing the party in Ann's home, with Rita and the two men as they smoke marijuana cigarettes and, under its influence, deport themselves in an obscene manner, is indecent and immoral. (3) The scene showing Rita dancing in an indecent fashion under the influence of the drug after smoking a marijuana cigarette is indecent and immoral. (4) The statement made by the dope peddler— "All that energy, beautiful; Let's not waste it in dancing"—is indecent and immoral. (5) The scene in which the dope peddler and Ann leave the room where the party has taken place and go into another room is indecent and immoral.

The owners of the film argued that *She Should'a Said No!* served a good purpose in depicting the evil results of narcotics and that it therefore was a good preachment against crime. The Board of Censors didn't accept this reasoning: "The evils of drug traffic and addiction shown as the theme of *She Should'a Said No!* are not sufficient of themselves to prevent such crime, or to discourage use of drugs, but rather in detailed dialogue and action show the use of the 'weed' leading to use of heroin, cocaine, and opium excites curiosity toward escape from reality to teenagers, frustrated men and women and weak characters, and actually leads to lives of sin, corruption, horror and murder and is indecent and immoral and, in the judgment of the Board, tends to debase and corrupt morals.''

The film's owners, Hallmark Productions, appealed the board's refusal to issue the exhibition permit, and the case finally reached the Pennsylvania Supreme Court in 1956 (*Hallmark Productions, Inc. v. Carroll*, 122 A. 2d 584 [1956]). The Pennsylvania Supreme Court, Chief Justice Stern delivering the Court's opinion, ruled that the state's motion picture censorship statute was unconstitutional because (1) the terms employed (indecent, immoral, etc.) were too vague and indefinite and (2) the entire scheme violated the First Amendment. Judge Stern: ''Any statute censoring motion pictures must be held to be unconstitutional on the theory that motion pictures are as much entitled to the protection of the constitutional guaranty of free speech as is now enjoyed by newspapers, magazines, books, theatrical exhibitions, radio and television scripts. It need hardly be added that even if all pre-censorship of motion picture films were to be held invalid this would not in and of itself affect the right to suppress objectionable films if exhibited, or to punish their exhibitor.''

Judge Musmanno dissented from this assault on Western civilization: ''The Pennsylvania Motion Picture Censorship Act is a fortress, armed originally with five cannon to protect the welfare of the people from the forces of immorality and intemperate greed. One of the cannon has been ruled out of action. The other four remain whole and strong and are in excellent firing condition. History has never shown in America a surrender, while artillery of this formidableness was fighting on the side of right. With this dissent I serve notice that I oppose hauling down the Flag.''

SHUTTLESWORTH v. CITY OF BIRMINGHAM (1969). Shuttlesworth, a black minister, helped organize and lead an orderly civil rights march in Birmingham, Alabama, in 1963. He was then arrested, tried, and convicted of violating § 1159 of the city's General Code (Birmingham [AL], Parade Ordinance*), which prohibited participation in any parade or procession on city streets or public ways without first obtaining a permit from the city commission. Section 1159 allowed the commission to refuse to issue a parade permit if its members believed ''the public welfare, peace, safety, health, decency, good order, morals or convenience require that it be refused.'' Shuttlesworth testified that he had been led to understand by a member of the commission that under no circumstances would Shuttlesworth and his group be allowed to demonstrate in Birmingham. The Alabama Supreme Court affirmed the conviction, seeing § 1159 as an ''objective, even-handed traffic regulation which did not allow the Commission unlimited discretion in granting or withholding permits.''

The U.S. Supreme Court did not agree with this reasoning and reversed the conviction: A law subjecting the right of free expression in publicly owned places to the prior restraint of a license, without narrow, objective, and definite standards is unconstitutional, and a person faced with such a law may ignore it and exercise his First Amendment rights.

In reversing Shuttlesworth's conviction, the Court offered the following comments: "It is argued, however, that what was involved here was not 'pure speech,' but the use of public streets and sidewalks, over which a municipality must rightfully exercise a great deal of control in the interest of traffic regulation and public safety. That, of course, is true. We have emphasized before this that the First and Fourteenth Amendments do not afford the same kind of freedom to those who would communicate ideas by conduct such as patrolling, marching, and picketing on streets and highways, as these amendments afford to those who communicate ideas by pure speech—governmental authorities have the duty and responsibility to keep their streets open and available for movement (*Cox v. Louisiana**). But our decisions have also made clear that picketing and parading may nonetheless constitute methods of expression, entitled to First Amendment protection. Wherever the title of streets and parks may rest, they have immemorially been held in trust for the use of the public and, time out of mind, have been used for purposes of assembly, communicating thoughts between citizens, and discussing public questions. Such use of the streets and public places has, from ancient times, been a part of the privileges, immunities, rights, and liberties of citizens. The privilege of a citizen of the United States to use the streets and parks for communication of views on national questions may be regulated in the interest of all; it is not absolute, but relative, and must be exercised in subordination to the general comfort and convenience, and in consonance with peace and good order; but it must not, in the guise of regulation, be abridged or denied. . . . Accordingly, although this Court has recognized that a statute may be enacted which prevents serious interference with normal usage of streets and parks, we have consistently condemned licensing systems which vest in an administrative official broad discretion to grant or withhold a permit upon broad criteria unrelated to proper regulation of public places (*Kunz v. New York,** *Saia v. New York,** and *Niemotko v. Maryland**). Even when the use of its public streets and sidewalks is involved, therefore, a municipality may not empower its licensing officials to roam essentially at will, dispensing or withholding permission to speak, assemble, picket, or parade, according to their own opinions regarding the potential effect of the activity on the 'welfare,' 'decency,' or 'morals' of the community." *Shuttlesworth v. City of Birmingham*, 394 U.S. 147 (1969).

SILK STOCKING MAGAZINE/SILK STOCKING STORIES. This strange case was an action brought by Ultem Publications (publisher of *Silk Stocking Stories*) against Arrow Publications (publisher of *Silk Stocking Magazine*). It appears that Arrow published a magazine similar in name, format, and content to the one published by Ultem, and Ultem wanted to prevent Arrow from continuing to publish. The New York judge, Judge Cotillo, denied the request for an injunction, for he thought both magazines were so vile and filthy and disgusting that the court should not protect either of them (*Ultem Publications, Inc. v. Arrow Publications, Inc.*, 2 N.Y.S. 2d 933 [1938]). There is usually not much humor in cases such as these, but Judge Cotillo made an unintentional attempt. Judge

Cotillo, writing in 1938: "Both litigants are publishers of magazines bearing a name the outstanding feature of which is the word 'stocking.' Neither one caters to the stocking trade and neither one is recognized or considered by the trade to be a trade paper. Upon reading the minutes of the trial and after an examination of the exhibits consisting of the magazines themselves, an entirely new atmosphere was thrown around the case. A prudent caution required that this examination of the exhibits be made in my own room, and the examination compelled me to place the exhibits under lock and key in order to prevent them from falling into the hands of my young daughter. Why was this necessary? Only a detailed description of the two magazines themselves can supply the reason. Each one of these issues bears on its cover the picture of a young and attractive woman in a state of deshabille, and permissible only in the sanctum of a woman's boudoir. Each picture features nakedness, particularly as to her lower limbs and the naked breasts. The table of contents partly published on the cover concerns stories each of which relates only to sex matters and bear names of double meaning such as 'Come and Get Me.' The pictures in the body of the magazine are confined to pictures of girls clad with nothing but underwear and stockings, and make a featured display of their arms and breasts, and thus there is an inordinate emphasis of these parts of the body [a good description of many of the advertisements that appear in the magazine section of the Sunday *New York Times*]. The stories are suggestive of illicit love affairs and some contain outright suggestions of sexual affairs between unmarried persons. Under the title 'Sheer Nonsense,' the magazine prints jokes and sayings each having a double-edged meaning and salacious ideas, such as 'We heard of an old maid who sued a hotel for mental cruelty. They gave her a room between two honeymooning couples.' The publishers set forth their policy as follows: 'Statement of Policy'— 'The Editors know what happens to a girl who wears cotton stockings—Nothing.' The make-up of the defendant's magazine differs from that of the plaintiff practically only in the matter of title. The front cover and the pictures in the magazine itself contain the same type of undressed women in suggestive poses. The stories have the same general theme of sex and sex relations. They contain the same type of double-meaning jokes and wisecracks. The pictures in both magazines are for the purpose of merely appealing to neurotic and moronic minds minus even the doubtful virtue of being exotic." Thus the description of *Silk Stocking Stories* and *Silk Stocking Magazine*.

Judge Cotillo then announced his reasons for not granting the injunction: "We face a current drive today against sex perverts, all forms of vice engendered by loose morals, and even positive degeneracy. Some portions of the public press print with almost gruesome detail sex practices involved in crimes for which the accused frequently are convicted after trial, and for which crimes the condemned often expiate with their lives. These descriptions of sex crimes under the guise of 'news' find avid readers among our youth, are even fed serially to their plastic minds, often being printed minus all condemnatory emphasis, so that the youth and unsophisticated might well secure the feeling that such abuses are more widespread than they actually are. Indeed, it would not be amiss to say that magazines of this character are actually more pernicious, definitely more harmful, than any newspaper which dares flagrantly to publish in untoward fashion current stories of sex crimes. In the case at bar, we do not have a criminal charge, but that is not the criterion. Courts of equity have and maintain moral standards based on social needs and demands both. The youth of this city require more than mere negative protection, if incumbuslike, the vices described above are not to spread. I wish our youth to learn safety in avoidance, but not by paying the bitter price of experience. Only by protracted exposure to that kind of literature where conspicuously absent are all forms of salaciousness and lewdness, and which are beyond any taint or suspicion of immorality, can this social objective be obtained. This is the price which any community must pay to protect its youth and which a policy of eternal vigilance requires, demands, and must exact. Only by such positive measures can we protect the minds of our growing boys and girls from this pestilence and noisome filth. These are not too strong words. . . . Here we have the pot calling the kettle black, and equity will furnish no aid in the furtherance of purposes unsound socially as well as tainted by depressed moral levels.''

SKOKIE (IL), PARADE PERMITS. The following ordinances were the ones involved in the attempt by the village of Skokie, Illinois, to prevent the American Nazi party from parading down the main streets of the village. Skokie, at the time of the clash with the Nazis, in 1978, had a large Jewish population, many of whom were survivors of the Nazi extermination camps in Europe. The ordinances basically prohibited certain kinds of parades (it was obvious to everyone that they were directed specifically at the Nazis) and required a permit before a parade could take place. Section 27-54 of Ordinance #994 (the ''Insurance'' ordinance) provided that: ''No permit shall be issued to any applicant until such applicant procures Public Liability Insurance in an amount of not less than Three Hundred Thousand Dollars ($300,000.00) and Property Damage Insurance of not less than Fifty Thousand Dollars ($50,000.00). Prior to the issuance of the permit, certificates of such insurance must be submitted to the Village Manager for verification that the company issuing such insurance is authorized to do business and write policies in the State of Illinois.'' Section 27-56(j) of #994 specifically required the village manager to deny a permit to anyone failing to comply with the insurance requirements and only a unanimous vote by the president and Board of Trustees of the village could waive the insurance requirement.

Ordinance #995 (the ''racial slur'' ordinance) provided the following: ''The dissemination of any material within the Village of Skokie which promotes and incites hatred against persons by reason of their race, national origin, or religion, and is intended to do so, is hereby prohibited.'' The term ''dissemination of materials'' was defined to include ''publication or display or distribution of posters, signs, handbills, or writings and public display of markings and clothing of symbolic significance.'' The village manager was also required to deny a permit for any assembly that would "portray criminality, depravity or lack of virtue in, or incite violence, hatred, abuse or hostility toward a person or group of persons by reason of reference to religious, racial, ethnic, national or regional affiliation.''

Ordinance #996 (the "military uniforms" ordinance) provided that "no person shall engage in any march, walk or public demonstration as a member or on behalf of any political party, while wearing a military-style uniform.'' A "political party" was defined to include "any organization existing primarily to influence government or politics," but the term "military-style uniform" was not defined in the ordinance.

These ordinances were found to be unconstitutional as an invalid restriction on the right of free speech in a long and convoluted court process (*Smith v. Collin**).

SMITH ACT. The Smith Act was originally enacted in 1940 (54 Stat. 670) and amended in 1948 (Title 18 U.S.C. § 2385). The relevant sections of the act read as follows: "Whoever knowingly or willfully advocates, abets, advises, or teaches the duty, necessity, desirability, or propriety of overthrowing or destroying the government of the United States or the government of any State, Territory, District or Possession thereof, or the government of any political subdivision therein, by force or violence, or by the assassination of any officer of any such government; or Whoever, with intent to cause the overthrow or destruction of any such government, prints, publishes, edits, issues, circulates, sells, distributes, or publicly displays any written or printed matter advocating, advising, or teaching the duty, necessity, desirability, or propriety of overthrowing or destroying any government in the United States by force or violence, or attempts to do so; or Whoever organizes or helps or attempts to organize any society, group, or assembly of persons who teach, advocate, or encourage the overthrow or destruction of any such government by force or violence; or becomes or is a member of, or affiliates with, any such society, group, or assembly of persons, knowing the purposes thereof—Shall be fined not more than $10,000 or imprisoned not more than ten years, or both, and shall be ineligible for employment by the United States or any department or agency thereof, for the five years next following his conviction.''

The validity of this act was upheld in 1951, in *Dennis v. United States**; the Supreme Court ruled that since Congress had the authority to protect the government from violent overthrow, it could then legitimately limit speech and press activities directed at inciting such a result (Sedition*). But a later decision, in 1957 (*Yates v. United States**), refined the advocacy section of the act: The Smith Act does *not* prohibit mere "advocacy" or teaching of any prohibited activities as an abstract principle, even if the advocacy or teaching is done with an "evil intent" and with the "hope" that a violent overthrow of the government might eventually occur. The urging of *action*—direct, immediate, imminent, clear and present danger action—can be punished; advocating or teaching the necessity or goodness of such action now falls within the area of "protected speech."

SMITH v. CALIFORNIA (1959). Smith, the owner of a bookstore in California, was convicted of violating a city ordinance (Los Angeles [CA], Possession of Obscene Matter*) for having in his store, with intent to sell, a book that was judicially determined to be obscene. Smith claimed that he had no knowledge of the book's content—he only sold the books, he didn't read them.

The U.S. Supreme Court reversed the conviction, holding it to be a form of censorship because the ordinance would restrict bookstores to selling only those books that were inspected for content. The Court's opinion is as follows: "We have held that obscene speech and writings are not protected by the constitutional guarantees of freedom of speech and the press (*Roth v. United States**). The ordinance here in question, to be sure, only imposes criminal sanctions on a bookseller if in fact there is to be found in his shop an obscene book. But our holding in *Roth* does not recognize any state power to restrict the dissemination of books which are not obscene; and we think this ordinance's strict liability feature would tend seriously to have that effect, by penalizing booksellers, even though they had not the slightest notice of the character of the books they sold. The [State of California] and the court below analogize this strict liability penal ordinance to familiar forms of penal statutes which dispense with any element of knowledge on the part of the person charged, food and drug legislation being a principal example. We find the analogy instructive in our examination of the question before us. The usual rationale for such statutes is that the public interest in the purity of its food is so great as to warrant the imposition of the highest standard of care on distributors—in fact an absolute standard which will not hear the distributor's plea as to the amount of care he has used. His ignorance of the character of the food is irrelevant. There is no specific constitutional inhibition against making the distributors of food the strictest censors of their merchandise, but the constitutional guarantees of the freedom of speech and of the press stand in the way of imposing a similar requirement on the bookseller. By dispensing with any requirement of knowlege of the contents of the book on the part of the seller, the ordinance tends to impose a severe limitation on the public's access to constitutionally protected matter. For if the bookseller is criminally liable without knowledge of the contents, and the ordinance fulfills its purpose, he will tend to restrict the books he sells to those he has inspected; and thus the State will have imposed a restriction upon the distribution of constitutionally protected as well as obscene literature. It has been well observed of a statute construed as dispensing with any requirement of scienter that: 'Every bookseller would be placed under an obligation to make himself aware of the contents of every book in his shop. It would be altogether unreasonable to demand so near an approach to omniscience.' And the bookseller's burden would become the public's burden, for by restricting him the public's access to reading matter would be restricted.

If the contents of bookshops and periodical stands were restricted to material of which their proprietors had made an inspection, they might be depleted indeed. The bookseller's limitation in the amount of reading material with which he could familiarize himself, and his timidity in the face of his absolute criminal liability, thus would tend to restrict the public's access to forms of the printed word which the State could not constitutionally suppress directly. The bookseller's self-censorship, compelled by the State, would be a censorship affecting the whole public, hardly less virulent for being privately administered. Through it, the distribution of all books, both obscene and not obscene, would be impeded." *Smith v. California*, 361 U.S. 147 (1959).

SMITH v. COLLIN (1978). This case concerned a clash of basic values in the United States—the right to free speech ran headlong into the right of privacy and the rights of individuals to be free from ethnic and religious slurs and hatred. The crux of the controversy was that Collin, then head of the American Nazi party, wanted to strut down the streets of Skokie, Illinois, with his men, dressed in the full regalia of the Nazis with swastikas and the Death Head; Skokie had a large Jewish population, many of whom were survivors of the Nazi extermination camps in Europe. This clash split well-meaning and intelligent people: Those who had spent a lifetime supporting the First Amendment principles protecting free speech just could not bring themselves to support Collin and his Nazi friends' right to march in Skokie; organizations such as the American Civil Liberties Union, who for decades fought against anti-Semitism, could not bring themselves to oppose the Nazis' claim to freedom of expression. This was a long and convoluted case; although the village of Skokie was eventually required to issue a parade permit, the Nazi march never did take place in Skokie; instead, it took place in Chicago, on June 24 and July 9, 1978.

The village received a stay of the injunction requiring it to issue a permit and went to the Supreme Court with an application to continue the stay. The Supreme Court refused to hear the appeal, certiorari was denied, and Collin and the Nazis eventually had their parade. The following comments were made by Justice Blackmun, joined by Justice White, in a dissent to the denial of certiorari (Justices Blackmun and White would have had the Court hear the entire case; their dissent does not necessarily mean that they would have granted the stay). Justice Blackmun, joined by Justice White: "It is a matter of regret for me that the Court denies certiorari in this case, for this is litigation that rests upon critical, disturbing, and emotional facts, and the issues cut down to the very heart of the First Amendment. The village of Skokie, Ill., a suburb of Chicago, in 1974 had a population of approximately 70,000 persons. A majority were Jewish; of the Jewish population a substantial number were survivors of World War II persecution. In March 1977, Collin and the National Socialist Party of America, which Collin described as a 'Nazi organization,' publicly announced plans to hold an assembly in front of the Skokie Village Hall. On May 2, the village enacted three ordinances [Skokie (IL), Parade Permits*]. The first established a permit system for parades and public assemblies and required applicants to post public liability and property damage insurance. The second prohibited the dissemination of material that incited racial or religious hatred with intent so to incite. The third prohibited public demonstrations by members of political parties while wearing military-style uniforms. On June 22, Collin applied for a permit under the first ordinance. His application stated that a public assembly would take place on July 4, would consist of persons demonstrating in front of the Village Hall, would last about a half hour, and would not disrupt traffic. It also stated that the participants would wear uniforms with swastikas and would carry placards proclaiming free speech for white persons, but would not distribute handbills or literature. The permit was denied.''

The narrative by Justice Blackmun continues below, after a discussion of what happened after the permit was denied. Collin went to a federal district court (*Collin v. Smith*, 447 F. Supp. 676 [1978]) and sought a decision that the ordinances were unconstitutional and that the village should be enjoined from enforcing them; the district court (later affirmed by an appeals court) agreed with Collin and ruled that the ordinances were unconstitutional and granted the injunction. The district court's decision was quite lengthy; the following represents only a small portion of it: "It is apparent that in enacting these ordinances, the Village government acted primarily to shield its citizens—and particularly its Jewish citizens—from the flaunting by plaintiffs of the symbols of a hated era and repugnant political philosophy. The ordinances adopted, however, do more than simply ban display of the swastika; they impose sweeping bans on the content of speech within Skokie and include provisions for which there is almost no precedent in constitutional law. The importance and novelty of the issues involved require a close re-examination of the basic principles of the First Amendment against which these ordinances must be measured. . . . It is obvious that this ordinance [the 'military uniforms' ordinance] is directed specifically at Nazi uniforms and regalia. If Skokie really meant to enforce the ordinance as written, it would prohibit, among other things, an appearance by members of the American Legion in support of the candidates of the Democratic or Republican party. . . . The use of symbolic forms of expression, including the wearing of distinctive clothing, is protected by the First Amendment (*Tinker v. Des Moines School District** [black arm bands]). This ordinance therefore imposes a restriction based on the content of 'speech' and must be supported by compelling governmental interests. The only reasons offered to support the ordinance are stated in the preamble: the wearing of military-style uniforms is 'repugnant' both to the 'tradition of civilian control of government' and to 'standards of morality and decency of the people of the Village of Skokie.' Defendants have sought to offer no other rationale for the ordinance. Both justifications are patently insufficient. The First Amendment embraces the freedom to advocate even that the government ought to be violently overthrown, let alone that it ought not be controlled by civilians. Thus the banning of a symbol which is repugnant to a 'tradition' which all Americans are free to reject and openly criticize is clearly unconstitutional. The reference to Skokie's standards of decency and morality is apparently an attempt to invoke the 'community standards' test applied in obscenity cases (*Miller v. California**). However, to be obscene, speech must in some way be erotically stimulating (*Cohen v. California**). Plaintiffs' wearing of uniforms is political speech, which, as the Court has often emphasized, 'need not meet standards of acceptability.' The court finds Ordinance #996 to be patently and flagrantly unconstitutional on its face, and there is no need to consider the prior restraint issue posed by its enforcement through Ordinance #994.'' That was the decision of the district court, which, as mentioned, was affirmed by an appeals court.

The narrative returns to the comments by Justice Blackmun, joined by Justice White: "A permit was then issued to respondent for a demonstration on the afternoon of June 25, 1978, in front of the Village Hall. Respondents, however, shifted their assembly from Skokie to Chicago where activities took place on June 24 and July 9. [Justice Blackmun then relates the long story of stays, injunctions, appeals, etc.] . . . These facts and this chronology demonstrate, I believe, the pervading sensitivity of the litigation. On the one hand, we have precious First Amendment rights vigorously asserted and an obvious concern that, if those asserted rights are not recognized, the precedent of a 'hard' case might offer a justification for repression in the future. On the other hand, we are presented with evidence of a potentially explosive and dangerous situation, enflamed by unforgettable recollections of traumatic experiences in the second world conflict. Finally, Judge Sprecher of the Seventh Circuit observed that 'each court dealing with these precise problems (the Illinois Supreme Court, the District Court, the U.S. Supreme Court) feels the need to apologize for its result.' I therefore would grant certiorari . . . [because] the present case affords the Court an opportunity to consider whether, in the context of the facts that this record appears to present, there is no limit whatsoever to the exercise of free speech. There indeed may be no such limit, but when citizens assert, not casually but with deep conviction, that the proposed demonstration is scheduled at a place and in a manner that is taunting and overwhelmingly offensive to the citizens of that place, that assertion, uncomfortable though it may be for judges, deserves to be examined. It just might fall into the same category as one's 'right' to cry 'fire' in a crowded theater, for 'the character of every act depends upon the circumstances in which it is done.' '' *Smith v. Collin*, 439 U.S. 916 (1978), *cert. denied.*

SMITH v. DAILY MAIL PUBLISHING CO. (1979). A West Virginia statute (West Virginia, Juvenile Privacy*) made it a crime for a newspaper to publish, without the written approval of a juvenile court, the name of any youth charged as a juvenile defendant. The statute was really not a prior restraint* because it only subjected newspapers to criminal punishment for what they print after the fact. The newspaper involved in this case, the *Daily Mail*, published articles containing the name of a juvenile who had been arrested for allegedly killing another youth. The newspaper learned the name by monitoring the police band radio frequency and by interviewing several eyewitnesses to the killing.

The Supreme Court reversed the newspaper's conviction and declared the statute to be an invalid restriction on the rights of a free press—a newspaper's First Amendment rights prevail over the state's interest in protecting juveniles. The Court ruled: (1) The state cannot punish the truthful publication of an alleged juvenile delinquent's name lawfully obtained by a newspaper. The asserted state interest in protecting the anonymity of the juvenile offender to further his rehabilitation cannot justify the statute's imposition of criminal sanctions for publication of a juvenile's name lawfully obtained. (2) Even assuming that the statute served a state interest, it does not accomplish its stated purpose, since it does not restrict the electronic media or any other form of publication from making public a juvenile's name. Only newspapers are singled out in the statute. *Smith v. Daily Mail Publishing Co.*, 443 U.S. 97 (1979).

SMITH v. GOGUEN (1974). Goguen, for wearing a small American flag sewn to the seat of his pants, was convicted of violating a provision of the Massachusetts flag-misuse statute (Massachusetts, Flag Desecration*) that subjected to a penalty anyone who "publicly treats contemptuously the flag of the United States." The Massachusetts Supreme Judicial Court affirmed the conviction, but the U.S. Supreme Court reversed. The Court found the statute to be too vague: (1) The challenged statutory language is void for vagueness, since by failing to draw reasonably clear lines between the kinds of non-ceremonial treatment of the flag that are criminal and those that are not, it does not provide adequate warning of forbidden conduct and sets forth a standard so indefinite that police, court, and jury are free to react to nothing more than their own preferences for treatment of the flag. (2) The phrase at issue is vague not in the sense of requiring a person to conform his conduct to an imprecise but comprehensible standard, but in the sense of not specifying any ascertainable standard of conduct at all. (3) That other words of the desecration and contempt portion of the statute address more specific conduct (mutilation, trampling, and defacing the flag) does not assist Goguen, since he was tried solely under the "treats contemptuously" phrase. *Smith v. Goguen*, 415 U.S. 566 (1974).

SMITH v. UNITED STATES (1977). In 1974, Smith mailed various material (issues of *Intrigue* magazine and two films entitled *Lovelace* and *Terrorized Virgin*) from Des Moines to post office box addresses in southern Iowa. The mailing was done after Smith received a written request for the material from post office inspectors using fictitious names. What Smith did was not a violation of any Iowa law, but he was duly indicted, tried, and convicted of violating 18 U.S.C. § 1461 (Postal Regulations, Mailing Obscene Material*). The Supreme Court affirmed the conviction, holding (1) It was not a form of entrapment for the postal inspectors to use fictitious names in requesting the material. (2) The fact that the state of Iowa decided not to make Smith's activities unlawful cannot compel the federal government to allow the mails to be used to send obscene materials within that state. *Smith v. United States*, 431 U.S. 291 (1977).

SNEPP v. UNITED STATES (1980). Snepp, a former agent with the Central Intelligence Agency (CIA), published a book (*Decent Interval*) about certain CIA activities in South Viet Nam. Snepp published the account without first submitting it to the CIA for pre-publication review (read censorship). As an express condition of his employment with the CIA in 1968, however, Snepp had signed an agreement (Central Intelligence Agency, Publishing Agreements*) promising that he would "not publish any information or material relating to the Agency, its activities or intelligence activities generally, either during or after the term of [his] employment without specific prior approval by the Agency." The promise was an integral part of Snepp's concurrent undertaking "not to disclose any classified information relating to the Agency without proper authorization." Snepp had thus pledged, without being under any apparent duress, not to divulge classified information and not to publish any information without pre-publication clearance.

The Supreme Court readily accepted the argument that Snepp's agreement was a prior restraint,* but such a restraint, as it deals with the CIA, is permissible in view of the national interest in maintaining an effective intelligence service. The Court ruled that Snepp had breached a fiduciary obligation, and imposed a constructive trust for the government's benefit on all profits Snepp might earn from publishing the book—the profits ran into thousands of dollars. The courts have been quite consistent in allowing prior restraints and prohibitions on publishing when the CIA is involved, as can also be seen in the cases of *McGehee v. Casey** and *United States v. Marchetti.** *Snepp v. United States*, 444 U.S. 507 (1980).

SNYDER v. MILWAUKEE (1939). Snyder, who was acting as a picket, stood in the street in front of a Milwaukee meat market and distributed to passing pedestrians handbills that pertained to a labor dispute with the meat market, explained organized labor's position in the dispute, and asked citizens not to do business with the market. Some of the handbills were thrown into the street by the recipients, and the result was that there was quite a bit of litter. Police then arrested Snyder and charged him with a violation of an ordinance (Milwaukee [WI], Distribution of Literature*) but did not arrest any of the people who actually threw the handbills in the street. There was testimony that this was the standard practice of the police under the ordinance—whenever the distribution of literature resulted in littering, the police would arrest the person who distributed the literature and not the person(s) who threw the material in the street. A Milwaukee County court found Snyder guilty, and his fine was affirmed by the Wisconsin Supreme Court; the U.S. Supreme Court reversed the conviction: (1) An ordinance designed to prevent litter is a justifiable and legitimate area of state activity and the police are empowered to arrest anyone who litters. (2) It is the person who throws the handbill in the street who is to be arrested and charged, not the person distributing the literature. (3) Enforcement of the ordinance against the distributor can lead to a form of censorship, since if anyone does not like the content of literature, he would throw it in the street, thus leading to the arrest of the distributor. *Snyder v. Milwaukee*, 308 U.S. 147 (1939).

SOUTH CAROLINA, BAR ASSOCIATION DISCIPLINARY RULES. Section 4(b) of the Supreme Court of South Carolina's Rule on Disciplinary Procedure defines "misconduct" as a "violation of any of the Canons of Professional Ethics as adopted by this Court from time to time." Some of these canons were employed in an attempt to limit the activities of the American Civil Liberties Union (ACLU) within the state by prohibiting the "soliciting" of clients by lawyers of such organizations as the ACLU. Some of the relevant bar association rules were as follows: "A lawyer shall not knowingly assist a person or organization that recommends, furnishes, or pays for legal services to promote the use of his services or those of his partners or associates." "A lawyer who has given unsolicited advice to a layman that he should obtain counsel or take legal action shall not accept employment resulting from that advice, except . . . " "If success in asserting rights or defenses of his client in litigation in the nature of a class action is dependent upon the joinder of others, a lawyer may accept, but shall not seek, employment from those contacted for the purpose of obtaining their joinder." These "anti-soliciting" rules were held to be inapplicable to attorneys working for such organizations as the ACLU in *In Re Primus*.*

SOUTH CAROLINA, BREACH OF THE PEACE. The state of South Carolina had a breach of the peace statute, and it employed that statute to convict Edwards, a leader of a civil rights demonstration. The Supreme Court reversed the conviction (*Edwards v. South Carolina**), for it was felt that the way in which the Supreme Court of South Carolina defined and applied the statute constituted an infringement of the right of free speech. In affirming the conviction, the South Carolina court said that the offense of breach of the peace "is not susceptible of exact definition," but that the "general definition of the offense" was as follows: "In general terms, a breach of the peace is a violation of public order, a disturbance of the public tranquility, by any act or conduct inciting to violence. It includes any violation of any law enacted to preserve peace and good order. It may consist of an act of violence or an act likely to produce violence. It is not necessary that the peace be actually broken to lay the foundation for a prosecution for this offense. If what is done is unjustifiable and unlawful, tending with sufficient directness to breach the peace, no more is required. Nor is actual personal violence an essential element in the offense. . . . By 'peace,' as used in the law in this connection, is meant the tranquility enjoyed by citizens of a municipality or community where good order reigns among its members, which is the natural right of all persons in political society."

SPEISER v. RANDALL (1958). The Speisers refused to sign an oath that they did not advocate the overthrow of any government within the United States by force or violence, and that they did not advocate the support of any foreign government against the United States in case of hostilities or war. For this refusal they were denied tax exemptions in California because the oath was required by a California statute (California, Property Tax Exemption*) before the tax exemptions would be given.

The U.S. Supreme Court struck down the entire process, holding that it was a blatant violation of the First Amendment guarantees of free speech. Justice Brennan delivered the opinion of the Court: "It cannot be gainsaid that a discriminatory denial of a tax exemption for engaging in speech is a limitation on free speech. . . . To deny an exemption to claimants who engage in certain forms of speech is in effect to penalize them for such speech. Its deterrent effect is the same as if the State were to fine them for this speech. . . . So here, the denial of a tax exemption for engaging in certain speech necessarily will have the effect of coercing the claimants to refrain from the proscribed speech. The denial is frankly aimed at the suppression of dangerous ideas."

Justice Black filed a concurring view, an opinion that emphasized the linkage of the California scheme to government censorship. Justice Black: "Here a tax is levied unless the taxpayer makes an oath that he does not and will not in the future advocate certain things; in Ohio those without jobs have been denied unemployment insurance unless they are willing to swear that they do not hold specific views; and Congress has even attempted to deny public housing to needy families unless they first demonstrate their loyalty. These are merely random samples; I will not take time here to refer to innumerable others, such as oaths for hunters and fishermen, wrestlers and boxers and junk dealers. I am convinced that this whole business of penalizing people because of their views and expressions concerning government is hopelessly repugnant to the principles of freedom upon which this Nation was founded and which have helped to make it the greatest in the world. As stated in prior cases, I believe 'that the First Amendment grants an absolute right to believe in any government system, [to] discuss all governmental affairs, and [to] argue for desired changes in the existing order. This freedom is too dangerous for bad, tyrannical governments to permit. But those who wrote and adopted our First Amendment weighed those dangers against the dangers of censorship and deliberately chose the First Amendment's unequivocal command that freedom of assembly, petition, speech and press shall not be abridged. I happen to believe this was a wise choice and that our free way of life enlists such respect and love that our Nation cannot be imperiled by mere talk.' "

Justice Douglas also added a concurring opinion: "When we allow government to probe his beliefs and withhold from him some of the privileges of citizenship because of what he thinks, we do indeed 'invert the order of things,' to use Hamilton's phrase. All public officials—state and federal—must take an oath to support the Constitution by the express command of Article VI of the Constitution. But otherwise the domains of conscience and belief have been set aside and protected from government intrusion. What a man thinks is of no concern to the government. The First Amendment gives freedom of mind the same security as freedom of conscience. Advocacy and belief go hand in hand. For there can be no true freedom of mind if thoughts are secure only when they are pent up.'' *Speiser v. Randall*, 357 U.S. 513 (1958).

SPENCE v. WASHINGTON (1974). Spence was convicted under Washington's ''improper use'' statute (Washington, Flag Desecration*), which prohibited the exhibition of a U.S. flag to which was attached or superimposed any figure, symbol, or other material. Spence's crime was that he hung a flag out his window upside down with the peace symbol attached as a protest against the then-recent actions in Cambodia and the fatal shootings at Kent State University; his purpose was not to desecrate the U.S. flag, but to associate it with peace instead of war and violence. The Supreme Court determined that his activity—a form of ''symbolic speech''*—was sufficiently imbued with elements of communication and therefore fell within the scope of the protections contained in the First and Fourteenth Amendments. The Court ruled that the Washington statute, as applied to Spence, impermissibly infringed a form of protected expression. *Spence v. Washington*, 418 U.S. 405 (1974).

STANLEY v. GEORGIA (1969). Stanley was a suspected bookmaker, and the police, while acting under a lawful search warrant in his house, looking for evidence of his bookmaking activities, found some films in his bedroom. The films were seized, viewed, and found to be obscene. Stanley was arrested for possession of obscene material in violation of a Georgia statute (Georgia, Possession of Obscene Material*), was tried and convicted, and had his conviction upheld by the Georgia Supreme Court.

The U.S. Supreme Court reversed the conviction in what has become a landmark decision: individuals may not have the right to produce, sell, distribute, transport, or give away obscene material, but there is a ''zone of privacy'' around an individual's home (a man's home is still his castle into which not even the king can enter) and the government has no right to determine what an individual can read or see within the privacy of his own home. Justice Marshall delivered the opinion of the Court: ''These are the rights that [Stanley] is asserting in the case before us. He is asserting the right to read or observe what he pleases—the right to satisfy his intellectual and emotional needs in the privacy of his own home. He is asserting the right to be free from state inquiry into the contents of his library. Georgia contends that [Stanley] does not have these rights, that there are certain types of materials that the individual may not read or even possess. Georgia justifies this assertion by arguing that the films in the present case are obscene. But we think that mere categorization of these films as 'obscene' is insufficient justification for such a drastic invasion of personal liberties guaranteed by the First and Fourteenth Amendments. Whatever may be the justifications for other statutes regulating obscenity, we do not think they reach into the privacy of one's own home. If the First Amendment means anything, it means that a State has no business telling a man, sitting alone in his own house, what books he may read or what films he may watch. Our whole constitutional heritage rebels at the thought of giving government the power to control men's minds. And yet, in the face of these traditional notions of individual liberty, Georgia asserts the right to protect the individual's mind from the effects of obscenity. We are not certain that this argument amounts to anything more than the assertion that the State has the right to control the moral content of a person's thoughts. . . . We hold that the First and Fourteenth Amendments prohibit making mere possession of obscene material a crime. *Roth* [*v. United States**] and the cases following that decision are not impaired by today's holding. As we have said, the States retain broad power to regulate obscenity; that power simply does not extend to mere possession by the individual in the privacy of his own home. Accordingly, the judgment of the court below is reversed.'' *Stanley v. Georgia*, 394 U.S. 557 (1969).

STAR CO. v. BRUSH (1918). The mayor and aldermen of Mount Vernon, New York, did not like the content of two certain newspapers—*New York American* and *New York Evening Journal*—and thus the town passed two ordinances (Mount Vernon [NY], Newspaper Licensing and Prohibiting Sale of Newspapers*) that prohibited the sale or distribution of the two newspapers anywhere within the town until after the then-current World War I. The two newspapers brought suit against the town, and Judge Giegerich (Supreme Court, New York County) struck down the sale or distribution statute: ''No other local authority has ever attempted this in this state. I am clearly of the opinion . . . that the local authorities had no power to ordain what they attempted to ordain in this case, and that their act is a nullity.''

Undaunted, the mayor and aldermen tried again by then passing an ordinance that prohibited the distribution of newspapers within the town without a license. The licensing ordinance permitted the town authorities to suppress the circulation of any newspaper that adversely criticized the town's official acts; a license, once issued, could be revoked at any time without notice, and allowed newspapers that approved the town's official acts to circulate freely. The ordinance was written in such terms that it was obvious to everyone concerned that the *New York American* and the *New York Evening Journal* would never receive such a license. This ordinance was also struck down as a violation of the First Amendment by Judge Donnelly (Supreme Court, New York County). *Star Co. v. Brush*, 170 N.Y. Supp. 987 (1918) (June) and 172 N.Y. Supp. 320 (1918) (September).

STAR v. PRELLER (1974). Star owned several bookstores in Baltimore that contained, among other things, coin-operated viewing machines that showed ''adult'' motion pictures. After a number of raids by the Baltimore vice squad in which these films were seized because they did not have a proper license from the Maryland State Board of Censors (Maryland, Motion Picture Censorship*), Star then went to court seeking an injunction against the enforcement of the film licensing requirements on the grounds that the scheme violated the First Amendment. The Supreme Court did not grant Star his request and upheld the Maryland censorship process. The Court was careful, however, to distinguish this case from *Freedman v. Maryland* (*Revenge at Daybreak**). In *Freedman*, the Maryland scheme was held to be unconstitutional because of certain defects; in *Star*, the Court concluded that these defects were remedied and thus held that the Maryland requirement that films be licensed before exhibition—and that obscene films need not be licensed—was constitutional.

Justice Brennan, from the denial of certiorari, repeated his view on the ability of the government to censor obscene material: "It is my view that at least in the absence of distribution to juveniles or obtrusive exposure to unconsenting adults, the First and Fourteenth Amendments prohibit the State and Federal Governments from attempting wholly to suppress sexually oriented materials on the basis of their allegedly 'obscene' contents." *Star v. Preller*, 419 U.S. 956 (1974), *cert. denied*.

STATE OF FLORIDA v. CLEIN (1951). Clein was indicted in Dade County, Florida, the indictment alledging that he "did then and there print, publish and distribute a certain written paper containing obscene written descriptions, of an act of unnatural sexual perversion between a male and a female person, manifestly tending to the corruption of the morals of youths." It appears that Clein published in *Miami Life* the following item: "White Girl, Negro Man, Face Morals Rap. The Moving Finger writes—for all interested in Segregation to see. This happened very early the other morning in Miami Beach. Address, south side of 12th Street, between Alton Rd. and Lenox Ave. Police Car 154 noticed a Cadillac auto parked there, with motor running. Officer Everett Walshon saw the Negro first. He was sitting up asleep, head lolling back on the top of the seat. Then the officer looked down, he saw the white girl. She was asleep, too—her head in the Negro's lap. The officer says the Negro was 'exposed.' The two were questioned separately. The Negro did not deny participating in an unnatural act. The evidence of it was irrefutable. The girl—who told the police she was a Jackson Memorial Hospital nurse and her name was Mary Connolly Premo— said she didn't remember what she had done. She only knew she had been 'drinking with Jimmy all that day' at an upper Miami Beach swank Bar."

The indictment of Clein was based on § 847.01 of the Florida code, making it unlawful for any person to print, publish, or distribute any printed paper concerning obscene language or descriptions manifestly tending to the corruption of the morals of youth. Clein attempted to have the indictment quashed, but a Florida court refused, holding that Clein must stand trial. In a concurring opinion, Judge Crosby stated: "This court would not be justified in assuming either that the morals of youth exposed to such a publication are so firmly elevated as to be immune to any possible adverse effect from it or, on the other hand, so sophisticated as to be beyond the possibility of further harm.'' *State of Florida v. Clein*, 93 So. 2d 876 (1951).

STATE OF NEW JERSEY v. HUDSON COUNTY NEWS COMPANY (1962). The state of New Jersey brought this suit against the Hudson County News Company for a violation of a statute that prohibited the sale and distribution of ''obscene and indecent'' books and publications. The targeted publications were about two dozen ''girlie'' and ''adventure for men only'' magazines (e.g., *Action for Men, Exposé for Men, Male, Untamed, Glamorgirl Photography*). The Essex County Court, Judge Matthews, described the magazines thusly: ''I have no hesitation in classifying each magazine as absolute trash. I am sure that a trained mind could not find diversion or entertainment in reading the contents of any of them. The obvious intent of these is to appeal to man's taste for bawdy things and to pander to the cult of pseudo-sophisticates represented by certain members of our male population who conceive the ultimate in values to be the perfect dry martini and a generously endowed, over-sexed female. The general make-up of these magazines consists of short stories involving rather obvious plots which invariably have as their denouement an illicit sexual relationship . . . and photographs of young women in scanty attire. To my mind they exist as forlorn evidence of the irresponsible efforts of the publishers concerned to contribute to the mediocrity of society. Many photographs depict women in various stages of dress and undress, and in scanty bathing suits. In many, the breasts and nipples of the model are exposed. Most of the poses are what might be described as provocative, and some, absolutely silly. All are obviously planned for the purpose of displaying in some manner or another the overabundance of certain physical attributes possessed by the model. These magazines are indicative of the fantasies which a large segment of our population has with regard to sex. The appeal of this type of magazine seems to be a reassurance to the illusion possessed by many of this group that somewhere, for somebody, sex can be a full-time activity.''

But Judge Matthews went on and ruled that the magazines were *not* obscene or pornographic under the statute and that the state could not prevent their sale or distribution. Judge Matthews gave an excellent statement on the rights guaranteed by the First Amendment: ''In a pluralistic society the courts, as I have stated heretofore, cannot and should not become involved in the attempts to improve individual morals, nor should they become involved as arbiters in the war between the *literati* and the philistines over the standards to which our literature is to adhere. The function of the courts and our law is clear: to provide, insofar as it is humanly possible, a climate free of unnecessary restraints in which our citizens will be able to express themselves without fear. It is, or should be apparent to all that everything we have been, are, or will be as a nation has or will come as the result of the unfettered expression of individual ideas. Responsible citizens should realize that our social freedoms are inextricably bound together so as to constitute a vital whole which is much more than a mere sum of its parts; and that whenever we deal with any area of freedom we are necessarily dealing with this living whole. If we cannot with reasonable certainty know every possible effect that will flow from the regulation of any specific area of social freedom when we consider the whole, self-restraint must be exercised, since unforeseen effects may follow, with the result that the regulation which seemed at the time sensible when viewed as to a part, now acts to harm irreparably the whole. The dangers of such consequences can not be overstated. Considered in this light, it must be agreed that if we are to continue to have the freedom of expression as it has been guaranteed, and which we have cherished since the days of the Revolution, the existence of the type of trash involved here must be tolerated as part of the price which we must pay." *State of New Jersey v. Hudson County News Company*, 183 A. 2d 161 (1962).

STATE OF OHIO v. MAZES (1966). Mazes was the operator of a newsstand, candy, and tobacco store in Clifton, a suburb of Cincinnati, Ohio. The court record says that the store enjoyed a "good reputation" in the community; that is, the store had a good reputation until the morning of November 7, 1962, when several officers of the Vice Control Bureau of the Cincinnati Police Department entered the store. One of the officers took a book, *Orgy Club*, from an open bookrack. The officer later testified that he read the flyleaf and excerpts chosen at random from about four pages. It appears that the vice bureau didn't like *Orgy Club*; the book was seized and Mazes was placed under arrest. Mazes was then tried for violating § 2905.34 of the Ohio Revised Code, which makes it an offense to "exhibit in a place which may be within the view of a minor" any book judged to be obscene. At Mazes' trial, it was shown that the book was on a rack on which a sign was placed reading "You must be over 21 to purchase one of these books." The arresting officer testified, however, that ":there were several young boys in the store" looking at the rack. Mazes was duly convicted and the decision was affirmed by the Ohio Supreme Court; the U.S. Supreme Court, in a per curiam decision (*Mazes v. Ohio*, 388 U.S. 453 [1967]), without written opinions, reversed Mazes' conviction. *State of Ohio v. Mazes*, 218 NE. 2d 725 (1966).

STATE OF WISCONSIN v. ARNOLD (1935). As the court record relates, Arnold ran a gas station in Milwaukee and, as usual, maintained a men's and a ladies' washroom. All was fine until December 19, 1933, when two detectives of the Milwaukee Police Department entered the station, asked to use the washroom, and entered; Arnold was arrested when the detectives came out of the men's room. It appears that there was a coin-operated vending machine in the men's room, and after placing ten cents in it, the detective received, as the court described it, "a cartridge containing a rubber article, commonly used for contraceptive purposes" (the court felt constrained to emphasize that "the purchase was made for purposes of evidence, and not for the purpose of illegal use").

On the vending machine was a sign stating, "Sold only for the prevention of disease" and "Minors are prohibited to operate this machine." Arnold was then tried for and convicted of violating a Wisconsin statute (Wisconsin, Display of Contraceptives*) that prohibited the sale of contraceptives except in limited circumstances (vending machines in gas stations were not listed among these exceptions).

In convicting Arnold, the Wisconsin court made the following comments: "It is claimed that subdivision (1), § 351.235, in defining indecent articles, appears to include many drugs, medicines, instruments, and devices which, while capable of use either as contraceptives or abortifacients, have many innocent and lawful common uses. Coming particularly to subdivision (3), under which defendant was prosecuted, it is claimed that this subsection is vague and indefinite in that it prohibits not the vending of indecent articles by a slot machine, but the manufacture, purchase, rent, or possession of any mechanism capable, by reason of its design and construction, of vending these articles. It is contended that if literally construed, this section, as well as subdivision (1), which is definitive of indecent articles, contains such broad and inclusive prohibitions of legitimate articles of commerce as to constitute an unreasonable, arbitrary, and unwarranted exercise of the police power. In support of this contention, it is urged that any antiseptic is capable of use as a contraceptive, including vinegar, sour milk, bichloride of mercury, as well as such proprietary antiseptics as Lysol, Listerine and Pepsodent. It is further contended that many drugs and devices having common legitimate uses are capable of being used as abortifacients, and that a law prohibiting their advertisement, display, or sale is an unwarranted interference with legitimate business. . . . The particular article involved [here] is as effective for contraceptive purposes as for disease prevention, and this is also true of drugs, the operation of which is antiseptic rather than mechanical. The difficulty with [Arnold's] position in this respect is the insistence that the protestations contained upon this slot machine that this is 'sold only for the prevention of disease' and that 'minors are prohibited to operate this machine,' are conclusive as to the intent. We think they are not. We think the sale of this particular device in a public toilet by a mechanical vending machine is a sufficient warrant for the inference that the purpose of its sale was contraception and not merely the prevention of disease." *State of Wisconsin v. Arnold*, 258 N.W. 843 (1935).

STATE v. APPLING (1857). Appling was indicted in the following terms: "That the defendant did, on the 25th of August, at the County of Laclede [Missouri], in a certain large assembly of males and females in said county, and in the hearing of said assembly of persons, unlawfully, wickedly and scandalously used vulgar, obscene and indecent language . . . and was then and there guilty of open and notorious acts of public indecency, grossly scandalous, to the manifest corruption of the morals of said assembly."

Appling was fined but appealed the conviction: There was no statute in Missouri that made the utterance of obscene words in public an act of public indecency. This claim was not accepted by the Missouri court hearing his appeal. Judge Tilghman: "We have no statute punishing a person for the use of vulgar, indecent and obscene words in public. There has not been an attempt to legislate on this particular offense. It was an offense at common law, because it was against good morals—against public decency." The court records are silent about the words Appling said in mixed company. *State v. Appling*, 25 Mo. 315 (1857).

STATE v. BROWN (1855). As the court record relates, Brown was indicted in Vermont for selling obscene publications that were described in the indictment as "certain lewd, scandalous and obscene printed papers, entitled *Amatory Letters, Ellen's Letter to Maria*, and *Maria's Letter to Ellen*, which such printed papers are so lewd and obscene, that the same would be offensive to the court here, and improper to be placed upon the records thereof, wherefore the jurors aforesaid do not set forth the same in this indictment." Brown was fined forty dollars but appealed, basing his argument on the claim that the indictment was not sufficient. The Vermont court did not agree, Judge Redfield delivering the opinion: "In a case like the present, if the publication be of so gross a character that spreading it upon the record will be an offence against decency, it may be excused, as all the English precedents show. Some of the precedents are much like the present, describing the obscene character of the publication in general terms. . . . If the paper is of a character to offend decency, and outrage modesty, it need not be so spread upon the record as to produce that effect." *State v. Brown*, 27 Vermont 619 (1855).

STATE v. KLAPPROTT (1941). Klapprott and others were convicted in a New Jersey court for violating a statute (New Jersey, Group Libel*) that made it a misdemeanor to make statements advocating hatred of any group of people by reason of race, color, religion, and that also made it a misdemeanor to permit any building to be used for the above purpose.

The convictions were reversed on appeal, the court holding the statutes in question to be an invalid prior restraint on the freedom of speech: "It would serve no purpose to reproduce and publish in this opinion the statements made by each plaintiff. It is sufficient to say that the individuals made statements containing unworthy and scurrilous references to the Jewish people. . . . That the statute tends to limit that which a speaker may say with impunity is obvious. Freedom of speech and of the press are not absolute rights; their abuse is subject to punishment by the State; and yet it would be a greater evil to our State and its people if the press was subject to censorship and the free speech of the individual dependent upon a censor's imprimatur. It is obvious that previous restraint of free speech or free press abridges the guaranteed liberties. And that is the sound reason why freedom of the press and freedom of speech are so zealously defended by courts and people alike even in the case of those who seem to desecrate that right. The abuse of these rights, however, need not go unpunished. There still remain the provisions of our laws regarding libel and slander. . . . In construing a statute strict regard must be had for all of its parts as well as its rigid enforcement. To particularize: Is the making of a statement in the presence of two or more persons in any language, which incites, let us say, 'hostility' towards a group by reason of religion or race, capable of being made into a misdemeanor? Suppose a father is instructing his children about the religion of a neighbor and such exposition excites hostility in the children towards those neighbors. This exposition or statement of view would result in the commission of a misdemeanor under the scope of this most sweeping statute. It is not required that the statement be made in a public place. Teachers in our high schools and colleges could be found to be violators of the law out of their lectures on the philosophy of history, or their dissertations on religion, or on the various cults which came into being through the years. Such consequences we do not think were intended by the Legislature.'' *State v. Klapprott*, 22 A. 2d 877 (1941).

STAUB v. CITY OF BAXLEY (1958). A city ordinance (Baxley [GA], Soliciting Ordinance*) made it an offense to solicit the citizens of Baxley to become members of any organization without first receiving a permit from the mayor and the town council. The permit would be granted or refused after a "consideration of the character of the applicant, the nature of the organization, and its effects upon the general welfare of the citizens." For soliciting applications for memberships in a labor union in the private homes of some people in Baxley without applying for the permit, Staub was convicted of violating the ordinance.

The U.S. Supreme Court reversed: The ordinance was invalid on its face because it made the enjoyment of the constitutionally guaranteed freedom of speech contingent on the will of the mayor and the town council and, as such, is a prior restraint. Justice Whittaker delivered the opinion of the Court: "It will also be noted that the permit is not to be issued as a matter of course, but only upon the affirmative action of the Mayor and Council of the City. They are expressly authorized to refuse to grant the permit if they do not approve of the applicant or of the union or of the union's 'effects upon the general welfare of the citizens of the City of Baxley.' These criteria are without semblance of definitive standards or other controlling guides governing the action of the Mayor and Council in granting or withholding a permit (*Niemotko v. Maryland**). It is thus plain that they act in this respect in their uncontrolled discretion. It is settled by a long line of recent decisions of this Court that an ordinance which, like this one, makes the peaceful enjoyment of freedoms which the Constitution guarantees contingent upon the uncontrolled will of an official—as by requiring a permit or license which may be granted or withheld in the discretion of such official—is an unconstitutional censorship or prior restraint upon the enjoyment of those freedoms." *Staub v. City of Baxley*, 355 U.S. 313 (1958).

STRANGE FRUIT. The General Laws of Massachusetts, c. 272, § 28 (Massachusetts, Obscenity Statute*) prohibit the sale or distribution of any publication that is "obscene, indecent, or impure, or manifestly tends to corrupt the morals of youth." One Isenstadt was found guilty under this statute in 1945 (*Commonwealth of Massachusetts v. Isenstadt*, 62 N.E. 2d 840 [1945]), when the court determined that *Strange Fruit* was not fit for public consumption in the state of Massachusetts.

The court described *Strange Fruit* in the following terms: "The scene is laid in a small town in Georgia. A white boy, Tracy Dean, who lacks the forcefulness to get ahead in the world, and an educated but compliant colored girl, Nonnie Anderson, fall genuinely in love, but because of race inhibitions and pressures they cannot marry. Nonnie supplies to Tracy the sympathy and nourishment of his self-esteem which his other associations deny him. Illicit intercourse occurs, resulting in pregnancy. Tragedy follows in the form of murder of Tracy committed by Nonnie's outraged brother and the lynching of an innocent colored man for that crime. Distributed through this book of 250 pages are four scenes of sexual intercourse, including one supposed to have been imagined. The immediate approaches to these acts and the descriptions of the acts themselves vary in length from a few lines to several pages. They differ in the degree of their suggestiveness. Two of them might be thought highly emotional, with strongly erotic connotations. In addition to these there is a fifth scene in an old abandoned cabin in which there are amatory attitudes, kissing, a loosened blouse, exposed breasts, and circumstances suggesting but perhaps not necessarily requiring an act of intercourse. In still another scene Tracy in a confused drunken frenzy 'saw somebody' (himself) tear off Nonnie's clothes 'until there was nothing between his hands and her body,' 'press her down against the floor,' 'press her body hard—saw him try and fail, try and fail, try and fail,' but he 'couldn't.' In addition to the scenes just mentioned there are distributed fairly evenly throughout the book approximately fifty instances where the author introduces into the story such episodes as indecent assaults upon little girls, an instance of, and a soliloquy upon, masturbation by boys, and references to acts of excretion, to 'bobbing' or 'pointed' breasts, to 'nice little rumps, hard, light, bouncy,' to a group of little girls 'giggling mightily' upon discovering a boy behind a bush and looking at his 'bared genitals.' We need not recite more of these. The instances mentioned will indicate the general character of the others. Some of these minor incidents might be dismissed as of little or no consequence if there were fewer of them, but when they occur on an average on every fifth page from beginning to end of the book it would seem that a jury or a judge might find that they had a strong tendency to maintain a salacious interest in the reader's mind and to whet his appetite for the next major episode."

After this description, the Massachusetts court did indeed rule that *Strange Fruit* was obscene, indecent, and impure within the meaning of the statute: "It is urged that this book was written with a serious purpose; that its theme is a legitimate one; that it possesses great literary merit; and that it has met with a generally favorable reception by reviewers and the reading public. We agree that it is a serious work. It brings out in bold relief the depth and the complexity of the race problem in the South, although, so far as we can see, it offers no remedy. We agree that the theme of a love which because of social conditions and conventions cannot be sanctioned by marriage and which leads to illicit relations is a permissible theme. That such a theme can be handled with power and realism without obscenity seems sufficiently demonstrated in George Eliot's *Adam Bede*, which we believe is universally recognized as an English classic. . . . Regarding the book as a whole, it is our opinion that a jury of honest and reasonable men could find beyond a reasonable doubt that it contains much that, even in this post-Victorian era, would tend to promote lascivious thoughts and to arouse lustful desire in the minds of substantial numbers of that public into whose hands this book, obviously intended for general sale, is likely to fall; that the matter which could be found objectionable is not necessary to convey any sincere message the book may contain and is of such character and so pervades the work as to give to the whole a sensual and licentious quality calculated to produce the harm which the statute was intended to prevent; and that that quality could be found to persist notwithstanding any literary or artistic merit.''

A STRANGER KNOCKS. This 1963 Danish film was directed by Johan Jacobsen and starred Birgitte Federspiel and Preben Lerdorff. The film was admitted into the United States after the Customs Service determined that it was not obscene (Tariff Act*). By early 1963, the film was exhibited in more than 150 theaters in twenty-three states and viewed by at least 250,000 persons without incident. When *A Stranger Knocks* was first exhibited in Denmark, it was awarded three "Bodils" (the equivalent of the American "Oscars") for best Danish picture, best leading actor, and best leading actress. In January 1964, the International Film Importers and Distributors of America gave Birgitte Federspiel its award for the best performance of the year by an actress in an imported foreign film.

A Stranger Knocks, however, ran into problems with the film censors in New York (New York, Motion Picture Censorship*) and in Maryland (Maryland, Motion Picture Censorship*). The film's plot is summarized by de Grazia and Newman (*Banned Films*, p. 279): "On a stormy evening, a woman admits a stranger to her isolated cottage near the sea, unaware that he is a wartime Nazi collaborator fleeing from Danish justice. Due to her lonely life-style, she welcomes his company and responds avidly to his lovemaking. In the course of their sexual intimacies, she discovers that he is the man who tortured and killed her husband during World War II. She struggles to resolve the dilemma presented by her attraction to this ruthless stranger and her desire for retribution.''† The woman finally shoots the stranger, and with the pistol still in her hand, she goes out the door of the cottage, walks slowly down the path, and casts the pistol to one side as the film ends.

---

†Reprinted from *Banned Films* with permission of the R. R. Bowker Company. Copyright © 1982 by Edward de Grazia and Roger K. Newman.

The New York Board of Regents, the agency charged by the statutes to review and issue exhibition permits for films, ordered the elimination of two specific scenes before a permit would be issued. The board determined that the two scenes were obscene. The first scene presented a man and a woman on a beach embracing and caressing each other and concluded with a view of the head and shoulders of the woman with facial expressions "indicative of orgasmic reaction." The second scene presented the woman astride the man on a bed. The movements were "unmistakably those of the sexual act and the woman's face again registers emotions concededly indicative of orgasm." The second scene is the dramatic climax of the film because of the "coincidence of the woman's passion with her sudden realization, through the exposure of a tell-tale scar, that the man is her husband's murderer."

The Appellate Division of the New York Supreme Court annulled the order of the board and directed that an exhibition permit be issued; on appeal, the New York Court of Appeals (*Trans-Lux Distributing Corp. v. Board of Regents of the University of the State of New York*, 248 N.Y.S. 2d 857 [1964]) reversed and ruled that the scenes in question were indeed obscene and that an exhibition permit need not be issued until and unless the scenes were deleted. Judge Burke delivered the opinion of the New York Court of Appeals: "This comparison between the acknowledged competence of the State to forbid public or semipublic sex displays and its power to exert similar control over similar conduct depicted on the screen is not intended to imply any broad theory of legal equivalence between real conduct and a filmed imitation. Indeed, the meaningful comparison exists only in a narrow range of cases. In most instances, the real conduct is illegal because of what is accomplished by the person, as in murder, forgery, or adultery. In such cases, the filmed dramatization obviously does not share the evil aimed at in the law applicable to the real thing. Where, however, the real conduct is illegal, not because of what is accomplished by those involved, but simply because what is done is shocking, offensive to see, and generally believed destructive of the general level of morality, then a filmed simulation fully shares, it seems to me, the evil of the original. In such cases the free expression protection of the First Amendment must apply to both or neither. It makes no sense at all to say that the conduct can be forbidden but not the play or film. . . . Lest we get too far away from the actual question, let us remind ourselves that the Regents did not refuse to license this picture but went no further than to direct elimination therefrom of the two scenes of sexual congress. If we were to hold that this Regent's determination was illegal we would be saying that there is a constitutional right to include in a motion picture a direct acting out of coitus. Therefore, what is involved here is not the description in a book of sexual acts but the actual performance of those acts in public. To fornicate in public or to exhibit the sexual organs in public has been considered obscene conduct at least since 1663 in the case of *King v. Sedley* (1 Keble 620) wherein Sir Charles Sedley was convicted of obscenity because, standing on a London balcony, he exhibited himself in the nude to the populace. The ban on such exhibitions is probably as old as human society and it has never disappeared from our law.''

A Stranger Knocks fared better in the Maryland courts after the Maryland State Board of Censors refused to issue an exhibition permit; the Maryland board wasn't interested in a couple of scenes—the entire film was determined to be objectionable. But the Maryland Court of Appeals (*Trans-Lux Distributing Corp. v. Maryland State Board of Censors*, 213 A. 2d 235 [1965]) reversed the board's order and directed that an exhibition license be issued. The court ruled that the film, which had favorable criticism from a number of critics, dealt with sex in a manner advocating ideas having artistic value and social importance and it did not go beyond the customary limits of candor in describing the sex. Judge Barnes delivered the majority opinion: ''The Board offered no evidence before the lower court of *any* expert or other opinion indicating that the film appealed to the prurient interest or was not a serious work of art. It only offered in evidence the film itself, contending that the two scenes complained of in the film met the burden of proof imposed upon it by the Act of 1965. We do not agree. In our opinion the weight of the testimony—including the film itself—establishes that the film is a serious work of art, dealing with a subject of social importance and does not appeal to the prurient interest. It most certainly is not 'utterly without redeeming social importance,' the film 'deals with sex in a manner which advocates ideas having artistic value and social importance,' and 'does not go beyond the customary limits of candor in the description of such matters.' The film may not constitutionally be denied a license for exhibition by the Board.''

There was a dissenting opinion from Judge Horney: ''It seems to me that the majority of the members of this Court, in approving a film portraying overt acts of illicit sexual intercourse, has gone further than even the majority of the Supreme Court of the United States has required, and, in so doing, has disregarded the Maryland statute which prohibits the showing of unlawful and immoral sexual relations. If such illicit acts are not obscene, it is difficult to envisage what, other than hard-core pornography, would constitute obscenity. In my opinion, the order of the lower court affirming the refusal of the State Board of Censors to license the motion picture, *A Stranger Knocks*, should not have been reversed. For, when these illicit acts of sexual gratification, the elimination of which, as the producer admitted, 'would virtually destroy the film as a serious motion picture,' are considered (either with or without the remainder of the film), it is clear that the dominant effect of the film, even assuming this was not its calculated purpose, is to arouse lascivious thoughts or desires which is expressly prohibited.''

De Grazia and Newman (*Banned Films*, p. 280) conclude the story of *A Stranger Knocks*: ''The U.S. Supreme Court's reversal of the New York ban on this film was without written opinion (*Trans-Lux Distributing Corp. v. Board of Regents*, 380 U.S. 259 [1965]); it simply cited its decision in the *Revenge at Daybreak** case [*Freedman v. Maryland*], holding that Maryland's film censorship law was procedurally defective and 'an invalid prior restraint.' As a result of the Supreme Court's action, the New York Court of Appeals declared New York's film censorship law invalid [*Trans-Lux Distributing Corp. v. Regents*, 209 N.E. 2d 558 (1965)]. Although Maryland enacted a new film censorship system designed to meet the Supreme Court's constitutional standards, the New York legislature has not resurrected any film censorship system for its state."†

STREET v. NEW YORK (1969). Street, after having heard a news broadcast of the shooting of James Meredith, a civil rights leader, took an American flag that he owned to a street corner near his home and ignited the flag. While the flag was burning, Street was quoted as saying, "We don't need no god-damn flag. If they let that happen to Meredith, we don't need an American flag." Street was then arrested, tried, and convicted in the New York courts for a violation of § 1425 of the New York Penal Law (New York, Flag Disrespect*), which makes it a crime "publicly to mutilate or publicly to defy or cast contempt upon any American flag either by words or act."

The Supreme Court reversed the conviction, holding that since Street was convicted of both burning the flag and speaking contemptuous words about the flag, and that since the statute allowed a prosecution just for words, the statute was seen to be an unconstitutional restriction on the right of free speech: "We come finally to the question whether, in the circumstances of this case, New York may constitutionally inflict criminal punishment upon one who ventures 'publicly to defy or cast contempt upon any American flag . . . by words.' In these circumstances, we can think of four governmental interests which might conceivably have been furthered by punishing [Street] for his words: (1) an interest in deterring appellant from vocally inciting others to commit unlawful acts; (2) an interest in preventing appellant from uttering words so inflammatory that they would provoke others to retaliate physically against him, thereby causing a breach of the peace; (3) an interest in protecting the sensibilities of passersby who might be shocked by appellant's words about the American flag; and (4) an interest in assuring that appellant, regardless of the impact of his words upon others, showed proper respect for our national emblem. In the circumstances of this case, we do not believe that any of these interests may constitutionally justify [Street's] conviction under § 1425 for speaking as he did. . . . We add that disrespect for our flag is to be deplored no less in these vexed times than in calmer periods of our history. Nevertheless, we are unable to sustain a conviction that may have rested on a form of expression, however distasteful, which the Constitution tolerates and protects." *Street v. New York*, 394 U.S. 576 (1969).

STROMBERG v. CALIFORNIA (1931). Stromberg was charged and convicted under California Penal Code § 403-a (California, Red Flag Statute*),

---

†Reprinted from *Banned Films* with permission of the R. R. Bowker Company. Copyright © 1982 by Edward de Grazia and Roger K. Newman.

which prohibited displaying a red flag in a public place or in a meeting place as (a) "a sign, symbol or emblem of opposition to organized government" or as (b) "an invitation or stimulus to anarchistic action" or as (c) "an aid to propaganda that is of a seditious character." The U.S. Supreme Court reversed the conviction, holding the statute to be too vague and indefinite: "The question is thus narrowed to that of the validity of the first clause, that is, with respect to the display of the flag 'as a sign, symbol or emblem of opposition to organized government.' This might be construed to include the peaceful and orderly opposition to a government as organized and controlled by one political party by those of another political party equally high minded and patriotic, which did not agree with the one in power. It might also be construed to include peaceful and orderly opposition to government by legal means and within constitutional limitations. The maintenance of the opportunity for free political discussion to the end that government may be responsive to the will of the people and that changes may be obtained by lawful means, an opportunity essential to the security of the Republic, is a fundamental principle of our constitutional system. A statute which upon its face is so vague and indefinite as to permit the punishment of the fair use of this opportunity is repugnant to the guaranty of liberty contained in the Fourteenth Amendment." *Stromberg v. California*, 283 U.S. 359 (1931).

STRUTHERS (OH), DISTRIBUTION OF HANDBILLS. The following ordinance was held to be an unconstitutional restriction on the First Amendment in 1943 by the Supreme Court in *Martin v. City of Struthers**: "It is unlawful for any person distributing handbills, circulars or other advertisements to ring the door bell, sound the door knocker, or otherwise summon the inmate or inmates of any residence to the door for the purpose of receiving such handbills, circulars or other advertisements they or any person with them may be distributing."

SUGARMAN v. UNITED STATES (1919). Sugarman was charged with having violated § 3 of the 1917 Espionage Act,* which punished "whoever, when the United States is at war, shall willfully cause or attempt to cause insubordination, disloyalty, mutiny, or refusal of duty, in the military or naval forces of the United States." Sugarman had made a speech at a Socialist meeting that was attended by many registrants under the Selective Service Act; the government claimed that the speech violated the act. Sugarman was tried and convicted.

He appealed to the Supreme Court, claiming that the trial judge refused to give certain instructions to the jury. One such requested instruction read as follows: "The Constitution of the United States provides that Congress shall make no law abridging the freedom of speech, or of the press, or the right of the people peaceably to assemble and to petition for a redress of greivances. This right has been deemed so essential and necessary to free institutions and a free people that it has been incorporated in substance in the constitutions of all the states of the Union. These constitutional provisions referred to are not abrogated, they are not less in force now because of war, as they are as vital during war as during times of peace, and as binding upon you now as though we were at peace." The Supreme Court, Justice Brandeis delivering the opinion, stated that the trial judge was under no obligation to adopt the language requested by Sugarman, and the Court dismissed Sugarman's appeal "for want of jurisdiction." *Sugarman v. United States*, 249 U.S. 182 (1919).

SUNSHINE AND HEALTH. The nudist magazine *Sunshine and Health* and several other magazines were involved in attempts to declare the publications obscene. In 1948, in *State of Ohio v. Lerner* (81 N.E. 2d 282 [1948]), Lerner was charged with having in his possession, with intent to sell, obscene literature in violation of an Ohio statute (Ohio, Obscenity Statute*). Lerner owned and operated the Bell Block News Shop in Cincinnati and carried issues of *Sunshine and Health*, the official publication of the American Sunbathing Association, Inc. The state of Ohio argued that the issues of the magazine "were not wholly obscene, but contained lewd and lascivious photographs and drawings." The Ohio court did not agree that the issues of *Sunshine and Health* were obscene and found Lerner not guilty. In the words of the Ohio judge, "an obscene book must be held to be one wholly obscene and that necessarily in testing a literary work for obscenity it must be viewed in its entirety and only when and if the obscene contents constitute the dominant feature or effect does it fall within the forbidden class. Is obscenity the dominant idea and aim of a literary work? If so it falls within the forbidden class, otherwise not."

The judge also made a statement that needs no additional comment: "These front views obscene? Well, they merely show humankind as God made them and does He not command 'Be ye fruitful and multiply and replenish the earth.' These front views, as well as the other views, are of God's own children as He made them in His own image. There can not be any obscenity in God's own handiwork."

Sunshine and Health and several other similar magazines (*Sunbathing for Health Magazine, Modern Sunbathing and Hygiene, Hollywood Girls of the Month*, and *Hollywood Models of the Month*) did not fare as well in New York City in 1952, however. New York City Commissioner of Licenses Edward T. McCaffrey sent a letter to newspaper distributors, stating in effect that their licenses would be suspended or revoked if they continued to display or offer for sale any of the above-named magazines. The publisher of *Sunshine and Health* then brought suit, seeking an injunction against McCaffrey's enforcement of his edict.

The Supreme Court, New York County, ruled that the threat to revoke the licenses of those who sold nudist magazines was a "reasonable regulation to aid the Commissioner of Licenses in performing the duties assigned to him by statute, and did not constitute a prior restraint" (*Sunshine Book Co. v. McCaffrey*, 112 N.Y.S. 2d 476 [1952]). Judge Corcoran delivered the opinion of the New York court: "In each of these issues there is a repletion of photographs of naked persons. These photographs have caused the present controversy. They generally fall into two categories. Some of them are action pictures, showing nudists in their camp activities, rowing, hitting volley balls, building fires, etc. In others, the editors are more subtle in their glorification of nudism. They show shapely and attractive young women in alluring poses in the nude. It is significant that the photographs of the second category are the ones selected for the covers of all issues without exception. These photographs are front views. They are cleverly colored to picture clearly the female breasts and pubic hair. They take up nearly all the space on the covers, leaving only enough for the title, price and issue identification. . . . [This is] the State of New York in the year 1952. Extreme and weird examples of deviations from our accepted standards can be found among the many races of mankind. Bizarre notions can also be found among civilized nations in man's long history. Such examples do not justify repetition in our society. It is interesting to note, nonetheless, that the authors on whom the plaintiffs rely so heavily fail to give examples of any civilized nations that accepted the practice of nudism as a general custom. It would appear that even they must concede that the use of clothing to cover one's sexual organs has been, throughout history, the practice of all humans except for the lowest grades of savages. Of course, nudity is not necessarily obscene. There are situations where no valid objection can be made to it. In the arts, in medicine, and in other sciences, we have ready examples. The fact that nudity in such instances may have the incidental effect of arousing sexual desires is not always sufficient reason for barring it. As to the conditions and circumstances under which nudity is permissible, reason sets the proper limits. Where the dominant purpose of nudity is to promote lust, it is obscene and indecent. The distribution and sale of the magazines in this case is a most objectionable example. The dominant purpose of the photographs in these magazines is to attract the attention of the public by an appeal to their sexual impulses. The sale of the magazines is not limited to any mailing list of members or subscribers. They are sold and distributed indiscriminately to all who wish to purchase the same. Men, women, youths of both sexes, and even children, can purchase these magazines. They will have a libidinous effect upon most ordinary, normal, healthy individuals. Their effect upon the abnormal individual may be more disastrous. Their sale and distribution are bound to add to the already burdensome problem of juvenile delinquency and sex crimes, and the Commissioner of Police properly arrested those who participated in this violation of our Penal Law."

The U.S. government even entered the fray, when, in 1957, both a district court and an appeals court ruled that *Sunshine and Health* was obscene and thus could be prohibited from the U.S. mail (*Sunshine Book Company v. Summerfield*, 249 F. 2d 114 [1957]). Judge Danaher of the appeals court cited the above remarks of Judge Corcoran in holding the magazine obscene. But one year later, in 1958, the Supreme Court (355 U.S. 372 [1958]) reversed the decision that

Sunshine and Health was obscene. This last decision was an unsigned per curiam decision, and the Court cited the *Roth v. United States** holding as the basis for their opinion.

SWEARINGEN v. UNITED STATES (1896). In 1895, Swearingen was indicted, under the provisions of § 3893 of the Revised Statutes (Postal Regulations, Mailing Obscene Material*), for "depositing in the post office of the United States, at Burlington, Kansas, to be conveyed by mail and delivered to certain named persons a certain publication or newspaper, entitled *The Burlington Courier*, dated September 21, 1894, and containing a certain article charged to be of an obscene, lewd, and lascivious character, and non-mailable matter." Some excerpts of the article follow: "About the meanest and most universally hated and detested thing in human shape that ever cursed this community is the red headed mental and physical bastard that flings filth under another man's name down on Neosho street. This black hearted coward . . . would pimp and fatten on a sister's shame with as much unction as a buzzard gluts in carrion. He has been known as the companion of negro strumpets and has revelled in lowest debauches. He is the embodiment of treachery, cowardice, and dishonor, and hasn't the physical nor moral courage to deny it. He is too little and rotten to merit the notice of men. We have been wrong in noticing the poltroon at all, and henceforth are done."

Swearingen received one year in jail and a fifty-dollar fine for sending the article through the mail, but the U.S. Supreme Court reversed the conviction, holding that the article was not obscene or lewd. Justice Shiras delivered the opinion of the Court: "The words 'obscene,' 'lewd' and 'lascivious,' as used in the statute, signify that form of immorality which has relation to sexual impurity, and have the same meaning as is given them at common law in prosecutions for obscene libel. As the statute is highly penal, it should not be held to embrace language unless it is fairly within its letter and spirit. Referring to this newspaper article, as found in the record, it is undeniable that its language is exceedingly coarse and vulgar, and, as applied to an individual person, plainly libellous. But we cannot perceive in it anything of a lewd, lascivious and obscene tendency, calculated to corrupt and debauch the mind and morals of those into whose hands it might fall." *Swearingen v. United States*, 161 U.S. 446 (1896).

SWEEZY v. NEW HAMPSHIRE (1957). In an investigation conducted by the New Hampshire attorney general, acting on behalf of the state legislature under a broad resolution (New Hampshire, Subversive Activities Act*) directing him to determine whether there were "subversive persons" in the state, Sweezy answered most of the questions put to him, but he refused to answer questions related to a lecture he delivered on March 22, 1954, to about one hundred students in a humanities course at the University of New Hampshire. He also refused to answer some questions related to his knowledge of the Progressive Party of the State. The questions he refused to answer included the following:

"What was the subject of your lecture?" "Didn't you tell the class . . . that Socialism was inevitable in this country?" "Did you advocate Marxism at that time?" "Did you . . . espouse the theory of dialectical materialism?" and "Do you believe in Communism?" Sweezy was then convicted of contempt, and the conviction was affirmed by the New Hampshire Supreme Court.

On appeal, the U.S. Supreme Court reversed the conviction, holding that the investigation and the questions asked violated Sweezy's rights of academic freedom and political expression. The Court's opinion made the following comments: "We believe that there unquestionably was an invasion of [Sweezy's] liberties in the areas of academic freedom and political expression—areas in which government should be extremely reticent to tread. The essentiality of freedom in the community of American universities is almost self-evident. No one should underestimate the vital role in a democracy that is played by those who guide and train our youth. To impose any strait jacket upon the intellectual leaders in our colleges and universities would imperil the future of our Nation. No field of education is so thoroughly comprehended by man that new discoveries cannot yet be made. Particularly is that true in the social sciences, where few, if any, principles are accepted as absolutes. Scholarship cannot flourish in an atmosphere of suspicion and distrust. Teachers and students must always remain free to inquire, to study and to evaluate, to gain new maturity and understanding; otherwise our civilization will stagnate and die. Equally manifest as a fundamental principle of a democratic society is political freedom of the individual. Our form of government is built on the premise that every citizen shall have the right to engage in political expression and association. This right was enshrined in the First Amendment of the Bill of Rights. Exercise of these basic freedoms in America has traditionally been through the media of political associations. Any interference with the freedom of a party is simultaneously an interference with the freedom of its adherents. All political ideas cannot and should not be channeled into the programs of our two major parties. History has amply proved the virtue of political activity by minority, dissident groups, who innumerable times have been in the vanguard of democratic thought and whose programs were ultimately accepted. Mere unorthodoxy or dissent from the prevailing mores is not to be condemned. The absence of such voices would be a symptom of grave illness in our society." *Sweezy v. New Hampshire*, 354 U.S. 234 (1957).

SYMBOLIC SPEECH. "Symbolic speech" is seen to be conduct done in order to communicate an idea, and the Supreme Court has generally afforded such "speech" the same constitutional protections afforded normal or usual speech. The Court, however, has punished people for conduct alone when the conduct could be separated from the element of communication. In this context, the Court upheld a conviction for intentionally destroying a draft card, holding that no "speech" was involved and that the conduct—burning the draft card—was not symbolic speech (*United States v. O'Brien**). But in other cases, the Court extended First Amendment protection to such symbolic speech as wearing black arm bands in a school to protest the Viet Nam war (*Tinker v. Des Moines School District**); wearing a jacket with the words "Fuck the Draft" on it (*Cohen v. California**); an actor wearing a military uniform and criticizing the military (*Schacht v. United States**); and several flag "misuse" cases (*Smith v. Goguen** and *Street v. New York**).

T

TALLEY v. CALIFORNIA (1960). Talley was arrested, tried, and convicted (a fine of ten dollars) in a Los Angeles municipal court for violating an ordinance (Los Angeles [CA], Anonymous Handbills*) that prohibited distribution, in any place under any circumstances, of any handbill or circular that did not have the name and address of the person who prepared or sponsored the handbill printed on it. Talley had distributed handbills on which was printed the following: "National Consumers Mobilization/Box 6533/Los Angeles 55 Calif./PLeasant 9-1576." The handbills urged readers to help the organization carry on a boycott against certain merchants and businessmen, whose names were given, on the grounds that, as one set of handbills said, they carried products of "manufacturers who will not offer equal employment opportunities to Negroes, Mexicans, and Orientals." On the handbill there was a space for a person to sign his name if he desired enrollment as a "member of National Consumers Mobilization." This space was preceded by the following statement: "I believe that every man should have an equal opportunity for employment no matter what his race, religion, or place of birth." The municipal court held that the identifying information printed on the handbills did not meet the requirements of the ordinance, and Talley was fined ten dollars.

The fine was affirmed on appeal in California, but the Supreme Court, ruling that the ordinance was void on its face under the First Amendment, reversed the conviction. Justice Black delivered the opinion of the Court: "This ordinance simply bars all handbills under all circumstances anywhere that do not have the names and addresses printed on them in the place the ordinance requires. There can be no doubt that such an identification requirement would tend to restrict freedom to distribute information and thereby freedom of expression. 'Liberty of circulating is as essential to that freedom as liberty of publishing; indeed, without the circulation, the publication would be of little value.' Anonymous pamphlets, leaflets, brochures and even books have played an important role in the progress of mankind. Persecuted groups and sects from time to time throughout history have been able to criticize oppressive practices and laws either anonymously or not at all. The obnoxious press licensing law of England, which was also enforced on the Colonies was due in part to the knowledge that exposure of the names of printers, writers and distributors would lessen the circulation of literature critical of the government. The old seditious libel cases in England show the lengths to which government had to go to find out who was responsible for books that were obnoxious to the rulers. John Lilburne was whipped, pilloried and fined for refusing to answer questions designed to get evidence to convict him or someone else for the secret distribution of books in England. Two Puritan ministers, John Penry and John Udal, were sentenced to death on charges that they were responsible for writing, printing or publishing books. Before the Revolutionary War colonial patriots frequently had to conceal their authorship or distribution of literature that easily could have brought down on them prosecutions by English-controlled courts. Along about that time the Letters of Junius were written and the identity of their author is unknown to this day. Even the Federalist Papers, written in favor of the adoption of our Constitution, were published under fictitious names. It is plain that anonymity has sometimes been assumed for the most constructive purposes. . . . There are times and circumstances when a State may not compel members of groups engaged in the dissemination of ideas to be publicly identified. . . . Identification and fear of reprisal might deter perfectly peaceful discussions of public matters of importance. This broad Los Angeles ordinance is subject to the same infirmity. We hold that it . . . is void on its face." *Talley v. California*, 362 U.S. 60 (1960).

TARIFF ACT. U.S. Customs regulations authorize the Customs Service to seize any "obscene" matter coming into the United States and then seek in a federal district court a judicial determination of the material's obscenity. If the court so rules, Customs can then destroy the material. The Tariff Act of 1930, 19 U.S.C. § 1305, provides, in part: "All persons are prohibited from importing into the United States from any foreign country . . . any obscene book, pamphlet, paper, writing, advertisement, circular, print, picture, drawing, or other representation, figure, or image on or of paper or other material, or any cast, instrument, or other article which is obscene or immoral, or any drug or medicine or any article whatever for the prevention of conception or for causing unlawful abortion. . . . No such articles whether imported separately or contained in packages with other goods entitled to entry, shall be admitted to entry; and all such articles and, unless it appears to the satisfaction of the collector that the obscene or other prohibited articles contained in the package were enclosed therein without the knowledge or consent of the importer, owner, agent, or consignee, the entire contents of the package in which such articles are contained, shall be subject to seizure and forfeiture as hereinafter provided. . . . Provided, further, That the Secretary of the Treasury may, in his discretion, admit the so-called classics or books of recognized and established literary or scientific merit, but may, in his discretion, admit such classics or books only when imported for noncommercial purposes. Upon the appearance of any such book or matter at any customs office, the same shall be seized and held by the collector to await the judgment of the district court as hereinafter provided; and no protest shall be taken to the United

States Customs Court from the decision of the collector. Upon the seizure of such book or matter the collector shall transmit information thereof to the district attorney of the district in which is situated the office at which such seizure has taken place, who shall institute proceedings in the district court for the forfeiture, confiscation, and destruction of the book or matter seized. Upon the adjudication that such book or matter thus seized is of the character the entry of which is by this section prohibited, it shall be ordered destroyed and shall be destroyed. Upon adjudication that such book or matter thus seized is not of the character the entry of which is by this section prohibited, it shall not be excluded from entry under the provisions of this section. In any such proceeding any party in interest may upon demand have the facts at issue determined by a jury and any party may have an appeal or the right of review as in the case of ordinary actions or suits.''

TEITEL FILM CORPORATION v. CUSACK (1968). The Teitel Film Corporation, permanently enjoined by the Illinois courts from showing certain motion pictures, filed a suit challenging the constitutionality of the Chicago film censorship scheme (Chicago [IL], Motion Picture Censorship*). The Supreme Court, relying on the *Freedman v. Maryland* decision (*Revenge at Daybreak**), ruled that the Chicago process violated First Amendment rights: ''The Illinois Supreme Court held 'that the administration of the Chicago Motion Picture Ordinance violates no consitutional rights of the defendants.' We disagree. In *Freedman v. Maryland* we held 'that a noncriminal process which requires the prior submission of a film to a censor avoids constitutional infirmity only if it takes place under procedural safeguards designed to obviate the dangers of a censorship system. To this end, the exhibitor must be assured, by statute or authoritative judicial construction, that the censor will, within a *specified brief period*, either issue a license or go to court to restrain showing of the film. The procedure must also assure a *prompt final judicial decision*, to minimize the deterrent effect of an interim and possibly erroneous denial of a license.' The Chicago censorship procedures violate these standards in two respects. (1) The 50 to 57 days provided by the ordinance to complete the administrative process before initiation of the judicial proceeding does not satisfy the standard that the procedure must assure 'that the censor will, within a specified brief period, either issue a license or go to court to restrain showing the film.' (2) The absence of any provision for a prompt judicial decision by the trial court violates the standard that 'the procedure must also assure a prompt final judicial decision.' Accordingly, we reverse the judgments of the Supreme Court of Illinois.'' *Teitel Film Corporation v. Cusack*, 390 U.S. 139 (1968).

TELEPHONE REGULATIONS, FEDERAL. Title 47 U.S.C. § 223 provides the following: ''Whoever—(1) in the District of Columbia or in interstate or foreign communication by means of telephone—(A) makes any comment, request, suggestion or proposal which is obscene, lewd, lascivious, filthy, or indecent; (B) makes a telephone call, whether or not conversation ensues, without disclosing his identity, and with intent to annoy, abuse, threaten, or harass any person at the called number; (C) makes or causes the telephone of another repeatedly or continuously to ring, with intent to harass any person at the called number; or (D) makes repeated telephone calls, during which conversation ensues, solely to harass any person at the called number; or (2) knowingly permits any telephone under his control to be used for any purpose prohibited by this section, shall be fined not more than $500 or imprisoned not more than six months, or both.''

Although the language in this statute is not that precise (''intent to annoy'' could cover a multitude of sins, as pointed out by Justice White [Telephone Regulations, State*]), this federal statute was upheld as constitutional in *United States v. Lampley* (573 F. 2d 783 [1978]), when an appeals court affirmed Lampley's conviction for making harassing interstate telephone calls. As the appeals court record relates, the facts in Lampley's case ''constitute a bizarre tale of a romantic obsession. In 1951 in Nashville, Tennessee, the appellant briefly dated Elizabeth Hatlen before her marriage, their relationship terminating after a few weeks. The relationship had an enduring effect on the appellant, however, for in the summer of 1969 he called Elizabeth in Evansville, Wisconsin, where she lived with her husband Richard Hatlen and their four children. The appellant told her that he could not get her out of his mind, that he had spent a rough 17 years for which she was at fault and that he wanted to see her again. When she refused, he told her that he would make life miserable for her. Thereupon, the appellant launched from his home in Pennsylvania a telephonic assault on the Hatlens and others, unleashing a barrage of incessant and subsequently abusive telephone calls. . . . Lampley would often make operator assisted calls, and while the operator placed the call, he would shout obscenities over the operator's voice. . . . Taking the stand . . . Lampley's defense was that his prosecution was the result of a plot on the part of the Hatlens, the United States Attorney, the Department of Justice, the Federal Bureau of Investigation, and the United States District Court to silence his activities in exposing corruption in government.''

More recently, in 1983, Congress passed legislation that would prohibit the rather lucrative commercial sex-over-the-phone services. The largest of these services was operated out of New York by the publisher of *High Society*, a magazine that mainly features pictures of nude women. Paying in advance by credit card, the caller can then hear recorded messages and stories and sounds about sex. The service is the equivalent of many other such telephone services—Dial-a-Prayer, Dial-a-Joke, Dial-the-Weather, Dial-the-Time, Sports Hot-Line; some libraries have Dial-a-Story for children. Representative Thomas J. Bliley, a Republican from Virginia, has dubbed this service ''Dial-a-Porn.'' The provisions in the bill dealing with sex over the phone authorize the Federal Communications Commission to impose fines, and the attorney general to seek criminal penalties, against any person or firm operating a telephone service determined to be "obscene or indecent" that is available to anyone under the age of eighteen. The "available to anyone under the age of eighteen" will probably put the dial-a-porn service out of business, since access to telephones cannot be controlled as neatly as, say, access to X-rated films.

TELEPHONE REGULATIONS, STATE. Most states have regulations dealing with the nature and content of telephone conversations that are similar to those at the federal level (Telephone Regulations, Federal*). The regulations all contain language to the effect that it is against the law to make a telephone call to another person with the "intent to annoy or to abuse" the recipient of the call. Several cases—none as yet has reached the Supreme Court for a definitive decision—have arisen in various states concerning the "intent to annoy or to abuse" the person called. One such case was in Connecticut, in *Gormley v. Director, Connecticut State Department of Probation* (632 F. 2d 938 [1980]),* in which Gormley was convicted of violating the Connecticut telephone statute that prohibits anyone from making a telephone call "with intent to harass, annoy . . . or in a manner likely to cause annoyance." It seems that Gormley had called the director and stated to him that his mother had gone to bed with Gormley's husband, that she had photographs to prove that the director's mother had been in bed with Gormley's husband, and that the director's entire family were a "bunch of nuts" and should all be under psychiatric care.

An appeals court affirmed Gormley's conviction and the U.S. Supreme Court refused to hear her appeal, thus keeping intact her conviction (449 U.S. 1023 [1981]). But Justice White filed a dissent to the denial of certiorari: "Telephone calls by irate citizens to their Congressmen, by collectors seeking payment of legitimate bills overdue, by customers voicing to a seller dissatisfaction with goods or services purchased, and calls of like tenor [perhaps even angry parents to children, jealous or stood-up lovers, publishers telling authors that their manuscripts are rejected, this list is most certainly endless!], are likely to be annoying, even harassing, to the recipients. Such calls are usually made to influence the person called. No one could seriously question the caller's free speech right under the First Amendment to engage in such telephone conversations. Yet, by prohibiting telephone calls made 'with intent to annoy' and 'in a manner likely to cause annoyance,' the Connecticut statute could be construed as prohibiting the exercise of this free speech. . . . It is no comfort to the citizen telephoning his Congressman or to the defrauded consumer calling the swindler to know that the statute was not intended to apply to their telephone calls if its language plainly does so. The mere existence of a statute prohibiting such obviously lawful exercise of a free speech right has a chilling effect, particularly if enforcement is threatened by the recipient of a call."

TENNESSEE, ANTI-EVOLUTION ACT. This statute was involved in the famous Scopes "monkey trial" in Tennessee, in 1927 (*Scopes v. State**). The Tennessee courts found nothing wrong with the act, and Scopes was found guilty as charged. The following description of the act is from the court records of the Scopes trial: "While the Act [Chapter 27 of the Acts of 1925] was not drafted with as much care as could have been desired, nevertheless there seems to be no great difficulty in determining its meaning. It is entitled: 'An act prohibiting the teaching of the evolution theory in all the Universities, normals and all other public schools in Tennessee, which are supported in whole or in part by the public school funds of the state, and to provide penalties for the violations thereof.' When the draftsman came to express this purpose in the body of the act, he first forbade the teaching of 'any theory that denies the story of the divine creation of man, as taught in the Bible'—his conception evidently being that to forbid the denial of the Bible story would ban the teaching of evolution. To make the purpose more explicit, he added that it should be unlawful to teach 'that man has descended from a lower order of animals.' The Act reads that it shall be unlawful for any teacher . . . 'to teach any theory that denies the story of the divine creation of man as taught in the Bible, and to teach instead [of the story on the divine creation of man as taught in the Bible] that man has descended from a lower order of animals.' ''

Such statutes can be found in states other than Tennessee. As late as 1968, Arkansas had its own anti-evolution statute (Arkansas, Anti-Evolution Statute*) that made it unlawful for a teacher in any state-supported school or university to teach or to use a textbook that taught "that mankind ascended or descended from a lower order of animals." The Arkansas statute was seen by the Supreme Court as a blatant violation of the First Amendment in *Epperson v. Arkansas*.*

TENNESSEE, OBSCENITY STATUTE. The Tennessee obscenity statute was seen as constitutional by the Supreme Court in *ABC Books, Inc. v. Benson* (1970).* Sections 39-3003 and 39-3007 of the Tennessee Code Ann. reads, in part: "It shall be a misdemeanor for any person to knowingly sell, distribute, display, exhibit, possess with the intent to sell, distribute, display or exhibit; or to publish, produce, or otherwise create with the intent to sell, distribute, display or exhibit any obscene material. . . . Every person who is convicted of violating this section shall be punished by imprisonment in the county jail or workhouse for not more than eleven (11) months and twenty-nine (29) days and a fine of not more than five thousand dollars ($5,000) in the discretion of the jury. . . . Obscene material: Any material, matter, object or thing, including but not limited to, any written or printed matter, film, picture, drawing, or any object or thing is obscene if, considered as a whole, its predominant appeal is to prurient interest, that is, a shameful or morbid interest in nudity, sex or excretion, and if in addition, (1) it is patently offensive to the public or if it goes substantially beyond customary limits of candor in describing or representing such matters, and (b) it is devoid of any literary, scientific or artistic value and is utterly without social importance. The phrase 'predominant appeal' shall be considered with reference to ordinary persons.''

TERMINIELLO v. CHICAGO (1949). Arthur Terminiello, a defrocked Catholic priest, gave a speech in a Chicago auditorium under the auspices of the Christian Veterans of America. The meeting received a lot of attention and publicity, and the auditorium was filled to capacity, with some 800 persons in the audience. Some excerpts from the good Father's speech follow: "Now, I am going to whisper my greetings to you, Fellow Christians. I will interpret it. I said 'Fellow *Christians*,' and I suppose there are some of the scum got in by mistake, so I want to tell a story about the scum/And nothing I could say tonight could begin to express the contempt I have for the slimy scum that got in by mistake/Now, let me say, I am going to talk about—I almost said, about the Jews. Of course, I would not want to say that. However, I am going to talk about some Jews. I hope that—I am a Christian minister. We must take a Christian attitude. I don't want you to go from this hall with hatred in your heart for any person, for no person/Now, this danger which we face—let's call them Zionist Jews if you will, let's call them atheistic communistic Jews or Zionist Jews, then let us not fear to condemn them. You remember the Apostles when they went into the upper room after the death of the Master, they went in there, after locking the doors; they closed the windows/So, my friends, since we spent much time tonight trying to quiet the howling mob, I am going to bring my thoughts to a conclusion, and the conclusion is this. We must all be like the Apostles before the coming of the Holy Ghost. We must not lock ourselves in an upper room for fear of the Jews. I speak of the Communistic Zionistic Jew, and those are not American Jews. We don't want them here; we want them to go back where they came from.''

In addition to the filled hall, a crowd of about 1,000 persons was outside the auditorium protesting the meeting and the speech. A cordon of Chicago policemen tried to maintain order, but there were several disturbances and the crowd was angry and turbulent. Father Terminiello was then charged with a violation of a city ordinance (Chicago [IL], Disturbing the Peace*). The trial judge instructed the jury that any misbehavior that "stirs the public to anger, invites dispute, brings about a condition of unrest, or creates a disturbance" violates the ordinance. Terminiello was convicted and his conviction was affirmed by an Illinois appeals court and by the Illinois Supreme Court. He argued throughout that the ordinance, as applied to him, violated his right of free speech as guaranteed by the First Amendment.

Terminiello then appealed to the U.S. Supreme Court. As is so often the case, important decisions defining and protecting First Amendment rights deal with some nasty people (*Near v. Minnesota ex rel. Olson**). Terminiello's conviction was reversed by the Supreme Court on the grounds that the state cannot punish someone whose speech "invites dispute" or "stirs people to anger," for in the Court's view, that is the very essence of speech and the communication of ideas. Justice Douglas delivered the opinion of the Court: "The vitality of civil and political institutions in our society depends on free discussion. As Chief Justice Hughes wrote in *De Jonge v. Oregon*,* it is only through free debate and free exchange of ideas that government remains responsive to the will of the people and peaceful change is effected. The right to speak freely and to promote diversity of ideas and programs is therefore one of the chief distinctions that sets us apart from totalitarian regimes. Accordingly a function of free speech under our system of government is to invite dispute. It may indeed best serve its high purpose when it induces a condition of unrest, creates dissatisfaction with conditions as they are, or even stirs people to anger. Speech is often provocative and challenging. It may strike at prejudices and preconceptions and have profound unsettling effects as it presses for acceptance of an idea. That is why freedom of speech, though not absolute, is nevertheless protected against censorship or punishment, unless shown likely to produce a clear and present danger of a serious substantive evil that rises far above public inconvenience, annoyance, or unrest. There is no room under our constitution for a more restrictive view. For the alternative would lead to standardization of ideas either by legislatures, courts, or dominant political or community groups. The ordinance as construed by the trial court seriously invaded this province. It permitted conviction of petitioner if his speech stirred people to anger, invited public dispute, or brought about a condition of unrest. A conviction resting on any of those grounds may not stand.''

This decision was not unanimous, however. Justice Jackson dissented from the majority, for he felt that the specific circumstances of the case justified a breach of the peace conviction. Justice Jackson: ''The Court reverses this conviction by reiterating generalized approbations of freedom of speech with which, in the abstract, no one will disagree. Doubts as to their applicability are lulled by avoidance of more than passing reference to the circumstances of Terminiello's speech and judging it as if he had spoken to persons as dispassionate as empty benches, or like a modern Demosthenes practicing his Philippics on a lonely seashore. But the local court that tried Terminiello was not indulging in theory. It was dealing with a riot and with a speech that provoked a hostile mob and incited a friendly one, and threatened violence between the two. When the trial judge instructed the jury that it might find Terminiello guilty of inducing a breach of the peace if his behavior stirred the public to anger, invited dispute, brought about unrest, created a disturbance or molested peace and quiet by arousing alarm, he was not speaking of these as harmless or abstract conditions. He was addressing his words to the concrete behavior and specific consequences disclosed by the evidence. He was saying to the jury, in effect, that if this particular speech added fuel to the situation already so inflamed as to threaten to get beyond police control, it could be punished as inducing a breach of peace. . . .

''As this case declares a nation-wide rule that disables local and state authorities from punishing conduct which produces conflicts of this kind, it is unrealistic not to take account of the nature, methods and objectives of the forces involved. This was not an isolated, spontaneous and unintended collision of political, racial or ideological adversaries. It was a local manifestation of a world-wide and standing conflict between two organized groups of revolutionary fanatics [Fascists and Communists], each of which has imported to this country the strong-arm technique developed in the struggle by which their kind has devastated Europe. Increasingly, American cities have to cope with it. One faction organizes a mass meeting, the other organizes pickets to harass it; each organizes squads to counteract the other's pickets; parade is met with counterparade. Each of these mass demonstrations has the potentiality, and more than a few the purpose, of disorder and violence. This technique appeals not to reason but to fears and mob spirit; each is a show of force designed to bully adversaries and to overawe the indifferent. We need not resort to speculation as to the purposes for which these tactics are calculated nor as to their consequences. Recent European history demonstrates both. . . .

"I am unable to see that the local authorities have transgressed the Federal Constitution. Illinois imposed no prior censorship or suppression upon Terminiello. On the contrary, its suffrance and protection were all that enabled him to speak. It does not appear that the motive in punishing him is to silence the ideology he expressed as offensive to the State's policy or as untrue, or has any purpose of controlling his thought or its peaceful communication to others. There is no claim that the proceedings against Terminiello are designed to discriminate against him or the faction he represents or the ideas that he bespeaks. There is no indication that the charge against him is a mere pretext to give the semblance of legality to a covert effort to silence him or to prevent his followers or the public from hearing any truth that is in him. A trial court and jury have found only that in the context of violence and disorder in which it was made, this speech was a provocation to immediate breach of the peace and therefore cannot claim constitutional immunity from punishment. Under the Constitution as it has been understood and applied, at least until most recently, the State was within its powers in taking this action. Rioting is a substantive evil, which I take it no one will deny that the State and the City have the right and the duty to prevent and punish. . . .

"This Court has gone far toward accepting the doctrine that civil liberty means the removal of all restraints from these crowds and that all local attempts to maintain order are impairments of the liberty of the citizen. The choice is not between order and liberty. It is between liberty with order and anarchy without either. There is danger that, if the Court does not temper its doctrinaire logic with a little practical wisdom, it will convert the constitutional Bill of Rights into a suicide pact." *Terminiello v. Chicago*, 337 U.S. 1 (1949).

TEXAS, LABOR UNION SOLICITING. A Texas statute requiring a person to register with a state official before making any public speech aimed at enlisting support for an organization, was declared a violation of the First Amendment guarantee of free speech by the Supreme Court, in *Thomas v. Collins* (1945).* The statute (House Bill No. 100, c. 104, General and Special Laws of Texas, Regular Session, 48th Legislature [1943], §§ 5 and 12) provided: "All labor union organizers operating in the State of Texas shall be required to file with the Secretary of State, before soliciting any members for his organization, a written request by United States mail, or shall apply in person for an organizer's card, stating (a) his name in full; (b) his labor union affiliations, if any; (c) describing his credentials and attaching thereto a copy thereof, which application shall be signed by him. Upon such applications being filed, the Secretary of State shall issue to the applicant a card on which shall appear the following: (1) the applicant's name; (2) his union affiliation; (3) a space for his personal signature; (4) a designation 'labor organizer'; and (5) the signature of the Secretary of State, dated and attested by his seal of office. Such organizer shall at all times, when soliciting members, carry such card, and shall exhibit the same when requested to do so by a person being so solicited for membership. The District Courts of this State and the Judges thereof shall have full power, authority and jurisdiction, upon the application of the State of Texas, acting through an enforcement officer herein authorized, to issue any and all proper restraining orders, temporary or permanent injunctions, and any other and further writs or processes appropriate to carry out and enforce the provisions of this Act.''

TEXAS, PUBLIC NUISANCE. The state of Texas, relying on a statute that authorized the abatement of "public nuisances," attempted to prohibit the future exhibition of motion pictures that had not yet been judged obscene on the basis that the theater had exhibited obscene films in the past. Employed rather routinely, the abatement procedure of a public nuisance was found by the Supreme Court (*Vance v. Universal Amusement Co., Inc.**) to be an invalid process when applied to areas protected by the First Amendment. Texas Rev. Civ. State. Ann., Article 466, defined the areas subject to abatement proceedings: "The habitual use, actual, threatened or contemplated, of any place or building or part thereof, for any of the following uses shall constitute a public nuisance and shall be enjoined at the suit of either the State or any citizen thereof: (1) For gambling, gambling promotion, or communicating gambling information prohibited by law; (2) For the promotion or aggravated promotion of prostitution, or compelling prostitution; (3) For the commercial manufacturing, commercial distribution, or commercial exhibition of obscene material; (4) For the commercial exhibition of live dances or exhibition which depicts real or simulated sexual intercourse or deviate sexual intercourse; and (5) For the voluntary engaging in a fight between a man and a bull for money or other thing of value, or for any championship, or upon result of which any money or anything of value is bet or wagered, or to see which any admission fee is charged either directly or indirectly, as prohibited by law.''

TEXAS STATE TEXTBOOK COMMITTEE. Largely through the lobbying efforts of Mel and Norma Gabler (Educational Research Analysts*) and other fundamental groups opposed to secular humanism and believing that everyone should be a religious fundamentalist—one who adheres to the literal interpretation of the book of Genesis and the theory of "scientific creationism"—the Texas

State Textbook Committee, in 1974, adopted a set of guidelines for determining which books would be approved for use in the public schools of Texas. The committee is composed of twenty-seven elected members, one from each of the state's congressional districts, and is a powerful and influential force in textbook publishing: It approves the books for all the public schools in Texas, and with about $65 million a year spent on texts, the state of Texas is the fourth largest market in the United States. Seventeen other states, mostly in the South and Southwest, have similar textbook approval systems, but the Texas process has received most of the attention. The 1974 guidelines were really messages to publishers on what had to be included in certain texts if the publishers wanted the committee to consider the text for adoption; they dealt with the anathema to the scientific creation school: Darwin's theory of evolution (*Scopes v. State** and *Epperson v. Arkansas**). The two guidelines were as follows: (1) "Textbooks that treat the theory of evolution shall identify it as only one of several explanations of the origins of humankind and avoid limiting young people in their search for meanings of their human existence," and (2) "Each textbook must carry a statement on an introductory page that any material on evolution included in the book is clearly presented as theory rather than fact."

Critics of the entire process have charged that certain publishers, wanting to maintain the Texas market, "watered down" their textbooks' treatment of evolution, thus not only satisfying the Texans, but also, more important, exporting the Texan ideology to the rest of the nation's schools. Several examples of this "as goes Texas, so goes the nation" are given in the magazine *Discover* (January 1984, p. 6): "In the only high school biology text published by one Doubleday division, even the word 'evolution' is now deleted. . . . As a spokesman for Doubleday explained, the firm's decision to delete the word evolution was intended 'to avoid the publicity that would surround a controversy.' . . . According to Gerald Skoog, a professor of education at Texas Tech University, Holt, Rinehart & Winston reduced the number of words relating to evolution in *Modern Biology*, the country's largest selling biology textbook, from 18,211 in 1973 to 12,807 in 1981. (The book carries on its introductory page . . . [the] disclaimer stating that the material on evolution is presented 'as theory rather than fact.') The 20,346 words about evolution in a 1974 Silver Burdett book were reduced to 4,313 words in the firm's 1981 edition." These anti-evolution guidelines were in effect for ten years, but on April 14, 1984, the textbook committee repealed them (26 to 1) and substituted a new provision that, without mentioning evolution, requires that "theories should be clearly distinguished from fact and presented in an objective educational manner."

According to the *New York Times* (April 15, 1984, Section 1, p. 1, 18), the guidelines were repealed because of a threatened lawsuit by People for the American Way,* a national anti-censorship group. The repeal did not really result from any fear by the Texans of People for the American Way; rather, it was the result of a ruling by the state's attorney general, Jim Mattox, who declared the anti-evolution guidelines to be an unconstitutional "intrusion" of the state into religious matters and stated that he would not defend the committee against any lawsuits. Attorney General Mattox was quoted as saying: "The inference is inescapable, from the narrowness of the requirement, that a concern for religious sensibilities rather than a dedication to scientific truth was the real motivation for the rules." The *New York Times* article also cited the committee's chairman, Joe Kelly Butler of Houston: "It [the repeal] was a proper reaction to the Attorney General's opinion, but I do not agree we were trying to put creationism into the books. The books are full of evolution, full of Darwin. All we were doing was being a referee between right and left."

Several representatives of textbook publishers were present in Austin for the vote, including Hank Watkins of Prentice-Hall (*Prentice-Hall Biology*). Watkins did not agree that the guidelines had led to the watering down of textbooks: "We have not changed our books in any way. The only thing we would have to do is not print the disclaimer." The Texas coordinator of People for the American Way, Michael Hudson, said that the repeal "undoes 10 years of creationist influence on textbook content and it will spill over into every state." He also linked the guidelines to a decline in scientific ability among U.S. schoolchildren.

The authors of the original guidelines, Mel and Norma Gabler, were not pleased with the repeal but didn't foresee any real difference for the future. Mrs. Gabler: "This is rule by intimidation and threat [the threatened lawsuit] . . . [but] textbooks had not changed much under the rule and still presented evolutionary theory. They still show hunched-over men moving up to man and fishes coming out of the water. If you want to believe you came from a monkey, that's fine, but I don't." The *Times* article concludes with a parting shot at the Texas educational system: "The vote came at a time of extraordinary turmoil in Texas public education. H. Ross Perot of Dallas, chairman of a Select Committee on Public Education appointed [in 1983] by Gov. Mark White, has been denouncing Texas schools as dominated by 'drill team, band and football' rather than academic interests."

THOMAS v. COLLINS (1945). A Texas statute (Texas, Labor Union Soliciting*) required any labor organizer, before soliciting members for a union in the state, to request an organizer's card from the Texas secretary of state. While under a court restraining order because he did not have the required card, Thomas made a speech before a group of workers and solicited them to join the union. He was then sentenced to a fine and imprisonment for contempt, but the Supreme Court reversed the conviction, holding the Texas statute to be an invalid prior restraint on the right of free speech. Justice Rutledge commented that, although a state may regulate labor unions in order to prevent fraud, coercion, or other abuses, such regulation must not infringe on the constitutional rights of free speech and free assembly, and that the requirement that one register with the state before making a speech to enlist support for a labor union imposed an unacceptable prior restraint on the rights of free speech. *Thomas v. Collins*, 323 U.S. 516 (1945).

THORNHILL v. ALABAMA (1940). An Alabama statute (Alabama, Loitering and Picketing*) made it unlawful for any person "without a just cause or legal excuse" to go near to or "loiter" about any place of lawful business for the purpose of or with the intent to influence other people not to buy from or be employed at such place of business, or to "picket" a business with the intent to interfere with the business. The complaint against Thornhill was that he "did go near to or loiter about the premises" of the Brown Wood Preserving Company with the intent of influencing others not to buy from the company, and that he "did picket" the works of the company "for the purpose of hindering, delaying or interfering with or injuring its lawful business." Thornhill was convicted of violating the statute and was sentenced to seventy-three days. The Alabama courts construed the statute as forbidding the publicizing of facts concerning a labor dispute, whether by printed sign, by pamphlet, by word of mouth, or otherwise, in the vicinity of the business involved, without regard to the number of persons engaged in such activity, the peaceful character of their conduct, the nature of the dispute, or the accuracy or restraint of the language used in imparting the information.

The Supreme Court reversed Thornhill's conviction, holding the statute to be violative of freedom of speech and of the press. Justice Murphy, delivering the Court's opinion, declared that the statute was invalid on its face: (1) Freedom of speech and of the press embraces at the least the liberty to discuss publicly and truthfully all matters of public concern without previous restraint or fear of subsequent punishment. (2) The dissemination of information concerning the facts of a labor dispute must be regarded as within the area of free discussion guaranteed by the Constitution. (3) Although the rights of employers and employees are subject to modification or qualification in the public interest, it does not follow that the state, in dealing with the evils arising from industrial disputes, may impair the effective exercise of the right to discuss freely industrial relations that are matters of public concern. (4) Although the state may take adequate steps to preserve the peace and to protect the privacy, the lives, and the property of its people, no clear and present danger of destruction of life or property, or invasion of the right of privacy, can be thought to be inherent in the activities of every person who approaches the premises of an employer and publicizes the facts of a labor dispute. (5) There is not here involved any question of picketing en masse, or otherwise conducted, that might occasion such imminent and aggravated danger to the community interests as to justify a statute narrowly drawn to cover the precise situation out of which the danger arises. *Thornhill v. Alabama*, 310 U.S. 88 (1940).

TIME, INC. v. HILL (1967). In 1952, members of the Hill family were held hostage in their home by some escaped convicts and were ultimately released without harm and without any violence happening. The family later changed residences and tried to discourage publicity about the event. A novel about a hostage incident later appeared and then was made into a play. *Life* magazine published an account of the play, related it to the Hill incident by describing it as a "re-enactment," and used photographs staged in the former Hill home. The Hills then brought suit against *Life*, claiming that the article gave the false impression that the play was based on their experiences; they sued for damages under a New York statute (New York, Civil Rights Law*) that prohibited anyone from using the name or picture of another person for advertising purposes without that person's consent. *Life* magazine maintained that the article dealt with a subject of general interest and was published in good faith.

The Supreme Court, reversing lower court decisions, ruled that damages could be awarded only if malice was present—the *New York Times* Rule* that reckless disregard of whether the information was true or false was present. The Court held that "erroneous statements about a matter of public interest, like the opening of a new play linked to an actual incident, which was the subject of the *Life* article, are inevitable and innocent or merely negligent. [Publications] must be protected if freedoms of expression are to have the breathing space that they need to survive."

Justice Fortas dissented from this view: "The courts may not and must not permit either public or private action that censors or inhibits the press. But part of this responsibility is to preserve values and procedures which assure the ordinary citizen that the press is not above the reach of the law—that its special prerogatives, granted because of its special and vital functions, are reasonably equated with its needs in the performance of these functions. For this Court to totally immunize the press in areas far beyond the needs of news, comment on public persons and events, discussion of public issues and the like would be no service to freedom of the press, but an invitation to public hostility to that freedom. This Court cannot and should not refuse to permit under state law the private citizen who is aggrieved by the type of assault which we have here and which is not within the specially protected core of the First Amendment to recover compensatory damages for recklessly inflicted invasion of his rights." *Time, Inc. v. Hill*, 385 U.S. 374 (1967).

TIME-PLACE-MANNER. "Time, place, and manner" refers to valid restrictions on the exercise of First Amendment rights in public forums/public places.* Such regulations must be reasonable restrictions in order to achieve a legitimate governmental interest. Restrictions that the Supreme Court have found to be valid time-place-manner restrictions include the non-use of military bases for political campaign speeches and the distribution of leaflets (*Greer v. Spock**); zoning requirements to limit the locations where "adult" movies can be exhibited (*Young, Mayor of Detroit v. American Mini Theatres, Inc.**); the ruling that indecent (but not obscene) material should not be broadcast at a time when children are likely to be in the listening audience ("Filthy Words"*). Other valid time-place-manner restrictions include keeping the streets and sidewalks passable for people and traffic and controlling litter and noise. The use of a marching band with dancing elephants to publicize a political candidate is fully protected by the First Amendment; however, it may not be a protected activity at 2:00 A.M. in a residential area.

TIMES FILM CORPORATION v. CITY OF CHICAGO (1961). The Municipal Code of Chicago, § 155-4 (Chicago [IL], Motion Picture Censorship*), required submission of all motion pictures for examination or censorship before their public exhibition and prohibited their exhibition unless they met certain standards. The Times Film Corporation applied for a permit to exhibit the film *Don Juan* and paid the required license fee but refused to submit the film itself to the censorship board for its examination; thus the board refused to issue the required permit. The film was not at issue; the sole reason the permit was denied was because the company refused to submit it along with the application. *Don Juan* was produced in Austria, in 1956, and was a film adaptation of Mozart's opera *Don Giovanni*; it "relates the story of the nobleman, Don Juan, who compulsively conquers and morally humiliates women and their menfolk" (de Grazia and Newman, *Banned Films*, p. 261).†

The Times Film Corporation then brought suit in a federal district court, asking for an order to the board to issue the permit without examining the film and to restrain the city officials from interfering with the film's exhibition. *Don Juan* was not submitted to the district court for examination either. The district court dismissed the complaint; an appeals court affirmed the dismissal; the Supreme Court affirmed the dismissal. In a close decision (5 to 4), the Supreme Court ruled that the provision requiring submission of motion pictures for examination or censorship before their public exhibition was not a violation of the First Amendment. This decision was an important one in the censorship process (Film Censorship*), for it did not deal, as did most other cases, with the standards or reasons for censoring a film; rather, this case dealt with the crux of the process— the requirement of submitting a film for examination or censorship before its exhibition. The Court apparently found this type of prior restraint not a violation of freedom of speech.

Justice Clark delivered the opinion of the majority of the badly divided Court: "Petitioner's narrow attack upon the ordinance does not require that any consideration be given to the validity of the standards set out therein. They are not challenged and are not before us. Prior motion picture censorship cases which reached this Court involved questions of standards. The films had all been submitted to the authorities and permits for their exhibition were refused because of their content. Obviously, whether a particular statute is 'clearly drawn,' or 'vague,' or 'indefinite,' or whether a clear standard is in fact met by a film are different questions involving other constitutional challenges to be tested by con-

†Reprinted from *Banned Films* with permission of the R. R. Bowker Company. Copyright © 1982 by Edward de Grazia and Roger K. Newman.

siderations not here involved. Moreover, there is not a word in the record as to the nature and content of *Don Juan*. We are left entirely in the dark in this regard, as were the city officials and the other reviewing courts. Petitioner claims that the nature of the film is irrelevant, and that even if this film contains the basest type of pornography, or incitement to riot, or forceful overthrow of orderly government, it may nonetheless be shown without prior submission for examination. The challenge here is to the censor's basic authority; it does not go to any statutory standards employed by the censor or procedural requirements as to the submission of the film.

"In this perspective we consider the prior decisions of this Court touching on the problem. Beginning over a third of a century ago in *Gitlow v. New York* (1925),* they have consistently reserved for future decision possible situations in which the claimed First Amendment privilege might have to give way to the necessities of the public welfare. It has never been held that liberty of speech is absolute. Nor has it been suggested that all previous restraints on speech are invalid. On the contrary, in *Near v. Minnesota ex rel. Olson* (1931),* Chief Justice Hughes, in discussing the classic legal statements concerning the immunity of the press from censorship, observed that the principle forbidding previous restraint 'is stated too broadly, if every such restraint is deemed to be prohibited. The protection even as to previous restraint is not absolutely unlimited. But the limitation has been recognized only in exceptional cases.' These included, the Chief Justice found, utterances creating 'a hindrance' to the Government's war effort, and 'actual obstruction to its recruiting service or the publication of the sailing dates of transports or the number and location of troops.' In addition, the Court said that 'the primary requirements of decency may be enforced against obscene publications' and the 'security of the community life may be protected against incitements to acts of violence and the overthrow by force of orderly government.'

"Some years later, a unanimous Court, speaking through Mr. Justice Murphy, in *Chaplinsky v. New Hampshire* (1942),* held that there were 'certain well-defined and narrowly limited classes of speech, the prevention and punishment of which have never been thought to raise any Constitutional problem. These include the lewd and obscene, the profane, the libelous, and the insulting or fighting words—those which by their very utterance inflict injury or tend to incite an immediate breach of the peace.' Thereafter, as we have mentioned, in [*The Miracle* case], we found motion pictures to be within the guarantees of the First and Fourteenth Amendments, but we added that this was 'not the end of our problem. It does not follow that the Constitution requires absolute freedom to exhibit every motion picture of every kind at all times and all places.' Five years later, in *Roth v. United States* (1957),* we held that 'in light of history, it is apparent that the unconditional phrasing of the First Amendment was not intended to protect every utterance.' Even those in dissent there found that 'Freedom of expression can be suppressed if, and to the extent that, it is so closely brigaded with illegal action as to be an inseparable part of it.' And . . .

in [the "Nights of Horror"* case], after characterizing *Near* as 'one of the landmark opinions' in its area, we took notice that *Near* 'left no doubts that liberty of speech, and of the press, is also not an absolute right . . . the protection even as to previous restraint is not absolutely limited.' . . .

"Petitioner would have us hold that the public exhibition of motion pictures must be allowed under any circumstances. The State's sole remedy, it says, is the invocation of criminal process under the Illinois pornography statute (Ill. Rev. State. [1959], c. 38, § 470), and then only after a transgression. But this position, as we have seen, is founded upon the claim of absolute privilege against prior restraint under the First Amendment—a claim without sanction in our cases. To illustrate its fallacy, we need only point to one of the 'exceptional cases' which Chief Justice Hughes enumerated in *Near*, namely, 'the primary requirements of decency [that] may be enforced against obscene publications.' Moreover, we later held specifically 'that obscenity is not within the area of constitutionally protected speech or press' (*Roth*). Chicago emphasizes here its duty to protect its people against the dangers of obscenity in the public exhibition of motion pictures. To this argument petitioner's only answer is that regardless of the capacity for, or extent of, such an evil, previous restraint cannot be justified. With this we cannot agree. We recognized that 'capacity for evil may be relevant in determining the permissible scope of community control,' and that motion pictures were not 'necessarily subject to the precise rules governing any other particular method of expression.' Each method . . . tends to present its own peculiar problems."

Justice Clark and the majority thus ruled in a seven-page opinion that although motion pictures are included within the free speech and free press guarantees of the First Amendment, there is no absolute freedom to exhibit publicly, at least once, every kind of motion picture. The minority view filed a twenty-eight-page dissent; it was written by Chief Justice Warren and joined by Justices Douglas, Black, and Brennan. Chief Justice Warren: "The decision presents a real danger of eventual censorship for every form of communication, be it newspapers, journals, books, magazines, television, radio or public speeches. The Court purports to leave these questions for another day, but I am aware of no constitutional principle which permits us to hold that the communication of ideas through one medium may be censored while other media are immune. Of course each medium presents its own peculiar problems, but they are not of the kind which would authorize the censorship of one form of communication and not others. I submit that at arriving at its decision the Court has interpreted our cases contrary to the intention at the time of their rendition and, in exalting the censor of motion pictures, has endangered the First and Fourteenth Amendment rights of all others engaged in the dissemination of ideas. . . . The censor is beholden to those who sponsored the creation of his office, to those who are most radically preoccupied with the suppression of communication. The censor's function is to restrict and to restrain; his decisions are insulated from the pressures that might be brought to bear by public sentiment if the public were given an opportunity to see that which the censor has curbed. The censor performs free from all of the procedural safeguards afforded litigants in a court of law. The likelihood of a fair and impartial trial disappears when the censor is both prosecutor and judge. There is a complete absence of rules of evidence; the fact is that there is usually no evidence at all. . . . The Court, in no way, explains why moving pictures should be treated differently than any other form of expression, why moving pictures should be denied the protection against censorship. . . . When pressed during oral argument, counsel for the city could make no meaningful distinction between the censorship of newspapers and motion pictures. . . . But, even if the impact of the motion picture is greater than that of some other media, that fact constitutes no basis for the argument that motion pictures should be subject to greater suppression. This is the traditional argument made in the censor's behalf; this is the argument advanced against newspapers at the time of the invention of the printing press. The argument was ultimately rejected in England, and has consistently been held to be contrary to our Constitution. No compelling reason has been predicated for accepting the contention now." *Times Film Corporation v. City of Chicago*, 365 U.S. 43 (1961).

TINKER v. DES MOINES SCHOOL DISTRICT (1969). Three public school pupils in Des Moines, Iowa, were suspended from school for wearing black arm bands as a symbolic protest against the government's policy in Viet Nam. The students then brought suit, seeking an injunction against the regulation passed by the school board banning the wearing of arm bands. A federal district court and an appeals court dismissed the students' complaint; the Supreme Court, however, was more sympathetic and ruled that the wearing of the arm bands was symbolic speech protected by the First Amendment. Justice Fortas delivered the opinion of the Court: "It does not concern aggressive, disruptive action or even group demonstrations. Our problem involves direct, primary First Amendment rights akin to 'pure speech.' The school officials banned and sought to punish petitioners for a silent, passive expression of opinion, unaccompanied by any disorder or disturbance on the part of petitioners. There is here no evidence whatever of petitioners' interference, actual or nascent, with the schools' work or of collision with the rights of other students to be secure and to be let alone. Accordingly, this case does not concern speech or action that intrudes upon the work of the schools or the rights of other students. . . . In our system, state-operated schools may not be enclaves of totalitarianism. School officials do not possess absolute authority over their students. Students in school as well as out of school are 'persons' under our Constitution. They are possessed of fundamental rights which the State must respect, just as they themselves must respect their obligations to the State. In our system, students may not be regarded as closed-circuit recipients of only that which the State chooses to communicate. They may not be confined to the expression of those sentiments that are officially approved. In the absence of a specific showing of constitutionally valid reasons to regulate their speech, students are entitled to freedom of expression of their views. As Judge Gewin, speaking for the Fifth Circuit, said, school officials cannot suppress 'expressions of feelings with which they do not wish to contend' (*Burnside v. Byars**). . . . Under our Constitution, free speech is not a right that is given only to be so circumscribed that it exists in principle but not in fact. Freedom of expression would not truly exist if the right could be exercised only in an area that a benevolent government has provided as a safe haven for crackpots. The Constitution says that Congress (and the States) may not abridge the right to free speech. This provision means what it says. We properly read it to permit reasonable regulation of speech-connected activities in carefully restricted circumstances. But we do not confine the permissible exercise of First Amendment rights to a telephone booth or the four corners of a pamphlet, or to supervised and ordained discussion in a school classroom.''

In a very, very uncharacteristic opinion, Justice Black dissented on the grounds that the majority's decision meant that teachers, parents, and elected school officials were surrendering control of the school system to the students—the inmates would have control of the asylum—and all the public school systems would now be subject to the whims and caprices of their loudest-mouthed, but maybe not their brightest, students. Justice Black's dissent: ''And I repeat that if the time has come when pupils of state-supported schools, kindergartens, grammar schools, or high schools, can defy and flout orders of school officials to keep their minds on their own schoolwork, it is the beginning of a new revolutionary era of permissiveness in this country fostered by the judiciary. . . . I deny that it has been the 'unmistakable holding of this Court for almost 50 years' that 'students' and 'teachers' take with them into the 'schoolhouse gate' constitutional rights to 'freedom of speech or expression.' The truth is that a teacher of kindergarten, grammar school, or high school pupils no more carries into a school with him a complete right to freedom of speech and expression than an anti-Catholic or anti-Semite carries with him a complete freedom of speech and religion into a Catholic church or Jewish synagogue. Nor does a person carry with him into the United States Senate or House or into the Supreme Court, or any other court, a complete constitutional right to go into those places contrary to their rules and speak his mind on any subject he pleases. It is a myth to say that any person has a constitutional right to say what he pleases, where he pleases, and when he pleases. Our Court has decided precisely the opposite. . . .

''In my view, teachers in state-controlled public schools are hired to teach there. Although Mr. Justice McReynolds may have intimated to the contrary in *Meyer v. Nebraska*,* certainly a teacher is not paid to go into school and teach subjects the State does not hire him to teach as part of its selected curriculum. Nor are public school students sent to the schools at public expense to broadcast political or other views to educate and inform the public. The original idea of schools, which I do not believe is yet abandoned as worthless or out of date, was that children had not yet reached the point of experience and wisdom which enabled them to teach all of their elders. It may be that the Nation has outworn the old-fashioned slogan that 'children are to be seen and not heard,' but one may, I hope, be permitted to harbor the thought that taxpayers send children to school on the premise that at their age they need to learn, not teach. . . .

"Change has been said to be truly the law of life but sometimes the old and the tried and true are worth holding. The schools of this Nation have undoubtedly contributed to giving us tranquility and to making us a more law-abiding people. Uncontrolled and uncontrollable liberty is an enemy to domestic peace. We cannot close our eyes to the fact that some of the country's greatest problems are crimes committed by the youth, too many of school age. School discipline, like parental discipline, is an integral and important part of training our children to be good citizens—to be better citizens. Here a very small number of students have crisply and summarily refused to obey a school order designed to give pupils who want to learn the opportunity to do so. One does not need to be a prophet or the son of a prophet to know that after the Court's holding today some students in Iowa schools and indeed in all schools will be ready, able, and willing to defy their teachers on practically all orders. This is the more unfortunate for the schools since groups of students all over the land are already running loose, conducting break-ins, sit-ins, lie-ins, and smash-ins. Many of these student groups, as is all too familiar to all who read the newspapers, have already engaged in rioting, property seizures, and destruction. They have picketed schools to force students not to cross their picket lines and have too often violently attacked earnest but frightened students who wanted an education that the pickets did not want them to get. Students engaged in such activities are apparently confident that they know far more about how to operate public school systems than do their parents, teachers, and elected school officials.

"It is no answer to say that the particular students here [Tinker] have not yet reached such high points in their demands to attend classes in order to exercise their political pressures. Turned loose with lawsuits for damages and injunctions against their teachers as they are here, it is nothing but wishful thinking to imagine that young, immature students will not soon believe it is their right to control the schools rather than the right of the States that collect the taxes to hire the teachers for the benefit of the pupils. This case, therefore, wholly without constitutional reasons in my judgment, subjects all the public schools in the country to the whims and caprices of their loudest-mouthed, but maybe not their brightest, students. I, for one, am not fully persuaded that school pupils are wise enough, even with this Court's expert help from Washington, to run the 23,390 public school systems in our 50 States. I wish, therefore, wholly to disclaim any purpose on my part to hold that the Federal Constitution compels the teachers, parents, and elected school officials to surrender control of the American public school system to public school students. I dissent." *Tinker v. Des Moines School District*, 393 U.S. 503 (1969).

TITICUT FOLLIES. In 1969, the Supreme Judicial Court of Massachusetts prevented the showing of the film *Titicut Follies* to any audience whatsoever except audiences of a specialized or professional character having a serious interest in the content of the film. This case really was a clash between two honorable objectives: the right of free speech and of the press against the right of individual privacy; the Massachusetts courts attempted to reconcile the two. De Grazia and Newman (*Banned Films*, p. 313) describe *Titicut Follies*: "This film is a documentary on the conditions in a state prison for the criminally insane at Bridgewater, Massachusetts, with scenes of a musical show put on by and for the inmates and the staff before and after the filming of several incidents of the inmates' lives in the prison. The film shows detailed close-ups of such episodes as the forced nose-feeding of an inmate on a hunger strike and his later death and burial; the explosive reaction of an inmate to repeated taunting by correction officers about his failure to keep his cell clean; the degrading process of subjecting inmates to stripping off their clothes publicly for a skin search conducted by correction officers for the purpose of discovering contraband; the questioning by a staff psychiatrist of a young paranoid husband and father committed for sex attacks on children; and the unhappy protests of a young, articulate schizophrenic to the effect that after one and a half years as an inmate he is being driven insane by the surroundings and the poor treatment or lack of treatment by the staff."†

The film was produced and directed by Frederick Wiseman. None of the scenes shown were staged or simulated—it was an accurate portrayal of the institution and the behavior of its inmates and staff. The following discussion of *Titicut Follies* comes from the Massachusetts Supreme Judicial Court's decision in *Commonwealth v. Wiseman* (249 N.E. 2d 610 [1969]). In 1965, Wiseman first requested permission from the superintendent and from the commissioner to make an educational documentary film concerning Bridgewater, but his request was denied. On January 28, 1966, permission was granted, subject to the receipt of a favorable opinion from the Massachusetts attorney general that the officials could grant permission and subject to four conditions: "(1) that the rights of the inmates and patients would be fully protected; (2) that there would be used only photographs of inmates and patients legally competent to sign releases; (3) that a written release would be obtained from each patient whose photograph is used in the film; and (4) that the film would not be released without first having been approved by the Commissioner and Superintendent." Attorney General Brooke gave his favorable ruling on March 21, 1966, and Wiseman began filming at Bridgewater in April 1966. Wiseman's film crew was given free access to all departments except the treatment center for the sexually dangerous, whose director made "strong objections" in writing to any photography there without compliance with explicit written conditions.

In three months, some 80,000 feet of film were exposed. Pictures were made of "mentally incompetent patients in the nude and in the most personal and private situations." The superintendent first saw the film on June 1, 1967, and objected "to the excessive nudity." The then attorney general, Elliot Richardson, also saw the film and raised several questions. At a conference in September 1967, Attorney General Richardson told Wiseman "that in his opinion the film constituted an invasion of the privacy of the inmates shown in the film; that mentally incompetent patients were shown . . . and that the releases, if any, obtained were not valid." The commissioner, on September 22, 1967, informed Wiseman "that the film could not be shown in its present form." But Wiseman had made an agreement with Grove Press to distribute the film, and *Titicut Follies* was exhibited to the public for profit in the fall of 1967; the state of Massachusetts then brought suit against Wiseman.

The trial court issued an injunction against the exhibition of the film and laid a "constructive trust" (as did the U.S. government against the profits of the book *Decent Interval* [*Snepp v. United States**]) against any profits that Wiseman might have realized from the film's exhibition. The trial judge commented that Wiseman requested permission to film under false pretenses: Wiseman had indicated that he planned a documentary about three people—an adult inmate, a youthful offender, and a correctional officer—and that the film would be "an effort to illustrate the various services performed—custodial, punitive, rehabilitative, and medical." The trial judge concluded, however, that although the film was to be "non-commercial and non-sensational . . . it was crass commercialism, a most flagrant abuse of the privilege [given], and instead of a public service project, the film was to be shown to the general public in movie houses."

The trial judge cited some examples of the alleged invasions of privacy: "The film is a hodge-podge of sequences depicting mentally ill patients engaged in repetitive, incoherent, and obscene rantings/the film is excessively preoccupied with nudity/naked inmates are shown desperately attempting to hide their privates with their hands/there is a scene of a priest administrating the last rites of the church to a dying patient and the preparation of the corpse for burial/a patient, grossly deformed by congenital brain damage, is paraded before the camera." The trial judge ruled (1) that the releases "as may have been obtained from the inmates are a nullity"; (2) that the film is an "unwarranted intrusion into the right of privacy of each inmate pictured, degrading these persons in a manner clearly not warranted by any legitimate public concern"; (3) that the "right of the public to know" does not justify the unauthorized use of pictures showing identifiable persons "in such a manner as to cause humiliation"; (4) that it was the responsibility of the state to "protect the inmates against any such exploitation"; and (5) that the state was under the "obligation to protect the right of privacy of those committed to its custody."

The trial judge did not impose a constructive trust on the profits already realized, and the state of Massachusetts was not pleased with this. The state appealed the decision to the Massachusetts Supreme Judicial Court in order to affirm the entire decision of the trial judge and to seek the constructive trust; the state did not receive what it wanted. Judge Cutter delivered the opinion:

"That injunctive relief may be granted against showing the film to the general public on a commercial basis does not mean that all showings of the film must be prevented. . . . The film gives a striking picture of life at Bridgewater and of the problems affecting treatment at that or any similar institution. It is a film which would be instructive to legislators, judges, lawyers, sociologists, social workers, doctors, psychiatrists, students in these or related fields, and organizations dealing with the social problems of custodial care and mental infirmity. The public interest in having such persons informed about Bridgewater, in our opinion, outweighs any countervailing interests of the inmates and of the Commonwealth (as *parens patriae*) in anonymity and privacy. The effect upon inmates of showing the film to persons with a serious interest in rehabilitation, and with potential capacity to be helpful, is likely to be very different from the effect of its exhibition merely to satisfy general public curiosity. There is possibility that showings to specialized audiences may be of benefit to the public interest, to the inmates themselves, and to the conduct of an important State institution. Because of the character of such audiences, the likelihood of humiliation, even of identifiable inmates, is greatly reduced. In any event the likelihood of harm seems to us less than the probability of benefits. . . . Mr. Wiseman, or those claiming through him [Grove Press], may make a charge for the use of the film, so far as showing it may be permitted by the modified degree [but] . . . a constructive trust will not be placed upon receipts for past showings of the film to general audiences."

This compromise of interests—the balancing of the First Amendment with the individual's right of privacy—was not accepted by Wiseman, and he appealed to the U.S. Supreme Court (*Wiseman v. Massachusetts*, 398 U.S. 960 [1970]). The Supreme Court refused to hear the appeal—only Justices Harlan, Brennan, and Douglas were willing to review it—thus affirming the compromise reached by the Massachusetts court. In a dissent filed from the Court's refusal to hear the case, Justice Harlan went to the crux of the matter: *Titicut Follies* "is at once a scathing indictment of the inhumane conditions that prevailed at the time of the film and an undeniable infringement of the privacy of the inmates filmed, who are shown nude and engaged in acts that would unquestionably embarrass an individual of normal sensitivity." The film highlighted the conflict "between the constitutional commitment to the principle that debate on public issues should be uninhibited, robust, and wide-open and the individual's interest in privacy and dignity."

TOLEDO NEWSPAPER CO. v. UNITED STATES (1918). This case concerned a contempt of court judgment against the Toledo Newspaper Co. for publishing, during an ongoing dispute, what a judge thought were uncomplimentary comments. The facts of the case were as follows: "One of the usual controversies between a street railroad and the city that it served had been going on for years and had culminated in an ordinance establishing three cent fares that was to go into effect on March 28th, 1914. In January of the year the people who were operating the [rail]road began a suit for an injunction on the ground that the ordinance was confiscatory. The plaintiffs, a newspaper and its editor, had long been on the popular side and had furnished news and comment to sustain it; and when, on March 24, a motion was made for a temporary injunction in the suit, they published a cartoon representing the [rail]road as a moribund man in bed with its friends at the bedside and one of them saying 'Guess we'd better call in Doc Killits.' Thereafter pending the controversy they published news, comment and cartoons as before. The injunction was issued on September 12. The Judge (Killits) who was referred took no steps until September 29, when he directed an information to be filed covering publications from March 24 through September 17. This was done on October 28. In December the case was tried summarily without a jury by the judge [Killits] who thought his authority contemned, and in the following year he imposed a considerable fine.''

The Court then asked itself whether it had acted within its powers under the statutes of the United States. The answer was that yes, indeed, Judge Killits had acted within his powers, and the Supreme Court upheld the contempt of court fine levied against the newspaper. The Supreme Court made the following comments: (1) The test of the power to punish for contempt is in the character of the acts in question; when their direct tendency is to prevent or obstruct the free and unprejudiced exercise of the judicial power, they are subject to be restrained through summary contempt proceedings. (2) Newspaper publications concerning injunction proceedings pending in a district court, and tending in the circumstances to create the impression that a particular decision would evoke public suspicion of the judge's integrity or fairness and bring him into public odium and would be met by public resistance, and tending in the circumstances to provoke such resistance in fact, are contemptuous, rendering the company owning the paper and its editor subject to summary conviction and punishment. (3) Such ''wrongful'' publications are not within the guarantee of freedom of the press. (4) As it is the reasonable tendency for such publications that determines their contemptuous character, it was irrelevant that they were not circulated in the courtroom or seen by the judge or that they did not influence his mind. This ''reasonable tendency'' test has since been overtaken by the ''clear and present danger'' test in deciding whether or not certain publications or statements interfere with the judicial process. *Toledo Newspaper Co. v. United States*, 247 U.S. 402 (1918).

TRENTON (NJ), SOUND TRUCKS. Ordinance No. 430 of the City of Trenton read as follows: ''That it shall be unlawful for any person, firm or corporation, either as principal, agent or employee, to play, use or operate for advertising purposes, or for any other purpose whatsoever, on or upon the public streets, alleys or thoroughfares in the City of Trenton, any device known as a sound truck, loud speaker or sound amplifier, or any other instrument known as a calliope or any instrument of any kind or character which emits therefrom loud and raucous noises and is attached to and upon any vehicle operated or standing upon said streets or public places aforementioned.'' Although the phrase ''loud and raucous noises'' was not as precise as some members of the Supreme Court would have liked, this ordinance was upheld by the Court in *Kovacs v. Cooper* (1949).*

TROPIC OF CANCER/TROPIC OF CAPRICORN. First published in Paris, in 1934, Henry Miller's *Tropic of Cancer*, along with his 1938 *Tropic of Capricorn*, was subject to censorship in the United States for thirty years; U.S. Customs first banned *Tropic of Cancer* in 1934 and it was not until 1964 that the Supreme Court ruled that the book was not obscene. U.S. Customs regulations (Tariff Act*) allow the Customs Service to seize any imported material that they consider to be obscene and then apply for a judicial determination as to the material's obscenity. *Tropic of Cancer* was seized in 1934, the court ruled the book obscene, the copies were destroyed, and until 1961, when Grove Press published an American edition of the book, the book became a standard item of contraband; U.S. tourists returning from Paris would have copies hidden under their raincoats or sewn into the linings of their suitcases, hoping that the Customs Service would not take them for drug smugglers and search their bags and find the prohibited books. This Customs ban on the importation of the books was upheld and reaffirmed in 1953, when the Customs Service did nab one unfortunate miscreant—he was caught with *Tropic of Cancer* and *Tropic of Capricorn*—and a U.S. district court ruled again that the books were obscene.

The literary smuggler appealed the decision to an appeals court (*Besig v. United States*, 208 F. 2d 142 [1953]), but the court ruled that Henry Miller's writings will ''incite to disgusting practices and to hideous crime.'' Judge Stephens delivered the following review of the books: ''The word 'obscene' is not uncommon and is used in English and American speech and writings as the word symbol for indecent, smutty, lewd or salacious reference to parts of the human or animal body or to their functions or to the excrement therefrom. Each of *The Tropics* is written in the composite style of a novel-autobiography, and the author as a character in the book carries the reader as though he himself is living in disgrace, degradation, poverty, mean crime, and prostitution of mind and body. The vehicle of description is the unprintable word of the debased and morally bankrupt. Practically everything that the world loosely regards as sin is detailed in the vivid, lurid, salacious language of smut, prostitution, and dirt. And all of it is related without the slightest expressed idea of its abandon. Consistent with the general tenor of the books, even human excrement is dwelt upon in the dirtiest words available. The author conducts the reader through sex orgies and perversions of the sex organs, and always in the debased language of the bawdy house. Nothing has the grace of purity and goodness. These words of the language of smut, and the disgraceful scenes, are so heavily larded throughout the books that those portions which are deemed to be of literary merit do not lift the reader's mind clear of their sticky slime. And it is safe to say that the 'literary merit' of the books carries the reader deeper into it. For this reason, *The Tropics* are far more dangerous than *Confessions of a Prostitute*. . . . There, the scenes depicted are obscene because of the scene itself which in its stark ugliness might well repel many. *The Tropics* lure on with the cleverness of scene, skillfulness of recital, and the use of worse than gutter words. . . . It is claimed that these books are not for the immature of mind, and that adults read them for their literary and informative merits, but, whether true or untrue, we cannot measure their importability by such a yardstick. The Congress probably saw the impracticality of preventing the use of the books by the young and the pure. And of course they knew that salacious print in the hands of adults, even in the hands of those whose sun is near the western horizon, may well incite to disgusting practices and to hideous crime.''

The smuggling had to continue until 1961, when Grove Press published the first U.S. edition of *Tropic of Cancer*. This led to an immediate nationwide controversy, for it was seen by many as the beginning of the breakdown of U.S. society by allowing the ''disgusting practices'' of Paris to enter the hearts and minds of Americans. There were many court cases against the books, most notably in California, Florida, Massachusetts, New York, and Wisconsin. *Tropic of Cancer* was, however, found *not* to be obscene in Wisconsin (*McCauley v. Tropic of Cancer*, 121 N.W. 2d 545 [1963]) and in California (*Zeitlin v. Arnebergh*, 383 P. 2d 152 [1963]). A Massachusetts trial court found the book obscene, for it was ''filthy, disgusting, nauseating and offensive to good taste— of the 318 pages of the book, there are sex episodes on 85 pages, some of which are described on two or more pages, and all of which are described with precise physical detail and four-letter words. The author's descriptive powers are truly impressive and he rises to great literary heights when he describes Paris. And suddenly he descends into the filthy gutter.''

Judge Goldberg concluded that the book was ''impure,'' but his decision was reversed by the Massachusetts Supreme Judicial Court (*Attorney General v. The Book Named Tropic of Cancer*, 184 N.E. 2d 328 [1962]). Judge Cutter held that the novel, portraying the experiences of an aspiring American writer who lived a down-and-out life in Paris, was ''the result of a conscious effort to create a work of literary art, it had significance, it was not obscene, and it was entitled to the protection of the First Amendment.'' Judge Cutter did not speak for a unanimous court, however; some Massachusetts judges were not impressed with the book: ''The book is pitched at the nadir of scatology. Indeed, its low level is relied upon as engulfing all obscene effect. We cannot bring ourselves to accept the thesis that the book . . . becomes endowed with constitutional protection. . . . It should be classified as pornography.''

In New York, the book was involved in a prosecution under a statute that prohibited the sale of any obscene book, and the New York Court of Appeals (*People v. Fritch*, 192 N.E. 2d 713 [1963]) ruled that *Tropic of Cancer* was obscene. Judge Desmond: ''If this book had not been written by a recognized author, if it did not contain some 'good writing' and if it were not approved by well-known reviewers, no one, I venture, would deny that it is obscene by any conceivable definition, narrow or tolerant. Its own cover blurb boasts of its 'unbridled obscenity.' From first to last page it is a filthy, cynical, disgusting narrative of sordid amours. Not only is there in it no word or suggestion of the romantic, sentimental, poetic or spiritual aspects of the sex relation, but it is not even bawdy sex or comic sex or sex described with vulgar good humor. No glory, no beauty, no stars—just mud. The whole book is 'sick sexuality,' a deliberate, studied exercise in the depiction of sex relations as debasing, filthy and revolting.''

Judge Dye of the New York Court of Appeals was a bit more sensitive: ''This so-called 'obscenity case' and those that preceded it all call to mind the book burning of eighteenth-century Europe and New England which fortunately did not stop the forces of the inquisitive and curious minds for long but, as might well have been expected and as we are now witnessing, released forces which today are demanding attention throughout the democracies of the world. To hold this book obscene necessarily places one in the role of the censor, a role which is incompatible with the fundamentals of a free society.''

The book was also judged to be obscene in Florida—a book ''into which filth was packed''—in *Grove Press v. Gerstein* (156 So. 2d 537 [1963]), and it was this Florida decision through which *Tropic of Cancer* finally reached the U.S. Supreme Court (*Grove Press, Inc. v. Gerstein, State Attorney*, 378 U.S. 577 [1964]). The Supreme Court granted certiorari, and by the barest of margins (5 [Justices Black, Brennan, Douglas, Goldberg, Stewart] to 4 [Chief Justice Warren and Justices Clark, Harlan, White]) in a per curiam opinion—there were no opinions given—the Supreme Court reversed the Florida finding and simply ruled that *Tropic of Cancer* was not obscene.

TUCKER v. TEXAS (1946). As the court record in the Justice Court of Medina County, Texas, relates, Tucker was charged with and found guilty of violating Article 479, Chap. 3 of the Texas Penal Code, Trespassing, which makes it an offense for any ''peddler or hawker of goods or merchandise willfully to refuse to leave premises after having been notified to do so by the owner or possessor thereof.'' Tucker argued that he was not a ''peddler'' or a ''hawker'' of merchandise, but a minister of the gospel engaged in the distribution of religious literature to willing recipients and that to apply the Texas statute would be a violation of his First Amendment guarantees of free speech and free press (and religion).

The Texas courts rejected his argument, but on appeal, the Supreme Court reversed. Justice Black, before giving the Court's opinion, first recited some additional information: ''[Tucker] is an ordained minister of the group known as Jehovah's Witnesses. In accordance with the practices of this group he calls on people from door to door, presents his religious views to those willing to listen, and distributes religious literature to those willing to receive it. In the course of his work, he went to the Hondo Navigation Village located in Medina County, Texas. The village is owned by the United States under a Congressional program which was designed to provide housing for persons engaged in National Defense activities (42 U.S.C. §§ 1521-1553). According to all indications the village was freely accessible and open to the public and had all the characteristics of a typical American town. The Federal Public Housing Authority had placed the buildings in charge of a manager whose duty it was to rent the houses, collect the rents, and generally to supervise operations, subject to over-all control by the Authority. He ordered [Tucker] to discontinue all religious activities in the village. Appellant refused. Later the manager orderd [Tucker] to leave the village. Insisting that the manager had no right to suppress religious activities, appellant declined to leave, and his arrest followed. At the trial the manager testified that the controlling Federal agency had given him full authority to regulate the conduct of those living in the village, and that he did not allow preaching by ministers of any denomination without a permit issued by him in his discretion. He thought this broad authority was entrusted to him, at least in part, by a regulation, which the Authority's Washington office had allegedly promulgated. He testified that this regulation provided that no peddlers or hawkers could come into or remain in the village without getting permission from the manager.''

The Court reversed Tucker's conviction for about the same reasons given in *Marsh v. Alabama*,* in which the managers of a company town attempted to prevent all distribution of religious literature within the town or conditioned the distribution on a permit issued at the discretion of the town's managers. Even though the town in Texas was "owned" by the U.S. government, it still had all the characteristics of a typical U.S. town, freely accessible and open to the public, and thus the Texas statute could not be applied in Tucker's case. *Tucker v. Texas*, 326 U.S. 517 (1946).

U

ULYSSES. U.S. Customs regulations (Tariff Act*) allow the Customs Service to seize any imported material that they deem to be "obscene" or "indecent." Customs then must bring the matter to the federal courts for a judicial determination as to its obscenity; if the court rules it not to be obscene or indecent, the material may then be imported into the United States; if the material is seen to be obscene, Customs is then mandated to destroy the material. In 1934, in accordance with the Tariff Act, a Customs collector seized *Ulysses*, the classic novel written by James Joyce, and attempted to have the courts rule it obscene so as to destroy the copies. The claimant was Random House, Inc., the U.S. publisher of James Joyce. Random House intervened in the suit and claimed that the book was not obscene and thus should be admitted freely into the United States. The case came before Judge Woolsey, whose decision became a landmark case in the history of censorship of obscenity: Judge Woolsey reacted against the current standard known as the Hicklin Rule*—an entire publication is obscene if isolated passages could corrupt the most susceptible mind that might come into contact with the book—and substituted the Ulysses Standard*—a book has to be evaluated, not in terms of a few isolated passages, but according to its dominant, overall effect on people of average sensitivities. The Ulysses Standard has really not been overruled; it has only been refined by later decisions and standards by the Supreme Court (Roth Standard*/Memoirs Standard*/Miller Standard*).

Judge Woolsey made his decision at the district court level and found that the book, taken as a whole, "did not tend to excite sexual impulses or lustful thoughts but that its net effect . . . was only that of a somewhat tragic and very powerful commentary on the inner lives of men and women." He then issued a decree adjudging *Ulysses* not to be obscene and thus eligible for admittance into the United States. Judge Woolsey made the following comments: "It may be that *Ulysses* will not last as a substantial contribution to literature, and it is certainly easy to believe that, in spite of the opinion of Joyce's laudators, the immortals will still reign, but the same thing may be said of current works of art and music and of many other serious efforts of the mind. Art certainly cannot advance under compulsion to traditional forms, and nothing in such a field is more stifling to progress than limitation of the right to experiment with a new technique. The foolish judgments of Lord Eldon about one hundred years ago, proscribing the works of Byron and Southey, and the finding by the jury under a charge by Lord Denman that the publication of Shelley's *Queen Mab* was an indictable offense are a warning to all who have to determine the limits of the field within which authors may exercise themselves. We think that *Ulysses* is a book of originality and sincerity of treatment and that it has not the effect of promoting lust.''

The U.S. government was not happy with this decision and appealed Judge Woolsey's ruling to an appeals court (*United States v. One Book Entitled Ulysses*, 72 F. 2d 705 [1934]), but Woolsey's ruling was left intact by the court of appeals. The court of appeals was not unanimous, however; the following two opinions reflect the differences. The first is by Judge Hand, who agreed with Woolsey's scrapping of the Hicklin Rule; the second is by Judge Manton, who felt that the reading public still required a censor to tell them what was acceptable literature and what was not acceptable. Judge Hand: ''James Joyce, the author of *Ulysses*, may be regarded as a pioneer among those writers who have adopted the 'stream of consciousness' method of presenting fiction, which has attracted considerable attention in academic and literary circles. In this field *Ulysses* is rated as a book of considerable power by persons whose opinions are entitled to weight. Indeed it has become a sort of contemporary classic, dealing with a new subject-matter. It attempts to depict the thoughts and lay bare the souls of a number of people, some of them intellectuals and some social outcasts and nothing more, with a literalism that leaves nothing unsaid. Certain of its passages are of beauty and undoubted distinction, while others are of a vulgarity that is extreme and the book as a whole has a realism characteristic of the present age. It is supposed to portray the thoughts of the principal characters during a period of about eighteen hours. We may discount the laudation of *Ulysses* by some of its admirers and reject the view that it will permanently stand among the great works of literature, but it is fair to say that it is a sincere portrayal with skillful artistry of the 'streams of consciousness' of all men and perhaps of only those of a morbid type, it seems to be sincere, truthful, relevant to the subject, and executed with real art. Joyce, in the words of *Paradise Lost*, has dealt with 'things unattempted yet in prose or rime'—with things that very likely might better have remained 'unattempted'—but his book shows originality and is a work of symmetry and excellent craftmanship of a sort. The question before us is whether such a book of artistic merit and scientific insight should be regarded as 'obscene' within section 305 (a) of the Tariff Act . . . [and the answer is 'no'].''

Judge Manton thought the only role of literature was to ''purify'' or ''ennoble'' the life of people, and he obviously regarded *Ulysses* as obscene. Judge Manton: ''Congress passed this statute against obscenity for the protection of the great mass of our people; the unusual literator can, or thinks he can, protect himself. The people do not exist for the sake of literature, to give the author fame, the publisher wealth, and the book a market. On the contrary, literature exists for the sake of the people, to refresh the weary, to console the sad, to hearten the dull and downcast, to increase man's interest in the world, his joy of living, and his sympathy in all sorts and conditions of men. Art for art's sake is heartless and soon grows artless; art for the public market is not art at all, but commerce; art for the people's service is a noble, vital, and permanent element of human life. The public is content with the standard of salability; the prigs with the standard of preciosity. The people need and deserve a moral standard; it should be a point of honor with men of letters to maintain it. Masterpieces have never been produced by men given to obscenity or lustful thoughts—men who have no Master. Reverence for good work is the foundation of literary character. A refusal to imitate obscenity or to load a book with it is an author's professional chastity. Good work in literature has its permanent mark; it is like all good work, noble and lasting. It requires a human aim—to cheer, console, purify, or ennoble the life of people. Without this aim, literature has never sent an arrow close to the mark. It is by good work only that men of letters can justify their right to a place in the world. Under the authoritative decisions and considering the substance involved in this appeal, it is my opinion that the decree should be reversed.''

James Joyce's *Ulysses* has since become a classic of English literature, and the number of university students over the past twenty years or so who have not been assigned the book are few and far between.

ULYSSES STANDARD. The concept of obscenity* has produced a variety of views from the courts, and there has been some difficulty in arriving at a unanimous and permanent definition of the term. It has been far easier for the courts to decide what obscenity is not than to decide what it is (e.g., sex and obscenity are not synonymous, nor is nudity alone synonymous with obscenity). The Hicklin Rule* was announced in 1868, in Great Britain, by Lord Chief Justice Cockburn. In dealing with a pamphlet entitled *The Confessional Unmasked*, Cockburn announced in *Regina v. Hicklin* (L.R. 3 Q.B. 360 [1868]): "The test of obscenity is this, whether the tendency of the matter charged as obscenity is to deprave and corrupt those whose minds are open to such immoral influences and into whose hands a publication of this sort may fall.''

This guide became the standard for practically all obscenity cases in Great Britain and in the United States. The Hicklin Rule basically declared a publication to be obscene if isolated passages (not the work taken as a whole) could "corrupt" the most susceptible person who might read it. One of the most trenchant comments on the Hicklin Rule was given by Judge Curtis Bok: "Strictly applied, this rule renders any book unsafe, since a moron could pervert to some sexual fantasy to which his mind is open the listings of a seed catalogue.'' The Hicklin Rule was in effect until 1934, when, in the *Ulysses** case (*United States v. One Book Entitled Ulysses*), Judge Woolsey formulated the "Ulysses" standard. Reacting against the Hicklin Rule, Woolsey ruled that obscenity was to be determined by the effect of a book read in its entirety on a person with average sex instincts: "We think the same immunity should apply to literature as to science, where the presentation, when viewed objectively, is sincere, and the erotic matter is not introduced to promote lust and does not furnish the dominant note of the publication. The question in each case is whether a publication taken as a whole has a libidinous effect.'' This standard has not been overruled; it has only been made more precise by the subsequent decisions in *Roth v. United States,* * *Memoirs,* * and *Miller v. California.* *

UN CHANT D'AMOUR. As the court records relate, *Un Chant d'Amour* is an 8 mm. silent film of about thirty minutes' duration made in the style of the short silent films of the 1920s and apparently deliberately ambiguous. No music or text accompanies the film. The actors are professionals. The film's writer, director, and producer was the well-known (and respected in certain circles) Jean Genet. The picture was made with artificial lighting on autochromatic film, which is blind to red, so that almost all the grays are eliminated. The resultant strong contrasts between dark and light create a particularly visual impact. The characters are a guard and four prisoners. At the outset, the guard is walking outside the prison walls. Each prisoner is alone in his cell, engaging in various acts, including masturbation. The prisoners are also shown communicating with one another by knocking on the walls and by the passage of a straw through a hole in the thick wall between the cells, and the blowing of smoke through a straw. Two of the prisoners are involved in a homosexual relationship. The guard, in the course of his duties, looks into each cell through peepholes and observes the prisoners. Their sexual acts, and particularly the conduct of one hairy-chested prisoner, arouse the guard's voyeuristic and latent homosexual tendencies. The film reaches a climactic ending with a beating of the hairy-chested prisoner by the sado-masochistic guard. In the latter half of the film, the realistic scenes in the prison are interspersed with three series of brief, recurring fantasy scenes that may or may not be the fantasy of some or only one of the characters. In the first series, two hands emerge from their individual barred cell windows, and one hand attempts unsuccessfully to throw a garland of flowers to the other. Toward the end of the film, the garland is caught. In the second series of fantasy scenes (most likely those of one or both of the homosexuals), the prisoners are playing together in a romantic sunlit wood. During the third series (most likely those of the guard during the beating), two male heads are seen passionately kissing; two male torsos appear in various positions depicting fellatio, sodomy, and oral copulation. The fantasy scenes increase in intensity during the film, and at several points, fantasy and reality appear to merge.

A California jury found *Un Chant d'Amour* to be obscene (California, Obscenity Statute*) and that any further exhibition of the film would be in violation of the penal code. The exhibitor appealed this decision to the California Supreme Court (*Landau v. Fording*, 54 Cal. Rptr. 177 [1966]), but the California court affirmed the finding of obscenity: "The trial court twice viewed the film and found that to the average person applying contemporary community standards, the predominant appeal of the film as a whole was to prurient interests, i.e., a shameful and morbid interest in nudity and sex, substantially beyond customary limits of candor in the description or representation of such matters. The court further found that the film explicitly and vividly revealed acts of masturbation, oral copulation, the infamous crime against nature (sodomy), voyeurism, nudity, sadism, masochism and sex and that it was 'nothing more than cheap pornography calculated to promote homosexuality, perversion, and morbid sex practices,' that it fell 'far short of dealing with homosexuality, perversion, masturbation or sex from the scientific, historical or critical point of view,' was completely lacking in the exposition of any ideas of social importance, and had no value as art or otherwise to give it redeeming social importance and thus obtain the benefit of the constitutional guarantees. . . . The fact that the writer, director and producer of the film, Jean Genet, is a French writer of renown does not settle the crucial question of whether the film contains sufficient artistic merit. Great artists can create the type of 'hard-core' pornography proscribed by our statute. Often, as in *Zeitlin v. Arnebergh*, the technical excellence and artistic merit redeem the work despite its obscene content [*Tropic of Cancer** by Henry Miller]. Unfortunately, that is not the case here. Even appellant's own literary witness admitted that the film was made at the beginning of Genet's career as a playwright and is a transitional work in his development from a novelist into a dramatist. The witness also testified that *Un Chant d'Amour* is much less complicated than his later works and is not easily recognizable as a work of Genet. The artistic merit of Genet's other works does not provide a carte blanche when he chooses to venture into the fields covered by the film. . . . As Mr. Justice Stewart noted in [the case of *Les Amants**], hard-core pornography is hard to define but he 'knew it when I see it.' We think we have seen it in *Un Chant d'Amour*. It is nothing more than hard-core pornography and should be banned. The judgment is affirmed.'' An appeal was taken to the U.S. Supreme Court (388 U.S. 456 [1967]), and the Court affirmed with a per curiam decision the California ruling that *Un Chant d'Amour* was obscene.

UNITED PUBLIC WORKERS v. MITCHELL (1947). Certain employees of the executive branch of the federal government and a union of such employees sued to enjoin the members of the U.S. Civil Service Commission from enforcing certain provisions of the Hatch Act,* which prohibited federal employees from taking ''any active part in political management or in political campaigns''; they also sought to have the entire Hatch Act ruled unconstitutional. The group of employees had not actually violated any of the provisions of the Hatch Act nor did they claim that they were threatened with any disciplinary action, but they stated that they wanted to engage in acts of ''political management and in political campaigns'' but they were afraid to do so by fear of dismissal from federal employment.

A federal district court dismissed their suit, and the dismissal was affirmed by the Supreme Court. This affirmation had the effect, in a roundabout fashion, of not preventing the Civil Service Commission from enforcing the provisions of the Hatch Act and not declaring the Hatch Act to be unconstitutional. The

Court held, among other things, that (1) Congress has the power to regulate, within reasonable limits, the political conduct of federal employees, in order to promote efficiency and integrity in the public service. (2) The fundamental human rights guaranteed by the First, Fifth, Ninth, and Tenth Amendments are not absolutes, and the Court must balance the extent of the guarantee of freedom against a congressional enactment to protect a democratic society against the supposed evil of political partisanship by employees of the government. (3) The Hatch Act permits full participation by federal employees in political decisions at the ballot box and forbids only the partisan activity deemed offensive to efficiency. (4) The Hatch Act does not restrict public and private expressions on public affairs, personalities, and matters of public interest, not an objective of party action, so long as the government employee does not direct his attention toward party success. (5) If political activity by government employees is harmful to the service, the employees, or the people dealing with them, it is hardly less so because it takes place after hours. (6) The determination of the extent to which political activities of government employees shall be regulated lies primarily with Congress, and the courts will interfere only when such regulation passes beyond the generally existing conception of governmental power. The provisions of the Hatch Act that restrict all sorts of overt partisan political activity have been upheld as constitutional in other cases, and civil servants in the United States—both at the federal and state levels—do not have as much freedom of speech or press as do people who are not government employees. *United Public Workers v. Mitchell*, 330 U.S. 75 (1947).

UNITED STATES CONGRESS, CONTEMPT. Title 2 U.S.C. § 192, "Contempt of Congress," reads as follows: "Every person summoned as a witness by the authority of either House of Congress to give testimony or to produce papers upon any matter under inquiry before either House, or any joint committee established by a joint or concurrent resolution of the two Houses of Congress, or any committee of either House of Congress, willfully makes default, or who, having appeared, refuses to answer any question pertinent to the question under inquiry, shall be deemed guilty of a misdemeanor, punishable by fine of not more than $1,000 nor less than $100 and imprisonment in a common jail for not less than one month nor more than twelve months."

This contempt power of the Congress has been involved in several cases with differing results. The contempt power was upheld by the Supreme Court in *Barenblatt v. United States*,* when Barenblatt was convicted of contempt of Congress, arising from his refusal to answer certain questions put to him by a subcommittee of the House Committee on Un-American Activities during the course of an inquiry concerning alleged Communist infiltration into the field of education. But in *Watkins v. United States*,* the Supreme Court ruled that Watkins, who refused to answer questions from the same subcommittee about other people's alleged association with Communist organizations, could not be convicted of contempt under the statute. The requirement "to produce papers

upon any matter'' was held by the Supreme Court (*United States v. Rumely**)
in 1953 as inapplicable to require someone to produce the subscription lists of
various publications.

**UNITED STATES POSTAL SERVICE v. COUNCIL OF GREENBURGH
CIVIC ASSOCIATIONS (1981).** Title 18 U.S.C. § 1725 (Postal Regulations,
Use of Letter Boxes*) prohibits the deposit of unstamped mailable matter in a
letterbox approved by the U.S. Postal Service; violations are subject to a fine.
A local postmaster notified the Greenburgh Civic Association that its practice
of delivering messages to residents by placing unstamped notices in the letterboxes of private homes violated § 1725 and advised that a fine could result if
the practice continued. The association brought suit, contending that the enforcement of § 1725 would inhibit their communication with local residents and
would thereby deny them the freedom of speech and press guaranteed by the
First Amendment. The Supreme Court held that § 1725 did not violate the First
Amendment, since it did not concern itself in any way with the content of the
message sought to be placed in the letterbox—a letterbox, once designated an
''authorized depository,'' does not at the same time transform itself into a ''public
forum''* to which the First Amendment guarantees access to all comers. Just
because it may be somewhat more efficient (and more economical) to place
messages in letterboxes does not mean that there is a First Amendment right to
do so. The regulation was characterized by Justice Brennan as a ''reasonable
time-place-manner''* regulation. This regulation may not have much impact on
the distribution of unstamped notices to private homes, for the message can be
left in another place—under the door, wedged in a crack, taped to the door—
but it most certainly does restrict such distribution to apartment buildings, where
the letterbox is the only receptacle for such messages. A strict reading of the
regulation, however, would permit the placing of unstamped obscene material
in the letterboxes, since such material is non-mailable (non-mailable matters*)
and § 1725 applies only to ''mailable'' matter. *United States Postal Service v.
Council of Greenburgh Civic Associations*, 453 U.S. 114 (1981).

UNITED STATES SUPREME COURT, REGULATIONS. In 1949, a statutory scheme was enacted to govern the protection, care, and policing of the
Supreme Court grounds. Title 40 U.S.C. § 13k provides: ''It shall be unlawful
to parade, stand, or move in processions or assemblages in the Supreme Court
Building or grounds, or to display therein any flag, banner, or device designed
or adapted to bring into public notice any party, organization, or movement.''
The Supreme Court, in 1983 (*United States v. Grace**), ruled that § 13k, as
applied to the public sidewalks surrounding the Supreme Court Building, was
an unconstitutional restriction on the right of free speech under the First
Amendment.

UNITED STATES v. ALPERS (1950). Certain regulations (Interstate Commerce Regulations, Transporting Obscene Material*) prohibit the interstate shipment by any means (including as part of one's personal possessions in the trunk of an automobile) of any obscene "book, pamphlet, picture, motion picture film, paper, letter, writing, print, or other matter of indecent character." Alpers was convicted under the regulations of transporting obscene/indecent phonograph records. He appealed to the Supreme Court because the statute in question did not specifically prohibit the shipment of "phonograph records." This apparent omission did not concern the Court very much—Alpers' conviction was affirmed: "We find nothing in the statute or its history to indicate that Congress intended to limit the applicable portion of the statute to such indecent matter as is comprehended through the sense of sight. True, this statute was amended in 1920 to include 'motion picture film.' We are not persuaded that Congress, by adding motion picture film to the specific provisions of the statute, evidenced an intent that obscene matter not specifically added was without the prohibition of the statute; nor do we think that Congress intended that only visual obscene matter was within the prohibition of the statute. The First World War gave considerable impetus to the making and distribution of motion picture films. And in 1920 the public was considerably alarmed at the indecency of many of the films. It thus appears that with respect to this amendment, Congress was preoccupied with making doubly sure that motion picture film was within the Act, and was concerned with nothing more or less. Upon this record we could not hold, nor do we wish to be understood to hold, that the applicable portion of the statute is all-inclusive. As we have pointed out, the same statute contains other provisions relating to objects intended for an indecent or immoral use. But the portion of the statute here in issue does proscribe the dissemination of matter which, in its essential nature, communicates obscene ideas. We are clear therefore that obscene phonograph records are within the meaning of the Act."

Justice Black was wary of this type of reasoning and extension, and he filed a dissent. Justice Black: "History is not lacking in proof that statutes like this may readily be converted into instruments for dangerous abridgments of freedom of expression. People of varied temperaments and beliefs have always differed among themselves concerning what is 'indecent.' Sculpture, paintings and literature, ranked among the classics by some, deeply offend the religious and moral sensibilities of others. And those which offend, however priceless or irreplaceable, have often been destroyed by honest zealots convinced that such destruction was necessary to preserve morality as they saw it. Of course there is a tremendous difference between cultural treasures and the phonograph records here involved. But our decision cannot be based on that difference. Involved in this case is the vital question of whether courts should give the most expansive construction to general terms in legislation providing for censorship of publications or pictures found to be 'indecent,' 'obscene,' etc. Censorship in any field may so readily encroach on constitutionally protected liberties that courts should not add to the list of items banned by Congress. In the provision relied on, as well as elsewhere in the Act, Congress used language carefully describing a number of 'indecent' articles and forbade their shipment in interstate commerce. This specific list applied censorship only to articles that people could read or see; the Court now adds to it articles capable of use to produce sounds that people can hear. . . . Since Congress did not specifically ban the shipment of phonograph records, this Court should not do so." *United States v. Alpers*, 338 U.S. 680 (1950).

UNITED STATES v. AUTO WORKERS (1957). Title 18 U.S.C. § 610 (Criminal Appeals Act* of 1907) prohibits any corporation or labor organization from making "a contribution or expenditure in connection with" an election for federal office. The Auto Workers Union was indicted under § 610 and charged with having used union dues to sponsor commercial television broadcasts designed to influence the electorate to select certain candidates for Congress in the 1954 elections. A federal district court dismissed the indictment, but the Supreme Court, without passing on any of the constitutional issues involved, reinstated the indictment and sent the case back to the district court.

The decision was not unanimous, however, and as was the situation in other decisions, the dissent is more relevant and significant than the majority opinion because the dissent eventually turns into accepted practice. The following dissent was written by Justice Douglas and joined by Chief Justice Warren and Justice Black: "We deal here with a problem that is fundamental to the electoral process and to the operation of our democratic society. It is whether a union can express its views on the issues of an election and on the merits of the candidates, unrestrained and unfettered by the Congress. The principle at stake is not peculiar to unions. It is applicable as well to associations of manufacturers, retail and wholesale trade groups, consumers' leagues, farmers' unions, religious groups and every other association representing a segment of American life and taking an active part in our political campaigns and discussions. It is as important an issue as has come before the Court, for it reaches the very vitals of our system of government. Under our Constitution it is We The People who are sovereign. The people have the final say. The legislators are their spokesmen. The people determine through their votes the destiny of the nation. It is therefore important—vitally important—that all channels of communication be open to them during every election, that no point of view be restrained or barred, and that the people have access to the views of every group in the community. . . .

"What the Court does today greatly impairs those rights. It sustains an indictment charging no more than the use of union funds for broadcasting television programs that urge and endorse the selection of certain candidates for the Congress of the United States. The opinion of the Court places that advocacy in the setting of corrupt practices. The opinion generates an environment of evil-doing and points to the oppressions and misdeeds that have haunted elections in this country. Making a speech endorsing a candidate for office does not, however, deserve to be identified with antisocial conduct. Until today political speech has never been considered a crime. The making of a political speech up to now has always been one of the preferred rights protected by the First Amendment. It usually costs money to communicate an idea to a large audience. But no one would seriously contend that the expenditure of money to print a newspaper deprives the publisher of freedom of the press. Nor can the fact that it costs money to make a speech—whether it be hiring a hall or purchasing time on the air—make the speech any the less an exercise of First Amendment rights. Yet this statute, as construed and applied in this indictment, makes criminal any 'expenditure' by a union for the purpose of expressing its views on the issues of an election and the candidates. It would make no difference under this construction of the Act whether the union spokesman made his address from the platform of a hall, used a sound truck in the streets, or bought time on radio or television. In each case the mere 'expenditure' of money to make the speech is an indictable offense. The principle applied today would make equally criminal the use by a union of its funds to print pamphlets for general distribution or to distribute political literature at large. . . .

"Can an Act so construed be constitutional in view of the command of the First Amendment that Congress shall make no law that abridges free speech or freedom of assembly? The Court says that the answer on the constitutional issue must await the development of the facts at the trial. It asks, 'Did the broadcast reach the public at large or only those affiliated with appellee?' But the size of the audience has heretofore been deemed wholly irrelevant to First Amendment issues. One has a right to freedom of speech whether he talks to one person or to one thousand. One has a right to freedom of speech not only when he talks to his friends but also when he talks to the public. It is startling to learn that a union spokesman or the spokesman for a corporate interest has fewer constitutional rights when he talks to the public than when he talks to members of his group. The Court asks whether the broadcast constituted 'active electioneering' or simply stated 'the record of particular candidates on economic issues.' What possible difference can it make under the First Amendment whether it was one or the other? The First Amendment covers the entire spectrum. It protects the impassioned plea of the orator as much as the quiet publication of the tabulations of the statistician or economist. If there is an innuendo that 'active electioneering' by union spokesmen is not covered by the First Amendment, the opinion makes a sharp break with our political and constitutional heritage. The Court asks, 'Did the union sponsor the broadcast with the intent to affect the results of the election?' The purpose of speech is not only to inform but to incite to action [and to influence]. As Mr. Justice Holmes said in his dissent in *Gitlow v. New York*,* 'Every idea is an incitement.' " *United States v. Auto Workers*, 352 U.S. 567 (1957).

UNITED STATES v. CHASE (1890). This early case concerned the question whether a sealed envelope on which was written only the name and address of the addressee and deposited in the U.S. mails, but whose content was an "obscene'' letter, was a violation of the statute against using the U.S. mails for sending "obscene, lascivious, or indecent writings" (Postal Regulations, Mailing Obscene Material*). The Supreme Court ruled that a sealed and addressed letter was not a "writing" within the meaning of the statute: "The contention on the part of the United States is, that the term 'writing' as used in this statute, is comprehensive enough to include, and does include, the term 'letter'; and it is insisted, therefore, that the offence charged is that of unlawfully and knowingly depositing in the mails of the United States an obscene, lewd and lascivious 'writing.' We do not concur in this construction of the statute. . . . We do not think it is a reasonable construction of the statute to say that the vast mass of postal matter known as 'letters' was intended by Congress to be expressed in a term so general and vague as the word 'writing,' when it would have been just as easy, and also in strict accordance with all of its other postal laws and regulations, to say 'letters' when letters were meant; and the very fact that the word 'letters' is not specifically mentioned among the enumerated articles in this clause is itself conclusive that Congress intended to exclude private letters from its operations.'' *United States v. Chase*, 135 U.S. 255 (1890).

UNITED STATES v. GRACE (1983). This case was decided along with *United States v. Zywicki*. In May 1978, Zywicki, standing on the sidewalk in front of the U.S. Supreme Court Building in Washington, D.C., distributed leaflets to passersby. The leaflets were reprints of a letter to the editor of the *Washington Post* from a U.S. Senator concerning the removal of unfit judges from the bench. A Supreme Court police officer approached Zywicki and told him that Title 40 U.S.C. § 13k (United States Supreme Court, Regulations*) prohibited the distribution of leaflets on the Supreme Court grounds, including the sidewalks, and Zywicki left. In January 1980, Zywicki again visited the sidewalk in front of the Court building and distributed pamphlets containing information about forthcoming meetings and events concerning "the oppressed peoples of Central America." He again was told by a police officer to stop or face arrest; Zywicki left. He reappeared in February 1980, distributing handbills concerning oppression in Guatemala. His by now friend the police officer told him that he would be arrested if he didn't stop the pamphleteering. Zywicki complained that he was being denied a right that others had—he pointed to the newspaper vending machines on the sidewalk—but he left anyway.

On March 17, 1980, Mary Grace was on the sidewalk in front of the Court; she was carrying a sign (4 by 2 feet) on which was inscribed the verbatim text of the First Amendment. She, too, was told to leave or face arrest for a violation of § 13k. Grace and Zywicki then brought suit in a federal district court, seeking an injunction against the enforcement of § 13k on the grounds that it was an unconstitutional abridgment of their rights of free speech and press. The district court dismissed their complaint for failure to exhaust the available administrative remedies, but on appeal, the court of appeals struck down § 13k as an unconstitutional restriction on First Amendment rights in a public forum.*

The government appealed the ruling, but the Supreme Court affirmed the court of appeals decision, ruling that § 13k, as applied to the public sidewalks surrounding the Court building, was unconstitutional under the First Amendment. Justice White delivered the opinion of the Court: (1) As a general matter, peaceful picketing and leafletting are expressive activities involving "speech" protected by the First Amendment. "Public places," such as streets, sidewalks, and parks, historically associated with the free exercise of expressive activities, are considered, without more, to be "public forums." In such places, the government may enforce reasonable time-place-manner* regulations, but additional restrictions, such as an absolute prohibition of a particular type of expression—the distribution of literature by a person was prohibited but the distribution of literature by a newspaper vending machine was permitted—would be upheld only if narrowly drawn to accomplish a compelling governmental interest. (2) The Court grounds are not transformed into "public forum" property merely because the public is permitted to enter and leave the grounds freely at practically all times and is admitted to the building during specified hours. But where the sidewalks forming the perimeter of the grounds are indistinguishable from any other sidewalks in Washington, D.C., they should not be treated any differently and thus they are public forums for First Amendment purposes. (3) Insofar as it banned specific communicative activity on the public sidewalks around the Court grounds, § 13k cannot be justified as a reasonable place restriction. A ban on carrying a flag, banner, or device on the public sidewalks does not substantially serve the purposes of the statute to provide for the maintenance of law and order on the Court grounds. In addition, the prohibitions in § 13k do not serve the purpose of protecting the Court from outside influence or of preventing it from appearing to the public that the Court is subject to such influence or that picketing or marching is an acceptable way of influencing the Court. *United States v. Grace* and *United States v. Zywicki*, 75 L. Ed. 2d 736 (1983).

UNITED STATES v. GRAY (1970). Certain military regulations (Military Regulations, Uniform Code of Military Justice,* Article 134) provide: "All disorders and neglects to the prejudice of good order and discipline in the armed forces, all conduct of a nature to bring discredit upon the armed forces . . . shall be punished at the discretion of [a] court." This article was employed to punish Claude Gray, a young Marine, who made what the military authorities deemed disloyal statements "to the prejudice of good order and discipline in the armed forces." The following is a segment of what Gray said and wrote: "We have not served in Vietnam but we have not been deaf or blind to the testimony of our brothers who have gone and were lucky enough to return. In the brig, one meets Vietnam veterans and conscientious objectors, and from them one gets a different view of the war. In the barracks we talk to each other; at demonstrations we have read leaflets and pamphlets. We have heard and encountered both sides of the war. We have heard the death tolls calmly announced over TV and radio. We have read of whole villages wiped out by our forces accidentally, and we have reason to believe our war there is a huge mistake made possible in part by inhumane and dictatorial practices within the military. We can no longer co-operate with these practices or with the war in Vietnam. We are not deserting; we are simply taking a stand to help others like us. Positively, we favor an immediate end to the war and the establishment of a voluntary military service to defend the nation, together with the needed reforms within the military to attract volunteers. Article 134 should be struck from the code [Uniform Code of Military Justice], free speech guaranteed and individual conscience respected; a conscientious objector's status should be easier to obtain for those with moral doubts about a war. In general, soldiers should have a greater say about the rules they live under, and certainly about a matter of life and death, and the destruction of another country. This is where we stand, and we hope that other men in the Armed Forces who know that we speak the truth will stand with us. Shalom.''

Gray might have been speaking the truth, but the military authorities perceived the statements (and other statements that Gray made but not reported here) as "disloyal statements" and, as such, conduct in violation of Article 134. The U.S. Court of Military Appeals (USCMA) cashiered Gray: (1) The public making of a statement disloyal to the United States, with the intent to promote disloyalty and disaffection among persons in the armed forces and under circumstances to the prejudice of good order and discipline, is not speech protected by the First Amendment and is conduct in violation of Article 134 of the Uniform Code of Military Justice. (2) A declaration of personal belief can amount to a disloyal statement if it disavows allegiance owed to the United States by the speaker. (3) A statement by Gray indicating that he was leaving his place of duty for some foreign country because of opposition to U.S. foreign policy and unjust rules of the Marine Corps and the government and characterizing the Constitution as a "farce," is seen as a disavowal of the allegiance that Gray owed the United States, and thus the statement was sufficient to prove a disloyal statement. (4) Successful propagation of disloyalty is not an essential element of the offense of making a disloyal statement—the statement itself is the violation (no clear and present danger test for the military!). (5) Although a "rough log" in which Gray wrote the disloyal statements was an informal, unofficial book containing such things as personal messages and jokes, the evidence was sufficient to support the finding that the statements were published with the intent to promote disloyalty and disaffection among the crew. Gray knew the crew members read the log as a regular practice, that the form of address used would ensure that the statement would be read and discussed, that Gray believed that the statement would be taken seriously, and that it was in fact read by other members of the crew. (6) The evidence with respect to a charge of making a disloyal statement was sufficient to support a finding of reasonably direct prejudice to good order and discipline where there was evidence of Gray's prior good conduct in the per-formance of his duties that would support an inference that his statements would be taken more seriously than those of a known malcontent. *United States v. Gray*, 20 U.S.C.M.A. 63 (1970).

UNITED STATES v. HARRISS (1954). The Federal Regulation of Lobbying Act,* among other provisions, contains the following section: "Any person who shall engage himself for pay . . . for the purpose of attempting to influence the passage or defeat of any legislation by the Congress of the United States shall . . . file with the Clerk . . . a detailed report under oath . . . the names of any papers, periodicals, magazines, or other publications in which he has caused to be published any articles or editorials; and the proposed legislation he is employed to support or oppose."

This case saw the Supreme Court deciding that the above requirement did not violate the freedom to speak or the freedom to publish as guaranteed by the First Amendment. Chief Justice Warren delivered the Court's majority opinion: "Present-day legislative complexities are such that individual members of Congress cannot be expected to explore the myriad pressures to which they are regularly subjected. Yet full realization of the American ideal of government by elected representatives depends to no small extent on their ability to properly evaluate such pressures. Otherwise the voice of the people may all too easily be drowned out by the voice of special interest groups seeking favored treatment while masquerading as proponents of the public weal. This is the evil which the Lobbying Act was designed to help prevent. Toward that end, Congress has not sought to prohibit these pressures. It has merely provided for a modicum of information from those who for hire attempt to influence legislation or who collect or spend funds for that purpose. It wants only to know who is being hired, who is putting up the money, and how much . . . to maintain the integrity of a basic governmental process. Under these circumstances, we believe that Congress, at least within the bounds of the Act as we have construed it, is not constitutionally forbidden to require the disclosure of lobbying activities. To do so would be to deny Congress in large measure the power of self-protection. . . . It is suggested, however, that the Lobbying Act, with respect to persons other than those [who are paid], may as a practical matter act as a deterrent to their exercise of First Amendment rights. Hypothetical borderline situations are conjured up in which such persons choose to remain silent because of fear of possible prosecution for failure to comply with the Act. Our narrow construction of the Act, precluding as it does reasonable fears, is calculated to avoid such restraint. But, even assuming some such deterrent effect, the restraint is at most an indirect one resulting from self-censorship, comparable in many ways to the restraint resulting from criminal libel laws. The hazard of such restraint is too remote to require striking down a statute which on its face is otherwise plainly within the area of congressional power and is designed to safeguard a vital national interest."

Justice Douglas, joined by Justice Black, was not happy with the Court's decision, which left open the possibility that a private citizen, in speaking or publishing whatever in an attempt to influence pending congressional legislation, could be open for prosecution for failing to register under the act. Justice Douglas: "I am in sympathy with the effort of the Court to save this statute from the charge that it is so vague and indefinite as to be unconstitutional. My inclinations were that way at the end of the oral argument. But further study changed my mind. I am now convinced that the formula adopted to save this Act is too dangerous for use. It can easily ensnare people who have done no more than exercise their constitutional rights of speech, assembly, and press. . . . The language of the Act is so broad that one who writes a letter or makes a speech or publishes an article or distributes literature or does many of the other things with which appellees are charged has no fair notice when he is close to the prohibited line. No construction we give it today will make clear retroactively the vague standards that confronted appellees when they did the acts now charged against them as criminal. Since the Act touches on the exercise of First Amendment rights, and is not narrowly drawn to meet precise evils, its vagueness has some of the evils of a continuous and effective restraint." *United States v. Harriss*, 347 U.S. 612 (1954).

UNITED STATES v. HOWE (1965). Howe, a commissioned officer in the U.S. Army, was convicted by court-martial of violating certain regulations (Military Regulations, Uniform Code of Military Justice,* Articles 88 and 133). Article 88 prohibits the use of "contemptuous words" against the president of the United States, and Article 133 prohibits "conduct unbecoming an officer and a gentleman." For using "contemptuous words" against President Johnson, and thus engaging in "conduct unbecoming an officer and a gentleman," Howe was dismissed from the service, forfeited all pay and allowances, and was confined in a military prison for one year "at hard labor." Howe's conduct would have been protected if he had been a civilian, but military justice being what it is, Howe was convicted.

On November 6, 1965, Howe, in civilian clothes, participated during off-duty hours in a public demonstration at San Jacinto Plaza, El Paso, Texas. For about thirty minutes Howe walked in a line of demonstrators. As he did, he carried a sign, one side of which read "LET'S HAVE MORE THAN A CHOICE BETWEEN PETTY FACISTS [sic] IN 1968" and the other side of the sign read "END JOHNSON'S FACIST [sic] AGRESSION [sic] IN VIET NAM." Some 500 to 1,500 spectators witnessed the demonstration, including at least three or four enlisted soldiers. At his court-martial, Howe argued that the First Amendment protected his right to have carried the sign and that he did not lose his right to free speech—out of uniform, off-duty, and at an off-base location—just because he was in the military.

The court thought otherwise: "We are aware of no legal authority, either military or civilian, who would view a constitutionally protected right of free speech as an absolute one without limitation. The constitutional guarantee of freedom of speech does not confer upon [Howe] an absolute right to speak and the law recognizes that there can be an abuse of such freedom. The Constitution does not confer unrestricted and unbridled license giving immunity for every possible use of language and preventing the punishment of those who abuse this freedom. . . . The right of free speech in the military is subject to reasonable limitations based on military necessity. In [this case], the limitations imposed upon [Howe's] conduct by Articles 88 and 133, Uniform Code of Military Justice, are constitutionally premised, reasonable and based upon military necessity. . . . The facts of record showed that [Howe], a commissioned officer, knowingly and purposely displayed a sign, the manifest import of which was to characterize the President of the United States as a petty, ignorant fascist and the President's policies in Viet Nam as fascist aggression. We find the use of such language by the appellant, under the circumstances here to be patently contemptuous in fact and in law. The military standard of discipline demands obedience to orders and respect for legally constituted authority. The ultimate purpose for the existence of the military establishment is to prepare for and to be successful in combat against the enemies of the United States, and its bedrock is order and discipline. The appellant may not contemptuously assail his Commander-in-Chief with impunity any more than he may behave himself with disrespect toward his superior officer. His relationship as an officer to the President, the highest source of military command authority, in this regard is significantly the same as his relationship to his superior officer—in both instances, respect is required and demanded. We cannot permit the very trust, fidelity and honor, reposed in the appellant by Presidential appointment and commission as a military officer, to be infamously compromised with privilege. The preservation of the necessary subordinate-superior relationship in the military service permits no such privilege or impunity, especially where, as here, a military officer notoriously and ignominiously vilifies the very superior authority to whom a duty of respect is owing and who appointed him to military office. Even the disciplined soldier, who would share appellant's view of privilege, could hardly be expected to willfully and cheerfully respond to the orders of the appellant where the latter has publicly manifested such disloyalty and contempt to his superior. Military discipline, in peace as well as in war, does more than expect obedience and respect—it demands it. . . . The privileges and status enjoyed by all military officers . . . carries with it correlative duties, responsibilities and standards of conduct peculiar to that status. We find Article 88 [using contemptuous words against the President] to be reasonable [and Howe's actions also a violation of Article 133—conduct unbecoming an officer and a gentleman]." Officer Howe's sentence of dismissal, forfeiture of all pay and allowances, and confinement at hard labor for one year was upheld by the Court of Military Review. *United States v. Howe*, 37 C.M.R. 555 (1965).

UNITED STATES v. JEWSON (1952). This case concerned the application of Article 133 of the Uniform Code of Military Justice (Military Regulations, Uniform Code of Military Justice*)—conduct "unbecoming an officer and a gentleman" can be punished as a court-martial sees fit. Officer Jewson was dismissed from a National Guard unit that had been called into federal service for attempting to organize a barracks party. The problem was that the main event of the party was to be the showing of an X-rated film; the military authorities didn't think that gentlemen should engage in such activities and Jewson was cashiered. The entire scenario reminds one of the behavior of teenage boys when their parents are absent and the blow-up when the mother and father return; the difference here is that a man's career in the National Guard was brought to an end. This case is best presented without additional comment; the reader is free to draw whatever conclusions are applicable to the facts.

The description of the case is from Judge Brosman of the U.S. Court of Military Appeals (USCMA): "This unfortunate case is the product of the following series of events. The commissioned officers and higher-ranking enlisted personnel of the 235th Field Artillery Observation Battalion, a National Guard unit called into federal service and stationed at Camp McCoy, Wisconsin, planned a stag party. [Jewson] was the commanding officer of the unit. Included within the plans was the showing of a pornographic motion picture. An enlisted man, who had access to such items, was detailed to secure the motion picture film. He did so, and at the agreed date and time the officers and men gathered for the battalion party. In the meantime, the commanding officer of Camp McCoy, a Colonel Bullard, received unofficial notice of the plans for the social event, including the film showing. There was a distressing background of friction between [Jewson's] National Guard unit and the regular complement of Camp McCoy. On the night scheduled for the party, Colonel Bullard, together with three of his subordinate officers, secreted themselves in a building adjoining that in which the film showing was to take place. When the lights were extinguished, indicating that the film was under way, they burst into the hall, switched on the lights, and ordered the showing halted. Colonel Bullard thereupon relieved Jewson of command . . . and ordered an investigation which culminated in these charges, in a trial by general court-martial, and in the findings of guilt with which we are now concerned."

The USCMA affirmed the finding that Officer Jewson engaged "in conduct unbecoming an officer and a gentleman" by "wrongfully and knowingly permitting, and assisting at, the showing of a lewd and obscene motion picture," and affirmed the verdict that led to Jewson's dismissal from the service. The court record does not contain any information as to the film that was at the center of this restriction on First Amendment rights. *United States v. Jewson*, 1 U.S.C.M.A. 652 (1952).

UNITED STATES v. KENNERLEY (1913). This case began the slow process of rejecting the Hicklin Rule* (the effect of isolated passages on the most susceptible minds) as a test or measure of obscenity; the process was not complete until 1934, when Judge Woolsey established the Ulysses Standard* (the effect of the work as a whole on the "average" mind). This case did not overrule the Hicklin Rule; the decision only stated that it no longer fit the times and that society should not limit itself to the weakest members; obscenity should be seen to "indicate the present critical point in the compromise between candor and shame at which the community may have arrived."

Mitchell Kennerley was indicted for sending an obscene book (*Hagar Revelly*) through the mails, a violation of certain statutes (Postal Regulations, Mailing Obscene Material*). The court record describes *Hagar Revelly* as "a novel of manners presenting the life of a young woman in New York compelled to earn her living. She is represented as impulsive, sensuous, fond of pleasure, and restive under the monotony and squalor of her surroundings. Her virtue is unsuccessfully assailed by a man she does not love and later successfully by one whom she does. After her seduction she has several amorous misadventures and ends with a loveless marriage and the prospect of a dreary future. In order to give complete portrayal to the girl's emotional character, some of the scenes are depicted with a frankness and detail which have given rise to this prosecution."

Judge Hand delivered the opinion of the Court: "Lord Cockburn laid down a test in *Regina v. Hicklin* (L.R. 3 Q.B. 360 [1968]) in these words: 'Whether the tendency of the matter charged as obscenity is to deprave and corrupt those whose minds are open to such immoral influences and into whose hands a publication of this sort may fall.' That test has been accepted by the lower federal courts until it would be no longer proper for me to disregard it. Under this rule, such parts of this book as pages 169 and 170 might be found obscene, because they certainly might tend to corrupt the morals of those into whose hands it might come and whose minds were open to such immoral influences. Indeed, it would be just those who would be most likely to concern themselves with those parts alone, forgetting their setting and their relevancy to the book as a whole. While, therefore, the demurrer must be overruled, I hope it is not improper for me to say that the rule as laid down, however consonant it may be with mid–Victorian morals, does not seem to me to answer to the understanding and morality of the present time, as conveyed by the words 'obscene, lewd, or lascivious.' I question whether in the end men will regard that as obscene which is honestly relevant to the adequate expression of innocent ideas, and whether they will not believe that truth and beauty are too precious to society at large to be mutilated in the interests of those most likely to pervert them to base uses. Indeed, it seems hardly likely that we are even to-day so lukewarm in our interest in letters or serious discussion as to be content to reduce our treatment of sex to the standard of a child's library in the supposed interest of a salacious few, or that shame will for long prevent us from adequate portrayal of some of the most serious and beautiful sides of human nature. That such latitude gives opportunity for its abuse is true enough; there will be, as there are, plenty who will misuse the privilege as a cover for lewdness and a stalking horse from which to strike at purity, but that is true to-day and only involves us in the same question of fact which we hope that we have the power to answer. Yet, if the time is not yet when men think innocent all that which is honestly germane to a pure subject, however little it may mince its words, still I scarcely think that they would forbid all which might corrupt the most corruptible, or that society is prepared to accept for its own limitations those which may perhaps be necessary to the weakest of its members. If there be no abstract definition, such as I have suggested, should not the word 'obscene' be allowed to indicate the present critical point in the compromise between candor and shame at which the community may have arrived here and now? If letters must, like other kinds of conduct, be subject to the social sense of what is right, it would seem that a jury should in each case establish the standard much as they do in cases of negligence. To put thought in leash to the average conscience of the time is perhaps tolerable, but to fetter it by the necessities of the lowest and least capable seems a fatal policy. Nor is it an objection, I think, that such an interpretation gives to the words of the statute a varying meaning from time to time. Such words as these do not embalm the precise morals of an age or place; while they presuppose that some things will always be shocking to the public taste, the vague subject-matter is left to the gradual development of general notions about what is decent.'' *United States v. Kennerley*, 209 F. 119 (1913).

UNITED STATES v. LEVINE (1936). Levine was indicted and convicted in a federal district court for sending certain obscene publications through the U.S. mails (Postal Regulations, Mailing Obscene Material*).Three publications were involved: *Secret Museum of Anthropology, Crossways of Sex*, and *Black Lust*. The court record describes *Secret Museum of Anthropology* as ''a reproduction of a collection of photographs, for the most part of nude female savages of different parts of the world; the legitimacy of its pretensions as serious anthropology is, to say the most, extremely tenuous, and while in the hands of adults it could not be considered obscene, it might be undesirable in those of children or youths.'' *Crossways of Sex* ''professes to be a scientific treatise on sexual pathology; again its good-faith is more than questionable; for example, the author, a supposititious scientist, remains anonymous. It could have no value to psychiatrists or others genuinely interested in the subject, and in the hands of children it might be injurious.'' *Black Lust* is a ''work of fiction of considerable merit, but patently erotic, describing the adventures of an English girl captured by the Dervishes at the fall of Khartoum and kept in a harem until the Battle of Omdurman, when she is killed. It purports to be a study in sadism and masochism, and would arouse libidinous feelings in almost any reader.''

Levine's conviction was overturned by an appeals court because the trial judge instructed the jury that the statute's purpose was ''to protect the young and immature and ignorant and those who were sensually inclined'' and that the jury ''should regard the effect of the books on their minds rather than on mature and highly intelligent people,'' and that the statute ''condemned any book which contained even a single passage which would excite lustful or sensual desires''— a classic statement of the Hicklin Rule.* But by 1936, the Hicklin Rule was just about discredited—the Ulysses Standard* was in vogue—and the appeals court reversed: ''This earlier doctrine [the Hicklin Rule] necessarily presupposed that the evil against which the statute is directed so much outweighs all interests of art, letters or science, that they must yield to the mere possibility that some prurient person may get a sensual gratification from reading or seeing what to most people is innocent and may be delightful or enlightening. No civilized community not fanatically puritanical would tolerate such an imposition, and we do not believe that the courts that have declared it, would ever have applied it consistently. As so often happens, the problem is to find a passable compromise between opposing interests, whose relative importance, like that of all social or personal values, is incommensurable.'' *United States v. Levine*, 83 F. 2d 156 (1936).

UNITED STATES v. LOCKS (1969). Article 92 of the Uniform Code of Military Justice subjects a member of the armed forces to punishment for failure to obey a lawful order. Airman Locks was convicted under this article for not obeying a general order not to wear his air force uniform when appearing in public at anti-Viet Nam activities (Military Regulations, Wearing Uniforms—Military Personnel*). For this breach of military discipline, Locks received a reduction in grade, forfeiture of all pay and allowances, a bad-conduct discharge, and confinement at hard labor for one year.

The conviction and sentence were affirmed by the Board of Military Review in 1969. If Locks had been a civilian, the First Amendment would have protected his activities, but military justice has its own interpretation of the First Amendment. In affirming the rather harsh sentence, the Military Board of Review made the following comments: ''Airman Locks on two separate occasions, while attired in his military uniform, appeared before the public in connection with anti-Viet Nam activities. These appearances were in direct and willful violation of an order from the Secretary of the Air Force, prohibiting such public appearances at this type of activity by military personnel while in uniform. At the core of this case lies the question of the constitutionality of the order issued by the Secretary. It is [Locks'] contention that the order is violative of his First Amendment right of freedom of speech per se, and of 'symbolic speech.' The issue was thoroughly litigated in the trial forum, and here on appeal. At trial, the law officer ruled that, as a matter of law, the order in question was lawful. Inherent in such determination is the conclusion that the order is constitutional, and specifically that it did not in any way unlawfully abridge or abrogate [Locks'] freedom of expression. We are in full agreement with the law officer's determination. If the Secretary of the Air Force commands that the uniform not be worn at events of the nature in question, the First Amendment does not command otherwise. To permit members of the military to display at will the primary symbol of their military service would be to permit the destruction of the very symbolic effectiveness which the uniform is intended to enjoy. This court does not find it violative of the First Amendment for the Secretary to limit the wearing of the uniform to contexts that will promote a sense, not just of membership in the Air Force, but of participation, allegiance, and achievement. The Air Force designs and furnishes the uniform according to its own criteria; the First Amendment does not forbid the Air Force from determining the uniform's *use* according to its own criteria." *United States v. Locks*, 40 C.M.R. 1022 (1969).

UNITED STATES v. MARCHETTI (1972). A former Central Intelligence Agency (CIA) employee, Marchetti, after his resignation from the CIA, published a novel entitled *The Rope Dancer*, concerning an agency called the "National Intelligence Agency." Marchetti had also published an article in the April 3, 1972 issue of *The Nation* entitled "CIA: The President's Loyal Tool." The article was critical of some policies and practices of the CIA. Marchetti appeared on television and radio shows and gave numerous interviews to the press. Before this case, he had submitted to a publisher (Alfred A. Knopf) an outline of a book he was planning to write about his experiences as an intelligence agent. In March 1972, Marchetti submitted to *Esquire* magazine and to six other publishers an article in which he recounted some of his experiences as an agent for the CIA.

The U.S. government claimed that the article submitted to *Esquire* and the proposed book "contained classified information concerning intelligence sources, methods, and operations." The U.S. government then brought suit against Marchetti, claiming that since Marchetti had signed various agreements (Central Intelligence Agency, Secrecy Agreement*) when he was employed by the agency, the CIA had the right to examine his writings before publication. Marchetti argued that his First Amendment rights prevented any prior restraint and that he could publish what he pleased about the CIA and its operations. Relying on the secrecy agreement that Marchetti signed when he first became an employee of the CIA and on a secrecy oath that he signed when he resigned, a federal district court ordered Marchetti to submit to the CIA at least thirty days in advance of release to anyone else any writing relating to the agency and not to publish any of this information unless and until the CIA approved it (i.e., censored the contents).

An appeals court affirmed this order, finding the agreement that Marchetti signed to be constitutional, but added some comments that recognized that some basic First Amendment rights were involved. In a section entitled "Marchetti's Rights," the appeals court decision noted the following: "As we have said, however, Marchetti by accepting employment with the CIA and by signing a secrecy agreement did not surrender his First Amendment right of free speech. The agreement is enforceable only because it is not a violation of those rights. We would decline enforcement of the secrecy oath signed when he left the employment of the CIA to the extent that it purports to prevent disclosure of unclassified information, for, to that extent, the oath would be in contravention of his First Amendment rights. Thus Marchetti retains the right to speak and write about the CIA and its operations, and to criticize it as any other citizen may, but he may not disclose classified information obtained by him during the course of his employment which is not already in the public domain. Because we are dealing with a prior restraint upon speech, we think that the CIA must act promptly to approve or disapprove any material which may be submitted to it by Marchetti. Undue delay would impair the reasonableness of the restraint, and that reasonableness is to be maintained if the restraint is to be enforced. We should think that, in all events, the maximum period for responding after the submission of material for approval should not exceed thirty days. Furthermore, since First Amendment rights are involved, we think Marchetti would be entitled to judicial review of any action by the CIA disapproving publication of the material. Some such review would seem essential to the enforcement of the prior restraint imposed upon Marchetti and other former employees." *United States v. Marchetti*, 466 F 2d 1309 (1972).

The U.S. Supreme Court was apparently satisfied by this "compromise," for it refused to hear Marchetti's appeal (409 U.S. 1063 [1972], *cert. denied*). But the story wasn't finished, because after the 1972 decision, Marchetti, in collaboration with John Marks, a former State Department employee who himself had signed an agreement not to disclose classified information acquired by him during his employment, prepared a book manuscript that was put under contract by Alfred A. Knopf, Inc. The manuscript, following the order of the above 1972 decision, was submitted to the CIA for pre-publication review and approval (read censorship). The CIA found, and requested deletion of, 339 items said to contain classified information. Later, after some discussion, the CIA agreed to "release" many of the items but stood fast and refused to permit the publication of some 168 items. The publisher, Alfred A. Knopf, Inc., joined by Marchetti and Marks, then filed suit, seeking an order that would permit the publication of the items that the CIA wanted deleted; the appeals court refused to issue the order.

This later case came before the same court and judge who had heard the 1972 case. Judge Haynsworth: "We decline to modify our previous holding that the First Amendment is no bar against an injunction forbidding the disclosure of classifiable information within the guidelines of the Executive Orders [Classified Information*] when (1) the classified information was acquired, during the course of his employment, by an employee of a United States agency or department in which such information is handled and (2) its disclosure would violate a solemn agreement made by the employee at the commencement of his employment. With respect to such information, by his execution of the secrecy agreement and his entry into the confidential employment relationship, he effectively relinquished his First Amendment rights." *Alfred A. Knopf, Inc. v. Colby*, 509 F. 2d 1362 (1975). And as was the situation with the original 1972 decision, the Supreme Court refused to hear the case on appeal (421 U.S. 999 [1975]), thus affirming the appeals court decision.

UNITED STATES v. NEW JERSEY LOTTERY (1975). A New Jersey radio station had sought, but was denied, permission from the Federal Communications Commission (FCC) to broadcast the winning numbers in the lawful, New Jersey state-run lottery. At the time, Title 18 U.S.C. § 1304 (Federal Communications

Commission Regulations, Lotteries*) prohibited such broadcasts. Subsequent to an appeals court reversal of the FCC's denial, Congress amended § 1304 by making the ban inapplicable to information concerning a state-authorized lottery broadcast in that state or an adjacent state also having a state-run lottery. The Supreme Court sent the case back to the court of appeals to consider whether the case was moot, as the government argued, or was not moot, as the state of New Hampshire argued. New Hampshire claimed that the amendment was in violation of the First Amendment because the regulation still prohibited Vermont radio stations (Vermont didn't have a lottery) from broadcasting the New Hampshire winning numbers.

Justice Douglas agreed with New Hampshire's argument and dissented from the Court's decision. Justice Douglas: "The United States now urges us to dismiss this case as moot. It points out that the only relief requested was by a broadcaster located in New Jersey, a state which conducts an authorized lottery, and therefore the type of broadcast at issue is now allowed by statute. Intervenor, the State of New Hampshire disputes the suggestion of mootness. New Hampshire argues that the amendment to § 1304 does not grant it full relief. It is noted that Vermont, an adjacent state, does not conduct a state-authorized lottery. Thus, Vermont broadcasters will not be allowed, under § 1304 as modified by § 1307, to broadcast to New Hampshire listeners the winning numbers in the New Hampshire state lottery. New Hampshire apparently believes that this limitation constitutes a denial of First Amendment rights. . . . With all respect, I do not believe that this case has become moot—certainly not for the reasons intimated by the Court. The First Amendment provides that Congress shall make no law abridging the freedom of the press. It is to me shocking that a radio station or a newspaper can be regulated by a court or by a commission, to the extent of being prevented from publishing any item of 'news' of the day. So to hold would be a prior restraint of a simple and unadulterated form, barred by constitutional principles. Can anyone doubt that the winner of a lottery is prime news by our press standards?" *United States v. New Jersey Lottery*, 420 U.S. 371 (1975).

UNITED STATES v. NIXON (1974). This case involved the request of Watergate Special Prosecutor Leon Jaworski for President Nixon to furnish certain tapes and documents relating to certain identified conversations and meetings between the president and other people. The president claimed executive privilege and refused to furnish the documents to the district court in order to have the court inspect them in private. The U.S. Supreme Court ruled (8 to 0) that the tapes had to be delivered to the district court; President Nixon complied with the order, and it was the beginning of the end of his tenure as president. The Court held: (1) Neither the doctrine of separation of powers nor the generalized need for confidentiality of high-level communications, without more, can sustain an absolute, unqualified presidential privilege of immunity from the judicial process under all circumstances. Absent a claim of need to protect military, diplomatic, or sensitive national security secrets, the confidentiality of a president's communications is not significantly diminished by producing material for a criminal trial under the protected conditions of *in camera* inspection, and any absolute executive privilege under Article II of the Constitution would plainly conflict with the function of the courts under the Constitution. (2) Since a president's communications encompass a vastly wider range of sensitive material than would be true of an ordinary individual, the public interest requires that presidential confidentiality be afforded the greatest protection consistent with the fair administration of justice. Material involving presidential conversations irrelevant to or inadmissible in the criminal prosecution must be accorded the high degree of respect due a president and such material must be returned under seal. *United States v. Nixon*, 418 U.S. 683 (1974).

UNITED STATES v. O'BRIEN (1968). O'Brien burned his Selective Service registration certificate (draft card) before a large crowd in order to influence others to adopt his anti-war and anti-Viet Nam beliefs. He was indicted, tried, and convicted for violating 50 U.S.C. App. § 462 (b), a part of the Universal Military Training and Service Act, punishing any person "who forges, alters, knowingly destroys, knowingly mutilates, or in any manner changes any such certificate." The words "knowingly destroys" and "knowingly mutilates" were added by a 1965 amendment. O'Brien argued that the amendment was unconstitutional because it was enacted to abridge free speech and served no legitimate legislative purpose.

The Supreme Court thought otherwise and affirmed O'Brien's conviction: "O'Brien first argues that the 1965 Amendment is unconstitutional as applied to him because his act of burning his registration certificate was protected 'symbolic speech' within the First Amendment. His argument is that the freedom of expression which the First Amendment guarantees includes all modes of 'communication of ideas by conduct,' and that his conduct is within this definition because he did it in 'demonstration against the war and against the draft.' We cannot accept the view that an apparently limitless variety of conduct can be labeled 'speech' whenever the person engaging in the conduct intends thereby to express an idea. However, even on the assumption that the alleged communicative element in O'Brien's conduct is sufficient to bring into play the First Amendment, it does not necessarily follow that the destruction of a registration certificate is constitutionally protected activity. This Court has held that when 'speech' and 'nonspeech' elements are combined in the same course of conduct, a sufficiently important governmental interest in regulating the nonspeech element can justify incidental limitations on First Amendment freedoms. . . . We find that the 1965 Amendment to § 12 (b)(3) of the Universal Military Training and Service Act [is constitutional] and consequently that O'Brien can be constitutionally convicted for violating it." *United States v. O'Brien*, 391 U.S. 367 (1968).

UNITED STATES v. ORITO (1973). Title 18 U.S.C. § 1462 (Interstate Commerce Regulations, Transporting Obscene Material*) prohibits the transportation of obscene material by common carrier in interstate commerce. The Supreme Court, in this case, upheld the constitutionality of this statute. The Court ruled that the *Stanley v. Georgia** decision, which established the right of every individual to possess obscene material in the privacy of one's home—the government cannot determine what a person may or may not have as reading material in his bookcase—did not extend beyond the privacy of one's home. The individual does not have a First Amendment right to receive obscene material, to transport obscene material, to sell obscene material, or to distribute obscene material. The Court ruled that Congress has the legitimate authority and power to prevent obscene material, material that is not protected by the First Amendment according to *Roth v. United States,** from entering the stream of interstate commerce and that the "zone of privacy" that *Stanley* created does not extend beyond the home. Thus, one may have and read obscene books at home; one should be circumspect about packing them up with the other household belongings and calling a moving van. *United States v. Orito*, 413 U.S. 139 (1973).

UNITED STATES v. PRIEST (1972). Article 134 of the Uniform Code of Military Justice (Military Regulations, Uniform Code of Military Justice*) provides for the punishment, as a court-martial may see fit, of "all conduct of a nature to bring discredit upon the armed forces." Priest, a member of the U.S. Navy, brought discredit on the armed forces by "printing and distributing with intent to promote disloyalty and disaffection among members of the armed forces, issues of a publication which, in its entirety, contained statements disloyal to the United States." The U.S. Court of Military Appeals affirmed his conviction and sentence of a reduction in grade and a bad-conduct discharge.

While on active duty in the navy, Priest edited, published, and distributed an "underground" newsletter entitled *OM*. Copies were left for free distribution to military personnel in the Navy Exchange, Washington Navy Yard, at a Pentagon newsstand, and were handed to individual members of the armed forces. The court-martial contained a description of some of the issues of *OM*: "The two issues of the newsletter with which we are concerned were issued in May and June, 1969. The lead article in the May issue is entitled 'A CALL TO RESIST ILLEGITIMATE AUTHORITY AN INDICTMENT AGAINST THE U.S. GOVERNMENT, THE ARMED SERVICES AND ITS INDUSTRIAL ALLIES.' This is specifically an attack on the United States for its involvement in Vietnam, in which the Government is accused of 'waging aggressive war crimes against humanity, and with specific violations of the laws of war.' The article portrays the United States as an aggressor, committing a horrendous crime 'against a peasant people fighting to expel foreign oppressors from their homeland.' The same issue contains an antiwar poem and various quotations attributed to well-known persons and to members of antiwar groups. They uniformly indicate opposition to the Vietnam war and militarism in America. Many are intemperate, and one suggests the abolition of our society. Other comments and articles attack career military personnel ('the lifers') and the trial of certain soldiers. The May issue also sets forth explicit information on how servicemen wishing to desert the armed forces may enter Canada and receive assistance from such groups as the American Deserters Committee, Toronto Anti-Draft Programme, and Vancouver Committee to Aid War Objectors. Another article points out that 53,357 servicemen have deserted the armed services and notes that the accused [Priest] would not himself desert but would stay and fight from within. The theme of the June issue is not unlike that of the May issue. Its language is somewhat more violent. For example, it suggests the velocity with which the Vice President would strike the pavement if he was pushed or fell from the Empire State Building. It quotes Che Guevara on the 'futility of maintaining the fight for social goals within the framework of civil debate.' ''

The Court of Military Appeals most definitely did not like this kind of free speech and cashiered Priest: (1) A declaration of personal belief can amount to a disloyal statement if it disavows allegiance owed to the United States by the declarant; the disloyalty involved, however, must be to the United States as a political entity and not necessarily to a department or other agency that forms a part of its operative administration. (2) The evidence presented was legally sufficient to support the fact finder's determination that two pamphlets, printed and distributed by Priest, each taken in its entirety, were statements disloyal to the United States, where the lead article in one pamphlet was an indictment of the United States and a call to resist its "illegitimate authority," wherein the accused suggested turning to the streets and the possibility of violent revolution, and expressly provided information encouraging desertions from the armed forces, and where, in the second pamphlet, the assassination of the president and the vice-president was advocated. (3) Where the accused's pamphlets suggested means by which the troops might actively demonstrate their own disloyalty and disaffection by deserting to Canada, refusing promotions, or themselves taking to the streets, such statements permitted an inference of the accused's intent to promote disloyalty and disaffection among the troops from the contents of the pamphlets and their free distribution to members of the armed services. (4) Veneration of constitutionally protected free speech values makes extraordinarily important the application of the standard of conduct punishable under Article 134 to publications and statements by military personnel. It is a standard by which such conduct, to be punishable, must be palpably and directly prejudicial to good order and discipline and not merely prejudicial in an indirect and remote sense. (5) The right of free speech in the armed services is not unlimited and must be brought into balance with the paramount consideration of providing an effective fighting force for the defense of the United States. (6) The accused's publication and distribution of two pamphlets tended palpably and directly to affect military order and discipline where the papers in question were directed primarily to other members of the armed services, and they expressly sought a breakdown in military discipline, called attention to methods by which members might safely flee from military control, heaped maledictions on the United States, called into disrespect all military superiors and particularly those who had chosen the defense of United States as their life's vocation, impliedly advocated assassination of the president and the vice-president, and appealed to readers to take to the streets in violent revolution. The lack of success was not the criterion, for the government is entitled to protect itself in advance against a calculated call for revolution. (7) It is not relevant that other writers and other publications have advocated measures similar to those espoused by the accused—Priest and no one else is on trial. (8) It is not relevant that other publications advocating the identical message were for sale at the Navy Exchange; the navy never sanctioned their contents and it is Priest, and not these other publications, who is on trial. *United States v. Priest*, 21 U.S.C.M.A. 564 (1972).

UNITED STATES v. RAMSEY (1977). Title 19 U.S.C. § 482 (Customs Regulations*) and implementing postal regulations authorize U.S. Customs officials to "inspect" incoming international mail if they have a "reasonable cause to suspect" that the mail contains illegally imported merchandise (including obscene material), although the regulations prohibit the reading of correspondence without a court-issued search warrant. The U.S. Supreme Court held that these regulations do not violate the First Amendment. The Court wrote that the opening of incoming international mail under the guidelines of the statute only when the Customs inspector has reason to believe that the mail contains something other than correspondence, while the reading of any correspondence inside is forbidden by the regulations, does not impermissibly chill the exercise of free speech under the First Amendment, and any "chill" that might exist under such circumstances is not only "minimal," but also wholly subjective. *United States v. Ramsey*, 431 U.S. 606 (1977).

UNITED STATES v. REIDEL (1971). Reidel was indicted for having violated 18 U.S.C. § 1461 (Postal Regulations, Mailing Obscene Material*) for mailing an illustrated booklet (*The True Facts About Imported Pornography*) to a postal inspector. The inspector had responded to a newspaper ad that stipulated that any recipient of the booklet had to be over twenty-one years of age. A federal district court dismissed the government's charge, holding § 1461 was unconstitutional, since a person had the right to receive and possess obscene material and since the booklet in question was not directed at children or at an unwilling or captive audience.

The U.S. Supreme Court did not agree with this reasoning, and it decided that § 1461 was constitutional as applied to the distribution of obscene materials to willing recipients who stated that they were adults: (1) The constitutional right of a person to possess obscene material in the privacy of his own home (*Stanley v. Georgia**) did not confer on another person a First Amendment right to sell or deliver such material. (2) Legislative and regulatory action could be validly taken to protect children and unwilling adults from exposure to obscene materials, and the mail-order distribution in Reidel's case did not have sufficient safeguards against receipt of the booklet by minors.

Justice Black, joined by Justice Douglas, dissented on the grounds that Congress did not have the power to determine what books people could read. Justice Black: "In my view the First Amendment denies Congress the power to act as censor and determine what books our citizens may read and what pictures they may watch. . . . For the foreseeable future this Court must sit as a Board of Supreme Censors, sifting through books and magazines and watching movies because some official fears they deal too explicitly with sex. I can imagine no more distasteful, useless, and time-consuming task for the members of this Court than perusing this material to determine whether it has 'redeeming social value.' This absurd spectacle could be avoided if we would adhere to the literal command of the First Amendment that 'Congress shall make no law . . . abridging the freedom of speech, or of the press.' " *United States v. Reidel*, 402 U.S. 351 (1971).

UNITED STATES v. RUMELY (1953). Rumely was secretary of an organization that, among other things, engaged in the sale of books of a political nature. He refused to disclose to a committee of Congress the names of those people who made bulk purchases of the books for future distribution, and he was convicted for a violation of 2 U.S.C. 192 (United States Congress, Contempt*), which reads, in part, that "every person who having been summoned as a witness by the authority of either House of Congress to give testimony or to produce papers upon any matter under inquiry" is subject to a fine or imprisonment or both if the witness refuses to give such testimony or to produce such papers. Rumely was convicted for refusing to produce the records of the Committee for Constitutional Government (CCG), showing the name and address of each person from whom a total of $1,000 or more had been received by CCG for any purpose, including receipts from the sale of books and pamphlets. He was also convicted for refusing to give the name of a woman from Toledo, Ohio, who gave him $2,000 for distribution of *The Road Ahead*, a book written by John T. Flynn.

The Supreme Court reversed Rumely's conviction, Justice Frankfurter writing that to construe the resolution as authorizing the committee to inquire into all efforts of private individuals to influence public opinion through books and periodicals, however remote the radiations of influence that they may exert on the ultimate legislative process, would raise doubts of constitutionality in view of the prohibitions contained in the First Amendment. Justice Douglas filed a concurring opinion that discussed fully the fears of the majority. Justice Douglas: "Of necessity I come then to the constitutional questions. [Rumely] represents a segment of the American press. Some may like what his group publishes; others may disapprove. These tracts may be the essence of wisdom to some; to others their point of view and philosophy may be anathema. To some ears their words may be harsh and repulsive; to others they may carry the hope of the future. We have here a publisher who through books and pamphlets seeks to reach the minds and hearts of the American people. He is different in some respects from other publishers. But the differences are minor. Like the publishers of newspapers, magazines, or books, this publisher bids for the minds of men in the market place of ideas. The aim of the historic struggle for a free press was 'to establish and preserve the right of the English people to full information in respect of the doings or misdoings of their government' (*Grossjean v. American Press**). That is the tradition behind the First Amendment. Censorship or previous restraint is banned (*Near v. Minnesota ex rel. Olson**). Discriminatory taxation is outlawed. The privilege of pamphleteering, as well as the more orthodox types of publications, may neither be licensed (*Lovell v. City of Griffin**) nor taxed (*Murdock v. Pennsylvania**). Door to door distribution is privileged (*Martin v. City of Struthers**). These are illustrative of the preferred position granted speech and the press by the First Amendment. The command that 'Congress shall make no law . . . abridging the freedom of speech, or of the press' has behind it a long history. It expresses the confidence that the safety of society depends on the tolerance of government for hostile as well as friendly criticism, that in a community where men's minds are free, there must be room for the unorthodox as well as the orthodox views. If the present inquiry were sanctioned, the press would be subjected to harassment that in practical effect might be as serious as censorship. A publisher, compelled to register with the Federal Government, would be subjected to vexatious inquiries. A requirement that a publisher disclose the identity of those who buy his books, pamphlets, or papers is indeed the beginning of surveillance of the press. True, no legal sanction is involved here. Congress has imposed no tax, established no board of censors, instituted no licensing system. But the potential restraint is equally severe. The finger of government leveled against the press is ominous. Once the government can demand of a publisher the names of the purchasers of his publications, the free press as we know it disappears. Then the spectre of a government agent will look over the shoulder of everyone who reads. The purchase of a book or pamphlet today may result in a subpoena tomorrow. Fear of criticism goes with every person into the bookstall. The subtle, imponderable pressures of the orthodox lay hold. Some will fear to read what is unpopular, what the powers-that-be dislike. When the light of publicity may reach any student, any teacher, inquiry will be discouraged. The books and pamphlets that are critical of the administration, that preach an unpopular policy in domestic or foreign affairs, that are in disrepute in the orthodox school of thought will be suspect and subject to investigation. The press and its readers will pay a heavy price in harassment. But that will be minor in comparison with the menace of the shadow which government will cast over literature that does not follow the dominant party line. If the lady from Toledo can be required to disclose what she read yesterday and what she will read tomorrow, fear will take the place of freedom in the libraries, book stores, and homes of the land. Through the harassment of hearings, investigations, reports, and subpoenas government will hold a club over speech and over the press.'' *United States v. Rumely*, 345 U.S. 41 (1953).

UNITED STATES v. THIRTY-SEVEN PHOTOGRAPHS (1971). Title 19 U.S.C. § 1305-a (Tariff Act*) authorizes the U.S. Customs Service to seize any incoming material that the service deems to be obscene. After seizure, the government must receive a judicial determination as to the material's obscenity. If the court rules that it is not obscene, the material is returned to the claimant and allowed to enter the United States; if the material is judged obscene, Customs then destroys it. This case concerned the seizure of thirty-seven photographs from the luggage of Milton Luros, who was returning from Europe. Luros testified that most of the thirty-seven photographs were intended to be incorporated in a new hardcover edition of *The Kama Sutra of Vatsyayana* a well-known and widely distributed book candidly describing a large number of sexual positions. Luros challenged the constitutionality of § 1305-a, but the Supreme Court held that the statute did not violate the First Amendment: Regardless of the right to possess obscene material for private use in one's home (*Stanley v. Georgia**), the government can properly prevent the importation of such obscene material, even when intended for the private use of an individual. Justice Black, joined by Justice Douglas, dissented: (1) The First Amendment denies Congress the power to act as a censor of books and pictures. (2) The recognized right to possession of obscene material in the privacy of one's home should be considered as including the right to carry such material privately in one's luggage when entering the United States. *United States v. Thirty-Seven Photographs*, 402 U.S. 363 (1971).

UNITED STATES v. TOOMEY (1968). A member of the U.S. Air Force, Toomey was convicted by a court-martial of violating certain military regulations (Military Regulations, Wearing Uniforms—Military Personnel* and Uniform Code of Military Justice*—Article 134, "Failure to Obey a Lawful Order"). He was sentenced to a reduction in grade to airman basic and a forfeiture of eighty-two dollars and received a bad-conduct discharge. This sentence was affirmed by a Military Board of Review.

On April 2, 1968, Toomey joined a group of approximately one hundred demonstrators assembled under the auspices of a group known locally as the "Resistance." The protest demonstration was at the Selective Service headquarters, housed in the Post Office Building, Albuquerque, New Mexico. It had as its theme resistance to the Selective Service System as a protest to the war in Viet Nam, which was described in pamphlet handouts as an "immoral, illegal and stupid war." Toomey, dressed in his air force blue uniform, in public view of a number of spectators, including representatives of the local news and television media, picketed the Post Office Building while carrying a sign bearing the words "Hell No, Don't Go." Toomey's participation continued until he was hauled off to the brig by a Kirtland Air Force Base security policeman.

Toomey argued in vain that the First Amendment protected his right to have engaged in the protest; the military authorities thought differently and gave him a bad-conduct discharge. The Military Board of Review made the following comments: "It has long been held that the right to free speech is not an indiscriminate right. Instead it is qualified by the requirements of reasonableness in relation to time, place, and circumstances. The character of every act depends upon the circumstances in which it was done. We should not deny to servicemen any right that can be given reasonably. But in measuring reasonableness, we should bear in mind that military units have one major purpose justifying their existence: to prepare themselves for war and to wage it successfully. That purpose must never be overlooked in weighing the conflicting interest between the right of the serviceman to express his views on any subject at any time and the right of the Government to prepare for and pursue a war to a successful conclusion. Embraced in success is sacrifice of life and personal liberties; secrecy of plans and movement of personnel; security; discipline and morale; and the faith of the public in the officers and men and the cause they represent. [We] have a great deal of difficulty in following an argument that those who serve should be entitled to express their views, even though by so doing they may destroy the spirit and morale of others which are so vital to military preparedness and success. Assuming arguendo that the privilege of free speech is a preferred right, we should not prefer it to such an extent that we lose all other benefits of our form of government. A demoralized and undisciplined military service could cost us all those we possess. It is unquestionable that the military services have the authority to regulate the wearing of their respective uniforms, and to prohibit the wearing of the uniform under inappropriate, service-demeaning circumstances. Nor can there be any doubt that the wearing of the uniform while participating in a demonstration protesting the Selective Service Act and its implementation, and advocating disobedience of its provisions, is highly injurious to the reputation of the military service. Worn in these circumstances, the uniform would be likely to attract much more attention and attribute greater significance to the purpose of the demonstration than would otherwise be the case and, additionally, would amount to an overt and simultaneous protest against the military establishment by one of its members. We have no hesitancy in [ruling that Toomey is guilty]." *United States v. Toomey*, A.C.M. (Military Board of Review) 20248 (1968).

UNITED STATES v. 12 200-FT. REELS OF SUPER 8MM. FILM (1973).

Title 19 U.S.C. § 1305-a (Tariff Act*) authorizes the U.S. Customs Service to seize allegedly obscene material and then turn to a federal district court for a judicial determination of the material's obscenity. The material is returned to the claimant and allowed to enter the United States if the court rules it not to be obscene; the material is destroyed by Customs if the court determines it to be obscene. In this case, the Supreme Court ruled that such seizure, forfeiture, and destruction is constitutional even when the obscene material is for the private and personal use and possession of the importer and not intended for any commercial purpose. The court record was silent as to the nature of the films involved in this case, but there was general agreement that they were, in fact, "obscene, lewd, lascivious, and indecent." The nature of the material did not concern Justice Douglas, and he dissented from the majority opinion: "I know of no constitutional way by which a book, tract, paper, postcard, or film may be made contraband because of its content. The Constitution never purported to give the Federal Government censorship or oversight over literature or artistic productions, save as they might be governed by the Patent and Copyright Clause of Article I, § 8, cl. 8, of the Constitution.'' *United States v. 12 200-Ft. Reels of Super 8mm. Film*, 413 U.S. 123 (1973).

UNITED STATES v. WAINWRIGHT (1970). A member of the military service, Wainwright was convicted of "communicating indecent language to a female." For this, he was reduced in rank to airman basic, confined at hard labor for three months, and, not least, received a bad-conduct discharge. The Court of Military Review, in affirming this punishment, first stated what the terms "indecent" and "obscene" meant in military parlance: "The terms 'indecent' and 'obscene' refer to that which is grossly offensive to modesty, decency or propriety, or shocks the moral sense, because of its vulgar, filthy, or disgusting nature, or its tendency to arouse lustful thoughts. The language used must violate community standards of decency and substantially exceed customary limits of candor." Airman Wainwright communicated to a female the following words: "I'll give you fifty dollars for a date." The military authorities were aghast at such vulgar, filthy, and disgusting language, and the full weight of military justice fell on Wainwright. The court commented: "In our view, that language does serve to convey an indecent message when reasonably interpreted . . . [and] dictates the conclusion that when compensation (particularly in the generous amount here alleged) is tendered to induce female company, it is understood that something more than scintillating conversation is the expectation of the solicitor. An illicit proposal was, of course, the plain and unmistakable implication of the language allegedly employed by the accused. That being so, we have no hesitation [in finding Wainwright guilty of the] offense of communicating indecent language to a female." *United States v. Wainwright*, 42 C.M.R. 997 (1970).

UNITED STEELWORKERS v. SADLOWSKI (1982). An unsuccessful candidate for a union office and several other individuals brought this suit challenging the union's "outsider rule"—candidates for union offices are prohibited from accepting campaign contributions from non-union members. A court of appeals found that the rule violated the free speech guarantee, but the U.S. Supreme Court reversed the decision. Justice Marshall delivered the opinion of the Court: Certain regulations within labor-management relations and union activities cannot be read as incorporating the entire body of the First Amendment. The scope of protection afforded candidates for union office is not the same as the protection afforded candidates for public political offices and the union rules are valid if they are reasonable—they need not pass the stringent tests demanded by the First Amendment. There was some dissent to this decision (the Court voted 5 to 4), the minority feeling that a union could not be allowed to impose a limitation that would confine a challenger to financial support garnered within the union. *United Steelworkers v. Sadlowski*, 457 U.S. 102 (1982).

UNPROTECTED SPEECH. "There are certain well-defined and narrowly limited classes of speech, the prevention and punishment of which have never been thought to raise any Constitutional problem. . . . It has been well observed that such utterances are no essential part of any exposition of ideas and are of such slight social value as a step to truth that any benefit that may be derived from them is clearly outweighed by the social interest and morality" (*Chaplinsky v. New Hampshire**). This "unprotected speech" means exactly what it says: Some forms of speech and press are *not* protected by the First Amendment, and under certain circumstances, they can be prevented or punished. These narrowly limited classes of speech include obscenity, child pornography (*New York v. Ferber**), fighting words,* clear and present danger* situations, libel-slander-defamation, and fraudulent-false-misleading commercial speech. The problem has not been what the classes of unprotected speech may be, but the description or definition of the class itself (Obscenity*).

A brief narrative on the development of this "unprotected speech," primarily dealing with obscenity, but also touching on other areas, was given by Justice Brennan, in *Roth v. United States.** Justice Brennan: "The dispositive question is whether obscenity is utterance within the area of protected speech and press. Although this is the first time the question has been squarely presented to this Court, either under the First Amendment or under the Fourteenth Amendment, expressions found in numerous opinions indicate that this Court has always assumed that obscenity is not protected by the freedoms of speech and press. . . . The guaranties of freedom of expression in effect in 10 of the 14 States which by 1792 had ratified the Constitution, gave no absolute protection for every utterance. Thirteen of the 14 States provided for the prosecution of libel, and all of those States made either blasphemy or profanity, or both, statutory crimes. As early as 1712, Massachusetts made it criminal to publish 'any filthy, obscene, or profane song, pamphlet, libel or mock sermon' in imitation or mimicking of religious services. [Acts and Laws of the Province of Mass. Bay, c. CV, § 8 (1712), Mass. Bay Colony Charters & Laws 399 (1814).] Thus, profanity and obscenity were related offenses. In light of this history, it is apparent that the unconditional phrasing of the First Amendment was not intended to protect every utterance. This phrasing did not prevent this Court from concluding that libelous utterances are not within the area of constitutionally protected speech (*Beauharnais v. Illinois**). At the time of the adoption of the First Amendment, obscenity law was not as fully developed as libel law, but there is sufficiently contemporaneous evidence to show that obscenity, too, was outside the protection intended for speech and press. The protection given speech and press was fashioned to assure unfettered interchange of ideas for the bringing about of political and social changes desired by the people. This objective was made explicit as early as 1774 in a letter of the Continental Congress to the inhabitants of Quebec: 'The last right we shall mention, regards the freedom of the press. The importance of this consists, besides the advancement of truth, science, morality, and arts in general, in its diffusion of liberal sentiments on the administration of Government, its ready communication of thoughts between subjects, and its consequential promotion of union among them, whereby oppressive officers are shamed or intimidated, into more honourable and just modes of conducting affairs.' All ideas having even the slightest redeeming social importance—unorthodox ideas, controversial ideas, even ideas hateful to the prevailing climate of opinion—have the full protection of the guaranties, unless excludable because they encroach upon the limited area of more important interests. But implicit in the history of the First Amendment is the rejection of obscenity as utterly without redeeming social importance.''

UPHAUS v. WYMAN (1959). In an investigation conducted by the attorney general of New Hampshire on behalf of the state legislature under a resolution directing him to determine whether or not there were ''subversive persons'' in the state (New Hampshire, Subversive Activities Act*), Uphaus testified about his own activities but refused to furnish the names of those who attended his camp during 1954 and 1955. Although Uphaus argued that to force him to produce the documents would violate his right of free speech, the New Hampshire courts convicted him of contempt and sentenced him to jail until he complied with the order.

The U.S. Supreme Court sustained the judgment. The Court commented: ''What was the interest of the State? The Attorney General was commissioned to determine if there were any subversive persons within New Hampshire. The obvious starting point of such an inquiry was to learn what persons were within the State. It is therefore clear that the requests relate directly to the Legislature's area of interest, i.e., the presence of subversives in the State, as announced in its resolution. Nor was the demand of the subpoena burdensome; as to time, only a few months of each of the two years were involved; as to place, only the camp conducted by the Corporation; nor as to the lists of names, which included about 300 each year. . . . The Attorney General had valid reason to believe that the speakers and guests at World Fellowship might be subversive persons within the meaning of the New Hampshire Act. The Supreme Court of New Hampshire found Uphaus' contrary position 'unrelated to reality.' Although the evidence as to the nexus between World Fellowship and subversive activities may not be conclusive, we believe it sufficiently relevant to support the Attorney General's action. The New Hampshire definition of subversive persons was born of the legislative determination that the Communist movement posed a serious threat to the security of the State. The record reveals that [Uphaus] had participated in 'Communist front activities' and that not 'less than nineteen speakers invited by Uphaus to talk at World Fellowship had either been members of the Communist Party or had connections or affiliations with it or with one or more of the organizations cited as subversive or Communist controlled in the United States Attorney General's list.' While . . . guilt by association remains a thoroughly discredited doctrine, it is with a legislative investigation—not a criminal prosecution—that we deal here. Certainly the investigatory power of the State need not be constricted until sufficient evidence of subversion is gathered to justify the institution of criminal proceedings." *Uphaus v. Wyman*, 360 U.S. 72 (1959).

UTAH, TOBACCO ADVERTISEMENTS ON BILLBOARDS. Section 2, of c. 145, Laws of Utah, 1921, as amended by c. 52, § 2, Laws of 1923, and c. 92, Laws of 1929, read as follows: "It shall be a misdemeanor for any person, company, or corporation, to display on any bill board, street car sign, street car, placard, or on any other object or place of display, any advertisement of cigarettes, cigarette papers, cigars, chewing tobacco, or smoking tobacco, or any disguise or substitute of either, except that a dealer in cigarettes, cigarette papers, tobacco or cigars or their substitutes, may have a sign on the front of his place of business stating that he is a dealer in such articles, provided that nothing herein shall be construed to prohibit the advertising of cigarettes, cigarette papers, chewing tobacco, smoking tobacco, or any disguise or substitute of either in any newspaper, magazine, or periodical printed or circulating in the State of Utah." The Supreme Court, in 1932 (*Packer Corporation v. Utah**), upheld this ban as a reasonable exercise of a state's power to regulate commercial speech and advertising.

V

VALENTINE v. CHRESTENSEN (1942). A New York City municipal ordinance (New York City [NY], Distribution of Commercial Material*) prohibited the distribution in the city streets of any handbills or circulars that contained any commercial material. Chrestensen attempted to get the courts to enjoin the city from enforcing the ordinance, and he was successful until he reached the Supreme Court. The Court ruled that the ordinance was not a violation of the First Amendment and that a commercial handbill remains a commercial handbill even after the distributor appends a short public interest message to it.

The question in front of the Court was whether the enforcement of the ordinance to Chrestensen's activity was an unconstitutional abridgment of the freedom of the press and of speech; the Court answered in the negative: "1. This Court has unequivocally held that the streets are proper places for the exercise of the freedom of communicating information and disseminating opinion and that, though the states and municipalities may appropriately regulate the privilege in the public interest, they may not unduly burden or proscribe its employment in these public thoroughfares. We are equally clear that the Constitution imposes no such restraint on government as respects purely commercial advertising. Whether, and to what extent, one may promote or pursue a gainful occupation in the streets, to what extent such activity shall be adjudged a derogation of the public right of user, are matters for legislative judgment. The question is not whether the legislative body may interfere with the harmless pursuit of a lawful business, but whether it must permit such pursuit by what it deems an undesirable invasion of, or interference with, the full and free use of the highways by the people in fulfillment of the public use to which streets are dedicated. If [Chrestensen] was attempting to use the streets of New York by distributing commercial advertising, the prohibition of the code provision was lawfully invoked against his conduct. 2. The respondent contends that, in truth, he was engaged in the dissemination of matter proper for public information, none the less so because there was inextricably attached to the medium of such dissemination commercial advertising matter. The court below appears to have taken this view, since it adverts to the difficulty of apportioning, in a given case, the contents of the communication as between what is of public interest and what is for private profit. We need not indulge nice appraisal based upon subtle distinctions in the present instance nor assume possible cases not now presented. It is enough for the present purpose that the stipulated facts justify the conclusion that the affixing of the protest against official conduct to the advertising circular was with the intent, and for the purpose, of evading the prohibition of the ordinance. If that evasion were successful, every merchant who desires to broadcast advertising leaflets in the streets need only append a civic appeal, or a moral platitude, to achieve immunity from the law's command.'' *Valentine v. Chrestensen*, 316 U.S. 52 (1942).

VANCE v. UNIVERSAL AMUSEMENT CO., INC. (1980). In 1973, King Arts Theatre operated an indoor, adults-only motion picture theater (it exhibited X-rated films). The landlord gave notice that the theater's lease would be terminated. The notice of termination from the landlord stated that the local county attorney had previously informed the landlord that the attorney, pursuant to a Texas statute (Texas, Public Nuisance*), intended to obtain an injunction to abate the theater as a "public nuisance" in order to prevent the future exhibition of allegedly obscene motion pictures. The theater then filed suit to prevent the county attorney from taking any action under the Texas nuisance statute. The Supreme Court agreed with the theater and affirmed an order preventing such action on the grounds that it would have been an unconstitutional prior restraint.* The Court, in a brief opinion, noted that the Texas public nuisance statute, "construed as authorizing state judges, on the basis of a showing that a theater exhibited obscene films in the past, to enjoin its future exhibition of films not yet found to be obscene, is unconstitutional as authorizing a prior restraint." *Vance v. Universal Amusement Co., Inc.*, 445 U.S. 308 (1980).

VILLAGE BOOKS v. STATE'S ATTORNEY FOR PRINCE GEORGE'S COUNTY (1971). This case involved a proceeding against eighteen books in order to have them judged obscene in violation of the Maryland obscenity statute and to prevent their sale. The Maryland statute (Ann. Code Md., Art. 27, § 418 and 418A) grants jurisdiction to the courts to enjoin the sale or distribution of any publication that is "obscene." Obscenity has been defined by the Maryland court by applying the various tests (Roth Standard*/Memoirs Standard*/Miller Standard*) enunciated by the Supreme Court over the years. The Maryland circuit court found all eighteen publications obscene; on appeal, the Maryland Court of Appeals found that only five of the books were obscene and that thirteen were not. Ten of the thirteen non-obscene books (*Fun and Games, New Directions, Nude Lark, One Plus One, Yum Yum No. 2, Love Date, Yum Yum, Naked Love, Eclipse I, No. 3*, and *Eclipse I, No. 4*) were described by the court: "The counsel for Village Books calls them 'garbage,' they are 'split-beavers' in the argot of the trade; photos of nude young adults; facial expressions range from utterly blank to lewd and lively; there is no depiction of actual sexual activity," but they are not obscene. The judge wrote that *The Boy Lovers* was a "close case," but it was not hard-core pornography. The other two non-obscene books (*Nudist Youth* and *Teen Nude*) were described as follows: "Nude young males; anyone examining these exhibits will be conscious of two things: these youngsters are generously endowed; their countenances reflect a smug awareness of that fact"; but they are not pornography. The remaining five books (*Sex Confidential, Masturbation and Youth, Ted and Blair, Allen and Jim*, and *Auto-Fellatio and Masturbation*) were not described, but the judge held them to be hard-core pornography. *Village Books v. State's Attorney for Prince George's County*, 282 A. 2d 126 (1971).

VILLAGE OF HOFFMAN ESTATES (IL), DRUG PARAPHERNALIA.

Village of Hoffman Estates, Ordinance No. 969-1978, "An Ordinance Amending the Municipal Code of the Village of Hoffman Estates by Providing for Regulation of Items Designed or Marketed for Use with Illegal Cannabis or Drugs," reads as follows: "Whereas, certain items designed or marketed for use with illegal drugs are being retailed within the Village of Hoffman Estates, Cook County, Illinois, and Whereas, it is recognized that such items are legal retail items and that their sale cannot be banned, and Whereas, there is evidence that these items are designed or marketed for use with illegal cannabis or drugs and it is in the best interests of the health, safety and welfare of the citizens of the Village of Hoffman Estates to regulate within the Village the sale of items designed or marketed for use with illegal cannabis or drugs. Now Therefore Be It Ordained by the President and Board of Trustees of the Village of Hoffman Estates, Cook County, Illinois, as follows: . . . the Municipal Code be amended by adding thereto an additional Section, Section 8-7-16, which additional section shall read as follows: . . . A. License Required: It shall be unlawful for any person or persons as principal, clerk, agent or servant to sell any items, effect, paraphernalia, accessory or thing which is designed or marketed for use with illegal cannabis or drugs, as defined by the Illinois Revised Statutes, without obtaining a license therefor. Such license shall be in addition to any or all other licenses held by applicant. B. Application. Application to sell any item, effect, paraphernalia, accessory or thing which is designed or marketed for use with illegal cannabis or drugs shall . . . be accompanied by affidavits by applicant and each and every employee authorized to sell such items that such person has never been convicted of a drug-related offense. C. Minors. It shall be unlawful to sell or give items as described . . . in any form to any male or female child under eighteen years of age." The Supreme Court, in *Village of Hoffman Estates v. Flipside, Hoffman Estates, Inc.** ruled that this ordinance was not unconstitutionally vague or overbroad.

VILLAGE OF HOFFMAN ESTATES v. FLIPSIDE, HOFFMAN ES-TATES, INC. (1982).

A village in the suburbs of Chicago enacted an ordinance (Village of Hoffman Estates [IL], Drug Paraphernalia*) requiring any business to obtain a license to sell any items that were "designed or marketed for use with illegal cannabis or drugs'' and made it a misdemeanor to sell such items, even with a license, to any minor under eighteen years of age. A store that sold such paraphernalia in the village brought suit, challenging the ordinance before its enforcement on grounds of vagueness and overbreadth*; a federal district court ruled the ordinance constitutional, an appeals court reversed, saying that the ordinance was impermissibly vague on its face.

On appeal, the U.S. Supreme Court ruled that the ordinance was neither vague nor overbroad and thus a valid regulation of commercial activity. The Court's decision was unanimous (8 to 0; Justice Stevens not participating), and Justice Marshall delivered the opinion: (1) "In a facial challenge to the overbreadth and vagueness of an enactment, a court must first determine whether the enactment reaches a substantial amount of constitutionally protected conduct. If it does not, the overbreadth challenge must fail. The court should then examine the facial vagueness challenge and should uphold such challenge only if the enactment is impermissibly vague in all of its applications." (2) "The ordinance here does not violate [Flipside's] First Amendment rights nor is it overbroad because it inhibits such rights of other parties. The ordinance does not restrict speech as such but simply regulates the commercial marketing of items that the labels reveal may be used for an illicit purpose and thus does not embrace noncommercial speech. With respect to any noncommercial speech implicated, the ordinance's restriction on the manner of marketing does not appreciably limit [Flipside's] communication of information, except to the extent it is directed at commercial activity promoting or encouraging illegal drug use, an activity which, if deemed 'speech,' is speech proposing an illegal transaction and thus subject to government regulation or ban. It is irrelevant whether the ordinance has an overbroad scope encompassing other persons' commercial speech, since the overbreadth doctrine does not apply to commercial speech." (3) "The ordinance's language 'designed for use' is not unconstitutionally vague on its face, since it is clear that such standard encompasses at least an item that is principally used with illegal drugs by virtue of its objective features, i.e., features designed by the manufacturer. Thus, the 'designed for use' standard is sufficiently clear to cover at least some of the items that [Flipside] sold, such as 'roach clips' and the specially designed pipes. As to the 'marketed for use' standard, the guidelines refer to the display of paraphernalia and to the proximity of covered items to otherwise uncovered items, and thus such standard requires scienter on the part of the retailer. Under this test, [Flipside] had ample warning that its marketing activities required a license, and by displaying a certain magazine and certain books dealing with illegal drugs physically close to pipes and colored rolling paper, it was in clear violation of the guidelines." *Village of Hoffman Estates v. Flipside, Hoffman Estates, Inc.*, 455 U.S. 489 (1982).

VILLAGE OF SCHAUMBURG v. CITIZENS FOR A BETTER ENVIRONMENT (1980).

The village of Schaumburg (twenty-five miles from Chicago) adopted, in 1974, an ordinance (Schaumburg [IL], Ordinance on Soliciting*) prohibiting door-to-door or on-street solicitation of contributions by charitable organizations that did not use at least 75 percent of the receipts for "charitable purposes." Citizens for a Better Environment, a non-profit environmental protection organization, was denied a permit to solicit contributions because it could not meet the ordinance's 75 percent requirement. The U.S. Supreme Court held that the ordinance was unconstitutionally overbroad in violation of the First Amendment: (1) "Charitable appeals for funds, on the street or door-to-door, involve a variety of speech interests—communication of information, dissemination and propagation of views and ideas, and advocacy of causes—that are within the First Amendment's protection. While soliciting financial support is subject to reasonable regulation, such regulation must give due regard to the reality that solicitation is characteristically intertwined with informative and perhaps persuasive speech seeking support for particular causes or for particular views on economic, political, or social issues, and to the reality that without solicitation, the flow of such information and advocacy would likely cease. Moreover, since charitable solicitation does more than inform private economic decisions and is not primarily concerned with providing information about the characteristics and costs for goods and services, it is not dealt with as a variety of purely commercial speech." (2) "The 75 per cent limitation is a direct and substantial limitation on protected activity that cannot be sustained unless it serves a sufficiently strong, subordinating interest that the Village is entitled to protect. Here, the Village's proffered justifications that such limitation is intimately related to substantial governmental interests in preventing fraud and protecting public safety and residential privacy are inadequate, and such interests could be sufficiently served by measures less destructive of First Amendment interests." *Village of Schaumburg v. Citizens for a Better Environment*, 444 U.S. 620 (1980).

VIRGINIA, ABORTION ADVERTISING STATUTE. Virginia Code Ann. § 18.1-63 (1960) read as follows: "If any person, by publication, lecture, advertisement, or by the sale or circulation of any publication, or in any other manner, encourage or prompt the procuring of abortion or miscarriage, he shall be guilty of a misdemeanor." The state of Virginia attempted to apply this statute to a newspaper published in Virginia that carried ads for abortions to be performed in New York, but the Supreme Court (*Bigelow v. Virginia**) ruled that the statute was an unconstitutional abridgment on the freedom of the press. Shortly after the statute was used in Bigelow's case (and before it was ever used again), the Virginia legislature amended it to make illegal such information about abortions to be performed in the state of Virginia, rather than, as the original read, wherever performed. The statute, as amended by Va. Acts of Assembly, 1972, c. 725, now reads: "18.1-63. If any person, by publication, lecture, advertisement, or by the sale or circulation of any publication, or through the use of a referral agency for profit, or in any other manner, encourage or promote the processing of an abortion or miscarriage to be performed in this State which is prohibited under this article, he shall be guilty of a misdemeanor."

VIRGINIA, CONFIDENTIALITY RULE. Virginia Code § 2.1-37.13 (1973) provided: "All papers filed with and proceedings before the [Judicial Inquiry and Review] Commission . . . including the identification of the subject judge as well as all testimony and other evidence and any transcript thereof made by a reporter, shall be confidential and shall not be divulged by any person to anyone except the Commission. . . . Any person who shall divulge information in violation of this section shall be guilty of a misdemeanor." The Supreme Court, in *Landmark Communications, Inc. v. Virginia,** ruled that although the state could punish people who had legitimate access to such information and then made it public, a recipient of the information—in this case, a newspaper—could not be prevented from publishing the information nor could the newspaper be punished after the fact.

VIRGINIA, LEGAL ETHICS. The state of Virginia, in an attempt to hamper, if not end altogether, the activities in Virginia of the National Association for the Advancement of Colored People (NAACP), passed legislation stating that it was against the state's code of legal ethics, and thus prohibited, for any person or organization to engage in activities "fomenting and soliciting legal business in which they are not parties and have no pecuniary right or liability, and which they channel to the enrichment of certain lawyers employed by them, at no cost to the litigants and over which the litigants have no control." Code of Virginia, 1950, §§ 54-74, 54-78, and 54-79, as amended by Acts of 1956, Ex. Sess., c. 33 (Repl. Vol. 1958). Penalty for violating the code of legal ethics was the revocation of the attorney's license to practice law in the state. The Supreme Court, in *National Association for the Advancement of Colored People v. Button,** ruled that such a statute was a violation of the expressive rights of such organizations. The Court ruled that it was a First Amendment right for organizations such as the NAACP and the American Civil Liberties Union (*In Re Primus**) to engage in litigation, for the litigation was a form of speech.

VIRGINIA PHARMACY BOARD v. VIRGINIA CITIZENS CONSUMER COUNCIL (1976). This case concerned the validity of a Virginia statute (Virginia, Prescription Drug Advertising*) that made it "unprofessional conduct" for a licensed pharmacist to advertise the prices of prescription drugs. The Supreme Court ruled the statute to be unconstitutional and stated that even commercial speech, if not fraudulent, misleading, or false (pure commercial speech such as "I will sell you product X at price Y"), does not lack First Amendment protection: (1) "That the advertiser's interest in a commercial advertisement is purely economic does not disqualify him from protection under the First and Fourteenth Amendments. Both the individual consumer and society in general may have strong interests in the free flow of commercial information." (2) "The ban on advertising prescription drug prices cannot be justified on the basis of the State's interest in maintaining the professionalism of its licensed pharmacists; the State is free to require whatever professional standards it wishes of pharmacists; and may subsidize them or protect them from competition in other ways, but it may not do so by keeping the public in ignorance of the lawful terms that competing pharmacists are offering.'' (3) ''Whatever may be the bounds of time, place, and manner* restrictions on commercial speech, they are plainly exceeded by the Virginia statute, which singles out speech of a particular content and seeks to prevent its dissemination completely.'' (4) ''No claim is made that the prohibited prescription drug advertisements are false, misleading, or propose illegal transactions, and a State may not suppress the dissemination of concededly truthful information about entirely lawful activity, fearful of that information's effect upon its disseminators and its recipients.'' *Virginia Pharmacy Board v. Virginia Citizens Consumer Council*, 425 U.S. 748 (1976).

VIRGINIA, PRESCRIPTION DRUG ADVERTISING. Section § 54-524.35 of the Virginia Code Ann. (1974) provided that a pharmacist licensed in Virginia was guilty of unprofessional conduct (with some resulting penalties) if he ''publishes, advertises or promotes, directly or indirectly, in any manner whatsoever, any amount, price, fee, premium, discount, rebate or credit terms for professional services or for drugs containing narcotics or for any drugs which may be dispensed only by prescription.'' The Supreme Court, in *Virginia Pharmacy Board v. Virginia Citizens Consumer Council*,* held that such a statute, even if applied to commercial speech, violated the First Amendment.

VIVA MARIA. The city of Dallas had an ordinance (Dallas [TX], Motion Picture Classification Board*) that established a film censorship board. The board was to classify films as either ''suitable'' or ''not suitable'' for young people (those under sixteen years of age). In classifying a picture as ''not suitable for young persons,'' the board had to follow standards set forth in the ordinance and find that, in its judgment, the film described or portrayed ''(1) brutality, criminal violence, or depravity in such a manner as likely to incite young persons to crime or delinquency or (2) sexual promiscuity or extra-marital or abnormal sexual relations in such a manner as . . . likely to incite or encourage delinquency or sexual promiscuity on the part of young persons or to appeal to their prurient interest.'' A film was to be considered likely to produce such results if, in the board's judgment, ''there is a substantial probability that it will create the impression on young persons that such conduct is profitable, desirable, acceptable, respectable, praiseworthy or commonly accepted.'' If the exhibitor did not accept the board's ''not suitable'' classification, the board had to file suit to enjoin the showing of the picture and the board's original determination was subject to a new review. The ordinance was enforceable by a misdemeanor penalty, an injunction, license revocation, or a combination of these.

Acting pursuant to the Dallas ordinance, the board, in 1966, without giving any reasons for its determination, classified the film *Viva Maria* as ''not suitable for young persons.'' The exhibitor did not accept this classification. The board then petitioned the Dallas court for an injunction against the film, claiming the classification was justified because the film portrayed "sexual promiscuity." Two board members testified at the hearing that several scenes portraying male-female relationships "contravened acceptable and approved behavior." The trial judge, concluding that there were "two or three features in the picture that look to me would be unsuitable to young people," issued the injunction. A Texas appeals court affirmed the injunction. The exhibitor and the distributor of the film appealed to the Supreme Court, but a brief description of the film follows before the Supreme Court's decision is presented.

Viva Maria was produced in France, in 1965, and was directed by Louis Malle. George Hamilton, Jeanne Moreau, and Brigitte Bardot were the stars. The film won the Grand Prix du Cinéma Français. *Viva Maria* was reviewed in such publications as *Life* and the *New York Times*. A synopsis of the plot is presented by de Grazia and Newman (*Banned Films*, pp. 291–292): "As British soldiers cross a bridge to close in on her wounded Irish anarchist father, Maria Fitzgerald O'Malley blows the bridge apart, with tears in her eyes. Fleeing, she stows away with a troupe of traveling players, is taken up by an older, worldly dancer also named Maria, inadvertently invents the striptease, and becomes the toast of the small, poor country of San Miguel, learning the ways of liquor and love. Having seen the few powerful men of San Miguel exploit the country's people, Maria O'Malley furiously shoots one looter of a marauding band, and the troupe is captured by evil Don Rodriguez. While imprisoned at the don's hacienda, the two Marias are attracted to Flores, the young, handsome leader of the country's revolt, who is bound with his arms tied to a wooden yoke across his shoulders. That night, having fallen for Flores, the more experienced, yet more romantic, Maria makes love to the chained leader while he is unable to move. The next morning, taken to Rodriguez for his pleasure before disposing of them, the two women destroy his magnificent salon, Maria O'Malley cutting loose with a captured machine gun. They escape the hacienda with the prisoners led by Flores. However, as Flores, shot in the fight, soon dies, the older Maria vows to lead the revolt in his place. The two raid and destroy the hacienda, leaving Rodriguez crawling through the brush in his underwear. With success after success, the older Maria leads the growing revolution and the two Marias are hailed as the country's saviors—until they are captured by San Miguel's billiard-playing president. Facing the firing squad, the two Marias are rescued by their revolutionary followers, who have just captured the country's capital, and, with a great celebration, are sent on their way to France. There, dancing with the troupe for the wealthy elite of Orleans, the two Marias take up again the explosive, revolutionary ways."†

The Supreme Court, in *Interstate Circuit, Inc. v. City of Dallas* and *United Artists Corp. v. City of Dallas*, 390 U.S. 676 (1968), ruled that the Dallas ordinance violated the First Amendment as being unconstitutionally vague, since it lacked "narrowly drawn, reasonable and definite standards for the officials to follow." Among the comments made by the Supreme Court were the following: "Motion pictures are protected by the First Amendment and cannot be regulated except by precise and definite standards. The vice of vagueness is particularly pronounced where expression is subject to licensing. Vague censorship standards are not cured merely by *de novo* judicial review and unless narrowed by interpretation only encourage erratic administration. The term 'sexual promiscuity' is not defined in the ordinance and was not interpreted in the State courts. The failure to limit that term or related terms used in the ordinance and the breadth of the standard 'profitable, desirable, acceptable, respectable, praiseworthy or commonly accepted' give the censor a roving commission. The evil of vagueness is not cured because the regulation of expression is one of classification rather than direct suppression or was adopted for the salutary purpose of protecting children."

WALKER v. CITY OF BIRMINGHAM (1967). On April 10, 1963, an Alabama circuit court judge issued a temporary injunction on the request of some Birmingham city officials enjoining Walker, and others, from participating in or encouraging mass street parades without the necessary permit (Birmingham [AL], Parade Ordinance*). The testimony by the city officials stated that demonstrations, parades, and picketing had been engaged in by Walker and the others for the previous seven days and were expected to continue. Some of the demonstrators, who had been served with copies of the injunction, announced in a press conference that they were going to disobey the injunction. No permit to parade was requested, but parades and demonstrations were held on April 12 and April 14. Walker and the others were then cited for contempt—they disobeyed the injunction not to parade without a permit—and the Alabama judge found them guilty. Walker's argument was that the injunction was unconstitutional on the grounds that it was vague, overbroad, and restrained free speech; the parade ordinance was also attacked on grounds of unconstitutionality and on the basis that it had been administered in an arbitrary and discriminatory fashion.

The Alabama Supreme Court affirmed the ruling, and on appeal, the U.S. Supreme Court, in one of the few post-1954 decisions (*Brown v. Board of Education*) that ruled against the civil rights movement, affirmed the conviction, holding that Walker and the other demonstrators could not bypass orderly judicial review of the temporary injunction before disobeying it. The Court offered the following argument: "We emphatically reject the notion . . . that the First and Fourteenth Amendments afford the same kind of freedom to those who would communicate ideas by conduct such as patrolling, marching, and picketing on streets and highways, as these amendments afford to those who communicate ideas by pure speech. Civil liberties, as guaranteed by the Constitution, imply the existence of an organized society maintaining public order without which liberty itself would be lost in the excesses of unrestrained abuses. The authority of a municipality to impose regulations in order to assure the safety and convenience of the people in the use of public highways has never been regarded as inconsistent with civil liberties but rather as one of the means of safeguarding the good order upon which they ultimately depend. The generality of the language contained in the Birmingham parade ordinance . . . would unquestionably raise substantial constitutional issues concerning some of its provisions. The petitioners, however, did not even attempt to apply to the Alabama courts for an authoritative construction of the ordinance. . . . The breadth and vagueness of the injunction itself would also unquestionably be subject to substantial constitutional question. But the way to raise that question was to apply to the Alabama courts to have the injunction modified or dissolved. The injunction in all events clearly prohibited mass parading without a permit, and the evidence shows that the petitioners fully understood that prohibition when they violated it.''

Justice Douglas dissented from the majority opinion, believing that the requirement of the permit was an invalid prior restraint and, therefore, Walker was justified in disobeying the injunction: ''The record shows that petitioners did not deliberately attempt to circumvent the permit requirement. Rather, they diligently attempted to obtain a permit and were rudely rebuffed and then reasonably concluded that any further attempts would be fruitless. The right to defy an unconstitutional statute is basic in our scheme. Even when an ordinance requires a permit to make a speech, to deliver a sermon, to picket, to parade, or to assemble, it need not be honored when it is invalid on its face. By like reason, where a permit has been arbitrarily denied, one need not pursue the long and expensive route to this Court to obtain a remedy. The reason is the same in both cases. For if a person must pursue his judicial remedy before he may speak, parade, or assemble, the occasion when protest is desired or needed will have become history and any later speech, parade, or assembly will be futile or pointless.'' *Walker v. City of Birmingham*, 388 U.S. 307 (1967).

WASHINGTON, DISRESPECT FOR THE LAW. The following statute (Wash. Code § 2564), ''Disrespect for the Law,'' was employed to convict, in 1915, one Fox (*Fox v. Washington**), who wrote a newspaper article extolling the benefits of nudism: ''Every person who shall wilfully print, publish, edit, issue, or knowingly circulate, sell, distribute or display any book, paper, document, or written or printed matter, in any form, advocating, encouraging or inciting, or having a tendency to encourage or to incite the commission of any crime, breach of the peace or act of violence, or which shall tend to encourage or advocate disrespect for law or for any court or courts of justice, shall be guilty of a gross misdemeanor.''

WASHINGTON, FLAG DESECRATION. Washington Rev. Code, § 9.86.020, provided the following: ''No person shall, in any manner, for exhibition or display: (1) Place or cause to be placed any word, figure, mark, picture, design, drawing or advertisement of any nature upon any flag, standard, color, ensign or shield of the United States or of this State . . . or (2) Expose to public view any such flag.'' The Supreme Court, in *Spence v. Washington* (1974),* ruled that this statute could not be applied to Spence, who hung a U.S. flag that had the peace symbol on it, upside down out his window.

WASHINGTON POST v. **CHALONER (1919).** On Saturday, April 3, 1909, the *Washington Post* published the following item: "John Armstrong Chaloner (Chanler), brother of Lewis Stuyvesant Chanler, of New York, and former husband of Amelie Rives, the authoress, now Princess Troubetskoy, is recuperating at Shadeland, the country home of Maj. Thomas L. Emry, near Weldon, N.C., where he had gone to recuperate following a nervous breakdown as a result of the tragedy at his home, Merry Mills, near Cobham, on March 15, when he shot and killed John Gillard, while the latter was abusing his wife, who had taken refuge at Merry Mills, Chaloner's home. Following the shooting, Chaloner suffered a nervous breakdown, and was ordered by his physician to take a long rest. He decided to visit his old friend, Maj. Emry, who, with Chaloner, was instrumental in founding Roanoke Rapids, a manufacturing town 5 miles from Weldon. Chaloner arrived at Weldon after travelling all night and was immediately hurried to Shadeland, where he received medical attention and temporary relief."

Be that all that it may, Chaloner did not like the article and brought a libel suit against the *Washington Post*, claiming damages on account of "shame, infamy and disgrace." The trial court judge told the jury that the article was a libel per se and that the only question for the jury to decide was the amount of damages; the jury awarded Chaloner $10,000, a grand sum at that time. The Supreme Court reversed the decision, ruling that the trial judge's instructions were wrong. Justice McReynolds delivered the opinion of the Court: (1) A news statement that Chaloner shot and killed Gillard while Gillard was abusing his wife who had taken refuge at Chaloner's home, is not libelous per se. (2) A publication claimed to be defamatory must be read and construed in the sense in which the readers to whom it is addressed would ordinarily understand it. If it is capable of two meanings, one of which would be libelous and the other not, it is for the jury to say, under all the circumstances surrounding its publication, including extraneous facts admissible in evidence, which of the two meanings would be attributed to it by those to whom it is addressed or by whom it may be read. (3) Irrelevant and scandalous matter may be stricken from the files of the Court. *Washington Post v. Chaloner*, 250 U.S. 290 (1919).

WATKINS v. UNITED STATES (1957). Watkins was convicted of a violation of 2 U.S.C. § 192 (United States Congress, Contempt*), which makes it a misdemeanor for any person summoned as a witness by either House of Congress or any congressional committee to refuse to answer any question "pertinent to the question under inquiry." Watkins was summoned to testify before a subcommittee of the House of Representatives' Committee on Un-American Activities. He testified freely about his own activities and associations but refused to answer any questions as to whether he had known certain other people to have been members of the Communist party. He was then cited for contempt of Congress.

Watkins appealed to the Supreme Court, and the Court ruled that the contempt citation was invalid. In a wide-ranging decision, the Court held: (1) The power of Congress to conduct investigations, inherent in the legislative process, is broad but not unlimited. (2) Congress has no general authority to expose the private affairs of individuals without justification in terms of the functions of Congress. (3) No inquiry is an end in itself—it must be related to, and in furtherance of, a legitimate task of Congress. (4) The Bill of Rights is applicable to congressional investigations, as it is to all forms of governmental action. (5) A congressional investigation is subject to the command that Congress shall make no law abridging freedom of speech or press or assembly. (6) When First Amendment rights are threatened, the delegation of power to a congressional committee must be clearly revealed in its charter. (7) A congressional investigation into individual affairs is invalid if unrelated to any legislative purpose, because it is beyond the powers conferred on Congress by the Constitution. (8) It cannot simply be assumed that every congressional investigation is justified by a public need that overbalances any private rights affected, since to do so would be to abdicate the responsibility placed by the Constitution on the judiciary to ensure that Congress does not unjustifiably encroach on an individual's right of privacy nor abridge his liberty of speech, press, religion, or assembly. (9) There is no congressional power to expose for the sake of exposure where the predominant result can be only an invasion of the private rights of individuals. (10) In authorizing an investigation by a committee, it is essential that the Senate or House should spell out the committee's jurisdiction and purpose with sufficient particularity to ensure that compulsory process is used only in furtherance of a legislative purpose. (11) The resolution authorizing the Un-American Activities Committee does not satisfy this requirement, especially when read in the light of the practices of the committee and subsequent actions of the House of Representatives extending the life of the committee. (12) Every reasonable indulgence of legality must be accorded to the actions of a coordinate branch of our government, but such deference cannot yield to an unnecessary and unreasonable dissipation of precious constitutional freedoms. (13) Protected freedoms should not be placed in danger in the absence of a clear determination by the House or Senate that a particular inquiry is justified by specific legislative need. (14) Congressional investigating committees are restricted to the missions delegated to them—to acquire certain data to be used by the House or Senate in coping with a problem that falls within its legislative sphere—and no witness can be compelled to make disclosures on matters outside that area.

The Court continued: ''Abuses of the investigative process may imperceptibly lead to abridgments of protected freedoms. The mere summoning of a witness and compelling him to testify against his will, about his beliefs, expressions or associations is a measure of governmental interference. And when those forced revelations concern matters that are unorthodox, unpopular, or even hateful to the general public, the reaction in the life of the witness may be disastrous. This effect is even more harsh when it is past beliefs, expressions or associations that are disclosed and judged by current standards rather than those contemporary with the matters exposed. Nor does the witness alone suffer the consequences. Those who are identified by witnesses and thereby placed in the same glare of publicity are equally subject to public stigma, scorn and obloquy. Beyond that, there is the more subtle and immeasurable effect upon those who tend to adhere to the most orthodox and uncontroversial views and associations in order to avoid a similar fate at some future time. That this impact is partly the result of non-governmental activity by private persons cannot relieve the investigators of their responsibility for initiating the reaction. . . . The mere semblance of legislative purpose would not justify an inquiry in the face of the Bill of Rights. The critical element is the existence of, and the weight to be ascribed to, the interest of the Congress in demanding disclosures from an unwilling witness. We cannot simply assume, however, that every congressional investigation is justified by a public need that overbalances any private rights affected. To do so would be to abdicate the responsibility placed by the Constitution upon the judiciary to insure that Congress does not unjustifiably encroach upon an individual's right to privacy nor abridge his liberty of speech, press, religion or assembly.'' *Watkins v. United States*, 354 U.S. 178 (1957).

WATTS v. SEWARD SCHOOL BOARD (1965). This is one case that the Supreme Court did not have a chance to decide—the state of Alaska changed the relevant statute—but it is informative nonetheless as an illustration of the degree to which governmental authorities have attempted to censor free speech and free press. The court record is as follows: Watts and Blue were dismissed from their positions as schoolteachers in Seward, Alaska, on grounds of ''immorality,'' which, under Alaska Statutes 1962, § 14.20.170 (Alaska, Teachers' Immorality*), was defined as ''conduct of the person tending to bring the individual concerned or the teaching profession into public disgrace or disrespect.''

The dismissals were upheld by both the Alaska Superior Court and the Alaska Supreme Court. The Alaska Supreme Court noted that ''the immoral conduct complained of as to the appellant Watts was his holding of private conversations with various teachers in which he solicited their support in an attempt to oust the school superintendent from his job. The allegedly immoral conduct of the appellant Blue was his making of a speech to a labor union at Seward in which he stated 'We have been unable to get rid of the [school] superintendent, so we are going to get rid of the Board,' or words to that effect.'' The Alaska Supreme Court held that this conduct ''had the tendency to bring the [Seward School Board] and the teaching profession into public disgrace or disrespect.'' Watts and Blue argued that their dismissals for engaging in their activities were an unconstitutional infringement on their rights to political expression guaranteed by the First Amendment.

The U.S. Supreme Court made the following comments: ''We need not consider petitioners' contentions at this time, for since their petition for certiorari was filed, Alaska has amended its statutes in this area. House Bill 27, adopted by the Alaska Legislature and signed by the Governor on March 31, 1965, now defines 'immorality' as grounds for revocation of a teaching certificate, as 'the commission of an act which, under the laws of the state, constitutes a crime involving moral turpitude.' . . . Accordingly, it is appropriate to allow the Alaska court to consider the effect of the new Alaska statutes upon this case. To that end, the petition for certiorari is granted, the judgment of the Supreme Court of Alaska is vacated, and this case is remanded to that court for such further consideration as may be deemed appropriate by that court under Alaska law.'' *Watts v. Seward School Board*, 381 U.S. 126 (1965).

THE WELL OF LONELINESS. This case involved a prosecution (*People v. Friede*, 233 N.Y.S. 565) in 1929, the defendants being charged with a violation of § 1141 of the New York Penal Law (New York, Obscenity Statute*)—they were charged with possession and sale of a book entitled *The Well of Loneliness*. New York City Magistrate Bushel described *The Well of Loneliness* in the following terms: ''The book here involved is a novel dealing with the childhood and early womanhood of a female invert. In broad outline the story shows how these unnatural tendencies manifested themselves from early childhood; the queer attraction of the child to the maid in the household, her affairs with one Angela Crossby, a normally sexed, but unhappily married, woman, causing further dissension between the latter and her husband, her jealousy of another man who later debauched this married woman, and her despair, in being supplanted by him in Angela's affections, are vividly portrayed. The book culminates with an extended elaboration upon her intimate relations with a normal young girl, who becomes a helpless subject of her perverted influence and passion, and pictures the struggle for this girl's affections between this invert and a man from whose normal advances she herself had previously recoiled, because of her perverted nature. Her sex experiences are set forth in some detail and also her visits to various resorts frequented by male and female inverts. . . . The unnatural and depraved relationships portrayed are sought to be idealized and extolled. The characters in the book who indulge in these vices are described in attractive terms, and it is maintained throughout that they be accepted on the same plane as persons normally constituted, and that their perverse and inverted love is as worthy as the affection between normal beings and should be considered just as sacred by society. The book can have no moral value since it seeks to justify the right of a pervert to prey upon normal members of a community, and to uphold such relationship as noble and lofty. Although it pleads for tolerance on the part of society of those possessed and inflicted with perverted traits and tendencies, it does not argue for repression or moderation of insidious impulses. An idea of the moral tone which the book assumes may be gained from the attitude taken by its principal character towards her mother, pictured as a hard, cruel, and pitiless woman, because of the abhorrence she displays to unnatural lust, and to who, because of that reaction, the former says: 'But what I will never forgive is your daring to try to make me ashamed of my love. I'm not ashamed of it; there's no shame in me.' The theme of the novel is not only antisocial and offensive to public morals and decency, but the method in which it is developed, in its highly emotional way attracting and focusing attention upon perverted ideas and unnatural vices, and seeking to justify and idealize them, is strongly calculated to corrupt and debase those members of the community who would be susceptible to its immoral influence.''

Magistrate Bushel obviously thought *The Well of Loneliness* was too perverted for public consumption, and he employed the Hicklin Rule* to judge the book obscene: ''Its [the Hicklin Rule] application and soundness are assailed by learned counsel for the defendants, who argues that it seeks to gauge the mental and moral capacity of the community by that of its dullest-witted and most fallible members. This contention overlooks the fact that those who are subject to perverted influences, and in whom that abnormality may be called into activity, and who might be aroused to lustful and lecherous practices are not limited to the young and immature, the moron, the mentally weak, or the intellectually impoverished, but may be found among those of mature age and of high intellectual development and professional attainment. I am convinced that *The Well of Loneliness* tends to debauch public morals, that its subject-matter is offensive to public decency, and that it is calculated to deprave and corrupt minds open to its immoral influences and who might come in contact with it and. . . . I hold that the book . . . is violative of the statute.''

WEST VIRGINIA, JUVENILE PRIVACY. West Virginia Code (1976), §§ 49-7-3 and 49-7-20, provided as follows: ''Nor shall the name of any child, in connection with any proceedings under this Chapter, be published in any newspaper without a written order of the court. . . . A person who violates . . . a provision of this Chapter for which punishment has not been specifically provided, shall be guilty of a misdemeanor, and upon conviction shall be fined not less than ten nor more than one hundred dollars, or confined in jail not less than five days nor more than six months, or both such fine and imprisonment.'' All fifty states have statutes that provide in some way for confidentiality in court proceedings involving juveniles, but other than this West Virginia statute, only four states imposed criminal penalties on parties not a participant in the proceedings— such as newspapers—for publishing the identity of the juvenile. The four other states were Colorado (Rev. State. § 19-1-107 [b] [1973]), Georgia (Code § 24A-3503 [g] [1] [1978]), New Hampshire (Rev. Stat. Ann. § 169: 27-28 [1977]), and South Carolina (Code § 14-21-30 [1976]). The Supreme Court, in *Smith v. Daily Mail Publishing Co.* (1979),* held that the West Virginia statute (and, by extension, the statutes in the other four states) violated the First Amendment rights of a newspaper to publish court proceedings.

WEST VIRGINIA STATE BOARD OF EDUCATION v. BARNETTE (1943).
A West Virginia statute made it compulsory for children in the public schools to salute the American flag and to recite the Pledge of Allegiance. The Supreme

Court, only three years before this case, in *Minersville School District v. Gobitis* (1940),* held that such forced utterances and expressions of opinion did not violate the First Amendment; this case overruled the *Gobitis* decision. Justice Jackson delivered the opinion of the Court: "There is no doubt that, in connection with the pledges, the flag salute is a form of utterance. Symbolism is a primitive but effective way of communicating ideas. The use of an emblem or flag to symbolize some system, idea, institution, or personality, is a short cut from mind to mind. Causes and nations, political parties, lodges and ecclesiastical groups seek to knit the loyalty of their followings to a flag or banner, a color or design. The State announces rank, function, and authority through crowns and maces, uniforms and black robes; the church speaks through the Cross, the Crucifix, the altar and shrine, and clerical raiment. Symbols of State often convey political ideas just as religious symbols come to convey theological ones. Associated with many of these symbols are appropriate gestures of acceptance or respect: a salute, a bowed or bared head, a bended knee. A person gets from a symbol the meaning he puts into it, and what is one man's comfort and inspiration is another's jest and scorn. . . . It is also to be noted that the compulsory flag salute and pledge requires affirmation of a belief and an attitude of mind. It is not clear whether the regulation contemplates that pupils forgo any contrary convictions of their own and become unwilling converts to the prescribed ceremony or whether it will be acceptable if they simulate assent by words without belief and by a gesture barren of meaning. It is now a commonplace that censorship or suppression of expression of opinion is tolerated by our Constitution only when the expression presents a clear and present danger of action of a kind the State is empowered to prevent and punish. It would seem that involuntary affirmation could be commanded only on even more immediate and urgent grounds than silence. But here the power of compulsion is invoked without any allegation that remaining passive during a flag salute ritual creates a clear and present danger that would justify an effort even to muffle expression. To sustain the compulsory flag salute we are required to say that a Bill of Rights which guards the individual's right to speak his own mind, left it open to public authorities to compel him to utter what is not in his mind." *West Virginia State Board of Education v. Barnette*, 319 U.S. 624 (1943).

WHITE v. NICHOLLS (1845). This was one of the earliest court decisions that dealt with libel of a public official. Nicholls (and others) wrote several letters to President Tyler and to the secretary of the treasury, alleging that White was unfit in his job as a Customs collector and requesting that one of the letter signers be appointed in White's place. The letter contained phrases such as "It is impossible that he [White] can ever regain the confidence of men whom he abandoned and vilified in the darkest hour of their existence." White brought suit, charging Nicholls and the others with publishing "false, malicious and defamatory libel" about his conduct in office, which led to his eventual removal from the position of Customs collector. The trial jury, under the direction of the judge, found Nicholls and the other defendants not guilty. White attempted to prove "express malice," but the judge refused to admit the evidence.

On appeal, the U.S. Supreme Court reversed the lower court's decision and remanded it for retrial, saying that "express malice" will render a publication libelous and "will subject the author and publisher thereof to all the consequences of libel" and the jury should have been allowed to determine whether "express malice" was present. Justice Daniel: "That every publication, either by writing, printing, or pictures, which charges upon or imputes to any person that which renders him liable to punishment, or which is calculated to make him infamous, or odious, or ridiculous, is *prima facie* a libel, and implies malice in the author and publisher. Proof of malice is not required of the complaining person—it is for the defendant to show absence of malice." But Justice Daniel continued, anticipating the 1964 *New York Times* Rule* as established by the Supreme Court in *New York Times Company v. Sullivan*,* that alleged libels against a "public official" were to be treated differently: The plaintiff is required to show "express malice" in order to render the publication a libel. *White v. Nicholls*, 3 How. 266 (1845).

WHITNEY v. CALIFORNIA (1927). Whitney had joined and assisted in the creation and organization of a Communist Labor party. For this activity, she was charged with violating a California statute (California, Criminal Syndicalism Act*) that defined "criminal syndicalism" as "any doctrine or precept advocating, teaching or aiding and abetting the commission of crime, sabotage (which word is hereby defined as meaning wilful and malicious physical damage or injury to physical property), or unlawful acts of force and violence or unlawful methods of terrorism as a means of accomplishing a change in industrial ownership or control, or effecting any political change."

The Supreme Court upheld Whitney's conviction, holding that her "advocacy" of the outlawed doctrine was as evil as the conduct itself. The Court offered two basic reasons: (1) The determination of the legislature that the acts defined involve such danger to the public peace and security of the state that they should be penalized in the exercise of the police power must be given great weight and every presumption be indulged in favor of the validity of the statute, which could be declared unconstitutional only if an attempt to exercise arbitrarily and unreasonably the authority vested in the state in the public interest. (2) The advocacy of criminal and unlawful methods partakes of the nature of a criminal conspiracy. Such united and joint action "involves even greater danger to the public peace and security than the isolated utterances and acts of individuals. We cannot hold that, as here applied, the Act is an unreasonable or arbitrary exercise of the police power of the State, unwarrantably infringing any right of free speech, assembly or association, or that those persons are protected from punishment by the due process clause who abuse such rights by joining and furthering an organization thus menacing the peace and welfare of the State." This decision, establishing that "advocacy" was equivalent to the act itself, was

a standard employed by the Supreme Court until the proponents of the "clear
and present danger"* view became the majority. In *Brandenburg v. Ohio*,* the
Supreme Court reversed *Whitney*, holding that mere "advocacy" without any
imminent or clear and present danger to the peace and security of the community
was protected under the First Amendment's guarantees of free speech and free
press. *Whitney v. California*, 274 U.S. 357 (1927).

WIDMAR v. VINCENT (1981). The University of Missouri at Kansas City,
a public state university, made the university's facilities generally available for
the activities of registered and recognized student groups. Such a recognized
and registered student religious group, who had previously received administrative permission to conduct some of its meetings in university facilities, was
informed that it could no longer do so because a university regulation (Missouri,
University Board of Curators, Building Use*) prohibited the use of the university
buildings and grounds "for purposes of religious worship or religious teaching."
Members of the group then brought suit, charging that the regulation violated
their rights to freedom of speech (and the free exercise of religion) under the
First Amendment. A federal district court upheld the regulation as not only being
justified, but required. A court of appeals reversed, viewing the regulation as
censorship based on the content of speech (religious speech could not use the
facilities but other types of speech could). The university, once opening its
facilities to student groups, had to abide by a policy of equal access.

The university was not pleased with this decision and appealed to the Supreme
Court; the Supreme Court affirmed the court of appeals decision and held that
the university's exclusionary policy violated the fundamental principle that state
regulation of speech should be content-neutral. Justice Powell delivered the
opinion of the Court: (1) Having created a forum generally open for use by
student groups, the university, in order to justify discriminatory exclusion from
the forum based on the (religious) content of a group's intended speech, must
satisfy the standard of review appropriate to content-based exclusions—it must
show that its regulation is necessary to serve a compelling state interest and that
it is narrowly drawn to achieve that end. (2) Although the university's interest
in complying with its constitutional obligations under the Establishment Clause
of the First Amendment may be characterized as compelling, an "equal access"
policy would not be in conflict with that clause. A policy will not violate the
Establishment Clause if it can pass the following test: (a) It has a secular legislative purpose; (b) its principal or primary effect would be neither to advance
nor to inhibit religion; and (c) it does not foster "an excessive government
entanglement with religion." It was conceded here that an "equal access" policy
would meet the first and third criteria of the test. In the context of this case and
in the absence of any evidence that religious groups would dominate the university's forum, the advancement of religion would not be the forum's "primary
effect." An "equal access" policy would satisfy the second criterion as well.
(3) The state's interest in achieving greater separation of church and state than

is already ensured under the Establishment Clause is not sufficiently compelling to justify content-based discrimination and censorship against religious speech of the student groups. *Widmar v. Vincent*, 454 U.S. 263 (1981).

WIEMAN v. UPDEGRAFF (1952). An Oklahoma statute (Ok. State. Ann., 1950, Tit. 51, §§ 37.1-37.8 [1952 Supp.]) required each state officer and employee, as a condition of employment, to take a "loyalty oath," stating, among other things, that the employee was not and had not been for the preceding five years, a member of any organization listed by the U.S. attorney general as "communist front" or "subversive." The Oklahoma Supreme Court interpreted the statute as excluding persons from state employment solely on the basis of membership in such listed organizations, regardless of their knowledge concerning the activities and purposes of the organizations to which they had belonged. This case concerned one Wieman, and others, who refused to subscribe to the loyalty oath. The Oklahoma courts sustained the constitutionality of the statute and enjoined payment of salaries to state employees who refused to take the oath.

Wieman appealed to the U.S. Supreme Court, his objections centering largely on the following clauses of the oath: "That I am not affiliated directly or indirectly . . . with any foreign political agency, party, organization or Government, or with any agency, party, organization, association, or group whatever which has been officially determined by the United States Attorney General or other authorized agency of the United States to be a communist front or subversive organization; . . . that I will take up arms in the defense of the United States in time of War, or National Emergency, if necessary; that within the five (5) years immediately preceding the taking of this oath (or affirmation) I have not been a member of . . . any agency, party, organization, association, or group whatever which has been officially determined by the United States Attorney General or other authorized public agency of the United States to be a communist front or subversive organization."

On appeal, the Supreme Court reversed, holding the oath requirement to be an unconstitutional infringement on a state employee's right of free speech, press, and association. As is true in many Supreme Court decisions, a concurring (or dissenting) opinion often is more significant and relevant than is the majority opinion; Justice Black wrote such a concurring opinion in this case, and it is his remarks rather than the Court's opinion that follow. Justice Black: "I concur in all the Court says in condemnation of Oklahoma's test oath. I agree that the State Act prescribing that test oath is fatally offensive to the due process guarantee of the United States Constitution. History indicates that individual liberty is intermittently subjected to extraordinary perils. Even countries dedicated to government by the people are not free from such cyclical dangers. The first years of our Republic marked such a period. Enforcement of the Alien and Sedition Laws by zealous patriots who feared ideas made it highly dangerous for people to think, speak, or write critically about government, its agents, or its policies, either foreign or domestic. Our constitutional liberties survived the ordeal of this regrettable period because there were influential men and powerful organized groups bold enough to champion the undiluted right of individuals to publish and argue for their beliefs however unorthodox or loathsome. Today, however, few individuals and organizations of power and influence argue that unpopular advocacy has this same wholly unqualified immunity from governmental interference. For this and other reasons the present period of fear seems more ominously dangerous to speech and press than was that of the Alien and Sedition Laws. Suppressive laws and practices are the fashion. The Oklahoma oath statute is but one manifestation of a national network of laws aimed at coercing and controlling the minds of men. Test oaths are notorious tools of tyranny. When used to shackle the mind, they are, or at least they should be, unspeakably odious to a free people. Test oaths are made still more dangerous when combined with bills of attainder which like this Oklahoma statute impose pains and penalties for past lawful associations and utterances. . . . Governments need and have ample power to punish treasonable acts. But it does not follow that they must have a further power to punish thought and speech as distinguished from acts. Our own free society should never forget that laws which stigmatize and penalize thought and speech of the unorthodox have a way of reaching, ensnaring and silencing many more people than at first intended. We must have freedom of speech for all or we will in the long run have it for none but the cringing and the craven. And I cannot too often repeat my belief that the right to speak on matters of public concern must be wholly free or eventually be wholly lost." *Wieman v. Updegraff*, 344 U.S. 183 (1952).

WILLIAM GOLDMAN THEATRES, INC. v. DANA (1961). This case was decided along with *Twentieth Century-Fox Film Corporation v. Boehm* and involved the motion picture censorship process in Pennsylvania (Pennsylvania, Motion Picture Control Act*). The suit by William Goldman Theatres sought to enjoin the members of the Pennsylvania State Board of Motion Picture Control from enforcing any of the provisions of the act (the board had to approve a film before an exhibition permit would be issued), and the second suit by Twentieth Century-Fox was a taxpayer's suit, seeking to enjoin any expenditures relating to the operation of the censorship board or the enforcement of the act.

Chief Justice Jones of the Supreme Court of Pennsylvania granted both motions, ruling that the Motion Picture Control Act was "clearly invalid" on its face. Justice Jones: "It is designed to effect, in violation of Article I, Section 7, of the Pennsylvania Constitution, a pre-censorship of the exercise of the individual's right freely to communicate thoughts and opinions. Section 3 of the Act expressly restrains the initial showing of a film for 48 hours after notice to the Board of its intended exhibition; and subsequent showings are likewise subjected to previous restraint for the reason that, if the motion picture is exhibited after the censors have disapproved it, the exhibitor may be criminally punished upon proof, not of showing a picture that is obscene or unsuitable for children, but merely upon proof of showing a picture the exhibition of which had been priorly restrained by the administrative action of the Board of Censors."

This decision did not sit well with Justice Musmanno, who filed a broadside dissent and, in the process, revealed his views as to the kinds of films that could be exhibited to the people of Pennsylvania. Justice Musmanno: "During the last five years this Court has dismantled the three most formidable dikes constructed by the people of Pennsylvania, through their representatives in Harrisburg, against the flood of cinematic filth always pounding at the borders of our Commonwealth. In 1956, in the *Hallmark* case (*Hallmark Productions v. Carroll*, 121 A. 2d 584) [*She Should' a Said No!**], this Court, by declaring an Act of 1915 unconstitutional, dissolved the Motion Picture Censorship Board which, for forty-one years, had faithfully served the people by keeping the theatres wholesome and clean of obscenity, vulgarity, blasphemy and profanity. At the time of that decision, the majority of this Court said that although its decision eliminated motion picture censorship this did not mean that objectionable films could not be suppressed since offending exhibitors could be prosecuted under the criminal code. Then, in 1959, in *Commonwealth v. Blumenstein* (153 A. 2d 227), this Court proceeded to strike down that section of the criminal code under which exhibitors of immoral pictures could be prosecuted. . . . And then, also in 1959, the majority of this Court in *Kingsley International Pictures Corp. v. Blanc* (153 A. 2d 254), ruled that a district attorney could be enjoined from seizing a film which he regarded as violating the laws of Pennsylvania, because of obscenity. I wrote a dissenting opinion in that case, as I did in the previous ones, and ended that dissent as follows: 'Unless the General Assembly comes to the aid of the people with renewed legislation and William Penn comes down from his pedestal atop City Hall to protect the State he founded against the forces of immorality at our borders, far more damaging to the welfare of the people than the Indians he encountered, the fair Commonwealth which he dedicated to religious freedom, civic liberties and moral purity, may well be on the way to a cinematic Gomorrah.' . . . In view of the fact that the highest tribunal in our State has now destroyed three statutes on the subject of motion picture sanitation, the people may well wonder what must be done to protect Pennsylvania from the evil of lascivous, pornographic, obscene and prurient motion pictures. As matters presently stand, the appalling prospect presents itself that films of the most degrading character, films revealing scenes of outright degeneracy, may be projected without legal hindrance in Pennsylvania. Dealers may traffick in pictures on subjects of the utmost depravity, pictures which cannot help but corrupt morals and weaken the will of immature minds, pictures which would make an ancient Pompeiian blush with shame—dealers may engage in this type of revolting merchandise and not be restrained. These four decisions of the Supreme Court of Pennsylvania have, in effect, bound prosecuting authorities hand and foot. Officials charged with standing guard over the moral health of the people have been disarmed. Every weapon which they could employ to stop the wicked and nefarious business of immoral films has been torn from their grasp. The armory in this field has been stripped bare. One of the most popular motion picture stars of the day, John Wayne, whose production *Alamo*—which for sheer visual beauty, patriotic theme, and its moving story of self-sacrifice must be rated among the classics of the screen—said: 'I don't like to see the Hollywood bloodstream polluted with immoral and amoral nuances. Fifthy minds, filthy words and filthy thoughts have no place in films, which I see as a universal instrument at once entertaining peoples and encouraging them to work toward a better world, a freer world.' So that there may be no misunderstanding about my position I want to add that I do not oppose motion pictures. On the contrary, I regard motion picture entertainment as the best form of relaxation extant. Color photography, the wide screen, and the miraculous equipment which reproduces music with such fidelity, volume and tone, that one can hardly believe that the orchestra is not actually in the theatre—all these magnificent features have made the motion picture theatre the rendezvous of relaxful diversion which even kings could not have dreamed of having fifty years ago. Classics in literature are being reproduced, educational subjects are attractively handled, history is made to live again before one's entranced vision. Faraway places, which the unwealthy person would never have the money to visit, are being brought to us in all their original charm, quaintness, and dramatic picturesqueness. Pictures like the *Alamo, Ben Hur, The Big Fisherman, The Big Country, The Ten Commandments* are more than entertainment; they are almost personal adventures and in many ways spiritual experiences. Masterpieces of this character, together with other dramatic gems are being endangered by the cheap, bawdy monstrosities. . . . Control such as that outlined in the Act before us will preserve films of this magnitude and artistic perfection as it will also protect children. The law-making body of this Commonwealth has tried a number of times to supply the motion picture control and protection which a decent, God-fearing, law-abiding, self-respecting and dignified people need, desire and demand. I hope and urge that it will not lose heart, but in the spirit of William Penn, try and try again.'' *William Goldman Theatres, Inc. v. Dana*, 173 A. 2d 59 (1961).

WINTERS v. NEW YORK (1948). The defendant Winters was convicted in a New York court on the following charge: ''The said defendant with intent did unlawfully offer for sale and distribution . . . a certain obscene, lewd, lascivious, filthy, indecent and disgusting magazine entitled *Headquarters Detective, True Cases from the Police Blotter, June 1940*, the same being devoted to the publication and principally made up of criminal news, police reports, and accounts of criminal deeds, and pictures and stories of deeds of bloodshed, lust and crime.'' The charge was based on subsection 2 of § 1141 of the New York Penal Law (New York, Crime Stories*), which prohibited distribution of a magazine principally made up of news and stories of criminal deeds of bloodshed or lust so massed as to become vehicles for inciting violent and depraved crimes against the person.

Winters' conviction was affirmed by the higher New York courts, but on appeal to the U.S. Supreme Court, the conviction was reversed. The Court held that the statute was too vague and indefinite and that it prohibited acts within the protection and guarantee of free speech and free press under the First Amendment. The Court opinion: "[Winters] contends that the subsection violates the right of free speech and press because it is vague and indefinite. It is settled that a statute so vague and indefinite, in form and as interpreted, as to permit within the scope of its language the punishment of incidents fairly within the protection of the guarantee of free speech is void, on its face, as contrary to the Fourteenth Amendment. A failure of a statute limiting freedom of expression to give fair notice of what acts will be punished and such a statute's inclusion of prohibitions against expressions, protected by the principles of the First Amendment, violates an accused's rights under procedural due process and freedom of speech or press. . . . We recognize the importance of the exercise of a state's police power to minimize all incentives to crime, particularly in the field of sanguinary or salacious publications with their stimulation of juvenile delinquency. Although we are dealing with an aspect of a free press in its relation to public morals, the principles of unrestricted distribution of publications admonish us of the particular importance of a maintenance of standards of certainty in the field of criminal prosecution for violation of statutory prohibitions against distribution. We do not accede to [New York's] suggestion that the constitutional protection for a free press applies only to the exposition of ideas. The line between the informing and the entertaining is too elusive for the protection of that basic right. Everyone is familiar with instances of propaganda through fiction. What is one man's amusement, teaches another's doctrine. Though we can see nothing of any possible value to society in these magazines, they are as much entitled to the protection of free speech as the best of literature."

It was this last statement of the majority— "Though we can see nothing of any possible value to society in these magazines, they are as much entitled to the protection of free speech as the best of literature"—that upset Justice Frankfurter. He filed a strong dissent, arguing that such magazines do incite morbid and immature minds to all sorts of criminal deeds and should be censored. Justice Frankfurter: "Not to make the magazines with which the case is concerned part of the Court's opinion is to play *Hamlet* without Hamlet. But the Court sufficiently summarizes one aspect of what the State of New York here condemned when it says 'we can see nothing of any possible value to society in these magazines.' From which it jumps to the conclusion that, nevertheless, 'they are as much entitled to the protection of free speech as the best of literature.' Wholly neutral futilities, of course, come under the protection of free speech as fully as do Keats' poems or Donne's sermons. But to say that these magazines have 'nothing of any possible value to society' is only half the truth. This merely denies them goodness. It disregards their mischief. As a result of appropriate judicial determination, these magazines were found to come within the prohibition of the law against inciting 'violent and depraved crimes against the person,' and the defendant was convicted because he exposed for sale such materials.

The essence of the Court's decision is that it gives publications which have 'nothing of any possible value to society' constitutional protection but denies to the States the power to prevent the grave evils to which, in their rational judgment, such publications give rise. The legislatures of New York and . . . other States were concerned with these evils and not with neutral abstractions of harmlessness. . . . 'Magazine thrillers' hardly characterizes what New York has outlawed. New York does not lay hold of publications merely because they are 'devoted to and principally made up of criminal news or police reports or accounts of criminal deeds' regardless of the manner of treatment. The aim of the publication must be to incitation to 'violent and depraved crimes against the person' and so massing 'pictures and stories of criminal deeds of bloodshed or lust' as to encourage like deeds in others. It would be sheer dogmatism in a field not within the professional competence of judges to deny to the New York legislature the right to believe that the intent of the type of publications which it has proscribed is to cater to morbid and immature minds—whether chronologically or permanently imma-ture." *Winters v. New York*, 333 U.S. 507 (1948).

WISCONSIN, DISPLAY OF CONTRACEPTIVES. The following statute (Section 351.235) was originally introduced in the Wisconsin legislature in 1933 as a bill providing an outright ban on birth control. The total prohibition did not pass and this statute appears to have been a compromise—the act of birth control was not prohibited, but most sales, distribution, etc. of any contraceptive was made a crime. The statute was upheld as not violating any rights in 1935, in *State of Wisconsin v. Arnold.** Section 351.235, "Advertising or display of indecent articles, sale in certain cases prohibited," provided: "(1) As used in this chapter, the term 'indecent articles' means any drug, medicine, mixture, preparation, instrument, article or device of whatsoever nature used or intended or represented to be used to procure a miscarriage or prevent pregnancy. (2) No person, firm or corporation shall publish, distribute or circulate any circular, card, advertisement or notice of any kind offering or advertising any indecent article for sale, nor shall exhibit or display any indecent article to the public. (3) No person, firm or corporation shall manufacture, purchase, or rent, or have in his or its possession or under his or its control, any slot machine, or other mechanism or means so designed and constructed as to contain and hold indecent articles and to release the same upon the deposit therein of a coin or other thing of value. (4) No person, firm or corporation shall sell or dispose of or attempt to offer to sell or dispose of any indecent articles to or for any unmarried person; and no sale in any case of any indecent articles shall be made except by a pharmacist registered under the provisions of chapter 151 or a physician or surgeon duly licensed under the laws of this state. (5) Any person, firm or corporation violating any provision of this section shall be deemed guilty of a misdemeanor and upon conviction thereof shall be punished by a fine of not less than one hundred nor more than five hundred dollars [quite a large sum in the Depression 1930s] or by imprisonment in the county jail for not to exceed six months, or by both such fine and imprisonment. In addition thereto, any license, permit or registration certificate issued under any law or ordinance to any such persons, firm or corporation, shall be canceled or revoked.''

WOLFF, WARDEN v. McDONNELL (1974). McDonnell, an inmate at a Nebraska prison, filed this complaint, on behalf of himself and other inmates, against the warden of the prison. It appears that the warden had instituted a scheme to examine the inmates' mail, and they claimed that the regulations were too restrictive under the First Amendment. One such regulation was that any letter to any inmate from an attorney had to have clear identification on the envelope that the letter did indeed come from an attorney and that the letters could be opened for inspection for contraband.

The Supreme Court held that these regulations were a proper exercise of the warden's power to prevent contraband from entering the prison. The Court ruled that prison officials can require that letters from attorneys to inmates be clearly identified as such and that, although the letters cannot be read by the prison officials, such letters could be opened by the officials in the presence of the inmates in order to search for contraband. Justice White delivered the opinion of the Court: ''[It is] certainly permissible that prison authorities require that a lawyer desiring to correspond with a prisoner, first identify himself and his client to the prison officials, to assure that the letters marked 'privileged' are actually from members of the bar. As to the ability to open the mail in the presence of inmates, this could in no way constitute censorship, since the mail would not be read. Neither could it chill such communications, since the inmate's presence insures that prison officials will not read the mail. The possibility that contraband will be enclosed in letters, even those from apparent attorneys, surely warrants prison officials opening the letters.'' *Wolff, Warden v. McDonnell*, 418 U.S. 539 (1974).

WOMACK v. UNITED STATES (1961). Womack was convicted of mailing information as to how obscene matter could be obtained and of mailing such obscene matter in violation of 18 U.S.C. § 1461 (Postal Regulations, Mailing Obscene Material*). Womack was convicted in a federal district court and then appealed to a court of appeals; Womack's conviction was affirmed. Judge Prettyman of the appeals court held that the photographs Womack was mailing were intended for purchase by homosexuals (they were photographs of nude boys and men in various and sundry poses) and were obscene. A postal inspector testified that Womack told him that the pictures ''were intended for or that the purchasers were homosexuals.'' The court record contains some of Womack's statements: ''A model, if he has been photographed properly, has the potential sex appeal and drawing power that is characteristic of so many of the models''; and ''In 1958, physique fans want their truck driver types already cleaned up, showered and ready for bed.''

The government's first witness was a thirteen-year-old boy who had received in the mail, without any solicitation or inquiry on the boy's part, one of Womack's advertisements for the photographs. The boy gave the material to his father, who then notified the postal inspectors. Other witnesses included boys from fifteen to nineteen years old who had also received the unsolicited advertisements. The advertising circular required the customer to sign a statement that he was an "art student or art teacher, or engaged in some occupation that would involve a professional need for such photographs." This "prospectus" added that, if the recipient did not feel qualified as an art student, a "home study course in figure drawing" would be recommended to him. Womack admitted on the witness stand that he sent two circulars to the boys' club in a certain town.

Judge Prettyman found the photographs to be obscene: "Whatever may be the precise meanings of 'obscene' and 'filthy,' or however broad or liberal community standards may be alleged to be, the photographs presented as Government exhibits in this case are within the definitions and outside the standards. No concept of art as art could include them. No concept of community standards could permit them. Mr. Wigmore says: 'all evidential sources . . . are divided into three classes, namely, Testimonial, Circumstantial, and Autoptical.' Concerning the latter he says: 'A fact is said to be evidence Autoptically when it is offered for direct perception by the senses of the tribunal without depending on any conscious inference from some other testimonial or circumstantial fact.' The photographs which are exhibits in this case are conclusive autoptical proof of obscenity and filth." *Womack v. United States*, 294 F. 2d 204 (1961).

WOMEN AGAINST PORNOGRAPHY. Founded in 1979 and with about 5,000 members, this group is a feminist organization established by author Susan Brownmiller and others that is seeking to change public opinion about pornography so that Americans no longer view it as "socially acceptable" or "sexually liberating." Women Against Pornography provided the following information about itself, found in the *Encyclopedia of Associations* (# 13091): "and offers tours of New York's Times Square district," which it "considers the porn capital of the country," to women and men of all ages and backgrounds. The tour is intended to show firsthand that "the essence of pornography is about the degradation, objectification, and brutalization of women." The group also offers adult and high school slide shows and lectures that show how "pornographic imagery pervades popular culture." It maintains a speaker's bureau and organizes anti-pornography protests.

WOMEN AGAINST VIOLENCE AGAINST WOMEN. Founded in 1976 and now with about 3,000 members, Women Against Violence Against Women describes itself as an "activist, feminist collective working to stop gratuitous use of images of physical and sexual violence against women in mass media and end the 'real world' violence it promotes. Sponsors public education, consciousness-raising, and mass consumer action. Current focus is on the movie industry, to press for policies of not using sexist-violent images of women in their advertising. Seeks to educate people about sexist and violent exploitation in media and advertising.'' *Encyclopedia of Associations* (# 13092).

WOMEN AGAINST VIOLENCE IN PORNOGRAPHY AND MEDIA.

Women Against Violence in Pornography and Media, founded in 1976 and now with about 4,800 members, describes itself as a: ''Feminist organization opposed to the association of violence with sexuality and to media portrayals encouraging abuse of women. Confronts pornography store and theatre owners, newspaper publishers who advertise pornographic material, and producers of record jackets portraying images of violence. Investigates trends in pornography; conducts public information and education programs; leads feminist tours of pornography districts; presents slide shows. Operates hotline to report media portrayals of violence against women. Coordinates national feminist letter-writing network, 'Write Back! Fight Back!,' protesting abusive images of women in the media. Maintains speakers bureau, library and anti-pornography display . . . and publishes 'Media Protest Packet' on how to write effective letters protesting abusive images in the media and educational packet on child pornography.'' *Encyclopedia of Associations* (# 13093).

WOODS v. DAGGETT (1976). This case concerned an application of the Publisher-Only Rule* that restricts prison inmates to receiving books directly from a bookstore, the publisher, or a book club. The rule has been upheld as necessary to preserve prison discipline and to prevent contraband from entering the prison, and it is not seen as a governmental censorship scheme over the reading materials of inmates. In this particular case, Woods, a federal prisoner, brought suit, claiming that his First Amendment rights were violated when the prison authorities refused to deliver to him copies of certain used law books mailed to him by his parents. A federal district court dismissed Woods' complaint, and he appealed to a court of appeals. The appeals court affirmed all but one of the district court's findings—one aspect of the case was remanded for further deliberations (the issue of whether or not the prisoner would be informed that certain books were being withheld or returned to the sender)—on the grounds that security considerations take precedence over any claimed First Amendment rights of the inmates. Judge Holloway delivered the court's opinion: (1) The prison's policy of prohibiting inmates from receiving books other than books sent directly from a publisher did not violate the prisoner's constitutional rights under the First Amendment. (2) Even though the prisoner was indigent and despite the fact that the policy might have discriminated to some extent against those inmates who could not afford to purchase new books directly from the publisher, the economic effect of the policy was sufficiently remote and inconsequential. (3) The prisoner failed to prove discrimination, particularly in view of the presence of a substantial prison library and in view of the prison's justification for the policy based on security reasons. (4) The fact that Woods would have permitted the prison authorities to inspect the books from his parents for contraband before receiving them is not relevant, for in the words of the prison authorities, if one person were allowed books from home, "they would be coming in by the box car load." *Woods v. Daggett*, 541 F. 2d 237 (1976).

WOOD v. GEORGIA (1962). In the midst of a local political campaign in Georgia, a county judge, in the presence of news media representatives assembled at the judge's request, issued a charge to a grand jury giving it special instructions to investigate rumors and accusations of alleged bloc voting by blacks and the rumored use of bribe money by political candidates to obtain the black vote. The next day, while the grand jury was in session, Wood, a candidate for reelection as sheriff, issued a press statement criticizing the judge's action and urged citizens to "take notice when their judges threatened political intimidation and persecution of voters under the guise of law enforcement." Wood was then cited for contempt by the judge on the grounds that Wood's statement was "calculated to be contemptuous of the Court and to obstruct the grand jury in its investigation and that it constituted a clear, present and imminent danger to the administration of justice." When Wood rejoined that all he had spoken was the truth, the judge cited him again for contempt.

The Supreme Court found this to be a violation of Wood's freedom of speech: "We start with the premise that the right of courts to conduct their business in an untrammeled way lies at the foundation of our system of government and that courts necessarily must possess the means of punishing for contempt when conduct tends directly to prevent the discharge of their functions. While courts have continuously had the authority and power to maintain order in their courtrooms and to assure litigants a fair trial, the exercise of that bare contempt power is not what is questioned in this case. Here it is asserted that the exercise of the contempt power, to commit a person to jail for an utterance out of the presence of the court, has abridged the accused's liberty of free expression. In this situation the burden upon this Court is to define the limitations upon the contempt power according to the terms of the Federal Constitution. . . . We are dealing here only with public expression. [Wood] was an elected official and had the right to enter the field of political controversy, particularly where his political life was at stake. The role that elected officials play in our society makes it all the more imperative that they be allowed freely to express themselves on matters of current public importance. Our examination of the content of [Wood's] statements and the circumstances under which they were published leads us to conclude that they did not present a danger to the administration of justice that should vitiate his freedom to express his opinions in the manner chosen." *Wood v. Georgia*, 370 U.S. 375 (1962).

WOOLEY v. MAYNARD (1977). New Hampshire statutes (New Hampshire, License Plates*) require that all non-commercial motor vehicles carry license plates embossed with the state motto ("Live Free or Die") and make it a misdemeanor to obscure the motto. The Maynards, Jehovah's Witnesses, viewed the motto as "repugnant to their moral, religious, and political beliefs" and, accordingly, covered up the motto on the license plates of their cars. Maynard received (and served) fifteen days in jail for refusing to pay the fine for the misdemeanor. The U.S. Supreme Court affirmed a district court ruling that enjoined the state of New Hampshire from arresting and prosecuting the Maynards (and, presumably, anyone else in the future) for covering up the motto on their license plates. In upholding the injunction, the Supreme Court ruled: (1) The state may not constitutionally require an individual to participate in the dissemination of an ideological message by displaying it on his private property in a manner and for the express purpose that it be observed and read by the public. (2) New Hampshire's statute, by forcing an individual, as part of his daily life—constantly while his automobile is in public view—to be an instrument for advocating public adherence to an ideological point of view he finds unacceptable, "invades the sphere of intellect and spirit which it is the purpose of the First Amendment to reserve from all official control." (3) New Hampshire's claimed interests in requiring display of the state motto on license plates (a) so as to facilitate the identification of passenger vehicles and (b) so as to promote an appreciation of history, individualism, and state pride, are not sufficiently compelling to justify infringement of individual First Amendment rights. The purpose of the first interest could be achieved by less drastic means, and the second interest cannot outweigh an individual's First Amendment right to avoid becoming the courier for the state's ideological message.

The Court's opinion contained the following comments: "We begin with the proposition that the right of freedom of thought protected by the First Amendment against state action includes both the right to speak freely and the right to refrain from speaking at all (*West Virginia State Board of Education v. Barnette**). A system which secures the right to proselytize religious, political, and ideological causes must also guarantee the concomitant right to decline to foster such concepts. The right to speak and the right to refrain from speaking are complementary components of the broader concept of 'individual freedom of mind.' . . . The Court in *Barnette* was faced with a state statute which required public school students to participate in daily public ceremonies by honoring the flag both with words and traditional salute gestures. In overruling its prior decision (*Minersville School District v. Gobitis**), the Court held that 'a ceremony so touching matters of opinion and political attitude may [not] be imposed upon the individual by official authority under powers committed to any political organization under our Constitution.' Compelling the affirmative act of a flag salute involved a more serious infringement upon personal liberties than the passive act of carrying the state motto on a license plate, but the difference is essentially one of degree. Here, as in *Barnette*, we are faced with a state measure which forces an individual, as part of his daily life—indeed constantly while his automobile is in public view—to be an instrument for fostering public adherence to an ideological point of view he finds unacceptable. In doing so, the State 'invades the sphere of intellect and spirit which it is the purpose of the First Amendment to our Constitution to reserve from all official control.' New Hampshire's statute in effect requires that [people] use their private property as a 'mobile billboard' for the State's ideological message—or suffer a penalty, as Maynard already has. As a condition for driving an automobile—a virtual necessity for most Americans—the Maynards must display 'Live Free or Die' to hundreds of people each day. The fact that most individuals agree with the thrust of New Hampshire's motto is not the test; most Americans also find the flag salute acceptable. The First Amendment protects the right of individuals to hold a point of view different from the majority and refuse to foster, in the way New Hampshire commands, an idea they find morally objectionable.'' *Wooley v. Maynard*, 430 U.S. 705 (1977).

Y

YATES v. UNITED STATES (1957). Yates and thirteen other people, all leaders of the Communist party in California, were indicted in 1951 for conspiring (1) to advocate and teach the duty and necessity of overthrowing the government of the United States by force and violence and (2) to organize, as the Communist party of the United States, a society of people who so advocate and teach, all with the intent of causing the overthrow of the government by force and violence as speedily as circumstances would permit (Smith Act*). Yates and the others were convicted in a federal district court and the convictions were affirmed by an appeals court.

The Supreme Court reversed the convictions of five of the defendants and ordered a retrial for the others. The Court ruled that the Smith Act does not prohibit advocacy* and teaching of the forcible overthrow of the government—only incitement to direct and immediate action and conduct can be punished—and thus this decision refined *Dennis v. United States.** Justice Harlan delivered the opinion of the Court: "We are thus faced with the question whether the Smith Act prohibits advocacy and teaching of forcible overthrow as an abstract principle, divorced from any effort to instigate action to that end, so long as such advocacy or teaching is engaged in with evil intent. We hold that it does not. The distinction between advocacy of abstract doctrine and advocacy directed at promoting unlawful action is one that has been consistently recognized in the opinions of this Court, beginning with *Fox v. Washington** and *Schenck v. United States.** This distinction was heavily underscored in *Gitlow v. New York,** in which the statute involved [New York, Criminal Anarchy*] was nearly identical with the one now before us, and where the Court, despite the narrow view there taken of the First Amendment, said: 'The statute does not penalize the utterance or publication of abstract doctrine or academic discussion having no quality of incitement to any concrete action. It is not the abstract doctrine of overthrowing organized government by unlawful means which is denounced by the statute, but the advocacy of action for the accomplishment of that purpose.' . . . In failing to distinguish between advocacy of forcible overthrow as an abstract doctrine and advocacy of action to that end, the District Court appears to have been led astray by the holding in *Dennis* that advocacy of violent action to be taken at some future time was enough. It seems to have considered that, since 'inciting' speech is usually thought of as something calculated to induce immediate action, and since *Dennis* held advocacy of action for future overthrow sufficient, this meant that advocacy, irrespective of its tendency to generate action, is punishable, provided only that it is uttered with a specific intent to accomplish overthrow. In other words, the District Court apparently thought that *Dennis* obliterated the traditional dividing line between advocacy of abstract doctrine and advocacy of action.''

Justice Black, joined by Justice Douglas, concurred in the reversal of the five convictions but dissented from the decision to have the remaining people tried again: ''I would reverse every one of these convictions and direct that all the defendants be acquitted. In my judgment the statutory provisions on which these prosecutions are based abridge freedom of speech, press and assembly in violation of the First Amendment to the United States Constitution. The kind of trials conducted here are wholly dissimilar to normal criminal trials. Ordinarily these 'Smith Act' trials are prolonged affairs lasting for months. In part this is attributable to the routine introduction in evidence of massive collections of books, tracts, pamphlets, newspapers, and manifestoes discussing Communism, Socialism, Capitalism, Feudalism and governmental institutions in general, which, it is not too much to say, are turgid, diffuse, abstruse, and just plain dull. Of course, no juror can or is expected to plow his way through this jungle of verbiage. The testimony of witnesses is comparatively insignificant. Guilt or innocence may turn on what Marx or Engels or someone else wrote or advocated as much as a hundred or more years ago. Elaborate, refined distinctions are drawn between 'Communism,' 'Marxism,' 'Leninism,' 'Trotskyism,' and 'Stalinism.' When the propriety of obnoxious or unorthodox views about government is in reality made the crucial issue, as it must be in cases of this kind, prejudice makes conviction inevitable except in the rarest circumstances. . . . In essence, petitioners were tried upon the charge that they believe in and want to foist upon this country a different and to us a despicable form of authoritarian government in which voices criticizing the existing order are summarily silenced. I fear that the present type of prosecutions are more in line with the philosophy of authoritarian government than with that expressed by our First Amendment. Doubtlessly, dictators have to stamp out causes and beliefs which they deem subversive to their evil regimes. But governmental suppression of causes and beliefs seems to me to be the very antithesis of what our constitution stands for. The choice expressed in the First Amendment in favor of free expression was made against a turbulent background by men such as Jefferson, Madison, and Mason—men who believed that loyalty to the provisions of this Amendment was the best way to assure a long life for this new nation and its Government. Unless there is complete freedom of expression for all ideas, whether we like them or not, concerning the way government should be run and who shall run it, I doubt if any views in the long run can be secured against the censor. The First Amendment provides the only kind of security system that can preserve a free government—

one that leaves the way wide open for people to favor, discuss, advocate, or incite causes and doctrines however obnoxious and antagonistic such views may be to the rest of us." *Yates v. United States*, 354 U.S. 298 (1957).

YOUNGER v. HARRIS (1971). Harris had been indicted for violating the California Criminal Syndicalism Act.* He then brought suit in a federal district court, asking the court to restrain the county district attorney from carrying out the prosecution, arguing that the California act was unconstitutional and that it prevented him from exercising his rights of free speech. Three other people joined Harris in seeking the injunction: Dan and Hirsch claimed that the prosecution of Harris would inhibit them from peacefully advocating the program of the political party to which they belonged, and Broslawsky, a university professor, claimed that the prosecution made him "uncertain" as to whether his teaching and reading practices would also subject him to prosecution. The district court issued the injunction, holding that the California act was void for vagueness and overbreadth, but on appeal, the Supreme Court reversed the decision and refused to enjoin the prosecution: "There is no basis for equitable jurisdiction based on the allegations of appellees other than Harris, who have not been indicted, arrested, or threatened with prosecution, and the normal course of a state criminal prosecution cannot be blocked on the basis of fears of prosecution that are merely speculative. Federal courts will not enjoin pending state criminal prosecutions except under extraordinary circumstances where the danger of irreparable loss is both great and immediate in that (unlike the situation affecting Harris) there is a threat to the plaintiff's federally protected rights that cannot be eliminated by his defense against a single prosecution." *Younger v. Harris*, 401 U.S. 37 (1971).

YOUNG, MAYOR OF DETROIT v. AMERICAN MINI THEATRES, INC. (1976). Two 1972 city of Detroit ordinances (Detroit, Anti–Skid Row Ordinances*) provided that an adult theater may not (apart from a special waiver) be located within 1,000 feet of any two other "regulated uses" or within 500 feet of a residential area. The term "regulated uses" was applied to various kinds of establishments in addition to adult theaters (adult bookstores, hotels, motels, pawnshops, pool halls, secondhand stores, shoeshine parlors, taxi dance halls). A theater was classified as an "adult" theater if it presented "material distinguished by an emphasis on matter depicting 'Specified Sexual Activities' or 'Specified Anatomical Areas.' " Although not attacking the definitions of sexual activities or anatomical areas, American Mini Theatres claimed that they could not determine how much of the described activity would be permissible before an exhibition would be "adult" and that the ordinances did not contain adequate procedures or standards for obtaining a waiver of the 1,000-foot restriction. The Supreme Court held that the ordinances were specific enough and that they were a valid time-place-manner* restriction on protected expression: "The ordinances are not invalid under the First Amendment as prior restraints on protected communication because of the licensing or zoning requirements. Though adult films may be exhibited commercially only in licensed theaters, that is also true of all films. That the place where films may be exhibited is regulated does not violate free expression; the city's interest in planning and regulating the use of property for commercial purposes being clearly adequate to support the locational restriction." Justice Stevens, while concurring in the decision, wondered if the city's approach was the best: "The line drawn by these ordinances is justified by the city's interest in preserving the character of its neighborhoods. . . . It is not our function to appraise the wisdom of its decision to require adult theaters to be separated rather than concentrated in the same areas." *Young, Mayor of Detroit v. American Mini Theatres, Inc.*, 427 U.S. 50 (1976).

YOUNGSTOWN (OHIO), OBSCENE LITERATURE. A Youngstown ordinance (Code 1925, No. 305) provided: "Any person who shall distribute, sell or expose for sale, or give away any books, papers, pictures and periodicals or advertising matter of any obscene or immoral nature, shall be fined in any sum not exceeding one hundred dollars or imprisoned not more than thirty days, or both." A federal district court, in *New American Library of World Literature, Inc. v. Allen* (1953),* ruled that the city police chief, acting on his own, could not determine what was and what was not "obscene."

APPENDICES

1.

CHRONOLOGY

1644   John Milton publishes his *Appeal for the Liberty of Unlicensed Printing*.

1712   The British Parliament imposes a tax on all newspapers and advertisements.

1749   John Cleland publishes his *Memoirs of a Woman of Pleasure*, also known as *Fanny Hill*.

1785   The Massachusetts legislature imposes a stamp tax on all newspapers; it is repealed one year later, in 1786.

1789   The First Amendment to the U.S. Constitution is proposed; it is ratified in 1791.

1798   Congress passes the Sedition Act, making it a crime to publish "scandalous or malicious writing against the government or the President," or to bring the government or the president into "contempt or disrepute," or to excite "hatred of the good people" against the government; the act expires in 1801.

1821   In one of the earliest recorded obscenity cases in the United States, John Cleland's *Memoirs of a Woman of Pleasure* is declared by a Massachusetts court to be "wicked and obscene" (*Commonwealth of Massachusetts v. Holmes*).

1825   The Supreme Court (*Commonwealth v. Blanding*) rules that the truth of a statement cannot be used as a defense against a libel suit.

1842   Congress passes the Tariff Act of 1842, forbidding the importation of "indecent and obscene" prints, paintings, lithographs, engravings, and transparencies; U.S. Customs is authorized to confiscate all such material.

1844   Anthony Comstock is born (d. 1915); Comstock becomes responsible for the 1873 Postal Act, which prohibits the use of the mails for any obscene, lewd, lascivious, indecent, vile, or disgusting matter, and later establishes the New York Society for the Suppression of Vice.

1845   The Supreme Court (*White v. Nicholls*) rules that a public official must prove "express malice" in a libel suit.

1865   Congress passes the Postal Act of 1865, making it a crime to deposit an "obscene book or other publication of a vulgar and indecent character" in the U.S. mails.

1868   Lord Chief Justice Cockburn, in *Regina v. Hicklin*, lays down what becomes known as the Hicklin Rule as a test for obscenity: A publication is obscene if isolated passages, not the work taken as a whole, could deprave and corrupt those whose minds are open to such immoral influences.

1873   Anthony Comstock founds and becomes secretary of the New York Society for the Suppression of Vice.

Congress passes the so-called Comstock Act, making it a crime to deposit any "obscene, lewd, or lascivious book or other publication of an indecent character" in the U.S. mails; the words "vile" and filthy" are added in 1909.

1875   The Supreme Court (*Pollard v. Lyon*) rules that although fornication by a married woman may not be nice, it is not slander for a third person to tell everyone else about her activities.

1876   The Boston-based New England Watch and Ward Society is established; its activities last well into the 1940s.

1877   The Supreme Court (*Ex Parte Jackson*) rules that Congress can prohibit information about lotteries from the U.S. mails.

1894   Anthony Comstock of the New York Society for the Suppression of Vice attempts to have several books (including Fielding's *Tom Jones* and Ovid's *Art of Love*) declared obscene but is rebuffed by a New York court.

1895   The Supreme Court (*Grimm v. United States*) rules that it is not a form of entrapment if someone mails obscene material or information on how to get such material as a response to a request from a government postal inspector posing as an interested customer.

1897   The Supreme Court (*Davis v. Massachusetts*) upholds the requirement that a permit is needed in advance from the mayor of Boston before making any public speech on the Boston Common.

1907   The Supreme Court (*Halter v. Nebraska*) upholds a Nebraska statute that prohibits the use of the U.S. flag for advertising purposes.

The Supreme Court (*Patterson v. Colorado*) sustains a conviction of contempt of court; Patterson impugns the motives of a judge, although there is no immediate danger to the administration of justice.

1913   Michael Kennerley is convicted of mailing an obscene book (*Hagar Revelly*), but Judge Hand remarks that the Hicklin Rule no longer reflects contemporary society and ought to be revised.

1915   A 1913 Ohio statute, establishing a board of censors over films and stating that only films "of moral, educational or amusing and harmless character" could be shown in the state, is seen to be constitutional by the Supreme Court on the grounds that films are not a form of speech or press, but a business, pure and simple; this sets the stage for decades of film censorship and suppression across the United States.

1917   Congress passes the Espionage Act, making it a crime to make false statements with the intent to interfere with the success of the war effort or to cause disloyalty or to obstruct the recruiting service; several people are convicted under the Espionage Act.

1919   American Socialist leader and 1920 presidential candidate Eugene Debs receives a ten-year jail term for violating the Espionage Act; President Harding commutes Debs' sentence in 1921.

1920   The Supreme Court (*Gilbert v. Minnesota*) affirms a conviction under a Minnesota statute that makes it a crime to discourage the war effort or to counsel against serving in the armed forces or to advocate pacifism as a political philosophy.

1921   The police chief of Cleveland, Ohio, attempts to prevent the sale of the *Dearborn Independent*, but a court rules that his actions are an unconstitutional prior restraint on the freedom of the press.

1922   A New York court rebuffs the claim of the New York Society for the Suppression of Vice that Théophile Gautier's *Mlle de Maupin* is obscene; in so ruling, the court discards the 1868 Hicklin Rule and announces that "no work may be judged from a selection of such [obscene] paragraphs alone."

The Motion Picture Association of America is established and imposes a strict moral code and censorship over U.S. films.

1925   The Supreme Court, in *Gitlow v. New York*, holds that the guarantees contained in the First Amendment are applicable to the states through the due process clause of the Fourteenth Amendment (Incorporation); the Court also rules that utterances involving a danger to the security of the nation can be punished, even though the danger is not immediate; the dissenting opinion states the "clear and present danger" test—press and speech cannot be censored unless there is a clear, immediate, present, and imminent danger to public order.

1927   Anita Whitney has her conviction affirmed by the Supreme Court: Advocacy of criminal syndicalism can be punished to the same extent as overt conduct.

The Tennessee Supreme Court affirms John T. Scopes' conviction for violating the state's Anti-Evolution Act in the famous "monkey trial," but Scopes' one-hundred-dollar fine is rescinded.

1928   Arkansas passes a statute prohibiting the teaching of Darwin's theory of evolution in any state-supported school; the prohibition remains in effect until 1968.

1929   A New York court rules the novel *The Well of Loneliness* to be obscene.

1930   Congress passes the Tariff Act of 1930, prohibiting the importation of any obscene or immoral thing and authorizes U.S. Customs to seize such material.

Schnitzler's classic *Hands Around (Reigen)* is banned in New York for being "disgusting, indecent, and obscene."

1931   Judge Woolsey rules that the books *Contraception* and *Married Love* are not obscene and that U.S. Customs cannot prevent their entry into the United States.

The Supreme Court (*Near v. Minnesota ex rel. Olson*) rules that a Minnesota statute aimed at preventing the publication of "scandalous and malicious publications" is an unconstitutional prior restraint on press freedom.

The Supreme Court (*Stromberg v. California*) reverses a California conviction of someone who displayed a red flag as a "sign, symbol or emblem of opposition to organized government."

1932   The state of New York attempts to ban the play *Frankie and Johnnie* as obscene but is rebuffed; the New York judge rules that the play's representation of prostitution does not "excite lustful and lecherous desire."

1934   Henry Miller's *Tropic of Cancer* is ruled obscene and its entry into the United
         States is prohibited; it is not until 1964 that the book is de-criminalized.

         The Roman Catholic Legion of Decency is established, pledging to rid America
         of all motion pictures that offend decency and Christian morality.

         Judge Woolsey rejects the 1868 Hicklin Rule as a test for obscenity regarding
         James Joyce's *Ulysses* and announces the *Ulysses* Standard: Obscenity is to be
         determined by the effect of a book, read in its entirety, on a person with average
         sex instincts.

1935   The New York Society for the Suppression of Vice attempts to have Gustave
         Flaubert's *November* declared obscene but is rebuffed by a New York court.

1936   The New York Society for the Suppression of Vice attempts to have André
         Gide's autobiography, *If I Die*, declared obscene but is rebuffed by a New York
         court.

         The Supreme Court (*Grossjean v. American Press*) refuses to sanction a Lou-
         isiana tax based on a newspaper's circulation, ruling the tax to be an unconsti-
         tutional restriction on the free press and as an unacceptable form of the odious
         knowledge tax.

1938   The Roman Catholic National Organization for Decent Literature is established,
         pledging to rid America of indecent and lewd literature.

         The Supreme Court, in *Lovell v. City of Griffin*, refuses to sanction an ordinance
         that requires permission from the city manager before distributing any pamphlets
         in the city; the ordinance is seen as an unconstitutional prior restraint on the rights
         guaranteed by the First Amendment.

1940   Congress passes the Smith Act, making it a crime to advocate or teach the
         desirability of overthrowing the government by force; the act is upheld in 1951
         (*Dennis v. United States*), but in 1957 (*Yates v. United States*), the Supreme
         Court rules that "mere advocacy" falls within the area of protected speech.

         Nudism in Modern Life, containing four small photographs of nude people, is
         declared not to be obscene and thus eligible for entry into the United States.

         The Supreme Court (*Minersville School District v. Gobitis*) rules that a state
         has the legitimate power to force schoolchildren to salute the flag and to recite
         the Pledge of Allegiance; this decision is overruled three years later, in 1943.

1942   The category of "fighting words"—words that by their very utterance inflict
         injury or tend to incite an immediate breach of the peace—is seen by the Supreme
         Court (*Chaplinsky v. New Hampshire*) to be unprotected by the First Amendment,
         and the Court affirms a conviction of someone who called police "damned
         Fascists."

1943   Only three years after the Supreme Court ruled to the contrary, the Court holds
         (*West Virginia State Board of Education v. Barnette*) that a state cannot force
         schoolchildren to salute the flag and recite the Pledge of Allegiance.

         The Supreme Court invalidates a Struthers, Ohio, ordinance that prohibits the
         ringing of doorbells or knocking on doors in order to distribute literature.

         A Dallas, Texas, ordinance prohibiting the distribution of handbills on the public streets, is seen by the Supreme Court (*Jamison v. Texas*) as an unconstitutional prior restraint on the First Amendment.

1944   *Lady Chatterley's Lover*, by D. H. Lawrence, is judged obscene by a New York court; it is not until 1960 that the book is de-criminalized.

1945   A Massachusetts court rules the novel *Strange Fruit* obscene.

The pamphlet *Preparing for Marriage* is ruled not to be obscene, and the postmaster general is ordered to carry it in the U.S. mails.

1946   The U.S. postmaster general decides that *Esquire* magazine doesn't "contribute to the public good and the public welfare" and attempts to revoke its second-class mailing permit; the Supreme Court refuses to allow the revocation.

1948   The Supreme Court lets stand a 1947 New York decision that Edmund Wilson's *Memoirs of Hecate County* (and especially the short story "The Princess with the Golden Hair") is obscene; the original suit was brought by the New York Society for the Improvement of Morals (formerly the New York Society for the Suppression of Vice).

A New Jersey court rules that *Mom and Dad*, a film showing conception and childbirth, is not obscene and orders the public safety director of Newark, New Jersey, to issue an exhibition permit.

The Supreme Court (*Winters v. New York*) rules that publications dealing with crime stories and criminal news are protected by the First Amendment.

1949   A defrocked Catholic priest, Arthur Terminiello, has his breach of the peace conviction set aside by the Supreme Court; Terminiello's Chicago speech incited hostility and anger in the crowd, but the Court rules that this is the function of speech.

1950   A Massachusetts court declares *God's Little Acre*, by Erskine Caldwell, to be obscene and prohibits its sale or distribution in the state.

1951   The Supreme Court (*Feiner v. New York*) affirms a breach of the peace conviction against Feiner; his speech in Syracuse stirs some of his listeners to anger.

The Supreme Court (*Kunz v. New York*) rules that New York City's system of requiring street preachers to have a permit before using the sidewalks is a form of unconstitutional prior restraint.

The 1940 Smith Act, making it a crime to advocate or teach the desirability of the overthrow of the government, is ruled to be constitutional (*Dennis v. United States*).

1952   Congress passes the Immigration and Nationality Act of 1952, authorizing the U.S. attorney general to refuse to issue a visa to any alien who writes or publishes on the "economic, international and governmental doctrines of world communism."

In ruling that New York cannot prevent the showing of the film *The Miracle* because of its alleged "sacrilegious" character, the Supreme Court states the general principle that films are a form of expressive communication and, as such, are protected by the First Amendment; this decision overturns the 1915 view that films are only a business and not a form of speech or press.

A New Jersey court orders the public safety director of Newark, New Jersey, to issue an exhibition permit for the film *Latuko*; the director had refused to issue the permit because he thought the film, a documentary about an African tribe that doesn't wear clothes, was obscene.

The Supreme Court (*Adler v. Board of Education*) rules that a New York statute that makes any person ineligible for public employment who is a member of any organization advocating the overthrow of the government by force, is constitutional; the ruling stays in effect until 1967.

In a rare departure from most past decisions, the Supreme Court (*Beauharnais v. Illinois*) rules that libelous speech directed at a group of people is not within the area of constitutionally protected speech.

1953   Otto Preminger produces, directs, and distributes the film *The Moon is Blue* without the Motion Picture Association of America's (MPAA's) Seal of Approval; this is the beginning of the end of the MPAA's censorship over the U.S. film industry and eventually leads to a new age classification rating scheme by the MPAA.

1954   The Ohio Board of Censors refuses to issue an exhibition permit for the film *Native Son* because it "undermines confidence that justice can be carried out and presents racial frictions at a time when all groups should be united against everything that is subversive"; the Supreme Court orders the board to issue the exhibition permit.

The Ohio Board of Censors refuses to issue an exhibition permit for the film *M* because it "leads to a serious increase in immorality and crime; serves no valid purpose; and the criminals are shown to be more efficient than the police"; the Supreme Court orders the board to issue the permit.

The New York Board of Motion Picture Censors refuses to issue an exhibition permit for the film *La Ronde*, the screen version of Schnitzler's *The Ring*, because the film "tends to corrupt morals"; the Supreme Court orders the permit to be issued.

1955   A Massachusetts ordinance, requiring the mayor of any city to first review and then issue a permit for any public event held on a Sunday in order to ensure that the activity is "in keeping with the character of the Lord's Day," is seen by a Massachusetts court to be an unconstitutional prior restraint on the First Amendment.

1956   Otto Preminger continues his assault on the MPAA's moral censorship over films by producing, directing, and distributing, without the MPAA's Seal of Approval, *The Man with the Golden Arm*.

With the objectives to weed out indecent and impure language in books and to uplift the moral character of the state's teenagers, the Rhode Island Commission to Encourage Morality in Youth is established; the entire enterprise is seen by the Supreme Court in 1973 to be an unconstitutional administrative censorship scheme.

1957   The Chicago police commissioner is ordered by the Supreme Court to issue an exhibition permit for the film *The Game of Love*; the commissioner thought the film was obscene.

The Supreme Court (*Konigsberg v. California*) rules that the California State Bar cannot refuse to license an attorney because of his failure to swear that he does not advocate the forcible overthrow of the government.

A Michigan statute that prohibits the sale of any book "tending to the corruption of the morals of youth" is seen as an unconstitutional restriction on the First Amendment by the Supreme Court (*Butler v. Michigan*) because "the incidence of this enactment is to reduce the adult population to reading what is only fit for children."

The Supreme Court rules that the 1940 Smith Act cannot be employed to punish someone who engages in "mere advocacy" of prohibited activities as compared with actual conduct (*Yates v. United States*).

A Maryland court orders the Maryland State Board of Motion Picture Censors to issue an exhibition permit for the film *Naked Amazon*, a documentary that includes scenes of naked Amazon Indians.

The Supreme Court (*Roth v. United States*) rules that obscenity is not protected speech or press and can be prohibited and punished; in so ruling, the Court lays down a new standard, the Roth Standard, of obscenity: "whether to the average person, applying contemporary standards, the dominant theme of the material appeals to prurient interest."

1958   The Supreme Court (*Speiser v. Randall*) rules that a California statute requiring the signing of a loyalty oath before receiving a standard property tax exemption violates the First Amendment.

1959   The Supreme Court rules that a radio station licensee cannot censor out alleged defamatory comments made by a political candidate and that the licensee cannot be held liable for any such defamatory comments (*Farmers Union v. WDAY*).

A bookseller cannot be held liable and punished for "possession with intent to sell" obscene books; the Supreme Court (*Smith v. California*) rules that this would lead to the bookseller censoring the books offered for sale.

The film version of *Lady Chatterley's Lover* (*L'Amant de Lady Chatterley*), by D. H. Lawrence, is judged not to be obscene, and the Supreme Court orders the New York authorities to issue an exhibition permit.

A California court (*Katzev v. California*) rules that it is not a crime to sell a comic book in which Bugs Bunny steals a carrot from Elmer Fudd's garden or in which Bluto abducts Olive Oyl away from Popeye.

1960   *Lady Chatterley's Lover*, by D. H. Lawrence, is judged not to be obscene, thus de-criminalizing the book.

1961   The Supreme Court (*Times Film Corporation v. City of Chicago*) rules that cities and states can require prior examination of a film before issuing an exhibition permit; films can be treated differently from books, magazines, newspapers, or dramatic presentations.

1963   Regarding a burlesque performance in a nightclub as "devoid of art and beauty as a garbage pail," a St. Louis court punishes the dancer and the owner of the nightclub for "lewd and indecent behavior" (*City of St. Louis v. Mikes*).

1964   In an extremely close vote (5 to 4), the Supreme Court rules that Henry Miller's *Tropic of Cancer* is not obscene, thus ending thirty years of suppression of the book.

Comedian Lenny Bruce successfully appeals his conviction by a Chicago court for having given an "obscene" nightclub performance.

The Supreme Court (*New York Times Company v. Sullivan*) announces the *New York Times* Rule: A public official who sues for defamation or libel must prove malice on the part of the defendant; malice is seen as the publishing of the material knowing it to be false or with a reckless disregard of whether it is true or false.

1965   The film *491* is judged obscene and is refused entry into the United States under the 1930 Tariff Act.

The Supreme Court rules that television cameras can be barred from a courtroom (*Estes v. Texas*).

A Connecticut statute prohibiting the use of any birth control device is seen by the Supreme Court to be unconstitutional (*Griswold v. Connecticut*).

The Supreme Court orders the Maryland and New York authorities to issue an exhibition permit for the film *A Stranger Knocks*.

The Supreme Court rules that certain postal regulations requiring an addressee to request that the post office deliver "communist political propaganda" violates the First Amendment.

1966   The Georgia House of Representatives is ordered by the Supreme Court (*Bond v. Floyd*) to seat Julian Bond; Bond was earlier denied his seat after making certain statements regarding the government's policies in Viet Nam and the operation of the Selective Service laws.

The Supreme Court rules that John Cleland's *Memoirs of a Woman of Pleasure/Fanny Hill* is not obscene and in so doing, lays down the Memoirs Standard as a test for obscenity: "Three elements must coalesce: it must be established that (a) the dominant theme of the material taken as a whole appeals to prurient interest in sex; (b) the material is patently offensive because it affronts contemporary community standards relating to the description or representation of sexual matters; and (c) the material is utterly without redeeming social value."

The Massachusetts Supreme Judicial Court reverses a lower court decision and rules that *Naked Lunch*, by William S. Burroughs, is not obscene and thus can be sold in the state.

The National Organization for Women is established and engages in various censorship attempts regarding the portrayal of women in society.

The Supreme Court (*Sheppard v. Maxwell*) rules that too much pre-trial publicity and the failure to shield jurors from media reports are not consistent with the right to a fair trial.

Congress passes the Freedom of Information Act, designed to make available to the public more information from most federal agencies.

Ralph Ginzburg is convicted of pandering: the leer of the sensualist, used to advertise and sell certain publications, is directed at appealing to the customer's erotic interest.

1967   The magazine *Hellenic Sun*, containing pictures of nude boys and men, is judged to be obscene and is refused entry into the United States.

The Supreme Court affirms a California ruling that the film *Un Chant d'Amour* is obscene.

The Supreme Court (*Keyishian v. Board of Regents*) rules that a New York statute making any person ineligible for public employment who is a member of any organization advocating the overthrow of the government by force, is a violation of the First Amendment.

1968   Ruling that different standards of obscenity can be applied to material distributed to children than those applied to material distributed to adults, the Supreme Court affirms (*Ginsberg v. New York*) a conviction of someone who sold a "girlie" magazine to a minor.

The Dallas, Texas, motion picture censorship process is ruled unconstitutional by the Supreme Court after the censorship board attempts to prevent the showing of *Viva Maria*.

Separating protected "symbolic speech" from unprotected conduct, the Supreme Court affirms a conviction for draft card burning (*United States v. O'Brien*).

The Arkansas anti-evolution statute, passed in 1928 and prohibiting the teaching that "mankind ascended or descended from a lower order of animals," is ruled to be a violation of the First Amendment.

1969   The Supreme Court (*Brandenburg v. Ohio*) rules that a state cannot punish advocacy of the use of force or of law violation unless such advocacy is directed to inciting or producing imminent lawless action and is likely to incite or produce such action; this is the "clear and present danger" doctrine.

The Supreme Court sanctions a Federal Communications Commission (FCC) order to implement the "fairness doctrine"—a radio station has to give air time to someone who is attacked on the station (*Red Lion Broadcasting Co. v. Federal Communications Commission*).

Although obscene material may be prevented from being transported, distributed, or sold, a state cannot punish a person who possesses such material in the privacy of his own home for his private use (*Stanley v. Georgia*).

Three schoolchildren in Des Moines, Iowa, win their suit to wear black arm bands in school as a symbolic protest against the war in Viet Nam; Justice Black offers an uncharacteristic dissent, believing the "inmates have taken over the asylum" (*Tinker v. Des Moines School District*).

1970   The Supreme Court lets stand a Massachusetts court ruling that the film *Titicut Follies* can be exhibited only to professional audiences.

A postal regulation that allows an individual addressee, if he thinks he is receiving "erotically arousing" or "sexually provocative" material, to have the postmaster stop the mailing of such material, is sanctioned by the Supreme Court.

The Supreme Court (*Schacht v. United States*) rules that the government cannot punish someone who criticizes the military while wearing a military uniform in a theatrical presentation.

The President's Commission on Obscenity and Pornography issues its *Report*, recommending the repeal of all federal, state, and local ordinances restricting the availability of explicit sexual material to consenting adults; Vice-President Agnew flays away at "radical liberals" and the "permissive society"; President Nixon calls the recommendations "morally bankrupt."

1971   The Supreme Court refuses to sanction the government's attempt to prevent the publication of *The Pentagon Papers* by the *New York Times* and the *Washington Post*, seeing it as a blatant and unconstitutional prior restraint on the freedom of the press.

The film *Carnal Knowledge* is judged not to be obscene; although the film contains occasional nudity, nudity alone is not sufficient to make a film obscene.

Congress passes the Federal Election Campaign Act, setting certain limits on campaign contributions and expenditures.

The Supreme Court affirms a lower court ruling that the film *I Am Curious—Yellow* is obscene.

The Supreme Court (*Cohen v. California*) rules that California cannot punish someone under an "offensive conduct" statute for wearing a jacket in public bearing the words "Fuck the Draft."

1972   A California statute prohibiting certain sexual activities and forms of entertainment in places licensed to serve alcohol does not violate the First Amendment; the Supreme Court (*California v. LaRue*) rules that the Twenty-first Amendment takes precedence over the First Amendment.

The Supreme Court sanctions Attorney General Kleindienst's refusal to grant a visa to Ernest Mandel, a Belgian journalist; the refusal is based on the fact that Mandel publishes on the "economic, international, and governmental doctrines of world communism."

The Central Intelligence Agency's (CIA's) insistence on pre-publication review and censorship of former agents' writings is sanctioned by the Supreme Court in *United States v. Marchetti*; Marchetti tries again in 1975 to publish without CIA permission but is again rebuffed by the courts.

1973   Various state statutes patterned after the federal Hatch Act that prevent certain kinds of political activity and free speech rights by state employees, are seen not to violate the First Amendment (*Broaderick v. Oklahoma*).

Although rude, the words "Get out of my way, you fucking prick-ass cops" are not seen as "fighting words" by the Supreme Court (*Cincinnati v. Karlan*).

The Supreme Court, in *Miller v. California*, lays down the Miller Standard as a test of obscenity: "The basic guidelines must be: (a) whether the average person, applying contemporary community standards, would find that the work, taken as a whole, appeals to the prurient interest; (b) whether the work depicts or describes, in a patently offensive way, sexual conduct specifically defined by the applicable state law; and (c) whether the work, taken as a whole, lacks serious literary, artistic, political, or scientific value."

1974   The Supreme Court lets stand a lower court ruling that although the University of Mississippi does not have to fund a campus publication and that it can place a disclaimer on the issues, saying the magazine is not an official university publication, the university cannot censor the contents of the magazine; the university administration did not like the use of a particular epithet referring to an "incestuous son."

The words "Look at the chicken-shit mother fucker" applied to a police officer are not seen as "fighting words."

A Florida "right of reply" statute requiring newspapers to print rejoinders from attacked political candidates, is seen to be an unconstitutional abridgment on the right of a free press (*Miami Herald Publishing Company v. Tornillo*).

A Jacksonville, Florida, ordinance prohibiting nudity in films shown at drive-ins is seen by the Supreme Court as too broad, for the ordinance would prevent the exhibition of a film showing a baby's buttocks or a picture of the nude body of a war victim.

An Indiana statute requiring a political party to furnish a loyalty oath before being placed on the ballot is seen to violate the First Amendment (*Communist Party of Indiana v. Whitcomb*).

In a unanimous (8 to 0) decision, the Supreme Court orders President Nixon to surrender the tapes of his secretly recorded conversations to Watergate Special Prosecutor Leon Jaworski.

A U.S. Army physician receives three years at hard labor and a dishonorable discharge for "conduct unbecoming an officer and a gentleman"; Dr. Levy's statements urging black enlisted men not to go to Viet Nam are not seen as protected speech, and the Supreme Court affirms the conviction (*Parker v. Levy*).

1975   A Chattanooga, Tennessee, municipal board refuses to issue an exhibition permit for the musical *Hair*, believing that the show is not in the best interests of the community; the Supreme Court orders the board to issue the permit.

The Supreme Court rules that topless dancing is a form of symbolic speech and is protected by the First Amendment (*Doran v. Salem Inn*).

1976   The commander of Fort Dix, New Jersey, refuses to give Benjamin Spock, a candidate for president of the People's party, permission to distribute campaign literature and to give a speech at Fort Dix; the Supreme Court sanctions this refusal, ruling that the loyalty, discipline, and morale of the troops take precedence over Spock's free speech rights (*Greer v. Spock*).

The X-rated all-time classic *Deep Throat* is judged obscene; the finding of obscenity doesn't prevent its exhibition in most places.

The Supreme Court (*Buckley v. Valeo*) rules that the 1971 Federal Election Campaign Act's limitations on political contributions are constitutional but that the expenditure provisions violate the First Amendment.

1977   Although such a display may offend some people, the Supreme Court rules that New York cannot make it a crime to advertise or display contraceptives.

The First Amendment guarantee of free speech is extended to advertising by attorneys (*Bates v. State Bar of Arizona*).

The Supreme Court rules that people do not have to display a government message on their private property if they are offended by the content of the message and prevents the state of New Hampshire from punishing anyone who covers up the state motto "Live Free or Die" on their automobile license plates (*Wooley v. Maynard*).

1978   The "Filthy Words" monologue by George Carlin is broadcast over a New

York radio station in the afternoon, and the Supreme Court sanctions an FCC ruling that reprimands the station for broadcasting indecent but not obscene material at a time when children are likely to be in the listening audience.

A Massachusetts statute prohibiting corporations from expressing their views on certain public policy questions is seen to be a violation of the First Amendment.

The village of Skokie, Illinois, attempts to prevent Frank Collin and his American Nazi party from parading down the village's main street, but the courts rule that the village's hastily passed parade ordinances are unconstitutional; the parade eventually takes place in Chicago.

1979   Senator William Proxmire is held liable for defamatory statements contained in various newsletters and press releases in conjunction with his "Golden Fleece" awards.

1980   For not submitting his book *Decent Interval* to the CIA for pre-publication review and clearance, former agent Frank Snepp sees the Supreme Court sanction the application of a constructive trust on the book's profits for the government.

1981   Former CIA agent Philip Agee has his passport revoked as punishment for disclosing the identity of several covert CIA operatives.

1982   The Board of Education of the Island Trees Union Free School District, in New York, is told by the Supreme Court (*Board of Education v. Pico*) that it cannot summarily remove from the school libraries a number of books thought to be "anti-American, anti-Christian, anti-Semitic, and just plain filthy"; among the books are *Slaughterhouse Five*, by Kurt Vonnegut, Jr., and *The Fixer*, by Bernard Malamud.

In an attempt to control child pornography, the Supreme Court (*New York v. Ferber*) rules that a state can prohibit and punish the dissemination of material depicting children engaged in sexual conduct whether or not the activity in question is obscene.

Congress passes the Intelligence Identities Protection Act, making it a crime to divulge the identity of any covert governmental agent or operative, even if such information is unclassified or is already part of the public record.

1983   The U.S. Senate votes 56 to 34 to delay a presidential scheme that would subject all federal employees who might have had access to classified material while employed to submit to government pre-publication review any writing the person may wish to do during his lifetime.

A federal court (*McGehee v. Casey*) reiterates that former CIA agents must submit their writings to the CIA for pre-publication review and approval.

The Supreme Court rules (*Bolger v. Youngs Drug Products Corporation*) that the U.S. Postal Service cannot prohibit the mailing of unsolicited advertisements for contraceptives.

1984   The Supreme Court rules that the film *Caligula* is not obscene, since it has serious artistic and political value and does not appeal to the prurient interest— it sickens and disgusts rather than arouses.

The Texas State Textbook Committee rescinds two ten-year-old guidelines for books sold in the state: (1) "Textbooks that treat the theory of evolution shall identify it as only one of several explanations of the origins of humankind and avoid limiting young people in their search for meanings of their human existence.'' (2) ''Each textbook must carry a statement on an introductory page that any material on evolution included in the book is clearly presented as theory rather than fact.''

2.

TABLE OF CASES

SELECTED BIBLIOGRAPHY

Abrams, Floyd. "The New Effort to Control Information." *New York Times Sunday Magazine* (September 25, 1983), 22–28.

Allen, Frederick L. *Frederick Baylies Allen: A Memoir*. Riverside Press, 1929.

Allen, Leslie H. *Bryan and Darrow at Dayton*. Lee, 1925.

Anderson, A. J. *Problems in Intellectual Freedom and Censorship*. R. R. Bowker, 1974.

Balio, Tino. *The American Film Industry*. University of Wisconsin Press, 1976.

Beale, Howard K. "Freedom for the School Teacher." 200 *Annals of the American Academy of Political and Social Science* (November 1938), 119–143.

Beman, Leman T. *Selected Articles on Censorship of Speech and the Press*. Wilson, 1930; Greenwood Press, 1971.

––––––. *Selected Articles on Censorship of the Theater and Motion Pictures*. Wilson, 1931.

Bent, Silas. *Newspaper Crusaders: A Neglected Story*. Whittlesey House, 1939.

Berns, Walter. *Freedom, Virtue and the First Amendment*. Louisiana State University Press, 1957.

Bickel, Alexander M. *The Morality of Consent*. Yale University Press, 1975.

Blackmur, R. P. *Dirty Hands or the True Born Censor*. Folcroft Library Editions, 1930.

Blanshard, Paul. *The Right to Read: The Battle Against Censorship*. Beacon Press, 1955.

Boles, Donald E. *The Bible, Religion, and the Public Schools*. Iowa State University Press, 1965.

Bolte, Charles G. "Security Through Book Burning." 2 *Annals of the American Academy of Political and Social Sciences* (July 1955), 87–93.

Bosmajian, Haig. *Censorship, Libraries and the Law*. Neal-Schuman, 1983.

Boyer, Paul S. "Boston Book Censorship in the Twenties." 15 *American Quarterly* (Spring 1963), 3–24.

––––––. *Purity in Print: The Vice-Society Movement and Book Censorship in America*. Scribner's, 1968.

Broun, Heywood, and Leech, Margaret. *Anthony Comstock: Roundsman of the Lord*. Boni, 1927.

Buranelli, Vincent. *The Trial of Peter Zenger*. New York University Press, 1957.

Busha, Charles H. *Freedom Versus Suppression and Censorship*. Libraries Unlimited, 1972.

Cairns, Huntington. "Freedom of Expression in Literature." 200 *Annals of the American Academy of Political and Social Science* (November 1938), 76–94.

Carmen, I. H. *Movies, Censorship, and the Law*. University of Michigan Press, 1966.

Carroll, Thomas F. "Freedom of Speech and of the Press During the Civil War." 9
    Virginia Law Review (April 1923), 516–551.
————. "Freedom of Speech and of the Press in the Federalist Period: The Sedition
    Act." 18 *Michigan Law Review* (May 1920), 615–651.
————. "Freedom of Speech and of the Press in War Time: The Espionage Act." 17
    Michigan Law Review (June 1919), 621–665.
Chafee, Zechariah, Jr. "Freedom of Speech in War Time." 32 *Harvard Law Review*
    (June 1919), 932–973.
————. *Free Speech in the United States*. Harvard University Press, 1941.
————. *Government and the Press: A Report from the Commission on Freedom of the
    Press*. University of Chicago Press, 1947.
Chambers, M. M. *The Colleges and the Courts: The Developing Law of the Student and
    the College*. The Interstate Printers and Publishers, 1972.
Clyde, William M. *The Struggle for the Freedom of the Press from Caxton to Cromwell*.
    Oxford University Press, 1934.
Comstock, Anthony. *Traps for the Young*. Funk & Wagnalls, 1883.
Countryman, Vern. *The Douglas Opinions*. Random House, 1977.
Daniels, Walter M. *The Censorship of Books*. H. W. Wilson, 1954.
De Grazia, Edward. *Censorship Landmarks*. R. R. Bowker, 1969.
————, and Newman, Roger K. *Banned Films: Movies, Censors, and the First Amend-
    ment*. R. R. Bowker, 1982.
Douglas, William O. *An Almanac of Liberty*. Doubleday, 1954.
————. *Freedom of the Mind*. Doubleday, 1964.
————. *The Right of the People*. Doubleday, 1958.
Dulles, Avery. *The Legion of Decency*. America Press, 1956.
Duniway, Clyde A. *The Development of the Freedom of the Press in Massachusetts*.
    Harvard University Press, 1906.
Edgar, Harold, and Schmidt, Benno C., Jr. "The Espionage Statutes and Publication of
    Defense Information." 73 *Columbia Law Review* (May 1973), 929–1087.
Emerson, Thomas I. *The System of Freedom of Expression*. Random House, 1970.
Emery, Walter B. *Broadcasting and Government: Responsibilities and Regulations*. Mich-
    igan State University Press, 1961.
Ernst, Morris L., and Lindey, Alexander. *The Censor Marches On: Recent Milestones
    in the Administration of the Obscenity Law in the United States*. Doubleday-
    Doran, 1940; Da Capo Press, 1971.
————, and Lorentz, Pare. *Censored: The Private Life of the Movies*. Jerome S. Ozer
    reprint, 1971.
Erskin, Hazel G. "The Polls: Freedom of Speech." 34 *Public Opinion Quarterly* (Fall
    1970), 483–496.
Farrer, James A. *Books Condemned to Be Burnt*. A. C. Armstrong, 1892.
Fellman, David. *The Censorship of Books*. University of Wisconsin Press, 1957.
Fiske, Marjorie. *Book Selection and Censorship*. University of California Press, 1959.
Ford, John. *Criminal Obscenity: A Plea for Its Suppression*. Revell, 1926.
Friedman, Leon. *Obscenity: The Complete Oral Arguments Before the Supreme Court
    in the Major Obscenity Cases*. Chelsea House, 1970.
Gallichan, Walter M. *The Poison of Prudery: A Historical Survey*. Stratford, 1929.
Galt, Thomas F. *Peter Zenger: Fighter for Freedom*. Crowell, 1951.
Gardiner, Harold C. *Catholic Viewpoint on Censorship*. Hanover House, 1958.

Gavin, Clark. *Foul, False and Infamous: Famous Libel and Slander Cases of History.* Abelard, 1950.

Gerald, J. Edward. *The Press and the Constitution, 1931–1947.* University of Minnesota Press, 1948.

Gillmore, Donald M. *Free Press and Fair Trial.* Public Affairs Press, 1966.

Ginger, Ray. *Six Days or Forever: Tennessee v. John Thomas Scopes.* Beacon Press, 1958.

Goodman, Paul. "Pornography, Art and Censorship." 31 *Commentary* (March 1961), 203–212.

Haight, Anne Lyon. *Banned Books, 387 B.C.–1978 A.D.* Updated and enlarged by Chandler B. Grannis. R. R. Bowker, 1978.

Haiman, Franklyn S. *Freedom of Speech: Issues and Cases.* Random House, 1965.

Haney, Robert W. *Comstockery in America: Patterns of Censorship and Control.* Beacon Press, 1960.

Hanson, Laurence. *Government and the Press: 1695–1763.* Oxford University Press, 1936; reprinted 1967.

Hart, Harold H. *Censorship, For and Against.* Hart Publishing Co., 1972.

Hays, Will H. *Memoirs.* Doubleday, 1955.

Hentoff, Nat. *The First Freedom: The Tumultuous History of Free Speech in America.* Dell, 1981.

Hopkins, Deian. "Domestic Censorship in the First World War." 5 *Journal of Contemporary History* (October 1970), 151–169.

Hoyt, Olga, and Hoyt, Edwin P. *Censorship in America.* Seabury Press, 1970.

Hudson, Edward G. *Freedom of Speech and Press in America.* Public Affairs Press, 1963.

Hunnings, Neville M. *Film Censors and the Law.* Allen & Unwin, 1967.

Hutchinson, E. R. *Tropic of Cancer on Trial: A Case History of Censorship.* Grove Press, 1968.

Inglis, Ruth A. *Freedom of the Movies: A Report on Self-Regulation.* University of Chicago Press, 1947; reprint Da Capo Press, 1974.

Jackson, Holbrook. *The Fear of Books.* Scribner's, 1932.

Jenkinson, Edward B. *Censors in the Classroom: The Mind Benders.* Southern Illinois University Press, 1979.

Kallen, Horace. *Indecency and the Seven Arts.* Liveright, 1930.

Kilpatrick, James J. *The Smut Peddlers.* Doubleday, 1960.

Konvitz, Milton R. *First Amendment Freedoms: Selected Cases on Freedom of Religion, Speech, Press, Assembly.* Cornell University Press, 1963.

Koop, Theodore F. *Weapon of Silence.* University of Chicago Press, 1946.

Kronhausen, Eberhard, and Kronhausen, Phyllis. *Pornography and the Law.* Ballantine, 1959.

Kuh, Richard H. *Foolish Figleaves: Pornography In and Out of Court.* Macmillan, 1967.

Kurland, Philip B. *Free Speech and Association: The Supreme Court and the First Amendment.* University of Chicago Press, 1961.

Lader, Lawrence. *The Margaret Sanger Story and the Fight for Birth Control.* Doubleday, 1955.

Lawrence, D. H. *Sex, Literature, and Censorship.* Viking, 1959.

Leary, William M., Jr. "Books, Soldiers and Censorship During the Second World War." 20 *American Quarterly* (Summer 1968), 237–245.

Levy, Leonard W. *Freedom of the Press from Zenger to Jefferson: Early American Libertarian Theories*. Bobbs-Merrill, 1966.

———. *Legacy of Suppression: Freedom of Speech and Press in Early American History*. Harvard University Press, 1960.

Liston, Robert A. *The Right to Know: Censorship in America*. Franklin Watts, 1978.

Lockhart, William B., and McClure, Robert C. "Censorship of Obscenity: The Developing Constitutional Standards." 45 *Minnesota Law Review* (November 1960), 5–121.

———. "Literature, The Law of Obscenity, and the Constitution." 38 *Minnesota Law Review* (March 1954), 295–395.

McCoy, Ralph E. *Freedom of the Press: An Annotated Bibliography*. Southern Illinois University Press, 1969.

Magee, James J. *Mr. Justice Black: Absolutist on the Court*. University Press of Virginia, 1979.

Makris, John N. *The Silent Investigators: The Great Untold Story of the United States Postal Inspection Service*. Dutton, 1959.

Miller, John C. *Crisis in Freedom: The Alien and Sedition Acts*. Little, Brown, 1952.

Minor, Dale. *The Information War*. Hawthorne Books, 1970.

Minow, Newton N. *Equal Time: The Private Broadcaster and the Public Interest*. Atheneum, 1964.

Mock, James R. *Censorship, 1917*. Princeton University Press, 1941.

———, and Larson, Cedric. *Words That Won the War: The Story of the Committee on Public Information, 1917–1919*. Princeton University Press, 1939.

Moon, Eric. *Book Selection and Censorship in the Sixties*. R. R. Bowker, 1969.

Moley, Raymond. *The Hays Office*. Bobbs-Merrill, 1945; Jerome S. Ozer reprint, 1971.

Mott, Frank L. *American Journalism: A History, 1690–1960*. Macmillan, 1962.

———. *Jefferson and the Press*. Louisiana State University Press, 1943.

———. *Journalism in Wartime*. American Council on Public Affairs, 1943.

Murphy, Terrence J. *Censorship: Government and Obscenity*. Helicon Press, 1963.

National Office for Decent Literature. *The Drive for Decency in Print*. Our Sunday Visitor Press, 1939.

Nelson, H. L. *Freedom of the Press from Hamilton to the Warren Court*. Bobbs-Merrill, 1967.

Nelson, Jack, and Roberts, Gene. *The Censors and the Schools*. Little, Brown, 1963; Greenwood Press reprint, 1977.

Nizer, Louis. *New Courts of Industry: Self-Regulation Under the Motion Picture Code*. Jerome S. Ozer, 1971.

Norwick, Kenneth P. *Lobbying for Freedom: A Citizen's Guide to Fighting Censorship at the State Level*. St. Martin's Press, 1975.

Oberholtzer, Ellis P. *The Morals of the Movie*. Penn Publishing Co., 1922; Jerome S. Ozer reprint, 1971.

Oboler, Eli M. *Defending Intellectual Freedom: The Library and the Censor*. Greenwood Press, 1980.

———. *The Fear of the World: Censorship and Sex*. Scarecrow Press, 1974.

Patterson, Giles J. *Free Speech and a Free Press*. Little, Brown, 1939.

Paul, James, and Schwartz, Murray L. *Federal Censorship: Obscenity in the Mail*. Free Press of Glencoe, 1961.

Perrin, Noel. *Dr. Bowdler's Legacy: A History of Expurgated Books in England and America*. Atheneum, 1969.

Phelan, John. *Communications Control: Readings in the Motives and Structures of Censorship*. Sheed and Ward, 1969.

Quigley, Martin. *Decency in Motion Pictures*. Macmillan, 1937.

Randall, Richard S. *Censorship of the Movies: The Social and Political Control of a Mass Medium*. University of Wisconsin Press, 1968.

Rembar, Charles. *The End of Obscenity: The Trials of Lady Chatterley, Tropic of Cancer, and Fanny Hill*. Random House, 1968.

Roebert, John. *The Wicked and the Banned*. Macfadden Publishing Co., 1963.

Rosenblatt, Albert M. "Flag Desecration Statutes: History and Analysis." 1972 *Washington University Law Quarterly* (Spring 1972), 193–237.

Schumach, Murray. *The Face on the Cutting Room Floor: The Story of Movie and Television Censorship*. Morrow, 1964; Da Capo Press reprint, 1975.

Schwartz, Bernard. *The Great Rights of Mankind: A History of the American Bill of Rights*. Oxford University Press, 1977.

Siebert, Frederick S. *Freedom of the Press in England, 1476–1776*. University of Illinois Press, 1952.

Singer, Richard G. "Censorship of Prisoners' Mail and the Constitution." 56 *American Bar Association Journal* (November 1970), 1051–1055.

Sjoman, Vilgot. *I Was Curious: Diary of the Making of a Film*. Grove Press, 1968.

Smith, James M. *Freedom's Fetters: The Alien and Sedition Laws and American Civil Liberties*. Cornell University Press, 1956.

Summers, Harrison B. *Radio Censorship*. Arno Press reprint, 1971.

Thomas, Donald. *A Long Time Burning: The History of Literary Censorship in England*. Praeger, 1969.

United States Department of the Air Force. *Armed Forces Censorship*. U.S. Government Printing Office, 1957.

United States President's Commission on Obscenity and Pornography. *The Report of the Commission on Obscenity and Pornography*. U.S. Government Printing Office, 1970.

Vizzard, Jack. *See No Evil: Life Inside a Hollywood Censor*. Simon & Schuster, 1970.

Walker, Alexander. *Sex in the Movies*. Penguin, 1968.

Watkins, Gordon S. "The Motion Picture Industry." 254 *Annals of the American Academy of Political and Social Science* (November 1947).

Widmer, Kingsley, and Widmer, Eleanor. *Literary Censorship: Principles, Cases, Problems*. Wadsworth, 1961.

Wiggins, James R. *Freedom or Secrecy*. Oxford University Press, 1964.

Williams, Bernard. *Obscenity and Film Censorship*. Cambridge University Press, 1982.

Wright, Charles A. "The Constitution on the Campus." 22 *Vanderbilt Law Review* (October 1969), 1027–1088.

INDEX

About the Author

LEON HURWITZ is Professor of Political Science at Cleveland State University, Ohio. His earlier works include *Contemporary Approaches to European Integration, The State as Defendant*, and *The Harmonization of European Public Policy* (Greenwood Press, 1980, 1981, 1983) as well as *Introduction to Politics* and *International Organizations* (with Werner J. Feld and Robert S. Jordan). He has also published articles in the *Journal of Common Market Studies, Comparative Political Studies*, and *Studies in Comparative Communism*.